Encyclopedia of World

MILITARY AIRCRAFT

Volume 2

Published by
Aerospace Publishing Ltd
179 Dalling Road
London W6 0ES
England

Published under licence in USA and
Canada by
AIRtime Publishing Inc.
10 Bay Street
Westport, CT 06880
USA

Aerospace ISBN: 1 874023 52 2
AIRtime ISBN: 1-880588-15-3

Distributed in the UK,
Commonwealth and Europe by
Airlife Publishing Ltd
101 Longden Road
Shrewsbury SY3 9EB
England
Telephone: 0743 235651
Fax: 0743 232944

Distributed to retail bookstores in the
USA and Canada by
AIRtime Publishing Inc.
10 Bay Street
Westport, CT 06880
USA
Telephone: (203) 226-3580
Fax: (203) 221-0779

US readers wishing to order by mail,
please contact
AIRtime Publishing Inc. toll-free at
1 800 359-3003

Publisher: Stan Morse

Editors: David Donald
Jon Lake

Associate Editors:
Robert Hewson
Sophearith Moeng
Tim Senior
Gordon Swanborough

Sub Editor:
Karen Leverington

Authors: David Donald
Robert F. Dorr
John Fricker
Bill Green
Bill Gunston
Robert Hewson
Paul Jackson
Jon Lake
Sophearith Moeng
Lindsay Peacock
Gordon Swanborough
Mike Verier

Artists: Chris Davey
Grant Race
Mark Styling
John Weal

Origination by
Imago Publishing Ltd

Printed in Singapore

**WORLD AIR POWER JOURNAL
is published quarterly and
provides an in-depth analysis
of contemporary military
aircraft and their worldwide
operators. Superbly produced
and filled with extensive colour
photography, World Air Power
Journal is available by
subscription from:**

**UK, Europe and
Commonwealth:**
**Aerospace Publishing Ltd
FREEPOST
PO Box 2822
London, W6 0BR
UK
Telephone: 081-740 9554
Fax: 081-746 2556
(no stamp required if posted in
the UK)**

USA and Canada:
**AIRtime Publishing Inc.
Subscription Dept
10 Bay Street
Westport, CT 06880
USA
Telephone: (203) 226-3580
Toll-free number in USA:
1 800 359-3003**

Encyclopedia of World

MILITARY AIRCRAFT

Volume 2: L to Z

Edited by David Donald and Jon Lake

Aerospace Publishing London
AIRtime Publishing USA

Lake LA-4 Buccaneer, LA-250 Renegade and Seawolf

Derived indirectly from the C 1 Skimmer of 1948, the **Lake LA-4 Buccaneer** is a four-seat amphibian for the general aviation market, more than 1,300 of which have been built in several versions. Two LA-4s serve the **Royal Thai navy** for general duties. The current standard version is the **LA-250 Renegade**, which features a lengthened six-seat cabin and an uprated engine. In 1985, Lake introduced a military version of the Renegade, with surveillance, patrol and SAR among its design roles. This variant was named **Seawolf** and introduced armament and radar options. Search radar can be fitted on the front of the (pusher) engine nacelle, and four Alkan wing hardpoints – one inboard and one outboard of each outrigger balance float – provide for up to 594 lb (270 kg) of stores such as SAR, ECM, gun, rocket or reconnaissance pods, external tanks, flares and practice bombs.

SPECIFICATION

Lake Seawolf
Wing: span 38 ft 4 in (11.68 m); aspect ratio 8.7; area 170.00 sq ft (15.79 m2)
Fuselage and tail: length 28 ft 4 in (8.64 m); height 10 ft 0 in (3.05 m); tailplane span 10 ft 0 in (3.05 m); wheel track 11 ft 2 in (3.40 m); wheel base 10 ft 3 in (3.13 m)

The Seawolf features a search radar mounted on the front of the engine.

Powerplant: one Textron Lycoming IO-540-C4B5 flat-six piston engine rated at 290 hp (216 kW)
Weights: empty 2,200 lb (998 kg); maximum take-off 3,450 lb (1565 kg)
Fuel and load: internal fuel 88 US gal (333 litres); external fuel up to two 31-US gal (117.3-litre) drop tanks; maximum ordnance 400 lb (181 kg)
Speed: never exceed speed 148 kt (170 mph; 274 km/h); maximum level speed 'clean' at 6,500 ft (1980 m) 139 kt (160 mph; 258 km/h); maximum cruising speed at 6,500 ft (1980 m) 132 kt (152 mph; 245 km/h); economical cruising speed at optimum altitude 110 kt (127 mph; 204 km/h)
Range: ferry range 1,500 nm (1,727 miles; 2780 km) with drop tanks; range 875 nm (1,008 miles; 1622 km) with standard fuel; endurance 14 hours 30 minutes with drop tanks or 8 hours 30 minutes with standard fuel
Performance: maximum rate of climb at sea level 900 ft (274 m) per minute; service ceiling 14,700 ft (4480 m); take-off run 880 ft (268 m) at maximum take-off weight on land, or 1,250 ft (381 m) at maximum take-off weight on water; landing run 755 ft (230 m) at normal landing weight on land and water

---

Learjet (Gates) Models 24/25/35/36 and C-21

Learjet Inc.
One Learjet Way, PO Box 7707,
Wichita, KS 67277, USA

Some 200 examples of different models of the Learjet corporate twin-jet transport currently serve with military air arms. The smallest in the range is the **Learjet 24**, and the **Model 25** introduced a 52-in (1.32-m) fuselage plug to increase maximum seating from eight to 10. Both versions are powered by General Electric CJ610 turbojets. The **Model 35** is based on the Model 25, with a further 13-in (33-cm) stretch, greater wingspan and TFE731-2 turbofans. The **Model 36** was adapted as a long-range Model 35, with extra fuel in the fuselage, reducing standard seating from eight to six passengers.

Eighty-four **C-21A**s were acquired by the USAF in 1984, based on the commercial **Learjet 35A** version. The C-21A is used as an Operational Support Aircraft to carry up to eight passengers or 3,153 lb (1593 kg) of cargo, and has a convertible interior for the casevac role.

The Learjet company (previously Gates, now a subsidiary of Bombardier in Canada) has developed several special mission versions of the Model 35/36, based on the basic designation **C-35/36**. The specialised variants include the **EC-35A** for EW training simulation and related roles; **PC-35A** for maritime patrol; **RC-35A** and **RC-36A** for photo and/or radar reconnaissance, surveillance and mapping, with long-range oblique cameras in the fuselage, other cameras or SLAR in external pods. The **UC-35A** is a utility version for transport, navaid calibration, medevac and target towing. Some earlier aircraft have also been converted for reconnaissance/mapping duties.

USAF Learjets are assigned to wings for high-speed staff and light cargo transport. This C-21A wears the 'OF' codes of the 55th Wing, the Learjet unit being the 11th Airlift Flight.

SPECIFICATION

Learjet 35A
Wing: span 39 ft 6 in (12.04 m) with tip tanks; aspect ratio 5.7; area 253.3 sq ft (23.53 m2)
Fuselage and tail: length 48 ft 8 in (14.83 m); height 12 ft 3 in (3.73 m); tailplane span 14 ft 8 in (4.47 m); wheel track 8 ft 3 in (2.51 m); wheel base 20 ft 2 in (6.15 m)
Powerplant: two Garrett TFE731-2-2B turbofans each rated at 3,500 lb st (15.57 kN)
Weights: empty equipped 9,838 lb (4462 kg); maximum take-off 18,300 lb (8301 kg)
Fuel and load: internal fuel 931 US gal (3524 litres); external fuel none; maximum payload 3,500 lb (1588 kg)
Speed: never exceed speed Mach 0.83; maximum level speed at 25,000 ft (7620 m) 471 kt (542 mph; 872 km/h); maximum cruising speed at 41,000 ft (12495 m) 460 kt (529 mph; 851 km/h); economical cruising speed at 45,000 ft (13715 m) 418 kt (481 mph; 774 km/h)
Range: 2,289 nm (2,634 miles; 4,239 km) with four passengers
Performance: maximum rate of climb at sea level 4,340 ft (1323 m) per minute; service ceiling 45,000 ft (13715 m); take-off balanced field length 4,972 ft (1515 m) at 18,300 lb (8301 kg); landing run 3,075 ft (937 m) at maximum landing weight

OPERATORS

Argentina: three 35As for survey and two 35As for calibration with 3ª Esc. de Fotografico at Parana. One 24D also on strength
Bolivia: one 25B for survey and one 35A for VIP transport
Brazil: three reconnaissance aircraft (locally designated **R-35A**) flown by 1ª Esq in No. 6 Wing at Recife. Three **C-35A** and six **VU-35A** transports also operated
Chile: two 35As with Servicio Aerofotogrametrico

Ecuador: one survey 24D operated by the army for the Instituo Geografico Militar
Finland: three 35As serve at Utti, equipped with a removable underbelly radar and underwing hardpoints, with facilities for target towing
Japan: one **U-36A** (described separately under ShinMaywa) aircraft operated by 81 Kokutai of 31 Kokugun at Iwakuni
Mexico: two 35A transports with air force, one 24D transport with navy
Peru: two 25Bs and two 36As for survey with Servicio Aerofotografico Nacional at Las Palmas
Saudi Arabia: two 35As serve as VIP transports with No. 1 Squadron, RSAF
Serbia/Yugoslavia: one 25B transport
Switzerland: two 35A transports
Thailand: two 35As for survey with 605 Sqn at Don Muang
USAF: in 1994 82 C-21As remained in USAF service, positioned at many USAF bases to

Several operators use Learjets in the photo-mapping role. This camera-equipped Lear 25 serves with Bolivia.

provide fast staff and light cargo transport. Major units are 1st FW, 24th Wing and 55th Wing within ACC, 12th FTW in AETC, 774th ALF in Space Command, 412th TW in AFMC, 89th AW and 375th AW in AMC, 374th AW in PACAF, USEUCOM and 86th AW in USAFE, and the 201st ALS/DC ANG
US Army: one 35A used for staff transport by OSAC at Andrews AFB, MD
Venezuela: one 24D for VIP transport
Other users: in several countries specially-equipped Learjets are flown by civilian contractors on behalf of the military, including Australia (target facilities/EW), China (two RC-35A and three RC-36A for survey, the 35As being equipped with SLAR for geological survey), Germany (four 35A and 36A target-tugs), Slovenia (VIP transport), Sweden (target facilities), UK (target facilities/EW) and USA (target facilities/EW)

Learjet 35A/C-21A

LET **L-410 Turbolet**

Let Akciová Spolecnost
Uherské Hradisté, CR-686 04 Kunovice
Czech Republic

First flown on 16 April 1969, the **LET L-410 Turbolet** was the first aircraft of indigenous design to emerge from the Kunovice factory of the LET concern, set up in 1950. Intended as a light commuter transport, the L-410 achieved considerable success after some early difficulties, and was adopted by Aeroflot as its standard feeder-liner, as well as being exported to several East European countries, and elsewhere. Between 1,000 and 1,100 L-410s were built, of which 318 were for the Soviet Union, primarily in the **L-410UVP** and **L-410UVP-E** versions. Some of these still fly with the **Russian** armed forces.

The L-410UVP, which was first flown on 1 November 1977, was distinguished by an increased wingspan and greater vertical tail area, dihedral on the tailplane, improvements to the control system and other modifications. The L-410UVP was powered by two Motorlet M601B turboprops, as used in the earlier **L-410M**. After production of 495 of the UVP model by late 1985, LET changed to the UVP-E variant which had first flown on 30 December 1984. This introduced M601E engines, provision for extra fuel in wingtip tanks and some further control system and equipment improvements.

About 50 examples of the L-410M and (mostly) UVP were delivered for military use in the light transport and communications role. These were delivered to the **Bulgarian air force, Czechoslovak air force** (20) and **army** (two), **East Germany** (12), **Hungarian air force** and the **Libyan Arab Jamahiriya air force** (18). In East Germany, four L-410 UVPs were delivered to VS14, a liaison squadron, and eight to the

Otto Lilienthal Air Academy for multi-engine conversion. Following German re-unification, some or all of these L-410s were absorbed into the Luftwaffe. They were subsequently withdrawn from service and at least one was sold to the **Latvian air force. Slovenia** operates one for parachute training.

SPECIFICATION

Let L-410UVP-E Turbolet
Wing: span 19.48 m (63 ft 11 in) without tip tanks and 19.98 m (65 ft 6.5 in) with tip tanks; aspect ratio 10.79; area 35.18 m2 (378.67 sq ft)

Fuselage and tail: length 14.424 m (47 ft 4 in); height 5.83 m (19 ft 1.5 in); tailplane span 6.74 m (22 ft 1.25 in); wheel track 3.65 m (11 ft 11.5 in); wheel base 3.67 m (12 ft 0.25 in)
Powerplant: two Motorlet (Walter) M 601E turboprops each rated at 559 kW (750 shp)
Weights: empty 3985 kg (8,785 lb); operating empty 4160 kg (9,171 lb); maximum take-off 6400 kg (14,109 lb)
Fuel and load: internal fuel 1300 kg (2,866 lb); external fuel none; maximum payload 1615 kg (3,560 lb)
Speed: never exceed speed 357 km/h (192 kt; 222 mph); maximum level speed 'clean' at 4200 m (13,780 ft) 311 km/h (168 kt; 193 mph); maximum cruising speed at 4200 m (13,780 ft) 380 km/h (205 kt;

Originally purchased by East Germany, this LET 410UVP now wears the colours of Latvia.

236 mph); economical cruising speed at 4200 m (13,780 ft) 365 km/h (197 kt; 227 mph)
Range: 1380 km (744 nm; 858 km) with maximum fuel or 546 km (294 nm; 339 miles) with maximum payload
Performance: maximum rate of climb at sea level 444 m (1,455 ft) per minute; service ceiling 6320 m (20,735 ft); take-off run 445 m (1,460 ft) at maximum take-off weight; take-off distance to 10.7 m (35 ft) 685 m (2,250 ft) at maximum take-off weight; landing distance from 9 m (30 ft) 480 m (1,575 ft) at normal landing weight; landing run 240 m (787 ft) at normal landing weight

---

Lisunov **Li-2 'Cab'**

The **Lisunov Li-2 'Cab'** is a Soviet version of the Douglas DC-3 (described separately) licensed before World War II. A few examples remain in service with the People's Liberation Army Air Force in **China** and in **Russia**. Initially designated **PS-84**, the aircraft was used by Aeroflot and the Red Army, which armed many of its

aircraft, sometimes with a dorsal gun turret. The original 671-kW (900-hp) Shvetsov M-62 radial engines were replaced by 746-kW (1,000-hp) Shvetsov ASh-62 engines on the post-war **Li-2P**, which became the major production variant and was supplied to the ADD (and later A-DVD) for short- and medium-range trooping in Eastern

Europe and the USSR. It was estimated that about 1,000 aircraft remained in service with the Soviet air forces during the 1950s, although many of these probably doubled their duties as back-up on domestic Aeroflot services. Variants included the **Li-2G** civil and **Li-2T** military freighters, **Li-2PG** convertible trooper/freighter, **Li-2D** paratrooper and the **Li-2V** high-altitude version with 895-kW (1,200-hp) radials. Some of the Li-2Ps and Li-2Gs appeared with wingspan reduced to 28.04 m (92 ft).

During the 1950s, as the Il-12 and Il-14 took over the majority of short-haul transport duties, the Li-2s underwent limited refurbishment for export among Communist Bloc air forces, the type being supplied in quantity to China, Poland, Bulgaria, Czechoslovakia, North Korea and Romania; in Hungary the type was named the **Teve** (Camel), reflecting its utilitarian transport role. A few examples may remain in service in **North Korea**.

Lockheed **C-5 Galaxy**

Lockheed Aeronautical Systems Company
86 South Cobb Drive, Marietta
GA 30063, USA

The **Lockheed C-5 Galaxy** heavy logistics transport is the workhorse of US strategic airlift and is flown by active, Reserve and Air National Guard units for the **US Air Force**'s Air Mobility Command. The C-5 originated with a 1963 USAF CX-HLS (Cargo Experimental – Heavy Logistics System) requirement for a capability to carry 250,000 lb (113400 kg) over 3,000 miles (2,606 nm; 4828 km) without air refuelling.

The Galaxy is a high-wing, T-tailed transport with four underwing pod-mounted TF39 turbofan engines and main undercarriage retracting into fuselage pods. The Galaxy's value for rapid deployment of large or heavy items of equipment has been demonstrated repeatedly. Key to the C-5's mission is its cavernous interior and 'roll-on/roll-off' capability with access to the vast cargo bay at both front and rear. The Galaxy has an upward-lifting visor nose which can be raised above the cockpit for loading/ unloading, while standard clamshell doors accommodate loading/unloading at the rear.

The Galaxy's primary mission is to carry equipment and vehicles, although it can be configured for up to 363 passengers (73 on the upper rear deck, 290 in the main compartment). The upper deck houses the flight crew of five (pilot, co-pilot, flight engineer and two load masters).

The **C-5A** first flew on 30 June 1968. The first operational C-5A was delivered on 17 December 1969, and deliveries were completed in May 1973. The C-5A suffered initially from wing crack problems and cost overruns, but has served well after a teething period. From 1981 to 1987, 77 C-5As underwent a rewinging programme, intended to increase service life to 30,000 hours. The wings are of virtually new design, apart from the moving surfaces, and incorporate new aluminium alloy for greater

strength and corrosion resistance.

In the mid-1980s, the production line was reopened to meet an urgent USAF demand for additional heavy airlift capacity. Fifty **C-5B** models were built, essentially similar to the C-5A but incorporating modifications and improvements resulting from operations with the C-5A. The C-5B dispensed with the C-5A's complex crosswind main landing gear and introduced improved AFCS (automated flight control system) and MADAR II (malfunction detection and analysis and

recording system). The first production C-5B was delivered on 8 January 1986 and deliveries were completed by April 1989.

On a typical mission, a Galaxy can carry 300,000 lb (136080 kg) to a range of 3,434 miles (5526 km). Typical loads include two M1A1 Abrams main battle tanks, four M551 Sheridan light tanks plus one HMMWV tactical vehicle, 16 ¾-ton trucks, 10 LAV-25 (light armoured vehicles), or a CH-47 Chinook helicopter. The aircraft provides the most ton-miles at the fastest speed of any

The C-5 Galaxy remains the USAF's most valuable airlift asset, serving with an Air Mobility Command wing on each coast and a training unit at Altus. The C-5's prodigious capacity and global reach make it crucial to the US rapid deployment forces.

Lockheed C-5 Galaxy

Lockheed C-5B Galaxy

The current camouflage scheme for Air Mobility Command airlifters is this 'proud grey'. This is considered to offer the best protection in the air and on the ground.

American airlifter. Although not usually assigned airdrop duties, the Galaxy can also drop paratroopers. On 7 June 1989, a C-5B air-dropped four M551 Sheridan tanks and 73 soldiers for a world record of 190,346 lb (86313 kg).

The C-5A/B serves with two Air Mobility Command wings, the 60th AW at Travis AFB, CA, and the 436th AW at Dover, DE. Two Reserve squadrons (68th AS at Kelly AFB, TX, and 337th AS at Westover AFB, MA) and one Air National Guard squadron (137th AS at Stewart IAP, NY) fly C-5As. Four further Reserve units (301st/312th AS at Travis and 326th/709th AS at Dover) support the active-duty force through the Associate programme. Training for the Galaxy

fleet is provided by AETC's 97th Air Mobility Wing at Altus AFB, OK.

Known to crews as 'FRED', for Fantastic Ridiculous Economic Disaster, the C-5A/B has served admirably and economically in airlifts supporting US operations in Vietnam, Israel during the October War of 1973, and the Desert Shield/Storm effort of 1990-91. During Operation Desert Shield, C-5A/Bs flew 42 per cent of cargo and 18.6 per cent of passenger missions in an effort which exceeded in 17 days the total tonnage of the 65-week Berlin Airlift, and totalled 15,800 missions with 498,900 passengers. One C-5A Galaxy of the 60th MAW (Travis AFB, CA) crewed by Reservists of the 433rd MAW (Kelly AFB, TX) crashed at Ramstein, Germany, on 29 August 1990, the only transport lost in the airlift.

Under the Pacer Snow project, two C-5s received a trial installation of ALE-40 flare dispensers and an AAR-47 missile warning system to provide a measure of self-

defence. The **C-5C** designation covers two Galaxies which have been modified with sealed front visor and strengthened interior for the carriage of satellites and space equipment.

In 1994, Lockheed is promoting an uprated **C-5D** variant, with new powerplant, to alleviate a projected shortfall in USAF strategic airlift capability.

SPECIFICATION

Lockheed C-5B Galaxy
Wing: span 222 ft 8.5 in (67.88 m); aspect ratio 7.75; area 6,200.00 sq ft (575.98 m²)
Fuselage and tail: length 247 ft 10 in (75.54 m); height 65 ft 1.5 in (19.85 m); tailplane span 68 ft 8.5 in (20.94 m); wheel track 37 ft 5.5 in (11.42 m); wheel base 72 ft 11 in (22.22 m)
Powerplant: four General Electric TF39-GE-1C turbofans each rated at 43,000 lb st (191.27 kN)
Weights: operating empty 374,000 lb (169643 kg);

maximum take-off 837,000 lb (379657 kg)
Fuel and load: internal fuel 332,500 lb (150815 kg); external fuel none; maximum payload 261,000 lb (118387 kg)
Speed: never exceed speed 402 kt (463 mph; 745 km/h) CAS; maximum level speed at 25,000 lb (7620 m) 496 kt (571 mph; 919 km/h); maximum cruising speed at 25,000 lb (7620 m) between 460 and 480 kt (552 and 564 mph; 888 and 908 km/h); economical cruising speed at 25,000 ft (7,620 m) 450 kt (518 mph; 833 km/h)
Range: 5,618 nm (6,469 miles; 10411 km) with maximum fuel or 2,982 nm (3,434 miles; 5526 km) with maximum payload
Performance: maximum rate of climb at sea level 1,725 ft (525 m) per minute; service ceiling 35,750 ft (10895 m) at 615,000 lb (278960 kg); take-off run 8,300 ft (2530 m) at maximum take-off weight; take-off distance to 50 ft (15 m) 9,800 ft (2987 m) at maximum take-off weight; landing distance from 50 ft (15 m) 3,820 ft (1164 m) at maximum landing weight; landing run 2,380 ft (725 m) at maximum landing weight

Lockheed **C-130 Hercules** transport versions

The **Lockheed C-130 Hercules** is the West's most popular and widely used military transport aircraft, in use for a wide range of airlift duties, and has been in production longer than any other aircraft type in history. Huge numbers remain in service on every continent, and many operators have replaced early variants with newer versions.

The **YC-130** prototype made its maiden flight on 23 August 1954, introducing the 3,250-eshp (2424-ekW) Allison YT56A-1 turboprop engine, which has itself evolved into the 4,900-eshp 3654-ekW) T56-A-15 used today on production **C-130H**s and other upgraded variants. Four decades later, the Hercules seems certain to remain in production into a new century. No newer aircraft design has proven more practical at hauling people, vehicles, equipment and supplies within a combat theatre. US Air Force, Navy and Marine Corps C-130s have served in

Vietnam, Grenada, Panama, the Persian Gulf, Somalia and Bosnia, while other operators, including the Royal Air Force, have added further combat experience to the aircraft's history. The number of countries operating C-130 variants now exceeds 60. The soundness of the basic Hercules design has led to numerous specialised versions optimised for gunship, rescue, tanker, drone control, reconnaissance and other missions.

The Hercules design employs a high wing, unobstructed cargo compartment, an integral 'roll-on/roll-off' rear loading ramp, a fully pressurised cargo hold which can rapidly be reconfigured for the carriage of troops, stretchers or passengers, and a floor at truck-bed height above the ground. The Hercules can be employed for air drops of troops or equipment and for LAPES (low-altitude parachute extraction system) delivery of heavy cargoes, and for the full range

of cargo, troop transport and medical evacuation duties. The standard unstretched Hercules can carry 78 troops (92 in a high-density configuration) or 64 paratroops, or up to 74 stretcher litters. Its capacious hold measures 41 ft (12.50 m) in length, 10.3 ft (3.14 m) in width, and is 9 ft (2.74 m) high at the lowest point.

The first two **YC-130A** prototypes came from the manufacturer's California 'Skunk Works', while more than 2,000 subsequent aircraft have been built in Marietta, Georgia. The first production **C-130A** flew on 7 April 1955, and deliveries to the US Air Force began in December of that year. All surviving C-130As now have four-bladed propellers, an extended tailcone housing a crash position indicator and AN/APN-59 radar in the reprofiled 'Pinnochio' nose, features originally associated with the later **C-130B**.

The oldest version of the Hercules in widespread use in the early 1990s was the C-130B, which introduced engine improvements for the type's original T56-A-1A engine, increased fuel capacity and Hamilton Standard Model 54H60-91 13-ft 6-in (4.17-m) four-bladed hydromatic propellers. The C-130B variant did not usually carry wing pylons for external fuel, and had better radius, range and endurance than other variants whose external wing tanks do not 'earn' their penalty in weight and drag. The Navy procured seven utility transport Hercules based on the C-130B, and designated these **GV-1U** and later **C-130F**.

In late 1961, production changed to the **C-130E** variant for the USAF and other operators, introducing 4,050-eshp (3020-ekW) T56-A-7 engines with increased power for improved 'hot-and-high' performance. Maximum take-off weight went up from 124,200 lb (56336 kg) in the C-130A to 175,000 lb (79379 kg), and required strengthened wing spars, thicker skins and a reinforced undercarriage to be fitted. The E model also introduced larger 1,360-US gal (5148-litre) external underwing tanks mounted between the inner and outer wing panels, and most Es have their forward cargo doors sealed. In service, the C-130E has been extensively upgraded and updated, with new avionics, a tactical precision approach system, and a self-contained navigation system.

The Navy's **C-130G** was a utility transport version based on the C-130E. The four aircraft were later modified as TACAMO communications relay aircraft and were redesignated **EC-130G**. After replacement by the E-6A, three aircraft were returned to

The Hercules is at its best operating into short, rough airstrips, proving its sturdiness and short-field ability. Seen during an airlift exercise, this is a C-130H of the Portuguese air force.

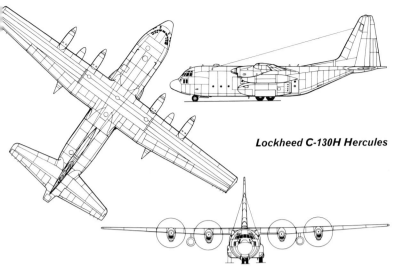

Lockheed C-130H Hercules

transport configuration (albeit with no cargo ramp) as **TC-130G**s, one now serving as the support aircraft for the 'Blue Angels' aerobatic team.

The current basic transport version, the C-130H, was developed for export customers, first flying in November 1964 and being delivered to the RNZAF in March 1965. The first delivery to the USAF occurred in April 1975. The new version has a redesigned and strengthened wing box, improved brakes and a new avionics suite, and is powered by improved T56-A-15 engines. Most lack provision for RATOG bottles. T56-A-15 powerplants and other features of the H model, including improved brakes and strengthened centre-wing design, have been retrofitted to many earlier Hercules airframes. Some C-130H transports can be fitted internally for medevac duties. Two Moroccan C-130Hs are fitted with SLAR pods on the port undercarriage fairing, and three USAF aircraft were extensively modified for participation in Operation Eagle Claw (the Iranian hostage rescue mission) with RATOG, aerodynamic improvements for better STOL performance and retro rockets for improved braking.

The C-130H served as the basis for a number of other variants, including the **C-130H(AEH)**, an airborne hospital aircraft used by Saudi Arabia, and the **C-130H-MP** maritime patroller supplied to Malaysia and Indonesia. The **C-130K** for Britain is essentially a C-130H with British avionics and equipment, incorporating some parts made by Scottish Aviation and fitted out by Marshall of Cambridge, which has become perhaps the world's leading Hercules refurbishing and modification centre, apart from Lockheed itself. The RAF's 66 C-130Ks were delivered as **Hercules C.Mk 1**s, although subsequent modification programmes have led to the allocation of new designations. During the Falklands War, 25 aircraft were fitted with inflight-refuelling probes to become **Hercules C.Mk 1P**s, and six others received a hose-drum refuelling unit and extra tanks in the hold to serve as tankers under the designation **Hercules C.Mk 1K**. Four of the tankers, and two C.Mk 1Ps used by No. 47 Squadron's Special Forces Flight, are equipped with wingtip-mounted Racal Orange Blossom ESM pods for surveillance tasks. The Special Forces support aircraft also have an extensive suite of defensive systems (including a Missile Approach Warning System) and an integrated INS/GPS. A single aircraft was converted for Meteorological Research duties under the designation **W.Mk 2**, and 30 have been stretched by the insertion of fuselage plugs to become **C.Mk 3**s. They are redesignated **C.Mk 3P** when retrofitted with an inflight-refuelling probe. The 15-ft (4.57-m) stretch (as used

The C-130 has been used for a huge variety of tasks other than the basic transport mission. Malaysia operates three C-130H-MPs for maritime patrol with a secondary transport tasking.

by the civilian **L-100-30**) increases maximum capacity from 92 to 128 troops. A prototype was converted by Lockheed, first flying on 3 December 1979, and was followed by aircraft converted by Marshall. Similarly stretched C-130Hs were built for Algeria, Cameroon, Colombia, Dubai, France, Indonesia, Nigeria and Thailand, as **C-130H-30**s, the initial designation of **C-130H(S)** having been dropped.

A number of military operators use the civilian version of the Hercules, which bears the company designation **L-100**. Certificated in February 1965, the basic L-100 was broadly equivalent to the C-130E, without pylon tanks or military equipment. The **L-100-20** was given plugs fore (5 ft/ 1.52 m) and aft (3.3 ft/1.02 m) of the wing. The L-100-30 has a full 15-ft (4.57-m) fuselage stretch and is operated by Dubai, Ecuador, Gabon, Indonesia and Kuwait.

On a 'real life' tactical mission, the Hercules can haul a payload of up to 38,702 lb (17555 kg) (C-130E) or 43,400 lb (19686 kg) (C-130H) to a range of 1,428 miles (2298 km) with a 45-minute fuel reserve and can make a tactical landing on an unprepared airstrip using 4,880 ft (1463 m) of landing roll. On famine relief missions into Somalia, C-130E/H transports with a reduced payload of 22,000 lb (9980 kg) routinely landed in 3,000 ft (930 m) of undeveloped airstrip. On other military missions, a Hercules can carry five HMMWV tactical vehicles, five 8,818-lb (4000-kg) rectangular palletised freight containers, or three Land Rover-type vehicles and two trailers.

For airborne operations, the C-130E carries 64 fully equipped paratroopers to a radius of up to 710 miles (1142 km) for a combat airdrop with a 45-minute fuel reserve. Most C-130 tactical airlift units are equipped with station-keeping equipment to facilitate formation flying in daylight on tactical missions. C-130Es of two USAF wings are equipped with AWADS (adverse weather aerial delivery system) to permit close formation flight during low-level air-

drop operations at night and in bad weather.

Lockheed is proceeding to develop a much-improved, high-technology Hercules designated **C-130J** and unofficially called **Hercules 2**. The C-130J proposal retains four engines rather than a twin-engined layout that was briefly contemplated, the new aircraft being powered by four Allison 2100 turboprop engines driving six-bladed, composite propellers. The C-130J, privately funded but responding to a US Air Force statement of need, will have a two-man automated cockpit with four flat-panel liquid crystal displays, eliminating navigator and flight engineer crew positions. The wing will have no pylons or provision for external tanks, a return to the 'slick wing' configuration of the C-130B model. Many existing Hercules users are considering the aircraft as a potential replacement for their first-generation C-130s, including the RAF and Australia. Lockheed is prepared to deliver a production C-130J in 1996 or 1997. Starting on 19 March 1994, an RAF Hercules C.Mk 1P was used for a 50-hour flight-test programme of the Allison AE2100D3 turboprop fitted in the inner port nacelle and driving a six-bladed Dowty R391 propeller.

Other sub-types closely based upon the above transport versions include the **TC-130A** trainer, the **JC-130A/B/F** and **NC-130A/B/E/H** test aircraft, the recce-configured **RC-130A**, the battlefield illumination **RC-130S**, the **VC-130B/H** VIP and staff transport, and the **WC-130B/E/H** weather reconnaissance ships.

Rescue, EW, gunship, special forces, tanker, and ABCC Hercules variants are described separately.

SPECIFICATION

Lockheed C-130F Hercules

Wing: span 132 ft 7 in (40.41 m); aspect ratio 10.09; area 1,745.00 sq ft (161.12 m²)

Fuselage and tail: length 97 ft 9 in (29.79 m); height 38 ft 3 in (11.66 m); tailplane span 52 ft 8 in (16.05 m); wheel track 14 ft 3 in (4.35 m); wheel base 32 ft 0.75 in (9.77 m)

Powerplant: four Allison T56-A-7 turboprops each rated at 4,050 ehp (3020 ekW)

Many C-130 operators have fire-fighting equipment for use in transport Hercules. This is a California ANG C-130E, demonstrating the MAFFS kit.

Weights: empty equipped 69,300 lb (31434 kg); maximum take-off 135,000 lb (61236 kg)

Fuel and load: internal fuel 5,050 US gal (19116 litres); external fuel two 450-US gal (1703-litre) underwing tanks; maximum payload 35,700 lb (16194 kg)

Speed: maximum cruising speed at 30,000 ft (9145 m) 321 kt (370 mph; 595 km/h)

Range: 4,210 nm (4,848 miles; 7802 km) with maximum fuel or 1,910 nm (2,199 miles; 3539 km) with maximum payload

Performance: maximum rate of climb at sea level 2,000 ft (610 m) per minute; service ceiling 34,000 ft (10365 m); take-off distance to 50 ft (15 m) 4,300 ft (1311 m) at maximum take-off weight

OPERATORS

1994 service status of transport-configured C-130s as follows (tanker and other versions detailed separately):

US Air Force (active-duty): approximately 200 C-130E/Hs serving with Air Combat Command (7th Wing – Dyess AFB, 23rd Wing – Pope AFB, 24th Wing – Howard AFB, and 314th Airlift Wing – Little Rock AFB), AFSOC (353rd SOG – Kadena AB), PACAF (3rd Wing – Elmendorf AFB, and 374th AW – Yokota AB) and USAFE (435th AW – Rhein Main AB).

US Air National Guard: over 200 C-130E/Hs serving with 19 ANG units from the following states: Alaska (144th AS), Arkansas (154th TS – training unit), California (115th AS), Delaware (142nd AS), Georgia (158th AS), Kentucky (165th AS), Maryland (135th AS), Minnesota (109th AS), Missouri (180th AS), New York (139th AS), North Carolina (156th AS), Ohio (164th AS), Oklahoma (185th AS), Rhode Island (143rd AS), Tennessee (105th AS), Texas (181st AS), West Virginia (130th and 167th AS) and Wyoming (187th AS).

US Air Force Reserve: over 100 C-130E/Hs assigned to 12 squadrons: 700th AS/94th AW, 731st AS/302nd AW, 815th AS/403rd AW, 95th AS/440th AW, 357th AS/908th AG, 757th AS/910th AG, 758th AS/911th AG, 327th AS/913th AG, 328th AS/914th AG, 711th SOS/919th SOW, 64th AS/928th AG and 96th AS/934th AG.

US Navy: VR-53 and VR-54 (USNR) operate the C-130T from Martinsburg RAP and NAS New Orleans,

Lockheed C-130 Hercules transport versions

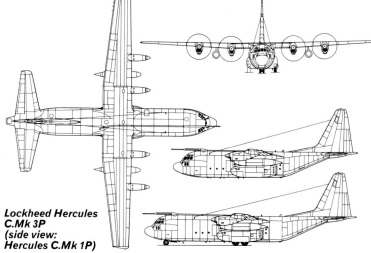

Lockheed Hercules C.Mk 3P (side view: Hercules C.Mk 1P)

For strategic airlift tasks, the stretched C-130H-30 offers far greater payload capacity but with reduced field performance. Indonesia has five with No. 32 Sqn.

respectively. VRC-50 flies the C-130F from Andersen AFB, Guam. The 'Blue Angels' display team has a single support TC-130G transport, operated with US Marine Corps titles.

Algeria: C-130H (10), C-130H-30 (8) serving with Escadrilles 31^e, 32^e, 33e and 35^e

Argentina: C-130B (2), C-130H (6), L-100-30 (1) serving with I Escuadrón, I Grupo

Australia: C-130E (12), C-130H (12) serving with Nos 36 and 37 Sqns at Richmond

Belgium: C-130H (12) serving with 20 Smaldeel/ Escadrille at Brussels

Bolivia: C-130A (5), C-130H (1) flying with Grupo Aéreo de Transporte 71 at La Paz

Brazil: C-130E (10), C-130H (4) serving with 1° Esq/1° GTT at Galeão and 2° Esq/1° GTT at Campo dos Alfonsos

Cameroon: C-130H (1)

Canada: CC-130E (19), CC-130H (11) serving with Nos 424 (SAR), 426 and 437 Sqns at Trenton, No. 413 Sqn at Greenwood (SAR), Nos 418 (SAR) and 435 Sqns at Namao. Five C-130Hs are KCC-130 tankers

Chad: C-130A (1), C-130H (1), C-130H-30 (1)

Chile: C-130B (4), C-130H (2) operated by Grupo de Aviación 10 at Santiago-Merino Benitez

Colombia: C-130B (5), C-130H (2) with the Escuadrón de Transporte at Bogota

Denmark: C-130H (3) flying with Eskadrille 721 at Vaerløse

Ecuador: C-130B (2), C-130H (1) serving with Ala de Transporte 11 at Quito-Mariscal Sucre

Egypt: C-130H (21), C-130H-30 (3). Two C-130Hs used in VIP role and two as electronic warfare platforms

France: C-130H (3), C-130H-30 (9) operated by Escadron de Transport 2/61 at Orléans-Bricy

Gabon: C-130H (1), L-100-20 (1)

Greece: C-130B (4), C-130H (11) with 356 Mira, 112 Ptérix at Elefsis

Honduras: C-130A (3)

India: order for 12 C-130H

Indonesia: C-130B (14), C-130H (3), C-130H-30 (5) flying with No. 31 Sqn at Jakarta-Halim and No. 32 Sqn at Malang

Iran: C-130H (approximately 10 believed serviceable)

Israel: C-130E (12), C-130H (9) serving with 131 Squadron which absorbed 103 Squadron's C-130Es

Italy: C-130H (12) with 50° Gruppo, 46ª Brigata at Pisa

Japan: C-130H (15) based with 401 Hikotai at Komatsu

Jordan: C-130B (2), C-130H (4) operated by No. 3 Sqn at Amman

Kuwait: L-100-30 (2) flown by No. 41 Sqn at Al al Salem

Libya: C-130H (7), L-100-20 (2), L-100-30 (2)

Malaysia: C-130H (5), C-130H-30 (1), C-130H-MP (3) serving with Nos 4 and 14 Sqns at Simpang

Mexico: C-130A (10) flying with Escuadrón Aéreo Transporte Pesado at Santa Lucia

Morocco: C-130H (17) based at Kenitra

Netherlands: C-130H-30 (2) with No. 334 Sqn at Eindhoven

New Zealand: C-130H (5) flying with No. 40 Sqn at Whenuapai

Niger: C-130H (2) based at Niamey

Nigeria: C-130H (6), C-130H-30 (3) based at Lagos

Norway: C-130H (6) serving with No. 335 Skvadron at Gardermoen

Oman: C-130H (3) operated by No. 4 Squadron at Muscat/Seeb

Pakistan: C-130B (7), C-130E (4), L-100 (1) serving with No. 6 Tactical Transport Squadron at Rawalpindi and the Transport Conversion Squadron at Chaklala

Peru: C-130A (3), L-100-20 (5) flying with Grupo de Transporte 41 at Lima-Jorge Chavez

Philippines: C-130B (2), C-130H (2) flown by 222 Squadron at Mactan

Portugal: C-130H (4), C-130H-30 (2) serving with Esquadra de Transport 501 at Montijo

Saudi Arabia: C-130E (7), C-130H (21), VC-130H (4), C-130H AEH (3), L-100-30 (6). Transports flown by Nos 4 and 16 Sqns at Jeddah, VIP aircraft and air ambulances (including L-100-30s) operated by Saudia/No. 1 Sqn based at Riyadh

Singapore: C-130H (5) flying with 122 Sqn at Changi

South Africa: C-130B (7) based with No. 28 Sqn at Waterkloof

South Korea: C-130H (8), C-130H-30 (4) based at Seoul

Spain: C-130H (6), C-130H-30 (1) flying with Ala 31 at Zaragoza

Sudan: C-130H (6) based at Khartoum

Sweden: C-130H/Tp 84 (8) based with F7 at Satenas

Taiwan: C-130H (12) with a further 12 on order

Thailand: C-130H (7), C-130H-30 (6) operated by 601 Squadron at Bangkok-Don Muang

Tunisia: C-130H (2) based at Bizerte

Turkey: C-130B (6), C-130E (5), C-130H (1) operated by 222 Squadron at Erkilet

United Arab Emirates: C-130H (4), C-130H-30 (1), L-100-30 (1) flying from Bateen AB and Mindhat AB

United Kingdom: C.Mk 1K (6), C.Mk 1P (25), C.Mk 3P (29). Most operated by the Lyneham Transport Wing, (pool of Nos 24, 30, 47 and 70 Sqns, with 57(R) Sqn), but two by 1312 Flt at Mount Pleasant. Single W.Mk 2 in use with DRA Boscombe Down

Uruguay: C-130B (2) based at Montevideo

Venezuela: C-130H (6) operated by Escuadrón 62 at Maracay-El Libertador

Vietnam: 13 C-130As put into use following North Vietnamese victory. A handful remain in open storage at Tan Son Nhut and Bien Hoa

Yemen: C-130H (2) based at Sana'a

Zaïre: C-130H (4) serving with 191^e Escadrille at Kinshasa

Lockheed AC-130A/E/H 'Spectre'

Lockheed Aircraft Services Company
1800 East Airport Drive, Ontario
CA 91761-0033, USA

From early experience in the Vietnam War, the **USAF** perceived a need for quick-reaction concentrated firepower for use against small targets, especially where defenders of isolated areas were subject to nocturnal attack. The first solution was the Gunship I conversion of the Douglas C-47 as the AC-47, known informally as 'Puff the Magic Dragon' or 'Spooky'. Initially fitted with three side-firing 7.62-mm (0.3-in) general-purpose machine-guns, they were soon refitted with three 7.62-mm multi-barrelled Miniguns.

With the system operational, there was a need to improve firepower, sensing equipment, targeting and armour. The Fairchild C-119 was adapted as the AC-119G Shadow and AC-119K Stinger with the 17th and 18th Special Operations Squadrons, respectively, while USAF's Aeronautical Systems Division began converting the 13th production C-130A (54-1626) to Gunship II standard in 1965. This involved installation of four 20-mm Vulcan cannon, four 7.62-mm Miniguns, flare equipment and improved sighting. This aircraft was tested operationally in Vietnam in late 1967, and LTV Electrosystems was awarded an immediate contract to modify seven JC-130A missile trackers to **Lockheed AC-130A** standard. Weaponry remained the same but these aircraft were fitted with an APQ-133 beacon tracker, an AN/APQ-136 MTI radar and a new analog computer, searchlight, sensors, target-acquisition and direct-view image intensifiers. Four were in service in Vietnam by the end of 1968 with the 14th Air Commando Wing operating from Ubon in Thailand. A further single C-130 was converted in the Surprise Package project with two 40-mm cannon replacing two of the 20-mm variety, and with computerised fire control. Nine more C-130A conversions were delivered to the same standards in the Pave Pronto programme, with Black Crow ignition sensor and a new AN/ASQ-24A Stabilised Tracking Set containing ASQ-145 LLTV and an AVQ-18 laser designator.

So successful was the project that 11 C-130Es were converted to **AC-130E** standard in the Pave Spectre programme. The aircraft were given heavier armour, bet-

ter avionics including APQ-150 beacon tracking radar, and provision for more ammunition; from 1973, the 10 survivors were brought to **AC-130H** standard with the installation of uprated T56-A-15 engines. The final developments for use in South East Asia were the fitting of a 105-mm howitzer and laser target designator in the Pave Aegis programme. At the end of the Vietnam War, remaining AC-130A/H aircraft returned to the US to serve with the 1st Special Operations Wing at Eglin AFB. AC-130Hs had their rear Miniguns deleted and do not usually carry forward Miniguns, either; from 1978, the aircraft were fitted with inflight-refuelling receptacles. The SOFI (Special Operations Force Improvement) programme of the early 1990s upgraded the sensors, fire control computers, ECM and nav/comms suite. The 1st SOW has renumbered as the 16th SOW.

The AC-130 was used operationally again with the US occupation of Grenada in October 1983, and was later involved in operations in Panama (1989) and the Gulf (1991). Five AC-130Hs were used in Desert Storm to conduct night operations against ground targets. One aircraft was lost in the Gulf and another during operations over Somalia in 1994. AC-130Hs have also been on night patrol over Bosnia, flying from Brindisi.

With the entry into service of the improved **AC-130U** model (described separately under Rockwell), the AC-130Hs, which number nine aircraft, are being cascaded to the Air Force Reserve's 711th Special Operations Squadron at Duke Field, FL, which currently operates the surviving AC-130As.

A Pave Pronto Plus AC-130A leaves a trail of smoke as it lets rip with its Miniguns.

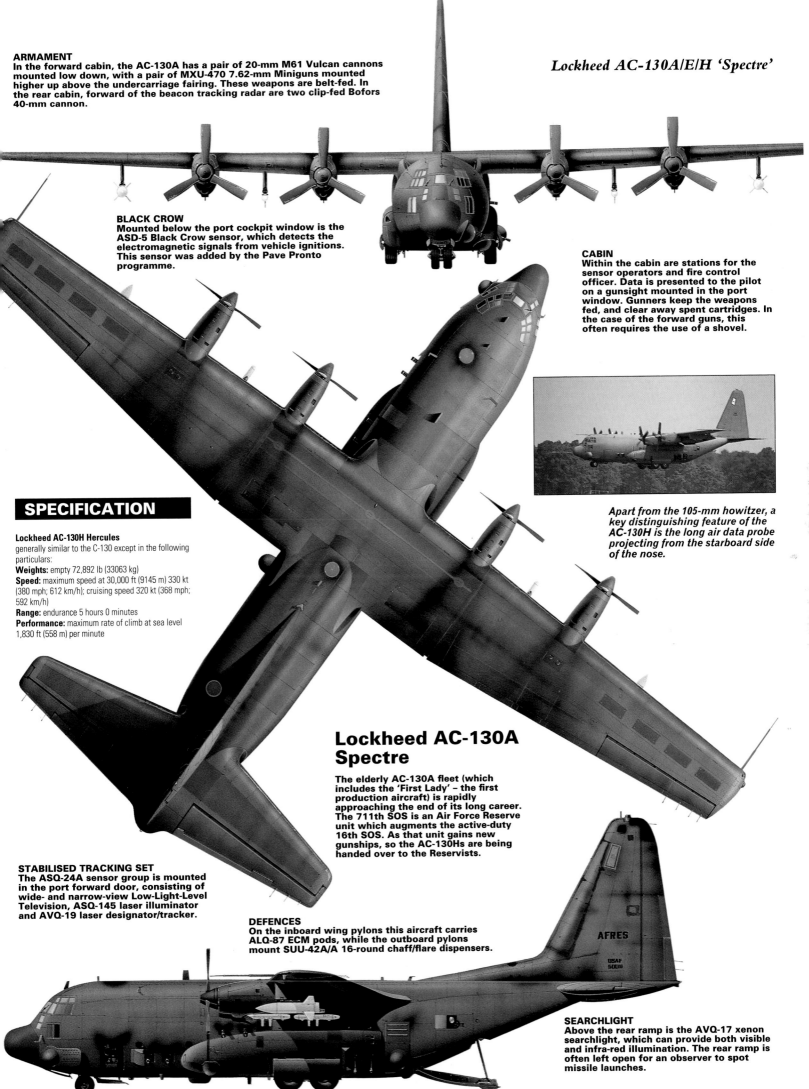

ARMAMENT
In the forward cabin, the AC-130A has a pair of 20-mm M61 Vulcan cannons mounted low down, with a pair of MXU-470 7.62-mm Miniguns mounted higher up above the undercarriage fairing. These weapons are belt-fed. In the rear cabin, forward of the beacon tracking radar are two clip-fed Bofors 40-mm cannon.

Lockheed AC-130A/E/H 'Spectre'

BLACK CROW
Mounted below the port cockpit window is the ASD-5 Black Crow sensor, which detects the electromagnetic signals from vehicle ignitions. This sensor was added by the Pave Pronto programme.

CABIN
Within the cabin are stations for the sensor operators and fire control officer. Data is presented to the pilot on a gunsight mounted in the port window. Gunners keep the weapons fed, and clear away spent cartridges. In the case of the forward guns, this often requires the use of a shovel.

Apart from the 105-mm howitzer, a key distinguishing feature of the AC-130H is the long air data probe projecting from the starboard side of the nose.

SPECIFICATION

Lockheed AC-130H Hercules
generally similar to the C-130 except in the following particulars:
Weights: empty 72,892 lb (33063 kg)
Speed: maximum speed at 30,000 ft (9145 m) 330 kt (380 mph; 612 km/h); cruising speed 320 kt (368 mph; 592 km/h)
Range: endurance 5 hours 0 minutes
Performance: maximum rate of climb at sea level 1,830 ft (558 m) per minute

Lockheed AC-130A Spectre

The elderly AC-130A fleet (which includes the 'First Lady' – the first production aircraft) is rapidly approaching the end of its long career. The 711th SOS is an Air Force Reserve unit which augments the active-duty 16th SOS. As that unit gains new gunships, so the AC-130Hs are being handed over to the Reservists.

STABILISED TRACKING SET
The ASQ-24A sensor group is mounted in the port forward door, consisting of wide- and narrow-view Low-Light-Level Television, ASQ-145 laser illuminator and AVQ-19 laser designator/tracker.

DEFENCES
On the inboard wing pylons this aircraft carries ALQ-87 ECM pods, while the outboard pylons mount SUU-42A/A 16-round chaff/flare dispensers.

SEARCHLIGHT
Above the rear ramp is the AVQ-17 xenon searchlight, which can provide both visible and infra-red illumination. The rear ramp is often left open for an observer to spot missile launches.

Lockheed DC-130 Hercules

The **Lockheed DC-130 Hercules** is a drone controller aircraft used for a variety of missions as a mother ship and launcher for RPVs, including some employed for reconnaissance in combat. These are carried on four underwing pylons.

Eight **DC-130A** aircraft (seven converted from C-130A, one converted from C-130D) were supplied to the US Air Force. DC-130As launched Combat Dawn reconnaissance RPVs in the Vietnam conflict and in a short-lived effort in Korea. Five of the USAF aircraft were subsequently transferred to the US Navy for drone target work. Three ex-**US Navy** DC-130As are operated by Tracor Flight Systems on behalf of the Naval Air Warfare Center at Point

Mugu, CA. These have AN/APN-45 tracking radar in an extended thimble nose, and can have an additional 'chin' radome for microwave guidance.

Seven similar **DC-130E**s were used for carrying reconnaissance drones during the Vietnam War, but all were subsequently converted back to transport configuration. A single **DC-130H** was converted from an HC-130H airframe during 1975-76, and was later redesignated **NC-130H**, although it continued to operate as a drone launcher and control aircraft. It now serves with the **USAF**'s 6514th Test Squadron at Hill AFB.

Three DC-130As are flown from Mojave in support of US Navy tests.

Lockheed EC-130E Hercules

Several **Lockheed C-130 Hercules** variants currently in service carry the nominal designation **EC-130E**. This has given rise to much confusion over roles and numbers of aircraft, which the USAF has never ventured to clarify. All of these Hercules have a special operations role about which little detail is known. The only aircraft actually built with the EC-130E designation was a single C-130 intended for the USCG as a calibration aircraft. It had no underwing fuel tanks and had additional radio operator and navigation stations for checking the US Navy's worldwide LORAN beacon system. It has since been retired.

Several C-130Es were operated by the 7405th Operations Squadron at Frankfurt/ Rhein Main to undertake Sigint, Comint and Elint missions, mainly along the Berlin corridors. Outwardly, they were almost indistinguishable from standard C-130Es but they gained the unofficial designation EC-130E. These aircraft have been retired.

Three further versions of 'EC-130E' are operational today. The first of these is the Airborne Battlefield Command and Control Center (**ABCCC**) variant. This aircraft is the least sensitive EC-130E and attempts have been made to sell it to foreign customers. It first appeared in Vietnam, where it solved the problem of co-ordinating all the tactical information supplied by forward air controllers, flare ships and the troops on the ground. Ten aircraft were converted to accommodate the ASC-15 battle staff module in the fuselage. Of these, seven are currently in service. Four aircraft have been re-engined with T56-A-15 engines and have inflight-refuelling capability. From the module, up to 16 personnel and a comprehensive communication fit can command and organise the battlefield situation. A ram air scoop, on the port side, is used to provide cooling for its systems and is the most obvious clue to this aircraft's role. Two new **ABCCC-III** capsules were delivered in January 1991. Fitted with satellite communication equipment, increased computer power and a JTIDS datalink, they controlled almost half the attack missions flown during Desert Storm, in addition to SAR co-ordination.

Five **EC-130E(CL)**s have been modified to undertake Elint (and probably jamming)

missions codenamed Senior Scout. There is little outward indication of their special role, since mission equipment uses antennas that are fitted to removable doors and fairings. These highly secretive aircraft are colloquially known as 'Comfy Levis' and are operated by the 193rd SOS, PA ANG. In the cargo hold, mission specialists are carried in a pressurised capsule, similar to the ABCCC variant. For operations, these aircraft are flown to Andrews AFB where mission equipment is installed and mission crews are picked up, both coming from the NSA at Fort Meade. Post-mission, the aircraft are demodified before they return to Harrisburg.

The 193rd SOS also operates a further C-130 variant alongside its EC-130E(CL)s. Four **EC-130E(RR)** 'Rivet Rider' aircraft are tasked with 'Volant Solo' Comint and Sigint missions. They have the ability to tap into and rebroadcast radio or TV transmissions, for 'aid to the civil power' in times of emergency or during natural disasters, or for propaganda/psy war tasks. The latter role was highlighted by the aircrafts' deployment during the Gulf War. Outwardly, they are the most obviously modified EC-130Es, having a huge blade antenna on the fin leading edge, and a pair of large 'axe-head' antennas under the wing. They are undergoing a major upgrading of their systems to allow colour TV broadcasting, and this upgrade has altered their appearance radically, adding two large bullet antennas on each side of the fin in place of the leading-edge blade, and large underwing pods. All 'Rivet Rider' aircraft currently wear an overall two-tone grey colour scheme.

Above: The EC-130E ABCC serves with the 355th Wing at Davis-Monthan AFB, AZ.

Below: The upgraded 'Rivet Rider' EC-130E is used for worldwide colour TV broadcasts.

SPECIFICATION

Lockheed EC-130E Hercules
generally similar to the C-130E except in the following particulars:
Weights: empty 72,892 lb (33063 kg); maximum payload 45,000 lb (20412 kg)
Speed: maximum speed at 30,000 ft (9145 m) 330 kt (380 mph; 612 km/h); cruising speed 320 kt (362 mph; 592 km/h)
Range: 4,080 nm (4,698 miles; 7560 km)
Performance: maximum rate of climb at sea level 1,830 ft (558 m) per minute

The Senior Scout Elint equipment is usually fitted to the EC-130E(CL)s of the 193rd SOS, but is seen here on a C-130H of a transport unit.

Lockheed EC-130H Compass Call

The EC-130H Compass Call carries a huge array of wire aerials supported by the fin surfaces and a large gantry. The main role is to jam hostile communications.

The **Lockheed EC-130H Compass Call** is the latest of several electronic warfare versions of the familiar Hercules, 10 of which serve the US Air Force for communications intrusion and jamming duties. In both missions, EC-130Hs supplement earlier EC-130E aircraft (described separately). The EC-130H Compass Call is used for stand-off jamming. It is distinguished exter-

nally from other Hercules variants by the antennas housed in a pair of blister fairings fitted to the rear fuselage, and an array of wire antennas connected to a gantry suspended beneath the tail. All EC-130H Compass Call aircraft are assigned to the 41st Electronic Combat Squadron at Davis-Monthan AFB, AZ, the 43rd ECS at Sembach, Germany, having now disbanded.

Lockheed EC-130V Hercules

Following experience in using borrowed E-2 Hawkeyes in the anti-drug trafficking role, the US Coast Guard decided to procure its own AEW platform by converting an HC-130H (1721) to **EC-130V** configuration, with the Hawkeye's APS-145 radar mounted above the fuselage and three palletised operator's consoles inside the cabin. General Dynamics undertook the conversion, which first flew on 31 July 1991.

The aircraft went into service with USCG Clearwater but, following extensive evaluations on interdiction patrols lasting up to 10 hours, the programme was considered too costly and was cancelled. The single EC-130V was handed over to the **US Air Force** on 1 October 1993, for use in an undisclosed 'black' programme in the hands of the 6545th Test Squadron at Hill AFB, Utah.

The EC-130V is now a USAF 'black' project. The USCG scrapped it on cost grounds.

Lockheed HC-130 Hercules

Intended as a long-range search and rescue aircraft, the **Lockheed HC-130 Hercules** has served with the **US Air Force** and **US Coast Guard**. The earliest model, the **HC-130B** (formerly designated **R8V-1G**), is now out of service, leaving five current variants. Most numerous of these are the 43 **HC-130H**s delivered to the USAF between 1965 and 1966. These snub-nosed Hercules are fitted with a large distinctive radome for the AN/ARD-17 Cook Aerial Tracker above the forward fuselage and a large observation window in the port fuselage to locate satellite capsules during re-entry from orbit. Some aircraft still retain the nose-mounted arms of the Fulton STAR (surface-to-air recovery) gear. Eighteen similar aircraft were delivered to the USCG, without the AN/ARD-17 radome or the Fulton STAR (although they retain the Fulton nose shape). A further 11 Hercules known as **HC-130H-7**s also carry Coast Guard colours. These are fitted with the standard C-130 'Pinnochio' nose but are otherwise identical to the HC-130H.

Intended as a combat-capable rescue aircraft, the **HC-130N** differed from the HC-130H in being equipped with inflight-refuelling HDUs underwing. Fifteen remain in USAF service. Soon after the introduction of this version came the **HC-130P**, which combines the appearance and ability of the HC-130H (including its Fulton STAR equipment and associated nose) with the air-to-air refuelling role of the HC-130N; 12 of these aircraft remain in squadron service with the USAF and are used primarily to refuel rescue and special operations heli-

copters. In 1991 the first of a new-build version, the **HC-130H(N)**, was delivered to the 210th RQS, Alaska ANG, differing primarily from earlier aircraft in having extensively modernised avionics. This version lacks Fulton gear and AN/ARD-17 equipment, but is equipped with underwing HDUs. Other ANG units which operate HC-130s are the 129th RQS, California ANG and the 102nd RQS, New York ANG. AFRes HC-130s are operated by the 301st, 304th and 305th Rescue Squadrons of the 939th Rescue Wing, respectively based at Portland, OR, Homestead, FL, and Selfridge, MI. Active-duty Combat Shadows (codename for HC-130 aircraft) fly with the 16th SOW, 352nd SOG and 353rd SOG.

The USCG's HC-130Hs are configured to carry the APS-137 radar on the side of the fuselage, greatly increasing search capability.

SPECIFICATION

Lockheed HC-130H Hercules
Wing: span 132 ft 7 in (40.41 m); aspect ratio 10.09; area 1,745.00 sq ft (162.12 m²)
Fuselage and tail: length 98 ft 9 in (30.10 m) with recovery system folded and 106 ft 4 in (32.41 m) with recovery system spread; height 38 ft 3 in (11.66 m); tailplane span 52 ft 8 in (16.05 m); wheel track 14 ft 3 in (4.35 m); wheel base 32 ft 0.75 in (9.77 m)
Powerplant: four Allison T56-A-15 turboprops each rated at 4,508 ehp (3362 ekW)
Weights: basic empty 72,611 lb (32936 kg); maximum normal take-off 155,000 lb (70307 kg); maximum overload take-off 175,000 lb (79379 kg)
Fuel and load: internal fuel 6,960 US gal (26344 litres); external fuel two 1,360-US gal (5146-litre) underwing tanks; maximum payload 43,811 lb (19872 kg)

Speed: maximum speed at 30,000 ft (9145 m) 325 kt (374 mph; 602 km/h); maximum cruising speed 318 kt (366 mph; 589 km/h); economical cruising speed 300 kt (345 mph; 556 km/h)
Range: with maximum internal and external fuel and 20,000-lb (9072-kg) payload 4,460 nm (5,135 miles; 8264 km); range with maximum payload 2,045 nm (2,356 miles; 3792 km)
Performance: maximum rate of climb at sea level 1,820 ft (555 m) per minute; service ceiling 33,000 ft (10060 m); take-off distance to 50 ft (15 m) 5,160 ft (1573 m) at maximum take-off weight; landing distance from 50 ft (15 m) 2,430 ft (741 m) at 100,000 lb (45360 kg)

Among the USAF's combat SAR assets are 10 HC-130N/Ps assigned to the Reserve's 939th Rescue Wing.

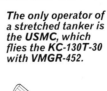

Lockheed KC-130 Hercules

The US Marine Corps required a tactical transport which could double as an inflight-refuelling tanker using the probe and drogue system. In August 1957 two US Air Force C-130As were borrowed and each fitted with two 506-US gal (1915-litre) fuel tanks in the fuselage and two underwing pods containing the hose equipment. So

successful were the trials that 46 **Lockheed KC-130F Hercules** were ordered for delivery from 1960. The KC-130F is based on the C-130B airframe, initially with Allison T56-A-7 engines but later re-engined with the T56-A-16. An easily removable fuselage tank holding 3,600 US gal (13627 litres) is fitted, and the two equipment pods enable

fuel transfer at the rate of 300 US gal (1136 litres) per minute. As well as the additional fuel, the tanker is able to transfer its own surplus fuel. Originally designated **GV-1**, the first production aircraft flew on 22 January 1960. The type currently equips VMGR-152, -252 and -352 of the USMC, and VR-22 of the USN.

To cope with attrition, the USMC ordered 14 **KC-130R** tankers based on the C-130H. These aircraft feature the T56-A-16 powerplant, pylon-mounted tanks with an addi-

tional 2,720 US gal (10296 litres) of fuel and single-point fuelling. Initial deliveries were to VMGR-352 at MCAS El Toro, CA. The most recent USMC variant is the **KC-130T**, 22 of which have been ordered for USMC service. This model has updated avionics, a new search radar and improved navigation systems. The most recent deliveries have been of the **KC-130T-30** variant, with stretched fuselage.

Although not in service with US forces, the **KC-130H** (similar in most respects to the KC-130R) has been successfully exported to several countries. Foreign interest in the tanker Hercules has been high, as detailed below.

In the UK, the Falklands War resulted in an urgent RAF demand for increased tanker

The only operator of a stretched tanker is the USMC, which flies the KC-130T-30 with VMGR-452.

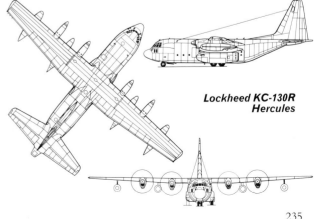

Lockheed KC-130R Hercules

OPERATORS

Users of tanker-configured Hercules in 1994 are:
Argentina: KC-130H (2) with Grupo I
Brazil: KC-130 (5) with 1°/1° GTT
Canada: KCC-130H(T) (5) with No. 435 Sqn
Indonesia: KC-130B (2) with No. 31 Sqn
Israel: KC-130H (3) with Nos 103/131 Sqn
Saudi Arabia: KC-130H (7) with Nos 4/16 Sqns
Singapore: KC-130B (4), KC-130H (1) with No. 122 Sqn
Spain: KC-130H (5) with Ala 31
United Kingdom: Hercules C.Mk 1K (6) with Lyneham Transport Wing and 1312 Flt
US Marine Corps: KC-130s are operated by the following USMC units:
VMGR-152 (KC-130R – MCAS Futenma),
VMGR-234 (KC-130T, KC-130T-30 – NAS Glenview),
VMGR-252 (KC-130F, KC-130R – MCAS Cherry Point),
VMGRT-253 (KC-130F – MCAS Cherry Point),
VMGR-352 (KC-130F, KC-130R – MCAS El Toro),
VMGR-452 (KC-130T, KC-130T-30 – Stewart ANGB)

The KC-130H is the standard export tanker version with an HDU pod under each wing. Brazil had two delivered as such, and subsequently converted several C-130H transports to tanker status.

support. Marshall of Cambridge, the UK support contractor for the Hercules, started work in May 1982 on converting a standard Hercules C.Mk 1 to tanker configuration. Four ex-Andover 900-Imp gal (4091-litre) tanks were fitted in the fuselage and a sin-

gle Flight Refuelling Ltd Mk 17B HDU was attached to the rear cargo ramp door. The first flight took place on 7 June 1982, and within three months four aircraft had been converted. Designated **Hercules C.Mk 1K**, six such aircraft are operated by the Lyneham Transport Wing. Four have been subsequently fitted with wingtip Orange Blossom ESM pods for surveillance duties.

Canada's CC-130H(T) tankers are basic H models with a 4,324-US gal (16365-litre) fuselage tank and FRL Mk 32B wing pods, installed by Northwest Industries.

SPECIFICATION

Lockheed KC-130F Hercules
generally similar to the C-130F Hercules except in the following particulars:
Powerplant: four Allison T56-A-16 turboprops each rated at 4,910 ehp (3661 ekW)
Fuel and load: maximum payload 3,600 US gal (13627 litres) of additional fuel in a removable cargo-hold tank
Speed: maximum cruising speed at 30,000 ft (9145 m) 330 kt (380 mph; 612 km/h); refuelling speed

Lockheed **LC-130F/H/R**

The **Lockheed LC-130F/H/R Hercules** transports are winterised aircraft designed for support operations (as denoted by the 'L' prefix) on the Antarctic ice shield and equipped with skis. LC-130F/H/R aircraft, with slightly redesigned fuselages, are intended for very long-range operations in polar environments. They can be distinguished by a nose fairing designed to hold the nose ski when retracted. All can be equipped with JATO (jet-assisted take-off) rockets for short-distance take-off from ice fields.

The C-130Ds were the first ski-equipped Hercules. These have been replaced by four **LC-130H** aircraft with the 139th Airlift Squadron, 109th Airlift Group, NY ANG at Schenectady. This is the only unit to operate LC-130s in the **USAF**.

The **LC-130F** was the first **US Navy**

variant for Antarctic operations (based on the C-130B variant). Four joined VXE-6 'Puckered Penguins' in 1969. The squadron recovered in 1987 one LC-130F which had spent 16 years buried in snow, and was scheduled to resume flying in the early 1990s. The **LC-130R** (six built) is the final ski-equipped Hercules and has joined the earlier version with VXE-6. It is powered by the 4,910-eshp (3663-ekW) T56-A-16 engine.

SPECIFICATION

Lockheed LC-130R Hercules
generally similar to the C-130F Hercules except in the following particulars:
Powerplant: four Allison T56-A-15 turboprops each rated at 4,508 ehp (3362 ekW)

Weights: empty equipped 78,492 lb (35604 kg); maximum take-off 175,000 lb (79380 kg)
Fuel and load: internal fuel 45,240 lb (20520 kg); external fuel up to 17,680 lb (8020 kg) in two 1,360-US gal (5148-litre) underwing tanks

VXE-6 is based at NAS Point Mugu, but its ski-equipped LC-130s perform their primary mission in the Antarctic, supporting US scientific establishments.

Lockheed **MC-130**

US Air Force interest in variants of the Hercules tailored to the support of Special Forces began in the Vietnam War, when 17 C-130Es were converted to **C-130E-I** standard, with Fulton STAR recovery gear on the nose for the mid-air retrieval of

agents from the ground. The system used a balloon which was inflated on the ground and sent aloft carrying a cable, to which the agent was attached. The C-130E-I snagged the cable between two forks which hinged forward from the nose, picking up the agent

who was then winched in to the rear ramp. Fulton was not used in combat, but the aircraft themselves undertook special missions in night and adverse weather.

The designation **MC-130E Combat Talon** was adopted as standard in the late 1970s for the Special Forces Hercules, although 'Skyhook' EC-130E, C-130H(CT) and HC-130E had also been applied to some aircraft at some point. The basic MC-130E

featured inflight-refuelling capability, uprated T56-A-15 engines, Omega and inertial navigation systems. There are three current sub-variants: the **MC-130E-C** (Clamp), which has Fulton STAR equipment and a nose radome extended downwards to house the radar in a lower position (below the Fulton gear); the **MC-130E-Y** (Yank), which has a standard 'Pinnochio' nose; and the **MC-130E-S** (Swap), which is reportedly used for Sigint work.

MC-130Es feature the APQ-122(V)8 weather avoidance and long-range navigation radar, to which a terrain-following function has been retrofitted. Combined with a forward-looking infra-red sensor in a retractable turret, this allows the aircraft to penetrate hostile air space at night or in adverse weather at very low level and to navigate accurately to a set position where Special Forces can be inserted by parachute, or supplied from the air. Makeshift landing strips can be used for the insertion of vehicles and retrieval of teams. An important task for the MC-130 is 'FARPing' (forward air refuelling point) for Special Forces helicopters, whereby the Hercules sets up at a landing strip and provides a fuel source for landing helicopters. MC-130Es can also

The MC-130H is the latest Special Operations version of the Hercules, readily identified by its enlarged radome. MC-130Hs from the Europe-based 352nd SOG have been used widely in Bosnia.

carry the inflight-refuelling pods used by MH-53s and MH-60s.

Entering service is the **MC-130H Combat Talon II**, 26 of which are on order to augment and eventually replace the MC-130E fleet. These have new radar (APQ-170) in a revised radome, with a FLIR turret mounted underneath. Specialist equipment includes a low-level aerial delivery and container release system, and comprehensive defensive countermeasures. The aircraft are manufactured by Lockheed with minimal equipment, and delivered to IBM Federal Systems Division for the installation of mission equipment.

The first aircraft flew in December 1987, and began equipment flight trials at Edwards AFB in spring 1988. The 8th Special Operations Squadron of the 1st SOW received its first MC-130H in June 1990. The 15th SOS has since formed to operate all operational US-based MC-130Hs. The 8th SOS retains MC-130Es, which also fly with the 1st SOS/353rd SOG at Kadena AB, Oki-

nawa, while the 7th SOS/352nd SOG at RAF Alconbury operates four MC-130Hs. The 58th SOW at Kirtland AFB is said to operate four MC-130Hs for training and the 418th TS (412th TW) at Edwards AFB has a few examples for test and trials duties.

An MC-130E-C kicks up the dust during a rough-field exercise. The Clamp variant has a drooped radome for terrain-following radar, and forks for the Fulton recovery system. Other MC-130E variants are far less conspicuous.

SPECIFICATION

Lockheed MC-130E Hercules
generally similar to the C-130E except in the following particulars:
Weights: empty 72,892 lb (33063 kg)
Speed: maximum speed 318 kt (366 mph; 589 km/h); speed for personnel airdrop at 50 ft (15 m) 125 kt (144 mph; 232 km/h)
Range: 2,000 nm (2,303 miles; 3706 km)

Performance: maximum rate of climb at sea level 1,600 ft (488 m) per minute

Lockheed **C-140 JetStar**

The **Lockheed JetStar** was produced as a private venture to meet the US Air Force UCX requirement for a utility jet for crew readiness training, navaid calibration, transport and other duties. The prototype was first flown on 4 September 1957, powered by two Bristol Orpheus turbojet engines. Production aircraft have four Pratt & Whitney JT12-8 turbojets, wings fitted with a high-lift leading edge, twin-wheel landing gear and engine thrust-reversers. External tanks at mid-span were intended to be optional, but became standard. In October 1959, the USAF selected the JetStar as the **C-140**; the aircraft was also developed for the civilian executive jet market. Five were used by the Special Air Missions wing, and others by the Airways and Air Communications Service for inspecting

overseas navaid calibration duties. The C-140 has been retired from USAF service, but JetStars continue to fly on VIP transport duties with **Indonesia** (two), **Iran** (two), **Mexico** (one) and **Saudi Arabia** (two).

SPECIFICATION

Lockheed Model 1329-25 JetStar II
Wing: span 54 ft 6 in (16.60 m); aspect ratio 5.27; area 542.50 sq ft (50.40 m²)
Fuselage and tail: length 60 ft 5 in (18.42 m); height 20 ft 5 in (6.23 m); tailplane span 24 ft 9 in (7.55 m); wheel track 12 ft 3.5 in (3.75 m); wheel base 20 ft 7 in (6.28 m)
Powerplant: four Garrett TFE731-3 turbofans each rated at 3,700 lb st (16.46 kN)
Weights: operating empty 24,178 lb (10967 kg);

Only a handful of JetStars are left in military service, operating as VIP/staff transports. Saudi Arabia still operates two. An unusual feature of the four-jet design was the use of flap sections on the mid-wing fuel tanks.

maximum take-off 44,000 lb (19844 kg)
Fuel and load: internal fuel 2,686 US gal (13953 litres); external fuel none; maximum payload 2,822 lb (1280 kg)
Speed: never exceed speed Mach 0.87; maximum level and maximum cruising speed 'clean' at 30,000 ft (9145 m) 475 kt (547 mph; 880 km/h); economical cruising speed at 35,000 ft (10670 m) 441 kt (508 mph; 817 km/h)
Range: range 2,770 nm (3,190 miles; 5132 km) with maximum fuel or 2,600 nm (2,994 miles; 4818 km) with maximum payload
Performance: maximum rate of climb at sea level 4,200 ft (1280 m) per minute; service ceiling 36,000 ft (10975 m); take-off distance to 50 ft (15 m) 4,950 ft

(1509 m) at maximum take-off weight; landing distance from 50 ft (15 m) 4,180 ft (1274 m) at normal landing weight

Lockheed **C-141 StarLifter**

First flown on 17 December 1963, the **Lockheed C-141A StarLifter** provided the **US Air Force** with a fast and capacious long-range jet transport with which it could replace the slow C-124 and narrow-cabin C-135 in service with the Military Air Transport Service. Drawing heavily on experience with the C-130 Hercules, the StarLifter featured a fuselage of similar cross-section (10 ft x 9 ft/3.05 m x 2.74 m), two large clamshell doors and a rear ramp that could be opened in flight for air-dropping, rear side parachute doors on both sides and an undercarriage housed in separate fairings.

Swept wings were adopted for high-speed cruise, with powerful high-lift devices provided for good low-speed field performance. The C-141A was also fitted with an all-weather landing system. Power came from four podded TF33 turbofans, and all

fuel was housed in integral wing tanks. The aircraft entered service in October 1964, and was soon engaged on the air bridge to South East Asia to supply the war effort in Vietnam, commencing squadron operations with MAC on 23 April 1965.

Not long after the StarLifter entered service, it became obvious that its maximum payload of 70,847 lb (32136 kg) (or 92,000 lb/41731 kg on aircraft configured to carry LGM-30 Minuteman ICBMs) was rarely achieved, the aircraft 'bulking out' in terms of volume long before its weight limit was approached.

During the 1970s, the entire fleet (minus four **NC-141A** aircraft used for test purposes) was returned to Lockheed for an ambitious programme that involved 270 aircraft. A considerable stretch to the fuselage (totalling 23 ft 4 in/7.11 m) allowed the resultant **C-141B** to carry loads much

closer to its design payload (overall cargo capacity has been increased by over 30 per cent). The programme added the equivalent of 90 new C-141s, in terms of capacity, at low relative cost. At the same time, Lockheed installed inflight-refuelling capability in a characteristic humped fairing above the flight deck, providing the StarLifter with true global airlift capacity. The prototype **YC-141B** made its first flight on 24 March 1977 and Lockheed completed the final C-141B on 29 June 1982.

Throughout its career the StarLifter has been the workhorse of the US Air Force, flying regular supply missions around the world in addition to special requirements. The latter have included disaster relief, evacuations, aid delivery and missions in support of combat operations. Perhaps the StarLifter's finest hour came in the second half of 1990, when the entire fleet was instrumental in transporting much of the equipment for Desert Storm.

Of inestimable value to the US Air Force is the StarLifter's sheer versatility. Like that of the Hercules, the C-141's main hold is fitted with tie-down points and floor cleats that allow it to be rapidly reconfigured for many missions. Palletised passenger seats can be fitted for 166 people, while by using canvas seats some 205 passengers or 168 paratroopers can be carried. For a medevac mission, the StarLifter can carry, for in-

stance, 103 litter patients and 113 walking wounded. Although most heavy equipment is moved by the C-5 Galaxy, the StarLifter can still carry a Sheridan tank, an AH-1 Cobra helicopter or five HMMWV vehicles. Thirteen standard cargo pallets can be admitted, and other loads can include aircraft engines, food supplies, fuel drums or nuclear weapons.

Thirteen C-141Bs of the 437th AW are being equipped for the Special Operations Low Level (SOLL) role with increased survivability measures, the most obvious being the addition of a FLIR turret beneath the nose.

Slated for replacement by the McDonnell Douglas C-17A, beginning with the 437th Airlift Wing, the C-141B serves with the following active-duty squadrons: 7th/86th Airlift Squadrons (60th AW, Travis AFB, CA), 4th/8th/36th AS (62nd AW, McChord AFB, WA), 20th/41st/76th AS (437th AW, Charleston AFB, SC), 6th/18th/30th AS (438th AW, McGuire AFB, NJ) and the 97th Air Mobility Wing (Altus AFB, OK) of AETC.

As active-duty units deactivate, the aircraft are being passed to reservist units. Currently equipped with the StarLifter are the 155th AS/164th AG of the Tennessee ANG at Memphis IAP, 183rd AS/172nd AG of the Mississippi ANG at Jackson MAP, 356th AS/907th AG (AFRes) at Wright-Patterson AFB, OH, 729th and 730th AS/452nd AMW at March AFB, CA, and the 756th AS/459th AW (AFRes) at Andrews AFB, MD. In addition, the Air Force Reserve provides crews for active-duty machines under the Associate programme at Travis, McChord, Charleston and McGuire. Finally, the 412th Test Wing at Edwards AFB, CA, still flies

Lengthening the StarLifter to produce the C-141B greatly increased the type's load-hauling capability, while the addition of a refuelling receptacle allowed global operations.

Lockheed C-141 StarLifter

Lockheed C-141B StarLifter

After initial service in white and grey, the C-141 fleet adopted a 'lizard' scheme (illustrated). Now the fleet is being painted in an overall light grey.

the short-fuselage NC-141A test aircraft, including one aircraft configured as an Advanced Radar Test Bed (ARTB) airborne laboratory to test sensors in a simulated ECM environment.

Of current major concern is the rapid ageing of the C-141 fleet. There are a num-

ber of reasons for this, most notably lower altitude operations imposed on certain special-missions and paradrop-tasked aircraft. The fatigue life of 45,000 hours specified in conversion to C-141B standard may be reduced due to wing cracks and other fatigue problems.

SPECIFICATION

Lockheed C-141B StarLifter
Wing: span 159 ft 11 in (48.74 m); aspect ratio 7.94; area 3,228.00 sq ft (299.88 m2)

Fuselage and tail: length 168 ft 3.5 in (51.29 m); height 39 ft 3 in (11.96 m); wheel track 17 ft 6 in (5.33 m); wheel base 66 ft 4 in (20.22 m)
Powerplant: four Pratt & Whitney TF33-P-7 turbofans each rated at 21,000 lb st (93.41 kN)
Weights: operating empty 148,120 lb (67186 kg); maximum take-off 343,000 lb (155580 kg)
Fuel and load: internal fuel 23,592 US gal (89305 litres); external fuel none; maximum payload 90,880 lb (41222 kg) at 2.25 g or 70,605 lb (32026 kg) at 2.5 g
Speed: maximum cruising speed at high altitude 492 kt (566 mph; 910 km/h); economical cruising speed at high altitude 430 kt (495 mph; 796 km/h)
Range: ferry range 5,550 nm (6,390 miles; 10280 km); range 2,550 nm (2,936 miles; 4725 km) with maximum payload
Performance: maximum rate of climb at sea level 2,920 ft (890 m) per minute; service ceiling 41,600 ft (12680 m); take-off distance to 50 ft (15 m) 5,800 ft (1768 m) at maximum take-off weight; landing distance from 50 ft (15 m) 3,700 ft (1128 m) at normal landing weight

Lockheed (General Dynamics) **F-16A/B Fighting Falcon**

Lockheed Fort Worth Co.
PO Box 748, Fort Worth
TX 761201, USA

The **Lockheed F-16 Fighting Falcon** is the most numerous fighter in the West. Many **F-16A/B**s have seen well over a decade's service, being modernised in operational capability upgrade programmes.

The Fighting Falcon was conceived as a lightweight 'no frills' fighter for air-to-air combat, but despite this, and despite its small dimensions and light weight, has evolved into a versatile and effective multi-role workhorse. First flown on 20 January 1974, the service-test **YF-16** defeated Northrop's YF-17 in a fly-off competition. The first of eight FSD F-16A airframes flew in 1975, the first FSD F-16B in 1977. The two-seat F-16B version remains fully combat capable and retains wing and fuselage dimensions of the single-seater, while sacrificing 1,500 lb (680 kg) of fuel.

Nicknamed the 'Viper', the F-16 cuts a unique silhouette, with its shock-inlet air intake located under the forward fuselage below its pilot. The Falcon's unusual shape features wing/body blending and large leading-edge root extensions to enhance lift at high angles of attack. While its high-Alpha capability is limited by comparison with that of the F/A-18 and the latest Soviet 'superfighters', its very high thrust-to-weight ratio, fast roll rate and high lift wing make it a very agile fighter. Among its once novel characteristics, the F-16 is statically unstable, relying upon a central computer and electronic FBW controls to remain controllable.

The F-16A pilot sits on a zero-zero ACES II ejection seat canted to recline 30°. This improves average g tolerance and necessitates provision of a limited-movement pressure-sensing sidestick controller in place of a conventional joystick. The cockpit has HUD and multifunction displays, and a one-piece canopy of blown polycarbonate with no windscreen and thus no framing forward of the pilot's shoulderline. This gives an incomparable all-round view and is the F-16's most radically new feature and a great boon for dogfighting.

The F-16A/B is armed with a General Electric M61A1 Vulcan 20-mm cannon with 511 rounds, located on the port side at the blend between wing and fuselage. On a typical mission, an F-16A/B can carry as much as 16,700 lb (7575 kg) of ordnance, including Mk 20 Rockeye and CBU-87 cluster bombs, Mk 83 and Mk 84 500-lb (227-kg) and 1,000-lb (454-kg) bombs, AGM-65 Maverick missiles, and GBU-10 and GBU-15 guided weapons. Except for ADF variants (described separately), all F-16A/Bs now have air-to-ground work as their primary duty, with air combat important but secondary. Still, pilots praise the manoeuvrability, high g tolerance, heat-seeking missiles and gun, all of which enable them to 'yank and bank' with an enemy fighter. Pilots are not pleased about what one flier calls "the conscious decision not to give it a radar missile" to fight beyond visual range, claiming that "we don't have a long enough spear to do battle with 'Floggers' and 'Fulcrums'."

Left: Tactical reconnaissance is the primary role of a few KLu aircraft, equipped with a centreline Orpheus camera pod.

Below: Like several overseas customers, Venezuela was offered the F-16/79, but eventually received F100-powered F-16A/B Block 15s.

NATO's search for an F-104 replacement led in June 1975 to the 'sale of the century' in which Belgium, Denmark, the Netherlands and Norway selected the F-16A/B. SABCA in Belgium was responsible for the manufacture of 221 aircraft, mainly for Belgium and Denmark, while Fokker in Holland built 300 aircraft primarily for the Royal Netherlands Air Force and Norway. Some Dutch aircraft are equipped with a centreline tactical reconnaissance pod, and are designated **F-16A(R)**. Subsequent OCUs have brought improvements to F-16A/Bs on both continents, while additional countries have taken the A model 'Viper' into their inventories. Many of these nations were initially offered the significantly inferior J79-powered **F-16/79**, but were able to buy the full-standard F100-engined F-16 when President Reagan relaxed some of the arms sales controls imposed by his predecessor.

Service entry

Delivery of operational USAF F-16A/Bs began in January 1979 to the 388th Tactical Fighter Wing at Hill AFB, UT. Despite teething troubles with engine malfunctions and structural cracks, the F-16 developed into a superb fighter-bomber. The F100-PW-100 engine encountered problems, including ground-start difficulties, compressor stalls, fuel-pump breakdowns and afterburner malfunctions, most of which were corrected early in the aircraft's career. The F-15, which shared a common powerplant, suffered similar problems, an ironic development when this commonality was a powerful factor in the selection of the F-16 over the rival Northrop YF-17.

Versions of the F-16A were tested with APG-65 radar and J79 and YJ101 engines. In December 1975, the first YF-16 was rebuilt with twin canards added, to become the USAF Flight Dynamics Laboratory's **CCV** (Control-Configured Vehicle). General Dynamics converted the fifth FSD F-16A into the **AFTI** (Advanced Fighter Technology Integration) aircraft, or **AFTI/F-16A**. The AFTI/F-16A has a triplex digital flight-control system, larger vertical canard surfaces at the air intake, and a thick dorsal spine; this aircraft was used in recent close air support studies before being laid up by funding constraints. The **SCAMP** (Supersonic Cruise and Maneuvering Prototype), or **F-16XL** (described separately), was yet another special version with a 'cranked delta' wing. Two F-16XLs, a single- and a two-seater, have participated in various research efforts.

The F-16A/B was built in distinct production blocks numbered 1, 5, 10 and 15. Forty-

The F-16B has similar dimensions to the single-seater, and gives away no combat capability other than reduced range. This Danish example carries the badge of Esk 726.

three F-16A/B Block 1s (21 F-16As and 22 F-16Bs) can be distinguished from later F-16s by their black radomes. F-16A/B Block 5s numbered 126 (99 F-16As and 27 F-16Bs). F-16A/B Block 10 consists of 170 aeroplanes, including 145 F-16As and and 24 F-16Bs, in addition to all surviving earlier machines which have been upgraded.

F-16A/B Block 15 introduced the first important changes to the F-16. Noteworthy in Block 15 is the extended horizontal stabilator, or 'big tail', now standard on these and all subsequent Fighting Falcons. Pilots prefer the small tail for dogfighting, but the big tail gives greater rudder authority when carrying a heavy ordnance load. Because of wing cracks and afterburner problems, the

USAF is expected to retire all of its pre-Block 15 'small tail' ships by the mid-1990s, making Block 15s the oldest F-16s in service. Block 15 comprises 457 US aircraft (410 F-16As, 47 F-16Bs), 270 of which were converted to **F-16A/B ADF** (described separately) with interceptor duties.

European upgrades

The OCU (Operational Capabilities Upgrade) programme, adopted by Belgium, Denmark, the Netherlands and Norway, improves the avionics and fire control systems, adds ring-laser INS and provides for the upgrading of the F100-PW-200 engine to F100-PW-220E. From 1988 exports were to Block 15 OCU standard, while surviving F-16A/Bs of the AFRes and ANG were upgraded with F100-PW-220Es. Further

improvements planned for the F-16A/B include the MLU (Mid-Life Update) which brings the cockpit to Block 50 standard with wide-angle HUD and NVG compatibility. New avionics include a modular mission computer, APG-66(V2A) radar and Navstar GPS. Options include wiring for intake-mounted FLIR and a helmet-mounted sight. The four European nations are customers for MLU aircraft, and the aircraft offered to Taiwan are also to this standard. USAF aircraft will adopt some of the MLU features.

The first F-16A/B aircraft to be taken directly from USAF inventory for an overseas customer were ex-'Thunderbirds' aircraft transferred to Singapore in 1993 but retained at Luke AFB, AZ, for training of Singaporean pilots.

In December 1992, Lockheed purchased General Dynamics Tactical Military Aircraft Division, which was renamed Lockheed Fort Worth Company on 1 March 1993.

WEAPON OPTIONS

Standard armament includes internal 20-mm M61A1 Vulcan cannon with 511 rounds, and wingtip launch rails for AIM-9L/M/P Sidewinder missiles. Alternatives to Sidewinder are MATRA Magic 2 or Rafael Python 3. Centreline pylon stressed for 2,200 lb (1000 kg) at 5.5g load or 1,200 lb (544 kg) at 9g, inboard wing pylons stressed to 4,500 lb (2040 kg)/ 2,500 lb (1134 kg), centre wing pylons stressed to 3,500 lb (1587 kg)/2,000 lb (907 kg) and outboard wing pylons (usually used for additional AIM-9 carriage) stressed to 700 lb (318 kg)/ 450 lb (204 kg). Most unguided weaponry is authorised for carriage, including Mk 82 bombs and cluster munitions on triple-ejector racks, or Mk 84 bombs carried singly on wing pylons. Guided weaponry includes AGM-65 Maverick anti-armour missile and Penguin anti-ship missile (Norway). Pakistani aircraft equipped with ATLIS laser-designator and Paveway LGBs. External fuel usually carried in 370-US gal (1400-litre) tanks on inboard pylons. ECM pods usually carried on centreline. KLu F-16A(R) carries Orpheus reconnaissance pod on centreline. GPU-5 Pave Claw cannon pod previously carried by NY ANG F-16As.

BLOCK 15
Also known as MSIP I, the Block 15 upgrades included a wider-span tailplane for greater control authority in out-of-control regimes and better stability, and a track-while-scan mode for the APG-66 radar giving better air-to-air capability.

Lockheed F-16A

Pakistan received 28 F-16As and 12 F-16Bs under the Peace Gate programme, the first being delivered in 1983. They are Block 15 aircraft powered by the F100-PW-200. This aircraft was used by Flt Lt Khalid Mahmood of No. 14 Squadron to shoot down an Afghan AF Sukhoi Su-22 on 3 November 1988. This was his third kill.

MARKINGS
Pakistani F-16s show a variation on the standard two-tone grey scheme, with a wide band around the centre of the aircraft and small patches on the tailplane. No squadron badges are worn.

ARMAMENT
In addition to the internal gun, this aircraft is armed with an air defence load of four Sidewinders. AIM-9Ls are carried on the wingtips, while the older-generation AIM-9P is carried on the outboard pylons.

ATTACK ARMAMENT
Pakistani F-16s are equipped for autonomous laser attacks using the French ATLIS acquisition/designation pod, allied to US Paveway II bombs.

84717

RADAR
The APG-66 operates in X-band and offers 10 modes covering air-to-air, air-to-ground and sea search. Some of the modes are frequency-agile to avoid jamming. The search angle is 120° in both azimuth and elevation.

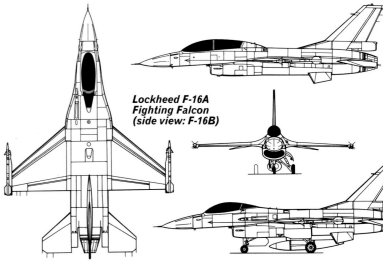

**Lockheed F-16A
Fighting Falcon
(side view: F-16B)**

Indonesia operates some of the most colourful F-16s. The aircraft were delivered to Block 15 OCU standard.

OPERATORS

Deliveries of F-16A/Bs are as follows:
USAF: F-16A (664), F-16B (121) – survivors remain with 704th FS/924th FG (Bergstrom AFS), 466th FS/419th FW (Hill AFB), 93rd FS/482nd FW (Homestead ARS), 89th FS/906th FG (Wright-Patterson AFB) of the Air Force Reserve. Air National Guard users are 160th FS/AL ANG, 184th FS/AR ANG, 162nd FG/AZ ANG, 121st FS/DC ANG, 170th FS/IL ANG, 107th FS/MI ANG, 182nd FS/TX ANG. Units slowly converting to F-16C/D or other types.
Belgium: F-16A (136), F-16B (24) – operated by 1, 2, 23, 31, 349 and 350 Sm/Esc
Denmark: F-16A (54), F-16B (16) – operated by 723, 726, 727 and 730 Esk
Egypt: F-16A (34), F-16B (7) – operated by Nos 72 and 74 Sqns
Indonesia: F-16A (8), F-16B (4) – flown by No. 3 Sqn
Israel: F-16A (67), F-16B (9) – flown by 147 and 253 Squadrons at Ramon
Netherlands: F-16A (177), F-16B (36) – flown by Nos 306, 311, 312, 313, 314, 315, 316, 322 and 323 Sqns
Norway: F-16A (96), F-16B (14) – flown by 331, 332, 334 and 338 Skv
Pakistan: F-16A (28), F-16B (3) – flown by Nos 9, 11 and 14 Sqns. Further 60 A/11 B subject to embargo
Portugal: F-16A (17), F-16B (3) – ADF F-16A/B standard aircraft, initial deliveries in 1994
Singapore: F-16A (6), F-16B (4) – flown by 140 Sqn. Nine aircraft leased from USAF for training.
Taiwan: F-16A/B (150) – scheduled for delivery in 1995
Thailand: F-16A (12), F-16B (6) – similar numbers on order for 1995 delivery
Venezuela: F-16A (18), F-16B (6) – operated by 161 and 162 Esc

SPECIFICATION

Lockheed (General Dynamics) F-16A Fighting Falcon

generally similar to the F-16C Fighting Falcon except in the following particulars:
Fuselage and tail: height 16 ft 5.2 in (5.01 m); tailplane span 18 ft 0.34 in (5.495 m)
Powerplant: one Pratt & Whitney F100-P-100 rated at 14,670 lb st (65.26 kN) dry and 23,830 lb st (106.0 kN) with afterburning
Weights: operational empty 14,567 lb (6607 kg); typical combat take-off 22,785 lb (10335 kg); maximum take-off 33,000 lb (14968 kg)
Fuel and load: internal fuel 6,972 lb (3162 kg); external fuel up to 6,760 lb (3066 kg) in three 300-, 370-, 450- and 600-US gal (1136-, 1400-, 1703- and 2271-litre) drop tanks; maximum ordnance 15,200 lb

Belgium is planning to put 48 of its F-16As through the MLU programme, with 24 further options depending on future defence budgets.

Lockheed (General Dynamics) ADF F-16A/B Block 15

The **Lockheed (General Dynamics) ADF F-16A Block 15 (Air Defense Fighter)** is the only interceptor assigned to air defence of the North American continent; with the collapse of the Soviet Union, it is almost certainly the last.

The **US Air Force** decided in October 1986 to convert 270 Block 15 F-16A/Bs to **ADF** standard. The Cold War drove military plans, which called for 14 ANG (Air National Guard) squadrons to receive the ADF to defend North America from bombers and cruise missiles. This combat role had not been foreseen when the F-16 Fighting Falcon was developed and no American unit had operated the F-16 with a radar-guided missile or on a long-range intercept profile.

The ADF conversion is centred primarily on upgrading the existing AN/APG-66 radar to improve small target detection and provide continuous-wave illumination (thus giving the ability to launch AIM-7 Sparrow BVR missiles). Further modifications include a night identification light in the port forward fuselage, advanced IFF, high-frequency, single side-band radio, improved ECCM and

provision for GPS and AIM-120 AMRAAM missile datalink. The ADF F-16 can carry up to six AIM-7 or AIM-9 Sidewinder missiles and retains the internal 20-mm M61 cannon of the F-16A. The first successful guided launch of a Sparrow missile from a Fighting Falcon took place in February 1989.

Actual conversion of the ADF F-16s (completed in early 1992) was undertaken by the USAF's Ogden Air Materiel Area at Hill AFB, Utah, with General Dynamics-sourced modification kits. Development of the ADF F-16 was conducted at Edwards AFB in 1990 and was followed by operational test and evaluation with the 57th Fighter Weapons Wing at Nellis AFB, Nevada. The first service aircraft were assigned to the 114th Fighter Squadron, Oregon ANG, at Kingsley Field in Klamath

Distinguishing features of the ADF F-16 are the bulge on the fin/fuselage fairing and the searchlight on the port side of the nose. This aircraft is from the 179th Fighter Squadron, Minnesota ANG.

AVIONICS
As part of the ADF upgrade, avionics were upgraded for the intercept mission. Bendix/King ARC-200 HF/SSB radio is added for long-range communications in the single-seat ADFs, and provision is made for Navstar GPS. An AMRAAM datalink is provided, and Teledyne/E-Systems Mk XII advanced IFF is carried.

Lockheed (General Dynamics) F-16A Air Defense Fighter

Conversion of F-16A Block 15 aircraft to ADF standard covered 272 airframes, for service with 13 squadrons, including the training unit at Klamath Falls, Oregon. The operational units provide a chain of air defence alerts around the periphery of the United States. In the light of the present near-zero threat, the force is a prime candidate for massive cutbacks or even complete dissolution.

Portugal's 20 F-16A/Bs are to Block 15OCU standard with F100-PW-220E engines. They also have the full ADF fit, as they are intended for a primary air defence mission.

in order to allocate resources elsewhere.

In addition to the ANG machines, the 17 F-16As and three F-16Bs supplied to Portugal for operation by 501 Esquadra are to ADF standard for the air defence mission.

ARMAMENT
The ADF can carry six air-to-air missiles on its outer pylons and wingtip launch rails. The standard load consists of four Sidewinders and two Sparrows, although AMRAAMs can be substituted for any of these. The internal M61A1 cannon is mounted in the port wingroot, with the ammunition housed in the central fuselage. The weapon is 6 ft 2 in (1.88 m) long and weighs approximately 265 lb (120 kg). Maximum rate of fire is 6,600 rounds per minute, and muzzle velocity is 3,400 ft (1036 m) per second.

Falls which trains ADF F-16A/B interceptor pilots. Operational ANG squadrons which fly the ADF are 194th FS/CA, 159th FS/FL , 169th FS/IL, 171st FS/MI, 179th FS/MN, 186th FS/MT, 119th FS/NJ, 136th FS/NY, 178th FS/ND, 198th FS/PR, 111th FS/TX and 134th FS/VT. In view of the lack of threat to the continental US, the Pentagon has been offering to disband them

WEAPON OPTIONS

Internal 20-mm M61A1 Vulcan cannon with 511 rounds. Wingtip and outboard wing pylons used for AIM-9 Sidewinder carriage. Often seen with AIM-9P on wingtip and AIM-9M on wing. Central wing pylon can carry AIM-7 Sparrow (ADF being only F-16 version with target illuminator for AIM-7). Inboard wing pylon usually reserved for fuel tanks. Alternatively six AIM-120 AMRAAM can be carried on the missile pylons, or a mix of any of the three missile types.

MARKINGS
The ADF wears the standard USAF two-tone grey camouflage. Most ANG units wear striking unit markings (none more so than this diving eagle of the 194th FS/144th FW/California ANG) and do not carry tailcodes. Those assigned to Puerto Rico and Illinois are outside the CONUS defence organisation, and wear ACC-style tailcodes.

SPOTLIGHT
Part of the ADF conversion was the fitment of a spotlight on the port side of the nose. This allows the ADF pilot to illuminate aircraft at night for visual identification or damage assessment purposes. The other main ADF distinguishing feature is the bulge on the fin/fuselage fairing. This houses the relocated rudder activators which were moved to make room for the HF radio.

RADAR
The ADF F-16A retains the Westinghouse APG-66, but this is uprated with a continuous-wave function to allow the launch of Sparrow missiles.

Lockheed (General Dynamics) F-16C/D Fighting Falcon

The **Lockheed (General Dynamics) F-16C** first flew on 19 June 1984. F-16C and two-seat **F-16D** models are distinguished by an enlarged base or 'island' leading up to the vertical fin, with a small blade antenna protruding up from it. This space was intended for the internal ASPJ (airborne self-protection jammer) which the USAF abandoned in favour of continuing use of external ECM pods.

Compared with earlier versions, the F-16C/D gives the pilot a GEC wide-angle HUD and a function keyboard control at the base of the HUD (located in a console to his left in earlier ships) and an improved data display with key items of information located at 'design eye' level for HOTAS flying. F-16C/Ds employ Hughes APG-68 multimode radar with increased range, sharper resolution and expanded operating modes, and have a weapons interface for the AGM-65D Maverick and AMRAAM missiles.

F-16C single-seat and combat-capable F-16D two-seat fighters introduced progressive changes, some installed at the factory and others as part of **MSIP II** (avionics, cockpit and airframe changes) and **MSIP III** (further systems installation) programmes, aimed at enhancing the Fighting Falcon's ability to fly and fight at night.

F-16C/D aircraft retain the unique, low-slung configuration of earlier Fighting Falcon variants, with fuselage-wing 'blending,' fly-by-wire controls, ACES II ejection seat, and a blown polycarbonate canopy which, in these later versions, has a gold tint because of its lining of radar-reflecting materials. F-16C/D models retain the General Electric M61A1 Vulcan 20-mm cannon with 511 rounds and a capability for up to 16,700 lb (7575 kg) of ordnance, including most bombs and missiles in inventory.

Block 25 aircraft entered production in July 1984 and totalled 319, 289 F-16Cs and 30 F-16Ds. With Blocks 30/32 came the configured (formerly 'common') engine bay, with options for the GE F110-GE-100 (Block 30) or P&W F100-PW-220 (Block 32).

F-16C Blocks 30 and 40 are powered by the General Electric F110-GE-100 offering 28,984 lb (128.9 kN), while F-16C Blocks 32 and 42 Falcons introduced 23,840-lb

(106.05-kN) thrust Pratt & Whitney F100-PW-220s. This powerplant change brought a need to alter the contours of the F-16's air intake to accommodate the larger amount of air ingested. Because the change was not made initially, early F-16C/D Block 30s are 'small inlet' aeroplanes, the 1-ft (0.30-m) wider air intake having become standard for GE power on 'big inlet' ships after deliveries began. USAF F-16C/D delivery totals slightly favour the GE engine.

The introduction of the F100-PW-220 engine marks a maturing of the original F-16 powerplant. While the improved P&W engine is not as powerful as the GE powerplant, it is lighter and crew chiefs consider it 'smarter' and more dependable than earlier P&W models. In addition, Block 30/32 aircraft have the capability to carry AGM-45 Shrike and AGM-88A HARM antiradiation missiles, and AIM-120 AMRAAM. Avionics hardware changes are also introduced with Block 30/32, which total 501 aircraft, comprising 446 F-16Cs and 55 two-seat F-16Ds. In addition to tactical squadrons, the F-16C/D Block 32 is flown by the USAF's Adversary Tactics Division on aggressor duties, and by the 'Thunderbirds' aerial demonstration team.

F-16C/D Block 40/42 **Night Falcons** began to come off the Fort Worth production line in December 1988. This version introduces LANTIRN navigation and targeting pods, Navstar GPS navigation receiver, AGM-88B HARM II, APG-68V radar, digital flight controls, automatic terrain following and, as a consequence, increased take-off weight. Greater structural strength raises the Night Falcon's 9g capability from 26,900 lb (12201 kg) to 28,500 lb (12928 kg). The heavier all-up weight and the need to accommodate LANTIRN has resulted in larger landing gear, bulged landing gear doors and the relocation of landing lights to the nose gear door. Block 40/42 Night Falcons have been delivered to the USAF, Israel, Egypt, Turkey and Bahrain. A Block 42 F-16D equipped with AMRAAMs became the first USAF 'Viper' to score an air-to-air victory by downing an Iraqi MiG-25 on 27 December 1992. In 1994 F-16s shot down four Serbian aircraft over Bosnia.

A total of 249 F-16 Fighting Falcons was deployed to Operation Desert Storm and flew almost 13,500 sorties, the highest sortie total for any aircraft in the war, while maintaining a 95.2 per cent mission-capable rate, 5 per cent better than the F-16's peacetime rate. F-16s attacked ground elements in the Kuwaiti Theatre of Operations, flew anti-'Scud' missions, and destroyed military and chemical production facilities, and airfields.

In December 1991, General Dynamics began delivering F-16C/D Block 50 and 52 aircraft. First flight date for Block 50 was 22 October 1991. The first Block 50s went to the 388th Fighter Wing at Hill Air Force Base, UT, in 1992, followed by delivery to USAFE's 52nd FW. Block 50/52 'Vipers' introduced the Westinghouse AN/APG-68 (V5) radar with improved memory and more modes, new NVG-compatible GEC HUD, and improved avionics computer. Numerous other additions to Block 50/52 include a Tracor AN/ALE-47 chaff/flare dispenser, ALR-56M radar warning receiver, Have Quick IIA radio, Have Sync anti-jam VHF and full HARM integration.

These latest F-16s are powered by the

IPE (Improved Performance Engine) versions of GE and P&W engines, the 29,588-lb (131.6-kN) F110-GE-229 and 29,100-lb (129.4-kN) F100-PW-220, respectively. Problems arose with developmental test ships for the Block 52 programme in July 1991, and these had to be refitted with older F100 variants until the P&W IPE's fourth fan blade could be redesigned.

Around 100 USAF F-16C/D Block 50/52 aircraft are being raised to Block 50/52D standard, with provision for the ASQ-213 pod carried under the starboard side of the intake. This pod is known as the HARM Targeting System, and provides the F-16 with a limited 'Wild Weasel' defence-suppression capability to augment the dwindling F-4G force. Further USAF programmes include the **RF-16** tactical reconnaissance aircraft carrying an IR/EO sensor pod, fitment of head-steered FLIR sensor and helmet-mounted sights and modifications of Block 30/32/40/42 aircraft for the close air support/battlefield air interdiction mission.

In 1991, the USAF began studying an MRF (Multi-Role Fighter) which would replace the F-16 in the 21st century. The future of MRF is doubtful, especially since USAF F-16C/Ds (in contrast to ageing F-16A 'small tail' Block 10s) have relatively low airframe hours and will not need early replacement. The proposed Block 60/62 F-16 would utilise some technology developed for the F-22 to answer the MRF requirement.

The F-16C/D has been widely exported, as detailed in the operators list. Licensed production is undertaken by TAI in Turkey and Samsung Aerospace in South Korea.

Many F-16Ds delivered to Israel have been subsequently fitted with a very bulged spine, housing unidentified indigenous avionics reportedly associated with the

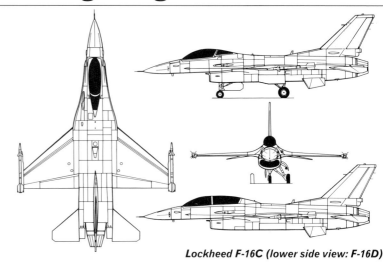

Lockheed F-16C (lower side view: F-16D)

Below: The Night Falcon features the LANTIRN system carried in two pods under the intake. This provides FLIR, laser designation and terrain-following radar for precision all-weather attack.

Above: Bahrain's small air force is spearheaded by a force of 12 F-16C/D Block 40s.

Below: The F-16C/D is firmly established in the ANG, this aircraft being a 162nd FS two-seater.

242

Above: An F-16C from the 432nd FW in Japan drops inert bombs on a range. The aircraft is armed with AIM-120 AMRAAM, and carries a centreline ALQ-184 ECM pod.

Right: F-16s of the 389th FS, 366th Wing carry Mk 82 bombs on triple-ejector racks. The wing is the USAF's power projection unit, also flying B-1s, F-15s and KC-135Rs,

'Wild Weasel'/SAM-suppression role. Several IDF/AF units operate an 'F-16D-heavy' mix of F-16Cs and F-16Ds.

WEAPON OPTIONS

F-16C/D basically similar to F-16A/B, but with greater accent on 'smart' weapons. Block 50/52 aircraft have full AGM-88 HARM capability, while LANTIRN-equipped aircraft can autonomously launch GBU-10 and GBU-12 laser-guided bombs.

SPECIFICATION

Lockheed (General Dynamics) F-16C Fighting Falcon
Wing: span 31 ft 0 in (9.45 m) without tip-mounted AAMs and 32 ft 9.75 in; (10.00 m) with tip-mounted AAMs; aspect ratio 3.09; area 300.00 sq ft (28.87 m²)
Fuselage and tail: length 49 ft 4 in (15.03 m); height 16 ft 8.5 in (5.09 m); tailplane span 18 ft 3.75 in (5.58 m); wheel track 7 ft 9 in (2.36 m); wheel base 13 ft 1.5 in (4.00 m)
Powerplant: (see text for sub-variant) one General Electric F110-GE-100 turbofan rated at 27,600 lb st (122.77 kN) with afterburning or one Pratt & Whitney F100-P-220 turbofan rated at 23,450 lb st (104.31 kN) with afterburning
Weights: empty 19,100 lb (8663 kg) with F110 turbofan or 18,335 lb (8316 kg) with F100 turbofan; typical combat take-off 21,585 lb (9791 kg); maximum take-off 25,071 lb (11372 kg) for an air-to-air mission without drop tanks or 42,300 lb (19187 kg) with maximum external load
Fuel and load: internal fuel 6,972 lb (3162 kg);

external fuel up to 6,760 lb (3066 kg) in three 300-, 370-, 450- and 600-US gal (1136-, 1400-, 1703- and 2271-litre) drop tanks; maximum ordnance 20,450 lb (9276 kg) for 5-g manoeuvre limit or 11,950 lb (5421 kg) for 9-g manoeuvre limit
Speed: maximum level speed 'clean' at 40,000 ft (12190 m) more than 1,146 kt (1,320 mph; 2124 km/h) and at sea level 795 kt (915 mph; 1472 km/h)
Range: ferry range more than 2,100 nm (2,418 miles; 3891 km) with drop tanks; combat radius 295 nm (340 miles; 547 km) on a hi-lo-hi mission with six 454-kg (1,000-lb) bombs
Performance: maximum rate of climb at sea level more than 50,000 ft (15240 m) per minute; service ceiling more than 50,000 ft (15240 m); typical take-off run 2,500 ft (762 m) at MTOW; typical landing run 2,500 ft (762 m) at normal landing weight
g limits: +9

OPERATORS

Deliveries of F-16C/D are as follows:
US Air Force: F-16C (1,009), F-16D (180) plus 229 F-16C/D Block 50/52 in process of delivery. Active-duty wings are the 20th FW (Shaw AFB), 23rd Wing (Pope AFB), 347th FW (Moody AFB), 366th Wing (Mountain Home AFB) and 388th FW (Hill AFB) in Air Combat Command (plus the 57th FWW at Nellis AFB and 79th TEG at Eglin AFB for test purposes), 58th FW (Luke AFB) in AETC, 8th FW (Kunsan AB), 51st FW (Osan AB), 354th FW (Eielson AFB) and 432nd FW (Misawa AB) in PACAF, and the 31st FW (Aviano AB), 52nd FW (Spangdahlem AB) and 86th Wing (Ramstein AB) in USAFE. Air Force Reserve units are the 457th FS/301st FW at Carswell AFB, 706th FS/926th FG at NAS New Orleans and 302nd FS/944th FG at Luke

AFB. Air National Guard units are 120th FS/CO, 124th and 174th FS/IA, 113th and 163rd/IN, 184th FG/KS, 188th FS/NM, 138th FS/NY, 112th and 162nd FS/OH, 125th FS/OK, 157th FS/SC, 175th FS/SD, 149th FS/VA and 176th FS/WI. Various test agencies also operate F-16s
Bahrain: F-16C Blk 40 (8), F-16D Blk 40 (4) – based at Sheikh Isa
Egypt: F-16C Blk 32 (36), F-16D Blk 32 (4), F-16C Blk 40 (40), F-16D Blk 40 (7) plus 46 TAI-built F-16C/D Blk 50 in process of delivery 1994
Greece: F-16C Blk 40 (34), F-16D Blk 40 (6) plus 40 F-16C/D in process of delivery 1994. Current squadrons are 330 and 346 Mira
Israel: F-16C Blk 30 (51), F-16D Blk 30 (24), F-16C Blk 40 (30), F-16D Blk 40 (30) – operated by 101 and 105 Sqns at Hatzor ('D-heavy' mix), 109, 110 and 117 Sqns at Ramat David and 102 and 105 Sqns at Nevatin
South Korea: F-16C Blk 32 (30), F-16D Blk 32 (10)

With its sophisticated weapon system, the F-16 can be used to replicate the latest Russian fighters for air combat training. This aircraft, painted to resemble a MiG-29, is one of a handful flown by the ATD/414th TS/57th Wing at Nellis AFB.

plus 120 F-16C/D Blk 52 on order – 12 built by Lockheed, 36 supplied as kits and 72 built by Samsung Aerospace
Turkey: F-16C Blk 30 (35), F-16D Blk 30 (9), F-16C Blk 40 (101), F-16D Blk 40 (15) plus 80 F-16C/D Blk 50. Local production by TAI. Current squadrons are 141, 142, 161 and 162 Filo with four more to form

A fully-armed Turkish F-16 patrols the skies over Bosnia during Operation Deny Flight.

The Block 50/52D F-16s are compatible with the ASQ-213 HARM Targeting System, carried on the intake. Around 100 are being produced to provide a stop-gap defence suppression capability.

Lockheed (General Dynamics) F-16N Fighting Falcon

Requiring a highly-manoeuvrable super-sonic aircraft for its adversary squadrons, the **US Navy** chose the F-16. Using the F-16C Block 30 as the basis, the **F-16N** is considerably downgraded, as it has no secondary operational function. The earlier APG-66 radar replaces the APG-68, and the cannon is removed. The wingtip rails can carry only AIS pods and AIM-9 acquisition rounds, although the other pylons remain available for stores. ALR-69 radar warning receivers are fitted, and there is some structural strengthening to resist the greater amount of high *g* forces encountered in the adversary mission.

Ordered in January 1985, 26 aircraft were delivered in 1987/88, for use with the Fighter Weapons School and VF-126 at NAS

Miramar, VF-43 at NAS Oceana and VF-45 at NAS Key West. VF-43 and VF-126 have since disbanded. Four of the 26 were **TF-16N** two-seaters. Most aircraft serve in a low-visibility three-tone air defence scheme with two-digit Soviet-style codes, but one was flown with a dark-green disruptive camouflage and Marine Corps titles.

Augmenting regular Navy types (A-4, F-14 and F/A-18) in the adversary role, the F-16Ns are the most exciting F-16s to fly, possessing the highest power/weight ratio of any variant. Titanium is used in key areas in place of aluminium to strengthen the airframe against the rigours of prolonged high-g flight.

Lockheed (General Dynamics) F-16XL/NF-16D/AFTI/F-16

The **Lockheed (General Dynamics) F-16XL** with its unique 'wedged' wing shape has flown intermittently at Edwards Air Force Base, CA, since 1982, first with the US Air Force and currently with **NASA**. The **SCAMP** (Supersonic Cruise and Maneuvering Prototype), or F-16XL, was conceived to increase weapons capacity, range and penetration speed of the F-16. The F-16XL's fuselage was lengthened to 54 ft 1.86 in (16.51 m) and grafted to a 'cranked-arrow' delta wing incorporating composite material to save weight while increasing area and allowing up to 17 stores stations. Tests confirmed greater lifting capability, range and manoeuvring capability with no corresponding penalty for the change in configuration which produced the design.

The two F-16XLs, a single- and a two-seater, are former F-16A FSD aircraft; the first made its initial flight as an F-16XL on 3 July 1982. During evaluations at Edwards in 1984, the standard F-16 undercarriage with a maximum weight limit of 37,500 lb (17010 kg) was replaced with strengthened units allowing 48,000 lb (21772 kg) gross weight. The first F-16XL is powered by a Pratt & Whitney F100 afterburning turbofan, the second by a General Electric F110.

The US Air Force abandoned development of the F-16XL in the late 1980s. The aircraft was revived to compete for the production contract that was eventually won by the McDonnell F-15E 'Strike Eagle'. Had it been successful, operational F-16XLs would have been designated **F-16E** (single-seat) and **F-16F** (two-seat).

NASA took delivery of the single-seater on 10 March 1989 and of the two-seat aircraft on 14 February 1991. To carry out laminar-flow flight tests at sustained supersonic speeds, NASA modified both aircraft with a Rockwell-designed titanium wing section or 'active suction glove', which

siphons away turbulent boundary-layer air through millions of tiny laser-cut holes. A foam and fibreglass fairing blends the raised 'glove' into the wing's upper surface. On 2 December 1991, the F-16XL single-seater achieved laminar flow over a swept-wing aircraft for the first time at speeds up to nearly 1,200 mph (1932 km/h) and at altitudes above 40,000 ft (12384 m).

Other research-dedicated F-16s include the **AFTI/F-16** (advanced fighter technology integration) and the **NF-16D VISTA** (variable-stability inflight simulator test aircraft). The AFTI/F-16 is used by the Air Force Flight Test Center at Edwards AFB to research many fighter/CAS-related systems, and features an enlarged spine to house more equipment. The NF-16D VISTA is currently in the **F-16 MATV** (multi-axis thrust-vectoring) testbed configuration, fitted with the AVEN (axisymmetric vectoring engine nozzle) to its F110 engine.

Above: Designated NF-16A, the AFTI/F-16 is fitted with a wide variety of avionics for close air support trials.

Below: The two-seat F-16XL displays the unique planform of the variant, together with the laminar-flow section on the starboard wing.

SPECIFICATION

Lockheed (General Dynamics) F-16XL Fighting Falcon

Wing: span 34 ft 2.8 in (10.43 m); aspect ratio 1.77; area 663.00 sq ft (61.59 m²)

Fuselage and tail: length 54 ft 1.86 in (16.51 m); height 17 ft 7 in (5.36 m); wheel track 7 ft 9 in (2.36 m)

Powerplant: one Pratt & Whitney F100-P-100 turbofan rated at 14,670 lb st (65.26 kN) dry and 23,830 lb st (106.0 kN) with afterburning, or one General Electric F110-GE-100 turbofan rated at 27,600 lb st (122.77 kN) with afterburning

Weights: design mission take-off 43,000 lb (19505 kg); maximum take-off 48,000 lb (21773 kg)

Fuel and load: maximum ordnance 15,000 lb (6803 kg)

Speed: maximum level speed 'clean' at 36,000 ft (10975 m) 1,147 kt (1,321 mph; 2126 km/h)

Range: more than 2,500 nm (2,875 miles; 4630 km)

***g* limits:** +9

Lockheed F-104 Starfighter

Some 2,221 single-seat **Starfighter**s were eventually built in the US, Canada, Europe and Japan in Lockheed's F-104 programme, which started in the early 1950s at C. L. 'Kelly' Johnson's renowned 'Skunk Works' at Burbank, CA. The first of two 10,200-lb (45.37-kN) Wright XJ65-W-6 (Sapphire)-powered **XF-104** prototypes started flying on 18 February 1954, in the hands of A. W. 'Tony' Le Vier. These were followed by 17 pre-production **YF-104A**s with definitive J79-GE-3A turbojets developing 14,800 lb st (65.83 kN) for take-off. The USAF procured 153 **F-104A**s and 77 **F-104C**s, although after at least 73 accident losses these were withdrawn from regular fighter units in 1968, and from the

Air National Guard in mid-1975. Most were transferred to the air forces of Jordan, Pakistan and Taiwan, all of whom used them in combat, but none now remains in service. Two-seat trainer variants of the F-104 are described separately.

Extensive modifications and installation of multi-role nav/attack systems and the improved 15,800-lb (70.28-kN) J79-GE-11A, coupled with US government-backed high-pressure salesmanship, secured for Lockheed in late 1958 an initial West German

A line-up of CF-104Gs of Turkey's 182 Filo. The Starfighter is in the process of being replaced by F-16s from local production.

contract for the new **F-104G** Starfighter, which spearheaded orders from other NATO countries in what quickly became known as 'the sale of the century'. This involved a massive European Starfighter licence-production programme by Belgium, Germany, Italy and the Netherlands, with

additional industrial participation from Canada, which also selected the **CF-104** as its next-generation fighter, and from Lockheed in the US. New **F/CF/RF-104G** Starfighters from this joint production were procured by Belgium (101), Canada (200), Denmark (40), the German Luftwaffe and

Within the ranks of RoCAF Starfighters are several RF-104G 'Stargazer' aircraft, serving with the 12th Special Missions Squadron, part of the 401st TCW at Taoyuan.

Marineflieger (749), Greece (45), Italy (125), the Netherlands (120), Norway (19), Spain (18), Taiwan (67) and Turkey (46). Starfighter production was also undertaken in Japan, where Mitsubishi built 210 Lockheed Model 683B **F-104J**s between 1962 and 1967 for the JASDF. These were retired from front-line service in March 1986, although four aircraft served until 1990 for trials duties. A number of F-104Js were stored and eight of these are being converted as target drones.

Many Starfighters were replaced in service from 1979 by more modern fighters, but large numbers were also transferred to US allies and other NATO countries. Major recipients included Greece, which eventually received at least 170 single-seat Starfighters from US and NATO sources, plus 60 ex-German F/RF-104Gs; Norway (18 surplus CAF CF-104s); Taiwan (53 ex-German/RDAF F-104Gs and at least 22 ex-JASDF F-104Js); and Turkey (230 F-104Gs/CF-104s, and 33 RF-104Gs). Some, particularly from Germany, were supplied in unairworthy condition for spares recovery, and most have since been retired.

In 1994, **Taiwan**'s RoCAF remained the biggest Starfighter operator, with seven tactical fighter squadrons and one reconnaissance unit using six so-called **RF-104G 'Stargazer'** aircraft. The F-104s form three wings at Hsinchu (41st, 42nd, 48th TFS), Ching Chuan Kang (7th, 8th, 28th and 35th TFS), and Taoyuan (12th Special Mission Sqn) air bases. In **Turkey**, the last F-104Gs were serving with 181 Filo at Diyarbakir and 193 Filo at Akhisar, while the CF-104G served with 182 Filo at Diyarbakir. Turkey also has one squadron of **F-104S**, a type which serves in numbers in **Italy**, and which is described separately under Alenia.

SPECIFICATION

Lockheed F-104G Starfighter
Wing: span 21 ft 11 in (6.68 m) without tip-mounted AAMs; aspect ratio 2.45; area 196.10 sq ft (18.22 m²)
Fuselage and tail: length 54 ft 9 in (16.69 m); height 13 ft 6 in (4.11 m); tailplane span 11 ft 11 in (3.63 m); wheel track 9 ft 0 in (2.74 m); wheel base 15 ft 0.5 in (4.59 m)
Powerplant: one General Electric J79-GE-11A turbojet rated at 10,000 lb st (44.48 kN) dry and 15,800 lb st (70.28 kN) with afterburning
Weights: empty equipped 14,082 lb (6387 kg); operating empty 14,903 lb (6760 kg); normal take-off 21,693 lb (9840 kg); maximum take-off 28,779 lb (13054 kg)

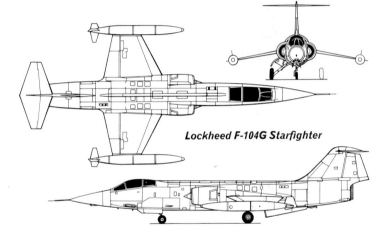

Lockheed F-104G Starfighter

Fuel and load: internal fuel 896 US gal (3392 litres); external fuel up to 955 US gal (3615 litres) in one 225-US gal (852-litre) drop tank, two 195-US gal (740-litre) drop tanks and two 170-US gal (645-litre) tip tanks; maximum ordnance 4,310 lb (1955 kg)
Speed: maximum level speed 'clean' at 36,000 ft (10975 m) 1,262 kt (1,453 mph; 2338 km/h); cruising speed at 36,000 ft (10975 m) 530 kt (610 mph; 981 km/h)
Range: ferry range 1,893 nm (2,180 miles; 3510 km) with four drop tanks; combat radius 648 nm

(746 miles; 1200 km) with maximum fuel or 261 nm (30 miles; 483 km) on a hi-lo-hi attack mission with maximum warload
Performance: maximum rate of climb at sea level 55,000 ft (16765 m) per minute; service ceiling 58,000 ft (17680 m); take-off run 2,960 ft (902 m) at 21,840 lb (9906 kg); take-off distance to 50 ft (15 m) 4,600 ft (1402 m) at 22,840 lb (10360 kg); landing distance from 50 ft (15 m) 3,250 ft (990 m) at 15,900 lb (7212 kg); landing run 2,280 ft (695 m) at 15,900 lb (7212 kg)

Lockheed **TF-104 Starfighter**

Following development and production for the USAF from 1956 of 26 tandem two-seat **F-104B** and 21 **F-104D** Starfighter conversion trainers, Lockheed undertook the output, from its Burbank and Palmdale factories in California, of most similar trainer versions of the later F-104G series in the NATO and Japanese programmes. These included 38 **CF-104D**s for Canada, 30 **F-104F**s and 137 **TF-104G**s for the FRG, 20 **F-104DJ**s for Japan, and 29 TFs for MAP contracts (Denmark, four; Greece, six; Norway, two; Spain, three; Turkey, six; Taiwan, eight). Lockheed built 191 TF-104Gs for NATO use, also including 12 each for Belgium and Italy and 18 for the Netherlands. Some 68 of these were assembled in Europe from Lockheed-supplied kits, an extra 16 being delivered from

Fiat for the AMI, increasing overall two-seat F-104 production to 359. The TF-104G retains the single-seat version's weapons systems and associated avionics, including its F-15A NASARR radar but not its 20-mm Vulcan cannon, which has been replaced by extra fuel. In 1994 TF-104Gs were still operated in **Italy**, **Turkey** and **Taiwan** (alongside F-104DJs).

SPECIFICATION

Lockheed TF-104G Starfighter
generally similar to the Lockheed F-104G Starfighter except in the following particulars:
Fuselage and tail: wheel base 14 ft 5.5 in (4.41 m)
Weights: empty equipped 14,181 lb (6432 kg); maximum take-off 26,364 lb (11959 kg)

Fuel and load: internal fuel 700 US gal (2650 litres); maximum ordnance 2,744 lb (1245 kg)
Range: combat radius 515 nm (593 miles; 955 km) with maximum fuel
Performance: take-off run 2,260 ft (960 m) at 18,900 lb (8573 kg); take-off distance to 50 ft (15 m) 3,500 ft (1067 m) at 18,900 lb (8573 kg); landing

distance from 50 ft (15 m) 3,190 ft (972 m) at 15,424 lb (6996 kg) weight; landing run 2,215 ft (676 m) at 15,424 lb (6996 kg)

Taiwan has many TF-104Gs in its inventory, most with the OCU but some with operational units.

Lockheed **F-117 Night Hawk**

Lockheed Advanced Development Company
1011 Lockheed Way, Palmdale
CA 93599-3740, USA

Stealth technology had been under low-key development since the 1940s, but it was the effects of the Vietnam and Yom Kippur Wars which spurred a DARPA request in 1974 for development of a stealth aircraft. This used a mix of radar-absorbent materials, radar-reflective internal structure (re-entrant triangles that scatter radar energy away from the transmitter) and a similarly 'reflective' configuration to dramatically decrease radar cross-section to the point at which defences have insufficient time to react to a threat, or do not 'see' it at all. Overall faceting reflects radar energy in all directions, making the aircraft virtually invisible even to AWACS platforms, and the concept extends to the wing itself, the aerofoil section of which consists of two flat surfaces on the underside and three on the top of the wing. The avoidance of straight lines is continued on access panels and doors, many of which have serrated edges for the same reason. Cockpit transparencies are coated with gold. Radio aerials are retractable, and during peacetime the aircraft carry external radar reflectors and transponders.

The Lockheed 'Skunk Works', famed builder of the U-2 and SR-71, was awarded a development order in April 1976 for two sub-scale technology demonstrators. Under the codename Have Blue, the first of these aircraft made its maiden flight in 1977 from the secret test base at Groom Dry Lake, NV, with Bill Park at the controls. Although both Have Blue aircraft were lost, experience gained was sufficient to win Lockheed a contract to develop a full-scale operational tactical fighter, awarded on 16 November

1978 under the Senior Trend codename. Lessons from the Have Blue prototypes led to some major changes, most notably to the configuration of the tailfins, which were canted outboard instead of inboard. The first of five FSD prototypes flew on 18 June 1981 under the command of Hal Farley. These aircraft were not originally painted in the black colour scheme which is now synonymous with the **F-117**, some being grey and others decorated in a two-tone disruptive camouflage. The aircraft also had smaller tailplanes than production aircraft.

To reduce costs and maintain secrecy, components and equipment from other in-service aircraft were used wherever possible, allowing many F-117 costs to be buried in 'spares' listings for other types. Thus, the aircraft has an A-10A nose gear, F-15E mainwheels, a standard ACES ejection seat, and cockpit displays from the F/A-18 Hornet. The aircraft's arrow-like configuration demands the use of a digital fly-by-wire control system. Lockheed selected the F-16's GEC Astronics quadruplex system to actuate two-section elevons and all-moving 'ruddervons'.

Tonopah base

As production continued at a low rate, the USAF began establishing a base at Tonopah Test Range, not far from Groom Lake and almost as secluded. In October 1983 the first unit was declared operational, with about five F-117s and 18 A-7D Corsairs, which were flown for proficiency and as a security 'cover'. All flights were undertaken at night, necessitating considerable upheavals to the lifestyles of the crews.

This factor was a contributory factor to the two F-117 losses in the 1980s. It was not until November 1988 that the F-117 was officially acknowledged by the Pentagon, allowing the 'Black Jet' to begin flying daylight missions.

As early as October 1979, the US Air Force began the task of picking pilots for F-117 operations, carefully selecting the personnel on the basis of flying skill, character and background. The 4450th Tactical Group was formed in 1980 at Nellis AFB as the operational unit, and the first cadre of pilots joined in mid-1982, at the same time as the first production aircraft arrived. The unit was divided into four units, known as P-unit (flying A-7Ds as cover and as chase aircraft), I-unit ('Nightstalkers'), Q-unit ('Goatsuckers') and Z-unit ('Grim Reapers'). Later these were formed as squadrons, 'I'

The F-117 presents an unmistakable silhouette from any angle. Fly-by-wire computer control is central to the ability to create a stealthy shape that is also an effective flying machine.

becoming the 4450th Tactical Squadron, 'P' the 4451st TS, 'Q' the 4452nd TS and 'Z' the 4453rd Test and Evaluation Squadron.

In October 1989, the 4450th TG was redesignated as the 37th Tactical Fighter Wing, taking this designation from the George-based 'Wild Weasel' Phantom wing, whose squadrons amalgamated with the 35th TFW. The F-117 units realigned into three squadrons, the 415th TFS 'Nightstalkers', 416th TFS 'Ghostriders' and 417th Tactical Fighter Training Squadron 'Bandits'. In October 1991 the 37th was redesignated as a Fighter Wing, and similarly all three subordinate units became Fighter Squadrons. The unit retained the bird of prey badge of the 4450th Tactical Group, but superimposed this on the famous cross of the 37th TFW.

On 19 December 1989, the F-117 finally went into action during a two-ship attack on the Rio Hato barracks during the invasion of Panama. This small baptism of fire was overshadowed by the type's contribution to Desert Storm, when an eventual total of 42 aircraft flew from Khamis Mushait in Saudi Arabia on nightly missions against Iraq and

Left: As the F-117 is a 'hot ship' on landing, a drag chute is deployed from between the F-117's tails to reduce the landing roll. This aircraft is a test example serving with the 412th TW at Edwards AFB.

Below: A 49th FW F-117A flies over White Sands, near the wing's base at Holloman AFB. The relocation to Holloman completed the move out of the 'black' world.

occupied Kuwait. Using its low observability to the full, the F-117 nightly penetrated the defences around Baghdad, and guided weapons with utmost precision against most of the key targets in the city, including the release of the first bomb of the war, against an air defence centre. As the availability of such targets dried up in the latter part of the war, the 'Black Jets' turned their sights on bridges and aircraft shelters. In a war that was a demonstration of Western technical capability, the F-117 was the undisputed star. Under the command of

Lieutenant Colonel Ralph W. Getchell, the 415th TFS was the first to deploy to the Gulf region, arriving at Khamis Mushait (known as 'Tonopah East') on 19 August 1990. The 416th TFS was sent out to Saudi Arabia in December, and the 37th TFW, commanded by Colonel Al Whitley, was further reinforced by a handful of aircraft and pilots from the 417th TFTS. A total of 1,271

A 412th TW F-117A displays the carriage of the GBU-27 2,000-lb class Paveway III laser-guided bomb.

FLY-BY-WIRE
The quadruplex flight control system is fed with precise air data from four nose probes.

ARMAMENT
The two weapon bays are equipped with a trapeze for the carriage of bombs up to 2,000 lb (907 kg). The laser-guided bomb is the standard weapon (either GBU-10 or GBU-27), but other weapons such as AGM-65 Maverick and AGM-88 HARM can be carried.

Lockheed F-117A Night Hawk

Arguably the best-known shape in the skies after Concorde, the F-117 equips the 49th Fighter Wing, serving with the 7th, 8th and 9th Fighter Squadrons. A handful are additionally used for test purposes. The force is intended for precision attacks against high-value targets, a capability it demonstrated with outstanding success in the Gulf War. The OCIP programme greatly improved the cockpit, adding full-colour MFDs and a moving-map display, while also adding an autothrottle and a pilot-activated 'panic' button that automatically restores the aircraft to straight and level flight from any attitude. Further immediate upgrades include a new FLIR/designator system, GPS and ring-laser gyro INS. In the future, radar may be added to improve bad-weather capability.

STEALTH FEATURES
Helped by its amazing shape, the F-117 defeats radars by the use of RAM over the entire surface. The use of mesh over the engine intakes and sensor ports make these appear as flat surfaces to radars, while dogtooth patterns are used to disrupt returns from doors and panels.

REFUELLING
The F-117 is equipped with a receptacle on the spine for boom refuelling. The small excrescence at the apex of the fuselage houses a small floodlight for illumination.

INFRA-RED SUPPRESSION
The exhaust nozzles are fashioned into narrow slits with vertical guide vanes to diffuse the hot efflux. These are surrounded by Space Shuttle-style heat tiles.

ACQUISITION/DESIGNATION SYSTEM
The F-117 pilot uses the highly-accurate INS for navigation to the target area, whereupon the forward-looking infra-red (mounted forward of the windscreen) is used to acquire the target from long range. Once the target has been locked-in to the system, the downward-looking infra-red system takes over, this sensor peering through a mesh in the lower side of the nose. The DLIR stays peering at the target throughout the attack phase, a boresighted laser designator supplying a 'sparkle' for the precision guidance of a laser-guided bomb.

Lockheed F-117 Night Hawk

In addition to having a tiny radar signature, the F-117 has a very low infra-red signature, due to the use of non-afterburning engines and a wide, diffusing exhaust slot.

combat missions was flown during Desert Storm. On their return from the battle zone, the Night Hawks became highly visible at many air shows, and in 1992 completed their move out of the 'black' world by moving to Holloman AFB, NM. In January 1992 the 37th FW changed its designation to 49th FW.

In US Air Force planning, the F-117 is used for attacks against what the service calls 'highly leveraged' targets. These are targets whose destruction would have a far greater effect on the defensive or offensive capability of the enemy than just the physical damage caused. Such targets include communications and command centres, air defence sector centres, key bridges, airfields and the like.

Target acquisition

In order to attack such targets, the F-117 uses a highly accurate inertial navigation system to put it in the right position to begin the attack. From there, the forward-looking infra-red is used to acquire the target. Once acquired, the pilot aligns cross-hairs on his FLIR screen over the target, and locks the point into the weapons computer. As the F-117 approaches its quarry, the target dips below the aircraft's nose, and the locked-in image is handed over to the downward-looking infra-red sensor mounted under the starboard side of the nose. This remains continuously pointed at the target image, using contrast auto-tracking techniques. Laser-guided bombs are released at a computed point, and at some time during their free fall in the general direction of the target a laser is used to designate the

impact point. This laser is boresighted with the DLIR. The reflected laser energy is picked up by the seeker head on the weapon, and guides it to a direct hit.

After the Gulf War, Lockheed began an Offensive Capability Improvement Program (OCIP) for the 57 remaining F-117s (of 59 production aircraft and five pre-series aircraft delivered) with the aim of increasing their combat effectiveness by reducing cockpit workload. Two colour multi-function displays are being added, together with a moving map display. An LCD unit is to provide for data entry. Auto-throttles are incorporated, tied in to the navigation system, which provide a time-over-target function for accurate timing of attacks. An auto-recovery facility is included to prevent spatial disorientation in bad weather. Since 1984 aircraft had been upgraded with IBM AP-102 computers in place of the Delco M362Fs. A third phase of the improvement programme will add a new infra-red acquisition and designation sensor in place of the existing FLIR and DLIR (test-flown in 1992), and will also provide a Honeywell ring laser gyro INS and Collins GPS.

RAF and Luftwaffe interest in the F-117 has been claimed, and RAF exchange pilots have flown the aircraft since 1987, perhaps in exchange for occasional permission to use British bases for the aircraft. A navalised derivative has been offered to the USN as an interim strike aircraft pending the introduction of the AX. Nicknamed 'Seahawk', this aircraft would be a derivative of the basic F-117A with reduced-sweep folding wings, trapezoidal F-22-style conventional tailplanes, provision to carry weapons externally, a Grumman F-14 undercarriage and carrier landing system, and with an arrester hook housed behind closing doors in the belly.

There is no two-seat trainer version of the F-117, although a crashed FSD F-117

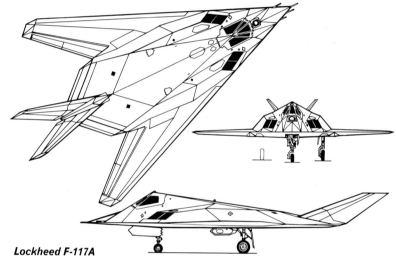

Lockheed F-117A

was proposed as the basis of a two-seat prototype. Instead, pilots rely on very sophisticated simulators and the use of a handful of T-38s for proficiency training.

WEAPON OPTIONS

Although able to carry many different weapons, the standard ordnance of the F-117 is the 2,000-lb (907-kg) LGB, either in GBU-10 Paveway II or GBU-27 Paveway III form. Each comes with two warhead options, the standard Mk 84 or the BLU-109 penetration with thicker, straight-sided walls. The GBU-27 was developed especially for the F-117 for, although it has the Paveway III guidance set, it has Paveway II-style fins that can fit in the internal weapons bays of the Night Hawk. The USAF is coy about the F-117's weapons options, answering all questions with a blanket "it can carry everything in the inventory",

refusing to discount the use of AAMs or even gun pods. Some sources suggest that the AGM-65 Maverick, AGM-88 HARM and AIM-9 Sidewinder are regularly carried, and there have been reports that there is a proposal to adapt the aircraft to carry a modified F-14-style TARPS pod internally.

SPECIFICATION

Lockheed F-117A Night Hawk
Wing: span 43 ft 4 in (13.20 m); aspect ratio about 4.3; area about 1,140.00 sq ft (105.9 m²)
Fuselage and tail: length 65 ft 11 in (20.08 m); height 12 ft 5 in (3.78 m)
Powerplant: two General Electric F404-GE-F1D2 non-afterburning turbofans each rated at 10,800 lb st (48.04 kN)
Weights: empty about 30,000 lb (13608 kg); maximum take-off 52,500 lb (23814 kg)
Fuel and load: maximum ordnance 5,000 lb (2268 kg)
Speed: maximum level speed 'clean' at high altitude possibly more than Mach 1; normal maximum operating speed at optimum altitude Mach 0.9
Range: combat radius about 600 nm (691 miles; 1112 km) with maximum ordnance
g limits: +6

Apart from the test aircraft, all F-117s are assigned to the 49th FW at Holloman, which operates three squadrons (7th/8th/9th FS), one of which is primarily a training unit. The small blades projecting from the back of this aircraft serve the communications suite, and are retractable for operations. For peacetime flying, F-117s usually carry radar reflectors to aid air traffic control.

Lockheed **L-188 Electra**

Having provided the basis for Lockheed's successful development of the P-3 Orion maritime reconnaissance aircraft, the **L-188 Electra** medium-range turboprop airliner itself entered service in a similar role late in its service life. This resulted from a modification programme to fit APS-705 search radar and other appropriate equipment in four ex-commercial **L-188A**s in **Argentina**. These serve in 1ª EAE (No. 1 Naval Reconnaissance Squadron) as part of the Argentine navy's 6ª Escuadra Aéronaval at Trelew, one Electra having been modified (by IAI in Israel) for operations in the Elint/Sigint role. Three ex-civil **L-188PF Electra Freighters** also are in service with 1ª EASLM (Logistical Supply Squadron) as part of 5ª Escuadra Aéronaval at Ezeiza. Several air forces have made use of Electras in the Presidential, VIP and general transport role, and single examples remain in service in this capacity in **Bolivia** (operated by the quasi-military TAM airline) and in **Honduras**. Airliner Electras are able to accommodate 98 passengers in high-density configuration.

SPECIFICATION

Lockheed L-188A Electra
Wing: span 99 ft 0 in (30.18 m); aspect ratio 7.54; area 1,300.00 sq ft (120.77 m2)
Fuselage and tail: length 104 ft 6 in (31.85 m); height 32 ft 10 in (10.01 m); tailplane span 42 ft 10 in (13.06 m); wheel track 31 ft 2 in (9.50 m); wheel base 29 ft 9 in (9.07 m)
Powerplant: four Allison 501D-13/13A turboprops each rated at 3,750 shp (2796 ekW) or 501D-15 each rated at 4,050 shp (3020 ekW)
Weights: empty 57,400 lb (26036 kg); typical operating empty 61,500 lb (27896 kg); maximum take-off 116,000 lb (52664 kg)
Fuel and load: internal fuel 37,500 lb (17010 kg); external fuel none; maximum payload 26,500 lb (12020 kg)
Speed: maximum level speed 'clean' at 12,000 ft (3660 m) 389 kt (448 mph; 721 km/h); maximum

cruising speed at 22,000 ft (6705 m) 352 kt (405 mph; 652 km/h); economical cruising speed at optimum altitude 325 kt (374 mph; 602 km/h)
Range: 2,180 nm (2,510 miles; 4040 km) with maximum fuel or 1,910 nm (2,200 miles; 3540 km) with maximum payload
Performance: maximum rate of climb at sea level 1,670 ft (509 m) per minute; service ceiling 27,000 ft

Argentina has a fleet of Electras for transport, Elint and maritime patrol. This example has APS-504 radar.

(8230 m); balanced take-off field length 4,720 ft (1439 m) at maximum take-off weight; balanced landing field length 4,300 ft (1311 m) at normal landing weight

Lockheed **L-1011 TriStar**

A total of nine **Lockheed TriStar 500** airliners was acquired by the UK Ministry of Defence in 1982/84 (six ex-British Airways and three ex-Pan Am) and these aircraft form the equipment of the **RAF**'s No. 216 Squadron at Brize Norton. In the first phase of a major programme handled by Marshall of Cambridge (Engineering) Ltd, four of the BA aircraft were converted to **TriStar K.Mk 1** tanker/transports. The conversion involves installation of underfloor fuel tanks in the fore and aft baggage compartments, providing an additional 100,000 lb (45360 kg) and increasing the aircraft's total fuel capacity to over 300,000 lb (136080 kg), paired Flight Refuelling Ltd HDUs in the lower rear fuselage, and a closed-circuit TV camera to monitor refuelling. The HDUs can transfer fuel at the rate of 4,000 lb (1814 kg) per minute. A refuelling probe is fitted above the forward fuselage and full passenger seating (all seats facing forwards) provided throughout the cabin. The first flight was made on 9 July 1985.

Two of the four K.Mk 1s remain in service, with the remaining two aircraft and two newly-acquired TriStars having been further modified as **TriStar KC.Mk 1** tanker/freighters. The KC.Mk 1 was first flown in 1988 and introduces a 104 x 140-in (264 x 356-cm) front fuselage port side cargo door and freight handling system, to carry palletised cargo and 35 passengers. The floor is strengthened for high-density loadings.

Two of the ex-Pan Am TriStars serve as **TriStar C.Mk 2** troop transports without probes. Planned modifications were abandoned to fit the third aircraft with under-wing Mk 32B pods containing HDUs as the **TriStar K.Mk 2** and it was delivered as a **TriStar C.Mk 2A** instead, with military avionics, a new interior and the troublesome digital autopilot replaced by an analog autopilot fitted to the K.Mk 1 and KC.Mk 1. All RAF TriStars are being fitted with AN/ALR-66 radar warning receivers, but plans to fit underwing FRL Mk 32B pods appear to have been abandoned. One other TriStar 500 (ex-Air Canada) has been converted by Marshall of Cambridge for Orbital Sciences Corp. in the USA to serve as a launcher for the Pegasus Air-Launched Space Booster, itself to be used to launch small satellites into low Earth orbit. One VIP-configured TriStar 500 serves as a part of the **Jordanian Royal Flight**.

SPECIFICATION

Lockheed L-1011 TriStar K.Mk 1
Wing: span 164 ft 4 in (50.09 m); aspect ratio 7.63; area 3,541.00 sq ft (328.96 m2)
Fuselage and tail: length 164 ft 2.5 in (50.05 m); height 55 ft 4 in (16.87 m); tailplane span 71 ft 7 in (21.82 m); wheel track 36 ft 0 in (10.97 m); wheel base 64 ft 8 in (19.71 m)
Powerplant: three Rolls-Royce RB211-524B4 turbofans each rated at 50,000 lb st (222.41 kN)
Weights: basic empty 242,684 lb (110163 kg); maximum take-off 540,000 lb (244944 kg)
Fuel and load: internal fuel 213,240 lb (96724 kg) plus provision for 100,060 lb (45387 kg) of transfer fuel in two fuselage tanks; external fuel none
Speed: never exceed speed 435 kt (501 mph; 806 km/h) CAS; maximum cruising speed at 35,000 ft (10670 m) 520 kt (599 mph; 964 km/h); economical cruising speed at 35,000 ft (10670 m) 480 kt (553 mph; 890 km/h)

Lockheed TriStar K.Mk 1

Range: 4,200 nm (4,836 miles; 7783 km) with maximum payload
Performance: maximum rate of climb at sea level 2,820 ft (860 m) per minute; service ceiling 43,000 ft (13105 m); take-off balanced field length 9,200 ft (2804 m) at maximum take-off weight; landing balanced field length 6,770 ft (2063 m)

A No. 216 Sqn TriStar K.Mk 1 refuels a Tornado F.Mk 3 from one of its fuselage HDUs. The TriStar is excellent for fighter deployments: not only can it refuel the fighters all the way, but it can also carry squadron personnel and supplies.

Lockheed **P-3A/B Orion**

In August 1957, Type Specification No. 146 was issued by the **US Navy**, calling for a new anti-submarine aircraft to replace the Lockheed P-2 Neptune. The Lockheed proposal was based on the company's L-188 Electra medium-range passenger airliner. In May 1958 Lockheed was awarded a contract largely on the basis of the strength of the aircraft's structure and its size, which was sufficient to house an extensive array of detection systems. Lockheed modified the third Electra airframe (N1883) as the prototype with a tail-mounted MAD boom and a ventral bulge simulating a weapons bay. Following extensive adaptations (including a shortening of the fuselage), the aircraft made a successful maiden flight as the **YP3V-1** (later redesignated **YP-3A**) on 25 November 1959. The Navy ordered an initial batch of seven aircraft in October 1960, and the first of these (BuNo. 148883) flew in April of the following year. In 1962 the type was redesignated **Lockheed P-3A** and named **Orion**.

Several nations are acquiring surplus US Navy P-3A/Bs. Chile has taken delivery of eight to patrol its extensive coastline.

Lockheed P-3A/B Orion

Iberian Orions: above is a Portuguese P-3P, while at left is a Spanish P-3A.

Many early Orions have had mission equipment removed (including the MAD sting) and transport interiors installed. This aircraft is a VP-3A staff transport.

The P-3A entered service in the summer of 1962, with Patrol Squadron Eight (VP-8); other units soon followed, and by December 1963 Lockheed had delivered over 50 Orions to eight squadrons. After the production of 109 P-3As, Lockheed incorporated the DELTIC (Delayed Time Compression) installation in an improvement programme. This doubled sonobuoy information-processing capability and also incorporated redesigned avionics. The first squadron to receive the new **P-3A DELTIC** was VP-46 at Moffett Field, and within a short time most aircraft had been retrofitted.

In the summer of 1965, after three years' experience and with 157 P-3As built, Lockheed began production of a new variant.

The **P-3B** was fitted with more powerful Allison T56-A-14 engines and was heavier than its predecessor, mainly through having provision for the AGM-12 Bullpup ASM, although it retained basically the same electronics fit. The P-3B secured the first export orders and became operational with the Royal New Zealand and Norwegian air forces (five aircraft each), and with the RAAF (10 aircraft). From 1977 the USN's P-3Bs have been updated with improved navigation and acoustic-processing equipment, and with provision for the AGM-84 Harpoon anti-ship missile. Production of the P-3B ceased in 1969, following the introduction of its successor, the **P-3C** (described separately).

P-3Bs have virtually been retired from USN service, although some remain with Reserve and trials units. P-3As were converted to **RP-3A** standard (three aircraft) for oceanographic reconnaissance use by VXN-8, and to **WP-3A** standard (four air-

craft) for weather reconnaissance by VW-4. Six early aircraft have been refitted for executive transport use as the **VP-3A**, while a handful serve as aircrew trainers under the designation **TP-3A**. Several early Orions have been converted for utility transport duties as **UP-3A**s and **UP-3B**s. Four P-3As were transferred to the US Customs Service under the **P-3A(CS)** designation, and others have been modified by Aero Union as civilian fire-bombers. Special-purpose variants are described separately.

New Zealand's aircraft have received an avionics upgrade (the first by Boeing, five more by Air New Zealand) and the new designation **P-3K**. The sixth was an ex-RAAF P-3B. **Norway** acquired two ex-USN P-3Bs in 1979 and one of these, plus one original aircraft, remain in service as **P-3N**s for pilot training, fishery protection and other duties. The other five were transferred to **Spain** to replace four leased USN P-3As and to augment the two surviving (of three originally) P-3As purchased by Spain.

One of Australia's P-3Bs was lost in service, and one was transferred to New Zealand in 1985. Four more were transferred to Lockheed in 1983, one becoming the P-3 AEW & C prototype (described separately). The six surviving Australian aircraft were upgraded to P-3C standard as **P-3P**s and subsequently transferred to **Portugal** in 1986. Australia plans to purchase three surplus USN P-3Bs for training duties.

A number of new customers may take delivery of surplus US Navy P-3As or P-3Bs, **Greece** being a likely candidate. Two P-3As and six UP-3As were held in storage against a **Chilean** contract and were subsequently

delivered from March 1993 for coastal patrol work. Three P-3As have been upgraded and redesignated **P-3T** (two) and **UP-3T** (one) for **Thailand** as replacements for the Grumman S-2 Tracker.

A summary of all Orion operators is provided in the following P-3C entry.

SPECIFICATION

Lockheed P-3B Orion
generally similar to the P-3C Orion except in the following particulars:
Weights: empty 60,000 lb (27216 kg); normal take-off 127,200 lb (57697 kg); maximum take-off 134,000 lb (60782)
Fuel load: internal fuel 9,200 US gal (34826 litres); maximum expendable load 15,000 lb (6804 kg) as 7,252 lb (3290 kg) in the weapon bay and 7,748 lb (3514 kg) under the wings
Speed: maximum level speed 'clean' at 15,000 ft (4575 m) 413 kt (476 mph; 766 km/h); economical cruising speed at 25,000 ft (7620 m) 345 kt (397 mph; 639 km/h); patrol speed at 1,500 ft (457 m) 200 kt (230 mph; 371 km/h)
Range: operational radius 2,200 nm (2,533 miles; 4076 km) with no time on station, or 1,680 nm (1,935 miles; 3114 km) with 3 hours on station; endurance at 1,500 ft (457 m) 12 hours 54 minutes on four engines or 17 hours on two engines
Performance: maximum rate of climb at sea level 3270 ft (997 m) per minute; take-off run 3,700 ft (1128 m) at maximum take-off weight; take-off distance to 50 ft (15 m) 4,900 ft (1494 m) at maximum take-off weight; landing distance from 50 ft (15 m) 2,420 ft (738 m) at design landing weight

Lockheed **P-3C Orion**

The **Lockheed P-3C Orion** is the US Navy's primary land-based, anti-submarine warfare patrol aircraft. It retains the airframe and powerplant installation of the earlier P-3B. The first service-test **YP-3C** 'prototype' was actually a converted P-3B and first flew on 18 September 1968. Since then, the P-3C has been exported to Australia, the Netherlands, Norway, Japan, Pakistan and South Korea.

With a crew of 10, the baseline P-3C carries out its mission of hunting submarines using a comprehensive package of ASW detection equipment. This includes APS-115B search radar, ASQ-81 magnetic anomaly detector, AQA-7 DIFAR (Directional Acoustics-Frequency Analysis and Recording) system, and AQH-4 multi-track sonar tape recorder. The P-3C introduced an integrated ASW and navigation avionics system, including the AN/ASQ-114 computer,

Iran received six P-3F Orions, which combined features of both the B and C models. Without a source of spares, the fleet has dwindled to just one or two airworthy specimens, kept aloft by raiding the others.

thus becoming the world's first ASW aircraft with a centralised computer. The first US Navy squadron to operate the P-3C was VP-30 in 1969. One hundred and eighteen 'baseline' aircraft have been succeeded by approximately 150 upgraded 'Update' versions. The P-3 has 10 stores stations (three under each outer wing panel and two on

each inner panel between the inner engine and fuselage) and a bomb bay which can carry a variety of ordnance including mines, torpedoes, destructors, nuclear depth charges, conventional bombs, practice bombs and rockets. Search stores include AN/ALQ-78 ESM pods, sonobuoys, smoke markers and parachute flares.

The **P-3C Update I** (31 built) introduced a sevenfold increase in computer memory and AN/ARN-99(V)-1 Omega navigation in place of the original LORAN. 'Baseline' and

Update I aircraft may be identified by an undernose camera fairing with windows. The **P-3C Update II** (37 built) featured the Cubic Corporation AN/ARS-3 Sonobuoy Reference System, provision for carrying and launching the AGM-84A Harpoon anti-shipping missile, an acoustic tape recording system and a Texas Instruments AN/AAS-36 IRDS (Infra-Red Detection System – a FLIR housed in a retractable turret at the nose radome). Since the AGM-84A Harpoon has been added to its armament, the Orion has

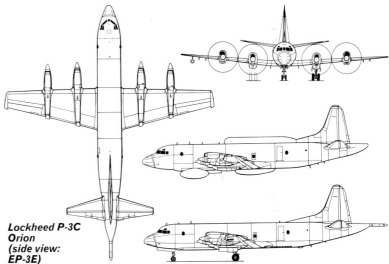

Lockheed P-3C Orion (side view: EP-3E)

Once highly colourful, the Orion fleet has surrendered to the drab grey Tactical Paint Scheme, as illustrated by this VP-16 aircraft from Jacksonville.

been given a secondary surface warfare role. This version was first delivered in August 1977. Update II.5 covered a further 24 US Navy P-3Cs with more reliable nav/comms suite, MAD compensation, standardised pylons and other improvements.

The definitive P-3C Orion variant is the **P-3C Update III**, fitted with an entirely new IBM AN/UYS-1 Proteus advanced acoustic signal processor and a new sonobuoy communications link. These enable the aircraft to monitor concurrently twice the number of sonobuoys as can the Update II.5 version. The Update III was the last production version and was first delivered in May 1984. Most baseline P-3Cs were later modified to **P-3C Update III Retrofit** standard.

Export P-3Cs included 10 Update IIs for Australia. These are equipped with the Anglo-Australian Barra acoustic data processor and indigenously developed Barra passive directional sonobuoys. Australia's second P-3C batch (a further 10 aircraft) comprised Update II.5s, but these are known locally as **P-3W**s. Ten of Australia's aircraft are receiving an Elta-developed ESM suite. The Netherlands (13) and Japan also received Update II.5s, a term also applied by the US Navy to embargoed Pakistani P-3Cs, although Lockheed calls these **Update II.75**s. P-3Cs for Norway and South Korea are Update IIIs.

Japan received three aircraft, plus a further four in component knocked-down kit form for assembly by Kawasaki (Japanese licence-built versions are described sepa-

rately). The Imperial Iranian Navy received six P-3Cs in 'baseline' standard (from an order placed in 1975) as **P-3F**s, and these were fitted with a receptacle for inflight refuelling. Due to chronic spares shortages, it is thought that only one or two are left airworthy. The Lockheed CP-140 Aurora, which resembles the P-3C externally, is built to Canadian specification with a different avionics fit. This variant is described separately.

The final P-3C for the US Navy was delivered on 17 April 1990. In 1991, Lockheed moved its Orion production line from Palmdale, CA, to Marietta, GA, with a start-up order announced on 10 December 1990 for eight P-3Cs for South Korea.

P-3C Orions have participated in all American military campaigns of their era. They played a key role in 1986 operations against Libya and in Operations Desert Shield/ Storm. In the war with Iraq, Orion detachments flew 3,787 hours in 369 combat sorties. One P-3C of VP-19 was modified under the Outlaw Hunter programme for the OASIS (OTH Airborne Sensor Information System) mission. This is an over-the-horizon targeting platform which provides an overall battlefield plot for commanders. Two further Orions, OASIS I and II, have since been modified for this role.

Proposals to further improve the Orion have fallen victim to programme management troubles and budgeting constraints. To replace some Orions, the US Navy intended in the late 1980s to procure 125 **P-7A** or **LRAACA** (Long-Range Air ASW-Capable Aircraft), originally designated **P-3G**. The P-7A also was expected to go to Britain and Germany, to replace Nimrod MR.Mk 2 and Atlantic ASW aircraft. Powered by four 5,000-shp (3730-ekW) General Electric GE38 free-turbine powerplants driving five-bladed Hamilton Standard 15WF modular

composite propellers, the P-7A was never built and the programme was cancelled on 20 July 1990 due to cost overruns.

The US Navy then sought to proceed with the **P-3C Orion Update IV** (the avionics package once envisioned for the P-7A), to introduce improved ASW electronics to cope with quiet, deep-running Soviet submarines. A 10 July 1987 contract to Boeing temporarily took this stage of Orion improvement work away from Lockheed. The Boeing-built P-3C Update IV aircraft made its first functional flight test on 16 December 1991. Update IV included IBM AN/UYS-2 processor with increased sonobuoy capability, APS-137 imaging radar, AAS-36 IRDS, ALR-66(V)5 ASM, GPS navigation, and improved stores and weapons management sub-systems. Following a brief flight test programme, development of the P-3C Update IV was suspended on 13 October 1992.

With both P-7A and P-3C Update IV removed from its future planning, in May 1992 the US Navy authorised developmental funding for yet another advanced Orion, now called the **P-3H Orion II**, a 'stretched' and largely new aircraft based on the P-3C.

VP-40 is based at NAS Barbers Point in Hawaii to cover the Pacific, with regular deployments to the Far East. The squadron operates one of the OASIS/Outlaw Hunter Orions.

The Orion II is to have a new 6,000-shp (4476-ekW) turboprop engine of unspecified type and six-bladed composite propellers to give the aircraft greater fuel economy, range and time on station. The Orion II is unlikely to advance to the hardware stage without a Pentagon go-ahead for 125 aircraft, and/or revival of interest by Britain and Germany.

WEAPON OPTIONS

The Orion has a large weapons bay forward of the wing and 10 underwing hardpoints. Standard ASW weapons are Mk 46 or Mk 50 torpedoes, various depth bombs and destructors, or B57 nuclear depth charges. For the ASV role some P-3Cs are equipped to launch AGM-84 Harpoon, while all can carry underwing rocket pods.

SPECIFICATION

Lockheed P-3C Orion

Wing: span 99 ft 8 in (30.37 m); aspect ratio 7.5; area 1,300.00 sq ft (120.77 m²)

Fuselage and tail: length 116 ft 10 in (35.61 m); height 33 ft 8.5 in (10.27 m); tailplane span 42 ft 10 in (13.06 m); wheel track 31 ft 2 in (9.50 m); wheel base 29 ft 9 in (9.07 m)

Powerplant: four Allison T56-A-14 turboprops each rated at 4,910 ehp (3661 ekW)

Weights: empty 61,491 lb (27890 kg); normal take-off

Lockheed P-3C Orion

Left: Australia purchased 20 P-3Cs in two batches, of which 19 still fly with 92 Wing, divided between Nos 10 and 11 Sqns. An ESM update used Israeli equipment, while local equipment includes the Barra sonobuoy. The second batch (Update II.5) is designated P-3W to avoid confusion with the earlier Update II aircraft.

Above: With a large slice of the North Sea and Atlantic to cover, the Netherlands purchased 13 P-3C Update II.5s to replace its elderly Neptunes. The force is concentrated at Valkenburg with the MARPAT (Maritime Patrol) group, although one aircraft is detached to Keflavik in Iceland on a rotational basis.

135,000 lb (61235 kg); maximum take-off 142,000 lb (64410 kg)
Fuel and load: internal fuel 62,500 lb (28350 kg); external fuel none; maximum expendable load 20,000 lb (9072 kg)
Speed: maximum level speed 'clean' at 15,000 ft (4575 m) 411 kt (473 mph; 761 km/h); economical cruising speed at 25,000 ft (7620 m) 328 kt (378 mph; 608 km/h); patrol speed at 1,500 ft (457 m) 206 kt (237 mph; 381 km/h)
Range: operational radius 2,070 nm (2,383 miles; 3835 km) with no time on station or 1,346 nm (1,550 miles; 2494 km) with 3 hours on station
Performance: maximum rate of climb 1,950 ft (594 m) per minute; service ceiling 28,300 ft (8625 m); take-off run 4,240 ft (1292 m) at maximum take-off weight; take-off distance to 50 ft (15 m) 5,490 ft (1673 m) at maximum take-off weight; landing distance from 50 ft (15 m) 5,490 ft (1673 m) at design landing weight

OPERATORS

The operators list covers all variants of the P-3.
US Navy: VP-1/4/9/17/47 (P-3C) NAS Barbers Point
VP-5/16/24/30/45/62 (P-3C) NAS Jacksonville
VP-8/10/11/23/26 (P-3C) NAS Brunswick
VP-46/91 (P-3C) NAS Moffett Field
VP-65 (P-3C) NAWS Point Mugu
VP-68 (P-3C) NAF Washington
VP-40/69 (P-3C) NAS Whidbey Island
VP-92 (P-3C) NAS South Weymouth
VP-30 (TP-3A, VP-3A, P-3C) NAS Jacksonville
VP-60/90 (P-3B) NAS Glenview
VP-64 (P-3B), VP-66 (P-3B, EP-3J) NAS Willow Grove
VP-67 (P-3B) NAS Memphis
VP-93/94 (P-3B) NAF Detroit
VP-94 (P-3B) NAS New Orleans
VPU-1 (P-3B) NAS Brunswick
VPU-2 (UP-3A, P-3B, P-3C) NAS Barbers Point
VQ-1 (UP-3A, UP-3B, EP-3E) NAS Agana

VQ-2 (UP-3B, EP-3E) NAS Rota
VRC-30 (UP-3A) NAS North Island
VX-1 (P-3C) NAS Patuxent River
ETD (TP-3A, UP-3A, VP-3A) NAS Barbers Point
NAS Bermuda (UP-3A)
NS Keflavik (UP-3A)
NAS Sigonella (VP-3A)
NRL (RP-3A, P-3B) NAS Patuxent River
NAWC-23 (P-3B, NP-3B, P-3C) Dallas-Love Field
NAWC-AD Patuxent River (P-3B, P-3C)
NAWC-AD Point Mugu (RP-3A)
NAWC-AD Warminster (UP-3A, P-3C)
US other agencies: US Customs Service (P-3A, P-3AEW) CSS Corpus Christi
US Forestry Service (P-3A) fire-bombers with Hawkins and Power, Black Hills Aviation and Aero Union
NASA (P-3B) Wallops Island
NOAA (WP-3D) Miami
Australia: P-3C (9), P-3W (10) – Nos 10 and 11 Sqns at RAAF Edinburgh
Canada: CP-140 (18), CP-140A (3) – aircraft of Nos

404, 405 and 415 Sqns pooled at CFB Greenwood, remainder at CFB Comox with No. 407 Sqn
Chile: P-3A (2), UP-3A (6)
Greece: expected to receive five P-3A and one UP-3A
Iran: six P-3Fs delivered, but only one or two remain airworthy
Japan: 109 P-3Cs procured for JMSDF. All but the first three built by Kawasaki (described under that manufacturer). Two converted to EP-3C and one to UP-3C
Netherlands: P-3C (13) – pooled under MARPAT Group for use by Nos 320 and 321 Sqns, and 2 OCU
New Zealand: P-3K (6) – serve with No 5 Sqn at Whenuapai
Norway: P-3C (4), P-3N (2) – operated by 333 Skvadron at Andoya
Pakistan: P-3C (3) – embargoed
Portugal: P-3P (6) – with Esquadra 601 at Montijo
South Korea: P-3C (8) – on order, first received 1994
Spain: P-3A (2), P-3B (5) – with Ala 22 at Jerez
Thailand: P-3T (2), UP-3T (1) – with 2 Sqn at U-Tapao

Lockheed **P-3 AEW**

Lockheed produced a prototype AEW & C (Airborne Early Warning & Control) aircraft as a private venture in 1984 using a **P-3B Orion** airframe reacquired from the RAAF. Flight testing began on 14 June 1984 with a 24-ft (7.32-m) rotodome mounted above the rear fuselage, and was continued in 1988 after installation of a full General Electric AN/APS-138 radar system. Export orders did not materialise, but the prototype conversion, initially fitted with AN/APS-125 radar, was delivered to the **US Customs Service** for anti-narcotics patrols on 17 June 1988. Options on three further aircraft were subsequently taken up by US Customs. These aircraft were also based on ex-RAAF P-3B airframes but were fitted with the AN/APS-138 system; deliveries took place in 1989, 1992 and 1993, respec-

In its fight against drug-smuggling, the US Customs Service employs eight Orions, four of them equipped with AEW radar as 'Blue Sentinel' aircraft. The 'slick' P-3s are fitted with the F-15's APG-63 fire control radar.

tively. These are augmented by four 'slick' P-3As equipped with APG-63 fire control radar on loan from the US Navy. The APG-63, as fitted to the F-15 Eagle interceptor, replaces the P-3A's AN/APS-80 radar in these **P-3A(CS)** aircraft.

SPECIFICATION

Lockheed P-3 AEW & C Orion
generally similar to the Lockheed P-3C Orion except in the following particulars:

Weight: maximum take-off 127,500 lb (57833 kg)
Fuel and load: maximum ordnance none
Speed: economical cruising speed at 30,000 ft (9145 m) 200 kt (230 mph; 370 km/h)
Range: endurance 14 hours

Lockheed **EP-3 Orion**

In order to maintain an up-to-date appraisal of the naval strengths of potentially hostile nations, the **US Navy** employs a fleet of specially-modified P-3s to perform the electronic intelligence-gathering role. These aircraft use receivers to gather data from foreign vessels and analyse the radars and other

electronic equipment in order to produce an electronic 'fingerprint' of the vessel. In this way, the vessel's warfighting capabilities can be catalogued, and it can be rapidly identified in the future. The electronic Orion fleet can also undertake regular Sigint duties against land-based and airborne targets.

The designation **EP-3A** has been applied to several airframes used for electronic research platforms in a variety of configurations (including a modified P-3A serving as an electronic aggressor). Two P-3As were converted to **EP-3B** standard in 1969 as Elint aircraft, known as 'Batrack'. These were fitted with direction-finding equipment and communications interception and recording equipment, replacing the ASW gear. Mission equipment was housed in a

large, retractable, ventral radome, dorsal and ventral 'canoe' fairings and a modified tailcone. EP-3Bs served with Fleet Air Reconnaissance Squadron (VQ-) 1 at NAS Agana, Guam, seeing service in Vietnam. Four **EP-3E** aircraft followed for VQ-1, these featuring improved systems, and six EP-3Es were converted for sister squadron VQ-2 at NAS Rota, Spain, operating in support of the Atlantic fleet. The EP-3E is easily distinguished by the large, flattened 360°

The EP-3E (and the similar replacement EP-3E-II) is the US Navy's principal Elint-gathering platform, tasked primarily with 'fingerprinting' foreign vessels.

radome under the forward fuselage, truncated tailboom, long dorsal and ventral canoes, and numerous additional small antennas. The array of antennas serves a comprehensive onboard suite, known collectively as the 'Aries' system. This has as its main constituent parts an ALD-8 radio direction finder, ALQ-110 signals-gathering system, ALR-52 frequency-measuring receiver and ALR-60 communications recorder. Both EP-3Bs were brought up to EP-3E standard.

As the elderly EP-3E airframes neared the end of their service lives, the US Navy opted for a CILOP (conversion in lieu of procurement) programme to update the fleet. Accordingly, 12 P-3Cs were stripped of ASW gear and had the original 'Aries' systems from the EP-3Bs and EP-3Es installed instead, together with some improvements. The aircraft emerged as **EP-3E-II**s, and continue to serve with both VQ-1 at Agana, Guam, and VQ-2 at Rota, Spain.

Additional Orions have carried the EP-3 designation for trials and EW aggressor work. At least one P-3A was converted as

an **EP-3A** to serve with various naval research facilities, including evaluation squadron VX-1, on trials work. Another EP-3A was converted to provide jamming for fleet exercises, this aircraft serving with VAQ-33 at NAS Key West. It has since been joined by an **EP-3J**, with internally- and pod-mounted jamming equipment. VAQ-33's Orions were used to provide heavy ECM environments in which naval defences could be exercised.

Both aircraft are now in EP-3J configuration, serving with VP-66 at NAS Willow Grove.

EP-3As which served the PMTC were redesignated as RP-3s, and are described separately.

SPECIFICATION

Lockheed EP-3E Orion

generally similar to the P-3C Orion except in the following particulars:
Speed: maximum level speed at 15,000 ft (4575 m) 380 kt (437 mph; 703 km/h); patrol speed 180 kt (207 mph; 333 km/h)
Range: operational radius 2,200 nm (2,533 miles; 4076 km) with no time on station
Performance: maximum rate of climb at sea level 2,175 ft (663 m) per minute; service ceiling 28,000 ft (8535 m)

Lockheed **NP-3/RP-3/WP-3**

In addition to the EP-3, TP-3, UP-3 and VP-3 described above, the **US Navy** and related agencies operate a small number of other special-mission Orions. The **RP-3A** designation is applied to seven PMTC (now Naval Air Warfare Center – Aircraft Division, NAWS Point Mugu, CA) Orions (four previously known as EP-3As), including two aircraft modified with SMILS (Sonobuoy Missile Impact Locating System) and three with 'Billboard' tail modifications (applied by Hayes International and Tracor during 1982/83). All seven aircraft have EATS (Extended Area Test System) gear, but the 'Billboard' tail adds a Raytheon Rotman-lens phased-array antenna in an extension of the fin leading edge, allowing the aircraft to receive and rebroadcast EATS data. Their

Three of NAWC-AD's RP-3A aircraft carry the 'billboard' antenna in a giant fin extension.

role is to monitor and support naval weapons trials over the Pacific. The US Navy's VXN-8 used a handful of **RP-3A**, **RP-3C** and **RP-3D** Orions on behalf of the US Naval Oceanographic Office for a variety of research programmes related to ocean currents, and acoustic and thermal properties, but these were retired in 1993.

A single **NP-3B** is used for trials by a Naval Air Systems Command test unit at Love Field, and a single P-3C has been modified with optical windows in the belly for a laser generator and receiver for the Tactical Airborne Laser Communication Program.

Two aircraft with an X-band radar in their tailcones and a C-band radar in a large ventral radome were built as **WP-3D**s using P-3C-type airframes and engines. These aircraft have extra observation windows and

new pitot static booms on nose and port wingtip, and are used by the **National Oceanic and Atmospheric Administration** for weather research and hurricane hunting from their Miami base.

Lockheed **CP-140 Aurora**

Externally closely resembling the US Navy's P-3C Orion (described separately), the **Lockheed CP-140 Aurora** is the version of the Orion purchased in 1976 by the **Canadian Armed Forces**. Internally, the 11-seat Aurora is configured to Canadian requirements, and is equipped with an avionics system based on that of the S-3A Viking, including APS-116 search radar, ASQ-501 MAD and AN/AYK-10 computer. Provision was also made in the weapons bay for Canadian-specified ordnance loads, including eight Mk 44/46 torpedoes. Lockheed flew the first CP-140 on 22 March 1979 and completed delivery of the 18 on

order in July 1981, allowing replacement of the CP-107 Argus in CAF service. The Auroras are flown by four squadrons: VP-404 (originally VT-404 for training), VP-405 and VP-415, all at Greenwood and sharing 14 aircraft, plus VP-407 at Comox with the remaining four. Paramax systems has submitted an unsolicited bid to the Department of National Defence for a C$750-million CP-140 upgrade covering acoustic sensors, radar, ESM and communications and navigation equipment, as well as a refurbishment/ SLEP to allow the fleet to operate to 2010 or beyond. Other Canadian companies are competing for the upgrade contract.

The CP-140A Arcturus is an austere version, described in the following entry.

SPECIFICATION

Lockheed CP-140 Aurora
Wing: span 99 ft 8 in (30.37 m); aspect ratio 7.5; area 1,300.00 sq ft (120.77 m²)
Fuselage and tail: length 116 ft 10 in (35.61 m); height 33 ft 8.5 in (10.29 m); tailplane span 42 ft 10 in (13.06 m); wheel track 31 ft 2 in (9.50 m); wheel base 29 ft 9 in (9.07 m)
Powerplant: four Allison T56-A-14 turboprops each rated at 4,910 ehp (3661 ekW)
Weights: empty 61,491 lb (27892 kg); normal take-off 135,000 lb

(61236 kg); maximum take-off 142,000 lb (64411 kg)
Fuel and load: internal fuel 9,200 US gal (34826 litres); external fuel none; maximum ordnance 20,000 lb (9071 kg)
Speed: maximum cruising speed at optimum altitude 395 kt (455 mph; 732 km/h)
Range: ferry range 4,500 nm (5,182 miles; 8339 km); operational radius 1,000 nm (1,152 miles; 1853 km) for an 8.2-hour patrol
Performance: maximum rate of climb at sea level 2,890 ft (881 m) per minute; service ceiling 28,250 ft (8610 m); take-off distance to 50 ft (15 m) 6,000 ft (1829 m) at maximum take-off weight; landing distance from 50 ft (15 m) 3,200 ft (975 m) at normal landing weight

Both pictures: The three Greenwood Aurora squadrons (404, 405 and 415) draw aircraft from a pool of 14 owned by the BAMEO. The remaining four are with 407 Sqn at Comox. Supporting the fleet are the Maritime Proving and Evaluation Unit, and the Aurora Software Development Unit, both at Greenwood.

Lockheed CP-140A Arcturus

Ordered by **Canada** in August 1989 and the last examples of the P-3 family built at Burbank before the final assembly line was transferred to Marietta, the **CP-140A Arcturus** is an austere special-duty variant of the CP-140 Aurora (described separately). Stripped of all ASW equipment, the Arcturus has two principal roles. The first is crew training for the Aurora fleet, and the second is environmental, Arctic sovereignty and fishery patrols, for which it carries AN/APS-134 radar and other appropriate sensors and flight systems. Delivery of three CP-140As to the BAMEO at Greenwood was completed in September 1991. The use of these aircraft releases the Aurora fleet to concentrate on their ASW activities.

Outwardly similar to the CP-140 Aurora, the Arcturus can be distinguished by the lack of certain antennas.

Lockheed S-3 Viking

A VS-32 S-3B lands carrying a D-704 refuelling pod.

The **Lockheed S-3 Viking** is the **US Navy**'s carrier-based, fixed-wing ASW aircraft. Designed to meet the US Navy's 1964 VSX (experimental carrier-based ASW aircraft) requirement, the first service-test **YS-3A** (of eight built) made its maiden flight on 21 January 1972 at Palmdale, CA. Conventional in design for a carrier-based warplane, the Viking is a high-wing, twin-turbofan aircraft with hydraulically-folding wings, and pressurised accommodation for its crew of four (comprising pilot, co-pilot, tactical co-ordinator and acoustic sensor operator). Based on an August 1969 contract, Lockheed manufactured the Viking in partnership with Vought, which designed and built wings, tail unit, landing gear and engine pods.

The original production **S-3A** variant is equipped with a Univac AN/AYK-10 digital computer, Texas Instruments AN/APS-116 radar and Texas Instruments OR-89 FLIR. The heart of the Viking's ASW suite is a Texas Instruments AN/ASQ-81 magnetic anomaly detector sensor housed in a retractable tailboom. The Viking carries 60 sonobuoys in its aft fuselage and has a ventral bomb bay and wing ordnance stations able to house bombs, torpedoes or depth charges. The first S-3A Viking went to VS-41 'Shamrocks', the first FRS for the type, located at North Island, CA, and was received in February 1974. VS-21 'Fighting Redtails', also at North Island, became the first fleet squadron to operate the type in July 1974. Lockheed built a total of 179 production S-3As, delivering the last aircraft in August 1978.

The improved **S-3B** variant is the result of a weapons system improvement pro-

Fleet ASW squadrons are equipped with the S-3B version, with improved systems and Harpoon anti-ship missile capability.

gramme launched in 1981, which retains the Viking airframe and engines but adds improved acoustic processing, expanded ESM coverage, increased radar processing capabilities, a new sonobuoy receiver system, and provision for AGM-84 Harpoon air-to-surface missiles. All but identical in outward appearance to the S-3A, the S-3B can be distinguished by a small chaff dispenser located on its aft fuselage. Nearly all existing S-3As have been upgraded to S-3B status at naval air depots. Except for a few S-3As scattered among the two training and two fleet air reconnaissance squadrons, the entire Viking force now consists of the upgraded S-3B model.

The seventh YS-3A was modified to become the **US-3A** carrier onboard delivery aircraft, envisioned as a replacement for the piston-engined Grumman C-1 Trader and first flown on 2 July 1976. In all, six US-3A Vikings, stripped of ASW equipment and transformed into 'people haulers', have been used to complement the turbine-powered Grumman C-2A Greyhound. Lockheed also modified the fifth YS-3A to test the aircraft as the **KS-3A** tanker. The dedicated tanker variant has not been produced, although operational Vikings have been adapted as part-time tankers with the same 'buddy-buddy' refuelling store.

Developed to meet the Cold War threat posed by the Soviet fleet of quiet, deep-diving nuclear submarines, the S-3 fought in Operation Desert Storm against an enemy which possessed no submarines. The S-3A/B Viking proved an exceedingly effective conventional bomber when employed against Iraqi radar stations, anti-aircraft batteries, small vessels in the Persian Gulf and other targets. On a typical mission on 20 February 1991, an S-3B of VS-32 'Maulers',

operating from USS *America* (CV-66), employed its own inverse SAR and FLIR, plus guidance from the cruiser USS *Valley Forge* (CG-50), to despatch an Iraqi combat vessel with a stick of three Mk 82 500-lb (227-kg) bombs.

Several special mission variants of the S-3B are in service or development. The **Outlaw Viking** is modified with OASIS III equipment to provide an over-the-horizon targeting and theatre control platform. The **Gray Wolf** S-3B features a Multi-Mode Radar System (comprising ISAR and SAR modes), laser ranger, digital camera system and infra-red. This is intended for littoral surveillance and tracking of 'Scud'-type missile launches. The deployed **Viking Beartrap** has an Elint processing capability in addition to its normal suite, while **Orca** is the name of one Viking used for testing advanced ASW systems such as the Intrum Extended Echo Ranger (IEER) and an ASW laser ranger integrated with some of the Gray Wolf's equipment, including a wing-mount-

ed synthetic aperture radar pod. Orca is believed to be able to detect minefields.

Several Vikings are currently involved in anti-drug trafficking duties in the Caribbean, using camera systems, FLIR and hand-held sensors. The **Calypso** S-3B is a proposal for a dedicated anti-smuggling variant, with many of the Gray Wolf systems including ISAR, SAR, IRST and cluster ranger. Finally, it has been reported that under the code-name Project Aladdin, so-called **Brown Boy** Vikings have been used to drop acoustic sensors to monitor ground movements in Bosnia, similar to the use of such sensors in the Igloo White programme in South East Asia.

WEAPON OPTIONS

The S-3B has two internal weapon bays on the 'corners' of its fuselage, able to carry four Mk 46 or 50 torpedoes, four Mk 36, 62 or 82 bomb/destructors, or two B57 nuclear depth charges (no longer carried on US carriers). A wing pylon outboard of each nacelle is able to carry two Mk 52, 55, 56 or 60 mines, six Mk 36, 62 or 82 destructor/bombs, six Mk 7 cluster dispensers, six ADM-141 decoys, six rocket pods, six flare dispensers or two AGM-84 Harpoons or AGM-84E SLAM. In the refuelling role the D-704 pod is carried under the port wing, with a 300-US gal (1135-litre) fuel tank to starboard.

SPECIFICATION

Lockheed S-3A Viking
Wing: span 68 ft 8 in (20.93 m); width folded 29 ft 6 in (8.99 m); aspect ratio 7.88; area 598.00 sq ft (55.56 m²)
Fuselage and tail: length overall 53 ft 4 in (16.26 m) and with tail folded 49 ft 5 in (15.06 m); height overall 22 ft 9 in (6.93 m) and with tail folded 15 ft 3 in (4.65 m); tailplane span 27 ft 0 in (8.23 m)
Powerplant: two General Electric TF34-GE-2 turbofans each rated at 9,275 lb st (41.26 kN) dry
Weights: empty 26,650 lb (12088 kg); normal take-off 42,500 lb (19277 kg); maximum take-off 52,540 lb (23832 kg)
Fuel and load: internal fuel 12,863 lb (5753 kg); external fuel two 300-US gal (1136-litre) drop tanks; maximum ordnance 7,000 lb (3175 kg) including 4,000 lb (1814 kg) carried internally
Speed: maximum level speed 'clean' at sea level 439 kt (506 mph; 814 km/h); maximum cruising speed

RADAR
The large nose radome houses the Texas Instruments APS-137(V)1 ISAR (inverse synthetic aperture radar). ISAR technology allows the long-range classification of ship types, while the radar uses pulse compression and a fast scan rate to eliminate sea clutter and therefore improve periscope detection capability. There are eight modes: small target detection, high-altitude long-range ocean surveillance, short-range search and rescue, medium-resolution ship classification, high-resolution classification and battle damage assessment, navigation/coast-mapping, weather detection and self-test.

Lockheed S-3 Viking

SONOBUOY LAUNCHERS
The 60 ejector ports are inclined backwards so that the buoys hit the surface below the point from which they were fired.

ASW SENSORS
In addition to the radar, the S-3B uses MAD and sonobuoys to detect and track submarines. The MAD 'sting' is deployed from the tailcone, while up to 60 sonobuoys are carried, ejected through ports in the lower fuselage. A Hazeltine ARR-78 system receives sonobuoy signals, which are processed by the AYS-1 Proteus system. ALR-76 ESM provides passive detection of hostile radar systems.

Lockheed S-3B Viking

The S-3 Viking is carried aboard each carrier to perform the outer-zone anti-submarine mission, patrolling at long distance from the carrier while the SH-60F Ocean Hawk or SH-3 Sea King handles the inner-zone defence. In addition to this primary role, the S-3B is tasked with secondary duties of inflight-refuelling (with the D-704 refuelling pod depicted here) and various forms of attack. These include anti-ship (with AGM-84 Harpoon), stand-off precision (with AGM-84E SLAM), surface attack (with general-purpose or cluster weapons) and mine-laying. ASW weapons include various destructors and depth charges, torpedoes, captive torpedoes and the B57 nuclear depth charge. The latter is no longer carried in the magazines of US Navy carriers, but remains available for contingencies.

CREW
The Viking is operated by a crew of four, all seated on McDonnell Douglas Escapac 1-E ejection seats. Two pilots sit side-by-side, handling flight control and navigation. Behind them sit the mission crew of Tactical Co-ordinator ('Tacco'), who controls the search and attack portion of the mission, and Sensor Operator ('Senso'). Both are provided with a small window in the cabin side.

FUEL
Internal fuel capacity (in the inner wing structure and top of the fuselage) is 1,900 US gal (7190 litres), which can be augmented by two 300-US gal (1136-litre) drop tanks. A retractable refuelling probe deploys from above the cockpit.

FLIR
One of the main attack sensors is the Texas Instruments OR-89/AA FLIR. This is mounted in a retractable turret located behind doors in the lower port fuselage beneath the flight deck.

WING-FOLDING
In order to take up the minimum amount of room on the carrier deck, and to fit the deck-edge elevators and hangars, the S-3 has a unique wing-folding arrangement. The wings hinge immediately outboard of the engine pylons, but stagger to lie against each other across the aircraft's back. The tall fin folds to port.

at optimum altitude more than 350 kt (403 mph; 649 km/h); patrol speed at optimum altitude 160 kt (184 mph; 296 km/h)
Range: ferry range more than 3,000 nm (3,454 miles; 5558 km); operational radius more than 945 nm (1,088 miles; 1751 km); endurance 7 hours 30 minutes
Performance: maximum rate of climb at sea level more than 4,200 ft (1280 m) per minute; service ceiling more than 35,000 ft (10670 m); take-off run 2,200 ft (671 m) at maximum take-off weight; landing run 1,600 ft (488 m) at 36,500 lb (16556 kg)

Six US-3A Vikings serve with VRC-50 in the Pacific on utility transport duties. Two were originally designated S-3A(COD). A dedicated tanker version was not proceeded with.

Lockheed ES-3A Viking

The **Lockheed ES-3A Viking** is a carrier-based Elint aircraft modified from the S-3A with over-the-horizon surveillance equipment similar to that fitted to the land-based Lockheed EP-3A Aries II. The **US Navy** has procured 16 ES-3As, converted by Lockheed at NAS Cecil Field, FL.

In the ES-3A, the co-pilot position is replaced by a third sensor station and the bomb bays have been modified to accommodate avionics. The ES-3A introduces a new radome, direction-finding antenna and other equipment in a dorsal 'shoulder' on the fuselage, an array of seven receiving antennas on its underfuselage, a cone-shaped omnidirectional Elint antenna on each side of the fuselage just forward of the horizontal stabiliser, and AN/ALR-76 ESM antennas forward and aft of the wingtips.

An ES-3A of VQ-6, the Atlantic Fleet carrierborne Sigint squadron. The US Navy was without a seagoing electronic surveillance aircraft from the withdrawal of the EA-3B in November 1987 until the arrival of the ES-3A in 1991.

Two US Navy squadrons deploy eight ES-3As each on carriers, generally in pairs. VQ-5 'Sea Shadows' stood up on 15 April 1991 at NAS Agana, Guam. VQ-6 'Black Ravens' was established in August 1991 at NAS Cecil Field.

Lockheed began the ES-3A programme with a 'proof of concept' aircraft lacking internal systems and, on 1 October 1990, began conversion of 15 ES-3As at Cecil. An ES-3A 'first flight' on 15 May 1991 involved the 16th aircraft, the sole production airframe modified by Lockheed at Palmdale, CA. The next 'production' ES-3A flew at Cecil on 21 January 1992.

Lockheed SR-71

Withdrawn from USAF service in 1990, the **Lockheed SR-71 Blackbird** reconnaissance aircraft, once the world's highest performance military aircraft, continues to play a role for research. Three SR-71s were originally placed in storage at Palmdale for the USAF, but these are believed to be no longer recoverable. A further three, comprising two **SR-71A**s and a dual-control **SR-71B**, were transferred to **NASA** and now form part of the research fleet at the Ames-Dryden Flight Research Facility based at Edwards AFB. In 1994 the possibility of returning the NASA aircraft to front-line USAF service was under review.

A proposal concerns the use of the SR-71 as a launch platform for lightweight space vehicles, using the aircraft as, in effect, a reusable first stage.

Although shrinking budgets forced the USAF to retire the SR-71, these three continue to fly from Edwards AFB with NASA-Dryden.

Lockheed T-33

With approximately 6,750 aircraft built, the **Lockheed T-33A** is by far the most successful jet trainer yet developed for service anywhere in the world, and it says much for the durability of the 'T-bird' that many aircraft remain airworthy around the world today, more than 40 years after the type first flew. The oldest aircraft in the USAF inventory is a much-modified **NT-33A** which is still flying at Wright-Patterson AFB on research tasks in mid-1994.

A logical development of the single-seat **F-80** (the first jet-powered fighter to become operational with the US Army Air Forces), the T-33A actually began life in the late 1940s as the **TF-80C**, a stretched tandem two-seater trainer version of the F-80.

Following introduction to service with the US Air Force in the closing stages of the 1940s, the 'T-bird' was soon being built in numbers that far outstripped those of the F-80, and it ultimately became the USAF's standard jet trainer type, equipping flying schools for several years. Just under 700 extensively modified examples of the T-33A were diverted to the US Navy, initially known as the **TO-2** and soon redesignated **TV-2 SeaStar** (**T-33B** from late 1962).

In addition to being extensively used by the USAF and US Navy, the T-33A found a ready market overseas, many of the aircraft built being supplied to friendly nations under the Military Assistance Program. Countries which acquired the T-33A in this way included France, Greece, Italy, the Philippines, Portugal, Spain, Taiwan, Thailand, Turkey and West Germany. Licence production was undertaken by Canada, which completed 656 Nene-engined **CL-30 Silver Star** aircraft, and by Japan, which assembled 210, many of them still engaged in training duties today.

Although viewed basically as a trainer, Lockheed's jet has performed other roles, a

Left: Thailand uses a large fleet of T-33s mainly for advanced training. A handful of RT-33s are on strength.

Right: In Europe both Greece and Turkey retain the T-33 for 'hack' and training work. This Turkish machine is on the strength of the Konya base flight.

Above: In JASDF service the T-33 is mainly assigned to HQ flights and in support of front-line units.

Above: Canada's surviving CT-133s are mostly used as either EW aggressors (illustrated) or in the target facilities role, serving with 414 Sqn.

Left: No. 2 Sqn, Pakistan air force, operates the camera-equipped RT-33A.

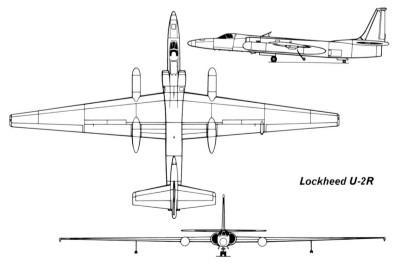

modest number of aircraft being fitted with a camera nose and electronic equipment in the aft cockpit in order to perform reconnaissance functions. Designated **RT-33A**, these single-seaters were produced mainly for MAP operators including France, Italy, the Netherlands, Pakistan, Thailand and Turkey. A version armed for interdiction and close support was the **AT-33A**, of which numbers are still in service.

Another important role was that of target drone, the US Navy being perhaps the major operator and destroyer of drone-configured 'T-birds'. Often controlled by a **DT-33** director, the **QT-33** took part in numerous weapons test projects, most of the converted aircraft meeting a fiery end over the range areas of the Pacific Missile Test Center and the Naval Weapons Center at Point Mugu and China Lake, respectively.

More recently, the Skyfox Corporation has proposed remanufacturing the T-33A as a twin-turbofan advanced trainer, employing externally-mounted Garrett TFE731 engines. Extensive redesign of the fuselage and empennage forms part of the modernisation process, but so far no customers have been found for the resulting **Skyfox**, the prototype of which flew in June 1983.

SPECIFICATION

Lockheed T-33A
Wing: span 38 ft 10.5 in (11.85 m); aspect ratio 6.44; area 234.00 sq ft (21.81 m²)
Fuselage and tail: length 37 ft 9 in (11.51 m); height 11 ft 8 in (3.55 m)
Powerplant: one Allison J33-A-35 turbojet rated at 5,400 lb st (24.02 kN)
Weights: empty equipped 8,365 lb (3794 kg); normal take-off 12,071 lb (5475 kg); maximum take-off 15,061 lb (6832 kg)
Fuel and load: internal fuel 353 US gal (1336 litres) plus provision for 460 US gal (1741 litres) in two tip tanks; external fuel none; maximum ordnance none

Speed: maximum level speed 'clean' at sea level 521 kt (600 mph; 966 km/h); cruising speed at optimum altitude 395 kt (455 mph; 732 km/h)
Range: ferry range 1,107 nm (1,275 miles; 2050 km) with tip tanks; range 890 nm (1,025 miles; 1650 km) with internal fuel
Performance: maximum rate of climb at sea level 4,870 ft (1484 m) per minute; service ceiling 48,000 ft (14630 m)

OPERATORS

T/AT-33s survive with the following air arms: Bolivia (32), Canada (local designation **CT-133**, 60 including about 30 in storage), Ecuador (23), Greece

Canada's test establishment, the AETE at Cold Lake, operates five CT-133s, including aircraft calibrated to act as chase planes. This example is used for ejection seat trials.

(about 40), Iran (10), Japan (over 100), Mexico (40), Pakistan (10 and four RT-33s), Philippines (3), South Korea (33), Thailand (over 30 and four RT-33s), Turkey about 50) and Uruguay (11 including six AT-33As).

Lockheed **U-2R**

In its original form, the **Lockheed U-2** first flew with Tony LeVier at the controls on 4 August 1955, from the secret Groom Dry Lake test facility in Nevada. A highly successful reconnaissance career for the early variants ensued, overshadowed by the shooting-down over Sverdlovsk of a CIA aircraft flown by Francis Gary Powers in May 1960. Despite the setback to the programme, the U-2 was still seen as a highly useful reconnaissance tool with its ability to loiter for hours at high altitude, making it an excellent platform for the gathering of electronic intelligence in addition to long-range oblique photographs.

As powered by the J75 engine, the first-generation U-2s were airframe-limited, so Lockheed began the development of a much larger aircraft to provide far greater sensor carriage on the same power. The result was the **U-2R**, which first flew from Edwards North Base on 28 August 1967. This closely resembled the early aircraft in layout, but was larger in overall dimensions, offering the ability to carry large amounts of

intelligence-gathering equipment and much greater range/endurance by way of large internal fuel carriage in the huge 'wet' wings. At the same time, the new design alleviated many of the aerodynamic flaws of the first generation, making the U-2R much less tricky to fly.

A first batch of 12 aircraft was completed, equally distributed between the **US Air Force** and the CIA. The former mostly flew in South East Asia, while the latter operated from Taiwan over Communist China. In 1974 the agency aircraft passed to the US Air Force, and joined a global reconnaissance effort that has been maintained ever since.

In November 1979, the production line reopened to provide 37 new airframes. The initiative for this was the **TR-1A** programme, which used the U-2R airframe as a platform for the ASARS-2 battlefield surveillance radar. The TR-1A was also seen as a platform for the PLSS radar location system, and for signals intelligence-gathering equipment as carried by the U-2R. TR-1As were

Lockheed U-2R

intended for use in Europe and deployed to RAF Alconbury and the 17th Reconnaissance Wing, but the presence was progressively withdrawn as the Cold War threat diminished. The TR-1A designation was

finally dropped to recognise the fact that the aircraft were virtually identical to the U-2Rs.

The new-build batch contained 25 aircraft designated TR-1A, and seven designated U-2Rs as attrition replacements from the

Lockheed U-2R

Lockheed began to replace J75 turbojets with GE F101-GE-F29 turbofans. First flown in a TR-1A in March 1989, this powerplant is derived from the B-2's F118 engine, and is in the 18,500-Lb st (83.9-kN) class. The F101 confers a 15 per cent increase in endurance, restores operational ceiling to above 80,000 ft (24380 m) and improves supportability across USAF bases, the U-2R being the last USAF aircraft to fly under J75 power.

SPECIFICATION

Lockheed U-2R

Wing: span 103 ft 0 in (31.39 m); aspect ratio 10.6; area about 1,000.00 sq ft (92.90 m2)

Fuselage and tail: length 62 ft 9 in (19.13 m); height 16 ft 0 in (4.88 m)

Powerplant: one Pratt & Whitney J75-P-13B turbojet rated at 17,000 lb st (75.62 kN) dry

Weights: basic empty without powerplant and equipment pods less than 10,000 lb (4536 kg); operating empty about 15,500 lb (7031 kg); maximum take-off 41,300 lb (18733 kg)

Fuel and load: internal fuel 7,649 lb (3469 kg); external fuel none; sensor weight 3,000 lb (1361 kg)

Speed: never exceed speed Mach 0.8; maximum cruising speed at 70,000 ft (21335 m) more than 373 kt (430 mph; 692 km/h)

Range: maximum range about 5,428 nm (6,250 miles); 10060 km); maximum endurance 12 hours

Performance: maximum rate of climb at sea level about 5,000 ft (1525 m) per minute; climb to 65,000 ft (19810 m) in 35 minutes; operational ceiling 80,000 ft (24385 m); take-off run about 650 ft (198 m) at MTOW; landing run about 2,500 ft (762 m) at maximum

NASA operates three ER-2s as high-altitude research and sensor platforms. These fly with NASA-Ames at Moffett Field.

Above: For the real-time global transfer of data, some U-2Rs are fitted with the Senior Span satellite communications equipment, housed in a teardrop fairing on a dorsal pylon.

Left: Three U-2RT trainers are on strength with the 9th Reconnaissance Wing for conversion training and check rides.

outset. Three two-seat trainers were included in the batch, these comprising two **TR-1Bs** and a single **U-2RT**. All three are identical, and the TR-1Bs have now adopted the U-2RT designation. Finally, two aircraft were completed as **ER-2s** for use as earth resources monitoring aircraft by NASA-Ames. These were later joined by an ex-TR-1A.

In configuration, the U-2R resembles a powered glider. The high aspect ratio wings confer extraordinary range and altitude performance, while the slender fuselage houses the engine, cockpit and bicycle undercarriage. The main undercarriage is retractable, but the wings are supported by plug-in 'pogo' outriggers. These fall free on take-off, leaving the aircraft to come to rest on one wingtip at the end of its landing run. The wingtips incorporate skids, above which are radar warning receivers.

Sensors are carried in the detachable nosecone (with different-shaped cones for different sensor fits), a large 'Q-bay' behind the cockpit for the carriage of large cameras, smaller bays along the lower fuselage and in two wing 'super pods', which are removable. Sensors include a wide range of recorders for Comint and Elint, imaging radars, radar locators and high-resolution cameras. A common configuration is the Tactical Reconnaissance System (TRS) fit, which features ASARS-2 radar in extended nosecone, side-looking radars in 'super pods' and a large farm of Sigint antennas on the 'super pods' and rear fuselage.

Recorded intelligence can be transmitted via datalink to ground stations, and at least three aircraft are equipped to carry the Senior Span satellite communications antenna in a huge teardrop radome mounted on a dorsal pylon. This allows the transmission of recorded intelligence across global distances in near real-time.

Missions vary according to requirements, but often reach 10 hours in duration. The standard profile is to fly racetrack patterns at altitudes around 75,000 ft (22860 m). On approach, the U-2R pilot is aided by another pilot in a Ford Mustang chase car (the 'mobile') who provides landing instruc-

tions as the U-2R settles back to earth. Despite the aerodynamic refinements applied to the second-generation U-2, it remains a particularly tricky aircraft to land, being very prone to weather-cocking due to the central main undercarriage and large fin, and with a high tendency to float due to the very low wing loading and high idle speed of the engine.

All U-2s serve with the 9th Reconnaissance Wing headquartered at Beale AFB, CA, where they previously shared the base with the Mach 3+ SR-71. The primary flying unit is the 99th Reconnaissance Squadron, augmented by the 1st RS(T) which undertakes training and flies the U-2RT trainers. This squadron previously flew the SR-71, while the U-2 training function was undertaken by the 5th SRTS. The 9th RW has

three theatre detachments to cover the Mediterranean, Far East and Europe. These are, respectively, at RAF Akrotiri, Cyprus (Det 2), Osan AB, South Korea (Det 3) and RAF Alconbury, England (OL-UK), each usually operating two aircraft. Additionally, U-2s have been stationed at Taif, Saudi Arabia (OL-CH – Operating Location-Camel Hump), since the first days of the Desert Shield military build-up following the Iraqi invasion of Kuwait in August 1990. In 1994 the U-2s were still regularly flying monitoring missions in that theatre, continuing an impressive record established before and during the war. Regular surveillance of Bosnia was also being maintained.

While new sensors are continually being developed for the U-2R fleet, airframe modifications were limited until 1992, when

Below: In common with other Air Combat Command aircraft, the 9th Wing's U-2Rs wear tailcodes and a unit fin-band.

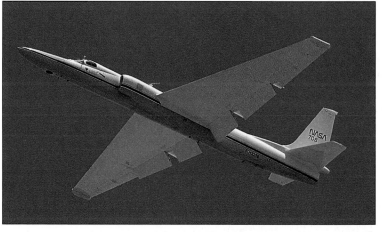

Lockheed/Boeing F-22

YF-22 originally Lockheed/General Dynamics/Boeing.
GD's fighter division at Fort Worth
subsequently purchased by Lockheed

The **Lockheed/Boeing F-22** is the **US Air Force**'s replacement for the F-15 Eagle. Intended to be the leading American air-to-air fighter in the early part of the 21st century, the F-22 meets a USAF requirement for long-range cruise at supersonic speeds without afterburning (supercruise), and makes use of low-observables (LO), or stealth technology, to defeat advanced radar defence systems.

The F-22 emerged from the free-spending Reagan years (1981-89) when the USAF sought an F-15 Eagle replacement. In 1984, the USAF formalised a requirement for a fighter capable of supersonic flight in the region of Mach 1.5 without afterburning, with a range greater than that of the F-15, and with vectoring and reversing engine nozzles for STOL performance.

Lockheed YF-22A and Northrop YF-23A candidates were developed for this ATF (Advanced Tactical Fighter) contest, initially in a 'black' programme accessible only to those with compartmentalised security clearances. Boeing and General Dynamics teamed with Lockheed; the former's company-owned Boeing 757 was modified to become an avionics flying laboratory for the F-22 programme. The first YF-22A, powered by General Electric YF120 engines, made its first flight on 29 September 1990. The second YF-22A, powered by Pratt & Whitney YF119 engines, flew on 30 October 1990. The competing Northrop YF-23 also

flew in both GE- and P&W-powered examples. On 23 April 1991, the USAF announced its choice of the F-22 for the ATF production contract. The decision in favour of the P&W engine came soon after.

The F-22 uses thrust vectoring to manoeuvre at high angles of attack in air-to-air combat: two-dimensional engine nozzles can be vectored 20 per cent up or down at any power setting. Coupled with large leading-edge wing flaps and overall low wing loading, the nozzles permit manoeuvre at low speeds and high flight angles.

The angular YF-22 has a comparatively large, diamond-shaped wing, splayed twin vertical tails and large horizontal tails. The wing is almost a delta, with 48° of sweep on the leading edge, a nearly straight trailing edge, and a very small tip chord. The wing blends into the fuselage to provide a lifting body area. Engine air intakes are located astride a short, tapered nose, which houses the cockpit and most of the avionics. The inlet ducts curve inward and upward, shielding the front faces of the engine from direct illumination by radar. Radar-absorbent materials are employed in the forward fuselage and cockpit canopy.

The pilot sits upright on a zero-zero ACES II seat beneath an unbroken bubble-style canopy and has a panel of liquid-crystal colour displays and HUD. Extensive use is made of VHSIC (very high-speed integrated circuits), common modules and high-speed

Lockheed/Boeing YF-22

data buses. The avionics suite makes use of voice command/control, VHSIC 1750 computer, shared antennas, advanced data fusion/cockpit displays, INEWS (integrated electronic warfare system), ICNIA (integrated communications, navigation, identification avionics) and fibre-optics data transmission. The integrated avionics suite maximises the pilot's situational awareness, allowing him to fully exploit the aircraft's

many high-technology systems.

The F-22 is intended to cruise at supersonic speed to a high-risk area and engage opposing aircraft beyond visual range but, if necessary, to be able to outmanoeuvre them at closer range. Details have not been released concerning the radar, which will be crucial to the F-22 in BVR engagements, although it will have a fixed, phased-array antenna. A 20-mm cannon is mounted internally in production F-22s for closer-in combat. The F-22's lower fuselage has a weapon bay with serrated edges to house four AIM-120 AMRAAM missiles. The aircraft also has lateral weapon bays just aft of the engine inlets for four AIM-9M

Left: The F119-powered YF-22 manoeuvres at speed. For the second stage of its flight trials a military serial was worn, in place of the civilian N22YX used for the first stage of Dem/Val. Note the Pratt & Whitney badge on the intake, and the 'Skunk Works' badge on the fin.

Below: Looking every inch a fighter, the F-22 design is a careful blend of manoeuvrability, performance, advanced avionics and stealthiness. The two YF-22 prototypes fully validated the design concept.

Sidewinders. Other planned production changes made in a desire for economy include a relaxation in rear hemisphere 'stealthiness'.

In September 1991, the USAF acknowledged that the F-22 would exceed its projected weight goal by 10,000 lb (4536 kg) and will weigh 20 per cent more than the target weight of 50,000 lb (22680 kg). A Martin-Marietta IRST for the F-22 was postponed due mainly to cost considerations. Flight testing of the YF-22 resumed on 30 October 1991 at Edwards AFB, but was discontinued after the second YF-22, the only example then flying, crashed at Edwards on 25 April 1992.

Engineering and manufacturing development work will occupy the period 1992-96. In the FSD F-22 programme, the manufacturers will produce seven single-seat **F-22A** aircraft and two two-seat **F-22B** aircraft, the first due to fly in 1996. The production aircraft will differ significantly from the YF-22s, with revised shapes applied to the nose, wings and tail surfaces. The all-important alignment of surfaces (for low radar cross-section) has been altered with leading-edge sweepback reduced from 48° to 42°, with an additional edge added to the wing planform. The tailplane is revised, although overall wing and tailplane areas remain unchanged. The engine intakes are moved farther back, and the nose profile enlarged to house the radar. The vertical tails are reduced in size and the wingroot thickness decreased. Air-to-ground capability is being added with provision to carry the Joint Direct Attack Munition and the Tri-Service Stand-off Attack Missile.

The USAF had planned originally to order 750 ATFs, with production from 1994. Following the 1990 Major Aircraft Review, production was to begin in 1996, saving $1.26 billion, for a total of 648 aircraft (one-third earmarked for air defence) with maximum production rate being changed from 72 per year in 1999 to 48 per year in 2001. By 1994 the figure stood at 442 aircraft for service entry in 2003/04. The 325th FW at Tyndall AFB, FL, may become the first F-22 operator for training, followed by the 1st FW at Langley AFB, VA, as the first front-line unit. Based on the F-22 design, the swing-wing **NATF** was proposed for the US Navy to replace the F-14 Tomcat. The programme was subsequently cancelled in 1993.

ALIGNMENT
Key edges of the F-22's shape are on the same alignment. This vastly reduces radar cross-section. The YF-22's principal alignment was 48°, that of the F-22A being 42°.

CONTROL SURFACES
The leading-edge flaps deflect 3° up and 35° down, the trailing-edge flaperons 20° up and 40° down, the ailerons +/- 20°, the tailplanes 30° up and 25° down, and the rudders +/- 30°.

AIR-TO-AIR ARMAMENT
The F-22 will have a primary armament of four AIM-120 AMRAAM missiles housed in two bays in the lower fuselage. The bay doors have serrated edges fore and aft to preserve the low radar cross-section. Short-range missiles are housed in two bays in the side of the engine intake trunks, again with dogtooth edges for the double doors. At present the AIM-9M would be carried, but under development is the AIM-9X, based on either the 'Boa' tail-control or 'Boxoffice' canard configurations. Missiles are carried on 'revolutionary' launch rails, which eject the weapon into the air stream from out of the bays before the motor fires. Gun armament, not fitted to the YF-22, will be a long-barrelled version of the trusty M61A1 20-mm Vulcan cannon.

AIR-TO-GROUND WEAPONS
The F-22 will have four underwing pylons for the carriage of fuel tanks or weapons. The main weapon will be the pylon-carried AGM-137 TSSAM, while the JDAM (Joint Direct Attack Munition) will be carried in the AMRAAM bays.

Lockheed/Boeing YF-22 PAV No. 1

Since the F-104, Lockheed has been out of the fighter business but now, with the F-22 programme and the purchase of GD's F-16 production facility, the company is at the forefront. Two YF-22s were built, along with two Northrop/McDD YF-23s, for the ATF Dem/Val competition. One aircraft of each pair was powered by the Pratt & Whitney YF119 and one by the General Electric YF120. This aircraft is the GE-powered PAV (prototype air vehicle) No. 1. The YF-22/YF119 combination was eventually selected, chiefly on the grounds of the least development risk factor, but also on cost. Nevertheless, the huge price tag of the F-22 has seen procurement totals tumble, and may yet see the programme cancelled or severely curtailed. Production aircraft will feature considerably revised surfaces, with double-cropped wing planform, smaller fins, wider nose profile and squarer tailplanes.

INTAKES
The diamond-shaped intakes follow the same alignments as the other surfaces to preserve stealth characteristics, while the serpentine trunks shield the compressor face from prying radars. A pronounced lip on the upper edge aids high-Alpha ingestion. Auxiliary doors are on top of the intakes.

AVIONICS TESTBED
Boeing is using the 757 prototype to test F-22 systems. It is currently being modified to 'Catfish' configuration with an F-22 wing section mounted at zero incidence above the forward fuselage, with an F-22 nose on the front.

With a large gantry mounting a spin recovery parachute, the General Electric YF120-powered YF-22 shows off its agility, and the complicated control surfaces. These include full-span leading-edge manoeuvring flaperons, small ailerons and larger flaperons. The horizontal tail surfaces are all-moving and are aided in pitch control by the vectoring nozzles. All surfaces, including the nozzles, are controlled by a digital triplex fly-by-wire system.

During the YF-22 Dem/Val phase, test pilot Jon Beesley launched an AIM-9 Sidewinder.

For longer-range engagements the AIM-120 will be carried, seen here being launched from the lower fuselage bay. JDAM air-to-ground munitions will also be carried in the lower weapon bays.

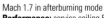

AVIONICS
The F-22 is the first aircraft with fully integrated avionics, with a Hughes common integrated processor at the heart of the system. The radar is a Westinghouse low probability-of-intercept unit which offers long-range detection without giving away the position of the F-22. A Sanders/General Electric EW system and TRW comm/nav/ident system are all controlled by the CIP. Data is presented to the pilot on four advanced liquid-crystal colour MFDs and a HUD.

POWERPLANT
The F-22 will be powered by two F119-PW-100 engines of roughly 35,000 lb (155 kN) thrust. These are low bypass ratio turbofans, with a two-shaft design. The fan has three stages, while the compressor is a multi-stage unit turning in the opposite direction. The turbine consists of single low- and high-pressure stages turning in opposition.

SPECIFICATION

Lockheed/Boeing YF-22A
Wing: span 43 ft 0 in (13.11 m); aspect ratio about 2.2; area about 840.00 sq ft (78.04 m²)
Fuselage and tail: length 64 ft 2 in (19.56 m); height 17 ft 7 in (5.36 m)
Powerplant: two Pratt & Whitney F119-P-100 turbofans each rated at 35,000 lb st (155.69 kN) with afterburning
Weights: empty more than 30,000 lb (13608 kg); maximum take-off 58,000 lb (26308 kg)
Speed: maximum level speed 'clean' at optimum altitude Mach 1.58 in supercruise mode and at 30,000 ft (9145 m)

Mach 1.7 in afterburning mode
Performance: service ceiling 50,000 ft (15240 m)
g limits: +7.9

Lockheed/Boeing F-22A
generally similar to the Lockheed/Boeing YF-22A except in the following particulars:
Wing: span 44 ft 6 in (13.56 m); aspect ratio 2.36
Fuselage and tail: length 62 ft 1 in (18.92 m); height 16 ft 5 in (5.00 m)
Weights: maximum take-off 60,000 lb (27216 kg)

AIRBRAKE
A dorsal airbrake was fitted to the YF-22, but will not be incorporated on production aircraft. Instead, the rudders will be differentially deployed to a maximum of 30° for aerodynamic braking.

Right: An artist's impression of the production F-22A displays the revised wing and tailplane plans, the fatter nose and the cut-back intakes.

EXHAUST
The exhaust nozzles are of the two-dimensional convergent-divergent type, incorporating vectoring to increase field performance and pitch/turn rate.

LTV (Vought) **A-7 Corsair II**

LTV renamed Vought Aircraft Company in 1992
9314 West Jefferson Boulevard, PO Box 655907
Dallas, TX 75265-5907, USA

First flying on 27 September 1965, the **A-7 Corsair II** was developed for the US Navy light attack mission, and early variants were active in the Vietnam War from carrier decks. The Corsair II is now out of front-line US Navy service. The type was adopted by the US Air Force for the close air support/battlefield air interdiction role as the **A-7D**, which differed primarily in being powered by a licence-built Rolls-Royce Spey turbofan (Allison TF41). The first A-7D flew on 26 September 1968, and this variant also saw service in South East Asia. A total of 459 was built.

After being replaced on active-duty service by the Fairchild A-10, A-7Ds were issued to Air National Guard units, where the type continued to have a productive career. In January 1981 the two-seat **A-7K** made its first flight, the 31 built being issued only to Guard units.

In order to keep the aircraft viable in the 1990s, Vought began development of the **A-7F** version, which involved a radical reworking of the ANG machines with P&W F100 afterburning turbofans, lengthened fuselage and updated avionics. This programme was cancelled after two prototype conversions had flown, and in the early

The pugnacious A-7 continues to provide sterling service, principally on anti-ship duties, to two Mediterranean NATO operators: the Greek and Portuguese air forces. Portuguese A-7Ps are equipped to carry the ALQ-131 ECM pod.

1990s the aircraft began a rapid withdrawal from Guard service. The last retired in 1993.

With the US Navy, 11 **TA-7C** trainers and **EA-7L** EW trainers survived a grounding order and continue to serve with test units at Point Mugu and Patuxent River.

Exports of the Corsair were limited, sales to Pakistan and Switzerland having been thwarted. **Portugal** received 50 aircraft in two batches from 1981 onwards. These are rebuilt Navy A-7A/Bs, and are designated in FAP service as the **A-7P** and **TA-7P**, the latter a two-seat derivative. The remaining 31 A-7Ps and six TA-7Ps are operated by Esquadra 302 and 304 at Monte Real with maritime strike as the primary role, using AGM-65 Maverick missiles. **Greece** purchased 60 **A-7H** and five **TA-7H** aircraft, and these are based on the Navy's **A-7E** variant with TF41 engine. Some 49 still serve, flying with 347 Mira at Larissa and 340/345 Mira at Soudha. Like Portuguese A-7Ps, the primary role is anti-shipping. The fleet has been bolstered by the transfer of 36 ex-US Navy aircraft, mostly A-7Es but also including a handful of TA-7C trainers. The sale of 18 ex-US Navy A-7Es to the **Royal Thai Navy** was agreed in 1994.

SPECIFICATION

Vought A-7D Corsair II
Wing: span 38 ft 9 in (11.81 m); width folded 23 ft 9 in (7.24 m); aspect ratio 4.0; area 375.00 sq ft (34.83 m²)
Fuselage and tail: length 46 ft 1.5 in (14.06 m); height 16 ft 0.75 in (4.90 m); tailplane span 18 ft 1.5 in

LTV (Vought) A-7D Corsair II (lower side view: A-7K)

(5.52 m); wheel base 18 ft 1.5 in (4.83 m)
Powerplant: one Allison TF41-A-1 turbofan rated at 14,500 lb st (64.50 kN)
Weights: basic empty 19,127 lb (8676 kg); operating empty 19,915 lb (9988 kg); maximum take-off 42,000 lb (19050 kg)
Fuel and load: internal fuel 9,263 lb (4202 kg); external fuel up to four 300-US gal (1136-litre) drop tanks; maximum ordnance 20,000 lb (9072 kg) theoretical, 15,000 lb (6804 kg) practical with reduced internal fuel and 9,500 lb (4309 kg) with maximum internal fuel
Speed: maximum level speed 'clean' at sea level 606 kt (698 mph; 1123 km/h); maximum speed at 5,000 ft (1525 m) 562 kt (646 mph; 1040 km/h) with 12

Mk 82 bombs or 595 kt (685 mph; 1102 km/h) after bomb release
Range: ferry range 2,485 nm (2,861 miles; 4604 km) with maximum internal and external fuel or 1,981 nm (2,281 miles; 3,671 km) with internal fuel; combat radius 620 nm (714 miles; 1149 km) on a hi-lo-hi mission
Performance: maximum rate of climb at sea level 15,000 ft (4572 m) per minute; service ceiling 42,000 ft (12800 m); take-off run 5,600 ft (1705 m) at MTOW

Vought A-7K
generally similar to the A-7D except in the following particulars:
Fuselage and tail: length 48 ft 11.5 in (14.92 m)

McDonnell Douglas **A-4 Skyhawk**

Initial design and manufacture of the A-4 by Douglas.
McDonnell Douglas Corporation formed
with McDonnell on 28 April 1967

A classic warplane by any criterion, the small and compact **A-4 Skyhawk** first flew in prototype form on 22 June 1954, and entered service with the **US Navy** in October 1956. It provided that service, and the **Marine Corps**, with their principal light attack platform for many years. Total production of all variants reached 2,960.

The early **A-4A/B/C** variants were powered by the Wright J65 turbojet and differed

in levels of avionics and engine power. The **A-4E** introduced the Pratt & Whitney J52 turbojet, and the **A-4F** featured a large dorsal hump to contain extra avionics, this being retrofitted to some earlier models. The **A-4G** was built for the Royal Australian Navy, while the **A-4H** was tailored to the requirements of the **Israeli air force**, featuring a revised fin and a braking parachute. The **A-4K** was supplied to **New Zealand** and the **A-4KU** to **Kuwait**, while the

The A-4K is the mainstay of the RNZAF, 14 single-seat aircraft serving with Nos 2 and 75 Sqns. The main improvement of the Kahu upgrade was the addition of APG-66NZ radar.

A-4L was a rebuilt A-4C for the US Navy Reserve. **A-4N**s were similar to the A-4H but featured uprated avionics, including an HUD. The last major production model was the **A-4M**, based on the A-4F but with numerous updates including the A-4H fin, brake chute and J52-P-408A engine. Most of the surviving aircraft have been updated to prolong their lives. The various two-seat variants are described separately.

With the original operator, there are few single-seat Skyhawks left, these mostly serving with aggressor squadrons. The major variant is the A-4F, which has been stripped of most of its attack avionics, including removal of the dorsal hump, and is known as the **'Super Fox'**. These serve, augmented by two-seat aircraft and the later stripped-down A-4M **'Super Mike'**, with adversary units, including the naval Fighter Weapons School ('Top Gun') at NAS Miramar. The A-4M model remains in use with three USMC Reserve squadrons (VMA-124, 131 and 322), but these are being phased out swiftly.

Overseas operators

In foreign service, there are seven operators. **Argentina** operates refurbished A-4B/Cs as the **A-4P** (air force) and **A-4Q** (navy), numbers remaining being 29 and five, respectively. The fleet has been bolstered by the transfer beginning in 1993 of 36 ex-USMC A-4Ms and two-seat OA-4Ms (described separately). **Indonesia** operates two squadrons of refurbished ex-Israeli A-4Es, one at Madiun (11 Sqn) and one at Pekanbaru (12 Sqn). Israel itself retains some 70 A-4Ns, probably now relegated to training or reserve use, and perhaps some A-4Hs, although most of these aircraft may be stored. Kuwait's A-4KU aircraft were used during the Gulf War in 1991, and it is thought 18 (of 30 delivered) remain in use, although these are likely to be sold in the near future, with Chile an interested party.

Malaysia has a fleet of Skyhawks designated **A-4PTM** (Peculiar To Malaysia). In 1979, the RMAF bought 88 former US Navy A-4C/Ls in storage, planning to overhaul and conduct an ambitious upgrade for 70 of them. This was later abandoned on cost grounds, and Grumman refurbished them to produce 40 A-4PTMs (comprising 34 single-seaters and six **TA-4S**s trainers). These aircraft can potentially carry AGM-65 Mavericks for air-to-surface missions, and AIM-9s for air-to-air combat. Two Kuantan-based squadrons (Nos 6 and 9) operate the 34 surviving aircraft, although these will probably be withdrawn as the RMAF receives its BAe Hawk 100s and 200s. Neighbour **Singapore** has the most capable Skyhawks, having substantially upgraded a large number of surplus A-4B/Cs as **A-4S**s. These

Israel still operates A-4N Skyhawks. They are fitted with lengthened jetpipes to reduce IR signature.

Grumman updated 40 ex-US Navy Skyhawks for Malaysia, which are designated A-4PTM. They serve with Nos 6 and 9 Squadrons at Kuantan on the east coast.

are described in greater detail under the heading Singapore Aerospace.

New Zealand is the final foreign user, flying 14 A-4Ks alongside two-seaters. These have been upgraded with new avionics under Project Kahu, including APG-66NZ radar, Ferranti HUD/WAC, ALR-66 RWR, ALE-39 chaff/flare dispenser, ring-laser gyro INS and HOTAS controls. The radar is similar to that fitted to the F-16, but with a reduced-size scanner to fit the Skyhawk's contours and an additional sea-search mode for anti-shipping attacks. New weapon options include AGM-65 Maverick, AIM-9 Sidewinder, GBU-16 LGB and CRV-7 rockets. A-4Ks serve with No. 75 Sqn at Ohakea, and No. 2 Sqn at RAN Nowra in Australia, where they provide a joint-national force for naval support. All foreign operators also fly two-seat trainer versions, which are described separately.

SPECIFICATION

McDonnell Douglas A-4M Skyhawk II
Wing: span 27 ft 6 in (8.38 m); aspect ratio 2.91; area 260.00 sq ft (24.155 m²)
Fuselage and tail: length 40 ft 3.5 in (12.27 m) excluding probe; height 15 ft 0 in (4.57 m); tailplane span 11 ft 3.5 in (3.44 m); wheel track 7 ft 9.5 in (2.38 m)
Powerplant: one Pratt & Whitney J52-P-408 turbojet rated at 11,200 lb st (50.0 kN) dry
Weights: empty 10,465 lb (4747 kg); normal take-off 24,500 lb (11113 kg)
Fuel and load: internal fuel 4,434 lb (2011 kg); external fuel up to three 300-US gal (1136-litre) drop tanks; maximum ordnance 9,155 lb (4153 kg)
Speed: maximum level speed 'clean' at 25,000 ft with a 4,000-lb (1814-kg) warload (7620 m) 560 kt (645 mph; 1,038 km/h) or 'clean' at sea level 595 kt

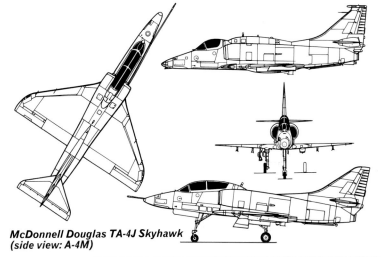

McDonnell Douglas TA-4J Skyhawk (side view: A-4M)

(685 mph; 1102 km/h)
Range: ferry range 1,785 nm (2,055 miles; 3,307 km); combat radius 295 nm (345 miles; 547 km) with a 4,000-lb (1814-kg) warload
Performance: maximum rate of climb at sea level 10,300 ft (3140 m) per minute; service ceiling 38,700 ft (11795 m); take-off run 2,730 ft (832 m) at 23,000 lb (10433 kg)

Above: US Navy use of the single-seat Skyhawk is restricted to a few examples with adversary units. This 'Super Mike' serves with VF-126.

Below: A-4Ms remain in the attack role with USMC Reserve, but are due for retirement in 1994/95.

McDonnell Douglas TA-4 Skyhawk

Although it was an easy aircraft to convert to, the Skyhawk was a natural basis for a two-seat trainer version, although such a variant was not introduced until some way into the production run. The first major Skyhawk trainer model was the **TA-4E/F**, which first flew on 30 June 1965, featuring two cockpits in tandem with a single canopy, and some combat capability (although the dorsal avionics hump could not be fitted). Related variants were the **TA-4G** for Australia, **TA-4H** for **Israel**, **TA-4K** for **New Zealand**, and **TA-4KU** for **Kuwait**. The **EA-4F** was an electronic warfare aggressor for US Navy squadron VAQ-33. The **OA-4M** was the sole two-seater based on the A-4M, and was used by the USMC for forward air control duties. Although retired from USMC service, some OA-4Ms are included in the 36-Skyhawk batch delivered to **Argentina** from 1994.

The definitive two-seater was the **TA-4J**, of which 292 were built new and several converted from TA-4Fs. This was a simplified version lacking cannon armament and combat capability. In **US Navy** service this is the major operational model, being used in the advanced training role, including carrier qualification, by squadrons VT-7 (NAS Meridian, MI), VT-21 and 22 (NAS Kingsville, TX), and VT-24 and 25 (NAS Chase Field, TX). The main training fleet is being replaced by the T-45 Goshawk. A small number of TA-4Js and Fs serve with utility composite squadrons, USMC units, and with adversary squadrons.

Overseas, the two-seaters remain with **Indonesia** (two TA-4Hs), Israel (30-plus TA-4Hs and ex-US Navy TA-4Js), Kuwait (one TA-4KU), **Malaysia** (10 TA-4PTMs), New Zealand (six TA-4Ks) and **Singapore** (12 **TA-4S**s). Many of these have been updated under the same programmes running for the single-seat aircraft. The trainers of Singapore are unique in so far as they are converted from single-seat aircraft with an additional, separate cockpit instead of the single two-place cockpit of the other trainer variants.

SPECIFICATION

McDonnell Douglas TA-4F Skyhawk
generally similar to the McDonnell Douglas A-4M Skyhawk II except in the following particulars:
Fuselage and tail: length 42 ft 7.25 in (12.98 m);
height 15 ft 3 in (4.65 m);
Powerplant: one Pratt & Whitney J52-P-8A turbojet rated at 9,300 lb st (41.3 kN)
Weights: empty 10,602 lb (4809 kg); normal take-off 15,783 lb (7159 kg)
Fuel and load: internal fuel 660 US gal (2498 litres)
Speed: maximum level speed 'clean' at sea level 586 kt (675 mph; 1086 km/h)
Range: ferry range 1,910 nm (2,200 miles; 3540 km); normal range 1,175 nm (1,353 miles; 2177 km)
Performance: maximum rate of climb at sea level 5,750 ft (1753 m) per minute; take-off run 3,380 ft (1030 m) at 23,000 lb (10433 kg)

McDonnell Douglas TA-4J Skyhawk
generally similar to the McDonnell Douglas TA-4F Skyhawk except in the following particulars:
Powerplant: one Pratt & Whitney J52-P-6 turbojet rated at 8,500 lb st (37.7 kN)

Above: Large numbers of TA-4Js serve the US Navy as advanced trainers. This aircraft serves with VT-7.

Below: Singapore's TA-4S conversion trainers are unique in having separate cockpits.

No. 2 Sqn RNZAF acts as the Skyhawk OCU and also undertakes the naval target facilities role, based at Nowra in Australia. It has three TA-4Ks on strength, all fully upgraded with the Kahu modifications, including APG-66NZ radar, a derivative of the unit fitted to the F-16.

McDonnell Douglas C-9 Nightingale/Skytrain II

Douglas Aircraft Company
3855 Lakewood Boulevard
Long Beach, CA 90846, USA

Experience gained in the early stages of American involvement in the Vietnam War highlighted the need for a medium-range aeromedical transport, and as a relatively low-cost expedient an initial order for eight 'off-the-shelf' commercial **McDonnell Douglas DC-9 Series 30** twin rear-turbofan airliners was placed, to be set aside for military conversion. Modifications included the provision of a special-care compartment, galleys and toilets fore and aft, and the addition of a third access door 11 ft 4 in (3.45 m) wide in the front fuselage with inbuilt hydraulic ramp to facilitate the loading of litters. Accommodation was provided for up to 40 litters and 40 ambulatory patients, two nurses and three aeromedical attendants.

With these features, the first **McDonnell Douglas C-9A Nightingale** was rolled out on 17 June 1968 and delivered to Scott AFB two months later; subsequent aircraft served with the 375th Aeromedical Airlift Wing of **USAF**'s MAC (now 375th AW of AMC), and later with the 55th AAS of the 435th Tactical Airlift Wing (now 86th Wing at Ramstein). Later orders brought the total deliveries to 21, in addition to three **C-9C** executive transports flown by the 89th Military Airlift Wing at Andrews AFB, MD. In addition to these operators, the C-9 is flown by the 374th AW at Yokota, while the 73rd AAS is an AFRes Associate unit at Scott, supplying aircrew to augment the active-duty crews.

A subsequent version of the DC-9 was developed as the **C-9B Skytrain II**, ordered by the **US Navy** as a fleet logistic transport. Combining features of both the DC-9 Series 30 and 40, a total of 19 aircraft was delivered for use by Navy logistic support squadrons in the USA and two to the **US Marine Corps**' Station Operations and Engineering Squadron at Cherry Point MCAS, NC. The US Navy subsequently purchased 10 similar DC-9-30s, the combined fleet serving with VR-46/51/52/55/56/57/58/59/60/61/62. Two similar military aircraft, which retain the **DC-9-32CF** designation, were delivered to the **Kuwaiti air force**, being convertible as either passenger or freight transports. One was lost during the Gulf War, but has since been replaced in No. 41 Squadron by a **McDonnell Douglas MD-83** aircraft, this much later variant featuring a stretched fuselage, updated cockpit and JT8D-219 engines. **Italy** operates two **DC-9-32s** on VIP transport duties.

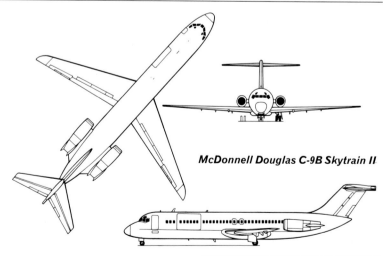

McDonnell Douglas C-9B Skytrain II

A pair of DC-9-32s serves with the AMI's 306° Gruppo, 31° Stormo for VIP transport duties. They are based at Roma-Ciampino.

SPECIFICATION

McDonnell Douglas C-9A Nightingale
Wing: span 93 ft 5 in (28.47 m); aspect ratio 8.71; area 1,000.70 sq ft (92.97 m²)
Fuselage and tail: length 119 ft 3.5 in (36.37 m); height 27 ft 6 in (8.38 m); tailplane span 36 ft 10.25 in (11.23 m); wheel track 16 ft 6 in (5.03 m); wheel base 53 ft 2.5 in (16.22 m)

Powerplant: two Pratt & Whitney JT8D-9 turbofans each rated at 14,500 lb st (64.5 kN)
Weights: empty 57,190 lb (25940 kg); maximum take-off 121,000 lb (54885 kg)
Fuel and load: internal fuel 3,679 US gal (13925 litres); external fuel none; maximum payload 31,125 lb (14118 kg)
Speed: never exceed speed 537 kt (618 mph; 995 km/h); maximum cruising speed at 25,000 ft (7620 m) 490 kt (564 mph; 907 km/h); economical cruising speed between 30,000 and 35,000 ft (9145 and 10670 m) 443 kt (510 mph; 821 km/h)
Range: ferry range 1,980 nm (2,280 miles; 3669 km); range at economical cruising speed at 30,000 m (9145 m) 1,670 nm (1,923 miles;

3095 km), or with full accommodation 1,290 nm (1,485 miles; 2390 km)
Performance: maximum rate of climb at sea level 2,900 ft (885 m) per minute; service ceiling 37,000 ft (11280 m); take-off distance to 35 ft (10.7 m) 7,400 ft (2256 m) at maximum take-off weight; landing distance from 50 ft (15 m) 4,720 ft (1439 m) at normal landing weight

The C-9 is used by the USAF for aeromedical duties, equipped for emergency treatment and evacuation. This example serves with the 20th Air Ambulance Squadron at Yokota.

McDonnell Douglas **KC-10A Extender**

The **McDonnell Douglas KC-10A Extender** strategic tanker/transport is based on the **DC-10 Series 30CF** commercial freighter/airliner and was obtained off the shelf to satisfy the ATCA (Advanced Tanker Cargo Aircraft) requirement. It emerged victorious in a competition with Boeing's Model 747 in December 1977 when the **USAF** indicated its intention to procure 16 examples, but the number on order rose substantially in December 1982, when the USAF placed a multi-year contract covering a further 44 aircraft. The first example of the Extender made its maiden flight on 12 July 1980 and deliveries to the Air Force at Barksdale, CA, commenced in March 1981, presaging a six-month period of operational testing in which all aspects were exhaustively evaluated. Just over seven years later, the 60th and last KC-10A was formally handed over on 29 November 1988.

Originally allocated solely to Strategic Air Command, the KC-10A was (and still is) frequently flown by Air Force Reserve crews under the so-called 'Associate' programme. The type was not fitted with thermal blast screens, nor 'hardened' against electromagnetic pulse effects, as it was not designed to to undertake Emergency War Order missions. Rather, the ATCA requirement was mainly concerned with supporting tactical rather than strategic forces.

The recent major USAF reorganisation that witnessed the elimination of SAC has resulted in examples of the Extender being redistributed among elements of Air Mobility Command and Air Combat Command. Apart from a single example that was destroyed in a fire on the ground in September 1987, all KC-10As continue to serve with units located at Barksdale AFB, LA, and March AFB, CA (both units with the 722nd Air Refueling Wing), and Seymour Johnson AFB, NC (4th Wing).

Changes from commercial DC-10 standard include provision of an inflight-refuelling receptacle above the cockpit, improved cargo-handling system and some military avionics. The most visible evidence of modification for the ATCA role is the McDonnell Douglas Advanced Aerial Refueling Boom (AARB) sited beneath the aft fuselage. The refuelling operator's station is equipped with a periscope observation system and rear window for wide field of view. The KC-10's boom is fitted with digital FBW control and provides greater capability than the type fitted in the KC-135. The boom is rated for a fuel transfer rate of 1,500 US gal

The KC-10 was procured primarily to support fighter deployments, being able to carry fuel, supplies and personnel. The type has proved extremely useful in both pure tanker and transport roles. These aircraft, demonstrating the previous charcoal grey and current mid-grey schemes, serve with the 4th Wing at Seymour Johnson AFB.

(5678 litres) per minute. The 'flying boom' is the preferred Air Force method of transferring fuel in flight, but the Extender is also fitted with a hose-and-reel unit in the starboard aft fuselage and can thus refuel Navy and Marine Corps aircraft during the same mission. This dual capability makes it much more versatile than the KC-135, which has to be configured for one or other option on the ground.

Twenty KC-10s are fitted with wing-mounted pods so that three receiver aircraft may be refuelled simultaneously with the probe-and-drogue system. Trials of this configuration were undertaken with the last Extender to be built, which was fitted with a pair of Flight Refuelling Ltd Mk 32B hose-drum units. Seven bladder fuel cells have been installed in the lower fuselage baggage compartments, and comprise three forward cells and four aft of the wing. These contain a total of 117,829 lb (53446 kg) of fuel, equivalent to approximately 18,125 US gal (68610 litres), and are interconnected with the aircraft's basic fuel system. Total onboard fuel is available either for transfer to other aircraft or for extended range. The KC-10 is able to transfer 200,000 lb (90718 kg) of fuel to a receiver 1,910 nm (2,200 miles; 3540 km) from its home base and return to base.

Other notable aspects are the 8 ft 6 in x 11 ft 8 in (2.59 m x 3.56 m) cargo door on the port side of the fuselage, a feature that allows the KC-10A to undertake conventional strategic transport missions carrying standard USAF pallets, bulk cargo or wheeled vehicles. In this role, maximum cargo ca-

pacity is 169,409 lb (76843 kg), which it can carry over an unrefuelled range of 3,797 nm (4,370 miles; 7031 km). Since it is also able to receive fuel in flight, it can effectively operate non-stop to any point on the globe, with the most important limiting factor likely to be crew duty restrictions. A modification introduced an onboard loading system to allow the KC-10 to operate from austere locations without the need for the prepositioning of ground loading equipment.

Finally, the aircraft may perform missions that call upon the Extender to undertake

aspects of both the tanker and transport functions in a single mission. For example, when accompanying deploying fighters, this is achieved during the transit by the provision of inflight-refuelling support. In addition, technicians, administrative staff and vital ground equipment can also be carried in the cabin, which is able to accommodate up to 75 personnel and 17 cargo pallets.

Two McDonnell Douglas DC-10s were procured secondhand from Martinair by the Royal Netherlands air force, but were temporarily leased back to the airline. These aircraft are being converted by McDonnell Douglas to **KDC-10** tanker configuration and will return to service in 1995 with 334 Squadron at Eindhoven.

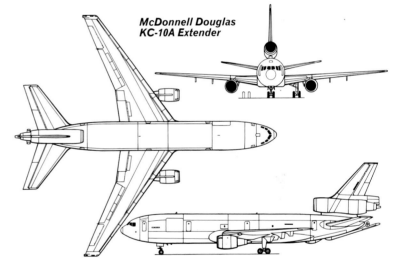

McDonnell Douglas KC-10A Extender

SPECIFICATION

McDonnell Douglas KC-10A Extender
Wing: span 155 ft 4 in (47.34 m); aspect ratio 6.8; area 3,861.00 sq ft (358.69 m²)
Fuselage and tail: length 181 ft 7 in (55.35 m); height 58 ft 1 in (17.70 m); tailplane span 71 ft 2 in (21.69 m); wheel track 34 ft 8 in (10.57 m); wheel

base 72 ft 5 in (22.07 m)
Powerplant: three General Electric CF6-50C2 turbofans each rated at 52,500 lb st (233.53 kN)
Weights: operating empty 240,065 lb (108891 kg) as a tanker or 244,630 lb (110962 kg) as a cargo transport; maximum take-off 267620 kg (590,000 lb)
Fuel and load: aircraft basic fuel system 238,236 lb (108062 kg); fuselage bladder fuel cells 117,829 lb (53446 kg); total internal fuel 356,065 lb (161508 kg);

external fuel none; maximum payload 169,409 lb (76843 kg) of cargo
Speed: never exceed speed Mach 0.95; maximum level speed 'clean' at 25,000 ft (7620 m) 530 kt (610 mph; 982 km/h); maximum cruising speed at 30,000 ft (9145 m) 490 kt (564 mph; 908 km/h)
Range: nominal range with 100,000 lb (45400 kg) payload 6,000 nm (6,905 miles; 11,112 km); maximum range with maximum cargo 3,797 nm (4,370 miles;

7032 km); ferry range 9,993 nm (11,500 miles; 18507 km)
Performance: maximum rate of climb at sea level 2,900 ft (884 m) per minute; service ceiling 33,400 ft (10180 m); take-off balanced field length 10,400 ft (3170 m) at maximum take-off weight; landing balanced field length 6,130 ft (1868 m) at maximum landing weight

McDonnell Douglas **C-17 Globemaster III**

On 29 August 1981 McDonnell Douglas was chosen to proceed with a design to fulfil the **USAF**'s **C-X** requirement for a new heavy cargo transport. Although the aircraft has suffered a protracted development programme – it is planned to achieve IOC in early 1995 – it is set to revitalise the US strategic airlift effort. The requirement called for the provision of intra-theatre and theatre airlift of outsize loads, including armoured vehicles, directly into a combat zone. This required an aircraft with a cabin

The C-17 entered service with the aptly-numbered 17th Airlift Squadron. The first aircraft wears the legend 'Spirit of Charleston'.

offering large-volume capacity, ease of loading/unloading for wheeled or tracked vehicles, and good short-field performance.

McDonnell's winning design was designated **C-17A** and named **Globemaster III**. It exhibits a classic military transport aircraft configuration – high wing, rear-fuselage loading ramp and undercarriage housings on each side of the fuselage. However, it has such advanced-technology features as winglets, supercritical wing section and high-performance turbofans. Short-field performance is aided to some extent by an externally-blown flap system similar to that demonstrated on the McDonnell Douglas YC-15 prototype, in which the trailing-edge flaps are extended into the exhaust flow

from the engines during take-off and landing to contribute to STOL performance. The usefulness of all these STOL features was negated to some extent when rough field capability was deleted as an economy measure. However, the C-17 can routinely operate from airfields previously denied to jet-powered transports. Reverse thrust on the F117 engines (similar to those which power the Boeing 757 airliner) allows the aircraft to reverse up a shallow slope or turn around on a narrow runway.

The C-17 has a flight crew of two, a loadmaster, and provision for 102 troops/paratroopers on stowable seats in the cabin, which can carry, for example, 48 litters, three AH-64A Apache helicopters, or air-

droppable platforms of up to 110,000 lb (49895 kg). The cockpit is state-of-the-art, with four multi-function displays and an HUD for each pilot. Flight control is effected by fly-by-wire, and the pilots have a control column rather than the conventional yoke.

After an earlier FSD schedule had been abandoned, the single prototype (T-1) of the C-17A flew on 15 September 1991, followed by the first three production examples comprising P-1 on 18 May, P-2 on 23 June and P-3 on 7 September 1992. A total of 10 aircraft was flying by February 1994. A symmetrical wing failure of the static test aircraft necessitated an extensive and costly stiffening and strengthening modification (with subsequent weight and performance penalties). An interim wing will be introduced to P-13 and subsequent aircraft and a new redesigned wing from aircraft between P-32 and P-38.

Deliveries to the 17th AS at Charleston AFB, SC, began in June 1993 to replace the C-141B StarLifter. Testing was continuing with the 412th Test Wing (417th TS) at Edwards AFB. Cold-weather trials were accomplished at Eielson AFB, AK. Total planned procurement is 120, although cancellation remains possible and further cutbacks in procurement are likely. By early 1994, 40 C-17s had been funded.

SPECIFICATION

McDonnell Douglas C-17A Globemaster III
Wing: span 165 ft 0 in (50.29 m) basic and 171 ft 3 in (52.20 m) between winglet tips; aspect ratio 7.16; area 3,800.00 sq ft (353.02 m²)

Below: Landing at Edwards, the first production C-17 displays the large flaps that are central to the aircraft's STOL performance.

PASSENGER CARRIAGE
The C-17 is equipped with 54 tip-up seats along the sides of the cargo hold, to which can be added a further 48 along the centreline for a maximum of 102 fully-equipped troops. Alternatively, the hold can be reconfigured with 100 pallet-mounted seats, for a maximum of 154 troops. In the medical evacuation role, 48 litters can be mounted on 12 four-litter stanchions.

McDonnell Douglas C-17 Globemaster III

AIRDROP
Paradropping capability from the rear ramp includes up to 110,000 lb (49895 kg) on multiple platforms, 60,000 lb (27215 kg) on a single platform or 102 paratroops. Eleven 463L pallets can be airdropped, including two carried on the rear ramp.

FUEL
Fuel is held in six main integral wing tanks, situated between the main spars and extending for virtually the full span of the wing. Total capacity is 27,108 US gal (102614 litres). A refuelling receptacle is located above the flight deck.

Fuselage and tail: length 174 ft 0 in (53.04 m); height 55 ft 1 in (16.79 m); tailplane span 65 ft 0 in (19.81 m); wheel track 33 ft 8.5 in (10.27 m); wheel base 65 ft 9.5 in (20.05 m)
Powerplant: four Pratt & Whitney F117-P-100 turbofans each rated at 41,700 lb st (185.49 kN)
Weights: operating empty 269,000 lb (122016 kg); maximum take-off 580,000 lb (263083 kg)
Fuel and load: internal fuel 27,108 US gal (102614 litres); maximum payload 172,200 lb (78108 kg); typical payload 124,000 lb (56245 kg) on an inter-theatre logistics mission at a 2.25-*g* load factor increasing to 153,300 lb (69535 kg) on a heavy logistics mission at a 2.5-*g* load factor
Speed: maximum cruising speed at low altitude 350 kt (403 mph; 648 km/h) CAS; airdrop speed at sea level between 115 and 250 kt (132 and 288 mph; 213 and 463 km/h) or at 25,000 ft (7620 m) between 130 and 250 kt (150 and 288 mph; 241 and 463 km/h)
Range: ferry range with maximum fuel and no payload 4,700 nm (5,412 miles; 8710 km); range with a 124,000-lb (56245-kg) payload 2,800 nm (3,225 miles; 5190 km), or with a 160,000-lb (72575-kg) payload 2,400 nm (2,765 miles; 4445 km); radius with an 81,100-lb (36786-kg) payload 500 nm (575 miles; 925 km) or with a 124,000-lb (56245-kg) payload 1,900 nm (2,190 miles; 3520 km)
Performance: service ceiling 45,000 ft (13715 m); take-off field length with 167,000-lb (75750-kg) payload 7,500 ft (2286 m); landing field length with 167,000-lb (75750-kg) payload 3,000 ft (914 m) with thrust reversal

MAIN CABIN
The main compartment measures 68 ft 2 in (20.78 m) in length, including the load-bearing rear ramp, and has a volume of 20,900 cu ft (592 m³). The height under the wing centre-section is 12 ft 4 in (3.76 m) and the maximum loadable width is 18 ft 0 in (5.49 m). An internal loading system runs the full length of the hold, and can be operated by the single loadmaster. In addition to outsize equipment, 18 standard 463L freight pallets can be carried.

POWERPLANT
The four F117-PW-100s give a total thrust of 166,800 lb (742.2 kN). The engine is similar to the PW2040 which powers several versions of the Boeing 757 airliner, offering high thrust with excellent fuel economy.

FLIGHT CONTROL
The General Electric quadruple-redundant fly-by-wire system controls outboard ailerons and eight overwing spoilers for roll control, two rudder sections for yaw, four elevator sections for pitch, and full-span leading-edge slats and trailing-edge hinged flaps for high lift.

FLAPS
The single-piece flaps employ propulsive-lift technology. Engine exhaust is blown back at the flap, and through the hinge slot, so that a sheet of air is deflected down either side of the flap. This allows steep approaches at 116 kt (215 km/h; 133 mph) with a 15 ft (4.5 m) per second sink rate.

McDonnell Douglas C-17A Globemaster III

The design of the C-17 was driven by the need to carry large items, such as tanks and helicopters, on strategic airlift tasks, while at the same time retaining the ability for tactical delivery profiles, including LAPES and short landings into austere airfields. Vital equipment can be delivered much closer to the front line than with existing strategic airlifters, which need full-length runways, while present tactical transports cannot carry such large items. Consequently, the C-17 has a voluminous and easily accessible cargo hold, but has outstanding STOL and ground-manoeuvring qualities. In the air the aircraft is far more responsive and agile than the C-141 and C-5, as it is required to operate closer to the front line.

CREW
The C-17 is flown and navigated by two pilots. The loadmaster has a work station at the forward end of the hold deck. Two additional seats are provided on the flight deck for observers or relief aircrew.

267

McDonnell Douglas **F-4D Phantom II**

McDonnell Aircraft Company
Box 516, St Louis
MO 63166, USA

The **F-4D** was the first purpose-designed USAF **Phantom II** variant. Specifically optimised for air-to-ground operations, it retained the basic airframe and engines of the **F-4C** but incorporated extensively modified avionics. A smaller, lighter, partly solid-state APQ-109 radar giving air-to-ground ranging replaced the F-4C's APQ-100 unit, and the ASN-63 replaced the ASN-48 inertial navigator. McDonnell manufactured a total of 825 F-4Ds.

The F-4C and F-4D have been retired from US service (all F-4Ds had been withdrawn from fighter intercept groups of the Air National Guard by 1992). The F-4D was exported to **Iran**, where some survivors of 32 delivered from 1968 are still flying, although serviceability is questionable. The final major user is **South Korea**, which has approximately 60 F-4Ds (the majority ex-USAF) as part of the 11th Fighter Wing at Taegu, comprising the 110th TFS (detached to Kunsan) and the 151st TFS. The last batch was equipped with Pave Spike laser designator pods for all-weather weapons delivery. Primary weapons comprise AIM-7E/AIM-7F Sparrow and AIM-9N AAMs for interception duties, and AGM-65A Maverick AGMs for air-to-surface tasks.

SPECIFICATION

McDonnell Douglas F-4D Phantom II
Wing: span 38 ft 4.875 in (11.71 m); aspect ratio 2.82; area 530.00 sq ft (49.24 m²)
Fuselage and tail: length 58 ft 3.25 in (17.76 m); height 16 ft 3 in (4.95 m); tailplane span 17 ft 11.5 in (5.47 m); wheel track 17 ft 10.5 in (5.30 m); wheel base 23 ft 4.5 in (7.12 m)
Powerplant: two General Electric J79-GE-15 turbojets each rated at 10,900 lb st (48.49 kN) dry and 17,000 lb st (75.62 kN) with afterburning
Weights: basic empty 28,976 lb (13144 kg); maximum

In addition to their primary air-to-ground tasking, armed with laser-guided bombs and Mavericks, the F-4Ds of the 11th TFW, RoKAF, undertake target-towing duties. The dart target is reeled out behind the Phantom.

take-off 59,247 lb (26874 kg)
Fuel and load: internal fuel 1,972 US gal (7465 litres); external fuel up to 8,830 lb (4005 kg) in one 600-US gal (2271-litre) and two 370-US-litre) drop tanks; maximum ordnance 16,000 lb (7257 kg)
Speed: maximum level speed 'clean' at 40,000 ft (12190 m) 1,290 kt (1,485 mph; 2390 km/h); cruising

speed at optimum altitude 510 kt (587 mph; 945 km/h)
Range: ferry range 1,520 nm (1,750 miles; 2816 km) with drop tanks; combat radius 730 nm (841 miles; 1353 km)
Performance: maximum rate of climb at sea level 48,000 ft (14630 m) per minute; service ceiling 59,400 ft (18105 m)

McDonnell Douglas **F-4E/F Phantom II**

The **McDonnell F-4E Phantom II** is the definitive version of the Phantom and currently serves half a dozen air arms in the strike role. While no longer the primary fighter in any air force, the F-4E retains some useful capabilities, although only Israel and South Korea are upgrading this version. The F-4E resulted from experience gained in air-to-air engagements over North Vietnam. It was first flown on 30 June 1967, and entered service in 1968. With 1,397 examples manufactured, the F-4E became the most numerous version, and serves with the air forces of Egypt, Greece, Iran, Israel, South Korea and Turkey. The F-4E has been withdrawn from the US Air Force (apart from the Luftwaffe training unit), AFRes and ANG, but some may be converted to drone configuration.

The F-4E is distinguished from other Phantom variants by its internal centreline General Electric M61A1 Vulcan or 'Gatling' 20-mm cannon with 640 rounds in an undernose fairing, and a new Westinghouse AN/APQ-120 solid-state radar fire control system housed in a longer nose. The F-4E also introduced a seventh 104-US gal (394-litre) fuselage fuel tank, although the impact of this is reduced by the addition of self-sealing to the fuel tanks, an innovation that reduces capacity from 1,364 to 1,225 US gal (5164 to 4636 litres). Powered wing folding was removed, and a slotted stabilator was added to increase tailplane authority. During production of the F-4E various improvements were added, including a leading-edge TISEO electro-optical sensor and leading-edge slats that dramatically improved instantaneous turn performance. Though outclassed by newer fighters such as the F-15, which have more capable and longer-range radar and greater manoeuvrability, the F-4E retains an air-to-air capability, with AIM-7 Sparrow and AIM-9 Sidewinder AAMs in addition to its cannon. It is now, however, more often used in the air-to-ground role carrying guided and unguided ordnance. Standard weapons include the AGM-65 Maverick. Korea uses the Phantom as an LGB launch platform, having been supplied with eight Pave Tack target acquisition/laser designation pods for all-weather precision attack. Some of Israel's Phantoms are believed to be equipped for the defence suppression role.

Israel's original **F-4E 'Super Phantom'** upgrade was to have been powered by Pratt & Whitney PW1120 engines. This aspect of the upgrade has not been proceeded with, but Israel has upgraded 50 of its surviving F-4Es under the designation **Kurnass 2000** (described separately under the heading IAI).

The multi-role F-4E served as the basis for the dedicated interceptor **Mitsubishi F-4EJ** (described separately) and the **F-4F**, unique to Germany. This was originally intended to be a lightweight single-seat version of the F-4E, and had the seventh fuel tank, Sparrow capability and inflight-refuelling equipment removed (the latter was later reinstated). The tailplane was unslot-ted. Although conceived as an interceptor, the F-4F was also employed in the fighter-bomber role by two wings. The F-4F first flew on 18 May 1973 and 175 were built. The Luftwaffe has pursued an ambitious upgrade programme to keep the F-4F competitive and has applied the first stage of the **ICE** (Improved Combat Efficiency, or **KWS** – Kampfwehrsteigerung) upgrade to 150 surviving F-4Fs. The upgrade adds a new laser inertial gyro, GEC CPU-143/A digital air data computer and a new databus. One hundred and ten interceptors (originally 75) are scheduled to receive the second phase with APG-65 radar, AEG radar displays, Hughes cockpit displays, an improved IFF system, Litton ALR-68(V)-2 RWR, smokeless engines, a new fire control computer and Frazer Nash ejector launchers for four belly-mounted AMRAAM missiles. The resulting **F-4F ICE** is AIM-120 AMRAAM capable, and the first guided firing was made on 22 November 1991. This upgraded variant has re-entered service with JG 71 and JG 74.

Left: An F-4E from 7 Ana Jet Üs touches down at Erhac. The wing has three Phantom squadrons, of which one (173 Filo) is the type OCU for the Turkish air force.

Below: Luftwaffe F-4Fs are being upgraded to ICE standard, with improved avionics, AIM-120 missiles and a modern radar (APG-65). A light grey camouflage is being adopted for air defence work, as demonstrated by this JG 74 aircraft.

WEAPON OPTIONS

Standard air-to-air load consists of internal M61A1 20-mm Vulcan cannon, four AIM-9 Sidewinders carried on shoulder rails either side of the inboard wing pylon and four AIM-7 Sparrows in semi-recessed bays under the fuselage. Luftwaffe ICE aircraft can carry AIM-120 AMRAAM in place of AIM-7. Fuel tanks usually carried on outboard wing pylons, leaving inboard pylon free for air-to-ground weapons carriage. Large variety of air-to-ground weapons available, including rocket pods, gun pods, 'iron' and cluster bombs, AGM-65 Maverick, laser-guided bombs (used in conjunction with AVQ-23 Pave Spike designator carried in forward Sparrow well or, for Korea, the AVQ-26 Pave Tack pod) and Shrike anti-radiation missiles. Israeli aircraft can launch Gabriel anti-ship missile.

SPECIFICATION

McDonnell Douglas F-4E Phantom II
Wing: span 38 ft 4.875 in (11.71 m); aspect ratio 2.82; area 530.00 sq ft (49.24 m²)
Fuselage and tail: length 63 ft 0 in (19.20 m); height 16 ft 5.5 in (5.02 m); tailplane span 17 ft 11.5 in (5.47 m); wheel track 17 ft 10.5 in (5.30 m); wheel base 23 ft 4.5 in (7.12 m)
Powerplant: two General Electric J79-GE-17A turbojets each rated at 11,810 lb st (52.53 kN) dry and 17,900 lb st (79.62 kN) with afterburning
Weights: basic empty 30,328 lb (13757 kg); mission empty 31,853 lb (14448 kg); combat take-off 41,487 lb (18818 kg); maximum take-off 61,795 lb (28030 kg)
Fuel and load: internal fuel 12,290 lb (5575 kg); external fuel up to 8,830 lb (4005 kg) in one 600-US gal (2271-litre) and two 370-US gal (1401-litre) drop tanks; maximum ordnance 16,000 lb (7258 kg)
Speed: maximum level speed 'clean' at 36,000 ft

Left: Two of the Greek Phantom squadrons are given a ground attack role, while the third is tasked with air defence.

Below left: Egypt received Phantoms from 1979, following the shift in allegiance from East to West. Orange stripes prevented confusion with Israeli F-4s.

(10975 m) 1,290 kt (1,485 mph; 2390 km/h); cruising speed at maximum take-off weight 496 kt (571 mph; 919 km/h)

Range: ferry range 1,718 nm (1,978 miles; 3184 km); defensive counter-air combat radius 430 nm (495 miles; 797 km); interdiction combat radius 618 nm (712 miles; 1145 km); area interception combat radius 683 nm (786 miles; 1266 km)

Performance: maximum rate of climb at sea level 61,400 ft (18715 m) per minute; service ceiling 62,250 ft (18975 m); take-off run 4,390 ft (1338 m) at maximum take-off weight or 3,180 ft (969 m) at 53,814 lb (24410 kg); landing run 3,780 ft (1152 m) at

maximum landing weight or 3,520 ft (1073 m) at 35,143 lb (15937 kg)

OPERATORS

Egypt: 32 F-4Es are in service with the 76th and 88th Squadrons of the 222nd TFB at Cairo-West
Germany: 150 F-4Fs fly with JG 71 (Wittmundhafen), JG 72 (Hopsten), JG 73 (Laage) and JG 74 (Neuburg). Some serve with the trials organisation ETD 61. The fleet is undergoing ICE/KWS upgrade
Greece: 48 F-4Es remain from the initial Greek procurement, being augmented by 28 ex-USAF aircraft. They serve with 337 Mira, 110 Ptérix at Larissa and 338/339 Mira, 117 Ptérix at Andravidha
Iran: 177 F-4Es were delivered prior to the Islamic revolution. About 40 Phantoms of all variants remain in service, many of which are F-4Es
Israel: 140 F-4Es fly with four squadrons. Aircraft are being updated to Kurnass 2000 standard
Japan: 129 F-4EJ Kais serve with 301 Hikotai (Hyakuri), 302 Hikotai (Naha), 306 Hikotai (Komatsu) and the Air Proving Wing at Gifu
South Korea: 59 F-4Es serve with the 152nd and 153rd TFS, assigned to the 17th TFW at Chongjiu
Turkey: 166 F-4Es with 111/112 Filo at Eskisehir, 131/132 Filo at Konya and 171/172/173 Filo at Erhac. Fleet due for upgrade, possibly to ICE standard with new radar and AIM-120 missile
United States: Seven F-4Es in use with the 20th FS/49th FW at Holloman AFB for training Luftwaffe crews

McDonnell Douglas **F-4G Wild Weasel V**

SPECIFICATION

McDonnell Douglas F-4G Phantom II
generally similar to the McDonnell Douglas F-4E Phantom II except in the following particulars:
Weights: empty equipped 29,321 lb (13300 kg); maximum take-off 62,390 lb (28300 kg)
Speed: maximum level speed 'clean' at 40,000 ft (12190 m) 1,290 kt (1,485 mph; 2300 km/h); cruising speed at maximum take-off weight 496 kt (571 mph; 919 km/h)
Range: ferry range 1,718 nm (1,978 miles; 3184 km); combat radius 520 nm (599 miles; 964 km)

Widespread use in Vietnam of Soviet-supplied SA-2 'Guideline' SAMs was only partly countered by the use of aircraft such as the Douglas EB-66 and Grumman EA-6B by the **USAF** and US Navy, respectively, and subsequent efforts were made to develop more capable anti-radar platforms. Greater success attended development of North American F-100s and Republic F-105s in the radar suppression role. This effort culminated in the adoption for a similar task of the **McDonnell Douglas F-4 Phantom II**, with its higher performance and strike capabilities. A total of 36 temporarily converted **F-4C Wild Weasel IV** aircraft were in service by 1972 (unofficially designated **EF-4C**), employing Westinghouse ECM pods in conjunction with AGM-45 Shrike anti-radiation missiles. Such aircraft frequently accompanied routine strike missions by standard F-4Cs.

In due course a much more extensive modification programme was undertaken. McDonnell produced a total of 116 **F-4G** aircraft (known initially as **Advanced Wild Weasel** or **Wild Weasel V**) by modifying F-4Es from production Block 42 onwards when they were returned for life-extension programmes. Changes included deletion of the integral M61A1 cannon and installation of a McDonnell Douglas APR-38 RHAWS, much of the component avionics for which are located in a long cylindrical fairing on top of the aircraft's fin. Associated with the APR-38 is a Texas Instruments computer, whose purpose is to accommodate varying future circumstances without demands for

additional electronic hardware in an already densely-packed aircraft (there are no fewer than 52 antennas distributed throughout the airframe).

Self-defence weaponry is confined to a pair of Sparrow AAMs in the rear fuselage recesses (and perhaps a pair of AIM-9s if pylon stations are available), one of the forward pair normally being occupied by an ECM pod such as ALQ-131. For the 'lethal SEAD' (suppression of enemy air defences) role, the APR-38 (and upgraded APR-47 system now carried) is compatible with the AGM-45 Shrike, AGM-65 Maverick EO-guided missile and AGM-88 HARM, and features automatic and blind weapon firing. Cockpit displays include annotated threat symbology, while reaction to priority threats is automatically initiated. Aircraft in service today have been re-equipped with LORAN, while restressing of the fuselage store mounting enables the McDonnell Douglas F-15-type centreline fuel drop tank to be carried; this is cleared to 5g when full, compared with 3g of the F-4's customary tank. The AGM-88 HARM, carried in pairs on the main wing pylon, is now the universal weapon of the F-4G, which remains the only aircraft that can employ all the operating modes of the missile.

After highly successful operations in Desert Storm, the F-4G will most likely remain in service with the USAF for some years. Only two squadrons remain operational with the type: the 561st FS at Nellis AFB, NV, and the 190th FS of the Idaho ANG at Boise. The 189th TF at the latter base undertakes training on the type. In 1994 the first of approximately 100 F-16C/F-16D Block 50/52Ds equipped with the ASQ-213 HARM Targeting System pod entered service, augmenting the dwindling F-4G force. Nevertheless, it will be some time before the F-4G's unique capabilities can be completely replaced.

The 190th FS/Idaho ANG began conversion to the F-4G in June 1991, and is now one of only two units operating the type. Both take turns manning detachments in the Middle East. Replacement of the F-4G is a hotly-debated issue, and neither the new F-16/HTS or planned F-15C/PDF combination provides the same capability as offered by the current F-4G. Both are hampered by single-pilot operation; one of the main reasons for the success of the F-4G is the dedicated and highly experienced EWO in the backseat.

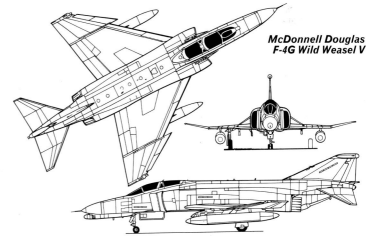

McDonnell Douglas F-4G Wild Weasel V

McDonnell Douglas RF-4 Phantom II

Representing a radical departure from the basic F-4B/C fighter, a reconnaissance version of the Phantom II was first flown as a **YRF-4C** demonstrator (of two prototypes) on 8 August 1963. This was followed on 18 May 1964 by the first flight of a production **RF-4C** aircraft. The RF-4C is a multi-sensor aircraft employed primarily for day reconnaissance and was used operationally in this role in Vietnam. McDonnell manufactured a total of 503 RF-4Cs.

Optical cameras, radar and electronic reconnaissance equipment and infra-red sensors are housed in a modified nose which increases the length of the aircraft by 33 in (84 cm) compared with the F-4B/C fighter versions. The F-4C's fire control radar was replaced by a smaller Texas Instruments AN/APQ-99 for mapping, and terrain and collision avoidance. Diverse sensors can be accommodated in the nose and forward fuselage. Twenty-four RF-4Cs were fitted with the AN/ALQ-125 TEREC (Tactical Electronic Reconnaissance) sensor for locating electronic emitters. Twenty-four others employ the LOROP suite, consisting of KS-127 optical camera with 66-in (167-cm) focal length. Other RF-4C/Es have carried various combinations of medium- to long-range and oblique reconnaissance cameras, including one KS-72 or KS-87 forward oblique-framing camera plus one KA-56A low-altitude and one KA-55A high-altitude panoramic camera. Unique to reconnaissance Phantoms is the AN/ARN-101 digital avionics navigation/reconnaissance system, supplemented recently by a new navigation/weapons delivery system and ring-laser gyro. Night capability was added with provision for photoflashes, with one or two ejectors on the upper rear fuselage.

On a typical mission, an RF-4 will cruise at medium altitude for a KS-127 LOROP day photographic 'sweep' of a target region, this camera providing a slant range of up to 55 miles (89 km) on missions flown at 30,000 ft (9144 m). Although the RF-4 is usually unarmed, some users have added AIM-9M/AIM-9P Sidewinder missiles for self-defence capability.

The RF-4C is the last dedicated fast-jet tactical reconnaissance aircraft in US service, where it operates with two **Air National Guard** squadrons in Alabama and Nevada. RF-4Cs from the Alabama ANG and the last active-duty squadron (from Zweibrücken in Germany) were used during Operation Desert Storm, flying from Sheikh Isa and Incirlik. The Alabama aircraft were equipped with KS-127 LOROP cameras with 66-in (168-cm) lenses. The RF-4C has been exported to two customers. Up to 27 have been delivered to **South Korea** from 1988, all aircraft having been transferred from USAF stocks, along with AN/ALQ-131 jamming pods. The RF-4C equips the 131st TRS/39th TRG of the 10th Tactical Fighter Wing at Suwon. **Spain** received a total of 12 RF-4Cs (locally designated **CR.12**), currently equipping 123 Escuadron at Torrejón within Ala 12. These have been steadily updated with AN/APQ-172 terrain-following radar, laser INS, new ECM systems, new electro-optical sensors and real-time datalinks, as well as inflight-refuelling probes similar to those installed on Israeli aircraft.

The **RF-4E** was developed as an export version of the RF-4C, primarily for the German **Luftwaffe**. The aircraft combines the airframe and engine of the early unslatted F-4E with the reconnaissance nose of the RF-4C, although some sensitive RF-4C systems were not installed. Its more fuel efficient J79-GE-17 engines improved range

and radius of action. The prototype was first flown on 15 September 1970 and a total of 150 aircraft was eventually built. German RF-4Es were retired in 1992. Additional operators comprise **Greece**, **Iran**, **Israel** and **Turkey**. Greece and Turkey each received eight new-build aircraft and these are being supplemented by surplus Luftwaffe RF-4Es. Israeli RF-4s are equipped with indigenous reconnaissance and avionics equipment and are armed with Shafrir, Python or Sidewinder missiles for self-defence. Under the Peace Jack codename, General Dynamics examined the use of the enormous HIAC-1 LOROP camera with the Phantom. Several USAF aircraft could carry a pod-mounted camera, but three Israeli F-4Es were converted to take the HIAC-1 in an enlarged nose. Redelivered to Israel in 1978 and designated **F-4E(S)**, one of these aircraft may still be in use. The **JASDF** purchased 14 reconnaissance Phantoms, actually built to a similar standard as the RF-4C. These were designated **RF-4EJ** and have been upgraded by Mitsubishi. Seventeen F-4EJ interceptors are being converted to a different RF-4EJ standard without camera noses but with pod-mounted camera, SLAR or Elint systems. Japanese RF-4Es

and RF-4EJs upgraded by Mitsubishi are described separately.

Now virtually obsolete despite a mid-life upgrade programme, which replaced AN/APQ-99 radar with AN/APQ-172, the RF-4C is no longer cost-effective, but the USAF has no ready substitute for its TEREC, LOROP and other capabilities. The overseas RF-4E fleet is more recent, so some examples will remain in service into the next century.

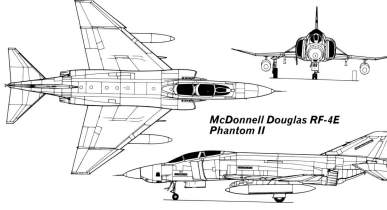

McDonnell Douglas RF-4E Phantom II

Spain received 12 ex-USAF RF-4Cs. Eight are still in use with Ala 12 at Torrejón.

In USAF service the RF-4C was largely flown by the ANG during the latter years of its service life. The 106th RS/AL ANG (illustrated) and 192nd RS/NE ANG still retained the type in mid-1994, but were due for a change of type and role. This aircraft carries self-defence AIM-9P Sidewinders.

SPECIFICATION

McDonnell Douglas RF-4C Phantom II
Wing: span 38 ft 4.875 in (11.71 m); aspect ratio 2.82; area 530.00 sq ft (49.24 m²)
Fuselage and tail: length 62 ft 11 in (19.17 m); height 16 ft 6 in (5.03 m); tailplane span 17 ft 11.5 in (5.47 m); wheel track 17 ft 10.5 in (5.30 m); wheel base 24 ft 9 in (7.54 m)
Powerplant: two General Electric J79-GE-15 turbojets each rated at 10,900 lb st (48.49 kN) dry and 17,000 lb st (75.62 kN) with afterburning
Weights: basic empty 28,276 lb (12826 kg); maximum take-off 58,000 lb (26308 kg)
Fuel and load: internal fuel 1,771 US gal (6704 litres); external fuel up to one 600-US gal (2271-litre) and two 370-US gal (1401-litre) drop tanks; maximum ordnance 16,000 lb (7257 kg), generally not carried
Speed: maximum level speed 'clean' at 40,000 ft (12190 m) 1,267 kt (1,459 mph; 2348 km/h) and at sea level 780 kt (898 mph; 1445 km/h)
Range: ferry range 1,520 nm (1,750 miles; 2816 km) with drop tanks; combat radius 730 nm (841 miles; 1,353 km)
Performance: maximum rate of climb at sea level 48,000 ft (14630 m) per minute; service ceiling 59,400 ft (18105 m)

348 Mira of the Elliniki Aeroporia (Greek air force) shares Larissa with two F-4E Phantom fighter squadrons. Greece operates seven of its original RF-4E batch, subsequently augmented by 18 ex-Luftwaffe aircraft.

McDonnell Douglas **F-15A/B Eagle**

The **McDonnell Douglas F-15 Eagle** air superiority fighter and interceptor is in service today in its original configuration and in two multi-stage improvement programme (MSIP) versions. The Eagle is widely viewed as setting the world standard for the primarily BVR air-to-air mission it performs, and has sufficient agility and the right armament to be able to hold its own in a close-in dogfight. Today, even unmodified early **F-15A/B** models remain among the world's most potent and capable fighters.

The F-15 Eagle programme dates from 1965 when the USAF issued its FX requirement for a long-range tactical air superiority fighter to replace the F-4. While the concept was being refined, hard-learned lessons from Vietnam were incorporated. In 1968, when the Required Operational Capability for the F-15 was issued, the aircraft was defined as a dedicated air-to-air fighter, a single-seat long-range BVR interceptor which would be able to dogfight. The F-15 was thus to be a fighter specifically tailored for the long-range air superiority role, marking a change in policy from the emphasis on multi-mission capabilities in earlier procurement of the F-4 and F-111. Vietnam experience pointed towards the need for twin engines, two crew (eventually not adopted) and an internal gun. The 1968 RFP added a requirement for a ferry range sufficient for deployment to Europe without tanker support and a maximum speed of at least Mach 2.5. This last inexplicable and very difficult requirement was technically achieved (albeit at huge cost), although an armed F-15 is limited to Mach 1.78.

McDonnell won the competition to build the F-15 (against proposals from North American and Fairchild-Republic), and the initial contract called for 10 single-seat development **F-15A**s (often erroneously referred to as **YF-15**s), two twin-seat development **TF-15A**s and eight Category II FSD aircraft. The first F-15 made its maiden flight on 27 July 1972, the first two-seater following on 7 July 1973. Initial plans called for the procurement of 729 more F-15A/Bs, 143 as attrition replacements. A total of 355 production F-15As was eventually built, together with 57 two-seat **F-15B**s. The F-15B is fully mission capable, but lacks the F-15A's AN/ALQ-135 ECM and is 800 lb (364 kg) heavier than the single-seater.

The weapon load, range and endurance requirements were resolved by adopting an aircraft of large overall dimensions. The large wings give a remarkably low wing loading and confer a surprising degree of agility. The wings employ conventional outboard ailerons and unblown inboard two-position flaps, but have no high-lift devices such as slats or computer-controlled combat flaps. The Eagle's aerodynamic design was very advanced by the standards of the day, and some modifications were needed to the original configuration flown on the first development aircraft. To reduce severe buffet encountered in transonic testing, the innovative spine-mounted airbrake (originally fitted with a small dorsal strake) was increased in size and its extension angle reduced. The trailing edges of the wingtips were cropped, while the tailplane was notched (equipped with dogtooth leading edges) to cure flutter problems.

More serious than these minor aerodynamic problems were difficulties experienced with the Eagle's Pratt & Whitney F100-PW-100 engine, and with the X-band

Hawaii's 199th Fighter Squadron is the principal air defence for the islands, flying the F-15A. The Guard unit is gained by PACAF in time of war. Two of the CONUS-based ANG Eagle squadrons (Massachusetts and Oregon) are dedicated to air defence, while the other three are battlefield air superiority units.

Hughes APG-63 coherent pulse-Doppler radar, both of which were designed specifically for the Eagle. To minimise asymmetric handling problems, the engines are mounted close together and, to prevent damage to one engine causing reciprocal damage to the other, they are separated by a titanium keel. This provides a very rigid, very simple engine mount and allows rapid engine changes to be achieved. An engine change under operational conditions has been demonstrated in some 20 minutes.

The F-15A has an advanced and sophisticated avionics system, with the main radar supplemented by an AN/ALR-56 RWR, and an AN/ALQ-128 EW warning system. These are backed up by a Northrop AN/ALQ-135 internal countermeasures set.

The F-15 pilot sits high up and well forward on a McDonnell Escapac IC-7 ejection seat under a large blown canopy, with excellent all-round view. The cockpit itself is well laid out, but is equipped only with analog instruments, with no CRT MFDs. An HUD and a variety of control column- and throttle-mounted controls give true HOTAS operation of all important systems. The Eagle was designed to fight in the HOTAS mode, the pilot receiving all necessary information from his HUD and cueing the weapons system without having to look down into the cockpit to make switch selections or monitor instruments.

Delivery to TAC

The operational career of the Eagle began with the first delivery of an F-15A to Tactical Air Command's 1st Tactical Fighter Wing at Langley AFB, VA, on 9 January 1976. The 36th TFW at Bitburg, Germany, received the Eagle in April 1977. Other operators have included the 21st FW (Elmendorf AFB, AK), 33rd FW (Eglin AFB, FL), 49th FW (Holloman AFB, NM), 57th Fighter Weapons Wing (Nellis AFB, NV) and 32nd FG (Soesterberg, Holland). Other wings have subsequently acquired the improved **F-15C/D** variant (described separately).

The first F-15s to engage in combat operations were blooded by Israel on 27 June 1979 when they claimed five MiG-21s of the Syrian air force. Four FSD F-15As were delivered to Israel during 1976 under Operation Peace Fox III, and these were later joined by 19 refurbished F-15As and a pair of F-15Bs. These serve with 133 Squadron at Tel Nov. Ten more ex-Louisiana ANG F-15As were supplied after Desert Storm in return for Israel's co-operation during the Gulf War. On 7 June 1981, Israeli Eagles escorted F-16 Fighting Falcons on the long-range strike against Iraq's Osirak nuclear reactor, and were heavily involved in the 1982 'turkey shoot' over the Bekaa Valley.

During the 1980s, the F-15A entered service with three TAC air defence squadrons in the interceptor role and was to have been the carrier aircraft for the ASAT (anti-satellite) weapon; development of the latter was cancelled, but aircraft continue to be

'wired' for it. The three fighter interceptor squadrons disbanded during 1988-91, passing their aircraft on to three ANG units (one in Hawaii) which fulfil the same role. Other ANG squadrons fly the F-15A in the tactical fighter role.

The original Eagle two-seater was modified to become the **SMTD** (STOL/Maneuver Technology Demonstrator), equipped with canard foreplanes and Pratt & Whitney two-dimensional vectoring nozzles that can deflect through 20° up and down and provide reverse thrust. The SMTD demonstrator flew on 7 September 1988. The aircraft used its vectored thrust and canards to improve low-speed performance. The result was an aircraft able to operate on a much shortened runway – an important consideration in wartime, when fixed airfields are likely to be cratered and under constant attack. After a three-year programme, the SMTD Eagle made its 138th and final flight on 12 August 1991, making a short night landing under a simulated 200-ft (61-m) ceiling in total darkness.

In the 1990s, with relatively few 'new-build' aircraft being ordered, the USAF is improving its F-15A/B fighters through an ambitious MSIP. This follows a far more modest MSIP of the early 1980s that resulted in only minor improvements to the aircraft. Developed jointly by the manufacturer and the Warner Robins Logistics Center in Georgia, the current MSIP endeavour for the F-15A/B (similar to, and carried out in conjunction with, MSIP for F-15C/D models) replaces the proven APG-63 with more advanced Hughes APG-70 look-down/shootdown radar, new avionics and digital central computers replacing the F-15A/B's original analog computers.

F-15A/B Eagles emerging from MSIP differ from F-15C/D models only in lacking the latter's radar warning receiver antenna located next to the horizontal stabiliser and

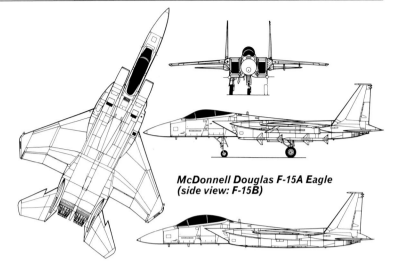

McDonnell Douglas F-15A Eagle (side view: F-15B)

the 2,000 lb (907 kg) of extra fuel carried by the F-15C. MSIP F-15A/B aircraft replaced non-MSIP F-15C/D models with the 32nd TFG, Soesterberg, Holland, in June 1992.

WEAPON OPTIONS

Standard Eagle weaponry is one M61A1 Vulcan 20-mm cannon with 940 rounds, four AIM-9M Sidewinders on wing pylon shoulder launchers and four AIM-7M Sparrows on the lower 'corners' of the fuselage. Older AIM-7/9 variants are still in use, while the AIM-120 AMRAAM is available to MSIP and F-15C/D aircraft. Secondary ground attack capability is virtually never employed.

SPECIFICATION

McDonnell Douglas F-15A Eagle
generally similar to the McDonnell Douglas F-15C Eagle except in the following particulars:
Powerplant: two Pratt & Whitney F100-PW-100 turbofans each rated at 14,670 lb st (65.26 kN) dry and 23,830 lb st (106.0 kN) with afterburning
Weights: operating empty 28,600 lb (12973 kg); normal take-off 41,500 lb (18884 kg) on an interception mission or 54,400 lb (24675 kg) with three 600-US gal (2271-litre) drop tanks; maximum take-off 56,000 lb (25401 kg)
Fuel and load: internal fuel 11,600 lb (5260 kg); external fuel up to 11,895 lb (5395 kg) in three 600-US gal (2271-litre) drop tanks; maximum ordnance 16,000 lb (7257 kg)
Range: ferry range more than 2,500 nm (2,878 miles; 4631 km) with drop tanks
Performance: landing run 2,500 ft (762 m) at normal landing weight with a brake parachute

OPERATORS

Israel: currently operates an estimated 35 F-15As and two F-15Bs with 133 Sqn at Tel Nov. Ten early Eagles

McDonnell Douglas F-15A/B Eagle

*An Israeli F-15A wears the badge of
133 Squadron, the unit which flies
the early variants from Tel Nov.
These aircraft were heavily
committed to the fighting over the
Bekaa Valley when the type claimed
40 kills over Syrian MiGs for no
losses. The eagle's head is a recent
addition to the inside of the fins.*

McDonnell Douglas **F-15C/D Eagle**

The **F-15C** followed the F-15A on the St
Louis production line and made its first
flight on 26 February 1979. It represents an
improved and updated derivative of the
basic fighter. The two-seat **F-15D** similarly

succeeds the F-15B trainer. F-15C/D Eagles
came off the production line with the
improved, lightweight Hughes APG-63
X-band pulse-Doppler radar with reprogrammable signal processing, and with provision

for 750-US gal (2389-litre) CFTs (conformal
fuel tanks) on the sides of the intakes.

Formerly known as FAST (fuel and sensor, tactical) packs, first demonstrated in
1974 and subsequently sold to Israel, the

CFTs cannot be jettisoned but their contents can be dumped, and the fuselage
Sparrow stations they displace are duplicated on the outside of the pack itself.
Plans for FAST packs containing 'Wild Weasel' avionics equipment, rocket motors and
recce equipment were eventually abandoned, and the CFT designation confirms
the change to fuel-only.

The prime armament of the baseline
F-15C/D remains the AIM-7/9 AAM combination, and the same 20-mm M61A cannon
is retained. The F-15C was intended to be
powered by the more powerful Pratt &
Whitney F100-PW-220 engine, although
early aircraft retained the -100 powerplant.
Minor changes were made to the undercarriage, allowing gross weight to be increased
to 68,000 lb (30845 kg). Software changes
increased the scope of the 9*g* envelope, an
important modification since F-15As had
effectively been limited to 7.33 *g* under

*Left: An F-15C of the RSAF's No. 13
Squadron leaves Dhahran during a
Desert Storm mission. Two Mirage
F1 kills were credited to a Saudi
pilot during the conflict.*

*Below: The 18th Wing is based at
Kadena on the Japanese island of
Okinawa, and is the main USAF unit
in the Pacific Rim region. It flies
three squadrons of F-15Cs,
alongside a KC-135 tanker squadron
and an E-3 Sentry unit.*

COCKPIT
The pilot sits on a McDonnell Douglas ACES II ejection seat, under a stretched acrylic canopy. Data is presented on a McDonnell Douglas AVQ-20 head-up display and a Honeywell vertical situation display including a CRT for presenting radar and attitude information.

McDonnell Douglas F-15C MSIP Eagle

The F-15 has been the USAF's premier fighter since the late 1970s, and has enjoyed ongoing improvements to keep it at the front of the air superiority race. The most recent development is the MSIP (Multi-Stage Improvement Program), which replaces the APG-63 radar with the APG-70, among a host of other improvements to aircraft and weapon systems. MSIP aircraft were available to the 58th TFS, 33rd TFW for their deployment to Desert Storm. Flying from Tabuk, the squadron was responsible for the majority of coalition kills over the Iraqi air force, claiming a total of 16 victories. This aircraft was marked for the wing commander, Colonel Rick Parsons, and wore the legend 'Gulf Spirit'. This was applied pre-war in recognition of the 33rd's base at Eglin, on the Gulf Coast of Florida. The three Iraqi flags marked the kills scored by the aircraft (one MiG-23 shot down by Captain David G. Rose on 29 January 1991 and two Su-22s shot down by Captain Anthony R. Murphy on 7 February). The single star marks the victory scored by Colonel Parsons over an Su-22 on the same day, when he was flying 85-0104.

FUEL
The basic internal capacity is 2,070 US gal (7836 litres), to which can be added 1,464 US gal (5542 litres) in the CFTs and three 610-US gal (2309-litre) drop tanks.

ARMAMENT
For many years, the standard missile armament comprised four AIM-9 Sidewinders on the wing launch rails and four AIM-7 Sparrows on the fuselage 'corner' stations. During the latter part of the Gulf War, the AIM-120 AMRAAM was carried (although not used), and this weapon is now used widely by the F-15C, replacing the Sidewinders on the wing launch rails. The internal M61A1 cannon is provided with 920 rounds.

MSIP
Apart from the addition of APG-70 radar, MSIP covers the replacement of the weapons control panel with a single colour display, enhanced ALQ-135 countermeasures and ALR-56C RWR, addition of ALE-45 chaff/flare dispenser and Magnavox EW warning system, provision for JTIDS and a four-fold increase in central computer memory, with three times the processing speed.

POWERPLANT
Early F-15Cs were fitted with F100-PW-100 engines, but most were delivered with F100-PW-220s, nominally rated at 23,830 lb (106 kN) thrust with afterburning.

Formerly an F-111F operator, the 48th FW at Lakenheath now flies F-15Cs and F-15Es.

most circumstances. Changes to the F-15C add about 600 lb (272 kg) to the aircraft's empty weight.

Initial F-15C deliveries were made to the 18th Tactical Fighter Wing at Kadena AB, Okinawa, commencing in September 1979. F-15C/D models later replaced F-15A/Bs with the 1st, 33rd and 36th TFWs and with the 32nd Fighter Squadron at Soesterberg, although the latter unit traded its F-15Cs for MSIP F-15As during 1991. The F-15C/D has also equipped the 57th Fighter-Interceptor

Squadron at NS Keflavik, Iceland.

First blood for the F-15C was drawn during a period of border tensions when two Saudi Arabian F-15Cs shot down two Iranian F-4E Phantoms over the Persian Gulf on 5 June 1984, possibly the only time one McDonnell fighter scored an aerial victory over another. Israeli F-15Cs may also have notched up kills prior to Desert Storm. When the US launched Operation Desert Shield on 6 August 1990, the 1st TFW at Langley AFB, VA, deployed F-15C/D Eagles

of its 27th and 71st Tactical Fighter Squadrons at very short notice. Forty-eight Eagles made the longest non-stop fighter deployment in history, flying between 14 and 17 hours from Langley to Dhahran with six to

eight inflight refuellings en route. The early arrival of the Eagles may have helped deter Iraq from moving immediately against Saudi oil fields.

In September 1990, the 33rd TFW from Eglin AFB, FL, deployed its 58th TFS with F-15C Eagles to Tabuk, Saudi Arabia. The 36th TFW at Bitburg, Germany, deployed F-15Cs to Tabuk and to Incirlik AB, Turkey. The 32nd TFS from Soesterberg, Holland, also deployed to Incirlik. When the war against Iraq began on 17 January 1991, the US had five F-15C air-to-air (and two F-15E strike) squadrons in the field. Most air-to-air

McDonnell Douglas F-15C/D Eagle

F-15s of the Alaska-based 3rd Wing display the old light grey scheme and the current 'Mod Eagle' darker grey low-visibility scheme.

engagements were fought by F-15Cs of the 58th TFS, part of the 33rd TFW, which scored 17 air-to-air victories, mainly during CAPs and fighter sweeps. Eagles also flew longer missions to escort strike aircraft. Quick turn-arounds were a major factor in achieving high sortie rates, and the F-15C exceeded expectations. No F-15C/Ds were lost during Desert Shield/ Storm. More than 2,200 missions totalling some 7,700 hours of combat time were logged, resulting in 32 aerial victories, two of them scored by a Saudi pilot of the RSAF's No. 13 Squadron. AMRAAM was sometimes carried, but was not used in combat.

During the 1990s, F-15 Eagles will continue to undergo staged improvements to radar and internal systems. Firmly committed to the F-22, the USAF appears to have abandoned plans for a scaled-down, improved Eagle known as **F-15XX**, but an MSIP for the F-15C/D, similar to that applied to earlier F-15A/B aircraft, is under way. This upgrade programme replaces the APG-63 with APG-70 radar, increases onboard computer memory to 1,000 K, trebles processing speed, multiplies central computer capacity by 300 per cent, and adds many improved avionics items. MSIP replaces the original weapons panel with a single Honeywell colour TV display. All F-15C/Ds are acquiring Tracor AN/ALE-45 chaff/flare dispensers located behind the nosewheel door, also found on the F-15E. Northrop AN/ALQ-135 enhanced internal countermeasures, Loral AN/ALR-56C RWR and a Magnavox EW warning system are all incorporated, and JTIDS 2 terminals are to be retrofitted. The MSIP F-15C/D is also compatible with the AIM-120 AMRAAM, which is belatedly replacing the AIM-7M Sparrow as the principal armament for the C/D model Eagle. The MSIP-II changes were flight-tested during December 1984, and were applied to production aircraft (beginning with 84-001) during June 1985. F-15C/D aircraft are projected to be operational in the fighter role until at least 2005.

When F-22s enter service in numbers, the displaced F-15Cs are scheduled to be reworked for the defence suppression role. This aircraft is known as **F-15/PDF (Precision Direction Finder)**, and the first contracts for this programme have been awarded. The aircraft is intended to supplement F-4Gs and F-16C/Ds in the 'Wild Weasel' role early in the next century.

The F-15C/D has been exported to favoured nations Israel, Japan and Saudi Arabia, as detailed under the operators. Japanese **F-15J** fighters (but not the two-seat **F-15DJ** trainers) are built by Mitsubishi and are described separately.

SPECIFICATION

McDonnell Douglas F-15C Eagle

Wing: span 42 ft 9.75 in (13.05 m); aspect ratio 3.01; area 608.00 sq ft (56.48 m²)
Fuselage and tail: length 63 ft 9 in (19.43 m); height 18 ft 5.5 in (5.63 m); tailplane span 28 ft 3 in (8.61 m); wheel track 9 ft 0.25 in (2.75 m); wheel base 17 ft 9.5 in (5.42 m)
Powerplant: two Pratt & Whitney F100-PW-220 turbofans each rated at 14,670 lb st (65.26 kN) dry and 23,830 lb st (106.0 kN) with afterburning

Weights: operating empty 28,600 lb (12793 kg); normal take-off 44,630 lb (20244 kg) on an intercept mission with four AIM-7 Sparrow AAMs; maximum take-off 58,470 lb (26521 kg) with three 610-US gal (2309-litre) drop tanks or 68,000 lb (30844 kg) with conformal fuel tanks
Fuel and load: internal fuel 13,455 lb (6103 kg); external fuel up to 9,750 lb (4423 kg) in two CFTs and 11,895 lb (5395 kg) in three 600-US gal (2271-litre) drop tanks; maximum ordnance 16,000 or 23,600 lb (7257 or 10705 kg) without or with CFTs respectively
Speed: maximum level speed 'clean' at 36,000 ft (10975 m) more than 1,433 kt (1,650 mph; 2655 km/h); cruising speed at optimum altitude 495 kt (570 mph; 917 km/h)
Range: ferry range with drop tanks more than 2,500 or 3,100 nm (2,879 or 3,570 miles; 4633 or 5745 km) without or with CFTs respectively; combat radius on an interception mission 1,061 nm (1,222 miles; 1967 km); endurance 5 hours 15 minutes with CFTs or 15 hours with flight refuelling
Performance: maximum rate of climb at sea level more than 50,000 ft (15240 m) per minute; service ceiling 60,000 ft (18290 m); absolute ceiling 100,000 ft (30480 m); take-off run 900 ft (274 m) at normal take-off weight; landing run 3,500 ft (1067 m) at normal landing weight without a brake parachute
g limits: -3 to +9

McDonnell Douglas F-15D Eagle
generally similar to the McDonnell Douglas F-15C Eagle except in the following particulars:
Weights: operating empty 29,400 lb (13336 kg)

OPERATORS

United States: 408 F-15Cs and 62 F-15Ds delivered. Current operators are 1st Fighter Wing (Langley AFB, VA), 33rd Fighter Wing (Eglin AFB, FL), 35th Wing (NS Keflavik, Iceland), 366th Wing (Mountain Home AFB, ID) of ACC, 325th Fighter Wing (Tyndall AFB, FL) of AETC, 3rd Wing (Elmendorf AFB, AK) and 18th Wing (Kadena AB, Okinawa) of PACAF, and 48th Fighter Wing (RAF Lakenheath, England) and 52nd Fighter Wing (Spangdahlem AB, Germany) of USAFE. Test and trials units include 57th FW (Nellis AFB, NV), 79th TEG (Eglin AFB, FL) and 412th Test Wing (Edwards AFB, CA)
Israel: 18 F-15Cs and eight F-15Ds supplied under Peace Fox III programme to equip 106 Sqn at Tel Nov. Five additional aircraft supplied in 1991. Israeli aircraft have the F-15A's IC-7 ejection seat in place of ACES II
Japan: two F-15J and 12 F-15DJ built by McDonnell, further single-seat aircraft built by Mitsubishi for a total of 223. These serve with 201/203 Hikotai at Chitose, 202 Hikotai/Hiko Kyodotai at Nyutabaru, 204/305 Hikotai at Hyakuri, 303 Hikotai at Komatsu, 304 Hikotai at Tsuiki
Saudi Arabia: 46 F-15Cs and 16 F-15Ds supplied under original Peace Sun programme. Total of 62 included two attrition replacments, as the US stipulated that no more than 60 F-15s could be operated by Saudi Arabia. This was rescinded during the Gulf War when 24 F-15C/Ds were hastily transferred from USAFE stocks. Peace Sun VI covered the delivery of a further nine F-15Cs and three F-15Ds from August 1991. Eagle units are No. 5 Sqn at Taif, No. 6 Sqn at Khamis Mushait, Nos 13 and 42 Sqns at Dhahran

Japanese two-seat F-15DJs are built by the parent company rather than by Mitsubishi. This example serves with the aggressor unit (Hiko Kyodotai) at Nyutabaru.

McDonnell Douglas **F-15E Eagle**

All F-15s were built with air-to-ground capability, and are wired for the carriage of air-to-ground ordnance. They were originally intended as dual-role aircraft, but the ground attack role was abandoned in 1975 and the relevant software was never incorporated. Trials of an air-to-ground F-15 began during 1982, when McDonnell Douglas modified the second TF-15A as the **'Strike Eagle'**, funding the project itself. The aircraft was conceived as an ETF (Enhanced Tactical Fighter) replacement for the General Dynamics F-111 and was cho-

sen in preference to the 'cranked wing' F-16XL Fighting Falcon. The 'Strike Eagle' demonstrator was joined by an F-15C and an F-15D which conducted trials with a variety of fuel and ordnance loads, usually with CFTs fitted. The resulting **F-15E** was given the go-ahead on 24 February 1984, and the first production aircraft made its maiden flight on 11 December 1986. McDonnell's 'Strike Eagle' name was not adopted, though some unofficial epithets such as 'Beagle' (Bomber Eagle) and 'Mud Hen' have been used on occasion.

In introducing new avionics and equipment for a 'mud-moving' role not assigned to earlier variants, the F-15E is very much a second-generation Eagle. The aircraft introduced redesigned controls, a wide field of vision HUD, and three CRTs that provide multi-purpose displays of navigation, weapons delivery and systems operations.

The F-15E has nuclear delivery capability in the form of the B61 tactical weapon, seen here on an Eglin test aircraft. The wing- and fuselage-mounted ciné cameras record the weapon separation.

COCKPIT
The F-15E has a state-of-the-art cockpit, the pilot having a wide-angle HUD and three MFDs. The WSO has four MFDs. All vital flight and attack inputs are made via an upfront controller and stick/throttle controls.

ARMAMENT
This F-15E is loaded for a close air support/battlefield air interdiction mission with 14 SUU-30H cluster bombs. The AIM-9s are for self-defence. Lakenheath F-15Es also carry AIM-120 AMRAAM from the outer launch rail, with Sidewinders on the inner.

McDonnell Douglas F-15E Eagle

Mirroring the USAF's quest for greater flexibility and efficiency in an era of vastly reduced expenditure, the F-15E is arguably the world's most capable operational warplane. In the air-to-ground role its superb avionics and sensors allow it to undertake precision attacks with heavy loads in any conditions, yet once it is relieved of the encumbrance of attack ordnance it handles just like any fighter Eagle. Strike/attack is its primary role, but its air-fighting prowess allows it to be far more survivable over hostile territory where there is a heavy air threat. F-15Es are based with theatre units in Alaska and Europe, with a rapid-reaction composite wing at Mountain Home and a dedicated F-15E wing at Seymour Johnson. The force is seen as a highly credible deterrent to meet quickly-evolving situations, and would be in the vanguard of any USAF deployment in a crisis. This aircraft is marked for the wing commander of the 48th Fighter Wing, which swapped its four squadrons of F-111Fs for two of F-15Es in 1992.

CFTs
The conformal fuel tanks each hold 723 US gal (2737 litres) of fuel, and have a continuous pylon (with three attachment points) and three stub pylons for the carriage of weapons.

LANTIRN NAV POD
The LANTIRN system consists of the AAQ-13 navigation pod on the starboard intake and AAQ-14 targeting pod on the port. The AAQ-13 consists of a wide-angle FLIR, which projects an image on the pilot's HUD, and a Texas Instruments terrain-following radar, which interfaces with the aircraft's autopilot system to provide safe low-level flight in all conditions.

LANTIRN TARGETING POD
The AAQ-14 is used for attacks, and contains a wide/narrow field-of-view forward-looking infra-red for target acquisition, laser designator/rangefinder, stabiliser system, multi-mode tracker and an automatic IR Maverick hands-off system. At the rear of both LANTIRN pods are air intakes to serve the cooling systems.

CANNON
The M61A1 cannon is mounted in the starboard wingroot, armed with 512 rounds. In the port wingroot is the refuelling receptacle.

RADAR
At the heart of the F-15E's capability is the APG-70 radar, a vastly-improved version of the F-15C's APG-63. As well as improved air-to-air modes, the APG-70 offers a high-resolution synthetic aperture mapping mode allowing highly accurate 'patch maps' to be taken of a target area, which in turn allow precise designation of the desired aimpoint.

POWERPLANT
Initial F-15E deliveries were powered by the P&W F100-PW-220 engine rated at 23,450 lb (104.3 kN) thrust. Later aircraft, like this one, are fitted with the F100-PW-229 IPE, offering 29,100 lb (129.4 kN) thrust.

This 412th TW F-15E displays the LANTIRN pods and the bomb carriage along the conformal fuel tanks.

The rear-cockpit WSO employs four multi-purpose CRT terminals for radar, weapon selection and monitoring of enemy tracking systems. The WSO also operates an AN/APG-70 synthetic aperture radar and Martin-Marietta LANTIRN navigation (AN/AAQ-13) and targeting (AN-AAQ-14) pods. The navigation pod incorporates its own terrain-following radar, which can be linked to the aircraft's flight control system to allow automatic coupled terrain-following flight. The targeting pod allows the aircraft to self-designate GBU-10 and GBU-24 laser-guided bombs. Basic flight controls are also

provided. Both pilot and WSO sit in tandem on ACES II zero-zero ejection seats.

Power for the new variant was initially provided by F100-PW-220 turbofans, as used by the F-15C, with a digital engine control system, but this was soon replaced under the Improved Performance Engine programme, whereby paired GE F110-GE-129 and P&W F100-PW-229 engines were flown in F-15Es under competitive evaluation; the Pratt & Whitney engine was eventually selected. Since August 1991 (F-15E serial 90-0233) the new engine has been fitted on the production line, and other aircraft

McDonnell Douglas F-15E Eagle

Powerplant: two Pratt & Whitney F100-P-220 turbofans each rated at 14,670 lb st (65.26 kN) dry and 23,830 lb st (106.0 kN) with afterburning or, in aircraft built after August 1991, two F100-PW-229s each rated at 17,800 lb st (79.18 kN) dry and 29,100 lb st (129.45 kN) with afterburning; option of two General Electric F110-GE-129s each rated at 17,000 lb st (75.62 kN) dry and 29,000 lb st (129.0 kN) with afterburning
Weights: operating empty 31,700 lb (14379 kg); maximum take-off 81,000 lb (36741 kg)
Fuel and load: internal fuel 13,123 lb (5952 kg); external fuel 21,645 lb (9818 kg) in two CFTs and up to three 610-US gal (2309-litre) drop tanks; maximum ordnance 24,500 lb (11113 kg)
Speed: maximum level speed 'clean' at high altitude more than 1,433 kt (1,650 mph; 2655 km/h); cruising speed at optimum altitude 495 kt (570 mph; 917 km/h)
Range: ferry range 3,100 nm (3,570 miles; 5745 km) with CFTs and drop tanks, or 2,400 nm (2,765 miles; 4445 km) with drop tanks; combat radius 685 nm (790 miles; 1270 km)
Performance: maximum rate of climb at sea level more than 50,000 ft (15240 m) per minute; service ceiling 60,000 ft (18290 m); landing run 3,500 ft (1067 m) at normal landing weight without braking parachute

The 366th Wing operates a mixed force of types as the USAF's rapid-reaction, power-projection 'super wing'. Offensive muscle comes from the B-52, F-16C and F-15E, the latter flown by the 'Bold Tigers' of the 391st Fighter Squadron.

will be retrofitted. To suit the F-15E for the rigours of the low-level role, the aircraft was structurally redesigned for a 16,000-hour life and loads of up to 9 *g*. More use was made of superplastic forming and diffusion bonding of titanium in the rear fuselage, engine bay and on some panels. The fuel tanks have been filled with reticulated foam, reducing capacity to 2,019 US gal (7643 litres).

In 1988, the 405th Tactical Training Wing at Luke AFB, AZ, became Tactical Air Command's replacement training unit for the F-15E Eagle aircraft, a role since taken over by the 58th Fighter Wing in Air Education and Training Command. The first operational F-15Es were delivered to the 4th TFW, Seymour Johnson AFB, NC, replacing F-4Es.

On 12 August 1990, as the US began Operation Desert Shield, F-15E Eagles from the 336th TFS, 4th TFW, deployed to Al Kharj air base, Saudi Arabia. F-15Es of that wing's 335th TFS followed. During Desert Storm, F-15Es were assigned strike missions against a variety of targets, including five/six-hour sorties in search of 'Scud' missile launch sites. Two F-15E Eagles were lost in combat during 2,200 sorties totalling 7,700 hours.

The USAF was authorised to procure 209 F-15Es, all of which have been delivered. In 1991, the Secretary of Defense overruled USAF leaders who wanted to keep the F-15E Eagle in production. Although the F-15E is an exceedingly potent warplane for the strike mission, critics point out that its low wing-loading produces a rough ride, especially for the backseater, and that the F-15E's payload is less than that of the 30-year-old F-111. The US Air Force wanted to

keep the production line open to 'bridge' a hoped-for additional purchase from Saudi Arabia directly from inventory.

WEAPON OPTIONS

The primary mission of the F-15E is air-to-ground strike, for which it carries a wide range of weapons on two underwing pylons, underfuselage pylons and 12 bomb racks mounted directly on the CFTs. The F-15E carries up to a maximum of 24,250 lb (11000 kg) of tactical ordnance, including Mk 82 500-lb (227-kg) (26) or Mk 84 2,000-lb (907-kg) (7) bombs; or GBU-10 (7), GBU-12 (15) or GBU-15 (2) guided weapons. GBU-15s are accompanied by an AN/AXQ-14 datalink pod carried on the centreline. The aircraft also carries 25 CBU-52, -58, -71, -87, -89, -90, -92 or -93 bombs. The AGM-65 Maverick can be carried, on single or triple launchers on the two underwing pylons only. The F-15E is also capable of carrying up to five B57 or B61 nuclear bombs. Specialist weapons include the AGM-

88 HARM for defence suppression, and the AGM-130, a powered version of the GBU-15 EO-guided bomb. As a dual-role warplane, the F-15E has air-to-air capability and, like its air-superiority predecessors, is able to engage enemy aircraft beyond visual range with four AIM-7M Sparrows or eight AIM-120 AMRAAMs. The F-15E also has four AIM-9 Sidewinder missiles and a 20-mm M61A1 Vulcan six-barrelled cannon with 512 rounds of ammunition. The centreline and wing pylons are often reserved for the carriage of 600-US gal (2270-litre) fuel tanks.

SPECIFICATION

McDonnell Douglas F-15E Eagle
Wing: span 42 ft 9.75 in (13.05 m); aspect ratio 3.01; area 608.00 sq ft (56.48 m²)
Fuselage and tail: length 63 ft 9 in (19.43 m); height 18 ft 5.5 in (5.63 m); tailplane span 28 ft 3 in (8.61 m); wheel track 9 ft 0.25 in (2.75 m); wheel base 17 ft 9.5 in (5.42 m)

OPERATORS

Air Combat Command: 4th Wing (Seymour Johnson AFB, NC), 57th Wing (Nellis AFB, NV), 366th Wing (Mountain Home AFB, ID), Air Warfare Center (Eglin AFB, FL)
Air Education and Training Command: 58th Fighter Wing (Luke AFB, AZ)
Air Force Materiel Command: 412th Test Wing (Edwards AFB, CA)
Pacific Air Forces: 3rd Wing (Elmendorf AFB, AK)
USAF Europe: 48th Fighter Wing (RAF Lakenheath, England)

The 46th Test Wing at Eglin uses F-15Es for weapons trial work with the 40th TS. This aircraft carries the AGM-130, essentially a GBU-15 electro-optical guided bomb with a rocket booster strapped on. For long-range guidance, the AXQ-14 datalink pod is carried on the centreline.

McDonnell Douglas **F-15F/H/I/S/XP** Eagle

McDonnell has proposed several versions of the F-15 Eagle which have not yet been ordered into production. A low-cost USAF alternative to the Lockheed F-22, the lightweight **F-15XX**, was abandoned in 1992. Other designations were applied to studies for export versions of the dual-role F-15E, primarily for **Saudi Arabia**.

The **F-15F** was a single-seater optimised for air-to-air duties, but based on the F-15E,

with the same airframe, engines, CRT-equipped cockpit and AN/APG-70 radar, although the latter has its attack and high-resolution synthetic aperture ground mapping modes deleted. No provision was made for LANTIRN pods. Saudi Arabia originally requested the supply of 24 of these aircraft, with 48 dual-role two-seaters.

The **F-15H** was probably the paper proposal for a dual-role aircraft, 48 of which

would have been delivered with the 24 F-15Fs. This was to have retained most of the capabilities of the F-15E without all of the latter's equipment, including the twin-podded LANTIRN system.

The **F-15XP** designation was applied to the F-15F and F-15H in the original Congressional notification documents, as a general term to cover new-generation Saudi F-15s. The term is no longer used, since Saudi Arabia is now to receive 72 examples of a new

two-seat, dual-role Eagle, under the designation **F-15S**. All will be two-seaters, again based on the F-15E airframe but with downgraded avionics and downgraded LANTIRN pods. The design calls for a simplified Hughes APG-70 radar without computerised radar mapping. CFTs are deleted, thereby reducing the F-15S's combat radius. A similar variant, designated **F-15I**, has gained an initial order for 26 from **Israel**, in the face of stiff competition from a modified, long-range strike version of the Lockheed F-16 Fighting Falcon.

McDonnell Douglas F/A-18A/C Hornet

Emerging victorious in the Navy's Air Combat Fighter programme that pitted the General Dynamics YF-16 against the **Northrop YF-17** in the mid-1970s, the **Hornet** was a more sophisticated navalised derivative of the Northrop contender (originally designed to meet the USAF's ACF requirement). It was at first intended to be produced in two distinct versions: specifically, the **F-18** fighter and the **A-18** for strike/attack tasks. Eventually, a single common aircraft was selected for both missions (replacing US Navy A-7s and US Marine Corps F-4s) and was given the designation **F/A-18**, although a land-based version, the **F/A-18L**, was to have been available for export. Under the original agreement, McDonnell was to have design leadership and the larger workshare of the naval versions, and Northrop that of the land-based versions. The export success of the naval F/A-18 to land-based customers eventually led to major disagreements and even a lawsuit between the partners.

These problems were eventually solved, and were never allowed to interfere with the aircraft itself. Responsibility for development and production of the F/A-18 has always been shared by McDonnell Douglas and Northrop, with the former company being the dominant partner. To speed the development process, a batch of 11 aircraft was ordered for trials purposes and nine of these were ultimately completed as single-seaters. The designation **YF/A-18A** has sometimes been unofficially applied, although technically the aircraft were not prototypes but pre-production aircraft. The first example made its maiden flight on 18 November 1978, and the remainder had all joined the test programme by March 1980.

Production of the initial **F/A-18A** version eventually totalled 371 and delivery of these began in May 1980, with early examples being allocated to the US Navy's operational test and evaluation force. Subsequent assignment to elements of the Navy and Marine Corps was spearheaded by the formation of a Navy training squadron at Lemoore, CA, but the first fully operational Hornet units were from the Marine Corps. Fighter-attack squadron VMFA-314 'Black Knights' led the way in August 1982, returning to El Toro from Lemoore and being declared operational on 7 January 1983.

The service entry of the new type made a huge impact that exceeded many expectations. The F/A-18 offered much greater weapons delivery accuracy than its predecessors, and was a genuinely multi-role aircraft, able to out-bomb the A-7 and to out-turn the F-14. Suddenly, the fleet's attack aircraft was in many ways also its finest fighter. The term 'Swing Fighter' has often been applied, referring to the pilot's ability to switch from the air-to-ground role to air-to-air or defence suppression duties literally at the push of a button. The aircraft's dogfighting capability is remarkable, the high-lift wing and leading-edge extensions conferring excellent high-Alpha capability and turn performance. Similarly, the APG-65 radar, which has become the benchmark fighter radar, is as effective at putting bombs on target as it is at detecting and engaging multiple airborne targets (fighter-sized targets can be picked up at ranges of over 80 nm/148 km). Air-to-air capability is enhanced by a well-designed cockpit with three multi-function CRT-type displays and true HOTAS controls, which help the pilot maintain situational awareness. In the air-to-ground role the F/A-18 can carry a Martin-Marietta laser spot tracker on the starboard underfuselage

Illustrating the Hornet's versatility, a pair of Marine Hornets carries iron bombs and AGM-88 defence suppression missiles. Both carry FLIR pods on the starboard intake pylons for night attack.

pylon, with a Ford Aerospace AN/AAS-38 FLIR or a Hughes AN/AAR-50 TINS to port.

Some of the Hornet's success may be attributed to its 16,000-lb st (71.2-kN) General Electric F404-GE-400 low-bypass turbofans, developed from the YJ101 engine of the YF-17. These have proved reliable and fuel-efficient, but are to be replaced by the derived 17,600-lb st (78.3-kN) F404-GE-402 EPE/IPE (Enhanced/Improved Performance Engine).

Navy service

The first US Navy squadron, VFA-113, soon followed VMFA-314 and accepted its first Hornet in August 1983. Accompanied by VFA-25, VFA-113 made the initial operational deployment as part of Carrier Air Wing 14 aboard USS *Constellation* during 1985. By the time they returned to the West Coast, several more squadrons were well advanced with conversion to the Hornet, the type replacing F-4 Phantoms with the Marines and A-7 Corsairs with the Navy.

Four Hornet squadrons aboard USS *Coral*

Right: Spain's Hornets serve with two wings (Ala 15 illustrated) for both air defence and attack roles. Specialist equipment includes Harpoon and HARM.

Sea (two Navy and two Marine Corps) participated in the El Dorado Canyon attack against targets in Libya in April 1986 when they were mainly employed in defence suppression. This marked the operational debut of both the F/A-18 and the AGM-88A HARM. Hornets from both the Navy (nine squadrons) and Marines (seven squadrons) were heavily committed to action during Desert Storm in 1991. Then, they were predominantly concerned with attack tasks, but they also flew combat air patrol missions. Two bomb-laden Hornets were responsible for the destruction of a pair of Iraqi F-7s on the first day of the war, continuing with their strike mission after despatching their enemies.

The F/A-18A was superseded on the St

Anti-ship capability is available thanks to the AGM-84 Harpoon missile, two of which can be carried. The AGM-84E SLAM version is available for long-range precision attack against ground targets.

Louis line by the **F/A-18C**, which remains the production single-seat model in 1994, some 355 examples having been ordered. The first F/A-18C (163427) made its maiden flight on 3 September 1986. Changes were made to weapons capability, so that the F/A-18C becomes the first Hornet variant compatible with the AIM-120 AMRAAM and with imaging infra-red Maverick missiles. The F/A-18C was also designed with provision for installation of the proposed (and

277

McDonnell Douglas F/A-18A/C Hornet

UNIT
VFA-87 'Golden Warriors' traded A-7s for F/A-18Cs in July 1987. In 1992 the squadron transitioned to Lot 14 Night-Attack Hornets. The squadron is shore-based at NAS Cecil Field, FL.

POWERPLANT
The basic F/A-18C featured the General Electric F404-GE-400 low-bypass turbofan, rated at 16,000 lb (71.2 kN) thrust with afterburning. From early 1992, the standard engine became the F404-GE-402 EPE (Enhanced Performance Engine), developing 17,600 lb (78.3 kN) thrust.

In addition to regular Fleet duties, the Hornet is routinely called upon to act in an aggressor role. Shown above is a VFA-37 aircraft carrying ALQ-167 ECM pods to provide an EW environment for realistic training, while below is a VFA-303 aircraft in an air combat adversary scheme, with black fin silhouette to represent a MiG-29.

cancelled) **RF-18A** interchangeable recce nose, with hardpoints, wiring and EMI shielding. It is fitted with a new CRT engine monitor display and has received an avionics upgrade with new AN/ALR-67 RHAWS. The type had provision for the cancelled AN/ALQ-165 airborne self-protection jammer (interchangeable with AN/ALQ-126B), and features revisions to mission computer equipment with enhanced built-in test facilities, increased memory and faster processing. These necessitated improvements to the ECS (Environmental Control System).

The new avionics give the F/A-18C its only external distinguishing characteristics, a five-pronged antenna array for the ALR-67 on the gun bay door, with small fairings on the sides of the nose and on the trailing edge of the fin, and similar ALQ-165 antennas on the gun bay access door, nose gear door, on top of the nose and behind the canopy. The F/A-18C also introduced the Martin-Baker NACES in place of the SJU-5/6 ejection seat and is fitted with small strakes above the LERXes designed to reduce buffet on the vertical tailfins and to improve yaw control at very high angles of attack. These strakes have since been retrofitted to virtually all surviving Hornets.

After 137 baseline F/A-18Cs had been delivered, production switched to a night-attack capable version (retaining the designation F/A-18C), the package of equipment including compatibility with GEC Cat's Eyes pilot's night vision goggles, a Hughes AN/AAR-50 TINS pod presenting its thermal picture of the terrain ahead in the Kaiser AN/AVQ-28 raster HUD, externally-carried Loral AN/AAS-38 targeting FLIR pod, and colour MFDs. The latter were joined by a new Honeywell colour digital moving map, which replaced the projected moving map display used previously, freeing the aircraft from having to be loaded with bulky film for projection. The first example (163985) was delivered to the NATC at Patuxent River, MD, on 1 November 1989.

Multi-mode radar

The Hornet's flexibility and versatility enable it to undertake interception, air superiority and strike/attack tasks with equal facility. One of the key factors in this flexibility is the radar. The Hughes AN/APG-65 multi-mode digital fire control unit has become a standard in fighter radars and can operate with equal effectiveness in air-to-air and air-to-surface modes. Future changes to the Hornet avionics suite include substitution of the Hughes AN/APG-73 radar in place of the same company's AN/APG-65 unit. This enhanced radar embodies new signal and data processors, a different bandwidth and an upgraded receiver/exciter. The first APG-73-equipped Hornet flew on 15 April 1992, and production aircraft have been fitted with the new radar since June 1994.

The F/A-18's unrivalled versatility makes it a real force multiplier in any carrier air wing, and current plans are increasing the type's importance, by deploying US Marine Corps F/A-18 squadrons on board US Navy carriers at the expense of A-6 and S-3 assets. The diminishing threat from cruise missile-carrying, very long-range strategic bombers means that carriers no longer have to stand-off so far from an enemy coast, and the F/A-18's relatively short range (often deliberately overstated by the aircraft's opponents) is less of a problem. In fact, a clean F/A-18 can out-distance a clean F-4, and even with fuel tanks can carry a greater bombload than the A-7, over the same range. The Hornet's accuracy also means that it can achieve more over the target on less fuel. In the air combat role, the F/A-18's high dry thrust means that it can outstay aircraft like the F-14, which rely more heavily on using afterburner. Hornet pilots seldom reach 'bingo' state (break off an engagement due to reaching minimum fuel) first.

The Hornet's versatility has led to substantial export sales. Canada was the first foreign customer and has taken delivery of 98 single-seaters. These are known as **CF-18A**s by McDonnell and as **CF-188A**s by the operator, although it should be noted that the name Hornet is used only unofficially, since the French language equivalent, 'Frelon', could be confused with the Aérospatiale helicopter of the same name. Deliveries were accomplished between October 1982 and September 1988. The Canadian aircraft are virtually standard F/A-18As, except in being fitted with a spotlight on the port side of the nose (for identifying aircraft during night intercepts), a new ILS and in having provision for the carriage of LAU-5003 rocket pods. These were followed by an Australian order negotiated in 1981, whereby local assembly, and later production, was undertaken of 57 **AF-18A**s by ASTA; these were handed over during 1985-90 as replacements for the Mirage. The aircraft are being updated to F/A-18C standard, and can launch AGM-85, AGM-88

and Paveway II laser-guided bombs. Spain originally evaluated the YF-17 but eventually opted to purchase 60 **EF-18A**s for the Ejercito del Aire, with delivery from 1986 to 1990. Spanish Hornets are operated under the local designation **C.15**. Like Australian Hornets, the Spanish EF-18As are being upgraded to near C model standard.

Subsequent export contracts have all been for the F/A-18C variant and comprise 32 for Kuwait, which were delivered by September 1993; 26 for Switzerland with deliveries due to start in 1995 (after a national referendum which endorsed the purchase); 57 for Finland, again with deliveries set to run from 1995. Finnish Hornets will be supplied in knock-down form by McDonnell Douglas and assembled locally by Valmet. Israel is continuing to look at the F/A-18 as a potential A-4/F-4 replacement, and has evaluated the type.

The F-18 has now entirely supplanted the A-7 and F-4 in US Navy and Marine Corps service. These two organisations currently possess more than 40 first- and second-line Hornet strike/fighter (VFA) and Marine fighter-attack (VMFA) squadrons. In addition, it also serves with several support squadrons in the adversary and electronic aggressor roles, and with test agencies. The F/A-18 has also been the mount for the Navy's 'Blue Angels' aerial display team since the end of the 1986 season.

WEAPON OPTIONS

In keeping with its multi-role capability, the Hornet is equipped with nine external stores stations, enabling it to carry a wide range of ordnance. For air-to-air missions, missile armament includes AIM-120 AMRAAM, AIM-7 Sparrow and AIM-9 Sidewinder, in addition to a nose-mounted Vulcan M61A1 20-mm cannon with 570 rounds of ammunition. For strike missions, options include precision-guided munitions

Left: Canada has four operational CF-188 squadrons, augmented by an OCU. The fleet has true dual-role taskings, including air defence alerts in the north of the country.

Below: Australian Hornets carry a wide variety of stores, and are able to carry the AAS-48 FLIR/laser designation pod.

RADAR
The present radar is the Hughes APG-65, a highly-capable multi-mode unit. From 1994 the radar will be upgraded to APG-73 standard with faster processing and larger memory. Air-to-air modes are velocity search, range while search, track while scan, and three air combat modes (gun acquisition, vertical acquisition and boresight acquisition). Air-to-ground modes include long-range mapping, sea search, terrain avoidance, moving target indication and air-to-surface ranging.

FLIGHT CONTROLS
The digital fly-by-wire system controls outboard ailerons and differential tailerons for roll control (aided by drooping flaperons at low speed), twin rudders for yaw and the tailerons for pitch. For take-off and landing the rudders are automatically toed-in to provide a nose-up pitch moment. Trailing- and leading-edge flaps are automatically programmed for optimum performance for both low-speed lift and high-speed manoeuvring.

AIR-TO-GROUND WEAPONS
A wide range of stores can be carried, depending on the nature of the mission. Here eight Mk 82 LDGP (low-drag general-purpose) bombs are carried, the twin yellow nose band distinguishing the fire-protected Navy version. The C model introduced the capability to launch imaging infra-red Maverick missiles.

INTAKES
As there was no Mach 2 requirement, the Hornet featured simple D-shaped intakes, with a large splitter plate. The advanced F/A-18E/F will have a wedge-shaped intake for better supersonic performance.

McDonnell Douglas F/A-18C Hornet

Procured primarily to replace the A-7 in light attack squadrons, and the last remaining F-4 Phantoms, the F/A-18 has now also taken over some of the F-14's fighter duties. In the attack role, the aircraft can undertake daylight close air support/battlefield air interdiction missions with 'dumb' weapons, but with the use of infra-red sensors and guided munitions has a measure of night and precision attack capability, including anti-ship strikes. In the air-to-air role it has excellent manoeuvrability for close-in work, while its radar and AIM-7/AIM-120 capability allows it to undertake long-range interception.

WING-FOLD
Incorporated in both carrier and land versions, the wing-fold reduces span by 12 ft 11 in (3.93 m).

AIR-TO-AIR WEAPONS
The wingtip launch rails are nearly always used for AIM-9 Sidewinders. For combat air patrol work the intake-side pylons can carry AIM-7 or AIM-120 missiles, these weapons (or twin AIM-9 launcher) also being carried on the outer wing pylons. The gun is the trusty M61A1 20-mm Vulcan cannon mounted in the nose, with 570 rounds in a drum tank mounted below the gun and aft of the radar.

such as the AGM-65 Maverick air-to-surface missile, AGM-84E stand-off land attack missile, AGM-62 Walleye EO-guided bomb and GBU-10/12/16 laser-guided bombs. 'Dumb' ordnance comprises the Mk 80 series of general-purpose bombs, CBU-59 cluster bomb units and fuel air explosives. For anti-ship attacks the F/A-18 can carry a pair of AGM-84 Harpoons. The Hornet is also fully able to deliver nuclear weapons, such as the B57 and B61 tactical devices. Finally, it is also frequently used as a 'Wild Weasel' in the defence suppression role, using the AGM-88A HARM to neutralise hostile radars.

PYLONS
The Hornet has nine external stations, comprising wingtip launch rails, four underwing pylons, two engine nacelle stations and a centreline hardpoint. Total load is 15,500 lb (7030 kg).

FUEL
Most of the internal fuel is housed in the swollen spine of the aircraft, total capacity being 1,600 US gal (6060 litres). Three 330-US gal (1250-litre) drop tanks can be carried, and a retractable refuelling probe is located in the starboard side of the nose.

SPECIFICATION

McDonnell Douglas F/A-18C Hornet
Wing: span 37 ft 6 in (11.43 m) without tip-mounted AAMs and 40 ft 4.75 in (12.31 m) with tip-mounted AAMs; width folded 27 ft 6 in (8.38 m); aspect ratio 3.5; area 400.00 sq ft (37.16 m²)
Fuselage and tail: length 56 ft 0 in (17.07 m); height 15 ft 3.5 in (4.66 m); tailplane span 21 ft 7.25 in (6.58 m); wheel track 10 ft 2.5 in (3.11 m); wheel base 17 ft 9.5 in (5.42 m)
Powerplant: two General Electric F404-GE-400 turbofans each rated at 16,000 lb st (71.17 kN) with afterburning or, in aircraft built from early 1992, F404-GE-402 turbofans each rated at 17,700 lb st (78.73 kN) with afterburning
Weights: empty 23,050 lb (10455 kg); normal take-off 36,710 lb (16652 kg) for a fighter mission or

51,900 lb (23541 kg) for an attack mission; maximum take-off about 56,000 lb (25401 kg)
Fuel and load: internal fuel 10,860 lb (4926 kg); external fuel up to 6,732 lb (3053 kg) in three 330-US gal (1250-litre) drop tanks; maximum ordnance 15,500 lb (7031 kg)
Speed: maximum level speed 'clean' at high altitude more than 1,033 kt (1,190 mph; 1915 km/h)
Range: ferry range more than 1,800 nm (2,073 miles; 3336 km) with drop tanks; combat radius more than 400 nm (460 miles; 740 km) on a fighter mission, or 575 nm (662 miles; 1065 km) on an attack mission, or 290 nm (340 miles; 537 km) on a hi-lo-hi interdiction mission
Performance: maximum rate of climb at sea level 45,000 ft (13715 m) per minute; combat ceiling about

50,000 ft (15240 m); take-off run less than 1,400 ft (427 m) at maximum take-off weight

McDonnell Douglas F/A-18A Hornet
generally similar to the F/A-18C Hornet except in the following particulars:
Weights: normal take-off 33,585 lb (15234 kg) for a fighter mission; maximum take-off 48,253 lb (21888 kg) for an attack mission

OPERATORS

In 1994 the units operating all Hornet variants (including two-seaters) were as follows:
US Navy (active-duty): VFA-15/37/81/82/83/86/87/105/106/131/132/136 NAS Cecil Field, FL

VFA-22/25/27/94/97/137/146/147/151 NAS Lemoore, CA
VFA-192/195 NAS Atsugi, Japan
VFA-127, NSWC NAS Fallon, NV
VX-4, NAWC-WD NAS Point Mugu, CA
VX-5, NAWC-WD NAS China Lake, CA
NAWC-AD, USN TPS NAS Patuxent River, MD
'Blue Angels' NAS Pensacola, FL
US Navy Reserve: VFA-203 NAS Cecil Field, FL
VFA-204 NAS New Orleans, LA
VFA-303 NAS Lemoore, CA
VFA-305 NAS Point Mugu, CA
US Marine Corps (active-duty): VMFA-115/122/251/312/451, VMFA(AW)-224/332/533 MCAS Beaufort, SC
VMFA-314/323, VMFAT-101, VMFA(AW)-121/225/242 MCAS El Toro, CA
VMFA-212/232/235 MCAS Kaneohe Bay, HI
US Marine Corps Reserve: VMFA-112 NAS Dallas, TX
VMFA-134 MCAS El Toro, CA
VMFA-142 NAS Cecil Field, FL

McDonnell Douglas F/A-18A/C Hornet

VMFA-321 NAF Washington, MD

Australia: 57 AF-18A and 18 AF-18B supplied for service with No. 2 OCU, Nos 3 and 77 Sqns at RAAF Williamtown, and No. 75 Sqn at RAAF Tindal
Canada: 98 CF-188A and 40 CF-188B supplied for service with Nos 410/416/441 Sqns/AETE at CFB Cold Lake, Alberta and Nos 425/433 Sqns at CFB Bagotville, Quebec
Finland: 57 F/A-18C and seven F/A-18D on order
Kuwait: 32 KAF-18C and eight KAF-18D delivered to Nos 9 and 25 Sqns
Malaysia: eight F/A-18Ds on order
Spain: 60 EF-18A and 12 EF-18B (local designation C.15 and CE.15) supplied for service with Ala de Caza 12 at Torrejón (Escuadrones 121 and 122) and Ala de Caza 15 at Zaragoza (Escuadrones 151 and 152)
Switzerland: 26 F/A-18C and eight F/A-18D on order

Eight F/A-18As and a single F/A-18B are assigned to the US Navy's 'Blue Angels' aerobatic team. The aircraft have civilian nav/comms gear, smoke-generating equipment and no cannon.

McDonnell Douglas F/A-18B/D/D(RC) Hornet

Development of a two-seat version of the Hornet was undertaken concurrently with that of the single-seater, following the McDonnell Douglas/Northrop contender's victory over the rival General Dynamics F-16 in the US Navy's Air Combat Fighter contest of the mid-1970s. In consequence, two examples of the **TF-18A** (initial designation, later replaced by **F/A-18B**) featured in the original contract which covered procurement of a batch of 11 prototype aircraft for RDT&E tasks.

Basically identical to the F/A-18A, the B model introduced a second seat in tandem for a modest six per cent penalty in fuel capacity. Otherwise, the F/A-18B was unaltered, possessing identical equipment and near-identical combat capability, with the latter being a factor in the change of designation.

Subsequent procurement of the F/A-18B for service with Navy and Marine Corps units ended with the 40th production example, and this version has never been employed by front-line forces. Apart from a few examples assigned to test agencies, the F/A-18B serves only with VFA-106.

The second two-seat Hornet version was the **F/A-18D**, which is broadly similar to the single-seat F/A-18C. Thirty-one baseline aircraft were procured before production changed to the night attack-capable F/A-18D, which has the same avionics improvements as the night-attack F/A-18C. All FY 1988 and subsequent F/A-18Cs and F/A-18Ds have been to this standard, the first night-attack F/A-18D going to Patuxent River on 14 Nov-

Left: Kuwait's Hornet order included eight KAF-18D two-seaters.

Below: The Marines use the F/A-18D for fast FAC duties in addition to training. This aircraft, from El Toro-based training outfit VMFAT-101 'Sharpshooters', lets fly with 5-in Zuni rockets. These weapons, carried in four-round LAU-10 pods, can be used for target-marking with white phosphorus warheads.

ember 1989. This variant is a special night-attack two-seat Hornet which has replaced the Grumman A-6 Intruder with the USMC's VMA(AW) units (All Weather Attack Squadrons). Originally dubbed **F/A-18D+**, the aircraft features 'uncoupled' cockpits, usually with no control column in the rear cockpit (although one can be refitted) and with two sidestick weapons controllers.

The Hornet was first proposed as a reconnaissance platform early in its career, and it was initially envisaged that single-seaters would be modified to accept an interchangeable recce package in the nose, occupying the space normally taken up by the M61A1 cannon. This contained a Fairchild-Weston KA-99 panoramic camera and a Honeywell AN/AAD-5 linescan, with provision for various other cameras. The first prototype was used as the aerodynamic prototype for the reconnaissance Hornet, with the bulged undernose sensor pallet and associated camera windows. An F/A-18A (161214) was modified more comprehensively, receiving full recce equipment, under the designation **RF-18** (or, more correctly, **F/A-18(R)**), first flying in its new configuration on 15 August 1984.

The increasing trend towards the use of digitised reconnaissance sensors, which

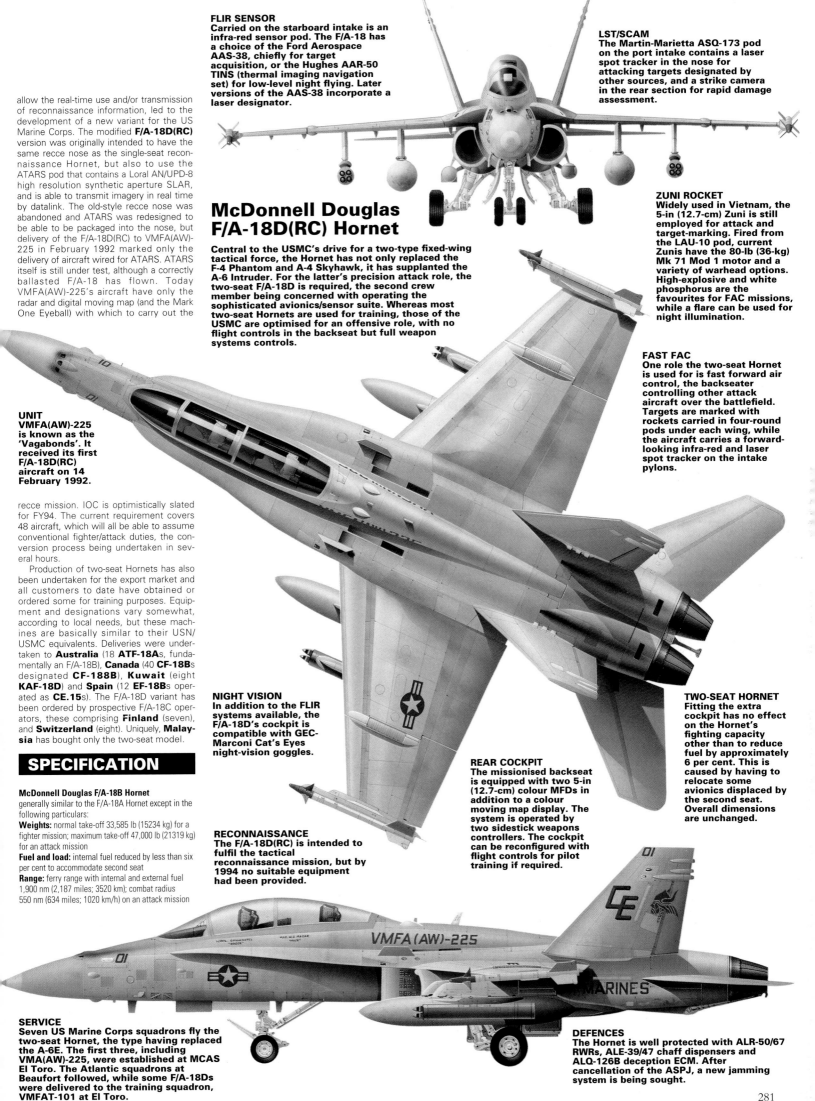

FLIR SENSOR
Carried on the starboard intake is an infra-red sensor pod. The F/A-18 has a choice of the Ford Aerospace AAS-38, chiefly for target acquisition, or the Hughes AAR-50 TINS (thermal imaging navigation set) for low-level night flying. Later versions of the AAS-38 incorporate a laser designator.

LST/SCAM
The Martin-Marietta ASQ-173 pod on the port intake contains a laser spot tracker in the nose for attacking targets designated by other sources, and a strike camera in the rear section for rapid damage assessment.

allow the real-time use and/or transmission of reconnaissance information, led to the development of a new variant for the US Marine Corps. The modified **F/A-18D(RC)** version was originally intended to have the same recce nose as the single-seat reconnaissance Hornet, but also to use the ATARS pod that contains a Loral AN/UPD-8 high resolution synthetic aperture SLAR, and is able to transmit imagery in real time by datalink. The old-style recce nose was abandoned and ATARS was redesigned to be able to be packaged into the nose, but delivery of the F/A-18D(RC) to VMFA(AW)-225 in February 1992 marked only the delivery of aircraft wired for ATARS. ATARS itself is still under test, although a correctly ballasted F/A-18 has flown. Today VMFA(AW)-225's aircraft have only the radar and digital moving map (and the Mark One Eyeball) with which to carry out the

McDonnell Douglas F/A-18D(RC) Hornet

Central to the USMC's drive for a two-type fixed-wing tactical force, the Hornet has not only replaced the F-4 Phantom and A-4 Skyhawk, it has supplanted the A-6 Intruder. For the latter's precision attack role, the two-seat F/A-18D is required, the second crew member being concerned with operating the sophisticated avionics/sensor suite. Whereas most two-seat Hornets are used for training, those of the USMC are optimised for an offensive role, with no flight controls in the backseat but full weapon systems controls.

ZUNI ROCKET
Widely used in Vietnam, the 5-in (12.7-cm) Zuni is still employed for attack and target-marking. Fired from the LAU-10 pod, current Zunis have the 80-lb (36-kg) Mk 71 Mod 1 motor and a variety of warhead options. High-explosive and white phosphorus are the favourites for FAC missions, while a flare can be used for night illumination.

FAST FAC
One role the two-seat Hornet is used for is fast forward air control, the backseater controlling other attack aircraft over the battlefield. Targets are marked with rockets carried in four-round pods under each wing, while the aircraft carries a forward-looking infra-red and laser spot tracker on the intake pylons.

UNIT
VMFA(AW)-225 is known as the 'Vagabonds'. It received its first F/A-18D(RC) aircraft on 14 February 1992.

recce mission. IOC is optimistically slated for FY94. The current requirement covers 48 aircraft, which will all be able to assume conventional fighter/attack duties, the conversion process being undertaken in several hours.

Production of two-seat Hornets has also been undertaken for the export market and all customers to date have obtained or ordered some for training purposes. Equipment and designations vary somewhat, according to local needs, but these machines are basically similar to their USN/USMC equivalents. Deliveries were undertaken to **Australia** (18 **ATF-18A**s, fundamentally an F/A-18B), **Canada** (40 **CF-18B**s designated **CF-188B**), **Kuwait** (eight **KAF-18D**) and **Spain** (12 **EF-18B**s operated as **CE.15**s). The F/A-18D variant has been ordered by prospective F/A-18C operators, these comprising **Finland** (seven), and **Switzerland** (eight). Uniquely, **Malaysia** has bought only the two-seat model.

SPECIFICATION

McDonnell Douglas F/A-18B Hornet
generally similar to the F/A-18A Hornet except in the following particulars:
Weights: normal take-off 33,585 lb (15234 kg) for a fighter mission; maximum take-off 47,000 lb (21319 kg) for an attack mission
Fuel and load: internal fuel reduced by less than six per cent to accommodate second seat
Range: ferry range with internal and external fuel 1,900 nm (2,187 miles; 3520 km); combat radius 550 nm (634 miles; 1020 km/h) on an attack mission

NIGHT VISION
In addition to the FLIR systems available, the F/A-18D's cockpit is compatible with GEC-Marconi Cat's Eyes night-vision goggles.

RECONNAISSANCE
The F/A-18D(RC) is intended to fulfil the tactical reconnaissance mission, but by 1994 no suitable equipment had been provided.

REAR COCKPIT
The missionised backseat is equipped with two 5-in (12.7-cm) colour MFDs in addition to a colour moving map display. The system is operated by two sidestick weapons controllers. The cockpit can be reconfigured with flight controls for pilot training if required.

TWO-SEAT HORNET
Fitting the extra cockpit has no effect on the Hornet's fighting capacity other than to reduce fuel by approximately 6 per cent. This is caused by having to relocate some avionics displaced by the second seat. Overall dimensions are unchanged.

SERVICE
Seven US Marine Corps squadrons fly the two-seat Hornet, the type having replaced the A-6E. The first three, including VMA(AW)-225, were established at MCAS El Toro. The Atlantic squadrons at Beaufort followed, while some F/A-18Ds were delivered to the training squadron, VMFAT-101 at El Toro.

DEFENCES
The Hornet is well protected with ALR-50/67 RWRs, ALE-39/47 chaff dispensers and ALQ-126B deception ECM. After cancellation of the ASPJ, a new jamming system is being sought.

McDonnell Douglas F/A-18E/F

Originally proposed during 1991 as a replacement for the abandoned A-12 Avenger project, the latest variants of the Hornet are presently under development with a view to flying for the first time in 1995 and attaining IOC in 1999. As with preceding variants, single- and two-seat versions have been proposed, with the respective designations **F/A-18E** and **F/A-18F**.

The resulting aircraft have been extensively redesigned and are fundamentally stretched versions of the current production F/A-18C/D models, featuring a 2-ft 10-in (86-cm) plug inserted in the fuselage, as well as increased span and wing area and enlarged horizontal tail surfaces. The LERXes have also been significantly increased in area. Gross weight is expected to rise by approximately 10,000 lb (4536 kg). These changes will allow an additional 3,000 lb (1361 kg) of internal and 3,100 lb (1406 kg) of external fuel capacity, resulting in an increase in range of approximately 38 per cent.

Further improvements are aimed at enhancing survivability and include measures intended to reduce radar cross-section. Performance benefits arising from the adoption of more powerful General Electric F414-GE-400 turbofan engines will be mainly related to payload capability, both new versions possessing two extra hardpoints (giving a total of 11) for the carriage of ordnance. As a result, maximum external payload will rise by some 2,250 lb (1020 kg)

to 17,750 lb (8050 kg). The F/A-18E/Fs have distinctive, sharply raked rectangular-section air intakes, which replace the old D-shaped intakes of previous models. The F414 is a derivative of the F404 and is closely related to the F412 developed for the ill-fated A-12. It will have a new afterburner with longer high-temperature life. With the current two-dimensional F/A-18E/F inlet, thrust growth will be limited to about 10-15 per cent, but an extra 30 per cent thrust could theoretically be provided.

Current avionics planning anticipates more than 90 per cent commonality with the F/A-18C version, but the primary radar sensor will be the Hughes AN/APG-73, an improved version of the APG-65 with enhanced data-processing capability. The radar entered flight tests in April 1992 and has also been installed in production F/A-18Cs and F/A-18Ds in place of the existing AN/APG-65 unit with effect from June 1994. In addition to its suitability for the fighter and strike/attack missions, the F/A-18E will be compatible with the pod-mounted Martin-Marietta ATARS for the recce role.

SPECIFICATION

McDonnell Douglas F/A-18E Hornet
Wing: (approximate) span 41 ft 10.25 in (12.76 m) without tip-mounted AAMs and 44 ft 8.5 in (13.62 m) with tip-mounted AAMs; width folded 30 ft 7.25 in

(9.32 m); aspect ratio 3.51; area 500.00 sq ft (46.45 m²)
Fuselage and tail: length 60 ft 1.25 in (18.31 m); height 15 ft 9.5 in (4.82 m)
Powerplant: two General Electric F414-GE-400 turbofans each rated at 22,000 lb st (97.86 kN) with afterburning
Weights: empty 30,600 lb (13880 kg); maximum take-off 66,000 lb (29937 kg)
Fuel and load: internal fuel 14,400 lb (6531 kg); external fuel up to 9,780 lb (4436 kg) in three 480-US gal (1818-litre) fuel tanks; maximum ordnance 17,750 lb (8051 kg)
Speed: maximum level speed 'clean' at high altitude more than 1,033 kt (1,190 mph; 1915 km/h)
Range: combat radius 591 nm (681 miles; 1095 km)

An artist's impression of the F/A-18E shows the lengthened fuselage, enlarged wings, greater-area LERX and extra pylons. Another major feature of the variant is the wedge-shaped engine intakes.

on a hi-hi-hi interdiction mission with four 1,000-lb (454-kg) bombs, two AIM-9 Sidewinder AAMs and two fuel tanks, or 486 nm (560 miles; 901 km) on a hi-lo-hi interdiction mission with the same stores, or 150 nm (173 miles; 278 km) on a 135-minute maritime air superiority mission with six AAMs and three fuel tanks
Performance: combat ceiling about 50,000 ft (15240 m)

McDonnell Douglas/British Aerospace AV-8B Harrier II

For all its attributes, the original BAe (Hawker Siddeley) Harrier was no more than an armed derivative of the original P.1127 technology demonstrator, and Kestrel trials aircraft. Strong USMC interest in the Harrier in 1968 was followed by an initial order for 12 AV-8As. (US use of these early-generation Harriers is described separately.) Service with four Marine Corps squadrons confirmed the Harrier's early promise, but also demonstrated the limitations of the basic design. Anglo-American design studies for a successor with a supercritical wing were eventually halted, BAe pulling out of the project in March 1975 citing 'insufficient common ground' as the reason. Eventually, the Marines backed a development of an advanced model of the Harrier, designated **AV-8B**, which was

The standard day-attack AV-8B is identified by a clean nose profile, this example serving with VMA-223. The USMC plans to upgrade these aircraft to Plus configuration with uprated engine and APG-65 radar.

intended to offer a larger warload and better range/endurance characteristics There followed considerable political wrangling and some revised thinking over future requirements on the part of the Marines before what was known for a time as the **'Super Harrier'** project became a reality in the early 1980s.

While the original designers of the Harrier concentrated on developing an enlarged, advanced metal wing, which could be retrofitted to existing Harrier airframes, the American former 'junior partner' on the AV-8A pressed ahead with its own second-generation new-build Harrier. This was intended as a new production aircraft from the outset, and not as an upgrade of existing AV-8As. The new design was based around a new, larger-area carbon-fibre supercritical wing, but also incorporating carbon-fibre in other airframe areas and completely revising the cockpit, with HOTAS controls and a higher seating position for the pilot, all without a significant increase in engine power, but with advanced aerodynamic devices to increase

lift. First flown on 9 November 1978, fitted to the 11th AV-8A (which thereby became the first of two **YAV-8B**s), the new wing had 14.5 per cent more area and 20 per cent greater span, with a reduced leading-edge sweep of 10°. The greater area allowed six hardpoints to be fitted. The carbon-fibre construction allowed a 331-lb (150-kg) weight saving by comparison with the original metal wing. More efficient air intakes and carbon-fibre fuselage sections allowed a further equivalent weight saving of 750 lb (340 kg). The British-built rear fuselage remains of metal construction, for heat resistance, and is virtually unchanged, as is the undercarriage.

Engine improvements

Following the testing of four pre-series FSD **AV-8B**s from November 1981, the USMC took delivery of the first production aircraft which were handed over during 1983. The first 12 (like the four FSD aircraft) were powered by F402-RR-404 engines and had double rows of inlet suction relief doors, while later aircraft had the 21,450-lb

st (95.42-kN) F402-RR-406 (Pegasus 11-21, equivalent to the RAF's Mk 105). From the 44th airframe (162747) a digital engine control unit was fitted to AV-8Bs and TAV-8Bs, while from the 197th (163874) the 23,800-lb st (105.87-kN) F402-RR-408 (Pegasus 11-61) is fitted. Procurement was cut from 342 to 336 and then to 328 aircraft. Later defence cuts reduced the total to 280 aircraft, although an additional purchase of six attrition replacements following Operation Desert Storm increased procurement to 286. Originally this figure did not include two-seat **TAV-8B** trainers (described separately), although these were subsequently incorporated on the McDonnell Douglas production line.

From the 167th airframe (163853), all USMC AV-8Bs were made capable of conducting night-attack operations with the installation of GEC FLIR, a head-down display, a colour moving map and an improved HUD. The terms **Night Attack Harrier II** or **Night Attack AV-8B** are sometimes applied unofficially. The first delivery of this variant was to VMA-214 on 15 September 1989. During Desert Storm, the AV-8B was operated by USMC squadrons VMA-231, 311 and 331, and by six aircraft operating as Detachment B of VMA-513. Seven AV-8Bs were lost in combat during Desert Storm, mainly to SAMs, the type having been heavily engaged on ground support strikes. VMA-331 was disestablished during 1992, but the remaining units will continue to play a vital part in US Marine Corps aviation. Plans to withdraw some of the US Navy's conventional carriers may well lead to an increased role for the AV-8B, which can provide air support from smaller platforms.

The 205th production single-seater (164129) was the first fully equipped example of the improved **AV-8B Harrier II Plus** variant, and the true prototype for the new variant. It made its inaugural flight on 22 September 1992, although 161397, the second FSD AV-8B, had already flown as an aerodynamic prototype, with a dummy radome and inert AIM-120 AMRAAM missiles. Equipped with the Hughes AN/APG-65 radar (with an antenna cropped by 2 in/5 cm

WORKSHARE
AV-8B construction is split roughly 60/40 in favour of McDD, which builds the forward and forward-central fuselage, tailplane, wing and underfuselage strakes. BAe builds the rear-central and rear fuselage, tail and reaction-control system.

ARMAMENT
This AV-8B carries a typical close air support load with two anti-armour Maverick missiles and two Mk 7 cluster bomb dispensers. The AIM-9M Sidewinders are standard for self-defence. Fire bombs (napalm) and fuel-air explosive weapons were also used during the Gulf War.

FLIGHT CONTROL
At normal airspeeds, the AV-8B has standard control surfaces comprising hydraulically-actuated ailerons and tailplane, and mechanically-actuated rudder. For high lift, the ailerons droop to augment single-slotted flaps. In very low-speed flight, control is effected by reaction control valves ('puffer jets') located in the nose, tail and wingtips and, of course, by the four thrust-vectoring nozzles. Extra lift is gained by creating a 'box' under the central fuselage out of the gun pods (or strakes), the airbrake and a retractable dam. This captures a cushion of jet air that bounces back off the ground, enabling the aircraft to take off vertically at the same weight at which it can hover.

McDonnell Douglas/ British Aerospace AV-8B Harrier II Night Attack

For direct support of troops on the ground, the US Marine Corps chose the AV-8B. The Harrier II is of great value, as it can happily operate from assault carriers or from makeshift landing strips on the beach-head, close to the fighting. This close proximity to the action allows a force of AV-8Bs to generate a large number of sorties, highly important to the task of close air support, where air power is required over the battlefield for as long a period as possible. Initial AV-8B deliveries were seen as daytime-only attack aircraft, but the Night Attack Harrier, as depicted here, introduced full low-light capability. The small protuberance ahead of the windscreen houses a GEC forward-looking infra-red, while the pilot is issued with night-vision goggles, the cockpit instruments then being made compatible with their use.

DISPENSERS
An unusual feature of the AV-8B is the upward-firing chaff/flare dispensers scabbed on to the upper fuselage. Further dispensers are located under the rear fuselage.

CANNON SYSTEM
Housed in the two underfuselage pods, the gun system consists of a pod containing a GAU-12/A Equaliser cannon, and the other a linear linkless 300-round feed system. A fairing crosses the fuselage to carry the rounds to the gun. The Equaliser has five barrels of 25-mm calibre, with a maximum rate of fire of 4,200 rpm. Muzzle velocity is 1097 m per second. Round options are APDS (armour-piercing discarding sabot), API (armour-piercing incendiary), HEI (high-explosive incendiary) and TP (training practice).

MARKINGS
The two-tone grey camouflage with low-visibility markings has been adopted as standard. This aircraft is from VMA-211 'Wake Island Avengers'.

to fit the AV-8B's fuselage cross-section), the Harrier II Plus retains the overnose FLIR sensor (although this is repackaged in a broader, squarer section fairing) and is otherwise externally identical to late production AV-8Bs. The provision of radar gives compatibility with the AIM-7 Sparrow and AIM-120 AMRAAM, endowing a BVR kill capability for the first time. It also allows the use of AGM-84 Harpoon missiles in the anti-shipping role. The last 27 aircraft of the US Marine Corps order were to have been built to this standard, but this total was reduced to 24, three of which will now be delivered to Italy. The first Plus (164542) was delivered in early 1993. In addition, 114 pre-

Night Attack AV-8Bs will be converted to Harrier II Plus configuration. These will retain only their existing wings, tail surfaces and undercarriage.

Foreign customers

Two other nations with a NATO maritime commitment have also purchased AV-8Bs, these countries being Spain and Italy. Since 1977 the Spanish navy has embarked the AV-8S Harrier (locally designated **VA.1 Matador**) on the carrier *Dedalo*. With the commissioning of the carrier *Principe de Asturias* in 1989, the Arma Aérea de la Armada embarked 12 **EAV-8Bs** as part of an expanded air group which included a mix

of AV/TAV-8Ss. The Spanish navy also ordered 13 AV-8B Harrier II Plus variants in November 1992, for initial delivery in late 1995, and the surviving EAV-8Bs are likely to be upgraded to the same standard. A two-seat TAV-8B had been ordered in March 1992 to supplement its two remaining TAV-8S models.

Italy's procurement of AV-8Bs followed a protracted political debate, but in May 1989 two TAV-8Bs were finally purchased, to enhance the main pilot training programme in the US by the Marine Corps. These aircraft were delivered in August 1991 and the first batch of three AV-8B Harrier II Plus aircraft was ordered in July 1991, followed by

a further 13 in November 1992. Italy has an option on eight more of these aircraft. Based at Luni, the Harriers will also embark on the carrier *Giuseppe Garibaldi*. In 1994, **Thailand** requested information on AV-8Bs for its new helicopter-carrier.

WEAPON OPTIONS

The AV-8B has three pylons under each wing, stressed to 2,000 lb (907 kg), 1,000 lb (454 kg) and 630 lb (286 kg) respectively. The outboard pylon is usually used for AIM-9 Sidewinder carriage, leaving the inner two for various air-to-ground weaponry, including Mk 7 cluster bomb dispensers, Mk 82/83 bombs, LAU-10/

The first operator of the AV-8B Plus is VMA-542 at Cherry Point. In addition to the radar, the nose also features FLIR in a flattened fairing.

68/69 rocket pods, AGM-65 Maverick, CBU-55/72 fuel-air explosive, Mk 77 fire bombs and GBU-12/16 LGBs, the latter requiring designation from another source. The centreline hardpoint is used for an ALQ-167 ECM pod. Two fuselage packs contain a five-barrelled 25-mm GAU-12 cannon (port) and ammunition tank for 300 rounds (starboard). These are replaced with aerodynamic strakes when not fitted. The Harrier II Plus adds two extra missile pylons for Sidewinders, and the ability to launch AMRAAM, Sparrow and Harpoon missiles.

SPECIFICATION

McDonnell Douglas AV-8B Harrier II
Wing: span 30 ft 4 in (9.25 m); aspect ratio 4.0; area 238.7 sq ft (22.18 m2) including two 4.35-sq ft (0.40-m2) LERXes or, in aircraft delivered from December 1990, 243.40 sq ft (22.61 m2) including two 6.70-sq ft (0.62-m2) LERXes
Fuselage and tail: length 46 ft 4 in (14.12 m); height 11 ft 7.75 in (3.55 m); tailplane span 13 ft 11 in (4.24 m); outrigger track 17 ft 0 in (5.18 m)

Powerplant: one Rolls-Royce F402-RR-406A turbofan rated at 21,450 lb st (95.42 kN) dry or, in aircraft delivered from December 1990, one Rolls-Royce F402-RR-408 turbofan rated at 23,800 lb st (105.87 kN)
Weights: operating empty 13,968 lb (6336 kg) including pilot and unused fuel; normal take-off 22,950 lb (10410 kg) for 7-g operation; maximum take-off 31,000 lb (14061 kg) for 1,330-ft (405-m) STO or 18,950 lb (8596 kg) for VTO
Fuel and load: internal fuel 7,759 lb (3519 kg); external fuel up to 8,070 lb (3661 kg) in four 300-US gal (1136-litre) drop tanks; maximum ordnance 10,800 lb (4899 kg) with -406A engine or 13,235 lb (6003 kg) with -408 engine
Speed: maximum level speed 'clean' at sea level 575 kt (662 mph; 1065 km/h)
Range: ferry range 1,965 nm (2,263 miles; 3641 km) with empty tanks dropped; combat radius 90 nm (103 miles; 167 km) with a 1-hour loiter after 1,200-ft (366-m) STO with 12 Mk 82 Snakeye bombs, or 594 nm (684 miles; 1001 km) on a hi-lo-hi attack mission after 1,200-ft (366-m) STO with seven 500-lb (227-kg) Mk 82 Snakeye bombs and two 300-US gal (1136-litre) drop tanks, or 627 nm (722 miles; 1162 km) on a deck-launched interception mission with two AIM-9 Sidewinders and two drop tanks; combat air patrol radius 100 nm (115 miles; 185 km) for a 3-hour patrol
Performance: maximum rate of climb at sea level 14,715 ft (4485 m) per minute; service ceiling more

than 50,000 ft (15240 m); STO run 1,437 ft (435 m) at maximum take-off weight; landing run 0 ft (0 m) at up to 19,937 lb (9043 kg)
g limits: -3 to +8

OPERATORS

US Marine Corps: VMA-223/231/542, VMAT-203 MCAS Cherry Point, NC
VMA-211/214/311/513 MCAS Yuma, AZ
US Navy: NAWC-AD NAS Patuxent River, MD

NAWC-WD NAS China Lake, CA
Italy: two AV-8B, 13 AV-8B Plus and three TAV-8B in the process of delivery. Option on eight more. Assembly of some aircraft undertaken by Alenia.
Spain: 12 EAV-8B for Eslla 9. One TAV-8B and eight EAV-8B Plus on order. Earlier aircraft to be brought to Plus standard.

Spain operates its Harrier fleet from the shore base at Rota, and aboard the carrier **Principe de Asturias.** *Note the GAU-12 cannon pod.*

McDonnell Douglas/British Aerospace TAV-8B Harrier II

Some while after the decision to go ahead with the AV-8B Harrier II programme, the **US Marine Corps** resolved that it would need a two-seat conversion

trainer version of the second-generation aircraft, to which the designation **TAV-8B** was allocated. The target for USMC acquisition was 28 aircraft, but only 26 were pro-

cured, all serving with the type conversion unit VMAT-203 at MCAS Cherry Point, NC. The other two aircraft were delivered to **Italy**. The first aircraft made its initial flight on 21 October 1986, and the first was delivered to the Marines in March 1987. A subsequent sale was made to **Spain** (one aircraft ordered in 1992). The RAF has ordered the similar **Harrier GR.Mk 10**, described separately.

Principal differences between the two-seat TAV-8B and the AV-8B involve the forward fuselage, which is 3 ft 11-in (1.2-m) longer to accommodate the two-man cockpit. The rear seat is considerably raised to provide excellent visibility for the instructor.

As part of Italy's Harrier II order, the AMI received a pair of TAV-8Bs from the USMC FY89 production. The single-seat aircraft are to radar-equipped 'Plus' standard.

To offset the reduced stability caused by the longer fuselage, the vertical fin is increased in area by adding 1 ft 5 in (0.43 m) to the height and widening the chord by straightening the lower portion of the leading edge. Internal fuel is reduced by 453 lb (205 kg). As the TAV-8B is intended purely as a conversion trainer, it has only one pylon under each wing for practice weapons, and routinely carries fuselage strakes in place of the cannon.

SPECIFICATION

McDonnell Douglas TAV-8B Harrier II
generally similar to the McDonnell Douglas AV-8B Harrier II except in the following particulars:
Fuselage and tail: length 50 ft 3 in (15.32 m)
Weights: operating empty 15,542 lb (7050 kg) including pilot and unused fuel
Fuel and load: internal fuel 7,306 lb (3314 kg)

McDonnell Douglas/British Aerospace T-45 Goshawk

In 1981, the US Navy selected a modified version of the **British Aerospace Hawk** trainer as its **T45TS** (Training System). This highly significant programme aims to produce up to 600 jet pilots annually throughout the 1990s and into the 21st century. Concurrent with the last phases of Hawk flight testing prior to its RAF service debut, the US Navy began a three-year study into new trainer requirements that would, ideally, combine the handling qualities of the intermediate T-2B/C Buckeye and the advanced TA-4J Skyhawk. A saving in flight hours and costs was seen to be possible with the right new aircraft and, in 1978, an evaluation of available types was made with the intention of undertaking what had become the VTXTS programme. The Hawk was judged to be superior to existing US Navy trainers and its rivals on a number of counts, including fuel consumption, and in November 1981 the British trainer was duly selected. FSD funding followed in 1984 and an engineering development contract was awarded in May 1986 to the prime US contractor McDonnell Douglas. The principal sub-contractor is British Aerospace, which retains responsibility for manufacture of wings, centre and rear fuselage, fin, tailplane, windscreen, canopy and flying controls.

As first proposed, there were to be two variants, a 'wet' **T-45A** model fitted for carrier operation and a 'dry' model **T-45B** restricted to land-based training and dummy carrier landing practice. Subsequent confirmation of the practicality of extending the lives of both the T-2 and TA-4J led to a decision for the US Navy to acquire only the T-45A, with full carrier qualification.

In order to tailor the basic **Hawk Mk 60** airframe to stringent US Navy requirements for operations from a carrier, a number of changes have been made. The airframe has been strengthened to withstand the inevitable stresses of carrier operations, including the severe sink-rates encountered on a pitching deck. The forward fuselage

The first T-45A demonstrates the considerable aerodynamic differences between it and basic Hawks, including full-span slats, twin airbrakes and 'smurfs' forward of the tailplane. The hefty nosewheel strut has a catapult launch bar and twin wheels.

has a deeper profile to accommodate a new strengthened twin nosewheel undercarriage unit, which is also compatible with the US Navy's steam catapults with catapult launch bar and holdback. The main gear is also redesigned, with longer-stroke oleos. The fin height has been increased by 6 in (15.2 cm), tailplane span has been increased by 4 in (10.2 cm) and a single ventral fin has been added. The Hawk's single ventral airbrake has been replaced by two fuselage side-mounted units (of composite construction), while 'smurfs' (side mounted unit horizontal root tail fins – small curved surfaces forward of each tailplane) eliminate airbrake-related pitch-down during low-speed gear-up manoeuvres. The T-45 has new electrically actuated and hydraulically operated full-span leading-edge slats and a new aileron/rudder interconnect. The aircraft is also provided with an arrester hook (deployable to 20° on each side of the centreline) and US Navy standard cockpit instrumentation and radios, the crew sit on Martin-Baker Mk 14 NACES ejection seats and the fuel system is revised. The aircraft's overall appearance is otherwise similar to other two-seat Hawks, apart from squared-off wing-tips, which do not alter overall span, and a broader-span square-tipped horizontal tail.

Although the strengthening programme was necessary for the carrier role, the T-45A (renamed **Goshawk** to avoid confusion with the US Army Hawk missile) will remain land-based, flying to a training carrier as required. The US Navy has stated that it expects each T-45A to undertake 38,000 field landings, 16,000 carrier landings and over 1,000 seaborne launchings. Initial carrier qualifications with the two Douglas-built, F405-RR-400L (Adour 861-49) engined FSD prototypes and McDonnell-built, F405-RR-401 (Adour 871) engined pre-production aircraft began aboard *John F. Kennedy* on 4 December 1991. The first St Louis-built T-45 made its maiden flight on 16 December 1991, and deliveries to the Navy began when the prototypes went to Patuxent River in October 1990. Even though the Adour 871 provides some 30 per cent more thrust than the original engine, there were for many years plans to re-engine the aircraft again, with a variety of American-built candidate engines. The 268 aircraft required (plus 24 simulators, and 34 computer-aided instruction devices) will be delivered to Naval Air Stations at Kingsville (VT-21/22/23

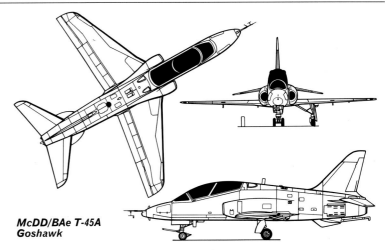

McDD/BAe T-45A Goshawk

of Training Wing 2) and NAS Meridian (VT-7 of Training Wing 1). It is planned to incorporate a digital, glass cockpit with two colour MFDs from the 97th aircraft, and a prototype will fly during 1995. Introduction of the T-45 will result in the training task being accomplished with 25 per cent fewer flying hours using 42 per cent fewer aircraft and 46 per cent fewer personnel.

WEAPON OPTIONS

Provision is made for a single pylon under each wing for the carriage of practice bomb rack, rocket pods or extra fuel. Centreline pylon can also carry stores for weapons training role. Rear cockpit has CAI gunsight.

SPECIFICATION

McDonnell Douglas/British Aerospace T-45A Goshawk
Wing: span 30 ft 9.75 in (9.39 m); aspect ratio 5.3; area 176.90 sq ft (16.69 m2)
Fuselage and tail: length 39 ft 3.125 in (11.97 m) including probe; height 14 ft 0 in (4.27 m); tailplane span 15 ft 0.75 in (4.59 m); wheel track 12 ft 9.5 in (3.90 m); wheel base 14 ft 1 in (4.29 m)
Powerplant: one Rolls-Royce/Turboméca F405-RR-401 turbofan rated at 5,845 lb st (26.00 kN)
Weights: empty 9,399 lb (4263 kg); maximum take-off 12,758 lb (5787 kg)
Fuel and load: internal fuel 2,893 lb (1312 kg);

Training Wing 2 received the first operational T-45As at Kingsville, the Goshawk replacing TA-4Js.

external fuel up to two 156-US gal (591-litre) drop tanks; maximum ordnance none
Speed: maximum level speed 'clean' at 8,000 ft (2440 m) 538 kt (620 mph; 997 km/h)
Range: ferry range on internal fuel 1,000 nm (1,152 miles; 1854 km)
Performance: maximum rate of climb at sea level 6,982 ft (2128 m) per minute; service ceiling 42,250 ft (12875 m); take-off distance to 50 ft (15 m) 3,744 ft (1189 m) at maximum take-off weight; landing distance from 50 ft (15 m) 3,900 ft (1189 m) at maximum landing weight
g limits: -3 to +7.33

McDonnell Douglas Helicopters **AH-64A/B Apache**

McDonnell Douglas Helicopter Company
5000 East McDowell Road, Mesa
AZ 85205-9797, USA

Formulated in the early 1970s, the US Army's requirement for an advanced attack helicopter (AAH) visualised an aircraft operating in a front-line environment and suitable for a day/night/adverse weather, anti-armour role. In the first part of a two-phase programme, Bell and Hughes were selected to build two flight-test prototypes for competitive evaluation, respectively the YAH-63 and **YAH-64A** (first flying on 30 September 1975). However, it was Hughes' **Model 77** submission that was declared the winning contender on 10 December 1976. A further four air vehicles (one ground test and three flight-test prototypes) were built for Phase 2, primarily concerned with full engineering development and evaluation of advanced avionics, electro-optical and fire-control systems, along with concurrent development of the airframe. Noteworthy modifications to production standard included swept tips on the main rotor blades, low-set (relocated) all-moving tailplane, increased-height vertical fin and adoption of 'Black Hole' infra-red suppression system. It was not until 26 March 1982 that final production approval was given with the issue of a US Army contract for an initial batch of 11 **Hughes AH-64A Apache** helicopters. The first production aircraft was subsequently delivered in January 1984, the same month Hughes became a division of McDonnell Douglas. The name was changed to McDonnell Helicopter Company on 27 August 1985.

The Apache is a tandem, two-seat conventional helicopter with advanced crew protection systems, avionics and electro-optics, plus weapon-control systems that include nose-mounted Martin-Marietta AN/AAQ-11 TADS/PNVS (Target Acquisition and Designation Sight/Pilot Night-Vision Sensor). TADS consists of a FLIR, TV camera, a laser spot tracker and a laser range-

Apaches make much use of the FARP (Forward Air Refueling Point) concept, ground-loitering close to the battle area. From the FARP they can rapidly re-enter the fray, fully armed and fuelled.

finder/designator, and is used for target search and designation, and as a back-up night-vision sensor for the pilot. PNVS is an articulated FLIR which permits nap-of-earth flight at night, providing thermal images to the pilot's monocular sight. The gunner sits in the front seat, with the pilot 19 in (49 cm) higher in the rear cockpit. Both use various sophisticated sensors and systems to detect and attack targets, including the IHADSS (Integrated Helmet And Display Sight System) which provides a monocular helmet-mounted designator/sight. The co-pilot/gunner has primary responsibility for firing both gun and missiles, but can be overridden by the pilot in the backseat. Teledyne Ryan is responsible for the manufacture of the Apache's fuselage, tail, wings, cowling, canopies and other components.

Terrain-masking flight

In combat, the AH-64A flies nap-of-the earth, using terrain masking. In some scenarios, OH-58C Kiowa or OH-58D Kiowa Warrior scout helicopters spot and designate targets and assist in communications to position AH-64As to engage armour and other ground forces. In joint exercises, Apaches have worked effectively with US Air Force A-10 'Warthogs', dividing up the tank-killing mission to make an adversary's task more difficult.

Survivability is enhanced by the use of armour, the design having been required to survive 12.7-mm hits fired from anywhere in the helicopter's lower hemisphere, plus 20°, and to remain airborne for 30 minutes after such a hit. Most critical systems are protected against 23-mm cannon hits. The crew is protected by lightweight boron armour shields, and the undercarriage, cockpit and seats are designed to give a 95 per cent chance of surviving ground impacts at sink rates up to 42 ft (12.9 m) per second. The gun mounting is designed to collapse into the fuselage between the pilots' seats in the event of a crash landing. The engines, which feature integral particle separators and integral exhaust cooling, are widely separated and the key components are armour protected. The Litton Precision Gear Divi-

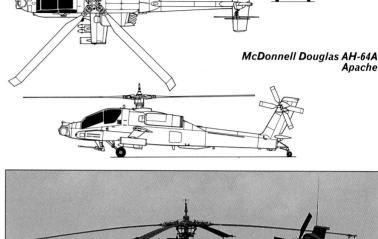
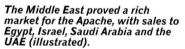

McDonnell Douglas AH-64A Apache

sion transmission can run for over an hour without oil, and the gearboxes and shafts are designed to run for a similar time after ballistic damage. The transmission is isolated from flight loads by a sleeve which contains the main rotor drive shaft. The helicopter is aerobatic and can be flown down to 0.5 g.

Total AH-64A procurement by the US Army stands at 813 helicopters (plus prototypes), comprising 807 planned production aircraft and six attrition replacements for AH-64As lost during Desert Storm. The US Army hoped to upgrade 254 AH-64As to **AH-64A+** or **AH-64B** standard, but this was cancelled in 1992. This was an interim step (coming ahead of the more advanced **AH-64D**, described separately), with modest, near-term improvements based on Operation Desert Storm experience. Modifications included addition of GPS for accurate navigation, SINCGARS radios, extended-range fuel tanks, and new rotor blades. TADS/PNVS and the M230 gun were to have been modified to improve reliability,

The Middle East proved a rich market for the Apache, with sales to Egypt, Israel, Saudi Arabia and the UAE (illustrated).

maintainability and accuracy. The AH-64B's in-the-field modification would have included retrofitted General Electric T700-GE-701C engines. These replaced the -701 in production AH-64s from aircraft 604 (89-0192).

The AH-64A demonstrated its capabilities on ferrying missions on a 4 April 1985 flight, carrying four 230-US gal (870-litre) fuel tanks and flying 1,175 miles (1891 km). On 22 June 1985, six Apaches were loaded into a C-5A Galaxy to demonstrate the capability, since used frequently, to deploy the battlefield helicopter overseas via strategic airlift. Two can be carried in a C-141 and three in the C-17.

The first fully-fledged Apache combat unit was the 3/6th Cavalry at Fort Hood, TX, beginning in July 1986. Soon afterwards, AH-64As were delivered to the 1/3rd Aviation Brigade, 2nd Armored Division, also at Fort Hood, followed by half a dozen more stateside units. In Europe, AH-64As joined the 3/1st Avn, 1st Armored Division at Hanau and the 3/227th Avn, 3rd Armored Division at Illesheim, plus other units. The Army National Guard became an operator of the AH-64A Apache, commencing with 1989 deliveries to the 1/130th Aviation Brigade at Raleigh-Durham, NC. Throughout its operational history, the AH-64A has suffered from adverse publicity, especially in 1987 after a fleet-wide grounding which followed a fatal 21 August 1987 crash at Fort Rucker. Questions of reliability have been raised several times by the General Accounting Office and other agencies.

Various air-to-air missiles have been test-launched from the Apache, including the AIM-9 Sidewinder (illustrated). AAMs have yet to be carried regularly. Another missile option is the visually similar AGM-122 Sidearm anti-radar weapon, which is derived from early AIM-9s.

The first combat deployment of the Apache came with the 82nd Airborne Division's 1st Aviation Battalion's participation in Operation Just Cause in Panama during December 1989/January 1990. More recently, Apaches were employed to devastating effect during Operations Desert Shield/Desert Storm. On 17 January 1992, AH-64s fired the first shots of the war, attacking Iraqi radar sites, and thus opening up a radar-free corridor for coalition air strikes against Baghdad and other targets. Several US Army units employed AH-64As successfully in the anti-tank role in the desert. During the final land offensive of the war, Apaches destroyed 81 tanks and 23 other vehicles and assisted in the capture of 3,200 Iraqi prisoners. Sadly, however, Apaches also figured in two friendly-fire incidents in which coalition troops were killed.

WEAPON OPTIONS

The Apache's principal payload consists of up to 16 AGM-114A Hellfire long-range, laser-guided anti-tank missiles, carried on four pylons under stub wings. Early plans to arm the AH-64 with TOW anti-tank missiles were halted when development of the Hellfire proceeded more rapidly than expected, the missile being adopted as the chosen weapon in 1976. The first successful Apache firing of an AGM-114 took place on 18 March 1979. Operations began at Fort Rucker, AL, and Fort Eustis, VA, in January 1985.

Other weaponry includes pods of 19 2.75-in (70-mm)

Apache on the warpath: this AH-64A displays a typical warload of eight Hellfires and two 19-round Hydra 70 rocket pods. Note the TADS/PNVS sensor array in the nose.

Hydra 70 rockets. Standard fixed armament comprises a 30-mm M230 Chain Gun cannon with 1,200 rounds, mounted under the forward fuselage. Normal rate of fire is 625 rounds per minute. NATO ADEN/DEFA 30-mm ammunition can be used in place of the normal HE or HEDP ammunition. Although US Army doctrine does not foresee the AH-64A engaging fixed-wing warplanes or opposing helicopters, the Apache has been tested with a variety of air-to-air weapons, including AIM-9L Sidewinder, AIM-92A Stinger and MATRA Mistral; the air-to-air capability of the M230 cannon is also being improved. For defence suppression, the Sidearm missile can be employed.

SPECIFICATION

McDonnell Douglas Helicopters AH-64A Apache
Rotor system: main rotor diameter 48 ft 0 in (14.63 m); tail rotor diameter 9 ft 2 in (2.79 m); main rotor disc area 1,809.56 sq ft (168.11 m²); tail rotor disc area 70.00 sq ft (6.13 m²)
Wing: span 17 ft 2 in (5.23 m) clean or 19 ft 1 in (5.82 m) over empty weapon racks
Fuselage and tail: length overall, rotors turning 58 ft 3.125 in (17.76 m) and fuselage 49 ft 1.5 in (14.97 m); height overall 15 ft 3.5 in (4.66 m) to top of air data sensor, 14 ft 1.25 in (4.30 m) over turning tail rotor and 12 ft 7 in (3.84 m) to top of rotor head; stabiliser

span 11 ft 2 in (3.40 m); wheel track 6 ft 8 in (2.03 m); wheel base 34 ft 9 in (10.59 m)
Powerplant: two 1,696-shp (1265-kW) General Electric T700-GE-701 turboshafts each derated for normal operations or, from 604th helicopter, two General Electric T700-GE-701C turboshafts each rated at 1,800 shp (1342 kW)
Weights: empty 11,387 lb (5165 kg); normal take-off 14,445 lb (6552 kg) at primary mission weight or 17,650 lb (8006 kg) at design mission weight; maximum take-off 21,000 lb (9525 kg)
Fuel and load: internal fuel 2,550 lb (1157 kg); maximum ordnance 1,700 lb (771 kg)
Speed: never exceed speed 197 kt (227 mph; 365 km/h); maximum level speed 'clean' and maximum cruising speed at optimum altitude 158 kt (182 mph; 293 km/h)
Range: ferry range 918 nm (1,057 miles; 1701 km) with drop tanks; range 260 nm (300 miles; 428 km) with internal fuel; endurance 3 hours 9 minutes with internal fuel
Performance: maximum vertical rate of climb at sea

level 2,500 ft (762 m) per minute; service ceiling 21,000 ft (6400 m); hovering ceiling 15,000 ft (4570 m) in ground effect and 11,500 ft (3505 m) out of ground effect
g limits: -0.5 to +3.5

OPERATORS

US Army: total procurement totals 813, including six Gulf War attrition replacements. Over 50 had been lost by 1994
Egypt: 24 aircraft on order with delivery commencing in 1994
Greece: 12 on order for delivery from 1995
Israel: 18 ordered from the manufacturer, delivered from September 1990. 24 ex-US Army aircraft delivered in 1993. Local name **Petan**
Saudi Arabia: 12 aircraft delivered from 1993
United Arab Emirates: 20 aircraft delivered 1993-94
Further interest: from Kuwait, South Korea and UK

McDonnell Douglas Helicopters **AH-64D/Longbow Apache**

In 1995 the **AH-64D Apache** is to become the third version of the US Army's principal attack helicopter to enter service, but will at first lack the Longbow radar/missile system fitted to the more advanced **AH-64D Longbow Apache** that is due to follow in 1997. The **AH-64C** designation was to have been applied to upgraded AH-64As that do not carry the Longbow radar. However, this was abandoned in early 1994, and all aircraft in the modernised fleet will be known as AH-64D.

The US Army's plan for an upgraded Apache fleet calls for conversion of 535 (or 750 according to some sources) existing AH-64A helicopters out of its total of 813 procured, of which 227 will be Longbow Apaches with the fire control radar fitted. In 1992, McDonnell Douglas converted four AH-64s with Longbow millimetric-wave fire control radar and Hellfire Longbow missile seekers to act as proof-of-concept aircraft for the AH-64D. Following completion of the Army's Longbow Apache critical design review in November 1991, and flight tests of an aerodynamically representative radome in March 1991, the prototype AH-64D Longbow Apache developmental aircraft made its first flight on 15 April 1992, although functioning radar was not flown until late 1993 (on the second prototype). The first RF Hellfire firing from an Apache followed soon after. Two AH-64C prototypes were also flown. Five aircraft will undergo a five-month Force Development Test and Evaluation during late 1994, and all six prototypes will then be used in the January-March initial operational test and evaluation.

McDonnell Douglas also has received limited funding to accelerate development of the AH-64D to enable production deliveries to begin in mid-1995, two years ahead of the fully-equipped Longbow Apache. The AH-64D and AH-64D Longbow Apache are identical except for radar and engine. The Longbow Apache will be distinguished by the mast-mounted location of its MMW radar and will also have 1,800-shp (1342-kW) General Electric T700-GE-701C engines in

place of the -701 now fitted. The -701C has an emergency rating of 1,940 shp (1447 kW).

The Longbow radar (also being fitted to some of the new RAH-66 Comanches) will be integrated with the helicopter's avionics and with a new RF (radio frequency) seeker-equipped version of the AGM-114 Hellfire ATGM. Some 13,000 of these are to be built, all but 2,000 earmarked for the AH-64. The new radar will allow missiles to be fired in an autonomous fire-and-forget mode. The current laser-guided Hellfire requires external designation (e.g. by an OH-58D scout) or can be used in conjunction with the TADS, in which case it is a line-of-sight, non fire-and-forget weapon. Longbow radar scans through 270°, in 90° sectors, or through 360° in the air-to-air mode. Twelve targets can be detected, classified and prioritised simultaneously, and targets will be classified by six categories: tracked vehicle, wheeled vehicle, air defence, rotary-wing aircraft, fixed-wing aircraft and unknown. The radar can see through the fog and smoke that currently foils IR or TV sensors. An improved Data Modem will be more efficient than the present Automatic Target Handover System. The rotating antenna weighs 300 lb (136 kg).

The AH-64D will also incorporate a range of improvements in targeting, battle management, communications, weapons and navigation systems, including Plessey AN/ASN-157 Doppler, a new integrated GPS/INS, and EMI protection, some of which are to be finalised as the programme progresses. The cockpit will be improved, with new glass displays and symbology, and electrical power generation will be doubled. The forward avionics bay is expanded, and the undercarriage fairings are extended forward to accommodate some of the new equipment. The AH-64D's terrain-profiling

Apart from the Longbow radar mounted on the rotor mast, the AH-64D is distinguished by the fuselage-side fairings, which are enlarged to cover the wingroot and extend to the nose.

feature will enable the crew to navigate nap-of-the-earth, and sensor cueing will allow precise pre-pointing of the target acquisition system in order to zero-in on targets for rapid identification. Additionally, the Longbow interferometer will sense enemy air defence threats from any angle and alert the crew.

The first batch of AH-64Ds (308 or 523 on present plans) will have provision for both -701C engines and Longbow radar, so that either or both can be retrofitted easily if funding permits. It will have the targeting element of the Longbow system, and will carry RF Hellfire, allowing it to operate in conjunction with the later, fully-equipped AH-64D for total fire-and-forget capability.

One potential export customer for the Longbow Apache is the British army, although the aircraft's very high price might mean that the basic AH-64A would be

more likely to be selected. Any Apache variant faces strong competition from the upgraded AH-1 Cobra Venom, and a host of other attack helicopters. Longbow Apache deliveries are expected to begin in mid-1996.

SPECIFICATION

McDonnell Douglas AH-64D Longbow Apache generally similar to the McDonnell Douglas AH-64A Apache except in the following particulars:
Fuselage and tail: height overall 16 ft 1 in (4.90 m) to top of mast-mounted radome and 14 ft 1.25 in (4.30 m) to top of turning tail rotor
Powerplant: two General Electric T700-GE-701C turboshafts each rated at 1,800 shp (1342 kW)
Performance: maximum vertical rate of climb at sea level 2,530 ft (771 m) per minute; hovering ceiling 17,210 ft (5245 m) in ground effect and 13,530 ft (4125 m) out of ground effect

McDonnell Douglas Helicopters (Hughes) Model 369/OH-6 Cayuse

Requiring a new light observation helicopter (LOH) to replace Bell and Hiller types then in service, the **US Army** drew up a specification in 1960. This stipulated high performance, turboshaft power, easy maintenance and low purchase cost. All the major manufacturers submitted proposals, but only three designs were evaluated: the Bell YHO-4, Hiller YHO-5 and **Hughes YHO-6**. Flown initially on 27 February 1963, the redesignated **YOH-6A Cayuse** was selected on 26 May 1965 after a seven-month evaluation. The LOH mission led to the type's popular 'Loach' nickname.

Although Hughes had little experience with helicopters (its Model 269 then being at an early production stage), the Model 369 offered some notable features, including an egg-shaped cabin and innovative four-bladed rotor that endowed excellent manoeuvrability. The use of four blades obviated the need for a heavy and complex control system by reducing rotor loads considerably.

First deliveries were made in September 1965 to the US Army, and the initial contract was for multi-year procurement of 714 aircraft. Production ended with 1,434 built in three slightly differing configurations. The production **OH-6A** was widely used in Vietnam, where 658 were lost in combat and a further 297 in accidents. The OH-6 could be armed with an XM27E1 7.62-mm machine-gun or an XM75 40-mm grenade launcher on the port side, with a flexibly mounted gun in the starboard cabin door. The US Army then reopened the LOH competition, which led to the Bell OH-58 Kiowa assuming the role (selected in preference to the **OH-6D**, a designation later used for a Japanese variant). This allowed wholesale transfers of OH-6As to the Reserve and National Guard. A package of modifications to airframe, transmission, avionics and equipment by the Mississippi AVCRAD led to the adoption of the designation **OH-6B** (or **Series IV**) for many modified aircraft. The modifications include re-engining with the 420-shp (313.32-kW) T63-A-720 engine with 'Black Hole' exhaust suppression, and provision of an undernose FLIR, wirestrike protection and an adjustable landing light. The prototype first flew during May 1988.

Some later airframes were manufactured to **MH-6B** and **MH-6C** configuration for Special Forces support, and as **EH-6B** Special Forces command and control and Elint/Sigint platforms and **AH-6C** light attack aircraft, all serving with the Army's 160th Special Operations Aviation Regiment. Twenty-three MH-6Bs were built as new, of which three were converted later to MH-6C configuration. Four EH-6Bs were built, and two were converted as MH-6Bs and one was later converted to AH-6C configuration. Approximately 14 AH-6Cs were built, comprising 11 delivered in May, August and October 1969, plus three converted MH-6Bs and a converted EH-6B.

This is an ex-US Army OH-6A now serving with Colombia's Escuadrón Aérotactico 511. This unit is one of the Fuerza Aérea Colombiana's most active participants in the unending war against the drug runners and growers. Unarmed OH-6As are augmented in Escuadrón 511 by armed versions of the MD500 and MD530, while rotary-wing training is carried out on the similar Model 500C.

These aircraft probably functioned as interim equipment pending delivery of the dedicated Special Forces AH/MH-6 variants of the **MD500** and **MD530** (described separately). All Special Forces H-6s were powered by the 400-shp (298.4-kW) Allison 250-C20 engine, with black hole IR suppressors, although retaining the V tail. They also had NVG-compatible cockpits and provision for a turret-mounted FLIR. The MH-6B and MH-6C had external pylons for two gun pods, or 'people platforms' seating up to four passengers. The AH-6C was usually equipped with an M27 cannon to port and a seven-round Mk 66 or Hydra rocket pod to starboard, but could carry two gun pods, up to four rocket pods or four BGM-71 TOW missiles. The early Special Forces variants are now out of service. Some surviving MH-6Bs were passed first to the 1/245th Aviation Battalion of the Oklahoma ArNG for continued Special Operations use, and then, stripped of special equipment, to A Company of the 1/132nd Aviation Battalion of the Oklahoma National Guard. They were finally retired in 1992.

The first-generation H-6 has now been declared obsolete, so its continued support receives no Army funding. Guard units can continue to operate the type by using state funds, some states having opted to do this. OH-6s are also operated by a number of Federal and State agencies, including the US Border Patrol and the State Department.

The Model 369/OH-6 is still operated by **Bahrain** (two), **Brazil** (four), **Colombia** (11), **Dominican Republic** (one), **Honduras** (four), **Nicaragua** (two) and **Taiwan** (six), and further aircraft may be exported as they are withdrawn from US Army National Guard service. Hughes became part of

McDonnell Douglas helicopters and its aircraft were accordingly renamed from August 1985, and were given new MD suffixes to their Hughes Model numbers.

SPECIFICATION

McDonnell Douglas Helicopters OH-6A Cayuse
Rotor system: main rotor diameter 26 ft 4 in (8.03 m); tail rotor diameter 4 ft 3 in (1.30 m); main rotor disc area 544.63 sq ft (50.60 m2); tail rotor disc area 14.19 sq ft (1.32 m2)
Fuselage and tail: length overall, rotors turning 30 ft 3.75 in (9.24 m) and fuselage 23 ft 0 in (7.01 m); height to top of rotor head 8 ft 1.4 in (2.48 m); skid track 6 ft 9 in (2.06 m)
Powerplant: one 317-shp (236.5-kW) Allison T63-A-5A turboshaft derated to 252.5 shp (188 kW) for take-off and 214.5 shp (160 kW) for continuous running
Weights: empty equipped 1,229 lb (557 kg); normal take-off 2,400 lb (1089 kg); MTOW 2,700 lb (1225 kg)
Fuel and load: internal fuel 61.5 US gal (232 litres)
Speed: never exceed and maximum level speed at sea level 130 kt (150 mph; 241 km/h); economical cruising speed at sea level 116 kt (134 mph; 216 km/h)
Range: ferry range 1,355 nm (1,560 miles; 2510 km); range at 5,000 ft (1525 m) 330 nm (380 miles; 611 km)
Performance: maximum rate of climb at sea level 1,250 ft (381 m) per minute; service ceiling 15,800 ft (4815 m); hovering ceiling 11,800 ft (3595 m) in ground effect and 7,300 ft (2225 m) out of ground effect

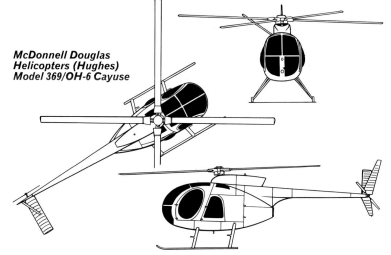

McDonnell Douglas Helicopters (Hughes) Model 369/OH-6 Cayuse

McDonnell Douglas Helicopters (Hughes) MD500

During the production run of the OH-6A for the US Army, Hughes also continued to build and market the aircraft for the civilian market, as the **Hughes 500**. The basic Model 500 was little more than a civilianised OH-6, spawning a sizeable family of related helicopters that has seen much service in military markings, although only a few examples have been operated by US services. The 500 differed primarily in having a more powerful engine, the 317-shp (236.5-kW) Allison 250-C18A turboshaft (derated to 243 shp/181.3 kW maximum continuous or 278 shp/207.4 kW for take-off), increased fuel and a revised interior. A dedicated 'hot-and-high' variant intended primarily for export was the **Model 500C**.

The first military variant was the **Model 500M Defender**, which was supplied initially (in 1968) to Colombia. This version was also licence-built for the **JGSDF** by Kawasaki as the **OH-6J** (subsequent Japanese versions are described separately), and by Nardi in Italy as the **NH500M** and the **NH500MC**, the latter a 'hot-and-high' variant. Spain bought a variant known as the **Model 500M/ASW** with MAD bird and the provision to carry torpedoes.

Hughes continued to develop the aircraft, producing an aircraft known simply as **'The Quiet One'** by fitting an early OH-6A with a five-bladed main rotor, a four-bladed tail rotor and a blanketed and muffled engine and exhaust. Airspeed was improved by 20 kt (23 mph; 37 km/h), payload was increased by 600 lb (272 kg) and the aircraft proved significantly quieter, running at 67 per cent of the usual rotor rpm. Its existence was revealed in April 1971. A second aircraft was fitted with a computer-controlled vibration-suppression system in 1982. Slightly later, a second early OH-6A was converted as the **OH-6C**, with an uprated 400-shp (298.4-kW) Allison 250-C20 turboshaft, a modified T-tail, and the five-bladed main rotor. It achieved a speed of 173 kt (200 mph; 322 km/h). Neither aircraft was put into production, but both tested features later incorporated into the Models 500, 520 and 530. The **MD520/530** series is described separately.

The next basic variant was the civilian **500D**, which introduced a slow-turning five-bladed rotor with the characteristic 'coolie hat' fairing over the rotor head, and a T-tail. Kawasaki manufactured this model under licence for the JGSDF under the designation **OH-6D**, the type also being licence-built in Argentina, Italy and Korea. Various military variants were developed from the 500D, the basic military equivalent being the **500MD Defender** with armour protection and IR exhaust suppression. This is available in several different configurations, each with a different designation. Thus, the **500D Scout Defender** has provision for rockets and gun pods, while the **500MD/ASW Defender** has nose-mounted search radar offset to port, a towed MAD bird on a fuselage-side pylon and a heightened undercarriage to allow the carriage of torpedoes. The **500MD/TOW**

Right: The Royal Jordanian air force uses eight Model 500Ds for rotary-wing training, after potential helicopter pilots have been graded and screened on the Scottish Aviation Bulldog. The type serves with No. 5 Squadron, part of the King Hussein Air College at Mafraq. Fixed-wing pilots move from the Bulldog to the T-37 or CASA C.101, which are also based at Mafraq.

Below: The Philippine air force operates both Model 500MGs and Model 530MGs, this aircraft serving with the 15th Strike Wing's 18th Tactical Air Support Squadron at Sangley Point. The 15th Strike Wing also includes Sikorsky S-76 gunships, and OV-10 Broncos, but the last armed T-28s have now been retired.

Defender is an anti-tank version with TOW missiles on outrigger pylons and a nose-mounted sight; the similar **500MD/MMS-TOW Defender** has equivalent missile capability but introduces a mast-mounted sight. The **500MD Quiet Advanced Scout Defender** had the same armament with a four-bladed quiet tail rotor and other noise reduction features.

A handful of the Special Operations aircraft used by the US Army's 160th Special Operations Aviation Regiment at Fort Campbell are understood to have been based on the MD500D and MD500MD with the 250-C30 engine of the MD530F. These are designated **EH-6E**, **MH-6E** and **AH-6F**, and may have been joined by the eight

MD500Es reportedly delivered to the US Army's Systems Command during early 1985. The EH-6E (four built, one converted to MH-6E) was an Elint/Sigint/command post aircraft, while the MH-6E (15 new builds and one ex-EH-6E) and AH-6F (nine built, plus one for evaluation by USAF SOCOM) designations reportedly cover an insertion and an attack version, respectively based upon the 500D (flown from the left-hand seat) and 500MD. Both are believed to retain (or to have reverted to) the original rounded nose contours of early MD500s, since this is felt to be more crashworthy and much better suited to NVG operations. The AH-6F has a mast-mounted sight and provision for the M230 Chain Gun, as used

by the AH-64. Pairs of Stinger air-to-air missiles can also be carried. Survivors are understood to have been converted to later marks, described separately under the MD520/530 entry. The **Model 500MD Defender II** is an uprated model available in all the above options but with a quieter, slow-turning four-bladed tail rotor.

Leading the next generation was the **Model 500E**, with a revised, pointed nose profile, improved tailplane endplate fins, more spacious interior and Allison 250-C20B engine. The specialist military models are designated **500MG Defender**. Further improvement led to the **MD530**, which is described separately.

SPECIFICATION

McDonnell Douglas Helicopters Model 500
Rotor system: main rotor diameter 26 ft 4 in (8.03 m); tail rotor diameter 4 ft 3 in (1.30 m); main rotor disc area 544.63 sq ft (50.60 m²); tail rotor disc area 14.19 sq ft (1.32 m²)
Fuselage and tail: length overall, rotors turning 30 ft 3.75 in (9.24 m) and fuselage 23 ft 0 in (7.01 m); height 8 ft 1.5 in (2.48 m) to top of rotor head; skid track 6 ft 9 in (2.06 m)
Powerplant: one 317-shp (236-kW) Allison 250-C18A turboshaft derated to 278 shp (207 kW) for take-off and 243 shp (181 kW) for continuous running
Weights: empty 1,088 lb (493 kg); normal take-off 2,550 lb (1157 kg); maximum take-off 3,000 lb (1361 kg)
Fuel and load: internal fuel 64 US gal (242 litres)
Speed: maximum level speed at 1,000 ft (305 m) 132 kt (152 mph; 244 km/h); economical cruising speed at optimum altitude 117 kt (135 mph; 217 km/h)
Range: 267 nm (307 miles; 606 km)
Performance: maximum rate of climb at sea level 700 ft (518 m) per minute; service ceiling 14,400 ft

(4390 m); hovering ceiling 8,200 ft (2500 m) in ground effect and 5,300 ft (1615 m) out of ground effect

OPERATORS

Argentina: 11 500Ds, two with the Coast Guard
Bahrain: 500Ds
Bolivia: 10 500Ms
Colombia: eight 500Ds, two 500s, two 500Es, and four or six 500MG NightFoxes
Costa Rica: two 500Ds
Cyprus: two 500s
Denmark: 12 500Ms of 15 delivered
El Salvador: four 500Ms plus three 500s delivered
Finland: two 500Ds
Greece: 20 NH500s
Indonesia: 12 500Cs
Iraq: impressed civilian 500Ds and 500F
Israel: 36 500MDs
Italy: 50 NH500s
Japan: six OH-6Ds with the JMSDF, 164 OH-6Ds and 65 OH-6Js with the JGSDF
Jordan: eight 500Ds
Kenya: two 500Ds, 15 500MDs, 15 500MD/TOWs, eight 500Es and eight 500MGs
Mauritania: five 500Ms
Mexico: four 500Es used for training by the navy
North Korea: 66 500Es, 20 500Ds and a single 300C were delivered via a West German dealer before the breach of US embargoes was discovered and halted
Philippines: 27 500MDs and 28 530MG Defenders now being delivered
South Korea: the survivors of 34 US-built 500MD/TOWs, plus some 25 locally-built 500M/ASWs with the navy and 144 500MDs and 50 500MD/TOWs with the army
Spain: 10 500M/ASWs, of 12 delivered from April 1972
Taiwan: 12 500MD/ASWs
United States: 4 US Army EH-6E, 16 MH-6E and 10 AH-6F all probably converted to later standards

McDonnell Douglas Helicopters **MD520/530 & MD520/530N**

The McDonnell Douglas MD500E formed the basis of a new family of 'Loach' variants. The first of these was the **MD530F Lifter**, which was first flown on 22 October 1982, primarily intended for civilian customers. Along with subsequent conventional 520 and 530 variants, it featured a fully articulated five-bladed main rotor, with 1 ft (30 cm) greater diameter, and a tail rotor with 2 in (5 cm) greater diameter. The 530 is powered by a 650-shp (484.9-ekW) Allison 250-C30 turboshaft engine derated to 425 shp (317 ekW). The **MD530F Lifter** is also assembled under licence by Korean Air (described separately). Since the first delivery on 20 January 1984, some have gone to military users such as the Chilean army. Dedicated military variants

derived from the MD530F include the **MD530MG Defender**, which was flown in prototype form on 4 May 1984, and which has subsequently been ordered by **Mexico** (10 for the air force), **Bolivia** (20), **Colombia**, and the **Philippines** (30). Those delivered to Bolivia are reportedly dubbed **MD530MG Black Falcon**.

In military guise, the MD530 is lightweight, versatile and highly survivable, and has both military and paramilitary (police, etc.) applications. Weapons and sensor fits are tailored to the point attack and anti-armour roles, and for scout and day/night surveillance duties. The integrated crew station offers the pilot a head-up mode called HOLAS (hands on lever and stick) giving the pilot head-up/hands-on control of all

weapons selection and delivery, communications and flight controls, essential in combat and similar to the HOTAS controls found in modern fast jets. The system is based around the Racal RAMS 3000, which also allows nap-of-earth and all-weather flight. A CDU (control and display unit) consisting of a high-definition monochrome MFD with keyboard can be used for flight planning, navigation and systems management, as well as for selecting frequencies. A three-seat front bench makes provision for a normal complement of two pilots and an observer.

The full standard MD530MG has options for a mast-mounted TOW sight, FLIR, RHAW gear, IFF and a laser rangefinder, and can be armed with Hughes TOW 2

missiles, 2.75-in unguided rockets, General Dynamic Stinger AAMs and a McDonnell Douglas Chain Gun. Avionics include a Decca Doppler navigator (with Racal Doppler velocity sensor), an Astronics Corporation autopilot, and a GEC/Ferranti FIN 1110 AHRS. A **Nightfox** version, with NVG-compatible cockpit and a FLIR Systems Series 2000 Thermal Imager, is available for low-cost night surveillance and attack missions, while a more austerely equipped **530MG Paramilitary Defender** is available for police, border patrol, narcotics interdiction and other roles.

Today the MD520 and MD530 are inevitably associated with the revolutionary NOTAR (No Tail Rotor) concept, although few production aircraft have been delivered

McDonnell Douglas Helicopters MD520/530 & MD520/530N

McDonnell Douglas Helicopters MD520 NOTAR

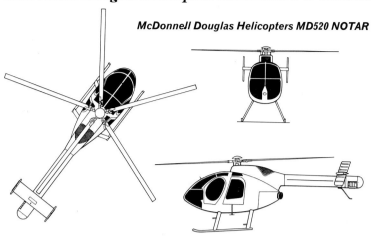

The Model 530MG, known as the 'Black Falcon', can carry rocket or gun pods, and may be fitted with exhaust suppressors. This aircraft serves with the Fuerza Aérea Colombiana.

with this type of tail and none has yet been delivered to military customers. The **MD520N** and the as-yet-unbuilt **MD530N** sub-variants both dispense with a conventional tail rotor in favour of the trademarked NOTAR system, an anti-torque tail boom that has experienced several design modifications. It has a variable-pitch fan mounted in the forward end, driven by a shortened tail rotor drive shaft and absorbing no more power. This produces an air stream which pressurises the boom interior to about 0.5 psi (0.034 bars) and vents pressurised air through a 0.33-in (0.85-cm) wide slot in the starboard side (a second slot was added later). This blown efflux unites with the main rotor downwash and is 'blown' down the side of the tailboom (the Coanda effect) as though it were a wing, generating a sideways thrusting force – 'lift' – which counteracts the main rotor's torque. A jet thruster with air exits to port and starboard allows pressurised air not vented through the slot to be ejected in either direction to provide control in yaw. This is operated via the pilot's 'rudder pedals', which move concentric fixed and moveable cones to block off one or other (or both) of the air exits.

The MD520N is the first widely-produced NOTAR variant, but owes its origin to a Hughes-initiated test programme employing an OH-6A. This testbed was first flown after conversion on 17 December 1981 as a testbed for the blown-air NOTAR system and subsequently has been modified several times, receiving an MD500E-type forward fuselage and eventually being upgraded to the current advanced NOTAR configuration. The NOTAR testbed was funded in part by DARPA and by the US Army Applied Technology Laboratory, and the original NOTAR boom was built by Aircraft Engineering Corporation of Paramount, CA.

The true MD520N prototype first flew 1 May 1990, with a production aircraft taking to the air on 28 June 1991. The MD530N prototype flew on 29 December 1989, but McDonnell Douglas did not proceed with certification of this variant, which has remained dormant, although it has formed the basis for military variants. The production MD520N is powered by a 450-shp (335.7-

ekW) Allison 250-C20R-2 turboshaft engine derated to 375 shp (279.75 ekW). Typically, the MD520N/530N offers a combat radius of around 160 miles (257 km) with a 1,600-lb (726-kg) payload for a variety of missions depending on configuration. The manufacturer has orders for about 160 examples, and many have been delivered to police forces.

Special variants

The US Army has taken delivery of a number of aircraft reportedly based on the non-NOTAR MD530FF with a unique part-glass instrument panel and a reinforced power train with a Kaflax shaft. They are reportedly equipped to a standard similar to the MD530MG, but with the original rounded nose contours of earlier MD500s. These are designated **MH-6H** (16 identified, all converted from EH-6E, MH-6E and AH-6F airframes) and **AH-6G** (five new build, seven converted from AH-6Fs) and are generically known as **'Little Birds'** They serve with the 160th Special Operations Aviation Regiment at Fort Campbell, and perhaps with 1 Battalion/245th Special Operations Aviation Group of the Oklahoma ArNG at Tulsa.

The AH-6G is a gunship, with a removable quick ordnance mounting system (known as a 'plank'), while the transport/insertion MH-6H has a so-called 'people plank' that allows the aircraft to carry three Special Operations soldiers externally on each side of the cabin. This is the same equipment as that fitted to the Kiowa Scout and is necessary because the rear cabin is occupied by radios and navigation systems, sometimes including Soviet-built GPS gear. In the MH-6, which is highly stable in the hover, the 'people plank' can also be used as a sniping platform by a Special Forces operative armed with a 0.50-calibre (12.7-mm) rifle.

All surviving 'Little Birds', perhaps including the AH-6Fs and MH-6Es, reportedly totalling 36 Model 500/520/530s, were to be upgraded to a common dual-role standard under the designation **MH-6J**. This was originally to have included conversion to NOTAR configuration, but this part of the

upgrade has reportedly been cancelled after trials of the first two NOTAR aircraft (perhaps designated **MH-6N** and **AH-6N**) showed that the new tailboom concept was less well-suited to the Special Operations role. A NOTAR allows the aircraft to hover 'tail-in-the-trees' and allows pedal turns at up to 90 kt, but limits maximum speed and dramatically increases fuel consumption.

The designation MH-6J may now apply to MH-6Es (currently at least four) brought up to the new standard, while **AH-6J** may be applied to new-build aircraft (at least seven). Many of the systems, avionics and equipment items reported for the MH-6J are already fitted to earlier 'Little Bird' variants, including a folding tailboom (to facilitate transport inside fixed-wing transport aircraft) and optional internal fuel tanks. These include a 29-US gal (110-litre) Robertson T-tank or a larger 62-US gal (236-litre) Goliath fuel tank package. These can be augmented by 30-US gal (114-litre) 'half tanks' carried externally. Armament can include M134 7.62-mm Miniguns, Aerocrafter 0.5-in (12.7-mm) machine-gun pods, or podded BEI Hydra 70-mm (2.75-in) rockets. A Litton AIM-1 laser designator and a Hughes AN/AAQ-16 FLIR can also be fitted, and the installations for these items of equipment are understood to be purpose-designed on the MH-6J, whereas earlier 'Little Birds' had them scabbed on at depot level in jury-rigged mountings. A FLIR-2000, similar to that carried by Britain's SAS Agusta 109s, can also be fitted.

The MD530N, with NOTAR features, offers about 40 per cent more power for hot-weather, high-altitude performance. McDonnell Douglas (which in any event

was seeking in mid-1994 to sell its Mesa, AZ, helicopter division) has indicated that it does not intend to proceed with the MD530N version and has instead launched the MD900 Explorer for the civil market.

SPECIFICATION

McDonnell Douglas Helicopters MD520N
generally similar to the McDonnell Douglas Helicopters Model 530MG Defender except in the following particulars:
Fuselage and tail: length overall, rotor turning 28 ft 6 in (8.69 m) and fuselage 25 ft 0 in (7.62 m); height overall 9 ft 10.75 in (3.01 m) to top of rotor head with extended skids or 9 ft 0 in (2.74 m) to top of rotor head with standard skids; stabilizer span 6 ft 9.5 in (2.07 m); skid track 6 ft 6 in (1.98 m)
Weights: empty 1,636 lb (742 kg); normal take-off 3,350 lb (1519 kg); maximum overload take-off 3,850 lb (1746 kg)
Fuel and load: internal fuel 404 lb (183 kg); external fuel none; maximum payload 2,214 lb (1004 kg)
Speed: never exceed speed 152 kt (175 mph; 281 km/h); maximum cruising speed at sea level 135 kt (155 mph; 249 km/h)
Range: range 217 nm (250 miles; 402 km) with standard fuel; endurance 2 hours 24 minutes
Performance: maximum rate of climb at sea level 1,850 ft (564 m) per minute; service ceiling 14,175 ft (4320 m); hovering ceiling 9,035 ft (2,755 m) in ground effect and 5,045 ft (1540 m) out of ground effect

With a crewman perched on its people platform, but without exhaust suppressors fitted, an MH-6 of the 160th Special Operations Aviation Regiment hover-taxis just above the runway.

Martin/General Dynamics **RB-57F**

The success of the **British Aerospace (English Electric, BAC) Canberra** (described separately) can be gauged not only by its long production run and many export customers, but also by the fact that it was selected by the US Air Force over indigenous American competitors and was manufactured under licence as the **Martin B-57**. The name **'Night Intruder'** was coined, but 'Canberra' was always more widely used. B-57s served the USAF for many years as nuclear-armed bombers,

night intruders, interdictors, target tugs, electronic aggressors, weather ships and survey and reconnaissance platforms. B-57s fought long and hard over Vietnam, and were exported to Taiwan (in small numbers) and to Pakistan, which added to the B-57's combat record by participating in the 1971 war with India. A handful of Pakistani B-57s served in the target facilities role into the 1980s, outlasting the final US Air National Guard **EB-57E**s (used in a similar role) by a handsome margin.

Remarkably, a pair of B-57s remains active today. Both are examples of the extensively modified **RB-57F**, production of which involved an almost complete redesign. Twenty aircraft were converted to **RB-57F** standard by General Dynamics for the weather and high-altitude reconnaissance roles, following the groundwork laid by the **RB-57D**, another dedicated high-altitude recce platform which had a similar long-span wing but which was otherwise less radically modified. The Canberra already had superb high-altitude performance, but this was improved by the addition of greater wing area and extra engine thrust. Four of the RB-57Fs were dedicated

reconnaissance platforms, but the others had a more limited reconnaissance fit and were also capable of sampling airborne radioactive particles. The RB-57F was powered by a pair of 18,000-lb st (80.1-kN) Pratt & Whitney TF33-P-11A turbofans, which gave almost twice the thrust of the original B-57 powerplant. These were augmented by a pair of underwing Pratt & Whitney J60-P-9 turbojets each rated at 3,300 lb st (14.7 kN), which were started after take-off and which 'cut in' at 42,000 ft (12800 m). They contributed 2,500 ft (760 m) to the aircraft's 64,000-ft (19507-m) ceiling. Four underwing pylons were provided for carriage of stores equipment pods, although two were usually used for the turbojets. The original wing was replaced by a completely new three-spar wing, incorporating honeycomb construction and with marked anhedral, and of almost doubled span at 122 ft 5 in (37.32 m). The fuselage fuel tank was deleted to accommodate equipment, all fuel being carried in the wings outboard of the engines, giving a typical mission range of 2,563 nm (2,950 miles; 4748 km). The tailfin was also increased in size to improve asymmetric handling and to damp out Dutch roll.

After retirement from the US Air Force, three RB-57Fs were taken on charge by **NASA** for high-altitude experiments from the Johnson Space Center at Ellington ANGB, TX. One was retired in September 1982, but the other two remain active, fulfilling a wide variety of roles. One is fitted with a NASA Universal Pallet System housing cameras, an X-band SLAR and a five-channel multi-spectral scanner, with a variety of other sensors and navigation aids. A handful of B-57s of other marks (including a B-57B used for gust response research) have now been retired by NASA.

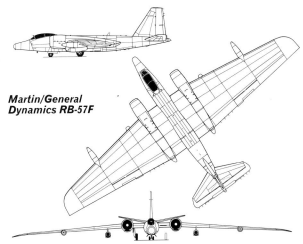

Martin/General Dynamics RB-57F

One of NASA's hardworking RB-57Fs flies near its Ellington ANGB home. The RB-57F's high-altitude performance and capacious fuselage make it a useful research tool.

Maule **M-4 to M-7**

Originating in 1968, the **Maule M-4** gave rise to a family of derivative designs in the classic high-wing single-engined lightplane configuration, featuring a fixed tailwheel undercarriage and 'razorback' glass-fibre fabric over a metal tube frame. The original M-4 was built in a number of forms, with various engine options, and with floats and cargo door options. The M-5 was introduced in 1975, with larger tail surfaces, extended flaps and other improvements. The M-6 was a one-off prototype which had new multi-position flaps and a larger cabin, while the M-7 introduced new engine options. Over 1,600 have been built, primarily for civil use, but with many being supplied to police, border patrol and other quasi-military operators. The contemporary, tricycle-undercarriage **MX-7-180 Star**

Rocket has been purchased by the **Royal Thai air force** (20) and the **Aviación de la Armada de Mexico** (Mexican navy) (12) for use in the basic training role.

SPECIFICATION

Maule MX-7-180 Star Rocket
Wing: span 30 ft 10 in (9.40 m); aspect ratio 6.0; area 157.90 sq ft (14.67 m²)
Fuselage and tail: length 23 ft 6 in (7.16 m); wheel base 15 ft 10 in (4.82 m) in tailwheel configuration
Powerplant: one Textron Lycoming O-360-C1F flat-four piston engine rated at 180 hp (134 kW)
Weights: basic empty 1,350 lb (613 kg); maximum take-off 2,500 lb (1134 kg)
Fuel and load: internal fuel 40 US gal (141 litres) plus provision for 30 US gal (113.5 litres) of auxiliary

fuel in outer wing fuel tanks; external fuel none
Speed: maximum level speed 'clean' at sea level 134 kt (154 mph; 248 km/h); maximum cruising speed at optimum altitude 126 kt (145 mph; 233 km/h)
Range: ferry range 977 nm (1,125 miles; 1810 km) with auxiliary fuel; range 560 nm (645 miles; 1038 km) with standard fuel

This aircraft is a Maule Patroller of the Georgia State Patrol.

Performance: maximum rate of climb at sea level 1,200 ft (366 m) per minute; service ceiling 15,000 ft (4570 m); take-off run 200 ft (61 m) at MTOW; landing run 500 ft (152 m) at maximum landing weight

Max Holste MH.1521M **Broussard**

The **Max Holste MH.1521M Broussard** is a single-engined, six-seat, general utility aircraft powered by a 450-hp (335.6-kW) Pratt & Whitney R-985 radial air-cooled engine. It is a high-wing, rigidly-braced monoplane with fixed tailwheel undercarriage and twin fins and rudders. At least nine former French territories in Africa

received Broussards for the use of their developing air forces upon the granting of independence. Of these, only **Burkina Faso** and, possibly, the **Central African Republic**'s air forces remain operators. Another serves in the communications role for the French **Aéronavale**, and two are used in **Argentina** for military parachute training.

DCAN, the French Board of Naval Dockyards and Weapons, operates a single MH.1521 Broussard for communications from Cuers.

Mikoyan-Gurevich MiG-15 'Fagot' and MiG-15UTI 'Midget'

The USSR's first operational swept-wing jet fighter, the **Mikoyan-Gurevich MiG-15** was built in huge numbers and became the Warsaw Pact's standard fighter. The estimated total of 3,000 included licence-built examples from Czechoslovakia and Poland, but not China, where large numbers of Russian-built aircraft were erroneously assumed to have been built as the Shenyang J-2, which in fact never existed. Made possible by Britain's short-sighted gift of examples of its latest turbojet engines (in particular the Rolls-Royce Nene with centrifugal-flow compressor) which were quickly copied and improved, the MiG-15 fought in Korea, where its poor showing was much more a reflection of pilot quality and training than of any inherent superiority of the US North American F-86 Sabre.

Production of a **MiG-15UTI** two-seat trainer (and limited conversion of single-seaters to this standard) totalled about 5,000 aircraft, and followed production of the improved single-seat **MiG-15bis**. The provision of an extra cockpit reduced internal fuel capacity, so external fuel tanks of various sizes are inevitably carried under the wing. Armament is not fitted as standard, although a single NR-23 23-mm cannon or UBK-Ye 12.7-mm machine-gun can be fitted, with 80 or 150 rounds of ammunition, respectively.

In 1994 the only positively confirmed operator of the Soviet-built MiG-15 was

Albania's Valona Air Academy still operates 12 single-seat Soviet-built MiG-15bis, of 26 delivered, together with 12 MiG-15UTI trainers.

Mikoyan-Gurevich MiG-15 'Fagot' and MiG-15UTI 'Midget'

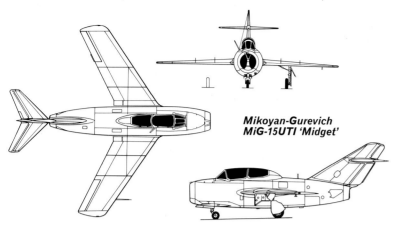

Mikoyan-Gurevich MiG-15UTI 'Midget'

Albania, whose Valona-based air academy operates 12 MiG-15bis and 12 MiG-15UTI trainers, although some of the latter were built in Czechoslovakia. Single-seat MiG-15s and MiG-15bis may continue to serve in **China, Cuba** and **Romania**, as advanced tactical trainers. The MiG-15UTI is believed to remain in service with **Algeria, Angola, Romania, Syria** and **Vietnam** for training duties, while one or two may remain on charge in the **Congo, Egypt, Guinea Bissau, Guinea Republic, Mali, Mongolia, Nigeria** and **Yemen** as hacks or as conversion trainers for MiG-17s.

SPECIFICATION

Mikoyan-Gurevich MiG-15UTI 'Midget'
Wing: span 10.085 m (33 ft 1 in); aspect ratio 4.93;

area 20.60 m2 (221.74 sq ft)
Fuselage and tail: length 10.11 m (33 ft 2 in); height 3.70 m (12 ft 1.7 in)
Powerplant: one Klimov RD-45F turbojet rated at 22.26 kN (5,004 lb st)
Weights: empty equipped 3724 kg (8,210 lb); maximum take-off 5400 kg (11,905 lb)
Fuel and load: internal fuel 900 kg (1,984 lb); maximum external load 1588 kg (3,500 lb)
Speed: maximum level speed 'clean' at 3000 m (9,843 ft) 1015 km/h (548 kt; 631 mph)
Range: ferry range 1054 km (569 nm; 655 miles) with drop tanks; range 680 km (367 nm; 423 miles) with standard fuel
Performance: climb to 5000 m (16,405 ft) in 2 minutes 36 seconds; service ceiling 14825 m (48,640 ft); take-off run 600 m (1,969 ft) at maximum take-off weight; landing run 740 m (2,428 ft) at normal landing weight

Mikoyan-Gurevich MiG-17 'Fresco'

Development of the **MiG-17** began in 1949 and was intended to address the shortcomings of the MiG-15, especially its high-speed handling characteristics. The production MiG-17 was preceded by a number of converted MiG-15s that acted as prototypes and introduced a larger tail unit, a lengthened rear fuselage, a thinner, more highly swept wing, revised airbrakes and other changes. The MiG-17 began to reach operational test units during late 1951 and soon demonstrated its superiority over the MiG-15, relegating the earlier aircraft to ground attack duties. The MiG-17 itself progressively went over to the ground attack role when newer fighters were introduced during the late 1950s. The basic MiG-17 was allocated the reporting name **'Fresco-A'**, while the improved **MiG-17F** with uprated engine became the **'Fresco-C'**. Interceptor variants equipped with radar included the cannon-armed **MiG-17PF 'Fresco-D'** with RP-1 'Scan Can' or RP-5 'Scan Odd' radar, and the **MiG-17PM 'Fresco-E'** with all guns removed, RP-2U radar, and an all-missile (RS-2U or AA-1 'Alkali') armament.

More than 8,000 MiG-17s were manufactured in the USSR. About 1,000 more were built in Poland under the local **LIM-5** and **LIM-6** designations, some variants having extensive modifications and improvements. The last Polish aircraft were retired from service during 1991/92. Although the decline of the MiG-17 has been very rapid, significant numbers remained in service well into the 1980s; East German MiG-17Fs, for example, were finally retired in 1986. Today,

Soviet-built MiG-17s may remain in service only with **Algeria**, the **Congo, Cuba, Guinea Bissau, Guinea, Madagascar, Mali, Mozambique, Romania, Syria, USA** (with the USAF's secret 'Red Hats' squadron at Groom Lake), **Vietnam** and **Yemen**.

SPECIFICATION

Mikoyan-Gurevich MiG-17F 'Fresco-C'
Wing: span 9.628 m (31 ft 7 in); aspect ratio 4.1; area 22.60 m2 (243.27 sq ft)
Fuselage and tail: length 11.264 m (36 ft 11.5 in); height 3.80 m (12 ft 5.5 in); wheel track 3.849 m (12 ft 7.5 in); wheel base 3.368 m (11 ft 0.5 in)
Powerplant: one Klimov VK-1F turbojet rated at 29.50 kN (5,732 lb st) dry and 33.14 kN (7,451 lb st) with afterburning
Weights: empty equipped 3930 kg (8,664 lb); maximum take-off 6069 kg (13,380 lb)
Fuel and load: internal fuel 1170 kg (2,579 lb); external fuel up to 655 kg (1,444 lb) in two 400- or 240-litre (106- or 63-US gal) drop tanks; maximum ordnance 500 kg (1,102 lb)
Speed: limiting Mach No. 1.03; maximum level speed 'clean' at 3000 m (9,845 ft) 1100 km/h (594 kt; 684 mph) or at 10000 m (32,810 ft) 1071 km/h (578 kt; 666 mph); 900 km/h (486 kt; 559 mph) limit with drop tanks
Range: ferry range 2020 km (1,091 nm; 1,255 miles) with drop tanks; combat radius 700 km (378 nm; 435 miles) on a hi-lo-hi attack mission with two 250-kg (551-lb) bombs and two drop tanks
Performance: maximum rate of climb at sea level 3900 m (12,795 ft) per minute; climb to 5000 m

Cuba is believed to maintain a small number of Russian-built MiG-17s in service, though they may recently have been grounded through spares shortages and economic problems. They are probably allocated to a reserve or advanced training unit.

Mikoyan-Gurevich MiG-17M 'Fresco'/LIM-6

(16,405 ft) in 2 minutes 36 seconds at dry thrust or 1 minute 48 seconds at afterburning thrust; service ceiling 15000 m (49,215 ft) at dry thrust and 16600 m (54,460 ft) at afterburning thrust;

take-off run 590 m (1,936 ft) at normal take-off weight; landing run 850 m (2,789 ft) at normal landing weight

Mikoyan-Gurevich MiG-19 'Farmer'

The **MiG-19** enjoyed a relatively short production run (about 2,500 aircraft) and a brief service life, having the misfortune to arrive on the scene between the MiG-17 and MiG-21. First flown on 5 January 1954, the MiG-19 was capable of supersonic level flight, reportedly achieving Mach 1.33 before the F-100 notched up its Mach 1.09 record. The aircraft entered service in early 1955. Successive variants included the **MiG-19S** with slab tailplane, more powerful engines and three NR-30 cannon; the **MiG-19SF** with uprated engine; the radar-equipped **MiG-19P**; the all-missile-armed **MiG-19PM**; and a host of research aircraft and testbeds. Most of the MiG-19s still in service worldwide are Chinese-built **Shenyang J-6s**, although a handful of Russian-built aircraft may still be in service in **China** itself, and perhaps also with a reserve unit in **Cuba**, although spares shortages may have grounded the latter.

SPECIFICATION

Mikoyan-Gurevich MiG-19SF 'Farmer-C'
Wing: span 9.00 m (29 ft 6.3 in); aspect ratio 3.24; area 25.00 m2 (269.11 sq ft)
Fuselage and tail: length 14.64 m (48 ft 0.4 in) including probe and 12.54 m (41 ft 1.7 in) excluding probe; height 3.885 m (12 ft 9.0 in); wheel track 4.156 m (13 ft 7.6 in)
Powerplant: two MNPK 'Soyuz' (Tumanskii) RD-9BM turbojets each rated at 25.50 kN (5,732 lb st) dry and 32.36 kN (7,275 lb st) with afterburning
Weights: nominal empty 5760 kg (12,698 lb); normal take-off 7600 kg (16,755 lb); maximum take-off 9100 kg (20,062 lb)
Fuel and load: internal fuel 1800 kg (3,968 lb) or 2170 litres (573 US gal); external fuel up to two 1520-, 800-, 300- or 200-litre (401.5-, 211-, 79- or 53-US gal) drop tanks; maximum ordnance 500 kg (1,102 lb)
Speed: maximum level speed 'clean' at 10000 m (32,810 ft) 1452 km/h (783 kt; 902 mph)

Range: ferry range 2200 km (1,186 nm; 1,366 miles) with two 800-litre (211-US gal) drop tanks; combat radius 685 km (370 nm; 426 miles) on a hi-hi-hi interception mission with maximum ordnance and two 800-litre (211-US gal) drop tanks

Performance: maximum rate of climb at sea level 6900 m (22,638 ft) per minute; service ceiling 17900 m (58,725 ft); take-off run 515 m (1,690 ft) with afterburning; landing run 600 m (1,969 ft) with brake parachute

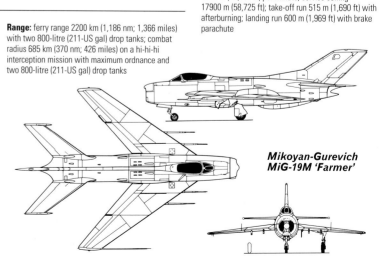

Mikoyan-Gurevich MiG-19M 'Farmer'

Mikoyan-Gurevich MiG-21 'Fishbed' early variants

The original concept of the **MiG-21** was for a simple, lightweight fighter, in which sophistication and considerations of endurance and firepower were sacrificed for outright performance. The production MiG-21 was preceded by a series of prototypes, some with swept wings and others with delta-wing planforms. The 40 pre-production **MiG-21F** (**Ye-6T** or **Type 72**) fighters were allocated the reporting name **'Fishbed-B'**, but the first full production version was the **MiG-21F-13 'Fishbed-C'**, or **Type 74**. The first 114 MiG-21F-13s had a narrow-chord vertical tail, but all had their armament reduced from two to one NR-30 cannon, on the starboard side, with underwing pylons for two guided AA-2 'Atoll' AAMs or rocket pods. Fuel capacity was increased from 2280 litres (602 US gal) to 2550 litres (674 US gal).

The **MiG-21P** (**Ye-7**) **'Fishbed-D'** dispensed with the cannon armament altogether, and introduced a modified fuselage, with a longer nose and larger inlet centrebody for its TsD-30T R1L 'Spin Scan' radar. The canopy and spine were also modified with a distinctive bulge immediately aft of the cockpit, narrowing to the standard early spine farther aft. Internal fuel was increased to 2750 litres (726 US gal). The MiG-21P was followed by the R-11F2-300-engined **MiG-21PF** (**Type 76**) with pitot probe relocated to the top of the nose. The MiG-21PF introduced a new system for controlling the variable intake centrebody, which accommodated the new RP-21 Sapfir radar. Late production sub-variants introduced a still broader-chord tailfin, with a brake chute fairing at the base of the rudder, and reintroduced a gun, in the shape of an external GP9 cannon pod. NATO allocated these aircraft the reporting name **'Fishbed-E'**. The **MiG-21FL** was primarily intended for export, and while it was externally identical to the late MiG-21PF it had less powerful R-2L radar and the original R-11F-300 engine. Fuel capacity was increased to 2900 litres (766 US gal). Approximately 200 were built under licence in India.

The final versions which can be considered part of the 'first generation' were the **Type 94** sub-variants, the **MiG-21PFS** and the **MiG-21PFM 'Fishbed-F'**, externally similar to the late MiG-21PF and MiG-21FL but having a two-piece canopy with a fixed windscreen instead of the single-piece forward-hingeing canopy which acted as a blast shield on ejection. They also introduced blown SPS flaps, a cruciform brake chute, and the R-11F2S-300 engine. Addition of the RP-21M radar gave compatability with the semi-active RS-2US (K-5M) missile.

A surprising number of early 'Fishbeds' remain in service. India, for example, retains large numbers of MiG-21FLs in at least three front-line squadrons. Many early 'Fishbeds' are presently being converted as unmanned target drones for use at the Akhtubinsk test centre in Russia.

SPECIFICATION

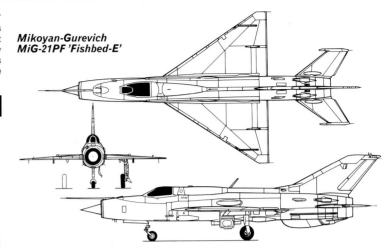

*Mikoyan-Gurevich
MiG-21PF 'Fishbed-E'*

Mikoyan-Gurevich MiG-21PFM 'Fishbed-F'
Wing: span 7.154 m (23 ft 5.7 in); aspect ratio 2.23; area 23 m2 (247.5 sq ft)
Fuselage and tail: length 15.76 m (51 ft 8.5 in) including probe; length 12.285 m (40 ft 3.9 in) excluding probe and centrebody; height 4.125 m (13 ft 6.2 in); wheel track 2.787 m (9 ft 1.75 in); wheel base 4.71 m (15 ft 5.5 in)
Powerplant: one MNPK 'Soyuz' (Tumanskii) R-11F2S-300 turbojet rated at 38.26 kN (8,600 lb st) dry and 60.57 kN (13,613 lb st) with afterburning, and provision for two SPRD-99 solid-propellant booster rockets each rated at 24.50 kN (5,511 lb st)
Weights: empty 5350 kg (11,795 lb); normal take-off 7820 kg (17,240 lb); maximum take-off 9080 kg (20,018 lb), or 8800 kg (19,400 lb) on rough strip
Fuel and load: internal fuel 2650 litres (700 US gal); external fuel up to one 490-litre (130-US gal) drop tank; maximum ordnance 500 kg (1,102 lb)

Speed: maximum level speed 'clean' at 11000 m (36,090 ft) 2125 km/h (1,146 kt; 1,320 mph)
Range: ferry range more than 1300 km (704 nm; 808 miles) with 800-litre (211-US gal) drop tank
Performance: maximum rate of climb at sea level with two missiles and 50 per cent fuel more than 7500 m (24,600 ft) per minute; service ceiling 19000 m

62,335 ft); take-off run 850 m (2,790 ft); landing run 550 m (1,800 ft) at normal landing weight with SPS and brake chute

This MiG-21FL of India's No. 8 Squadron wears a temporary dark green fin for ACM training.

Mikoyan MiG-21 'Fishbed' second-generation models

Later MiG-21 variants moved progressively further away from the original lightweight fighter concept, gaining more internal fuel, heavier armament and increasingly more sophisticated avionics. All had R-11F2S-300 and or R-13-300 engines, blown SPS flaps, pitot probes offset to the right of the centreline, two-piece canopies and broad-chord tailfins, as seen on some earlier aircraft. For the first time, all also had four underwing pylons, although initially only two of these were compatible with guided AAMs.

The first of the new generation was the **MiG-21R** (**Type 94R**), a dedicated recce aircraft based on the MiG-21PFM, but with a new, enlarged dorsal fairing and with provision for carrying a variety of centreline reconnaissance pods, containing either optical or TV cameras, IR and laser sensors or SLAR. Codenamed **'Fishbed-H'** by NATO, some examples of the MiG-21R have ECM/ESM equipment in wingtip pods.

The **MiG-21S** (**Type 95**) was a fighter based on the MiG-21R airframe, with new RP-22 radar and with a GP-9 gun pod under the belly instead of a recce pod. It was followed by the R-13-300-engined **MiG-21SM** (**Type 15**), which also introduced a gunsight optimised for manoeuvring in high-*g* combat, and the improved GSh-23L cannon in a fixed installation recessed into the belly, instead of in the removable GP-9 gondola. Small rectangular fences were fitted below the auxiliary intakes in front of the wingroots to prevent gun gas ingestion. The **MiG-21M** (**Type 96**) was an export version of the SM, with the older R-11F2S-300 engine. The aircraft was built under licence

The MiG-21M was built only for export, first by the Moscow Znamaya Truda factory, and then under licence by HAL in India. This aircraft wears the markings of No. 101 Squadron 'Falcons'.

in India. The **MiG-21MF 'Fishbed-J'** (**Type 96F**) was a MiG-21M derivative for VVS use, powered by the R-13-300 engine, and fitted with the SMs RP-22 radar. It introduced AAM capability on all four underwing pylons, and was initially identifiable by

the rear-view mirror above the canopy, although this was later retrofitted to many MiG-21Rs, MiG-21SMs and MiG-21Ms. The **MiG-21MT** (**Type 96T**) introduced the more-powerful R-13F-300 engine but only 15 were built.

This Czech air force MiG-21R carries a centreline optical reconnaissance pod.

The **MiG-21SMT 'Fishbed-K' (Type 50)** was fitted with a unique dorsal spine of huge dimensions, holding some 900 litres

(238 US gal) of fuel, although this reduced stability so much that capacity had to be reduced by 50 per cent.

Large numbers of MiG-21Rs, MiG-21Ms and MiG-21MFs remain in service, including many with the non-Soviet air forces of the former Warsaw Pact. In the CIS itself it

would seem likely that these variants, and the MiG-21SMT, have all been retired, although one or two may still be in use at trials or experimental establishments. More are almost certainly in storage, and some may have been converted as unmanned target drones. Many of the proposed Western retrofit programmes for the MiG-21, promoted by companies like IAI and GEC, would be most likely to be applied to these MiG-21 variants.

Note: We use only those designations used by the Mikoyan OKB and Russian air force, and have ignored speculative Western designations like PFMA. All MiG-21 operators (all variants) are listed in the MiG-21bis entry.

SPECIFICATION

Mikoyan Gurevich MiG-21MF 'Fishbed-J'
Generally similar to the MiG-21PFM except in the following particulars:

Powerplant: one MNPK 'Soyuz' (Tumanskii/Gavrilov) R-13-300 turbojet rated at 39.92 kN (8,972 lb st) dry and 63.66 kN (14,307 lb st) with afterburning
Weights: empty 5350 kg (11,795 lb); normal take-off 8150 kg (17.967 lb) with four AAMs and three 490-litre (129-US gal) tanks; maximum take-off 9400 kg (20,723 lb)
Fuel and load: internal fuel 2200 kg (4,850 lb) or 2600 litres (687 US gal); external fuel up to 1470 litres (387 US gal) in three drop tanks; maximum ordnance 2000 kg (4,409 lb)
Speed: maximum level speed 'clean' at 11000 m (36,090 ft) 2230 km/h (1,203 kt; 1,385 mph); maximum level speed at sea level 1300 km/h (703 kt; 807 mph)
Range: ferry range 1800 km (971 nm; 1,118 miles) with three drop tanks; combat radius 370 km (200 nm; 230 miles) on a hi-lo-hi attack mission with four 250-kg (551-lb) bombs, or 740 km (400 nm; 460 miles) on a hi-lo-hi attack mission with two 250-kg (551-lb) bombs and drop tanks
Performance: maximum rate of climb at sea level 7200 m (23,622 ft) per minute; service ceiling 18200 m (59,711 ft); take-off run 800m (2,625ft)

Mikoyan-Gurevich MiG-21bis

The third generation **MiG-21bis** is the most advanced and most capable production variant, although by modern standards its lack of BVR missile capability, limited radar range, mediocre low-speed handling and poor endurance limit its usefulness. Various upgrades are being offered for the aircraft, most of them centred around replacing the radar and modernising the cockpit. A similar proposed indigenous upgrade, shown in mock-up form in 1992, would add a new pulse-Doppler radar and AA-10 'Alamo' and AA-11 'Archer' AAM compatibility.

The MiG-21bis was developed as a multi-role fighter for Frontal Aviation, with better close combat capability through improved avionics and the ability to carry the new R-60 AA-8 'Aphid' AAM. It was optimised for air combat at lower altitudes, against slower, more agile opponents, and had an enhanced ground attack capability. It can carry four UV-16-57 rocket pods, or four 240-mm (9½-in) rockets, or two 500-kg (1,102-lb) and two 250-kg (551-lb) bombs. Equipped with improved Sapfir-21 radar and powered by the 69.65-kN (15,653-lb) Tumanskii R-25-300 engine, the MiG-21bis features a completely redesigned dorsal spine which looks little different from that fitted to most second-generation 'Fishbeds', but which holds nearly as much fuel as even the huge spine of the MiG-21SMT.

The NATO reporting name **'Fishbed-L'** was allocated to the first version of the MiG-21bis, which entered service in February 1972. **'Fishbed-N'** was applied to later production aircraft (retaining the same Soviet designation) which had an undernose 'Swift Rod' ILS antenna and improved avionics. The 'Fishbed-N' was built under licence in India between 1980 and 1987. Another version of the MiG-21bis was optimised for the nuclear strike role, but no designations or NATO reporting name are known.

It is believed that about 60 MiG-21bis remain in service with a Russian tactical reconnaissance regiment, having replaced older 'Fishbed-Hs', and reportedly carrying the same reconnaissance pods. Other aircraft may still be in service in an advanced training role. Elsewhere, the MiG-21bis enjoys a much firmer hold on life, serving in large numbers with many operators.

SPECIFICATION

Mikoyan-Gurevich MiG-21bis 'Fishbed-L'
generally similar to the Mikoyan-Gurevich MiG-21MF 'Fishbed-J' except in the following particulars:
Powerplant: one MNPK 'Soyuz' (Tumanskii) R-25-300 turbojet rated at 40.2 kN (9,038 lb st) dry and 69.65 kN (15,653 lb st) with afterburning, with an emergency

regime rating of 97.12 kN (21,825 lb st) above Mach 1 and at heights up to 4000 m (13,123 ft) for periods of up to three minutes. Provision for two 24.52-kN (5,511-lb st) SPRD-99 solid rocket boosters
Weights: empty 5450 kg (12,015 lb); normal take-off 8725 kg (19,235 lb); maximum take-off 9800 kg (21,605 lb) or 8800 kg (19,400 lb) on rough strip, or 10400 kg (22,928 lb) with KT-92D wheels and 058 tyres
Fuel and load: internal fuel 2880 litres (760 US gal); external fuel up to 1750 litres (462 US gal) in three drop tanks; maximum ordnance 2000 kg (4,409 lb)
Speed: maximum level speed 'clean' at 13000 m (42,650 ft) 2175 km/h (1,177 kt; 1,351.5 mph)
Range: 1470 km (795 nm, 913 miles) at 10000m (32,800 ft) with one 800-litre (211-US gal) drop tank
Performance: maximum rate of climb at sea level with two missiles and 50 per cent fuel more than 13800 m (45,275 ft) per minute; service ceiling 17500 m (57,415 ft); take-off run 830 m (2,720 ft);

landing run 550 m (1,800 ft) at normal landing weight with SPS and brake chute

OPERATORS

Operators of all MiG-21 variants are listed below:

Afghanistan: 322 Regiment at Bagram may have as many as four squadrons of MiG-21s on charge, with up to 65 aircraft. Large numbers of late-mark MiG-21s, including examples of the MiG-21bis, transferred from the Soviet air force
Albania: Albania's MiG-21s are all believed to be obtained from Chinese sources
Algeria: Three regiments operated examples of the MiG-21F, MiG-21M and MiG-21bis
Angola: Up to 70 MiG-21U, MiG-21M and MiG-21bis
Azerbaijan: Less than 10 MiG-21s are in use
Bangladesh: A handful of MiG-21MFs may remain in use with No. 5 Squadron, alongside Chinese-built aircraft from Pakistan
Byelorussia: Late series MiG-21s may remain active, at least for advanced training
Bulgaria: Bulgaria's air force includes at least one MiG-21 regiment, Polk 28000 at Graf Ignatievo. This operates the MiG-21bis and MiG-21UM. Other variants are still in service with regiments at Balchik, Jambol East and Uzundjovo and with training units at Dolna Metropolija, Kamen and Ruse, including the MiG-21M (18), MiG-21U (17) and MiG-21R (6)
Burkina Faso: About eight MiG-21s were delivered during the mid-1980s
Cambodia: The MiG-21bis fighters and MiG-21U trainers of Unit 701 are believed to have been grounded
Congo: About a dozen of the 16 MiG-21s delivered in 1986 remain in service
Croatia: Two MFs and a bis were acquired when JRV pilots defected to Croatia, at least one of these having subsequently been lost. Twenty more from Ukrainian sources are believed to be based at Pula
Cuba: Analysts believe that Cuba still operates the MiG-21F (30), MiG-21M/MF (35), MiG-21PFM (40), MiG-21bis (80), and MiG-21U/UM (18)
Czech Republic: Czechoslovakia received large numbers of early MiG-21s, many being built under licence by Aero. These included an estimated 150 MiG-21F-13s (62 survivors wfu in the late 1980s), 30

India's Hindustan Aeronautics Ltd built the Mikoyan MiG-21bis under licence and it continues to form the backbone of Indian air defence, equipping seven or eight squadrons. An ambitious upgrade with modern radar, ECM and other systems is planned. This aircraft, wearing yellow stripes for similar-type air combat training, serves with No. 24 Squadron 'Hunting Hawks' at Ambala, midway between Delhi and Amritsar.

MiG-21PFs (15 survivors wfu in the late 1980s), 50 MiG-21PFMs (35 survivors wfu in 1991), 25 MiG-21Rs (21 operational in 1993) and 120 MiG-21MFs (about 106 operational in 1993). These single-seaters were augmented by an unknown number of MiG-21Us (all retired by 1992), eight MiG-21USs and 30 MiG-21UMs. Before the division of Czechoslovakia, the country's air order of battle included the 9th Fighter-Bomber Regiment at Bechyne, the 47th Reconnaissance Regiment with MiG-21Rs and Su-22s at Hradec Kralove, with further MiG-21 squadrons at Zatec (part of the 1st Fighter Regiment) and Mosnov (82nd Independent Attack Squadron). After division, following reorganisation, all MiG-21MFs, Rs and USs and UMs were combined within a single regiment at Prerov, but may be retired by mid-1995

Ethiopia: The collapse of the Mengistu regime in May 1991 left the air force in tatters, many aircraft having flown to neighbouring states with their defecting aircrew, and others being abandoned on their airfields where they fell victim to vandalism, souvenir hunting or simple neglect. Before the collapse, Ethiopia had an estimated 60 MiG-21Ms, with five MiG-21U trainers

Finland: The first export customer for the MiG-21, Finland replaced its MiG-21F-13s with new MiG-21bis airframes delivered during 1980-81. Fourteen single-seaters serve with HavLlv 31 at Kuopio Rissala

Germany: The MiG-21s inherited from East Germany have now been retired, even from test and evaluation units, and are being scrapped or retired to museums under the terms of the CFE treaty

Guinea Republic: Seven MiG-21s may be in service with a fighter squadron at Conakry. These aircraft were supplied in return for landing rights for Tu-95 and Tu-142 'Bears'

Guinea Bissau: There are reports that MiG-21s have replaced MiG-17s with the sole combat unit at Bissalanca

Hungary: Although Kécskemet's two MiG-21MF squadrons are now re-equipping with the MiG-29, the MiG-21bis remains in service with one squadron of the Stromfeld Aurel Regiment at Pápa and with both squadrons of the Kapos Regiment at Taszár. An upgrade is likely

India: Despite the influx of more modern fighters like the MiG-29 and Mirage 2000, the MiG-21 remains the backbone of India's fighter strength with 830 (including 580 built locally) having been delivered. The MiG-21bis serves with Nos 3, 4, 15, 21, 23, 24, 26 and 37 Squadrons, the MiG-21M with Nos 17, 32, 35, 45, 101 and 108 Squadrons, and the MiG-21FL (and perhaps PFM) with Nos 8, 29, 30, 51 and 52 Squadrons. A variety of types serves with MOFTU at Tezpur for advanced training, and each squadron usually includes a handful of two-seat trainers

Indonesia: Indonesia operated MiG-21s before its break with the USSR during the 1960s

Iran: Believed to operate only Chinese-built 'Fishbeds'

Iraq: Before the Gulf War, Iraq's air force included 70 single-seat Soviet-built MiG-21s (probably MiG-21Ms and PFMs) with a dozen two-seaters and some 75 Chengdu F-7s. The number remaining is uncertain

Kazakhstan: Late series MiG-21s may remain active,

This battered-looking MiG-21bis is typical of those now serving with the Vietnamese People's Air Force. A handful are camouflaged in blue and grey, but most wear an overall scheme of light grey, often with faded, peeling insignia and serial numbers.

at least for advanced training

Laos: Two squadrons of MiG-21bis fighters operated from Wattay (Vientiane) but have now been grounded by lack of spares and support problems

Mongolia: Twelve 'Fishbeds', probably MiG-21MFs, are believed to be in use

Mozambique: Despite having been offered for sale, the 30-strong MiG-21 force, once split between squadrons at Beira, Nacala and Nampula, continues to fly from Nampula

Myanmar: Believed to operate only Chinese-built 'Fishbeds'

Nigeria: A fleet of about 28 MiG-21bis or MF fighters and two trainers is in service

North Korea: North Korea operates some 150 MiG-21s, believed mainly to be PFs and PFMs

Pakistan: Operates only Chengdu F-7Ps

Poland: Before the dissolution of the Warsaw Pact, Poland had nine MiG-21-equipped fighter regiments (1 PLM, 2 PLM, 9 PLM, 10 PLM, 11 PLM, 28 PLM, 34 PLM, 41 PLM, 62 PLM, and one tactical reconnaissance regiment, 32 PLRT), with more MiG-21s in use for advanced training with 23 Flying School at Deblin. 2 PLM and 34 PLM have now disbanded, but large numbers remain in use

Romania: Romania is the first MiG-21 user to have placed a contract for the upgrade of its aircraft (with Elbit). About 100 single-seaters remain in use, with some 12 or more trainers, in two to four air defence regiments. These include 86 Regiment at Borcea Baraganu and another at Caracal-Deveselu

Russia: Late series MiG-21s may remain active, at least for advanced training and perhaps for reconnaissance

Slovakia: Seventy Slovak MiG-21MFs, USs and UMs (and perhaps a handful of MiG-21PFs and even F-13s) serve with the Sliac-based 1st Fighter Regiment's second and third squadrons, alongside MiG-29s

Somalia: Six MiG-21MFs and a pair of MiG-21UMs remained active until grounded by the recent civil war, of an unknown number of aircraft delivered from 1974

Sri Lanka: Operates only Chengdu F-7s

Sudan: Nine MiG-21s (perhaps PFs) may be in

Sudanese service

Syria: Despite very heavy losses (especially over the Bekaa), Syria continues to be a major 'Fishbed' operator, with about 250 on charge

Tanzania: Believed to operate only Chengdu F-7s

Uganda: Five surviving MiG-21Ms may be in storage.

Ukraine: A handful of late series MiG-21s may remain active, for advanced training, but most Ukrainian MiG-21s (which totalled 195 in early 1994) are in storage or being scrapped under the terms of the CFE agreement

United States of America: The USAF's 4477th Fighter Squadron ('Red Hats') at Groom Lake has operated a variety of MiG-21 variants, acquired from Israel, Egypt and other sources

Vietnam: The MiG-21bis and MiG-21UM serve with the 920th Fighter Training Wing at Phu Cat, and with the 921st, 925th, 927th, 929th, 931st, 933rd and 935th

Fighter Wings, respectively based at Da Phuc, unknown, Kep, unknown, Yen Bai, unknown, Phu Cat and unknown. These are split between three divisions, the 370th 'Hai Van' Fighter Division, headquartered at Da Nang, the 371st 'Thang Long' Fighter Division, headquartered at Da Phuc, and the 372nd Fighter Division, headquartered at Tho Xuan

Yemen: The merger of North and South Yemen in 1990 resulted in a fleet of 70 MiG-21M and MiG-21bis fighters from North Yemen forming the backbone of the new combined air arm

Yugoslavia: Most of Yugoslavia's MiG-21R, MiG-21M and MiG-21bis aircraft were inherited by the federal (Serbian) air force

Zambia: Zambia's 16 aircraft, delivered in 1980-82, are believed to be MiG-21MFs

Zimbabwe: Believed to operate only Chengdu F-7s

Mikoyan-Gurevich MiG-21bis 'Fishbed-L'

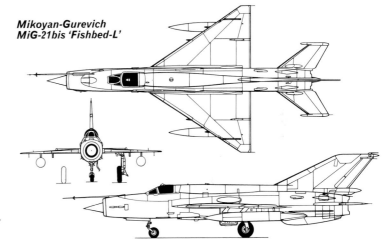

Mikoyan-Gurevich MiG-21U/US/UM 'Mongol'

Proposed two-seat trainer versions of the MiG-19 and MiG-17 did not reach production, but it soon became apparent that the MiG-15UTI would be inadequate for the conversion training of MiG-21 pilots. Mikoyan accordingly designed a two-seat trainer version, based on the MiG-21F-13 'Fishbed-C'. Armament and radar were deleted, although provision was made for a ventral gun pack and it also had two under-wing pylons. The aircraft was fitted with a one-piece airbrake below the forward fuselage and the pitot boom was repositioned above the nose. The instructor's cockpit was added behind the normal cockpit, and both were covered by separate sideways-hinge-ing canopies. Internal fuel was reduced to 2,350 litres (620 US gal).

The new trainer first flew, as the **Ye-6U**, on 17 October 1960, and entered production as the **MiG-21U (Type 66)**. Early produc-

tion aircraft had the original narrow-chord fin and had a brake chute at the rear of the ventral fin. The basic MiG-21U received the ASCC reporting name **'Mongol-A'** and was built by Znamya Truda between 1964 and 1968.

On the **MiG-21US 'Mongol-B' (Type 68** or **Ye-66B)**, built at Tbilisi between 1966 and 1970, the increased-chord tailfin was introduced from the start, along with the fin trailing-edge brake chute fairing, improved ejection seats, a bigger spine rais-

ing internal fuel capacity to 2450 litres (647 US gal), a retractable periscope and SPS flaps. The **MiG-21UM (Type 69)** introduced updated instruments, autopilot and

This is a late series MiG-21U of No. 8 Squadron, Indian Air Force. The basic MiG-21U equates to early single-seaters like the MiG-21F-13 and MiG-21FL.

Mikoyan-Gurevich MiG-21UM 'Mongol'

This Hungarian MiG-21UM is seen after a post-overhaul test flight, before the reapplication of camouflage and serial number. The nose-mounted AoA sensor and instructor's periscope are evident.

avionics (as fitted to the MiG-21R and subsequent single-seaters), and was fitted with an AoA sensor on the starboard side of the nose. It was built at Tbilisi from 1971.

Today MiG-21 trainers serve with most operators of the single-seat 'Fishbed' (see operators list with MiG-21bis entry) as conversion and continuation trainers,. However, in India and in the former USSR, MiG-21 trainers also serve as dedicated advanced flying training, pre-OCU/OTU aircraft.

SPECIFICATION

Mikoyan-Gurevich MiG-21US 'Mongol-B'
generally similar to the Mikoyan-Gurevich MiG-21PFM

except in the following particulars:
Fuselage and tail: length 14.41 m (47.27 ft), 12.18 m (39 ft 11.5 in) without probe and inlet centrebody; wheel track 2.69 m (8 ft 10 in); wheel base 4.81 m (15 ft 9.2 in)
Weights: normal take-off 8000 kg (17,636 lb)
Fuel and load: internal fuel 2030 kg (4,475 lb); maximum ordnance 1000 kg (2,204 lb)
Speed: maximum level speed 'clean' at 13000 m (42,650 ft) 2175 km/h (1,175 kt; 1,352 mph)
Performance: maximum rate of climb at sea level 6900 m (22,638 ft) per minute; service ceiling 17700 m (58,070 ft); take-off run 900 m (2,953 ft); landing run 550 m (1,800 ft) at normal landing weight with SPS and brake chute
Range: 1460 km (790 nm; 907 miles) with 800-litre (211-US gal) drop tank

Mikoyan-Gurevich MiG-23S/M/MF/MS 'Flogger-A/B/E'

Widely dismissed in the West as obsolete and ineffective, the remarkable **MiG-23/-27 'Flogger'** family has proved extremely versatile and robust, with an impressive performance. Its reputation has been severely damaged by a number of actions in which downgraded export variants, flown by ill-trained pilots using inflexible tactics, have been shot down without inflicting any loss themselves, most notably over the Bekaa Valley in 1982. Recent evaluations of the aircraft by Western pilots have led to some revised opinions, and the more recent versions of the aircraft have emerged with a much enhanced reputation.

Development of the MiG-23 began during the early 1960s, as a replacement for the MiG-21. Greater payload, range and firepower were clearly needed, along with more powerful onboard sensors to free the pilot from the constraints imposed by tight GCI control. The new fighter would clearly be larger and heavier, but the USSR was determined that this should not impose longer take-off distances.

Two approaches to the problem of giving their new fighter a degree of STOL capability were explored, both producing flying prototypes. A prototype with a delta wing and two 23.05-kN (5,180-lb st) Koliesov RD-36-35 lift jets, and with SPS flaps and a 76.52-kN (17,195-lb st) R-27F-300 primary engine, was designated **Model 23-01** (**MiG-23PD** NATO reporting name **'Faithless'**), while the **Model 23-11** was a version with variable-geometry wings. The 'swing-wing' concept was adopted to satisfy the conflicting requirements of high-speed flight and good low-speed airfield performance. Powered by a Tumanskii R-27F-300 turbojet, the 23-11 made its maiden flight on 10 April 1967, one week after the 23-01. The 23-11 had a multitude of high-lift devices, includ-

ing full-span four-section trailing-edge flaps, leading-edge slats and two-section spoilers, and these, in conjunction with the powerful engine, gave a useful STOL performance. The 23-11 demonstrated take-off runs of 320 m (1,050 ft) and a landing roll of 440 m (1,444 ft).

The 23-11 was ordered into production as the **MiG-23S** with a more powerful 98.1-kN (22,046-lb st) R-27F2M-300 engine, but without the intended Sapfir radar. Instead, the RP-22 'Jay Bird' of the MiG-21S was fitted, giving a very recognisable short radome and removing BVR capability. The aircraft was also fitted with a TP-23 IRST. Fifty were built between mid-1969 and the end of 1970 and were used for operational trials before production switched to the **MiG-23M**, dubbed **'Flogger-B'** by NATO. This featured the intended pulse-Doppler Sapfir-23 ('High Lark') radar and new fire control system and autopilot. The MiG-23M could fire the R-23 AA-7 'Apex' semi-active radar-homing missile. A new 122.63-kN (27,557-lb st) Soyuz (Tumanskii) R-29-300 (with shorter jetpipe) was fitted, while at the same time the aircraft's horizontal tail surfaces were moved aft, giving a very different appearance. A fourth fuel tank was added in the rear fuselage. A new Type 1 wing, with an extended leading edge, was introduced, this having a pronounced 'dogtooth' inboard. Leading-edge slats were deleted (the Type 2 wing), then reintroduced in 1973 with the Type 3 wing.

MiG-23Ms were delivered to Frontal Aviation as MiG-21 replacements, operating mainly in the battlefield air superiority role, but with an important secondary ground attack capability. Others went to the IA-PVO, where they augmented MiG-21s, Su-9s, Su-11s and Su-15s in the air defence role. Two downgraded export versions of the

Mikoyan-Gurevich MiG-23M 'Flogger-B'

Above: Romanian MiG-23MFs wear a wide variety of colour schemes, and equip three front-line interceptor regiments. They are augmented by a single squadron of MiG-29 'Fulcrums'.

Below: The MiG-23M and MF can be identified by their large dorsal fin fillet and full-size 'High Lark' radar. This aircraft belongs to No. 224 Squadron, Indian Air Force, based at Adampur.

MiG-23M were produced, the second gaining the new reporting name **'Flogger-E'**. The **MiG-23MS** was a substantially downgraded version with MiG-21-type 'Jay Bird' radar in a short radome, with no BVR missile capability. The **MiG-23MF** was less radically sanitised and retained the 'High Lark' fire control radar, AA-7 'Apex' missile capability and 'Flogger-B' reporting name of the MiG-23M, and was delivered to Russia's Warsaw Pact allies, then later to Syria, Angola, Iraq, India and Libya.

Operators of all fighter/interceptor variants are listed in the MiG-23ML/P/MLD 'Flogger-G/K' entry.

SPECIFICATION

Mikoyan-Gurevich MiG-23MF 'Flogger-B'
Wing: span swept 7.779 m (25 ft 6.5 in); span spread 13.965 m (45.9 ft); area swept 34.16 m² (367.7 sq ft); area spread 37.35 m² (402 sq ft)
Fuselage and tail: length 16.7 m (54.8 ft); wheelbase 5.772 m (18.9 ft); wheel track 2.658 m (8.8 ft); height 4.82 m (15.8 ft)
Powerplant: one Soyuz (Tumanskii) R-29-300 turbojet rated at 78.45 kN (17,635 lb), 112.76 kN

Originally designed as a substantially downgraded export aircraft, with MiG-21-type 'Jay Bird' radar (note the small white radome), the MiG-23MS 'Flogger-E' was also used in small numbers by Frontal Aviation, probably for advanced training. Today, the recipients of front-line Russian-built fighters tend to receive almost full-standard versions, and the kind of radically downgraded export version typified by the MiG-23MS is no longer produced.

(25,348 lb) with afterburner
Weights: empty 8200 kg (18,077 lb); normal take-off 15750 kg (34,722 lb); maximum take-off 20670 kg (45569 lb) with three external tanks
Fuel and load: internal fuel 4700 litres (1,242 US gal); external fuel 2370 litres (626 US gal); maximum ordnance 1600 kg (3,527 lb)

Speed: maximum level speed at 12500 m (41,010 ft) 2490 km/h (1,348 kt; 1,547 mph); maximum speed with 16° sweepback 935 km/h (506 kt; 581 mph)
Range: estimated ferry range 2996 km (1,624 nm; 1,864 miles); estimated hi-lo-hi radius of action 323 nm (600 km; 372 miles)
Performance: estimated service ceiling 17500 m

(57,414 ft); estimated take-off run 580-600 m (1,902-1,968 ft); estimated landing run at normal landing weight with brake chute 750 m (2,460 ft); estimated time to 11000 m (36,084 ft) 1 minute 24 seconds
g limits: +8 up to Mach 0.85; +7 above Mach 0.85

Mikoyan-Gurevich MiG-23ML/P/MLD 'Flogger-G/K'

Like most Soviet fighters, the MiG-23 has been subject to a constant programme of improvements and refinements, resulting in a succession of variants. The **MiG-23ML 'Flogger-G'** (allocated the OKB designation **23-12**) was intended to have improved handling, especially at high angles of attack, enhanced manoeuvrability and higher g limits. It featured a lightened airframe, with the fourth fuselage fuel tank removed and with the dorsal fin fillet deleted. More power was provided by installing the Soyuz (Tumanskii) R-35-300 engine. Strengthened three-section leading-edge slats were fitted.

Airframe and engine improvements were accompanied by an improved radar, the lightweight SP-23L, which had a new dog-fight mode, and improvements to the defensive avionics suite. A new IRST was also fitted. The MiG-23ML has been delivered to Frontal Aviation and to a number of export customers including Syria, North Korea, Czechoslovakia and East Germany. A very similar aircraft, designated **MiG-23P** (**23-14**), is used by the PVO and has a new digital computer that allows the aircraft to be automatically steered onto its target from the ground, cueing the pilot to engage afterburner and launch weapons. Israeli evaluation of a defecting Syrian MiG-23ML showed the aircraft to be a match for the F-16 in some respects.

Super 'Flogger'

The MiG-23ML also serves as the basis for the further improved **MiG-23MLD**, codenamed **'Flogger-K'** by NATO, and known as the **23-18** to the OKB. The new version, reportedly produced by conversion of MiG-23ML airframes, incorporates vortex generators on the pitot probe and notches in its vestigial leading-edge root extensions. These notches generate powerful vortices at high angles of attack, improving high-Alpha handling and increasing Alpha limits. New automatic leading-edge slats are also fitted, these deploying to optimise handling and manoeuvrability at all angles of attack. Large chaff/flare dispensers can be fitted above the rear fuselage, and these are linked to the new RWR system. A new IFF system is fitted, and a missile-firing simulator allows economic training. Further modifications include swivelling pylons under the outboard wing panels, which move to remain aligned with the airflow even when the wings are swept. On other

MiG-23 variants these pylons can only be used with the wings fully forward, and are thus rarely fitted.

Some reports suggest that the 'Flogger-K' is compatible with the new R-73 AA-11 'Archer' IR-homing missile, or perhaps even with the long-range AA-10 'Alamo', but this cannot yet be confirmed. Either of these missiles would represent a major increase in capability over the armament of previous MiG-23 variants. No MiG-23MLDs have been exported.

SPECIFICATION

Mikoyan-Gurevich MiG-23ML 'Flogger-G'
generally similar to the MiG-23MF except in the following particulars:
Fuselage and tail: length 15.65 m (51 ft 3.7 in) excluding probe (0.08 m/3 in shorter than MiG-23M)
Powerplant: one Soyuz (Tumanskii) R-35-300 turbojet rated at 83.88 kN (18,849 lb st) dry and 127.5 kN (28,660 lb st) with afterburning
Weights: normal take-off 14700 kg (32,407 lb); maximum take-off 17800 kg (39,242 lb)
Fuel and load: internal fuel 4250 litres (1,122 US gal); external fuel 2400 litres (632 US gal); maximum ordnance 2000 kg (4409 lb)
Speed: maximum speed at 72° sweepback 2500 km/h

Mikoyan-Gurevich MiG-23MLD 'Flogger-K'

(1,349 kt; 1,553 mph); at 16° sweepback 940 km/h (507 kt; 584 mph)
Range: ferry range 2820 km (1,521 nm; 1,752 miles) with drop tanks
Performance: service ceiling 18000 m (59,055 ft); take-off run 1200-1300 m (3,937-4,265 ft); time to 11000 m (36,089 ft) 1 minute 12 seconds
g limits: +8.5 below Mach 0.85 and +7.5 above Mach 0.85

OPERATORS

Afghanistan: Reports of Afghan MiG-23s may refer to Soviet aircraft stationed in that country, and perhaps temporarily operated with Afghan markings, although there are persistent reports that MiG-23MFs equipped the 322nd Fighter Interceptor Regiment at Bagram

A MiG-23ML on alert at the Peenemünde base of JFG-9 'Heinrich Rau'. It carries a pair of R-23 (AA-7 'Alamo') missiles under the wing gloves, IR-homing to port and semi-active radar-homing to starboard. Two short-range R-60 (AA-8 'Aphid' missiles) are carried below the fuselage. The small blue 'Q' is a quality award, given to the crew chief to acknowledge the excellent condition of his charge.

Mikoyan-Gurevich MiG-23ML/P/MLD 'Flogger-G/K'

This fully modified MiG-23MLD of the 83rd Fighter Regiment is based at Altes Lager in Germany. Chaff/flare dispensers are carried above the rear fuselage.

Algeria: Algeria operates some 20 MiG-23 fighters, (MiG-23MFs or MSs), alongside UB trainers

Angola: Angola's 80-strong MiG-23 fleet includes MiG-23MLs, and, reportedly, MFs and MSs as well as BN fighter-bombers and UB trainers

Byelorussia: The Byelorussian republic has 50 MiG-23s at Machulisch and Baranovich

Bulgaria: Eighty MiG-23MFs (and reportedly some MiG-23MLs delivered as attrition replacements) serve with the fighter regiment at Dobroslavtzi (which may be designated Polk 24900). Other MiG-23s serve at Bozhurishte

China: China is believed to have received between two and four (and perhaps many more) MiG-23s from Egypt in return for spares support for that nation's MiG-21s after its break with the USSR. They were minutely examined, and technology acquired in the process was used in the J-8 and stillborn J-9 programmes

Cuba: Cuba is believed to have received about 20 MiG-23MS 'Flogger-Es' in 1977, together with a few MiG-23MLs, and perhaps later augmented by a number of MiG-23MFs

Czech Republic: Czechoslovakia took delivery of 12 MiG-23MFs and 18 MiG-23MLs for the 1st Fighter Regiment at Ceske Budejovice. Ten MiG-23UBs were also delivered. Slovakia did not take its allocated one-third of the MiG-23s on the division of Czechoslovakia into separate Czech and Slovak Republics. The Czech Republic is reportedly making its MiG-23s compatible with the MATRA Magic missile, and is actively looking to upgrade the aircraft further. With the withdrawal of the nine MiG-29s (judged too small a number to be viable) in late 1994, the MiG-23MFs will form the backbone of Czech air defence

Egypt: About 16 MiG-23s were delivered in 1974, but were passed to the USA and China following the split with the USSR

Ethiopia: A handful of MiG-23UBs were delivered to support Ethiopia's fighter-bomber MiG-23BMNs (which may actually be BMs or BKs)

Germany: An original batch of MiG-23MFs (delivered in 1978) and eight MiG-23UBs were augmented by 28 MiG-23MLs delivered during 1982 and 1983. Twelve MFs remained in use at reunification. Several aircraft were flown by the Luftwaffe for evaluation following the reunification of the two Germanies, and others were supplied to the RAF and US Air Force for evaluation

Hungary: Nine of the 12 MiG-23MFs delivered remain in service with the Saman squadron of the Stromfeld Aurel wing at Pápa, with three of four MiG-23UBs transferred from Frontal Aviation

India: Forty MiG-23MFs were acquired in 1982 as interim fighters pending the delivery of MiG-29s. The survivors remain in use with No. 224 Squadron, No. 223 having converted to the MiG-29 in 1989. Fifteen MiG-23UBs were delivered primarily to support the MiG-23BN and MiG-27 fighter-bomber force

Iraq: Iraq's MiG-23 fleet, severely depleted by the Gulf War, included MiG-23MS, MF(?) and ML fighters, and UB trainers. Eight were shot down during the war, eight fled to Iran, and many more were destroyed on the ground

Libya: Libya has received more than 150 MiG-23s, some of which were transferred to Sudan. About 85 fighters (MS, MF and ML) remain in use, with 15 trainers

North Korea: An initial 1984 batch of eight MiG-23MLs has been augmented by further deliveries, giving a total force of about 60 MiG-23s, including a handful of MiG-23UBs

Poland: About 28 survivors of 45 MiG-23MFs serve with 28 PLM at Slupsk, with about four MiG-23UBs

Romania: Some 30 MiG-23MFs and eight MiG-23UBs are in service with the 32nd and 57th Fighter Regiments at Timisoara and Constanta

Russia: Despite the widespread introduction of the MiG-29, MiG-23s remain in service in large numbers. Air forces withdrawn from Czechoslovakia, Germany and Poland all included MiG-23MLD fighter regiments, which joined other MiG-23 regiments in Russian-based Frontal Aviation, and Russian-based PVO regiments

Sudan: Libyan MiG-23s transferred to Sudan during 1987 may have been fighter-bombers or fighters. Between six and 12 remain in use

Syria: Many of the initial batch of MiG-23MS fighters were lost to the IDF/AF (especially over the Bekaa in 1982) and replacements have included MiG-23MFs and MLs. MiG-23UB trainers are also in service. About 100 fighter/trainer 'Floggers' are in service

Turkmenistan: Turkmenistan has a number of MiG-23s, some of which it has tried to sell to raise foreign currency. Whether its single combat squadron will have MiG-23s remains uncertain

Ukraine: About 230 MiG-23s remain active with the air defence force in the new republic, but not with the air force itself, apart from a handful of MiG-23UBs used as trainers by MiG-29 regiments. The air defence force, the PVO during USSR days, has Southern, Western and Central Regions, and MiG-23s serve with the 737th IAP at Chervanoglinskoe (Southern Region), and with the 179th IAP and 894th IAP at Stryy and Ozernoe (Western Region)

United States of America: The USAF's ex-Egyptian MiG-23s, augmented by three ex-East German aircraft (three MiG-23MLs), serve in the adversary tactics development role

Vietnam: About 30 MiG-23s were delivered to replace MiG-19s in the interceptor role during 1985/86. These may be MiG-23MLs

Yemen: Ex-South Yemeni MiG-23s have been described by different sources as MiG-23BN fighter-bombers and as MiG-23ML fighters. About 25 remain in use

Mikoyan-Gurevich **MiG-23UB 'Flogger-C'**

Because the handling characteristics of the MiG-23 were so different from those of other aircraft in the Soviet inventory, development of a two-seat trainer version was authorised in May 1968, six months after the the go-ahead had been given for the single-seat aircraft. Photographs of the second prototype, often described as a simple two-seat conversion of the MiG-23S, seem to show an aircraft with the definitive rear fuselage contours of the MiG-23M but with the original wing, and with no 'dogtooth' on the leading edge. The **MiG-23UB** prototype (allocated the NATO reporting name **'Flogger-C'**, and known to the bureau as the **23-51**) made its maiden flight in May 1969, three years before the first MiG-23M. This may perhaps indicate that the two-seater's rear-located tailplane and short jetpipe were adopted for the new single-seater.

Although never intended to have the Sapfir radar, the MiG-23UB was always supposed to be used for both pilot conversion and weapons training, and even to have a restricted combat capability, within the limitations imposed by the weapons carried. Accordingly, a separate guidance and illuminator pod for the AA-7 'Apex' missile was fitted in a conical fairing on the starboard wingroot. Production aircraft all have the 'clawed' No. 3 wing (compatible with the carriage of outboard underwing fuel tanks on non-swivelling pylons), and the two tandem cockpits are covered by separate upward-hinging canopies. The instructor is provided with a retractable periscope to give a better view forward on approach. All

This MiG-23UB served as a trainer with the 33rd IAP at Wittstock, one of the MiG-29-equipped fighter regiments assigned to the Group of Soviet Forces in Germany. These tended to use MiG-23UBs to augment their MiG-29UB trainers.

two-seaters are fitted with an AoA limiter or an AoA warning system, together with a comprehensive avionics suite featuring improved navaids and a sophisticated system which allows the backseater to simulate emergencies and threats for the student pilot in the front cockpit.

All MiG-23, 23BN and MiG-27 operators also use the MiG-23UB, and the type, which was phased out of production at Irkutsk in 1978, also serves with many Russian MiG-29 and Su-27 units.

SPECIFICATION

Mikoyan-Gurevich MiG-23UB 'Flogger-C'
generally similar to the Mikoyan-Gurevich MiG-23MF 'Flogger-B' except in the following particulars:
Fuselage and tail: length 16.64 m (54.6 ft); 15.66 m (51ft 4.5 in) without probe
Powerplant: one Soyuz (Tumanskii) R-27F2M-300 turbojet rated at 67.67 kN (15,212 lb st) dry and 98.07 kN (22,046 lb st) with afterburning

Weights: empty 8700 kg (19,179 lb); normal take-off 15740 kg (34,700 lb); maximum take-off 18000 kg (39,682 lb)
Fuel and load: internal fuel 4000 kg (8,818 lb); external fuel 2400 litres (634 US gal)
Range: radius of action 700 km (377 km; 434 miles)
Performance: service ceiling 18000 m (59,055 ft); take-off run 1200-1300 m (3,837-4,265 ft); landing roll 1200-1300 m (3,837-4,265 ft)
***g* limit:** +7

A Mikoyan MiG-23UB of No. 10 Squadron, Indian Air Force, takes off in full burner. No. 10 Squadron operates MiG-23BN fighter-bombers. There are no external differences between the two-seaters used by fighter and fighter-bomber squadrons, but there may be equipment changes.

Mikoyan-Gurevich **MiG-23B/BK/BM/BN 'Flogger-F/-H'**

Mikoyan began studies of a 'jet *Shturmovik*' during 1969, to meet a Frontal Aviation requirement for a cheap, mass-produced attack aircraft offering the same level of capability as the Anglo-French SEPECAT Jaguar. Mikoyan assumed that an entirely new subsonic design would be necessary. The resulting MiG-27-11 combined the basic airframe of the MiG-21bis with an ogival delta wing (as used on Mikoyan's A-144 Analog and Tupolev's Tu-144) and side-mounted intakes. An alternative supersonic design, the MiG-27Sh, used a wing similar to that of the Jaguar. Economic constraints forced Mikoyan to examine the possibility of using a derivative of the MiG-23S, whose supersonic dash capability was felt to be a useful bonus. How the new design fitted in with the Su-25 'Frogfoot' being developed by Sukhoi to meet essentially the same role remains unclear. Mikoyan allocated a new designation (**Model 32**) but the air force retained a MiG-23 designation, perhaps feeling that funding for a new aircraft would be harder to obtain.

The original MiG-23 had been developed as a multi-role tactical fighter, and the ability to operate from primitive, semi-prepared airstrips had been stressed from the start. The aircraft's rugged airframe, strong under-

The MiG-23BN was essentially an attack derivative of the basic 'Flogger-B' fighter, with the same airframe and engine.

carriage, powerful engine and variable-geometry wing thus made it extremely suitable for conversion or adaptation to the fighter-bomber role. The use of a swing wing, in particular, allowed high straight line performance (with wings swept aft), while also endowing excellent low-speed handling characteristics, turn performance and short take-off/landing distances.

The basic **MiG-23B** (**32-24**) was based on the airframe of the MiG-23S, but with a new, more sloping nose giving the pilot an improved view forward and downward, and with a 112.78-kN (25,353-lb st) Lyul'ka AL-21F-300 powerplant in a shortened rear fuselage, again with the horizontal tailplane shifted rearward, as on the MiG-23M. Also like the MiG-23M, the new ground attack variant featured the No. 2 wing and was later fitted with the the No. 3 wing. Radar was not installed, and instead the new aircraft had a PrNK Sokol 23S nav/attack system. Armour was scabbed on to the sides of the forward fuselage, to protect the pilot, and the fuel tanks were fitted with an inert gas injection fire protection system. A missile illuminator (starboard) and a TV camera (port) were housed in bullet-like fairings on the wingroot gloves. The TV camera was later removed from most MiG-23 fighter-bombers. Piotr Ostapenko flew the first prototype on 20 August 1970, making the aircraft the third production version to fly, after the MiG-23S and MiG-23UB.

Twenty-four MiG-23Bs were built before

production finally switched to an improved variant. The **MiG-23BN** (**32-23**), featured an upgraded PrNK Sokol 23N nav/attack system, and was powered by a slightly derated

Above: The nose contours of a MiG-23BN reveal the undernose 'Swift Rod' and laser rangefinder window in the 'chisel nose'.

Mikoyan-Gurevich MiG-23B/BK/BM/BN 'Flogger-F/-H'

With the canopy cracked open for ventilation, an East German MiG-23BN taxis out for a mission at Drewitz. JBG 37 'Klement Gottwald' disbanded on the reunification of the two Germanies, although a handful of its aircraft were briefly retained for evaluation.

version of the Soyuz (Tumanskii) R-29B-300 engine. The MiG-23BN was intended to have been the first attack version, but was delayed by equipment and engine problems. It introduced the leading-edge bullet fairings on the fixed wing gloves that are usually associated with the AS-7 'Kerry' ASM. The MiG-23B and MiG-23BN share the NATO reporting name **'Flogger-F'**, and all seem to have a simplified jetpipe, which is more like that fitted to the MiG-27 than the standard MiG-23M jetpipe.

The MiG-23B and MiG-23BN proved disappointing in service, and many were subsequently upgraded to **MiG-23BK (32-26)** or **MiG-23BM (32-25)** standards, or exported, mainly to Third World customers. Cuban attack MiG-23s are 'Flogger-Fs', without the intake-mounted RWR fairings, for example, while German and Czech aircraft, designated MiG-23BNs, have these fairings and are thus 'Flogger-Hs'. Improved avionics were desperately needed, and two new fighter-bombers were quickly developed, both sharing the same **'Flogger-H'** reporting name. This was assigned because they

had new RWR fairings on the lower 'corners' of the fuselage, just ahead of the nose-wheel bay. The first of the new variants was the MiG-23BK, which had the same nav/attack system and laser rangefinder as the MiG-27K. The MiG-23BM was similar, but with the same PrNK Sokol 23M nav/attack system as the MiG-27D. Confusingly, the MiG-23BN designation seems to have been adopted as an overall service designation, sometimes being applied to aircraft designated BM or BK by the bureau. Many of the export 'Flogger-Hs' are usually described as MiG-23BNs, and were perhaps built as such, but are actually to MiG-23BK standards. Such aircraft include East Germany's MiG-23BKs, whose documentation described them as **MiG-24BNs**. Bulgarian, Czech, Indian and Iraqi 'Flogger-Hs' look identical, although many of the latter have fixed inflight-refuelling probes above the nose, almost identical to those fitted to the Mirage F1, and perhaps supplied by the same French manufacturer.

WEAPON OPTIONS

The MiG-23B series can carry a variety of guided and unguided weapons on underwing and underfuselage pylons. The aircraft also has a secondary reconnaissance capability, using podded sensors which are most frequently attached to one of the under-intake pylons. Hardpoints are provided under the forward fuselage, on the bottom 'corners' of the

rear fuselage and under the wing gloves. These can be used to carry the full range of podded and unpodded rockets, the UV-32-57 and newer S-8 rocket pods (respectively containing 32 57-mm rockets and 20 80-mm rockets) being favourite MiG-23BN weapons. The KMG-U bomblet dispenser can be carried, together with 50-kg (110-lb), 100-kg (220-lb), 250-kg (551-lb) or 500-kg (1,102-lb) freefall bombs. The bullet fairing on the starboard wing glove is believed to house a command guidance antenna for guided ASMs like the AS-7 'Kerry'. Internal armament consists of a GSh-23L 23-mm twin-barrelled cannon, as fitted to earlier fighter versions. This is carried in a semi-conformal gondola below the fuselage, just aft of the nosewheel bay. For strafing missions, this weapon can be augmented by UPK-23-250 cannon pods, or the SPPU-22 with traversible barrels.

SPECIFICATION

Mikoyan MiG-23BN 'Flogger-F'
generally similar to the MiG-23MF except in the following particulars:
Fuselage and tail: length 15.35 m (50.36 ft); wheelbase 5.9 m (19.35 ft); wheel track 2.73 m (2.9 ft)
Powerplant: one Soyuz (Tumanskii) R-29B-300 turbojet rated at 77 kN (17,310 lb) or 110 kN (24,728 lb) with afterburner
Weights: empty 10700 kg (23,589 lb); normal take-off 16750 kg (36,926 lb); maximum take-off 18850 kg (41,556 lb)
Fuel and load: internal fuel 5380 litres (1,421 US gal); maximum external fuel 2370 litres (626 US gal); maximum ordnance 3000 kg (6,613 lb)

Speed: maximum level speed at 11000 m (36,089 ft) 1900 km/h (1,025 kt; 1,180 mph); maximum level speed at sea level 1350 km/h (728 kt; 838 mph)
Range: ferry range 1350 km (728 nm; 838 miles); radius of action 550 km (296 nm; 341 miles)
Performance: service ceiling 16800 m (55,118 ft); take-off run 650-700 m (2,132-2,296 ft); landing run at normal landing weight with brake chute 800-850 m (2,262-2,788 ft); time to 11000 m (36,089 ft) 1 minute 42 seconds
g limits: +7 up to Mach 0.85; +6 above Mach 0.85

OPERATORS

Algeria: Algeria operates some 40 MiG-23BNs (which may actually be, or have been upgraded to, MiG-23BM or BK standards) in two squadrons
Angola: Angola's 80-strong MiG-23 fleet includes MiG-23 BN fighter-bombers (which may actually be, or have been upgraded to, MiG-23BM or BK standards)
Bulgaria: About 40 MiG-23BNs (which may actually be, or have been upgraded to, MiG-23BM or BK standards, and which are certainly 'Flogger-Hs') serve the 25th Bomber Regiment at Sadovo (which may alternatively be known as Polk 38790)
Cuba: Cuba is believed to operate 35 MiG-23BNs 'Flogger-Fs' in three squadrons at Guines and Santa Clara
Czech Republic: On the division of Czechoslovakia into separate Czech and Slovak Republics, the new Czech Republic retained all 28 surviving MiG-23BNs (of 32 delivered) for the 28th Fighter-Bomber Regiment at Caslav
Egypt: About 16 MiG-23s, including an unknown number of fighter-bombers, were delivered in 1974, and were later passed to the USA and China
Ethiopia: Ethiopia operates about 36 fighter-bomber MiG-23BNs (which may actually be BMs or BKs) with the 3rd Air Regiment at Dire Dawa and Debre Zeit
Germany: Eighteen MiG-23BNs (which may actually be, or have been upgraded to, MiG-23BM or BK standards, and which were reportedly known locally as MiG-24s) remained in service at reunification. Some were briefly flown in Luftwaffe markings for evaluation.
India: Ninety-five MiG-23BNs were delivered from December 1980, allowing the re-equipment of Nos 10, 31, 220 and 221 Squadrons, which remain active
Iraq: Iraq's MiG-23 fleet included about 70 MiG-23BNs, but four fled to Iran during the Gulf War, several were impounded while on overhaul in Yugoslavia and Germany, and many more were destroyed on the ground. Many were fitted with Mirage F1-style refuelling probes and were compatible with the AS-14 'Kedge' ASM
Libya: Libya took delivery of some 40-50 MiG-23BNs (which may actually be, or have been upgraded to, MiG-23BM or BK standards), 35-38 of which remain in service with a regiment at El Adem. These may have been fitted with Mirage F1-style refuelling probes
Nigeria: Reports that Nigeria received some 40 MiG-23BNs and 10 UBs cannot be confirmed
Russia: MiG-23Bs, MiG-23BNs, BMs and BKs have been retired from front-line service, but a handful may be in use for test or trials duties
Sudan: Libyan MiG-23s transferred to Sudan during 1987 may have been fighter-bombers or fighters. Between six and 12 remain in use
Syria: Some sources suggest that Syria has about 60 MiG-23BNs (which may actually be, or have been upgraded to, MiG-23BM or BK standards)
United States of America: The USAF's ex-Egyptian MiG-23s included some MiG-23BNs
Yemen: 25 ex-South Yemeni MiG-23s have been described by different sources as MiG-23BN fighter-bombers and as MiG-23ML fighters. About 25 remain in use

This Indian Air Force MiG-23BN carries four UV-16-57 rocket pods, giving a total of 64 57-mm rockets. It wears the tiger's head insignia of No. 220 Squadron 'The Desert Tigers'.

Mikoyan-Gurevich MiG-25 fighter variants

The **MiG-25** was developed as a panic response to the American North American XB-70 Valkyrie strategic bomber, whose Mach 3 performance and very high altitude capability threatened to present Soviet air defences with almost insoluble problems. When development of the Valkyrie was halted in 1961, work on the MiG-25 was well advanced, and the USSR continued with the project, perhaps knowing that a Mach 3-capable reconnaissance aircraft, the Lockheed A-11 (later SR-71), was about to begin flight tests.

In designing an aircraft for sustained flight at Mach 3, the biggest problem facing the design bureau was the so-called heat barrier. It had been estimated that while a MiG-21 flying at Mach 2.05 with an outside air temperature of 0°C (32°F) would encounter nose temperatures of 107°C (225°F), the air friction of an aircraft flying at Mach 3 would generate temperatures of almost 300°C (572°F), well above the maximum temperature (130°C/266°F) that aluminium could withstand.

Those parts of the airframe which would have to withstand the greatest heat, such as the nose and leading edges, had to be of titanium construction, but many other areas that could theoretically have been made of riveted aluminium, such as the wing skins (which served as fuel tanks and were thus cooled by their contents) had to be made of welded steel because no suitable heat-resistant sealant could be found, and because there was a shortage of skilled riveters. Structural design of a Mach 3 aircraft posed enormous problems and demanded the use of advanced metallurgy and new welding processes to develop heat-resistant alloys and to avoid cracking and other problems. Eventually, 80 per cent of the aircraft was of tempered steel, 11 per cent of aluminium alloys and eight per cent of titanium. Similarly, no less than 76.5 per cent of assembly was by different types of welding, with conventional riveted joints making up only 23.5 per cent.

The aerodynamic problems posed by an aircraft designed to operate at sustained Mach 3 speeds were no less acute. In order to achieve satisfactory levels of stability and good manoeuvrability without sacrificing speed or altitude performance, the design bureau selected a novel configuration with large, highly-swept thin wings, sophisticated variable lateral air intakes, and canted twin tailfins. The wing leading-edge sweepback angle is not constant, with slightly more inboard (42°30') than outboard (41°). In order to provide adequate range and endurance, about 70 per cent of the aircraft's volume consists of fuel tanks, giving the prototype an internal capacity of 17660 litres (4,666 US gal).

Advanced cooling and insulation systems had to be developed for the engines, avionics and cockpit. The success of these features can be gauged by the fact that at maximum speed the pilot remains comfortable, yet the canopy above him is too hot to touch with the naked hand. Development of the **Ye-155P** interceptor was finally approved in February 1962, and the prototype **Ye-155P-1** made its maiden flight on 9 September 1964, after the first MiG-25 reconnaissance version, which had been designed after it. The aircraft was powered by a pair of 100-kN (22,500-lb) Mikulin (later Tumanskii) R-15B-300 turbojets with a life of 150 hours, and fitted with a Smertch-A radar, known to NATO as 'Fox Fire'. This

With twin cruciform brake chutes streamed, a MiG-25PU taxis in after a training mission. The instructor sits in the forward cockpit, displacing the radar, giving the pupil exactly the same view as he would have in the single-seat MiG-25.

The lack of an undernose IRST sensor identifies this Libyan MiG-25 as a 'Foxbat-A'. Libya has some 60 MiG-25 fighters, augmenting a smaller number of recce aircraft. These serve with a three-squadron regiment at Tripoli.

had a detection range of 54 nm (100 km; 62 miles) and a tracking range of 27 nm (50 km; 31 miles). The aircraft carried two R-40 air-to-air missiles, in mixed pairs of R-40R and R-40T semi-active radar- and IR-homing versions. Look-down capability was virtually non-existent.

Performance was up to expectations, and in March 1965, under the cover designation **Ye-266**, an early aircraft was used to shatter several of the records set by the Lockheed SR-71. Between 1965 and 1977, the Ye-266 and **Ye-266M** eventually made 21 FAI-notified record-breaking flights, setting nine records which still remained unbroken in 1994.

For the production **MiG-25P 'Foxbat-A'** the tailfin area was reduced and planned canard foreplanes were abandoned, as were the small wingtip tanks and winglets. Armament was increased from two to four R-40 (AA-6 'Acrid') missiles, comprising two each with infra-red and radar-homing seeker heads. The landing weight was so high that twin brake chutes had to be fitted, production aircraft eventually using either 60-m^2 (646-sq ft) conical or 50-m^2 (538-sq ft) cruciform chutes. Production began in 1969, but the aircraft did not enter full air force service until 1973, having been plagued by engine and control problems. Even in service, the MiG-25 was subject to severe operating limitations, which strictly constrained the amount of time that could be spent at very high speeds, and which limited the use of full engine power.

The ultimate **MiG-25PD 'Foxbat-E'** fighter variant entered production in 1978, and featured a new RP-25 look-down/shoot-down radar (similar to that fitted to the MiG-23M) and an undernose IRST. The engines were replaced by more powerful R-15BD-300s whose lives were extended to 1,000 hours, and provision was made for a 5300-litre (1,400-US gal) belly tank. Surviving Soviet 'Foxbat-As' were brought up to the same standard from 1979, under the designation **MiG-25PDS**. Some of the latter aircraft received a 250-mm (10-in) plug in front of the canopy to allow a retractable IFR probe to be fitted, although inflight refuelling was not (and is still not) a regular part of front-line PVO operations. Normal armament comprises two R-40s and four R-60 (AA-8 'Aphid') AAMs. The PD/PDS upgrade has restored the MiG-25's viability, however, and some are expected to serve into the next millennium.

Right: The MiG-25PD 'Foxbat-E' prototype lacks an undernose IRST and is currently in storage at the Zhukhovskii Flight Research Centre. Red stars along the intake represent successful missile firings.

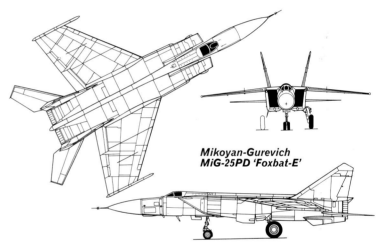

Mikoyan-Gurevich MiG-25PD 'Foxbat-E'

The added fuselage plug of the **MiG-25PDS** can clearly be seen ahead of the windscreen in this view of 'Red 45'. The 'scallop' below the nose is a black-painted anti-glare patch which surrounds the **IRST** sensor in order to maintain a constant temperature, and to not transmit reflections to the **IRST**.

Gulf War. Fuller user details are given in the operators section of the MiG-25R entry.

The **MiG-25PU 'Foxbat-C'** two-seat conversion trainer was rolled out in 1968. It lacks radar and has no combat capability. The type features a new forward cockpit for the instructor stepped down in front of the standard single-seat cockpit. The MiG-25P and MiG-25PU have been exported to Algeria, Iraq, Libya and Syria. Remarkably, an Iraqi MiG-25 is believed to have shot down a USN F/A-18 during the

This MiG-25 serves as an ejection seat testbed, with an open rear cockpit surrounded by a built-up blast screen. Based at Zhukhovskii, it serves alongside other MiG-25s used in test and research roles.

SPECIFICATION

Mikoyan-Gurevich MiG-25PDS 'Foxbat-E'
Wing: span 14.015 m (45 ft 11.75 in); aspect ratio 3.2; area 61.40 m² (660.93 sq ft)
Fuselage and tail: length 23.82 m (78 ft 1.75 in) or, in aircraft modified with IFR capability, 24.07 m (78 ft 11.67 in); height 6.10 m (20 ft 0.25 in); wheel track 3.85 m (12 ft 7.5 in); wheel base 5.14 m (16 ft 10.5 in)
Powerplant: two MNPK 'Soyuz' (Tumanskii) R-15BD-300 turbojets each rated at 109.83 kN (24,691 lb st) with afterburning
Weights: normal take-off 36720 kg (80,952 lb) with four R-40s and 100 per cent internal fuel
Fuel and load: internal fuel 14570 kg (32,121 lb); external fuel up to 4370 kg (9,634 lb) in an underbelly tank; maximum ordnance 4000 kg (8,818 lb)
Speed: maximum level speed 'clean' at 13000 m (42,650 ft) Mach 2.8 or 3000 km/h (1,619 kt; 1,864 mph) and at sea level 1200 km/h (647 kt; 745 mph)
Range: with internal fuel 1730 km (933 nm; 1,075 miles) subsonic or 1250 km (675 nm; 776 miles) supersonic; endurance 2 hours 5 minutes
Performance: climb to 20000 m (65,615 ft) in 8 minutes 54 seconds; service ceiling 20700 m (67,915 ft); take-off run 1250 m (4,101 ft) at normal take-off weight; landing run 800 m (2,624 ft) at normal landing weight with brake chutes
g limits: +4.5 supersonic

Mikoyan-Gurevich **MiG-25 reconnaissance variants**

Although the MiG-25 was originally designed as an interceptor, it had obvious potential as a reconnaissance platform. The prototype recce aircraft, the **Ye-155R-1**, made its maiden flight six months before the prototype fighter, on 6 March 1964. During flight trials of the three Ye-155Rs, the original wingtip tanks with vertical finlets were soon discarded and replaced by smaller anti-flutter masses, and 'letterbox'-shaped dielectric panels on the nose were made deeper and more square. Tail surfaces were also enlarged and the R-15B-300 engines were replaced by R-15BD-300s.

As the **MiG-25R**, the reconnaissance version passed its state acceptance tests in 1969, and series production began at Gorky in April 1969. The MiG-25R had five camera ports in the nose, one vertical and four oblique, with small square flush antennas further forward on the sides of the nose, probably serving some kind of SLAR. Three cameras would usually be carried, one vertical and two oblique, the latter having 300-mm and 650-mm lenses, allowing them to cover swathes of land equal to two-and-a-half times and five times the aircraft altitude, respectively.

Even before the aircraft entered front-line service, a trials unit with four MiG-25Rs was deployed to Egypt for operational reconnaissance missions over Israel. These operated under the cover designation **X-500**, flying at speeds of up to Mach 2.83 (flight at this upper limit was officially limited to eight minutes), although one pilot took his aircraft to Mach 3 to avoid Israeli SAMs and the time

The Indian Air Force's No. 102 Squadron operates five MiG-25RBs (of six delivered) and also has a pair of MiG-25RU trainers.

limit was frequently broken. The aircraft enjoyed a four-year immunity from interception, between their deployment in 1971 to their withdrawal in 1975, despite a lack of security which meant that the IDF/AF was forewarned of virtually every mission.

The original MiG-25R was replaced on the production line by the **MiG-25RB 'Foxbat-B'** in 1970, this type remaining in production until 1982. The MiG-25RB was a dual-role reconnaissance bomber, with a new Peleng automatic bombing system, the Soviet Union's first operational inertial navigation system, and a Doppler to measure speed and drift. These allowed the aircraft to release its bombs from altitudes in excess of 20000 m (65,617 ft) at supersonic speeds. Four underwing hardpoints were provided for 500-kg (1,102-lb) bombs, with another two under the fuselage. Alternatively, a single nuclear weapon could be carried. The standard camera bay remained but the SRS-4A Elint system was slightly

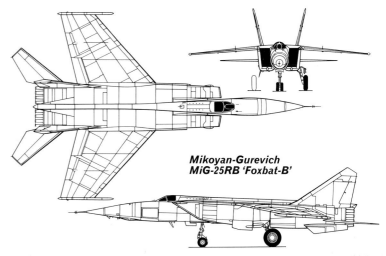

Mikoyan-Gurevich MiG-25RB 'Foxbat-B'

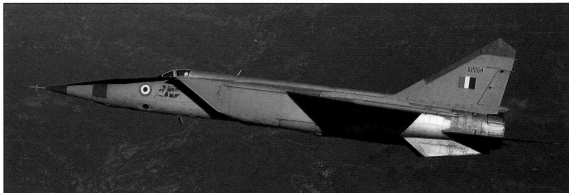

This MiG-25RBF, identifiable by the small dielectric panels in place of camera ports, served with the Soviet Forces in Germany, based first at Werneuchen and later at Welzow.

improved. All surviving Soviet MiG-25Rs were brought up to MiG-25RB standards. Further models which are understood to have retained their cameras included the **MiG-25RBS** with the new Sabla radio location system. This variant entered service in 1972, and was produced until 1977. From 1981 many of these aircraft received new equipment and were allocated a new designation of **MiG-25RBSh**. The MiG-25RBS was replaced on the production line by the **MiG-25RBV**, with further improved equipment, and by the MiG-25RBV with SRS-9 Virazh Elint equipment. From observation of an aircraft described as a MiG-25RBV in Germany during 1992, this variant appears to have all but its vertical camera port faired over, but is otherwise externally identical to the MiG-25RB and MiG-25RBS.

The basic MiG-25RB also formed the basis of a model dedicated to Elint duties, with its optical sensors replaced by a variety of passive receivers and active SLAR systems. It is unclear whether the NATO **'Foxbat-D'** reporting name covers all such versions, or just those with an enlarged SLAR antenna on the side of the nose, further aft. The first 'camera-less' 'Foxbat' was the **MiG-25RBK**, which has the usual flush antennas and cameras removed and replaced by much larger, longer dielectric panels on the sides of the cockpit stretching forward from a point immediately under the windscreen. These antennas reportedly serve the new Kub SLAR. The aircraft lacks even the vertical camera port, and the underside of the nose is completely smooth. The MiG-25RBK entered service in 1972 and remained in production until 1980.

The final variant is the **MiG-25RBF**, variously described as an RB brought up to RBK standards, or as a new production aircraft which replaced the RBK on the production line, with expanded jamming capability.

There is less doubt about the MiG-25RBF's appearance, fortunately. The aircraft lacks the large SLAR antennas of the RBK, instead having reverted to the small dielectric panels farther forward, as carried on the MiG-25RB and other variants. In place of oblique camera windows, the RBF has four small, symmetrically arranged, rectangular dielectric panels. The vertical camera window seems to be retained.

Unusually, the reconnaissance 'Foxbat' has its own dedicated two-seat trainer, designated **MiG-25RU**. This has no operational equipment, but does seem to have a constant-sweep wing leading edge. By comparison with 'fighter' MiG-25s, all reconnaissance aircraft have slightly reduced wingspan and a leading edge with constant sweep, instead of the fighter's 'cranked' leading edge. Camera-equipped MiG-25RBs have been exported to Algeria, Bulgaria, India, Iraq, Libya and Syria.

SPECIFICATION

Mikoyan-Gurevich MiG-25RB 'Foxbat-B'
generally similar to the Mikoyan-Gurevich MiG-25PDS 'Foxbat-E' except in the following particulars:
Wing: span 13.42 m (44 ft 0.25 in)
Weights: normal take-off 37000 kg (81,570 lb); maximum take-off 41200 kg (90,829 lb)
Fuel and load: internal fuel 15245 kg (33,609 lb); maximum ordnance 3000 kg (6,614 lb)
Range: ferry range with underbelly tank 2400 km (1,295 nm; 1,491 miles) subsonic or 2130 km (1150 nm; 1,323 miles) supersonic; range with internal fuel 1865 km (1,006 nm; 1,158 miles) subsonic or 1635 km (882 nm; 1,015 miles) supersonic
Performance: climb to 19000 m (41,885 ft) in 6 minutes 36 seconds 'clean' or 8 minutes 12 seconds with 2000 kg (4,409 lb) of bombs; service ceiling 21000 m (68,900 ft)

OPERATORS

Algeria: A single squadron is understood to operate some 16 MiG-25P interceptors and four MiG-25RB recce aircraft, although some reports estimate a total of 36 MiG-25s delivered

Azerbaijan: The Azeris seized several unserviceable MiG-25PD interceptors left behind when Russia withdrew from Nasosnaya air base, and also took over five MiG-25RBs. Their status is uncertain
Byelorussia: About 60 MiG-25PDs and MiG-25Rs of various types are believed to be in service
Bulgaria: Spares shortages and economic considerations have grounded Bulgaria's Tolbukhin/Dobritch-based MiG-25RBs since July 1991
Egypt: Egyptian markings were applied to Soviet MiG-25RBs operating from Egyptian bases during the early 1970s, but the type was never officially on charge
India: Five of the six MiG-25RBs delivered still serve with No. 102 Squadron, along with two MiG-25RUs
Iraq: Some 20 MiG-25s may have survived the Gulf War, several having been destroyed on the ground, two in the air, and at least one more lost to the USAF after the war, in January 1993
Kazakhstan: MiG-25RBs and other recce variants serve with the 39th RAP at Balkesh

A MiG-25RBK 'Foxbat-D' gets airborne, followed by a camera-equipped MiG-25RB 'Foxbat-B'. The MiG-25RBK has a large dielectric panel on each side of the nose, serving a SLAR, and has no undernose camera ports.

Libya: Libya's fleet of MiG-25s includes 60 fighters (MiG-25Ps and PDs), with five trainers and five RBs
Russia: Russia retains a number of MiG-25 regiments, especially in the reconnaissance role. MiG-25R squadrons were among the last units withdrawn from both Poland and Germany
Syria: Thirty MiG-25Ps are augmented by some five MiG-25PUs and six MiG-25RBs
Ukraine: MiG-25RBs and other recce variants serve with the 48th RAP at Kolomyya, while MiG-25PDs serve with the Air Defence Force's 933rd IAP at Dnepropetrovsk (Voloskoye)

Mikoyan-Gurevich MiG-25BM 'Foxbat-F'

The **MiG-25BM** is a dedicated defence suppression aircraft, based on the airframe of the MiG-25RB and designed for high-level, long-range, stand-off, anti-radar missions. This unusual approach was chosen because the traditional 'low down and dirty' close-in tactics used by American 'Wild Weasel' defence suppression aircraft were felt to impose an unacceptable and unnecessary degree of vulnerability. Development began in 1972, and the aircraft was produced between 1982 and 1985.

The primary armament of the MiG-25BM is the Kh-58 (NATO AS-11 'Kilter'), four of which are carried on the underwing pylons.

The 'Kilter' is a conventional-looking anti-radiation missile, with cruciform clipped-delta wings and smaller moving tailfins of similar shape. The missile has a passive radar-homing head, a 129-kg (285-lb) blast fragmentation warhead, and a solid fuel rocket motor which gives a range in excess of 30 miles (48 km). The new anti-radar Kh-31 may be a suitable replacement, offering higher speed and a longer reach.

MiG-25BMs observed in service have their noses painted to represent the radomes of fighter MiG-25s, and when the first photos of the aircraft emerged this led some Western analysts to assume that a large nose radar was fitted. More recent photos show that a MiG-25R-type nose is fitted, with similar flush dielectric antennas on the sides. It is now almost certain that these cover passive emitter location devices. The aircraft often carry the huge (5300-litre; 1,400-US gal) underfuselage auxiliary fuel tanks often associated with the MiG-25PD 'Foxbat-E'.

Clad in partial pressure suits, the crew of a MiG-25BM stand in front of their high-altitude defence suppression aircraft. The nose is painted to simulate an AI radome.

Mikoyan MiG-27 'Flogger-D/-J'

Because it was seen by Western intelligence agencies first, the **MiG-27** was for many years regarded as the first ground attack derivative of the 'Flogger' family, and the MiG-23B variants were regarded as later, less sophisticated, cheaper versions. In fact, the MiG-23B/BN/BK/BM were interim types which filled the gap until the definitive MiG-27 could enter service. The earlier aircraft actually gained a later NATO codename because it was not recorded by Western observers until after the MiG-27, largely because it had never reached squadron service with the front-line Group of Soviet Forces in Germany, where Soviet tactical aircraft were usually first sighted.

The MiG-27 designation was originally applied to a number of clean-sheet-of-paper studies drawn up by the Mikoyan OKB to meet the requirement eventually fulfilled by the Su-25. During the 1950s and 1960s the advent of the tactical nuclear weapon had apparently removed the need for dedicated close-support aircraft, Frontal Aviation instead relying on supersonic fighter-bombers delivering single weapons against troop concentrations, bridges or other high-value targets. US experience in Vietnam showed the limitations of such aircraft when forced to operate with conventional weapons, and the *Shturmovik* role was rediscovered. The September 1967 Exercise Dneipr showed that the elderly subsonic MiG-17 was a more effective conventional close air support/battlefield air interdiction aircraft than the MiG-21 or Su-7, although the supersonic fighters clearly had a role to play in attacking targets farther behind enemy lines. The OKB simultaneously worked on two designs under the MiG-27 designation, drawing up a subsonic **MiG-27Sh** (similar in configuration to the Anglo-French Jaguar) and a supersonic delta-winged MiG-27. In the event Sukhoi produced the Su-25 to fulfil the *Shturmovik* role, and financial considerations forced the OKB to produce a MiG-23-based fighter-bomber reusing the MiG-27 designation.

The new aircraft featured simplified, but slightly larger, 'bulged' air intakes, without the large variable intake ramps of previous 'Flogger' variants. The simplified two-position afterburner nozzle is externally similar to the nozzle fitted to MiG-23BMs and BKs. These modifications improve fuel economy and dramatically reduce weight, at the expense of absolute top speed performance. To improve the aircraft's warload, an extra (seventh) hardpoint was added on the centreline, and the original underfuselage

pylons were moved out to the intake ducts to allow wider stores to be carried. The two pylons on the sides of the rear fuselage, behind the main undercarriage, first fitted on the MiG-23B series, were retained, and may have been stressed to carry heavier stores. They are seldom used, however, since they impose a limit on the amount of fuel that can be carried because of centre of gravity considerations. A new six-barrelled GSh-6-30 30-mm cannon with 260 rounds of ammunition replaced the 23-mm cannon, which had often been described as inadequate for strafing ground targets and which carried only 200 rounds. The new mounting imposed a greater drag penalty than a podded gun, but had some advantages. Access for armourers and maintenance personnel was improved, and the risk of dangerous gases building up within the fuselage was completely avoided.

Further cannon armament can be added in underwing pods, including the UPK-23 23-mm cannon pod and the SPPU-22 gun pod that contains a 23-mm cannon with barrels which can be depressed for strafing ground targets in level flight. The full range of guided and unguided bombs and rockets

can be carried, including the new KMG-U bomblet dispenser and various tactical nuclear weapons. Mikoyan is not coy about this capability, listing the option between references to 500-kg (1,102-lb) bombs and napalm tanks. The aircraft can also be used in the tactical reconnaissance role, and some front-line Soviet MiG-27s have been

The original MiG-27K introduced a laser rangefinder in the nose, but retained the undernose 'Swift Rod' ILS antenna.

photographed with a reconnaissance pod on the starboard under-intake pylon. Plans are afoot to add a measure of defence suppres-

Above: The MiG-27 usually uses a single cruciform brake chute, as seen here. The MiG-27 can operate from rough, semi-prepared strips, thanks to its variable-geometry wing and strong undercarriage.

Left: Wearing a Guards badge on the intake, and carrying an unidentified pod below the starboard intake (perhaps a guidance/ datalink pod for an ASM?), a Lärz-based, yellow-coded MiG-27D 'Flogger-J' taxis in after a mission.

sion capability, with the Kh-31 anti-radar missile having been spotted on some test and trials aircraft. Heavier than any other 'Flogger' variant, the MiG-27 required a redesigned undercarriage and large, high-pressure tyres. This necessitated the provision of new bulged main undercarriage doors.

The original MiG-27 and similar **MiG-27K 'Flogger-D'** were ordered into production directly off the drawing board, and the prototype (a converted MiG-23BM airframe) made its maiden flight during 1972 in the hands of Valery Menitsky, later to become OKB chief test pilot. Early examples were soon in service with the Group of Soviet Forces in Germany, equipping regiments at Mirow, Finsterwalde and Altenburg. Eventually, the MiG-27 equipped four of the 16th Air Army's fighter-bomber regiments, at Lärz, Grossenhain, Finsterwalde and Brand. The MiG-27 also served with the 59th Air Army in Hungary. The 'straight' MiG-27 (perhaps delivered without cannon armament) was very soon replaced by the MiG-27K, equipped with the PrNK-23K nav/attack system and a Fone laser rangefinder/target tracker mounted behind a small window in the nose. The MiG-27K was capable of automatic night or bad weather blind bombing with a very high degree of accuracy. RWR and ECM equipment is highly automated, and a new stores management system gives the pilot greater flexibility in selecting and using weapons.

There are several sub-variants of the aircraft known to NATO as **'Flogger-J'**, all equipped with the PrNK-23M nav/attack system, and 'Pelenga' weapons system giving compatability with PGMs and guided ASMs. All have wing glove bullet fairings removed and with extended wing leading-edge root extensions. The latter were added to serve as a location for the forward hemisphere RWR antennas, but also have the beneficial side effect of improving high-Alpha handling. All 'Flogger-Js' have a new Klen (maple) laser rangefinder in place of the MiG-27K's Fone unit. The 'Swift Rod' ILS antenna was moved from below the nose to the port side of the nose, opposite the pitot. Maximum take-off weight is increased to 20670 kg (45,569 lb).

There is some confusion as to the Soviet designations of some of the aircraft. The first of the 'Flogger-Js' was the new-build **MiG-27M**, which has an enlarged laser window in the nose, below a dielectric 'pimple' which protrudes forward from its upper 'lip'. Some externally identical aircraft (reportedly produced through conversion of ordinary MiG-27s) allegedly bear the Soviet air force designation **MiG-27D**. This variant incorporates the RSBN-6S navigation system, which is associated with the nuclear strike role. The twin pitot probes which serve the nav/attack system are mounted

high on the nose, providing the main recognition features between the basic MiG-27D/ MiG-27K 'Flogger-J' and the **MiG-27K 'Flogger-J2'**. The latter variant was produced as a new-build aircraft, and by conversion of MiG-27s, MiG-27Ds and perhaps MiG-27Ms. It has a noticeable fairing below the nose, with a broad rectangular window for a FLIR system, and an upper window for the laser target designator. The new system is a member of the Kaira family, equivalent to the equipment used on the Su-24M. The twin pitots are mounted low on the nose and the 'pimple' radome is enlarged.

The Soviet Union exported its most capable bombers and strike aircraft only to a handful of its most-trusted Warsaw Pact allies and a few most-favoured client states. Thus, like the Su-24 'Fencer', the MiG-27 has not been made widely available to foreign customers. The only exception so far has been India, which actually builds the MiG-27 under licence, operating a version which it calls the MiG-27M or **Bahadur** (Valiant), but which Mikoyan refers to as the **MiG-27L**. The aircraft has the same nose contours as the MiG-27M/D, with only a single window in the undernose fairing, and shares the same 'Flogger-J' reporting name, and not the 'Flogger-J2' reporting name of the MiG-27K. The first Indian-assembled example was rolled out in October 1984, and the first MiG-27L using Indian-built sub-assemblies was rolled out on 11 January 1986. India's requirement is for 165 aircraft to equip six squadrons, five of which had formed by the end of 1992. All are now operational with the type.

The MiG-27 received its baptism of fire in Afghanistan where a regiment of MiG-27Ds was deployed to Shindand for offensive operations against Mujahideen guerrilla positions. Flying their first mission on 31 October 1987, the MiG-27s flew intensively until withdrawn on 15 February 1989. Over-wing chaff/flare dispensers were hurriedly fitted as a result of this combat experience. The MiG-27 is said to be much more capa-

ble than its main rival, the Su-17M-4 'Fitter-K', but its more demanding handling characteristics, relative fragility and less easy maintenance reportedly make it less popular. The drawdown in defence spending following the end of the Cold War has affected Russia as much as any other nation, and the MiG-23BN and MiG-27 are likely to be casualties of the current policy of reducing the number of different aircraft types in service, which will see older single-engined types like the MiG-27 and Su-17 replaced by newer, twin-engined aircraft like the Su-24, MiG-29 and Su-27.

SPECIFICATION

Mikoyan MiG-27 'Flogger-D'

Wing: span 13.97 m (45 ft 9.8 in) spread and 7.78 m (25 ft 6.25 in) swept; aspect ratio 5.22 spread and 1.77 swept; area 37.35 m² (402.05 sq ft) spread and 34.16 m² (367.71 sq ft) swept
Fuselage and tail: length 17.08 m (56 ft 0.25 in) including probe; height 5.00 m (16 ft 5 in); tailplane span 5.75 m (18 ft 10.25 in); wheel track 2.66 m (8 ft 8.75 in); wheel base 5.772 m (18 ft 11.25 in)
Powerplant: one MNPK 'Soyuz' (Tumanskii) R-29B-300 turbojet rated at 78.45 kN (17,637 lb st) dry and 112.77 kN (25,353 lb st) with afterburning
Weights: empty equipped 11908 kg (26,252 lb); normal take-off 18100 kg (39,903 lb); maximum take-off 20300 kg (44,753 lb)
Fuel and load: internal fuel 4560 kg (10,053 lb); external fuel up to three 790-litre (209-US gal) drop tanks; maximum ordnance more than 4000 kg (8,818 lb)
Speed: maximum level speed 'clean' at 8000 m (26,245 ft) 1885 km/h (1,017 kt; 1,170 mph) or at sea level 1350 km/h (728 kt; 839 mph)
Range: combat radius 540 km (291 nm; 335 miles) on a lo-lo-lo attack mission with two Kh-29 ASMs and three drop tanks, or 225 km (121 nm; 140 miles) with two Kh-29 ASMs
Performance: maximum rate of climb at sea level 12000 m (39,370 ft) per minute; service ceiling 14000 m (45,930 ft); take-off run 950 m (3,117 ft) at maximum take-off weight; landing run 1300 m (4,265 ft) at normal landing weight without brake

chute or 900 m (2,953 ft) at normal landing weight with brake chute
g limits: +7.0

OPERATORS

Byelorussia: Five MiG-27s are believed to be in service in Byelorussia, though they may be scrapped to comply with CFE limitations
India: MiG-27s serve with Nos 2, 9, 18, 22, 31 and 222 Squadrons, which are nominally based at Hindan, Halwara and Hashimara. India has ordered 165, progressively incorporating more and more local content (and eventually being fully licence-built) to replace the Su-7, Marut and Ajeet
Kazakhstan: The 11th Fighter-Bomber Division augments its Su-24 strike regiment with two MiG-27 units, the 129th IBAP at Taldy Kurgan and the 134th IBAP at Zhang Iztobe
Turkmenistan: MiG-27s were among the aircraft offered for sale by Turkmenistan, and probably will not be among the 32 aircraft retained for the air arm's planned single fighter regiment
Russia: The MiG-27M remains in service in significant numbers, although it is being rapidly withdrawn from use to comply with CFE treaty limitations and to allow the air force to standardise on more modern, twin-engined tactical aircraft. Large numbers of MiG-27s were withdrawn to European Russia and the Far East from both Hungary (regiments at Debrecen and Kunmadaras) and East Germany (the 19th IBAP at Lärz, the 116th IBAP at Brand, the 296th IBAP at Grossenhain and the 339th at Finsterwalde), joining significant numbers of regiments already based in Russia
Ukraine: In 1992 Ukraine tried to sell 27 surplus MiG-27Ks for $16 million each, at which time it had 49 of these aircraft on strength, all reportedly withdrawn from front-line service and held at the 117th Aircraft Repair Factory at Lvov, the 562nd Aircraft Repair Factory at Odessa or, more ominously, at the 6221st Aircraft Destruction Base
Uzbekistan: A regiment of MiG-27s at Chirchik has been used to support government forces engaged in the civil war in neighbouring Tadjikistan and remains under central CIS control

Mikoyan MiG-29 'Fulcrum-A' (9-12)

Comparisons between the **MiG-29** (initially allocated the internal OKB designation **9-12**) and the American Lockheed (General Dynamics) F-16 are perhaps inevitable, since both fulfil the same broad tactical fighter role, both are extremely agile high-performance aircraft optimised for dogfighting, both have been widely exported, and both were designed to meet requirements for a 'lightweight fighter'.

The MiG-29 which is recognised today was derived from a study for a heavier fighter (also designated MiG-29) designed to counter the F-15 under the Perspektivnyi Frontovoi Istrebeitel ('prospective frontal fighter') competition. The Mikoyan OKB proposed following the US example, with both heavy and light fighters complementing each other to meet the requirement. Its arguments were accepted and the requirement was redrafted to cover two quite separate aircraft. The new Soviet air forces' requirement for a Logkii Frontovoi Istrebityel ('lightweight front-line fighter') was issued in 1972, and Mikoyan successfully submitted a smaller version of the original design, the **MiG-29D** (Dubler – double), while Sukhoi submitted the T-10 proposal to meet the Tyazholyi Frontovoi Istrebityel requirement.

The new Soviet air force LFI requirement detailed a replacement for Frontal Aviation's MiG-21s and MiG-23s, Su-7s and Su-17s. The new fighter was to be capable of destroying enemy fighters in air combat, destroying enemy bombers and reconnaissance aircraft, and escorting friendly bombers and attack aircraft. The aircraft would also have an important secondary ground attack role. A production order was placed at the same time as the Technical Assignment was issued, meaning that the MiG-29 never received an in-house I- ('Ye-') designation.

The increasing importance of low-level penetration by attack aircraft made lookdown/shoot-down capability vital, while the growing importance of ECM made a capacity for independent action similarly important. The aircraft was from the start designed to be able to beat the new generation of US fighters (the F-14, F-15, YF-16 and YF-17) in air combat, and to restore the tarnished reputation of Soviet fighters incurred by heavy losses in the Middle East. Finally, a measure of rough-field/dispersed site capability was felt to be essential. Detailed design work began in 1974, the year that the F-15 entered service and that the YF-16 first flew.

While the MiG-29's configuration is superficially similar to those of the F-14, F-15, YF-17 and Su-27, it is different in many important ways, although common problems make some common solutions inevitable. Starting with a blended high-lift, low-drag wing and forebody, Mikoyan added twin canted fins, widely flared wing leading-edge root extensions and widely spaced twin engines with carefully tailored intakes to maximise high angle-of-attack capability. The original MiG-29 had been broadly similar, but with a faired-in MiG-25-type cockpit and with MiG-25-type engine intakes on each side of a conventional fuselage, with no inter-engine tunnel.

While some have criticised the MiG-29 for its supposedly crude finish in places, there can be no doubt that its aerodynamic design is extremely advanced, giving unmatched low-speed and high-Alpha handling characteristics, which can be invaluable

The earliest production MiG-29s had ventral fins below the vertical fins and tailplanes, and lacked the fin leading-edge extension chaff/flare dispensers fitted to later MiG-29s. These early aircraft were retrofitted with broad-chord rudders and pitot-mounted vortex generators after entry into service.

Above: Trailing its distinctive cruciform drag chute, a MiG-29 lands at Rissala during an exchange visit to Finland during 1986. The aircraft represents the initial definitive production standard. It has no ventral fins, and has narrow-chord rudders and an undernose 'Swift Rod' ILS antenna, but does have the fin leading-edge flare dispensers.

Right: The very first production series MiG-29s had an unusual debris deflector ahead of the nosewheels. Some are still used for trials, like this aircraft, which has a MiG-29M-type embedded radio compass antenna in the canopy.

in a 'close-in' engagement. The electro-mechanical flight control system has no 'hard limits', allowing the pilot briefly to override pitch and g limiters when tactically necessary, by deliberately pulling through a stick stop to enter that area of the flight envelope where departure becomes progressively more likely. Ample aerodynamic warning is given before the aircraft departs. When it does, the MiG-29 is reluctant to spin and recovers when pro-spin controls are released. Sophisticated aileron/rudder interconnects gradually phase out aileron at increasing angles of attack.

Flying controls are mainly conventional, and are hydraulically controlled. Computer-controlled full-span manoeuvre flaps occupy the wing leading edge, with plain flaps inboard and ailerons outboard on the trailing edge. The horizontal tail surfaces are all-moving.

To allow the aircraft to operate from primitive forward airfields, the low-mounted intakes are fitted with large doors that close on start-up, open only after the aircraft has rotated on take-off, and close again when the mainwheels touch on landing. These prevent the ingestion of mud, snow or other debris. While the main intakes are closed, air is drawn in through spring-loaded louvres in the top of the wingroots. Flight is possible at speeds of up to 800 km/h (432 kt; 500 mph) with the main intakes closed.

The MiG-29 broke much new ground for Mikoyan, with advanced aerodynamics, avionics, systems and even materials. The new aircraft made extensive use of advanced, lightweight aluminium-lithium alloys, which allowed fewer fasteners and bolts to be used, with savings in weight and production complexity. The operational life of the MiG-29

airframe, however, is believed to be significantly shorter than equivalent Western aircraft types.

The MiG-29 is powered by a pair of Sargisov (Leningrad/Klimov, formerly Isotov) RD-33 afterburning turbofans. These produce considerably more augmented thrust than equivalent Western aircraft types, but slightly less in dry power. This can make the aircraft more reliant on using afterburner in some circumstances, increasing fuel consumption. The latest versions of the engine have a full-authority digital engine-control system, and a sophisticated stall prevention/relight system. The engine is understood to have a four-stage fan (with fixed stator vanes) and a nine-stage high-pressure compressor (with variable stators on the first three stages). The time between overhauls is reportedly 350 hours.

This quartet of Indian MiG-29s is drawn from Nos 28 and 47 Squadrons. Coloured tail units are used to differentiate friend from foe during non-dissimilar air combat training. Each aircraft carries an R-60 AA-8 'Aphid' acquisition round.

Eleven prototypes (9-01 to 9-11) were built, the first flying initially on 6 October 1977. Two of them were lost in engine-related accidents. Spotted by a US satellite at Ramenskoye in November 1977, the aircraft was allocated the provisional reporting name **'Ram-L'**. The prototypes were followed by eight pre-production aircraft (9-12 to 9-19). Frontal Aviation evaluation commenced in 1983, and the aircraft began to enter service soon afterwards, initially with the Kubinka and Ros regiments. Early reliability problems were soon solved, and MTBF figures rose from 2.3 hours to 5.7 hours by 1988, while mission-capable rates rose from 65 per cent to 90 per cent over the same period.

The 'bald' MiG-29 designation covers most of the single-seat fighters delivered so far, although a host of improvements have been incorporated, some of them giving the aircraft involved a distinctive appearance and which might have been expected to lead to allocation of a new service designation (see **'Fulcrum-C'** entry). Small ventral fins, initially fitted to the prototype after its first flight, were deleted after a small batch of production aircraft (probably about 100) had been completed, at the same time as overwing chaff/flare dispensers were fitted in extensions to the tailfin leading edges. Extended-chord rudders and pitot-mounted vortex generators were adopted in the late 1980s, and were retrofitted to all service aircraft (including some of the earliest standard ventral-finned machines which remained in use even in 1994).

In the fighter role, the MiG-29 carries six underwing missiles, with two BVR R-27R/AKU-470 AA-10 'Alamo-As' inboard (usually both semi-active radar homing, but sometimes with one IR-homing 'Alamo-B') and four R-60/AA-8 'Aphid' or AA-11 'Archer' short-range IR-homing AAMs outboard. These are backed up by an internal lightweight GSh-301 single-barrelled 30-mm cannon, which replaced a twin-barrelled weapon on the first prototype.

The fire-control system is a sophisticated sensor, with data gathered by the aircraft's sensors being datalinked to a ground station or AWACS aircraft. The radar is extremely powerful and can easily overwhelm the pilot with information, and filtering and software techniques are inadequate for on-board threat prioritisation. The need to keep contact with an external agency limits the MiG pilot's capacity for independent action, and imposes a degree of inflexibility. ('Freelance' operations and independent search are, however, seen as desirable, and are stressed much more in current doctrine.)

The MiG-29 has two sensors for target acquisition. The first is the N-019 pulse-Doppler radar, which has previously been misidentified as the HO-93, the HO-193 and the NO-193, confusion arising because the Cyrillic letter 'H' is in fact an English 'N', and the '3' is an 'E' (for export), and because on a Farnborough demonstrator a hyphen was misplaced. The radar is known to NATO as 'Slot Back'. A measure of passive target acquisition capability is afforded by the IRST, which has a collimated laser rangefinder. This can be used to detect, track and engage a target while leaving the radar in a passive (non-emitting) mode, ready to be 'turned on' if contact is lost (if the target goes into cloud, for instance) or to fire a semi-active radar-homing missile. All the while, the target aircraft's RWR will not detect the MiG-29's unwelcome attentions.

For close-in engagements, a helmet-mounted sight (which works by sensing the pilot's head position) can be used to cue IR-homing missiles onto an off-boresight target. This is extremely useful in conjunction with the very agile R-73 (AA-11 'Archer') AAM, although firing at an angle well off the nose dramatically reduces missile range.

Primarily designed for fighter/air superiority duties, the MiG-29 nonetheless has an important secondary ground attack role. It is therefore able to carry a variety of bombs, rockets and missiles on the inboard and central underwing pylons, although the outboard pylons are believed to be reserved for the carriage of R-60 (AA-8 'Aphid') or R-73 IR-homing AAMs. Many Frontal Aviation MiG-29 regiments are believed to incorporate a nuclear strike squadron, whose aircraft can carry a single 30-kT RN-40 nuclear bomb on the port inboard pylon. A handful of MiG-29 regiments have even been assigned a primary air-to-ground role, including at least one of the units now under Ukrainian command. For ferrying, fuel tanks can be carried under the inboard

A Soviet air force MiG-29 undergoes servicing; with its radome removed, the unusual twist-cassegrain antenna of the 'Fulcrum's' N-019 'Slot Back' radar is revealed. The MiG-29 is remarkably maintainable but operators have to suffer a short time-between-overhauls, plus poor after-sales support and spares availability.

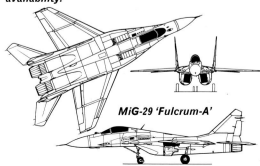

MiG-29 'Fulcrum-A'

Mikoyan MiG-29 'Fulcrum-A' (9-12)

A Czech MiG-29 reefs into a 'burner climb. The Czechoslovakian and East German air forces had their MiG-29s delivered in brown and green camouflage, applied to only a handful of Soviet MiG-29s. The Czech Republic is selling the MiG-29s it inherited on the division of Czechoslovakia.

underwing pylons, augmenting the tank carried on the centreline, which is stressed to 9 *g*.

About 450 'Fulcrums' are estimated to be in service with the VVS (more than 300 were in service with the Soviet air forces in East Germany alone during 1990), with 50 more in AV-MF service. Byelorussia, Kazakhstan, Moldova and Ukraine account for some 350 more. An estimated 380 have been delivered to export customers. Total production, including UBs and 'Fulcrum-Cs', probably stands at 1,250-1,350.

The Moscow Aircraft Production Organisation is presently offering a programme of modifications to MiG-29 operators that is aimed at improving the aircraft's combat potential. This programme would bring any 'Fulcrum-A' to virtual MiG-29S or MiG-29SE standard. These variants are described separately under the 9-13 'Fulcrum-C' entry. The modifications include making the inboard underwing pylons compatible with a pair of 1150-litre (304-US gal) fuel tanks (this modification has already been applied to some 40 per cent of Russian MiG-29s, including the factory demonstrators and most of those aircraft based in Germany and Hungary). Other improvements include the provision of compatibility with the new

This MiG-29 wears old-style Yugoslav markings, which have been replaced on some aircraft by a horizontally banded roundel on the intake (blue, white and red, descending) and a similar fin flash on the tail.

R-77 (AAM-AE) active radar homing missile and simultaneous two-target engagement capability. The flight control system is modified to allow the aircraft to reach higher angles of attack (30°+), and Western navaids can be installed. A new radio with the standard international emergency frequency of 243 MHz is also provided. Finally, the inboard underwing pylons are restressed for the carriage of up to four 500-kg (1,102-lb) bombs each, in tandem side-by-side pairs.

MAPO hopes to offer a retrofitted in-flight-refuelling probe, a ground mapping radar mode and compatibility with anti-radar, TV- and laser-guided ASMs in 1995.

WEAPON OPTIONS

In service, the MiG-29 is used primarily in the air-to-air fighter role. Its primary BVR armament is the R-27 (AA-10 'Alamo'), two of which may be carried on the inboard underwing pylons. The 'Fulcrum' usually carries the short-burn semi-active radar-homing R-27R ('Alamo-A') sometimes with one example of the similar IR-homing R-27T ('Alamo-B'), or sometimes as a pair of semi-active radar-homing missiles. The 'Fulcrum' is believed to be compatible with later long-burn versions of the R-27, but these have not been noted in released photographs and may have been given to long-range PVO interceptor Su-27s as a priority. Early reports that the MiG-29 could carry the AA-9 'Amos' are completely unfounded. When it first entered service, the MiG-29 usually carried R-60 (AA-8 'Aphid') short-range IR-homing missiles on the centre and outboard underwing pylons, but these have largely been replaced by the more capable R-73 RM2D (AA-11 'Archer'), a short-range IR-homing dogfight missile of exceptional agility, which has been rated by some experts as being superior to any Western equivalent. Some MiG-29s, especially those supplied to Warsaw Pact export customers, have been seen with 'cheap' AA-8s outboard, a pair of AA-11s on the centre pylons and AA-10s inboard. Some foreign customers (Cuba, Iran, Iraq and Syria, for example) may not have received AA-11s at all. In the future, MiG-29s will probably receive the active-homing R-77 ('AMRAAMski'), if it enters service, but

this will require some modifications. In the fighter-bomber role, MiG-29s have been seen carrying the B-8W 20-round 80-mm rocket pod and the older UV-32-57 32-round 57-mm rocket pod on inboard and/or centre underwing pylons. The S-24 240-mm rocket can be carried singly on the same pylons. The MiG-29 is believed to be compatible with the B-13 five-round 130-mm rocket pod, although use of this pod has not yet been confirmed. 'Fulcrum' ground attack weapons which can be confirmed include FAB-250ShN and -500ShN, FAB-250M-46 and -500M-46 and FAB-250M-62 and -500M-62 general-purpose bombs, and a range of specialised weapons. These included cluster bombs like the RBK-250 and -500, containing AO-2.5 RTM fragmentation munitions, BETAB concrete penetrators, PTAB-1M anti-armour munitions, ShOAB-0.5 anti-personnel mines, or SPBE anti-armour bomblets. The reusable KMGU-2 sub-munition dispenser carries AO-2.5 fragmentation bombs, which are dispensed through the container's rotary doors downwards, or to either side, depending on how the KMGU-2 container is mounted. BETAB-250 or -500 concrete-piercing bombs, BRAB-200, -220 and -500 armour-piercing bombs, FOZAB-500 incendiary bombs, ODAB-500 FAE bombs, and the deadly OFZAB-500 fragmentation/incendiary bomb are also compatible with the MiG-29.

SPECIFICATION

Mikoyan MiG-29 'Fulcrum-A'
Wing: span 11.36 m (37 ft 3.25 in); aspect ratio 3.4; wing area 38.00 m² (409.04 sq ft)
Fuselage and tail: length 17.32 m (56 ft 9.85 in) including probe; height 4.73 m (15 ft 6.2 in); tailplane span 7.78 m (25 ft 6.25 in); wheel track 3.10 m (10 ft 2 in); wheel base 3.67 m (12 ft 0.5 in)
Powerplant: two Klimov/Leningrad (Isotov/Sarkisov) RD-33 augmented turbofans each rated at 49.42 kN (11,111 lb st) dry and 81.39 kN (18,298 lb st) with afterburning
Weights: operating empty 10900 kg (24,030 lb); normal take-off 15240 kg (33,598 lb); maximum take-off 18500 kg (40,785 lb)
Fuel and load: internal fuel 3200 kg (7,055 lb) 4300-4365 litres (1,136-1,153 US gal); external fuel one 1500-1520 litre (396-402 US gal) centreline tank and (on some Soviet aircraft) two 1150-litre (303-US gal) underwing ferry tanks; maximum ordnance 3000 kg (6,614 lb)
Speed: maximum level speed 'clean' at 11000 m (36,090 ft) 2445 km/h (1,319 kt; 1,519 mph) or at sea level 1500 km/h (810 kt; 932 mph)
Range: ferry range 2100 km (1,134 nm; 1,305 miles) with three tanks; range 1500 km (810 nm; 932 miles) with internal fuel
Performance: maximum rate of climb at sea level 19800 m (64,961 ft) per minute; service ceiling 17000 m (55,775 ft); take-off run 250 m (820 ft) at normal take-off weight; landing run 600 m (1,969 ft) at normal landing weight with brake-chute
g limits: +9 below Mach 0.85 and +7 above Mach 0.85

An Iraqi MiG-29 takes off before Desert Storm. Iraqi 'Fulcrum' strength was severely depleted by the Gulf War, with losses in air-to-air combat and on the ground to coalition airfield attacks, together with the non-return of aircraft which fled to Iran for sanctuary.

OPERATORS

Afghanistan: Before the fall of the Kabul regime, there were negotiations for the supply of MiG-29s
Byelorussia: At least one MiG-29 regiment has been based in Byelorussia, at Minsk for many years, and this has been joined by the 787th IAP from Finow in Germany, which withdrew to Ros. A further regiment is based at Baranovich
Bulgaria: The MiG-29 equips two fighter regiments at Rawnetz and Jambol. An estimated 22 (including four two-seaters) were delivered in 1990
China: There are persistent reports that China intends ordering MiG-29s to augment its Su-27s. It has already bought RD-33 engines to upgrade its J-7s
Cuba: An initial batch of seven MiG-29s was delivered to San Antonio de los Banos during 1990. Deliveries are believed to have reached about 16 aircraft. A requirement for 36 MiG-29s is unlikely to be fulfilled
Czechoslovakia: Eighteen MiG-29s and two MiG-29UBs were delivered to Czechoslovakia for the 11th Fighter Regiment at Zatec. Delivery of the rest of the 40-aircraft order was halted by economic problems. On the division of Czechoslovakia, the MiG-29s were divided evenly between the new Czech and Slovak Republics
Czech Republic: With only nine MiG-29s and a single UB (since written off) remaining after the split with Slovakia, the Czech Republic assessed that this was not sufficient to form a viable unit and moved the aircraft from Zatec to Ceske Budejovice to join the air arm's MiG-23s. It was eventually decided to sell the MiG-29s to Slovakia, Israel or Iraq, and the aircraft were grounded from 1 July 1994 pending disposal
Germany: Twenty MiG-29s and four MiG-29UBs were delivered to the first and second *Staffeln* of JFG 3 'Vladimir Komarov' at Preschen from May 1988. An order for 32 more MiG-29s was cancelled after reunification, on payment of a massive penalty clause. The aircraft were absorbed into the Luftwaffe (as a redesignated single-*Staffel* JG-3) and will eventually move to Laage to join a squadron of Phantoms as JG 73. MiG-29s also flew with WTD 61 for evaluation and trials, and some aircraft were loaned to friendly air forces for evaluation. A front-line fighter squadron, JG 3 has also operated successfully as an adversary unit, and was heavily involved in preparing coalition aircrew for Operation Desert Storm
Hungary: Twenty-two MiG-29s and six MiG-29UBs were delivered to Hungary in lieu of debt repayments from October 1993. These will re-equip the 'Puma' and 'Wasp' squadrons of the Kécskemet-based Vitez Szenfgyörgyi Deszo Regiment, and will be declared operational in September 1994
India: An initial batch of 45 single-seat MiG-29s (sometimes referred to as MiG-29Bs) and five UBs (not 42 single-seaters and eight UBs reported elsewhere)

was delivered to equip Nos 28 and 47 Squadrons at Poona. A second batch of 20 MiG-29s (all single-seaters) went to No. 223 Squadron at the same base. An attrition/top-up batch of 10 aircraft has now reportedly been ordered, and an order for up to 30 MiG-29Ms is under consideration

Iran: Iran received 14 MiG-29s in 1990, and gained either four or eight more when Iraqi aircraft fled to Iran for sanctuary during Desert Storm

Iraq: An estimated 36 MiG-29s (of some 50 delivered) survived the Gulf War, though spares shortages and the withdrawal of Russian advisors leave their status in some doubt. Five were shot down during Desert Storm and one during Southern Watch, and others were destroyed on the ground. Iraq claims that eight MiG-29s fled to Iran, while Iran admits to receiving four

Kazakhstan: Air force units in Kazakhstan remain under CIS (Russian) command and control and include the 715th IAP with MiG-29s at Lugovaya

Kyrgizia: The independent republic of Kyrgizia declared its sovereignty over Frunze-Lygovaya near the capital at Rishkek. This was used for MiG-29 conversion training for pilots from foreign customer nations and may have a based regiment

Malaysia: Malaysia has ordered 18 MiG-29s (including six two-seaters) which are expected to be variants of the MiG-29S, although pre-conditions set by the Malaysians would seem to exclude anything less capable than the MiG-29M

Moldova: Moldova took over some 34 MiG-29s from the 86th IAP (an AVMF fighter regiment) but had only four MiG-29-qualified pilots. The aircraft were used in bombing attacks on the breakaway Pridnestrovskaya Republic, and one was lost to a SAM. Moldova wishes to exchange its MiGs for more useful attack helicopters and has approached Russia and Romania

Turkmenistan: Turkmenistan includes the Mary training range complex, which may have a based MiG-29 regiment

North Korea: The 57th Fighter Regiment at Onchon operates an estimated 30 MiG-29s (delivered in 1988)

Poland: The first squadron of No. 1 PLM operates nine single-seat MiG-29s and three UBs from its Minsk-Mazowiecki base. These were delivered in 1989 and 1990

Romania: The 57th Fighter Regiment's 2nd Esquadrilla operates 14 single-seat MiG-29s and a pair of UBs from Constanta-Mihail Kogalniceanu. These were delivered in 1989

Russia: A number of MiG-29 regiments are based in Russia. The 234th 'Proskurovskii' Guards IAP at Kubinka includes one expanded squadron of MiG-29s (of almost regimental strength and including the 'Swifts' aerobatic team). Other Russia-based regiments include the 176th IAP at Ruslan AB, Tskhakaya, and another at Primorsko-Akhtarsk. Six of the eight MiG-29 regiments formerly based in Germany have also returned to bases in Russia, the other two flying to bases in Byelorussia

and Ukraine. The 33rd IAP at Wittstock and the 733rd IAP at Pütnitz-Damgarten returned to Anreapol, while the 31st 'Nilopolskyi' Guards IAP from Alt Lonnewitz returned to Zernograd. The destinations of the 35th IAP from Zerbst, the 73rd 'Sevastapolski' IAP from Merseburg and the 968th Guards IAP from Altenburg are unknown. The 19th Guards Fighter-Bomber Regiment replaced its MiG-27s with MiG-29s when it returned from Germany and is based at Milerovo near Rostov. At least 14 regiments were equipped with the 'Fulcrum-A' by 1989

Serbia: Serbia inherited all 14 MiG-29s and both MiG-29UBs from the former Yugoslavia. These still equip the 204th Fighter Regiment's 127th Fighter Squadron at Batajnica, near Belgrade

Slovakia: Slovakia took over nine single-seat MiG-29s and a single UB on the division of Czechoslovakia. These were assigned to the 1st Fighter Regiment's 1st Fighter Squadron at Sliac and have been augmented by five ex-Ukrainian MiG-29s (including a single UB). Slovakia may buy further MiG-29s (from the Czech Republic or from Ukraine) or may take more from Russia in lieu of debt repayments

Syria: Twenty-four MiG-29s delivered in 1987 have reportedly been joined by two or three further batches of 24 aircraft each, and some 50 more are on order

Ukraine: The Ukrainian air force controls three air armies, with 185 MiG-29s in four regiments. The 5th Air Army, headquartered at Odessa, controls the 85th

IAP at Starokonstantinov (which returned from Köthen in Germany) and the 642nd IBAP (a fighter-bomber unit) at Marlynovskoye, while the Lvov-headquartered 14th Air Army includes the 114th IAP at Ivano-Frankovsk. The autonomous air defence force's Western Region includes the 92nd IAP at Mukochevo. A handful of aircraft have been sold (e.g. to Slovakia). More MiG-29s are based at Mirgorod and Valsilkov

USA: The USAF evaluated two or three MiG-29s borrowed from the Luftwaffe, and there have been reports that secondhand MiG-29s may be procured for adversary training and tactics development

Yugoslavia: Fourteen single-seat MiG-29s and two UBs were delivered to the the 204th Fighter Regiment's 127th Fighter Squadron at Batajnica, near Belgrade, during October 1987 (see under Serbia)

Zimbabwe: A 1987 £125 million order for 12 MiG-29s was reportedly allowed to lapse

Others: The MiG-29 has been evaluated by Finland, Jordan, South Korea, Switzerland and a number of other nations. In Finland and Switzerland the MiG-29 lost out to the F/A-18, largely through its perceived lack of support infrastructure, and Jordan was unable to fund its intended purchase. A Taiwanese order was reportedly refused by the Russian government

Mikoyan **MiG-29UB** 'Fulcrum-B' (9-51)

Due to its performance and handling characteristics, the MiG-29 clearly needed a two-seat conversion trainer variant. The extra weight of the second cockpit and the reduction in internal fuel tankage made it operationally limited, so the N-019 radar was deleted. Instead, the **MiG-29UB** (OKB designation **9-51**) trainer has a sophisticated weapons system and emergencies simulator, allowing the instructor to generate appropriate HUD and radar scope symbology in the front cockpit.

To minimise drag, the rear seat is not raised significantly. It was felt that an unobstructed view forward for the instructor was not a priority, with a small retractable periscope making up the deficiency.

The relatively low ratio of two-seat trainers delivered can be explained by the ease

of conversion to the MiG-29 from other Soviet Bloc fighters, and by the practice of converting aircrew from customer nations in the Soviet Union itself. Most operators have a few two-seat aircraft, usually assigned to front-line units.

A MiG-29UB 'Fulcrum-C' trainer wearing East German markings takes off from its Preschen base.

SPECIFICATION

Mikoyan MiG-29UB 'Fulcrum-B'
generally similar to the Mikoyan MiG-29 'Fulcrum-A' except in the following particulars:
Fuselage and tail: length 17.42 m (57 ft 2 in)

NATO allocated the new reporting name 'Fulcrum-C' for aircraft fitted with a bulged and extended spine, which reportedly houses both fuel and avionics, and which may also be applied through retrofit. Internal fuel is increased by provision of a larger No. 1 fuel tank, though different sources disagree as to the size of the increase (75, 130, 175 or 240 litres/20, 34, 46 or 63 US gal, according to different Mikoyan documents). Soviet sources suggest that the 'Fulcrum-C' is still simply designated **MiG-29**, although the nickname 'Gorbatov' (hunchback) is commonly used.

The first 'fatbacked' MiG-29 was **9-13**, the second pre-production aircraft, which first flew on 23 December 1980, in the hands of V. M. Gorbunov. At one time the 'Fulcrum-C' seemed to be slowly replacing the 'Fulcrum-A' in **VVS** service, but the two types continued in production alongside one another and often serve in the same units (occasionally with the very early ventral-finned MiG-29s). Pilots report that apart from endurance, there is no difference in flying/operating characteristics, although some sources suggest that the 'Fulcrum-C' has an enhanced ground attack capability and/or provision for an active jammer. Certainly the 9-13 has redesigned wingtips which appear to accommodate new RWR antennas. No 'hunchbacked' 'Fulcrum-Cs' have been exported yet, though Malaysia's MiG-29s may prove to be based on the 'Fulcrum-C'.

The 9-13 forms the basis of the improved **MiG-29S** (**9-13S**), which was designed as an increased-capability version of the standard MiG-29. According to Mikoyan, the MiG-29S represents "what happened when we squeezed all we could from the basic MiG-29 airframe." The new variant has a modified flight control system, using small computers to improve stability and controllability, and the control surfaces have greater deflection. Alpha and *g* limits are increased. All MiG-29S features can be incorporated by upgrading existing 'Fulcrum-Cs', and MAPO is aggressively marketing a similar upgrade for export 'Fulcrum-As'.

The MiG-29S introduces revised radar/weapons system algorithms and software (and it is believed that processing capacity has been increased) to allow for the simultaneous tracking and engagement of multiple targets. The modified radar is redesignated N-019M. Operational capability has been enhanced by fitting a new sighting system, and more recently by making provision for the active homing AAM-AE 'AMRAAMski'. The first MiG-29S made its maiden flight during 1984, and three prototypes were followed by new production aircraft and conversions. Two *polk* (squadrons) are in service.

The designation **MiG-29SE** has been applied to an export version of the MiG-29S. This has a slightly downgraded radar (the

Right: One of the MiG-29S prototypes, this aircraft has a modified flight control system and upgraded radar, plus provision for Western avionics and underwing fuel tanks. A staged programme of modifications will allow the aircraft to carry up to 4000 kg of external stores. An inflight-refuelling probe and laser-, TV- and radar-guided ASMs will be added from 1995.

Right: The unique contours of the 'Fulcrum-C's enlarged fuselage spine led to the allocation of a new NATO reporting name, although the OKB designation is unchanged.

N-019ME) which retains multiple-target tracking and which may give compatibility with AAM-AE. An aircraft displayed at Le Bourget in June 1993 was not a MiG-29SE, but was a standard MiG-29 serving as a testbed, with a full standard MiG-29SE cockpit, new navaids and English language captions. Some sources have suggested that the MiG-29S was the first MiG-29 variant plumbed for the carriage of underwing fuel tanks, but this is untrue, since many Soviet 'Fulcrum-As' have been seen carrying these for ferry flights. The MiG-29S may, however, be the first variant stressed to carry underwing tanks in combat, or to have provision for extra pylons (like the MiG-29M and MiG-29K, which are described separately) to allow tanks to be carried without sacrificing weapons, and is the first export model offered with underwing tanks. External warload is doubled by the simple expedient of restressing the inner underwing pylons to carry up to four 500-kg (1,102-lb) bombs in side-by-side tandem pairs.

The end of the Cold War has led to a dramatic down-scaling of MiG-29 production, both for the VVS and for export customers. Production in Moscow (at the Labour Banner factory) and in Nizhny Novograd continues at a very low rate, adding to a June 1993 stockpile which totalled about 100 unsold aircraft. A July 1993 Malaysian order for the MiG-29 may have been for some of these aircraft upgraded to MiG-29SE standards, or for MiG-29Ms. The 18 aircraft on order include some two-seaters (perhaps as

Right: Although the spine of the 'Fulcrum-C' is considerably enlarged, it contains only 75-240 litres of extra fuel.

many as six). Hungary's MiG-29s have been described as MiG-29Ss by some sources, but are actually standard 'Fulcrum-As'.

SPECIFICATION

Mikoyan MiG-29S
generally similar to the Mikoyan MiG-29 'Fulcrum-A' except in the following particulars:
Weights: normal take-off weight 15300 kg (33,730 lb): maximum take-off weight 19700 kg (42,680 lb)
Fuel and load: internal fuel 4440-4540 litres (976-998 US gal), external fuel 3,800 litres (1,004 US gal): maximum ordnance load 4000 kg (8,818 lb)
Range: ferry range 2900 km (1,566 nm; 1,802 miles) with three drop tanks

Below: The brown and green ground attack colour scheme worn by some Russian and Ukrainian MiG-29s (mainly 'Fulcrum-Cs', but including some early ventral-finned 'Fulcrum-As') is very similar to that applied to Czech and East German air force aircraft. This Russian 'Fulcrum-C' carries a Guards badge, perhaps indicating previous service at Kubinka, but was photographed at Zhukovskii, where it serves the LII Gromov Flight Research Centre as a development and test aircraft.

Below: This unusual two-tone green camouflage, seen on a pair of MiG-29s (this one a 'Fulcrum-C') departing from Ribnitz-Damgarten during May 1994, may be the latest MiG-29 fighter-bomber colour scheme, or may have been entirely experimental and applied at unit level. One of the 733rd IAP's three squadrons was believed to have a primary fighter-bomber role.

Mikoyan MiG-29M (9-15)

Many Western analysts initially attributed the **MiG-29M** (**9-15**) designation to the big-spined MiG-29 fighter known to NATO as 'Fulcrum-C'. In fact, although the MiG-29M does incorporate a similar, large fuselage spine, the designation is applied to a completely new multi-role 'Fulcrum' variant that incorporates a quadruplex analog FBW control system (triplex in roll and yaw) and a modernised cockpit with two CRT displays. A heavier analog system was selected in preference to a digital system for simplicity and to provide greater protection from electro-magnetic damage.

The aircraft has a new N-010 radar (related to the Zhuk) with a new flat plate antenna like that of the AN/APG-65 in place of the original aircraft's cassegrain antenna. The new radar has a 400 per cent improvement in data processing capability and provides many new modes, especially for air-to-ground use, and gives automatic terrain-following capability. The MiG-29M also has a refined and updated IRST, similar to that fitted to the naval 'Fulcrum'. This reportedly has better sensor cooling, giving much increased detection range, and is collimated with a TV camera and powerful laser for designating targets for 'smart' air-to-air and air-to-ground weapons. The MiG-29M was once described as a one-off technology demonstrator, but in fact six prototypes have been built and are intended to lead to a new production variant.

Described by the bureau as being "based around the aerodynamically stable MiG-29 airframe, but different in every respect," the MiG-29M incorporates a number of major airframe changes and innovations. The leading-edge root extensions are redesigned, with a sharp leading edge, and overwing intake louvres are omitted, with the old solid anti-FOD doors in the main intakes being replaced by meshed grilles. This has allowed a dramatic increase in fuel capacity, with a 2550-litre (674-US gal) welded aluminium-lithium alloy tank replacing the original No. 1 and No. 2 tanks, and the space occupied by the old overwing intakes and their ducts, and by part of the cannon ammunition tank, which is of reduced capacity.

Equipped with four hardpoints under each wing, the MiG-29M can carry a wide range of weapons. This aircraft is seen carrying eight of the new Vympel R-77 'AMRAAMskis'. The R-77 is a medium-range AAM with active radar homing, giving true fire-and-forget capability. By comparison with the standard MiG-29, the MiG-29M has aerodynamic refinements and is structurally redesigned, with a recontoured radome and reshaped spine.

The integral wing tanks are also increased in capacity. Interestingly, the auxiliary air intakes have been painted on to some prototypes to confuse observers. Welded Al-Li is also used in the forward fuselage. Such structures do not require fasteners, resulting in increased volume that is used either for fuel or avionics black boxes. Greater use is also made of composites, with new engine intake ducts and access covers, and a new increased-area dorsal airbrake, of honeycomb construction. The new airframe has a design life of 2,500 flying hours, extendable to 4,000 hours. The overhaul interval has been extended to 1,000 hours.

The new spine accommodates a new chaff/flare dispenser, leading to the deletion of the leading edge extensions fitted to the standard aircraft's fins. The fins themselves have a slightly modified trailing edge, giving improved low-speed handling characteristics. The bulged spine continues to a new, slightly flattened tailcone, which still contains the braking parachutes. The twin upper and lower airbrakes have been replaced by a much larger one-piece airbrake on the

spine. The opportunity has also been taken to raise the pilot's seat, and this has necessitated a slight redesign of the canopy, which is slightly longer and rather more bulged. An antenna for the ARK radio compass is embedded in the canopy aft of the pilot's K-36D ejection seat.

The original MiG-29 was always hampered by its short range and endurance, and was sometimes unkindly referred to as a "fighter for use over the airfield beacon." The MiG-29M has an increase in internal fuel capacity of over 33 per cent (to a similar tankage to the McDonnell Douglas F/A-18C Hornet), giving a 33 per cent improvement in operational radius. The increased weight of the MiG-29M demands a reinforced (but externally unchanged) undercarriage, and the provision of twin braking parachutes, each of 13 m² (140 sq ft) area, replace the original 17 m² (183 sq ft) chute.

The MiG-29M features a slightly modified wing which shares the same span as the original MiG-29 wing but with new wingtips housing a different ECM/RWR system. The ailerons are of extended span. The tailplane

is more radically modified, with a significant increase in chord (and area) on the trailing edge but no increase in span. The tailplane has a small dogtooth on the leading edge, but this is much less prominent than has been shown in some Western artists' impressions. Other external changes include an extended and reconfigured rear fuselage (this allowing the centre of gravity to be moved aft), removal of the undernose sensor/equipment fairing and a recontoured (and possibly shortened) radome which lacks the distinctive double curvature on its leading edge.

The bulged spine of the MiG-29M is not the same as that fitted to the 'Fulcrum-C' and terminates in an entirely new 'beaver tail'. The aircraft also features increased-span ailerons, which extend out almost to the wingtips. The lack of overwing auxiliary intake louvres and the sharp-edged leading-edge root extensions (LERXes) are also noteworthy.

Mikoyan MiG-29M (9-15)

The first MiG-29M prototype may have been converted from the pre-production aircraft 9-15, and first flew in its new guise on 25 April 1986. The MiG-29M is now powered by uprated RD-33K engines, which first flew on 1 November 1989. These have a new four-stage fan, and second-stage compressor with variable stators in front of the first stage. These give a useful increase in thrust to 86 kN (19,400 lb st) with afterburning. To provide greater mass flow on take-off the intakes have small downward-hinging sections on the lower lip. Engine life and TBO figures have also been improved. Performance figures for the MiG-29M are little changed, although the new flight control system has significantly improved the aircraft's already formidable high angle-of-attack capability.

Like the MiG-29K, the aircraft has eight underwing hardpoints, and these are used to carry the new long/medium-range AAM-AE ('AMRAAMski') and a variety of other weapons, including for the first time laser-guided and TV-guided air-to-surface missiles

like the Kh-25 and Kh-31. The two inboard pylons on each wing are each stressed to carry stores of up to 1000 kg (2,204 lb), and the outboard pair to carry 500 kg (1,102 lb) of stores. New 2500-litre (660-US gal) fuel tanks (of the same length and width as standard tanks, but deeper and more slab-sided) are reportedly under development, together with auxiliary missile launch rails for the fuel tank pylons. Ammunition capacity for the internal 30-mm cannon has been reduced to 100 rounds.

During 1990 the VPK commission reportedly refused certification because of radar problems, although earlier FBW control system problems have apparently now been solved, and the aircraft has reportedly successfully completed state acceptance trials, unlike the troubled Su-35, production of which has temporarily ceased. Central funding for the MiG-29M may not have been obtained (although 1994 reports suggested that a small batch would be obtained by the **Russian air forces** in place of some of the more expensive Su-35s), and Mikoyan

is therefore actively looking for an international partner to put the aircraft into production. Recent orders by **Malaysia** and **India** may be for the MiG-29M, and India would be an obvious production partner. The 28 January 1993 Indian contract reportedly covered 30 single-seat MiG-29Ms and six MiG-29M two-seaters with the same CRT-equipped cockpit, and perhaps with radar. These were to be built by MAPO and supplied complete and in kit form for assembly by HAL. Negotiations reportedly took place with Lucas Aerospace for the provision of FADEC systems for the Indian MiG-29Ms. By June 1994, further details emerged of a $750 million Russian offer to supply these 36 aircraft, funding the first 10 through a state bank loan, and the remaining aircraft through a commercial loan. If finalised, this deal will allow development of the MiG-29M to be completed. The $385 million Malaysian contract incorporated with it a number of stringent conditions and requirements that seem to be impossible to fulfil except with a modified MiG-29M, although these

aircraft are expected to be MiG-29SEs which may not even be based on the 'Fulcrum-C'. The designation **MiG-33** may be applied to such an aircraft if it reaches production and Russian air force service, but the most senior bureau personnel aver that to use the designation now is incorrect.

SPECIFICATION

Mikoyan MiG-29M
generally similar to the Mikoyan MiG-29 'Fulcrum-A' except in the following particulars:
Fuselage and tail: length 17.37 m (57 ft 0 in) including probe
Powerplant: two Leningrad/Klimov (Isotov/Sarkisov) RD-33K turbofans rated at 53.95 kN (12,125 lb st) dry, 86.33 kN (19,400 lb st) with afterburning, and with an 'emergency regime' rating of 92.22 kN (20,725 lb st)
Fuel and load: internal fuel 5000 kg (6,250 litres; 1,651 US gal); maximum ordnance 4500 kg (9,921 lb)
Range: 2000 km (1,080 nm; 1,243 miles) with internal fuel; 3200 km (1,728 nm; 1,988 miles) with external fuel tanks

Mikoyan MiG-29K (9-31), MiG-29KU and MiG-29KVP

Because it shares so many features and systems with the MiG-29M, the development programme of the **MiG-29K** (**9-31**) has been achieved using only two prototypes, although a handful of early 'Fulcrum-As', including some with ventral fins, have received arrester hooks and a carrier landing system for trials, and for training naval pilots at the naval airfield at Saki in the Crimea. Designated **MiG-29KVP**, these aircraft lack folding wings and do not have the MiG-29K's fully strengthened undercarriage, so cannot routinely operate from a carrier, where a pitching deck can dramatically increase landing loads. One of these aircraft was also involved in the early trials, probably making a series of touch-and-go landings to familiarise test pilots with the deck of the *Tbilisi*. Some sources have suggested that the MiG-29KVP was originally developed as a naval fighter in its own right, although it quickly became apparent that greater fuel capacity and wing area, and improved high lift devices, would be desirable, and a new start was made using the MiG-29M airframe as a basis.

The Mikoyan design bureau claims to have been working on a naval MiG-29 derivative for some 10 years, in order to provide a multi-role fighter to serve aboard the *Kuznetsov* and her sister carriers. The first of two MiG-29K prototypes made its

maiden flight on 23 June 1988, in the hands of Takhtar Aubakirov. Based on the airframe of the MiG-29M, the big-spined MiG-29Ks similarly lack the usual 'Fulcrum' overwing chaff/flare dispensers, and have a similar, single large airbrake further forward on the spine. Like the MiG-29M, the naval variant also has revised tailfins.

The heavy intake door system has been removed (presumably to save weight) and has been replaced by lighter meshed grilles. The overwing auxiliary intakes have also gone, allowing the space they previously occupied to be taken by a large fuel tank of aluminium-lithium construction, of approximately 2550-litre (674-US gal) capacity.

The MiG-29K prototypes were 'navalised' by the substitution of an arrester hook for the braking parachute, and by the provision of a strengthened undercarriage. Maximum braking deceleration is 4.5 g. Equipment changes seem to include a new defensive ECM system (with bulged wingtips apparently housing passive receivers) and a new IRST sensor (which may be different in detail to that fitted to the MiG-29M). The prototypes have a solid IRST ball with a small window, this housing a test camera to record carrier approaches. The radome is of more curved profile, without the slightly concave conical leading edge of the 'Fulcrum-A' radome. This is more aerodynamically efficient and indicates that the new N-010 radar is fitted.

A retractable inflight-refuelling probe is fitted below the port side of the windscreen and the aircraft apparently incorporates various corrosion-protection measures.

The MiG-29K also has an entirely new wing, of slightly greater chord at the root and with slightly reduced leading edge sweep. The aircraft retains the extended-span ailerons of the MiG-29M, and has extended wingtips, giving greater overall span. New, broader-chord, double-slotted trailing-edge flaps are fitted, these projecting farther aft than the ailerons even when retracted. The aircraft has eight underwing hardpoints that can carry the same range of air-to-air and air-to-ground weapons as the MiG-29M, as well as the anti-ship version of Kh-31 or the new Kh-35 'Harpoonski' anti-ship missile.

For trials aboard the *Tbilisi* (as it then was) '311' initially made 20 launches (using the vessel's 15° ski jump, and running up against the unique deck restrainers, since no catapults are fitted). The MiG-29K landed

The MiG-29KVP served primarily as a trials aircraft for ski-jump and arrester gear development.

on *Tbilisi* after the first Su-27K, but did make the first fixed-wing launch from the new ship. Approaches are flown at some 130 kt (150 mph; 241 km/h) (also quoted as 124 kt/143 mph/230 km/h) and about 14° of Alpha, some 25 kt (29 mph; 46 km/h) lower and 3° higher than a normal approach. The usual glide slope is 4°. The RD-33K engine provides useful extra thrust, making the missed approach/go-around case less criti-

The second MiG-29K wore an overall dark grey camouflage. The increased-span, increased-chord wing of the -29K can be seen in this view of the aircraft.

The first MiG-29K prototype is about to take the wire on the carrier Kuznetsov. The square-section arrester hook and large double-slotted flaps are clearly evident.

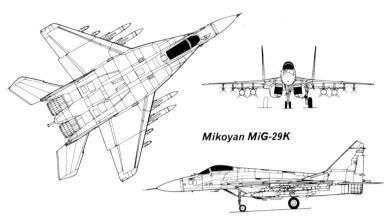

Mikoyan MiG-29K

cal. The third and fourth proposed carriers have now been abandoned, or scrapped. The second, *Varyag*, is almost complete, but its fate remains uncertain. China and India have both been quoted as possible purchasers and Russia itself still wants to take the vessel into service, but cannot do so while Ukraine contests the ownership of the vessel. The sudden reduction in carrier numbers, coupled with funding problems, has reduced the requirement for carrier-based fighters, and the original plan to have a mix of multi-role **MiG-29K**s and dedicated Su-27K interceptors may now have been abandoned in favour of using a single type. If this is the case, the MiG-29K would have been the most useful type, by virtue of

its multi-role capability and small size. Politics, however, always favoured the Sukhoi aircraft, which was selected for production (although this has now ceased, and the MiG-29K is reportedly being reconsidered).

Since the view from the rear cockpit of the MiG-29UB is inadequate for operations from aircraft-carriers (even without the increased angle of attack used on a carrier approach), Mikoyan proposed a new two-seat trainer variant for naval training. Designated **MiG-29KU**, the aircraft incorporated the same naval modifications as the MiG-29K (folding wings, removal of the intake doors, corrosion resistance, etc.) with a new stepped cockpit, covered by separate bubble canopies, with the instructor's cock-

pit forward, in the former radar bay as in the MiG-25U. The MiG-29KU reached model stage but has since been abandoned.

India is a possible export customer for both the MiG-29K and the MiG-29KU, since it hopes to acquire a third (conventional) aircraft-carrier. A second possible export customer is China, which continues to show interest in acquiring the *Varyag*. The future of the MiG-29K seems to have been dealt a fatal blow by recent moves to standardise Soviet tactical aircraft production on the Su-27, although the MiG-29K's relatively untroubled development, multi-role capability and smaller size (allowing more aircraft to be carried in the hangar deck or spotted on the main deck) make it the navy's preferred option and the natural choice if only one carrierborne fighter is to be procured. The recent cessation of Su-27/Su-27K/Su-35 production at Komsomolsk may lend credence to early 1994 reports that the aircraft's future had been reconsidered.

The view shows the second MiG-29K prototype at the LII Gromov Flight Research Centre at Zhukhovskii. It is laden with X-31 anti-radar missiles inboard and R-73 AAMs outboard, and has its IFR probe extended.

SPECIFICATION

Mikoyan MiG-29K
generally similar to the Mikoyan MiG-29M except in the following particulars:
Wing: span 12.00 m (39 ft 4 in); span (folded) 7.80 m (25 ft 7 in); area 41.6 m2 (447.77 sq ft)
Fuselage and tail: length 17.27 m (56 ft 8 in)
Weights: normal take-off 18480 kg (40,705 lb); maximum take-off 22400 kg (49,340 lb)
Speed: maximum level speed 'clean' at 11000 m (36.089 ft) 2300 km/h (1,242 kt; 1,430 mph)
Range: 1600 km (866 nm; 994 miles) with internal fuel; 2900 km (1,570 nm; 1,802 miles) with external fuel tanks

Mikoyan MiG-31 'Foxhound'

The **MiG-31** (Item 01) was developed as part of an overall programme to revitalise Soviet air defences to meet the threat posed by NATO low-level strike aircraft and cruise missiles. It was clear that Frontal Aviation's MiG-29s and the PVO's Su-27s would not be in service before the mid-1980s, and as an interim measure several existing aircraft were upgraded with new radar and weapons systems. The MiG-31 has often been assumed to be a similar low-risk upgrade of the MiG-25 but, actually, the new aircraft was always intended to complement the Su-27 in service, providing ultra-long-range intercept capability

and filling the gaps in Russia's ground-based radar chain. In fact, the MiG-31 nearly had a very different configuration to the MiG-25, since the original E-155MP design was a swing-wing, single-finned aircraft similar in configuration to the MiG-23, but with a large, square-section fuselage similar to that of the MiG-25, and with large folding ventral fins below the rear fuselage. This design, and an even more ambitious tailless

This MiG-31 development aircraft is armed with four R-33s in the belly recesses and two older R-40Rs underwing.

Mikoyan MiG-31 'Foxhound'

The MiG-31M features a wraparound one-piece windscreen, a neat retractable inflight-refuelling probe and underfuselage missile recesses for up to six R-37 missiles. This prototype also carried finned wingtip ESM/ECM pods.

delta (still secret because it eventually formed the basis of the 1-42's aerodynamic configuration) were eventually rejected in favour of a configuration more closely based on the MiG-25. This design, the **Ye-155M**, was a MiG-25 derivative intended to explore ways of improving the 'Foxbat's' speed and range. The aircraft served as a testbed for the 132-kN (29,762-lb) R-15BF-2-300 engine, and later the Soloviev D-30F-6, a high by-pass turbofan used by the MiG-31, but plans to incorporate structural improvements were dropped. Several records were beaten by the aircraft during 1975, operating under the cover designation **Ye-266M**.

The new interceptor was closely based on this trials aircraft, originally bearing the designation **Ye-155MP**, and was expected to enter service as the **MiG-25MP**. A two-seater, the new interceptor also featured a new undercarriage, with side-by-side nosewheels and offset tandem mainwheels. The rear wheel on each oleo was located out-board of the oleo, so that on snow it did not follow in the furrow of compacted snow left by the front wheel. This arrangement also spread the weight and reduced wear on un-hardened runways. New airbrakes were fitted, located ahead of the undercarriage and opening diagonally downwards from the 'corners' of the fuselage. The wing planform was subtly changed, with small leading-edge root extensions and no wingtip anti-flutter weights.

The basic Ye-155MP trials aircraft was originally one of a family of variants. The unbuilt **Ye-155MF**, for example, was a similar aircraft with side-by-side seats in a broader nose, intended for the defence suppression role, and there is also believed to have been a reconnaissance version.

The Ye-155MP interceptor made its maiden flight on 16 September 1975, and was clearly the two-seat 'Super Foxbat' described by defecting MiG-25 pilot Victor Belenko in 1976. He claimed that this was strengthened for supersonic flight at low level and fitted with a new look-down/shoot-down radar giving genuine anti-cruise missile capability.

During 1977, a satellite observed the new aircraft destroy a low-flying target while itself flying at 20,000 ft (6096 m), and in a later test despatching an RPV at 70,000 ft (21336 m) while itself at 55,000 ft (16764 m). Series production of the MiG-31 began

at Gorki (now Nizhny Novgorod) in 1979, the new designation having been adopted to acknowledge that this was a very new air-craft, with new capabilities. Production air-craft began entering PVO service during 1982. The production aircraft had refined leading-edge slats and relocated airbrakes. Some very long-range flights were demon-strated during operational trials, including a gruelling five-hour CAP and a flight over the North Pole during tests of the navigation system. This included the Omega-equiva-lent Marshrut and the LORAN-like Tropik.

At the heart of the MiG-31 is its SBI-16 (S-800) 'Zaslon' radar, codenamed 'Flash Dance' by NATO. This uses a unique, fixed, phased-array antenna, which points its beam electronically. This allows the full fuselage diameter to be used, increasing radar range, and provides faster and more accurate beam pointing. Mikoyan claims rear hemisphere coverage to 120° on each side of the centreline. Ten targets can be tracked simultaneously, and four can be engaged at once. These can be automati-cally selected by the mission computer, which assigns priorities to all threats. Mik-oyan claims a detection range of 200 km (125 miles) for a fighter-sized target, and a tracking range of 120 km (75 miles).

Even more impressively, groups of four MiG-31s can operate together, with only the leader linked to the AK-RLDN ground-based automatic guidance network, joined to his wingmen by datalink and covering a swathe of territory 900 km (560 miles) across. The formation leader can automatically control his wingmen, assigning them to engage threats according to the tactical situation. The air-craft also features a sensitive IRST to pro-vide an emission-free alternative to radar.

The MiG-31 is fitted with a GSh-6-23 six-barrelled 23-mm Gatling-type cannon, with 260 rounds of linkless ammunition, scabbed on to the rear fuselage, just behind the star-board main undercarriage unit, and can carry two R-40 (AA-6 'Acrid') or four R-60 (AA-8 'Aphid') missiles under the wing. Its primary armament is the R-33 (AA-9 'Amos'), a long-range semi-active radar homing missile which bears some resemblance to Hughes' AIM-54 Phoenix AAM. Fully armed and fully fuelled, at its maximum take-off weight of 100,000 lb (45360 kg) the MiG-31 grosses as much as three AV-8B Harrier IIs.

Some improvements were added during the course of production (which amounted to 280 aircraft) at Gorky's IGAZ Sokol plant. Later MiG-31s are fitted with a semi-retractable inflight-refuelling probe just below the windscreen on the port side, and the two underwing pylons have been increased to four. Some sources suggest that plans exist for the outer pair to be

'plumbed' for the carriage of underwing drop tanks, as on the MiG-31D.

The **MiG-31M** (Item 05), which has yet to receive a production order, is an im-proved interceptor variant built only in proto-type form (eight aircraft, at least some con-verted from production MiG-31s), in at least two configurations. All feature a new radar, whose recontoured radome droops by 7° by comparison with the old aircraft, and whose scanner has a diameter of 1.4 m (4 ft 6 in) (compared with 1.1 m/3 ft 6 in). This new radar may have a conventional scanner in place of the original Zaslon's fixed, phased array antenna.

The new variant also has new R-37 mis-siles (up to six of which can now apparently be carried below the fuselage), and can simultaneously engage up to six targets, but the cannon has been removed. All aircraft also have provision for a non-retractable IRST below the nose, and have lost their intake-mounted RWR antennas. Develop-ment began in 1983 under K. Vasilichenko, and the first MiG-31M (a converted produc-tion MiG-31) was delivered to Zhukhovskii for flight trials in March 1984.

MiG-31M modifications

All MiG-31Ms have a redesigned rear cockpit, with no periscope or control col-umn (a sidestick is provided for emergency use), but with three colour CRT MFDs. There are two wingtip configurations, one with rounded tips and one with finned ECM pods. The MiG-31M features a host of aero-dynamic and structural refinements and modifications, which increase maximum take-off weight to 52000 kg (114,638 lb). A fully retractable inflight-refuelling probe is mounted on the starboard side, and large cylindrical pods can be carried on the wing-tips, with upper and lower vertical winglet fins or blade antennas. The tail unit is of raised height, and there are a number of aerodynamic improvements to the tailfin trailing edge/fuselage intersection. Fin LERXes were also revised, although these are now understood to have reverted to the original shape. The nose gear doors have been redesigned, with a pair of side-hing-ing doors and no forward-hinging front door. Handling at high angles of attack has been improved by the addition of longer, curving extensions to the wingroot leading edge, and the aircraft reportedly features a new digital flight control system. The overwing fences have been reduced in height. The MiG-31M also has a deeper, more bulged spine, with increased fuel capacity in three saddle tanks (an extra 300 litres/79 US gal), smaller windows for the rear cockpit and a one-piece canopy over the pilot's cockpit. A new one-piece windscreen has also been

provided. It is believed that at least eight prototypes have been constructed (or per-haps converted from earlier aircraft).

The big spine, new cockpit and non-retractable IRST of the MiG-31M have all been adopted on the new **MiG-31D** (Item 12), which retains the original 1.1-m (3-ft 6-in) radar diameter, and which has inter-changeable wingtips (rounded or podded). The new variant, designed under the lead-ership of A. Belosvet, is also compatible with the new R-37 missile, a round-nosed derivative of the R-33 (AA-9 'Amos') with folding stabilisers, and can carry four R-77s ('AMRAAMski') under the wing. The out-board underwing pylons are plugged for the carriage of 2250-litre (594-US gal) fuel tanks. It seems likely that the MiG-31D will never become a production aircraft, but has already been produced by conversion of existing MiG-31s since 1991 under the des-ignation **MiG-31BS** (Item 01BS). One last MiG-31 sub-variant which reached proto-type stage was the Item 07, a dedicated satellite killer which was to have been arm-ed with a Soviet equivalent of the US ASAT missile. Two prototypes were converted from production MiG-31s, with flat bellies, no underwing pylons, and a shortened, bal-lasted nose that lacked radar. They were produced during 1987.

SPECIFICATION

Mikoyan MiG-31 'Foxhound'

Wing: span 13.464 m (44 ft 4 in); area 61.6 m2 (663 sq ft)

Fuselage and tail: overall length 22.688 m (74 ft 6 in); height 6.2 m (20.3 ft)

Powerplant: two PNPP (Soloviev) D-30F6 turbofans each rated at 93.19 kN (20,944 lb st) or 152.06 kN (34,171 lb st) with afterburner

Weights: empty 21825 kg (48,115 lb); normal take-off 41000 kg (90,388 lb); maximum take-off 46200 kg (101851 lb)

Fuel and load: internal fuel 16350 kg (36,045 lb); maximum external fuel 5000 litres (1,320 US gal)

Speed: maximum level speed at 17500 m (57,400 ft) 3000 km/h (1,620 kt; 1,865 mph); maximum level speed at sea level 1500 km/h (810 kt; 932 mph); economical cruising speed Mach 0.8; limiting Mach No. 2.83

Range: ferry range 3300 km (1,780 nm; 2,050 miles); Mach 2.35 radius of action 720 km (388 nm; 447 miles) unrefuelled; Mach 0.85 radius of action 1200 km (648 nm; 745 miles) unrefuelled, 2200 km (1,185 nm; 1,365 miles) with one inflight refuelling

Performance: service ceiling 20600 m (67,585 ft); take-off run 1200 m (3,937 ft) at maximum take-off weight; landing run at normal landing weight with brake chutes 800 m (2,624 ft); time to 1000 m (3,280 ft) 7 minutes 45 seconds

g limits: +5 at supersonic speed

Mikoyan 701 and 1-42

These **Mikoyan 701** and **1-42** designations were revealed in 1988 by Rostislav Belyakov, Designer General of the Mikoyan OKB, although since then he has both denied and admitted them. The 1-42 was said to be broadly equivalent to the EFA and Rafale in concept, role, weight, configuration and size, and was developed (perhaps from one of the Ye-155 designs discarded during the development of the MiG-31) to meet the air force's requirement for an MFI, or Mnogofunkstsionalniy Istrebityel (multi-role fighter). The Sukhoi Su-37 (described

separately), which has reportedly been abandoned, may have been intended as a competitor to this aircraft. Rumours suggest that one, and perhaps two, 1-42 prototypes are in an advanced stage of construction in the factory at Nizhny Novgorod, but that funding problems and the non-availability of the intended Saturn/Lyul'ka engines have prevented their completion. The Russian air force has stated that it remains fully committed to the programme and will attempt to make available additional funding, but Lyul'ka remains coy about the progress of

the unnamed engine. A brochure released at the 1993 Paris air show revealed a very crude sketch of a tailless twin-finned fighter with side-by-side engines, and this may represent the 1-42 basic configuration. Other earlier artists' impressions showed an aircraft which more resembled the F-22, but with inward-canted tailfins.

The Mikoyan 701 was developed to meet the MDP, or Mnogofunkstsionalniy Dalniy Perevkhvatchik (multi-role long-range interceptor) requirement, perhaps in competition with a Sukhoi design known as the Su-32.

The aircraft is a long, slender, tailless delta-winged aircraft with intakes mounted above the fuselage and internal weapons bays. The fighter version has tandem cockpits, while a bizjet derivative has a side-by-side flight deck. Neither are believed to have progressed beyond the drawing board.

Although both Mikoyan and Sukhoi have hinted that they have flown aircraft more advanced than the MiG-29 and Su-27, they have on other occasions also claimed that the MiG-29M and Su-33 are their most advanced flying aircraft.

Mil Mi-1 'Hare'

Moskovskii Vertoletnay Zavod Imieni M.L. Milya,
2 Sokolnichyesky Val,
107113 Moscow, Russia.

The **Mil Mi-1** three/four-seat light liaison helicopter first flew in 1948 and is similar in size and configuration to the Sikorsky S-51. Also built under licence in Poland, the Mil Mi-1 appeared in several different variants, including a dual-control trainer. Powered by an AI-26 radial engine, driving a three-bladed wooden main rotor, the Mil Mi-1 proved a popular light utility and train-

ing helicopter, and was widely exported. A handful may remain in service in the states of the former **USSR**, in **Cuba** and in **China**.

SPECIFICATION

Mil Mi-1 'Hare'
Rotors: main rotor diameter 14.3 m (46.9 ft); main

rotor disc area 161.56 m² (193.32 sq ft)
Fuselage and tail: length overall 16.95 m (55.6 ft); height 3.30 m (10.8 ft)
Powerplant: one Ivchenko AI-26W piston engine rated at 422 kW (566 hp)
Weights: empty 1800 kg (3,968 lb); normal take-off 2300 kg (5,070 lb); maximum take-off 2400 kg (5,291 lb)
Fuel and load: internal fuel 260 litres (68.6 US gal);

external fuel 160 litres (42.2 US gal); maximum payload 300 kg (661 lb)
Speed: maximum level speed at 2000 m (6,561 ft) 185 km/h (99 kt; 114 mph); maximum level speed at sea level 170 km/h (91 kt; 105 mph)
Range: ferry range 620 km (334 nm; 385 miles);
Performance: maximum rate of climb at sea level 6.5 m (21.3 ft) per second; service ceiling 3000 m (9,842 ft)

Mil Mi-4 'Hound'

Design of the **Mil Mi-4 'Hound'** transport helicopter was initiated in 1951 and the first example was flown in August 1952. It was soon put into production, initially for Aeroflot, as the passenger-carrying **Mil Mi-4P**, and later for use by the Soviet armed forces in assault and troop transport roles. Of conventional design, the Mi-4 has rear clamshell doors to simplify loading of vehicles and cargo and a radial piston engine mounted in fuselage nose, similar to the contemporary Sikorsky S-55/Westland Whirlwind. The initial four-bladed wooden rotor caused many problems, and it was not until 1954 that blade life was extended to 300 hours; in 1960, all-metal parallel-chord blades were introduced.

Several military versions of the Mil Mi-4 were built. The basic **'Hound-A'** assault transport could carry 14 fully-equipped troops, 1600 kg (3,527 lb) of stores, or underslung loads. Many 'Hounds' were converted to other roles, including armed assault versions fitted with a ventral cannon gondola (initially designed for an observer or naviga-

tor), the ASW-configured **'Hound-B'**, and the **'Hound-C'** ECM platform. When production ended in 1969, about 3,500 of all variants had been built in the USSR, mostly for military service, and an additional 1,000 were produced in China as the **Harbin Z-5** (described separately). Small numbers of 'Hound-As' remain active, with **Albania** and perhaps with **Afghanistan**, **Algeria**, **Angola**, **Bangladesh**, **Bhutan**, **China**, **Cuba**, **Egypt**, **Ethiopia**, **Guinea**, **Iraq**, **Mongolia**, **North Korea**, **Sudan**, **Syria**, **Vietnam** and **Yemen**.

SPECIFICATION

Mil Mi-4 'Hound-A'
Rotor system: main rotor diameter 21.00 m (68 ft 11 in); main rotor disc area 349.49 m² (3,761.88 sq ft)
Fuselage and tail: length overall, rotors turning 25.02 m (82 ft 1 in) and fuselage 16.80 m (55 ft 1 in); height overall 4.40 m (14 ft 5.25 in)
Powerplant: one Shvetsov ASh-82V radial piston engine rated at 1,700 hp (1268 kW)

Weights: empty 4900 kg (10,802 lb); normal take-off 7150 kg (15,763 lb); maximum take-off 7550 kg (16,645 lb)
Fuel and load: internal fuel 960 litres (254 US gal) plus provision for 500 litres (132 US gal) of auxiliary fuel in cabin tank; maximum payload 1000 kg (2,204 lb)
Speed: maximum level speed at 1000 m (3,281 ft) 200 km/h (108 kt; 124 mph); maximum level speed at sea level 175 km/h (94 kt;109 mph); maximum cruising speed at optimum altitude 160 km/h (65 kt; 99 mph)
Range: 650 km (351 nm; 404 miles)

Performance: service ceiling 5500 m (18,045 ft); hovering ceiling 700 m (2,295 ft) out of ground effect

Albania operates a mix of Russian-built Mi-4s and Chinese Harbin Z-5s, all of which have been retrofitted with Chinese metal rotor blades. This Mi-4, now in use as an air ambulance with Albania's Sixth Regiment, used to be dictator Enver Hoxha's personal aircraft.

Mil Mi-6 'Hook-A'

Development of the **Mil Mi-6** began in 1954 in response to Aeroflot and VVS requirements for a large transport helicopter. When it made its maiden flight in late 1957, it was the world's largest rotary-wing aircraft, but despite this size it retained the basic helicopter configuration. More significantly, it was also the first turbine-powered helicopter to enter production in the USSR. The Mi-6 immediately began to demonstrate its capabilities by demolishing records, and by becoming the first helicopter to exceed 162 kt (300 km/h; 186 mph). The Mi-6 featured

an optional detachable stub wing, which offloaded the rotor by some 20 per cent in cruising flight, with attendant benefits on fuel consumption and endurance. Five prototypes were followed by an initial production batch of 30, most of which went to the air force.

The standard **Mil Mi-6T 'Hook-A'** can carry 65 passengers on tip-up seats along the cabin sides and additional bench seats along the centreline, or 75 in a high-density configuration of 15 five-abreast forward-facing rows. In the medevac role, up to 41

stretchers can be carried. Clamshell doors are provided at the rear, with hydraulically operated loading ramps and an 800-kg (1,764-lb) capacity internal winch for cargo handling. The floor is stressed for loads of up to 2000 kg/m² (409 lb/sq ft). The hold is 11.72 m (38 ft 6 in) long and 2.65 m (8 ft 7 in) wide, with height varying between 2.00 and 2.64 m (6 ft 6 in and 8 ft 6 in). A maximum load of 12000 kg (26,455 lb) can be carried internally. Alternatively, an external cargo hook allows underslung loads of up to 9000 kg (19,800 lb) to be carried. A total of 800 'Hooks' had been built when production ended in 1981.

There are various civilian variants, including the **Mil Mi-6P** with square windows, and fire-fighting and flying crane versions. Special military versions are described separately under the Mi-6VKP heading.

All military 'Hooks' fly with a flight crew of five, comprised of two pilots, a flight engineer, a radio operator and a navigator (who sits in the glazed nose). The latter doubles as a gunner, since military Mil Mi-6s

are fitted with a nose-mounted 12.7-mm Afansanayev machine-gun, and some (notably some Peruvian 'Hook-As') have a podded weather radar below the nose. The aircraft has reportedly been exported to **Algeria**, **Angola**, **Egypt**, **Ethiopia**, **Iraq**, **Indonesia**, **Laos**, **Peru**, **Pakistan**, **Poland**, **Syria**, **Vietnam** and **Zambia**. Although the Mi-6 has been withdrawn from service in Ethiopia, Indonesia, Pakistan, Poland and Vietnam, many remain operational elsewhere. Even in **Russia**, where the much newer, even larger Mil Mi-26 'Halo' is in service, the ageing 'Hook' remains highly prized.

SPECIFICATION

Mil Mi-6A 'Hook'
Rotor system: main rotor diameter 35.00 m (114 ft 10 in); tail rotor diameter 6.30 m (20 ft 8 in); wing span 15.30 m (50 ft 2.5 in); main rotor disc area 962.11 m² (10,356.43 sq ft); tail rotor disc area 31.17 m² (335.55 sq ft); wing area 35.00 m² (376.75 sq ft)
Wing: span 15.30 m (50 ft 2.5 in); area 35.00 m² (376.75 sq ft)
Fuselage and tail: length overall, rotors turning 41.74 m (136 ft 11.5 in) and fuselage 33.18 m (108 ft 10.5 in) excluding nose gun and tail rotor; height

This Mil Mi-6 'Hook' was assigned to the Group of Soviet Forces in Germany, based at Oranienburg, near Berlin.

overall 9.86 m (32 ft 4 in); wheel track 7.50 m (24 ft 7.25 in); wheel base 9.09 m (29 ft 9.75 in) **Powerplant:** two PNPP 'Aviadvigatel' (Soloviev) D-25V (TV-2BM) turboshafts each rated at 4101 kW (5,500 shp) **Weights:** empty 27240 kg (60,055 lb); normal take-off 40500 kg (82,285 lb); maximum take-off 42500 kg

(93,700 lb) for VTO **Fuel and load:** internal fuel 6315 kg (13,922 lb) plus provision for 3490 kg (7,965 lb) of auxiliary fuel in two cabin tanks; maximum external fuel 3490 kg (7,965 lb) in two auxiliary tanks; maximum payload 12000 kg (26,455 lb)

Speed: maximum level speed 'clean' at optimum altitude 300 km/h (162 kt; 186 mph); maximum cruising speed at optimum altitude 250 km/h (135 kt; 155 mph) **Range:** ferry range 1450 km (782 nm; 900 miles) with auxiliary fuel; range 1000 km (539 nm; 621 miles) with

external tanks and a 4500-kg (9,921-lb) payload or 620 km (334 nm; 385 miles) with internal fuel and an 8000-kg (17,637-lb) payload **Performance:** service ceiling 4500 m (14,765 ft); hovering ceiling 2500 m (8,200 ft) in ground effect

Mil **Mi-6VKP 'Hook-B' & Mil Mi-22 'Hook-C'**

Possessing excellent performance, ready availability and capacious fuselage, the Mil Mi-6 has been adapted in small numbers for special duties. Two separate versions have been identified to date, both being described as airborne command posts. It may be more accurate to call the aircraft air-mobile command posts, since it seems likely that they function as command posts only on the ground. The nose-mounted Afanaseyev 12.7-mm machine-gun is deleted in both versions.

The Mi-6VKP 'Hook-B' is an airborne command post and has a cluster of 'swept-T' blade antennas around the tailboom, with a tubular antenna further forward and a heat exchanger pod on the starboard cabin side. This aircraft has a vertical (fold down?) rod-like antenna below the engine exhaust.

The first such variant is the **Mil Mi-6VKP 'Hook-B'**, which is packed with electronic equipment and bristles with unidentified antennas. Four blade antennas are arranged round the corners of the rear part of the tailboom, and in front of these is a large rectangular, tubular antenna frame which hangs below the forward part of the tailboom. The aircraft has a number of extra blade and whip antennas above and below the fuselage, and some examples are also fitted with a vertical upright rod antenna projecting from the port side of the fuselage, just aft of the forward entrance door. This may 'fold down' to a horizontal position when in use. The 'Hook-B' also has a small, horizontal drum-like fairing on the starboard side, just ahead of the former clamshell door hinge line, and just behind the entrance door. The extensive electronic equipment inside the cabin necessitates the provision of a heat exchanger, which is mount-

ed on the starboard side of the fuselage, forward of the main undercarriage, and this seems to prevent the aircraft from carrying an auxiliary fuel tank on that side.

'Hook-C', which is apparently designated **Mil Mi-22** by the manufacturers, is a second command post variant and features an entirely different antenna array. It more closely resembles the standard 'Hook-A', with auxiliary fuel tanks on both sides, but with a new underfuselage antenna farm, and with a single large swept blade antenna above the rear fuselage, roughly level with the top corner of the clamshell door, closest to the hinge line. Some 'Hook-Cs' have been seen carrying horizontally a large 'spear-like' device on the main under-

carriage legs. Some sources suggest that this might be a separate antenna designed to be erected on the ground. It is believed that both command post 'Hooks' have their clamshell doors sealed, and it is thought that neither can easily be reconfigured for transport duties. Neither 'Hook-B' nor 'Hook-C' has been exported, all aircraft serving in **Russia**, and in the states of the former **Soviet Union**.

The 'Hook-C' has a single large blade antenna above the tailboom, with an antenna farm below the cabin. This aircraft also carries an unidentified antenna on the starboard undercarriage outrigger.

Mil **Mi-8/17 'Hip-C' and 'Hip-H' – transport variants**

Combat proven in the Middle East, East Africa, Afghanistan, Angola, Mozambique and Nicaragua, the 'Hip' has proved rugged and dependable, and large numbers remain in use today. Design of the **Mi-8** was initiated in 1960 as a second-generation, turbine-engined derivative of and replacement for the Mil Mi-4, using the same tailboom, main rotor and tail rotor. The small size of the Isotov turboshaft engine permitted the engine to be moved from the nose to a position above the cabin, allowing the cockpit to be relocated to the nose and making possible a simpler transmission system. The cabin was much bigger, even though external dimensions were little changed, and could seat twice as many passengers (28 instead of the Mi-4's 14).

The single-engined prototype ('Hip-A') was powered by a 2,700-shp (2013-kW) Soloviev turboshaft and made its maiden flight during 1961, but proved slightly underpowered and was quickly followed by a twin-engined prototype (**'Hip-B'**), which introduced the Isotov TV2 turboshafts. The production **'Hip-C'** introduced a new five-bladed main rotor, essentially a scaled-down copy of the Mi-6 rotor. The first production version was the **Mil Mi-8P**, a civilian passenger/freight transport which retained the rectangular cabin windows of the prototype, as did the **Mi-8S**, a passenger-carrying airliner with armchair-style seats, a toilet and galley. The Mi-8S has also seen service with many air forces as a VIP transport, and some have their clamshell doors removed and

replaced by a one-piece fairing to improve soundproofing and reduce draughts.

More popular with military customers is the **Mil Mi-8T**, the standard utility transport. This introduced small, circular cabin windows, and had rail-mounted seats (like the Mi-8P) that allowed the interior to be rapidly reconfigured. Early Mi-8Ts were fitted with 1,500-shp (1119-kW) engines, but most were powered by the 1,700-shp

(1268-kW) Isotov TV2-117A. The Mi-8T can be equipped with outriggers carrying four pylons, each capable of carrying a UV-16-57 rocket pod. Many aircraft have had these outrigger pylons strengthened to carry the larger UV-32-57 pod, or bombs of up to 250 kg (551 lb).

Mi-8Ts have been fitted with various other items of equipment. Finnish aircraft have an undernose weather radar and

pylon-mounted searchlight, while Egyptian aircraft have British-made sand filters. Angolan and Ethiopian Mi-8Ts, on the other hand, have the same PZU filters as are normally fitted to the Mi-17.

To improve performance, especially under 'hot-and-high' conditions, or with an engine out, the Mi-8 was re-engined with 1,950-shp (1454-kW) Isotov TV3-117MT engines to produce the **Mil Mi-17**, dubbed

This standard Soviet air force 'Hip-C' is equipped with a winch above the cabin entry door and with outriggers for the carriage of weapons. Unusually, the aircraft does not have chaff/flare dispensers. Despite the introduction of the up-engined Mi-17 'Hip-H', the Mi-8 remains in widespread service with the air force and with army aviation, in a very wide variety of roles.

'Hip-H' by NATO. With one engine inoperative, the other can produce up to 2,200 shp (1641 kW). The new aircraft has PZU dust filters in the engine intakes, and the tail rotor is relocated from starboard to port, changing its direction of rotation and becoming a tractor rather than a pusher unit. The aircraft also has a new titanium alloy rotor hub and an all-new gearbox. Payloads remain unchanged at 4000 kg (8,818 lb) (internal) or 3000 kg (6,614 lb) (underslung), but performance is considerably improved, and fuel consumption is reduced. Export customers often use the civilian Mil Mi-17 designation, but the CIS and Russian air forces have retained the **Mil Mi-8MT**, or **Mi-8TV** designations depending on equipment fit. Former Soviet military 'Hip-Hs' are often fitted with extra cockpit armour, IR jammers, chaff/flare dispensers, and even bulky EVU exhaust gas diffusers. The 'Hip-H' can also carry the same six-pylon outrigger as the **'Hip-E'** and **'Hip-F'** armed variants (described separately), and some have been fitted with machine-guns in flexible nose mountings.

Because of its relatively capacious cabin, availability, reliability and performance, the Mil Mi-8 and Mil Mi-17 have been adapted to fulfil a number of different roles, boosting the numbers in service. Examples of the 'Hip' have been exported widely, to virtually every country which operates an aircraft of Soviet origin. Operators of all 'Hips', including EW and specialised sub-types, are detailed in the operators section below.

SPECIFICATION

Mil Mi-8T 'Hip-C'
Rotor system: main rotor diameter 21.29 m (69 ft 10.25 in); tail rotor diameter 3.91 m (12 ft 9.875 in); main rotor disc area 356.00 m² (3,832.08 sq ft); tail rotor disc area 12.01 m² (129.25 sq ft)
Fuselage and tail: length overall, rotors turning

25.24 m (82 ft 9.75 in) and fuselage 18.17 m (59 ft 7.375 in) excluding tail rotor; height overall 5.65 m (18 ft 6.5 in); wheel track 4.50 m (14 ft 9 in); wheel base 4.26 m (13 ft 11.75 in)
Powerplant: two Klimov (Isotov) TV2-117A turboshafts each rated at 1104 kW (1,481 shp)
Weights: typical empty 7160 kg (15,784 lb); normal take-off 11100 kg (24,471 lb); maximum take-off 12000 kg (26,455 lb)
Fuel and load: standard fuel 1870 litres (494 US gal); external fuel 980 litres (258 US gal); maximum payload 660 kg (1,455 lb)
Speed: maximum level speed at sea level 250 km/h (134 kt; 155 mph)
Range: ferry range 930 km (501 nm; 577 miles); radius of action 350 km (188 nm; 217 miles)
Performance: maximum rate of climb at sea level 4.5 m (14.7 ft) per second; service ceiling 4500 m (14,760 ft); hovering ceiling 1900 m (6,235 ft) in ground effect and 800 m (2,625 ft) out of ground effect

OPERATORS

All Mi-8 variants:
Afghanistan: Mi-8s and Mi-17s serve with 375 and 377 Combat Helicopter Regiments at Bagram and Mazar-E-Sharif, under the control of disparate warlords.
Algeria: Mi-8 (12) and Mi-17?
Angola: 40+ survivors of 42 Mi-8 and 18 Mi-17 delivered.
Armenia: Mi-8 or Mi-17, small numbers.
Bangladesh: In No. 1 Squadron at Chittagong, five Mi-8s are being replaced by five new Mi-17s. Another Mi-8 serves in the VIP role with No. 31 Squadron at Dhaka.
Byelorussia: Large numbers remain in service. Most variants are in use.
Bhutan: Mi-8 (2)
Bulgaria: Bulgaria operates Mi-8s (7) and Mi-17s (19) with a transport regiment at Krumovo.
Cambodia: Cambodia is believed to have been an Mi-8/-17 operator.
China: Mi-8 (30)
Congo: Mi-8 (2)

Croatia: Croatia may have inherited some Mi-8s from the former Yugoslavia, and is understood to have purchased more (perhaps including Mi-17s) from the Ukraine.
Cuba: Mi-8 (20 of 40 delivered) and Mi-17 (16)
Czech Republic: After the division of Czechoslovakia the Czech Republic retained 32 Mi-8 and 31 Mi-17 transports, together with two Mi-8PPAs and a single Mi-9. These serve with the 3rd DLP at Kbely and the 11th VRP at Line, and with the border police.
Egypt: Mi-8 (50+ of 120 delivered)
Ethiopia: Mi-8 (35) – status uncertain since fall of Mengistu.
Finland: Seven surviving Mi-8s serve with the Kuljetuslentolaivue at Utti.
Germany: The Luftwaffe has now retired the last of the Mi-8s which it inherited from East Germany. LSK/LV Mi-8s were operated with KG-3 at Cottbus, KG-5 at Basepohl (mainly Mi-8TBKs), MHG-18, THG-34 at Brandenburg-Briest, LTG-65 at Marxwalde and MFG-28 at Perow.
Guinea Bissau: Mi-8 (single aircraft now w/o?)
Guyana: Mi-8 (3)
Hungary: 29 Mi-8s and eight Mi-17s (including a single Mi-9 and two Mi-17P EW aircraft) fly with the Bakony Combat Helicopter Wing at Szentkirályszabadja and the Szolnok transport brigade at Szolnok.
India: The survivors of 140+ Mi-8s and Mi-17s serve with Nos 107, 109, 110, 111, 117, 118, 119, 120, 121, 128, 129, 130, 151 and 152 helicopter units.
Iraq: Mi-8 (100)
Kazakhstan: Large numbers remain in service. Most variants are in use.
Laos: Mi-8 (9 of 10 delivered)
Libya: Mi-8 (7 of 12 delivered)
Madagascar: Mi-8 (2)
Mali: Mi-8 (1)
Moldova: Small numbers (8) in service.
Mongolia: Mi-8 (10-12)
Mozambique: Mi-8 (6 of 15 delivered)
Nicaragua: Mi-8TBK (10 delivered), Mi-17 (15 delivered)
North Korea: Mi-8/-17 (20 to 70)
Pakistan: Pakistan's Army Aviation Corps operates 10 Mi-8s (of 12 delivered), these serving No. 4 Squadron at Dhamial, Rahwali and Gilgit.

This fully equipped Russian air force 'Hip-H' features scabbed-on cockpit armour, IR jammer and chaff/flare dispensers, and is armed with 80-mm rocket pods.

Paraguay: At least one Mi-8 delivered for the army
Peru: The survivors of 51 Mi-8s and 27 Mi-17s serve with the army, and with the air force's Escuadróns 332 and 441 at Lima-Callao.
Poland: 50+ Mi-8s and -17s serve with the 103 PL at Warszawa-Bemowo, with the 37th PST at Leznica-Wielka, and with the 36th SPLT at Warsaw-Okecie.
Romania: 25 Mi-8Ps and Mi-17s serve with the MAI/Polita at Baneasa, and with a FAR unit at Alexini.
Russia: Large numbers remain in service. Most variants are in use.
Slovakia: After the division of Czechoslovakia, Slovakia retained nine Mi-8 and 19 Mi-17 transports, together with an Mi-8PPA. These serve with squadrons at Sliac, Piestany, Malacky and Prerov.
Sri Lanka: Mi-17 deliveries (3?) have reportedly commenced recently.
Sudan: Mi-8 (4 of 10 delivered)
Syria: Mi-8/-17 (100+ including 'Hip-J/-K')
Tadjikistan: 10 Mi-8 ordered
Turkmenistan: One Mi-8 in government service, perhaps more with air force?
Ukraine: Large numbers remain in service, although some have been offered for sale. Most variants are in use.
United States of America: The US Army operates some Soviet-built helicopters, with at least one Mi-8.
Uzbekistan: One Mi-17 in government service, perhaps more with air force
Vietnam: Between 30 and 50 Mi-8s and Mi-17s serve with the 916th Helicopter Transport Regiment at Hoa Lac.
Yemen: Unification of the two Yemens brought together 25 North Yemeni 'Hips' and 30 South Yemeni examples. The type was used by both sides in the 1994 civil war.
Yugoslavia: 50 Mi-8s with 780th TRE and 787th TRE, under Serbian command.
Zambia: Seven Mi-8s were delivered, but at least five have have been withdrawn from use.

Mil **Mi-8TB 'Hip-E' and Mi-8TBK 'Hip-F'**

Early experience with the 'Hip-C' armed assault version of the Mi-8 validated the airborne assault concept, and Mil subsequently developed a dedicated 'Hip' variant. The **Mi-8TB** is a minimum-change derivative of the basic Mi-8T transport helicopter, with a 12.7-mm Afanasayev machine-gun in a flexible mounting in the bottom of the nose, operated by the flight engineer. This

replaces the lower of the central two transparencies in the nosecone. The aircraft is also fitted with redesigned braced outriggers that each have three underslung pylons capable of carrying a UV-32-57 rocket pod, 250-kg (557-lb) bomb or equivalent. Above the outer two pylons are launch rails for the 9M17 Falanga (AT-2 'Swatter') anti-tank missile, which is aimed by the co-pilot

via a gyro-stabilised sight. When fully armed, the 'Hip-E' can carry only 14 troops and a limited fuel load, but packs an impressive punch. With a full attack load of six UV-32-57 rocket pods (192 57-mm rockets) and four 'Swatters', the Mi-8TB is more heavily armed than the Mi-24 'Hind'. Former **Soviet** Mil Mi-8TBs have now largely been replaced by similarly armed 'Hip-Hs'.

The related **Mil Mi-8TBK** was built for export to **East Germany**, because the Falanga missile had not been cleared for export. Instead, **'Hip-F'** had six 'overwing' launch rails for the 9M14M Malyutka (AT-3 'Sagger') anti-tank missile on its six-pylon outriggers. The aircraft served with the East German air force and navy, and some transferred to the **Luftwaffe** after reunification.

317

Mil Mi-8TB 'Hip-E' and Mi-8TBK 'Hip-F'

Others were exported to **Nicaragua**. Some **Yugoslav** Mil Mi-8s may also have been locally modified to carry the AT-3.

SPECIFICATION

Mil Mi-8TB 'Hip-E'
generally similar to the Mil Mi-8 'Hip-C' except in the following particulars:
Weights: empty 7422 kg (16,362 lb); normal take-off 11564 kg (25,494 lb)
Fuel and load: maximum auxiliary fuel 915 litres (242 US gal); maximum ordnance 1821 kg (4,015 lb)
Speed: maximum speed at sea level 245 km/h (132 kt; 152 mph)
Range: ferry range 930 km (502 nm; 578 miles); radius of action 200 km (108 nm; 124 miles)

This is one of the Mi-8TBK 'Hip-Fs' used by the East German navy (Volksmarine). 'Hip-Fs' transferred to the Luftwaffe after reunification have now all been retired.

Mil **Mi-8/9/17 'Hip-D/G/J/K'**

The Mi-8's performance and capacious cabin, plus the plentiful availability of surplus airframes, make it a natural choice for conversion to other roles. Many 'Hips' of various types are in front-line service with the air forces of the former Soviet Union, acting as ECM jamming platforms, command posts and Elint aircraft. The first special-purpose Mi-8 variant identified by NATO was the **Mi-8PS 'Hip-D'**. Fitted with long rectangular boxes on its outriggers, the aircraft also has a pair of canted tubular antennas above the rear fuselage, and a V-shaped antenna mast under the tailboom supporting an unusual twin wire antenna. The aircraft has been described as a radio relay platform, or as an airborne command post. The tubular antennas above the fuselage bear some resemblance to one of the aerials carried by the 'Hook-B' command post.

The **Mil Mi-9 'Hip-G'** is a further command post and radio relay aircraft, and may have been designed as a replacement for the 'Hip-D', although both remained in front-line service with the Group of Soviet Forces in Germany until their departure in 1994. Alternatively, the 'Hip-G' may have been intended primarily for export, since it was delivered to **East Germany**, **Hungary** and **Czechoslovakia**. The Mil Mi-9 has the smaller clamshell doors (with vertical hinge line) associated with the Mi-8S and earlier Mi-8 variants. It also has an unusual 'hockey stick' antenna under the tailboom, with another under the port clamshell door.

The **Mil Mi-8SMV** bears the NATO reporting name **'Hip-J'** and is believed to operate in the ECM jamming role. Clearly based on the standard Mi-8T airframe, 'Hip-J' has a small bulge under the co-pilot's window, and has two vertical 'handle' antennas and two box-like fairings on the fuselage sides. The **Mil Mi-8PPA 'Hip-K'** is a dedicated communications jammer, and is very distinctive in appearance. Very large but quite shallow box fairings are fitted on the fuselage sides, and a complex antenna array is mounted behind these, adjacent to the former clamshell doors. These antenna arrays consist of a fine square mesh on a rectangular tubular framework, with six cross dipole antennas, in three vertical rows of two, projecting from short plinths which

Above: The Mi-8PS 'Hip-D' is a dedicated airborne command post/relay aircraft, and usually operates in conjunction with the Mi-9 in many army aviation regiments.

Right: The Mi-9 is a command post and bristles with antennas, including two distinctive 'hockey sticks' under the tailboom and rear fuselage. Several have been exported, to Czechoslovakia, Hungary and East Germany.

stand proud from the tubular framework. A side-by-side row of six heat exchangers is located below the forward fuselage. The Mi-8PPA is in service in **Russia** and the **Czech Republic**.

Right: Hungary may be the only operator of the 'Hip-H (EW)', an Mi-17 airframe carrying equipment based on that used by the Mi-8PPA, but with a new antenna array.

Below: This Czech Mi-8PPA is a dedicated communications jamming aircraft.

This is one of the Czech air force's two unidentified special-purpose Mi-17s. The purpose of the four drum-like fairings is unknown.

Although it bears obvious similarities to the Mi-8PPA 'Hip-K', the **Mil Mi-17P** or **Mil Mi-17PP** is known to NATO simply as the **'Hip-H (EW)'**. Based on the Mil Mi-17 airframe, this communications jammer has the same row of heat exchangers under the forward fuselage, and the same box-like fairings on the fuselage sides. In place of the mesh and dipole antenna array, the new variant has a solid array which seems to consist of shallow circular drum antennas set into a slightly square concave fairing. The solid array is slightly larger than that fitted to 'Hip-K' and has eight vertical rows of four drum antennas, with four more drums set in a smaller square mounted on the tailboom, adjacent to the Doppler box.

The **Czech Republic** operates two radically modified Mil Mi-17s which have no NATO reporting name and no known designation. These carry two huge drum-like fair- ings, mounted one behind the other. Both are carried vertically upright on special outriggers on each side of the fuselage. There are several blade antennas above the tailboom, and the cabin contains two operator's stations, each with a large display screen, keyboard and oscilloscope.

SPECIFICATION

Mil Mi-9 'Hip-G'
generally similar to the Mil Mi-8 'Hip-C' except in the

The Mi-8SMV 'Hip-J' is an ECM and Elint platform. The Soviet Group of Forces in Germany included six of these aircraft, based at Cochstedt, close to the inter-German border.

following particulars:
Weights: empty 7500 kg (16,534 lb); normal take-off 11000 kg (24,250 lb)
Fuel and load: internal fuel 2615 litres (691 US gal)
Range: 480 km (259 nm;298 miles); radius of action 200 km (108 nm; 124 miles)

Mil **Mi-10 'Harke'**

The **Mil Mi-10 'Harke'** is a specialised flying crane version of the Mil Mi-6 'Hook'. First flown in 1960 as the **V-10** prototype, the Mil Mi-10 **'Harke-A'** in production form has the same powerplants, transmission system and rotors as the Mi-6, with a shallower fuselage. This supports a very tall, very wide track (6.01 m/19.7 ft front, 6.92 m/22.7 ft rear) quadricycle landing gear which allows the helicopter to be taxied with almost any load carried underslung between the undercarriage units (ground/ underfuselage clearance is 3.75 m/12.3 ft). Alternatively, wheeled loading platforms can be rolled under the aircraft and clipped to the undercarriage units. Twenty-eight passengers can be carried internally, or freight can be loaded via a door on the starboard side. The **Mil Mi-10K 'Harke-B'** has a shortened, narrower-track undercarriage, but has a ventral gondola with a backward-facing seat, allowing a second pilot to hover the aircraft accurately over a load and to operate the hoist. Small numbers of both types may remain available to the **Russian military**.

SPECIFICATION

Mil Mi-10K 'Harke-B'
Rotor system: main rotor diameter 35.00 m (114 ft 10 in); tail rotor diameter 6.30 m (20 ft 8 in); main rotor disc area 962.11 m² (10,356.43 sq ft); tail rotor disc area 31.17 m² (335.55 sq ft)
Fuselage and tail: length overall, rotors turning 41.89 m (137 ft 5.5 in) and fuselage 32.86 m (107 ft 9.75 in); height overall 7.80 m (25 ft 7 in); wheel track 5.00 m (16 ft 4.75 in); wheel base 8.74 m (28 ft 8 in)

Powerplant: two PNPP 'Aviadvigatel' (Soloviev) D-25VF turboshafts each rated at 4847 kW (6,500 shp)
Weights: empty 24680 kg (54,409 lb); maximum take-off 38000 kg (83,774 lb)
Fuel and load: internal fuel 8670 litres (19,114 lb) including auxiliary fuel in two cabin tanks; external fuel none; maximum payload 14000 kg (30,864 lb)
Speed: maximum cruising speed at optimum altitude

Mil Mi-10 flying cranes are nominally operated by Aeroflot, but are often tasked by the Russian military.

250 km/h (135 kt; 155 mph)
Range: ferry range 795 km (429 nm; 494 miles) with auxiliary fuel
Performance: service ceiling 3000 m (9,845 ft)

Mil **Mi-14PL 'Haze-A'**

It soon became apparent that the Mil Mi-8 could form the basis of a replacement for the many Mi-4 'Hounds' in service with the AV-MF in the ASW and SAR roles. Accordingly, a new version was developed with a boat-like hull, flotation gear and other improvements, resulting in the **Mil Mi-14**, which was allocated the new NATO reporting name **'Haze'**. Development commenced in 1968, resulting in a prototype, the **V-14**, in 1973. The production **Mil Mi-14PL** (NATO **'Haze-A'**) is a dedicated ASW platform, with a towed APM-60 MAD, OKA-2 dipping sonar, sonobuoys and a retractable Type 12-M search radar. Early Mi-14PLs had undercarriage doors, but these were soon deleted. To improve controllability in hovering flight, the more powerful TV3-117 engine of the Mi-17 was adopted during production, and the tail rotor changed sides from starboard to port. However, there was no change of reporting name or designation. The latest 'Haze-As' have a relocated APM-60D MAD and various other improvements, including a new IFF system, and are designated **Mi-14PLM**.

The Mi-14PL has been exported to **Bulgaria**, **Cuba**, **Libya**, **Poland** and **Syria**. One Polish aircraft has been modified for SAR training under the designation **Mi-14PX**.

SPECIFICATION

Mil Mi-14PL 'Haze-A'
Rotor system: main rotor diameter 21.29 m (69 ft 10.25 in); tail rotor diameter 3.91 m (12 ft 9.875 in); main rotor disc area 356.00 m² (3,832.08 sq ft); tail rotor disc area 12.01 m² (129.25 sq ft)
Fuselage and tail: length overall, rotors turning 25.32 m (83 ft 1 in) and fuselage 18.37 m (60 ft 3.0 in); height overall 6.93 m (22 ft 9 in); wheel base 4.13 m (13 ft 6.5 in)
Powerplant: two Klimov (Isotov) TV3-117A turboshafts each rated at 1268 kW (1,700 shp) in earlier helicopters, or two Klimov (Isotov) TV3-117M turboshafts each rated at 1417 kW (1,900 shp) or TV3-117MT turboshafts each rated at 2245 kW (1,950 shp) in later helicopters
Weights: empty 8902 kg (19,625 lb); maximum take-off 14000 kg (30,864 lb)
Fuel and load: standard fuel 1450 kg (3,197 lb) or 3530 litres (933 US gal) in one internal and two external tanks; auxiliary fuel up to 1420 kg (3,131 lb) or 465 litres (123 US gal) in one or two cabin tanks
Speed: maximum level speed 'clean' at optimum altitude 230 km/h (124 kt; 143 mph); maximum cruising speed at optimum altitude 215 km/h (116 kt; 133 mph); economical cruising speed at optimum altitude 205 km/h (110 kt; 127 mph)
Range: ferry range 1135 km (612 nm; 705 miles) with

Above: The Mi-14PLM has a revised avionics fit, and its APM-60 towed magnetic anomaly detector (MAD) bird is mounted lower on the rear fuselage. Revealed in 1989, it retains the NATO ASCC 'Haze-A' reporting name. The Mi-14PLM may be a new-build aircraft, or may have been produced by conversion of redundant Mi-14PLs. No Mil Mi-14PLMs have been exported.

auxiliary fuel; range 925 km (499 nm; 575 miles) with standard fuel; endurance 5 hours 56 minutes
Performance: service ceiling 4000 m (13,123 ft); initial rate of climb 468 m (1,535 ft) per minute; time to 1000 m (3,281 ft) 2 minutes 18 secs

Above: This German Mi-14PL is painted in dark blue maritime camouflage. The 'Haze-A' has an internal heat exchanger for its air conditioning system.

Mil Mi-14BT 'Haze-B'

The **Mil Mi-14BT 'Haze-B'** is a dedicated minesweeping helicopter, delivered only to the **AV-MF** and the **Volksmarine** but then transferred to the Luftwaffe. About 25 'Haze-Bs' were built, six of these going to the East German navy. Mine-sweeping trials were carried out in 1983, and production Mi-14BTs were deployed on multinational mine clearing operations during the early 1980s. The aircraft has never been widely deployed, however, the Russian navy and its allies preferring to use surface vessels for the mine countermeasures (MCM) role.

Externally, the Mil Mi-14BT can be distinguished by its lack of a towed MAD, and by having its SKW heating and ventilation system mounted in a pod on the starboard side of the cabin, above the windows. A further distinguishing feature is a broad strake running below the windows on the same side. The aircraft also has a small box under the tailboom, forward of the Doppler box, which houses a searchlight designed to illuminate the mine-clearing sled's launch and recovery at night. Some Mil Mi-14BTs have small windows in the lower part of the rear fuse-

The Mi-14BT is a dedicated mine countermeasures helicopter, equipped to tow various types of mine-clearing sled. On the Mi-14BT the SKW heating system is relocated to a pod scabbed on to the starboard side of the cabin. This East German Mi-14BT was converted to SAR duties but retains the external configuration of the 'Haze-B'. The Mi-14 has not been retained by the Luftwaffe.

lage, to allow the MCM operator to watch the mine-clearing sled.

The Mi-14BT 'Haze-B' can tow at least three different types of sled, usually doing this while flying at between 15 and 20 m (50 and 65 ft). An electromagnetic sled towing electrical cables is used against magnetic mines, while a noise-generating sled is used against acoustic mines and a sled tow-

ing small detonators is used against contact mines. Several of the East German Mi-14BTs were withdrawn from mine countermeasures duties and were converted for SAR duties prior to reunification, and all were offered for sale shortly after their transfer into Luftwaffe hands. Their fate remains uncertain. Some have emerged as civilian water-bombers for use in the fire-fighting role.

SPECIFICATION

Mil Mi-14BT 'Haze-B'
generally similar to the Mil Mi-14PL 'Haze-A' except in the following particulars:
Weights: empty 8800 kg (19,400 lb)

Mil Mi-14PS 'Haze-C'

The **'Haze-C'** is a dedicated search and rescue variant for the **AV-MF**, based on the airframe of the Mil Mi-14BT, with the same external air conditioning/heat exchanger pod and fuselage strake, but also with a widened cabin entry door, an increased capacity rescue winch and pop-out articulated searchlights in the nose. No MAD is fitted, but the Mil Mi-14BT's MCM sled illuminating searchlight is retained. Some Polish aircraft have an extra downward-shining searchlight in a nose 'beak',

and some former Soviet aircraft carry a survey camera in a third box under the tailboom. Poland is the only export customer.

SPECIFICATION

Mil Mi-14PS 'Haze-C'
generally similar to the Mil Mi-14BT 'Haze-B' except in the following particulars:
Fuselage and tail: fuselage length 18.78 m (61 ft 7.5 in)

This Russian AV-MF Mi-14PS has the unusual nose-mounted searchlight 'beak' fairing fitted to late production examples. The main cabin entry door (on the port side) is of much increased width, and is equipped with a swing-out internal rescue winch. Some aircraft have a camera box below the rear part of the tailboom.

Mil Mi-24 'Hind-A', 'Hind-B' and 'Hind-C'

The original **Mil Mi-24** was developed as a flying armoured personnel carrier, carrying a squad of soldiers and providing its own defensive and suppressive fire, and relying on speed for protection. It was optimised for moving troops forward quickly, either in support of an armoured push or participating in independent airborne assaults. The Mil Design Bureau carefully studied US experience in Vietnam, and concluded that speed and firepower were essential in a battlefield helicopter.

To hasten development, the Mil Mi-24 was designed around the same 1,700-shp (1268-kW) TV2-117A engines and dynamics system as the Mil Mi-8, but with a new airframe and a new smaller tail rotor, which turned at higher speed. The new cabin seated eight, in two back-to-back rows of four, with access via horizontally split outward-opening doors. The windows could be opened and incorporated firing supports for the occupants' AK-47 assault rifles. The crew were housed in an extensive greenhouse, with an engineer/gunner forward to aim the 12.7-mm machine-gun, and pilot and navigator side-by-side further aft.

From the start, the Mil Mi-24 was fitted with stub wings (similar to those fitted to the Mi-6 'Hook'), the purpose of which was to generate lift in forward flight, thereby offloading the main rotor and leaving more power available to carry weapons and provide greater speed. The wings also reduced turning radius and acted as a convenient

point to mount weapons of various types.

The prototype made its maiden flight during 1970 and was designated **V-24** or **A.10**. It, and two pre-production aircraft (also A.10s), had wings with no anhedral and were codenamed **'Hind-B'** by NATO because their existence was discovered after that of the production Mil Mi-24. One of the pre-production aircraft is reported to have tested an enclosed fan or fenestron tail rotor, like that fitted to the Aérospatiale Gazelle. The A.10s established a number of rotary-wing world speed, altitude and time-to-climb records, in the hands of both male and female pilots, by eventually reaching a remarkable 198.8 kt (368.4 km/h; 228.9 mph).

The production **'Hind-A'** entered frontline service with the **Group of Soviet Forces in Germany** during 1973, and was fitted with anhedral stub wings. These retained underwing pylons, but also had vertical endplates which served as the mounting for two missile launch rails for the 9M117P Falanga (AT-2 'Swatter') missile. A missile guidance/illuminator pod was mounted below the fuselage and a camera gun was recessed into the leading edge of the port inner pylon. During the production run of the 'Hind-A', the TV3-117 engine (as used by the Mil Mi-17) was introduced, and this led to the tail rotor being repositioned from the starboard side of the tailboom to the port. Late-model 'Hind-As' also received a panel with seven external strengthening ribs on the rear fuselage. An unarmed ver-

sion of the aircraft used for training, with no gun, undernose blister and missile rails, was dubbed **'Hind-C'** by NATO.

Only a handful of these early 'Hinds', if any, remain in service, and those that do serve as trainers or hacks. Early Mil Mi-24s were not widely exported, but examples were noted in service in **Afghanistan**, **Algeria**, **Libya** and **Vietnam**. Some of these export aircraft have even been photographed with PZU intake filters, normally associated with later variants.

A more comprehensive list of current op-

erators of early 'Hinds' is given in the Mil Mi-24D 'Hind-D' operators section.

SPECIFICATION

Mil Mi-24 'Hind-A'
generally similar to the Mil Mi-24 'Hind-D' except in the following particulars:
Speed: maximum level sspeed 'clean' at optimum altitude 320 km/h (173 kt; 199 mph)
Performance: maximum rate of climb at sea level 900 m (2,953 ft) per minute

This early Mil Mi-24 'Hind-A' is fully armed with rocket pods and wingtip AT-2 'Swatter' ATGMs. Early aircraft had a starboard side tail rotor.

Mil Mi-24D 'Hind-D' and Mi-24V 'Hind-E'

Operational experience with the initial Mil Mi-24s soon showed that the original concept was slightly flawed. The type's ground attack potential was clearly reduced when carrying troops, and it was realised that this task was better suited to less agile helicopters like the Mil Mi-8. As the Mi-24's transport role declined in importance, anti-tank capability became progressively more important. It soon became apparent that the greenhouse canopy of the 'Hind-A' gave less than perfect all-round visibility, and yet offered the crew little protection. To develop another new battlefield helicopter was unnecessary, since in many respects the basic Mi-24 design had proved outstanding.

The solution was to redesign the Mi-24 with an entirely new nose, with heavily armoured tandem cockpits for the pilot (rear) and gunner (front). These were covered by bubble canopies, with bullet-proof armoured glass windscreens. The pilot's cockpit canopy incorporated a large door which opened to starboard, while the front canopy hinged sideways to port. Besides ease of access, the new arrangement gave a much smaller frontal area, improved visibility and reduced drag.

Under the nose was fitted a stabilised turret housing a completely new four-barrelled JakB 12.7-mm Gatling gun. This has a very high rate of fire (about 4,000 rpm), and in its new turret could be traversed through 70° on each side of the centreline, elevated by 15° and depressed through 60°. The gun is normally aimed from the front cockpit, but the turret can be locked fore-and-aft, allowing the pilot to fire the gun using a fixed sight.

New sensors

Beside the new gun turret were a missile guidance pod (to port) and an electro-optical device, normally covered by armoured doors, but apparently serving as a laser rangefinder and designator. Further inputs to the weapons system come from the sensitive pitch and yaw vanes mounted on the long air data boom projecting from the forward cockpit. These sense sideslip and relative wind, allowing accurate weapons aiming. Aft of the cockpit the aircraft was unchanged, the flight engineer sitting in the narrow 'corridor' between the cockpit and the cabin. The cabin itself retained its seats and horizontally-split doors, but came to be regarded as a space for stowing missile reloads rather than for carrying passengers. The new variant received the bureau designation **Mil Mi-24A**, but some sources suggest a military designation of **Mil Mi-24D**. Export variants are designated **Mil Mi-25**. The NATO reporting name is **'Hind-D'**.

The 'Hind-D' was soon replaced in service by the outwardly similar **Mil Mi-24V 'Hind-E'**, which introduced wingtip launch rails for the tube-launched AT-6 'Spiral' missile. This accelerates faster than the older missile, has a range about 1000 m (3,280 ft) greater, and generates less smoke and flare on launch and in flight. It also necessitated the fitting of a new enlarged missile guidance pod. A HUD replaced the pilot's reflector gunsight. The Mil Mi-24V is the major current production version, and its export sub-variants are designated **Mil Mi-35**. The Mil Mi-24V also forms the basis for the **Mil Mi-24P**, **Mil Mi-24RCh** and **Mil Mi-24K** variants (described separately). Since the war in Afghanistan, Mil Mi-24Vs have been fitted with a variety of defensive systems, including IR jammers, dispensers for IRCM flares and chaff cartridges, and even exhaust suppressors to reduce the aircraft's IR signature. These, however, impose a significant drag penalty, and are not usually fitted in peacetime.

An unarmed version of the 'Hind-D' has been developed for training purposes. Reportedly designated **Mil Mi-24DU**, its gun turret has been faired over.

SPECIFICATION

Mil Mi-24D 'Hind-D'
Rotor system: main rotor diameter 17.30 m (56 ft 9 in); tail rotor diameter 3.908 m (12 ft 10 in); main rotor disc area 235.00 m² (2,529.52 sq ft); tail rotor disc area 11.99 m² (129.12 sq ft)
Wing: span 6.536 m (21 ft 5.5 in)
Fuselage and tail: length overall, rotors turning 19.79 m (64 ft 11 in) and fuselage 17.51 m (57 ft 5.5 in) excluding rotors and gun; height overall 6.50 m (21 ft 4 in) with rotors turning and 4.44 m (14 ft 6.75 in) to top of rotor head; stabiliser span 3.27 m (10 ft 9 in); wheel track 3.03 m (9 ft 11.5 in); wheel base 4.39 m (14 ft 5 in)
Powerplant: two Klimov (Isotov) TV3-117 Series III turboshafts each rated at 1640 kW (2,200 shp)
Weights: empty 8400 kg (18,519 lb); normal take-off 11000 kg (24,250 lb); maximum take-off 12500 kg (27,557 lb)
Fuel and load: internal fuel 1500 kg (3,307 lb) or 2130 litres (563 US gal) plus provision for 1000 kg (2,205 lb) or 850 litres (225 US gal) of auxiliary fuel in a cabin tank; external fuel (instead of internal auxiliary tank) up to 1200 kg (2,646 lb) in four 500-litre (132-US gal) drop tanks; maximum ordnance 2400 kg (5,291 lb)
Speed: maximum level speed 'clean' at optimum altitude 310 km/h (168 kt; 192 mph); maximum cruising speed at optimum altitude 260 km/h (140 kt; 162 mph)
Range: 750 km (405 nm; 466 miles) with internal fuel; combat radius 160 km (86 nm; 99 miles) with maximum military load, or 250 km (135 nm; 155 miles) with two drop tanks, or 288 km (155 nm; 179 miles) with four drop tanks
Performance: maximum rate of climb at sea level 750 m (2,461 ft) per minute; service ceiling 4500 m (14,765 ft); hovering ceiling 2200 m (7,220 ft) out of ground effect

OPERATORS

Afghanistan: 60 Mi-24s currently operational; 'Hind-As', '-Ds', '-Es' and '-Fs' (some of them export Mi-25/-35 variants) served with the 332nd CHR at Jurum, the 375th CHR at Mazar-e-Sharif and the 377th CHR at Kabul. They now serve with unknown units supporting varying factions
Algeria: about 30 Mi-24s operational, including 'Hind-A', '-D' and possibly 'Hind-E' models
Angola: about 30 Mi-24s operational, including 'Hind-E' and '-F' models
Armenia: 13 Mi-24s operational
Azerbaijan: less than 10 'Hinds' in service
Bulgaria: 45 Mi-24s operational with CHRs at Stara Zagora and Targoviste
Byelorussia: 80 Hinds operational with OVPs at Pruzhany, Luninets and Borovtsy
Croatia: seen at Pula – believed to be ex-Ukranian
Cuba: at least 12 Mi-24s operational
Czech Republic: 20 'Hind-Ds' with the 51st VRP at Prostejov and 20 Mi-24Vs with the 11th VRP at Line
Ethiopia: 11 survivors, probably fled after the fall of the Mengistu regime
Germany: operated Mi-24s with the following units: 20 Mi-24Ds with KHG-3 at Cottbus, 12 Mi-24Vs and 18 Mi-24Ds with KHG-5 at Basepohl, these units transferring briefly to the Luftwaffe after reunification
Hungary: 'Hinds' serve with the Bakony combat helicopter wing at Szentkirályszabadja, eight Mi-24Ds and eight Mi-24Vs with 1 CHS 'Phoenix', and 16 Mi-24D Mods with 2 CHS 'Falcon'
India: No. 125 HU at Pathankot has Mi-25 'Hind-Ds', while Mi-35 'Hind-Es' are operated by No. 116 HU (base unknown) and No. 104 HU at Pathankot
Iraq: at least 40 Mi-24s operational, including Hind-Ds' and probably 'Hind-Es' and '-Fs'
Kazakhstan: in service with the 486th OVP at Ucharal
North Korea: at least 50 Mi-24s operational
Krygyzstan: some Mi-24s at Frunze
Laos: unconfirmed operator of eight 'Hind-Ds' (Mi-25s?)
Libya: 26 Mi-24s operational, including 'Hind-As', '-Ds' and possibly '-Es'
Mozambique: 15 'Hinds' in service
Nicaragua: six Mi-25s operational
Pakistan: some Afghani defectors evaluated
Peru: 24 Mi-25s operational
Russia: in service with the following units in East Germany, which all returned to Russia during 1991-

This Russian Mi-24D is one of the few 'Hind-Ds' remaining in front-line service during 1993/94, when this aircraft was in use by the Group of Soviet Forces in Germany. Russian army aviation regiments generally use the 'Hind-E'.

The Mi-24V is fitted with endplate launch rails for the 9M114 Shturm (AT-6 'Spiral') ATGM, and has a new command guidance antenna below the port side of the nose. This aircraft carries S-8 80-mm rocket pods underwing.

Mil Mi-24D 'Hind-D' and Mi-24V 'Hind-E'

The Mi-24DU is a little-known trainer version of the Mi-24D, with full dual controls permanently installed, and with no nose-mounted gun turret.

1994: 172nd VP from Parchum, 178th OVP from Borstel, 225th OVP at Allstedt, 336th OVP at Nohra, 337th OVP at Mahlwinkel, 439th OVP from Parchum, 440th OVP from Borstel, 485th OVP from Brandi, 486th OVP from Altes Lager, and 487th OVP from Gross-Dolln. The 55th OVP from Bagisz in Poland returned to Krasnodar in 1992. Many other Mi-24 units already served in Russia

Syria: over 50 Mi-24s in service, including Mi-25s and Mi-35s

United States: the US Army has at least one ex-Libyan 'Hind-D' and possibly also some captured Iraqi and ex-East German Mi-24s for evaluation

Vietnam: received 'Hind-As' which may be wfu

Yemen: delivered to South Yemen c. 1981, and absorbed by the unified Yemeni armed forces on the merger of the two countries

Slovakia: eight Mi-24Ds, one Mi-24DU and 10 Mi-24Vs serve with the 4th Vrtulnikovy Pluk at Presov

Poland: 16 Hind-Ds' with 49 PSB at Proszcz-Gdansk and 16 Mi-24Vs with 56 PSB at Howrozclaw

Ukraine: 270 'Hinds' operational with 111 CHS and 119th OVP at Brody, 287th OVP at Rankhovka, 513th OVP at Berdichev, 441st OVP at Korosten, 442nd OVP at Zhovtnevoe, 335th OVP at Kalinov, and 488th OVP at Vapnyovka. Handfuls of 'Hind-Gs' serve with other Ukranian units

OVP – Independent Combat Helicopter Regiment
CHS/R – Combat Helicopter Squadron/Regiment
HU – Helicopter Unit

Mil **Mi-24P** 'Hind-F'

The development of the **Mil Mi-24P** was spurred by combat experience in Afghanistan. The 12.7-mm machine-gun had proved ineffective against some targets, but the use of rockets or guided missile was deemed wasteful. The obvious answer was a larger-calibre cannon. Interim solutions included a variety of podded cannon for carriage underwing, and the little-known **Mil Mi-24VP**, a 'Hind-E' with a twin-barrelled GSh-23L in its nose turret, may have dated from this time. The GSh-23L proved too big for the 'Hind's' turret mechanism, and ammunition stowage was also a problem, dropping to 300 rounds or less from the 1,470 carried by the 'Hind-D' and 'Hind-E' for their 12.7-mm machine-guns.

A better solution was to delete the nose turret altogether, and to rigidly mount a GSh-30-2 twin-barrelled 30-mm cannon, with 750 rounds of ammunition, on the star-board side of the forward fuselage of a basic 'Hind-E'. This modification resulted in the Mil Mi-24P **'Hind-F'**. The new aircraft is often deployed in mixed regiments along-side Mi-24V 'Hind-Es', and the two types can usefully operate in concert.

Export versions of the 'Hind-F' are designated **Mil Mi-25P** and **Mil Mi-35P**. These are believed to have been supplied to **Angola** and **Iraq**.

SPECIFICATION

Mil Mi-24P 'Hind-F'
generally similar to the Mil Mi-24D 'Hind-D' except in the following particulars:
Fuselage and tail: overall length 19.19 m (62 ft 11.5 in)
Powerplant: two Klimov (Isotov) TV3-117 Series III turboshafts each rated at 1545 kW (2,072 shp)

Weights: empty 8550 kg (18,849 lb); normal take-off 11200 kg (24,691 lb); maximum take-off 11800 kg (26,014 lb)
Fuel and load: maximum ordnance 2400 kg (5,291 lb)
Speed: maximum level speed 'clean' at optimum altitude 335 km/h (180 kt; 208 mph); maximum cruising speed at optimum altitude 270 km/h (145 kt; 168 mph); economical cruising speed at optimum altitude 217 km/h (117 kt; 135 mph)
Range: ferry range 1200 km (648 nm; 746 miles) with auxiliary fuel; range 500 km (270 nm; 310 miles) with internal fuel
Performance: hovering ceiling 1500 m (4,920 ft) out of ground effect

The Mi-24P has a twin-barrelled 30-mm cannon fixed to the starboard side of the forward fuselage to give heavier firepower. This colourful example wears Luftwaffe markings.

Mil **Mi-24RCh** 'Hind-G' and Mi-24K 'Hind-G2'

At least two 'Hind' reconnaissance variants have been produced for **Russia**, each carrying out different tasks over the battlefield. The first model to be identified by NATO was the **Mil Mi-24RCh** (OKB **Mi-24RKR**) **'Hind-G'**, which was seen in press and TV reports during the aftermath of the Chernobyl disaster. Equipped with 'clutching hand' devices at the bottom of the wing's vertical endplates in place of missile launch rails, and with no missile guidance pod or laser/electro-optical pods under the nose, the aircraft's role was correctly assumed to be 'connected with radiation sampling'. In fact, the aircraft is deployed in small numbers throughout the former Soviet armed forces, and is charged with NBC reconnaissance, picking up soil samples to ascertain the spread of fallout and of chemical and bacteriological agents. The aircraft is also fitted with a rearward-firing marker flare dispenser mounted on the tail-skid, and has an unusual cylindrical device projecting down from the port side of the forward fuselage. The aircraft retains its undernose 12.7-mm gun turret, and sometimes carries rocket pods, although fuel tanks and box-like pods are also carried.

The second reconnaissance Mil Mi-24 version is the **Mil Mi-24K 'Hind-G2'**, used for fire correction. This is based on the airframe of the Mi-24RCh, but with a large, bulky camera housing under the nose, off-set to starboard, in place of the laser/electro-optical package fitted to most late-model 'Hinds'. The housing clearly includes a moving section, presumably allowing the camera lens to be 'pointed'. 'Hind-G2' also has a square-shaped camera window set into the starboard side of the fuselage, where the lower half of the starboard cabin door would be, had the door not been faired over.

At least one Mil Mi-24V has been modified for environmental and ecological monitoring, and was displayed at an international 'Exhibition for Ecology and Resources' at Nizhny Novgorod. It featured a large, box-like pod on the starboard outer pylon, reportedly developed by the Polet Scientific Production Association and the Scientific Research Radiophysics Institute. This aircraft also has a tongue-like flat 'board' projecting ahead of the front cockpit from the position where the top of the gun turret would have been (if fitted). This device may or may not be re-tractable, and its purpose is unknown. Other one-off research helicopters based on the Mi-24RC hvae been identified.

Below: About half the front-line Russian army aviation independent helicopter regiments include single mixed flights of two Mi-24RKRs and two Mi-24Ks in each of their three constituent squadrons. More of these specialised aircraft serve with units attached directly to fronts and to manoeuvre groups.

Above: The Mi-24K is a dedicated artillery fire-correction helicopter, equipped with a huge oblique camera in the cabin. A smaller electro-optical or video device replaces the usual Mi-24D/V EO package.

Mil Mi-26 'Halo'

The **Mil Mi-26 'Halo'** was designed as a replacement for the Mil Mi-6, but was intended to offer 50-100 per cent greater capability. Designed around a cabin broadly equivalent to that of the Lockheed C-130 Hercules, the Mil Mi-26 is the world's most powerful helicopter. A prototype was first flown on 14 December 1977, and squadron-strength military evaluations began in 1983, with full service entry in 1985.

Although dimensionally slightly smaller than the Mil Mi-6, and with a 3-m (9.8-ft) smaller rotor diameter, the Mil Mi-26 uses advanced gearbox design and makes extensive use of composites and advanced aluminium-lithium alloys to save weight, resulting in an empty weight less than 1000 kg (2,204 lb) greater than the Mi-6. Its two D-136 turboshafts are more than twice as powerful as those fitted to the 'Hook', and its advanced eight-bladed rotor allows it to lift almost twice the payload.

In addition to its crew of five, the Mil Mi-26's fuselage can accommodate up to 80 fully-equipped troops or 60 stretchers. There is a permanent four-seat passenger compartment aft of the flight deck, but the main hold can be reconfigured for passenger transport, air ambulance or freight duties.

This Mil Mi-26 belongs to India's No. 126 Helicopter Unit, the ironically named 'Feather-weights', which is based at Chandigarh. Ten were delivered to the unit.

Loading of the 'Halo' is achieved using a downward-hinged lower door, with an integral folding ramp, and the two clamshell upper doors. Two 2500-kg (5,511-lb) capacity electric overhead hoists and a 500-kg (1,102-lb) capacity winch are provided for freight handling, together with roller conveyors in the floor.

While command post versions of 'Halo' are expected, only one sub-variant has so far been announced: the **Mi-26TZ** tanker. An advanced transport version, with uprated engines and composite rotor blades, is also believed to be under development. A Russian air force Mil Mi-26 observed clandestinely at Mil's Moscow airfield during 1992 was described as having a nose-mounted gun (or possibly an inflight-refuelling probe).

The basic Mil Mi-26 is operated by both Aeroflot and the **Russian air force**, and has been exported to **India** (serving with No. 126 Helicopter Unit at Chandigarh). Some may also serve with **Ukrainian** armed forces, although this cannot be confirmed.

SPECIFICATION

Mil Mi-26 'Halo-A'
Rotor system: main rotor diameter 32.00 m (105 ft 9 in); tail rotor diameter 7.61 m (24 ft 11.5 in); main rotor disc area 804.25 m² (8,657.13 sq ft); tail rotor disc area 45.48 m² (489.60 sq ft)
Fuselage and tail: length overall, rotors turning 40.025 m (131 ft 3.75 in) and fuselage 33.727 m (110 ft 8 in) excluding tail rotor; height overall 8.145 m (26 ft 8.25 in) to top of rotor head; wheel track 7.17 m (23 ft 6.25 in); wheel base 8.95 m (29 ft 4.5 in)
Powerplant: two ZMDB 'Progress' (Lotarev) D-136 turboshafts each rated at 8380 kW (11,240 shp)
Weights: empty 28200 kg (62,170 lb); normal take-off 49600 kg (109,347 lb); maximum take-off 56000 kg (123,457 lb)
Fuel and load: internal fuel 12000 litres (3,170 US gal); external fuel none; maximum payload 20000 kg (44,092 lb)
Speed: maximum level speed at optimum altitude 295 km/h (159 kt; 183 mph); normal cruising speed at optimum altitude 255 km/h (137 kt; 158 mph)
Range: ferry range 2000 km (1,080 nm; 1,240 miles) with auxiliary fuel; range 800 km (432 nm; 497 miles) with standard fuel
Performance: service ceiling 4600 m (15,090 ft); hovering ceiling 1800 m (5,905 ft) out of ground effect

Mil Mi-28 'Havoc'

Despite its reported defeat by the Kamov Ka-50 'Hokum', Mil claims to have received an order for the **Mil Mi-28** from the **Russian armed forces**, and continues to market the aircraft actively. The **'Havoc'** is of conventional 'helicopter gunship' configuration, with an undernose cannon and stepped armoured cockpits accommodating pilot (rear) and gunner (forward). The first of three Mil Mi-28 prototypes made its maiden flight on 10 November 1982.

A conventional three-bladed tail rotor was abandoned and replaced on the second and third prototypes by a 'scissors'-type tail rotor, with two independent two-bladed rotors on the same shaft. These are set at approximately 35° to each other and form a narrow X shape. The prototypes also had different exhaust suppressors.

The Mil Mi-28 is armed with a single-barrelled 2A42 30-mm cannon under the nose, with twin 150-round ammunition boxes co-mounted to traverse, elevate and depress with the gun itself, reducing the likelihood of jamming. The gun traverses through 110° on each side of the centreline, elevates to 13° and depresses through 40°. Two rates of fire are available for the gun: 300 rpm for air-to-ground use, and 900 rpm for air-to-air.

A total of four pylons is mounted under the stub wings. Each hardpoint can carry 480 kg (1,058 lb), typically consisting of four tube-launched AT-6 'Spiral' missiles or a variety of rocket pods. These can be loaded using a hand crank and built-in winch. The wingtip houses a chaff/flare dispenser.

The cockpit is covered by flat, non-glint panels of armoured glass, and is protected by titanium and ceramic armour. Vital components are heavily protected and duplicated, and shielded by less important items. In the event of a catastrophic hit, the crew are protected by energy-absorbing seats, which can withstand a 12 m (40 ft) per second crash landing. An emergency escape system is installed which blows off the doors and inflates air bladders on the fuselage sides. The crew members roll over these before pulling their parachute ripcords.

A hatch in the port side, aft of the wing, gives access to the avionics compartment and to an area large enough to accommodate two or three people (in some discomfort). This is intended to allow an Mi-28 to pick up the crew of another downed helicopter. The production **Mil Mi-28N** will feature FLIR and LLLTV in the nose, on each side of the laser rangefinder/designator turret, and will have an NVG-compatible cockpit. Above this is a radome for missile illumination/guidance. A transport derivative of the Mi-28, apparently designated **Mi-40**, is said to be under development.

The Mi-28 is of broadly conventional configuration, with stepped tandem cockpits for pilot and WSO/gunner.

SPECIFICATION

Mil Mi-28 'Havoc-A'
Rotor system: main rotor diameter 17.20 m (56 ft 5 in); tail rotor diameter 3.84 m (12 ft 7.25 in); main rotor disc area 232.35 m² (2,501.10 sq ft); tail rotor disc area 11.58 m² (124.66 sq ft)
Wing: span 4.87 m (16 ft 0 in)
Fuselage and tail: length overall, rotors turning 19.15 m (62 ft 10 in) and fuselage 16.85 m (55 ft 3.5 in); wheel track 2.29 m (7 ft 6.25 in); wheel base 11.00 m (36 ft 1 in)
Powerplant: two Klimov (Isotov) TV3-117 turboshafts each rated at 1640 kW (2,200 shp)
Weights: empty 7000 kg (15,432 lb); maximum take-off 10400 kg (22,928 lb)
Fuel and load: internal fuel about 1900 litres (502 US gal); maximum ordnance about 1920 kg (4,233 lb)
Speed: maximum level speed 'clean' at optimum altitude 300 km/h (162 kt; 186 mph); maximum cruising speed at optimum altitude 270 km/h (146 kt; 168 mph)
Range: 470 km (253 nm; 292 miles) with standard fuel; endurance 2 hours 0 minutes
Performance: service ceiling 5800 m (19,025 ft); hovering ceiling 3600 m (11,810 ft) out of ground effect

Mil Mi-34 'Hermit'

The **Mil Mi-34 'Hermit'** was designed as an Mi-1/Mi-2 replacement, both as a civil light helicopter and, more importantly, as a military trainer and liaison aircraft. It has seating for two pilots, with space behind for a bench seat for two passengers or for cargo. The first Soviet helicopter capable of executing a loop or roll, the Mil Mi-34 was flown initially during 1986. It is sparsely equipped and has unboosted mechanical controls, but incorporates some use of composites in the rotor and tail rotor.

The **Mil Mi-34V** or **Mi-34VAZ**, built by the VAZ motor car works at Togliatigrad, is a twin-engined version of the 'Hermit' and is powered by two 164-kW (220-hp) VAZ-430 twin-chamber rotary engines. A prototype flew during 1993. The Mi-34VAZ also features a totally new rotor head designed around a carbon-fibre star plate and giving very good control response. The new variant offers improved range, endurance and performance characteristics.

SPECIFICATION

Mil Mi-34 'Hermit'
Rotor system: main rotor diameter 10.00 m (32 ft 9.75 in); tail rotor diameter 1.48 m (4 ft 10.25 in); main rotor disc area 78.54 m² (845.42 sq ft); tail rotor disc area 1.72 m² (18.51 sq ft)
Fuselage and tail: length of fuselage 8.71 m (28 ft 7 in); skid track 2.06 m (6 ft 9.25 in)
Powerplant: one VMKB (Vedeneyev) M-14V-26 nine-cylinder air-cooled radial engine rated at 242 kW (325 hp)
Weights: normal take-off 1080 kg (2,381 lb) for aerobatic use or 1200 kg (2,646 lb) for normal use; maximum take-off 1350 kg (2,976 lb)
Fuel and load: internal fuel 120 kg (265 lb); external fuel none

Speed: maximum level speed at optimum altitude 210 km/h (113 kt; 130 mph); maximum cruising speed at optimum altitude 180 km/h (97 kt; 112 mph); economical cruising speed at optimum altitude 160 km/h (86 kt; 99 mph)
Range: 450 km (243 nm; 280 miles) with a 90-kg (198-lb) payload or 180 km (97 nm; 112 miles) with a

The basic Mi-34 shows enormous potential as a training and light utility/liaison helicopter.

165-kg (353-lb) payload
Performance: service ceiling 4500 m (14,765 ft); hovering ceiling 1500 m (4,920 ft) in ground effect

Mil **Mi-38**

The **Mil Mi-38** was conceived as a replacement for the Mil Mi-8 and Mil Mi-17 in Aeroflot and Soviet air force/army service. Of similar configuration to the EH.101, but powered by a pair of 1753-kW (2,350-shp) Klimov TV7-117V turboshafts, the Mil Mi-38 was shown in model form at the 1989 Paris air show and in mock-up form at the 1992 Mosaero show at Zhukhovskii. Fuel is carried in bag-type tanks below the cabin floor, and auxiliary external tanks may also be provided. Seating up to 32 passengers or accommodating up to 5000 kg (11,020 lb) of cargo, the Mil Mi-38 will be cleared for single-pilot operation in the cargo role. Provision is to be made for running the aircraft on liquid gas instead of kerosene.

A first flight was once expected in 1993, with production provisionally scheduled to begin during 1996, but these dates have apparently 'slipped'. The sophisticated new helicopter has a six-bladed main rotor, with non-linear twist and swept tips, a delta 3-type (narrow X) tail rotor like that of the Mil Mi-28 and AH-64, FBW controls and EFIS instruments with five colour CRTs, and makes extensive use of composites and lightweight aluminium-lithium alloys. The aircraft has an entrance door at the front of the cabin to port, with a hatch in the floor, below the rotor drive shaft, for airdropping or underslung loads. This can be replaced by a camera window for survey work. Large clamshell doors are provided at the rear of the cabin, with an integral remotely controlled, hydraulically actuated loading ramp. A roller-conveyor and a powered 'travelling crane' hoist are provided to improve cargo handling.

Various advanced avionics systems will be available as customer options, together with sensors for weighing the cargo and finding the centre of gravity. A closed circuit TV system will be installed for monitoring cargo loading and underslung loads, and there may be a low-cost version of the helicopter with Mi-8-style electromechanical instrumentation.

SPECIFICATION

Mil Mi-38
Rotor system: main rotor diameter 21.10 m (69 ft 2.75 in); tail rotor diameter 3.84 m (12 ft 7.25 in); main rotor disc area 349.67 m² (3,763.91 sq ft); tail rotor disc area 11.58 m² (124.66 sq ft)
Fuselage and tail: length of fuselage 19.70 m (64 ft 7.5 in); stabiliser span 3.60 m (11 ft 9.75 in); wheel track 3.30 m (10 ft 10 in); wheel base 6.61 m (21 ft 8.25 in)
Powerplant: two Klimov (Isotov) TV7-117V turboshafts each flat-rated at 1753 kW (2,350 shp)
Weights: normal take-off 13460 kg (29,674 lb); maximum take-off 14500 kg (31,966 lb)
Fuel and load: external fuel none; maximum payload 5000 kg (11,023 lb)
Speed: maximum level speed 'clean' at optimum altitude 275 km/h (148 kt; 171 mph); maximum cruising speed at optimum altitude 250 km/h (135 kt; 155 mph)
Range: range 1300 km (700 nm; 808 miles) with a 1800-kg (3,968-kg) payload, or 800 km (430 nm; 497 miles) with a 3500-kg (7,716-lb) payload, or 530 km (286 nm; 329 miles) with a 4500-kg (9,921-lb) payload or 325 km (175 nm; 202 miles) with a 5000-kg (11,023-lb) payload
Performance: service ceiling 6500 m (21,325 ft); hovering ceiling 2500 m (8,200 ft) out of ground effect

---

Mitsubishi **F-1**

Mitsubishi Jukogyo Kabushiki Kaisha
5-1, Marunouchi 2-chome, Chiyoda-ku,
Tokyo 100, Japan

Following the successful development of its **T-2** supersonic twin-turbofan two-seat advanced trainer (described separately), Mitsubishi proceeded with a close-support fighter version, designated **F-1**, and tasked primarily with anti-shipping missions. The second and third T-2 prototypes were modified to single-seat configuration, the first such conversion making its maiden flight on 3 June 1975. After a year's evaluation by the **JASDF**'s Air Proving Wing at Gifu, the F-1 was accepted for service and ordered into production as Japan's first indigenous supersonic fighter. The first production F-1 made its maiden flight on 16 June 1977.

Dimensionally, the single-seater is similar to the T-2, but the space behind the pilot's (front) cockpit of the trainer has been replaced by a 'solid' fairing which contains an avionics compartment with a Mitsubishi Electric J/ASQ-1 fire-control system and bombing computer, Ferranti 6TNJ-f INS and a radar warning and homing sub-system (the sensors of which are located at the top of the fin). The F-1 retains the T-2's Lear Siegler 5010BL attitude and heading reference system, but introduces a strike camera system. The principal anti-shipping weapon is the indigenously developed Mitsubishi ASM-1 (Type 80) solid-propellant missile with active radar terminal seeker, compatible with the J/ASQ-1 FCS. From 1982, a Mitsubishi J/AWG-12 air-to-air and air-to-ground radar replaced the J/AWG-11 search and ranging radar in the nose for compatibility with the ASM-1. The J/AWG-12 operates in conjunction with the retained Mitsubishi Electric (Thomson-CSF) HUD.

A total of 77 F-1s was produced for the JASDF, the last aircraft being delivered in March 1987. Original plans were for the production of about 160 aircraft but, as a result of budgetary constraints, procurement was halted at the 77th aircraft. The F-1 entered service in April 1978, replacing elderly F-86 Sabres with 3 Hikotai of 3 Kokudan at Misawa. Further units comprise 8 Hikotai (also of 3 Kokudan at Misawa) and 6 Hikotai of 8 Kokudan at Tsuiki.

As a result of delays to the FS-X fighter programme, the F-1s are expected to remain in service until at least 1999/2000, and are undergoing a service life extension programme that extends airframe life from 3,500 to 4,000 hours.

WEAPON OPTIONS

The F-1 retains the T-2's single JM61 Vulcan 20-mm rotary cannon in the lower port side of the nose. The F-1 is equipped with four underwing stores stations and a centreline fuselage hardpoint. Two radar-guided ASM-1s may be carried on the inboard wing pylons.

The 4.0-m (13 ft 1.5-in) long medium-range missile has a launch weight of 610 kg (1,348 lb) and a range of 50 km (27 nm; 31 miles). The longer-ranged ASM-2 (Type 88) IIR-guided missile is planned to enter service in 1995, carried by P-3 Orion maritime patrol aircraft and JASDF fighters, including the F-1. Development of this 150-km range missile began in 1987, with flight trials commencing in 1990. In the air combat role the principal weapon is the AIM-9L Sidewinder produced under licence by Mitsubishi. The AIM-9L was first tested with an F-1 in 1986 and issued to units in late 1987. Four of these may be carried on the outboard wing pylons and on the wingtip stations. Further stores options comprise bombs of 500 lb (227 kg) or 750 lb (340 kg) and rocket pods such as the 19 x 70-mm JLAU-3A, 7 x 70-mm RL-7 and 4 x 125-mm RL-4. Three auxiliary fuel tanks can also be carried under the fuselage and wings for long-range missions.

SPECIFICATION

Mitsubishi F-1
Wing: span 7.88 m (25 ft 10.25 in); aspect ratio 2.87; area 21.17 m² (227.88 sq ft)

Fuselage and tail: length 17.86 m (58 ft 7 in) including probe; height 4.39 m (14 ft 5 in); tailplane span 4.33 m (14 ft 2.5 in); wheel track 2.82 m (9 ft 3 in); wheel base 5.72 m (18 ft 9 in)
Powerplant: two Ishikawajima-Harima TF40-IHI-801 (Rolls-Royce/Turboméca Adour Mk 801A) turbofans each rated at 5,115 lb st (22.75 kN) dry and 7,305 lb st (32.49 kN) with afterburning
Weights: operating empty 6358 kg (14,017 lb); normal take-off 12800 kg (28,219 lb); maximum take-off 13700 kg (30,203 lb)
Fuel and load: internal fuel 3823 litres (1,010 US gal); external fuel up to three 821-litre (217-US gal) drop tanks; maximum ordnance 6,000 lb (2722 kg)
Speed: maximum level speed 'clean' at 36,000 ft (10975 m) 917 kt (1,056 mph; 1700 km/h)
Range: ferry range 1,402 nm (1,616 miles; 2600 km); combat radius 189 nm (218 miles; 350 km) on a hi-lo-hi attack mission with eight 500-lb (227-kg) bombs, or 300 nm (345 miles; 555 km) on a hi-lo-hi attack mission with two anti-ship missiles and two drop tanks
Performance: maximum rate of climb at sea level 35,000 ft (10670 m) per minute; service ceiling 50,000 ft (15240 m); take-off run 4,200 ft (1280 m) at maximum take-off weight

The F-1 serves with three squadrons, mainly in the anti-shipping role. The tan and green camouflage seen here has been replaced on some aircraft by various toned-down colour schemes.

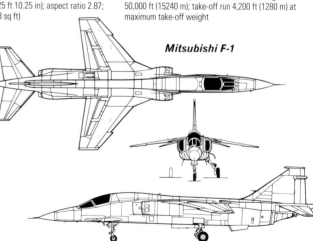

Mitsubishi F-1

Mitsubishi/McDonnell Douglas **RF/F-4EJ Kai Phantom II**

The **McDonnell Douglas F-4E Phantom II** was selected by the **JASDF** as a replacement for the F-86 and F-104 in the air defence role. Designated **F-4EJ**, Japan's variant is optimised for the air defence role, with the bombing computer deleted and without inflight-refuelling capability (although this feature was later retrofitted). Many items of avionics equipment were of Japanese design, including an indigenous RWR. In a bid to save money, Japan's aircraft were delivered with unslatted wings and stabilators. Four F-4EJs were built by McDonnell Douglas, followed by 11 kits which were assembled by Mitsubishi, before Mitsubishi manufactured a further 125. The last of these was also the very last Phantom built. The designation **EF-4EJ** has been applied (perhaps unofficially) to some Japanese Phantoms used in an ECM role with underwing AN/ALQ-6 jammer pods.

Ninety-six of the 125 surviving F-4EJs are being extensively upgraded and modernised for service into the next century under the designation **F-4EJ Kai**. Airframe life is being extended from 3,000 to 5,000 hours and the aircraft is being fitted with an all-new avionics suite. The original Westinghouse APQ-120 radar is replaced by the same company's APG-66J, with much improved look-down/shoot-down capability.

The aircraft also has a new central computer, a Kaiser HUD, a Hazeltine APZ-79A IFF, a licence-built Litton LN-39 INS and indigenous J/APR-6 RWRs. The F-4EJ Kai can be identified by its distinctive twin RWR fairings on the fin and wingtip, by a taller blade antenna for the AC-164 UHF and by small conducting strips on the radome.

The F-4EJ Kai is compatible with the ASM-1 anti-ship missile, and some may be used in the maritime strike role. Three 22-aircraft squadrons will be retained. Of the remaining 29 F-4EJs, 12 will be retired and 17 adapted for the reconnaissance role.

Mitsubishi F-4EJ Kai

Japan's 14 dedicated **RF-4E** reconnaissance Phantoms are often wrongly identified as RF-4EJs, but were built by McDonnell. They are now being upgraded to Kai standard with a Texas Instruments AN/APQ-172 radar, a new INS, an IR reconnaissance system, digital cockpit displays and new defensive avionics. It is unclear as to whether the **RF-4E Kai** designation will be officially applied to these aircraft after conversion.

After conversion, the **RF-4EJ** designation is applied to 17 very different recce-tasked aircraft which are being modified from F-4EJ fighter airframes. These gain digital avionics (including RWRs and taller UHF antenna) but retain their APQ-120 radar and gun, carrying a variety of podded sensors, including the Thomson-CSF ASTAC, a Raphael-based SLAR and a LOROP pod. The RF-4EJs wear the same three-tone camouflage as the original RF-4Es, serving alongside them with the 501st Hikotai at Hyakuri.

SPECIFICATION

Mitsubishi (McDonnell Douglas) RF-4E
generally similar to the McDonnell Douglas RF-4C Phantom II except in the following particulars:
Powerplant: two General Electric J79-GE-17A turbojets each rated at 11,810 lb st (52.53 kN) dry and 17,900 lb st (79.62 kN) with afterburning
Fuel and load: internal fuel 12,290 lb (5575 kg); external fuel up to 8,830 lb (4005 kg) in one 600-US gal (2271-litre) and two 370-US gal (1401-litre) drop tanks; maximum ordnance none
Speed: maximum level speed 'clean' at 36,000 ft (10975 m) 1,290 kt (1,485 mph; 2390 km/h)

The F-4EJ Kai can be distinguished from unconverted Japanese Phantoms by its new blade antennas and double RWR antenna fairings on the wingtips and fin trailing edge. Internally, the differences are more marked.

Mitsubishi/McDonnell Douglas **F-15J/DJ Eagle**

The **Mitsubishi F-15J/DJ Eagle** is the principal air superiority fighter operated by the **Nihon Koku Jietai**, or **JASDF**. Japanese pilots evaluated the F-15A/B at Edwards AFB, CA, in 1975, and in April 1978 Mitsubishi was selected as the prime contractor for Japanese F-15J/DJ Eagles. These differ from US F-15C/D Eagles only in the deletion of sensitive items of ECM, radar warning, and nuclear delivery equipment. The AN/ALQ-135 is replaced by indigenous J/ALQ-8 and the AN/ALR-56 RHAWS is replaced by J/APR-4. The aircraft is also fitted with a datalink compatible with the Japanese GCI network.

The first two F-15Js and 12 F-15DJs were manufactured by McDonnell Douglas under Project Peace Eagle. The first Japanese aircraft, a single-seater, flew at St Louis on 4 June 1980. These were followed by eight F-15DJs delivered as knocked-down kits for assembly by Mitsubishi. Subsequent Japanese Eagles have been assembled in Japan from largely indigenously manufactured sub-assemblies and equipment. Mitsubishi is responsible for forward and central fuselage sections, with Kawasaki making wings and tails. Further manufacturers include Shinmaywa (drop tanks), Sumitomo (landing gear), Fuji (landing gear doors) and Nippi (missile pylons and launchers). IHI produces the F100 engines under licence.

The Rinii F-15 Hikotai (Temporary F-15 Squadron) received the first operational Eagles at Nyutabaru in December 1981. A year later, this conversion unit was given permanent status as No. 202 Hikotai. Initial plans for the JASDF to operate 123 Eagles in five 18-aircraft squadrons have been enlarged, and total F-15J/DJ procurement for seven 22-aircraft front-line squadrons is now to be 191 aircraft, including 173 locally built. These equip Nos 201 and 203 Hikotai of the Northern Air Defence Force's 2nd Kokudan at Chitose, No. 303 Hikotai of the Central Air Defence Force's 6th Kokudan at Komatsu, Nos 204 and 305 Hikotai of the Central ADF's 7th Kokudan at Hyakuri, and No. 202 Hikotai (the OCU) of the 5th Kokudan at Nyutabaru, and the 8th Kokudan's 304 Hikotai at Tsuiki. The 5th and 8th Kokudan form part of the Western Air Defence Force, which also controls the six-aircraft Hiko Kyodotai, a dedicated aggressor unit flying six F-15DJs, which wear two-tone camouflage schemes.

Mitsubishi/Lockheed (General Dynamics) **FS-X**

Japan's search for a replacement for the Mitsubishi F-1 support fighter ended in October 1987 with the selection of a developed version of the Lockheed (General Dynamics) F-16C. Identified as the **FS-X** at present, but likely to acquire the service designation **F-2**, the new close-support fighter will differ from the F-16C in several important respects. The FS-X will feature a 41-cm (16-in) aft fuselage extension, a larger wing of all-composites, co-cured construction to be designed and produced in Japan, a larger tailplane, a lengthened nose to accommodate Mitsubishi Electrics (MELCO) phased-array radar, and a full FBW system. The FS-X will be powered by the 29,000-lb st (129-kN) General Electric F110-GE-129 turbofan assembled in Japan by IHI, with Mitsubishi responsible for airframe assembly using components contributed by Kawasaki and Fuji. With AAMs (Sidewinder or Mitsubishi AAM-3) mounted at the wingtips, the FS-X will have six wing stores pylons – including two 'plumbed' for long-range tanks – and provision for various weaponry, including the Mitsubishi ASM-2 (Type 88) anti-shipping missile currently under development. The ASM-2 is a long-range ASM with an imaging infra-red (IIR) seeker for terminal guidance and a range of approximately 150 km (81 nm; 93 miles). Fixed armament on the FS-X will comprise a single 20-mm cannon.

The FS-X programme has suffered delays and cost escalation since it was first announced, and may undergo further changes to schedule or production quantities. The first of four prototypes, including one two-seat **TFS-X** conversion trainer, is expected to fly by mid-1995, followed by production orders in time for service entry in 1999. The JASDF has a requirement for up to 130 aircraft, including some two-seat TFS-Xs, to replace the F-1s currently serving in Nos 3, 6 and 8 Hikotais. However, due to slippage in the FS-X timescale, two squadrons of the upgraded F-4EJ Kai may be used as interim F-1 replacements.

Mitsubishi/Sikorsky **SH-60J Seahawk**

The **SH-60J** is a dedicated ASW helicopter produced under licence by Mitsubishi. Closely based on the SH-60B Seahawk, it is intended to replace the HSS-2B (a licence-built Sea King) in service with the **JMSDF** and is fitted with indigenous Japanese avionics. These include an HQS-103 sonar, HPS-104 search radar and HLR-108 ESM, plus indigenous displays, datalink, flight management system and ring-laser gyro/attitude and heading reference system. Imported systems include a Texas Instruments AN/ASQ-81D2(V) MAD, a General Instruments AN/ALR-66(VE) RWR and an Edmac AN/ARR-75 sonobuoy receiver.

The first two **XSH-60J** prototypes were built by Sikorsky but were delivered 'green', to be reassembled and fitted out by Mitsubishi. Following the first flight on 31 August 1987, the XSH-60Js were subsequently evaluated by the 51st Air Development Kokutai of the JMSDF at Atsugi, this process being completed in early 1991. A total of 56 production SH-60Js (designated S-70B-3 by Sikorsky) has been ordered. The first production aircraft made its maiden flight on 10 May 1991 and was delivered three months later.

SPECIFICATION

Mitsubishi-Sikorsky SH-60J
generally similar to the Sikorsky S-70B (SH-60B Seahawk) except in the following particulars:
Powerplant: two Ishikawajima-Harima (General Electric) T700-IHI-401C turboshafts each rated at 1,900 shp (1417 kW)

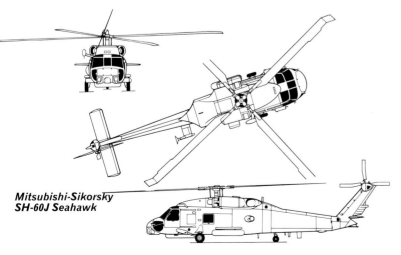

*Mitsubishi-Sikorsky
SH-60J Seahawk*

A JMSDF SH-60J is seen in flight. The SH-60J is a Mitsubishi-built variant of the SH-60B with Japanese avionics, including search radar, sonar and ESM.

Mitsubishi/Sikorsky UH-60J

The **Mitsubishi-Sikorsky UH-60J** is intended to replace Kawasaki-Vertol KV-107IIA5s with the Air Rescue Wing of the **JASDF** and Mitsubishi-Sikorsky S-61As serving with **JMSDF** rescue units. Designated **S-70A-12** by Sikorsky, the UH-60J is a dedicated SAR version of the **Sikorsky UH-60L** helicopter (described separately) with increased internal fuel capacity and indigenous avionics, notably a nose-mounted radar. The aircraft has a Sikorsky-integrated self-contained navigation system, a turret-mounted FLIR and bubble windows in the sides of the cabin.

The first two aircraft were manufactured by Sikorsky, and were followed by a further two supplied in kit form for licence-assembly by Mitsubishi. Total requirements are 46 for the JASDF and 18 for the JMSDF. The first Mitsubishi-built UH-60J was delivered on 28 February 1991 and UH-60Js became operational with the JMSDF in March 1992. Three units are planned ultimately, serving six bases at Atsugi, Hachinoe, Kanoya, Azuki, Shimofusa and Tokoshima. With the JASDF, UH-60Js will be based at Iruma, with detachments as required.

The UH-60J is replacing the KV-107 in the SAR role with both the JMSDF and the JASDF. The aircraft is a rescue-optimised UH-60L derivative, with indigenous search radar and a turret-mounted FLIR. Mitsubishi is manufacturing 22 of the 28 currently on order, and assembled the third and fourth aircraft delivered from components supplied by Sikorsky. The eventual requirement for the UH-60J will be for 64 aircraft.

SPECIFICATION

Mitsubishi/Sikorsky UH-60J
generally similar to the Sikorsky S-70A (UH-60L Black Hawk) except in the following particulars:
Powerplant: two Ishikawajima-Harima (General Electric) T700-IHI-701A turboshafts each rated at 1,723 shp (1285 kW) in JASDF helicopters or, for JMSDF aircraft, two Ishikawajima-Harima (General Electric) T700-IHI-401C turboshafts each rated at 1,940 shp (1447 kW) for take-off and 1,662 shp (1239 kW) for continuous running

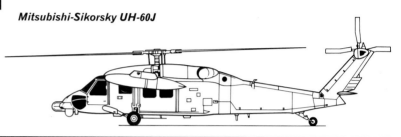

Mitsubishi-Sikorsky UH-60J

Mitsubishi MU-2

In 1959, Mitsubishi initiated design of a light twin-turboprop STOL utility transport designated **MU-2**. The aircraft emerged as a compact high-wing monoplane with a circular-section fuselage seating seven to nine passengers, and with wingtip tanks as standard. Designed primarily to serve as a light business transport, the majority of the 831 built were sold to civilian customers in this role. First flown on 14 September 1963, the Astazou-engined **MU-2A** prototype and initial production Garrett-engined **MU-2B** were fitted with pressurised fuselages for commercial use. The civil **MU-2G** was based on the MU-2B, but featured a 1.9-m (6.2-ft) fuselage stretch seating nine to 11 passengers, larger vertical tail, external undercarriage fairings to provide greater internal cabin volume, and uprated engines. Military sales of the MU-2 were limited to Japanese forces as a result of a policy towards the export of defence material. A total of 53 MU-2s was delivered to the **JASDF** and **JGSDF**, the majority of which remain in service.

Two MU-2 versions were ordered by the JGSDF as the sole fixed-wing assets for the liaison and photo-reconnaissance role. These comprised four **MU-2C**s, an unpressurised variant of the basic MU-2B (first flown on 11 May 1967), and 16 **MU-2K**s, developed from the **MU-2F**, but fitted with uprated turboprops for higher cruising speed. The wingtip tanks on the first MU-2C were removed in favour of an additional fuel tank carried aft of the cabin. Military equipment included one vertical and one swing-type oblique camera for reconnaissance, and the provision for side-looking radar, underwing stores (bombs and rockets), and two 12.7-mm (0.5-in) machine-guns. Both versions received the service designation **LR-1**. Seventeen remain in service, assigned to the HQ Aviation Squadron of each Air Command (at Okadama, Kasuminome, Takayubaru, Tachikawa and Yao), HQ Flight of 1 Helicopter Brigade at Kisarazu

and the Air Training School at Utsonomiya.

To serve in the search and rescue role, the JASDF began to acquire MU-2s concurrently. The air force designation **MU-2S** was applied to a version with the Mitsubishi designation **MU-2E**. First flown on 15 August 1967, this unpressurised variant introduced extensive additional navigation and communications equipment, Doppler search radar in an extended 'thimble' nose radome, bulged observation windows in the fuselage sides below the wing and a port-side sliding entry door for dropping rafts. The wingtip tanks were enlarged to increase maximum fuel capacity to 1389 litres (367 US gal) and maximum take-off weight to 4560 kg (10,053 lb). Delivery of a batch of 27 began in December 1967, with a further two aircraft in 1987 after the Mitsubishi production line had closed. They remain in service with the Air Rescue Wing at Iruma, plus detachments. The **MU-2J** was based on the MU-2G, but introduced

more powerful TPE331-6-251M engines giving a cruising speed of 600 km/h (324 kt; 373 mph). Following a maiden flight on 31 January 1975, four MU-2Js were delivered to the Hiko Tenkentai (Flight Check Group) of the JASDF at Iruma in 1975-79 for navaid calibration duty.

SPECIFICATION

Mitsubishi MU-2C
Wing: span 39 ft 2 in (11.94 m) with tip tanks; aspect ratio 7.71; area 178.15 sq ft (16.55 m²)
Fuselage and tail: length 33 ft 3 in (10.13 m); height 12 ft 11 in (3.94 m); tailplane span 15 ft 9 in (4.80 m); wheel track 7 ft 9 in (2.36 m); wheel base 14 ft 10 in (4.52 m)
Powerplant: two Garrett TPE331-6-251M turboprops each rated at 724 ehp (540 kW)
Weights: empty equipped 5,920 lb (2685 kg); maximum take-off 9,920 lb (4500 kg)
Fuel and load: internal fuel 366 US gal (1387 litres); external fuel none
Speed: maximum cruising speed at 15,000 ft (4575 m) 318 kt (367 mph; 590 km/h); economical cruising speed at 25,000 ft (7620 m) 270 kt (311 mph; 500 km/h)

Mitsubishi MU-2

Range: 1,460 nm (1,681 miles; 2706 km)
Performance: maximum rate of climb at sea level 3,100 ft (945 m) per minute; service ceiling 33,200 ft (10110 m); take-off distance to 50 ft (15 m) 1,705 ft (520 m) at maximum take-off weight; landing distance from 50 ft (15 m) 1,495 ft (455 m) at normal landing weight

This MU-2J is one of those operated in the calibration role by the Hiko Tenkentai. Others serve in the SAR and liaison roles.

Mitsubishi T-2

In a fine exercise of farsighted ergonomics, Japan's first excursion into supersonic military aircraft design was a two-seat combat trainer which would, it was argued, double as an aircraft in which **JASDF** pilots

could be trained for the F-104J and F-4EJ combat aircraft, and which would provide design experience for a subsequent indigenous supersonic fighter. In the event, the **Mitsubishi T-2** itself proved readily adaptable to become that fighter, the **F-1** (described separately).

First flown on 20 July 1971 as the **XT-2**, the trainer superficially resembles the F-4

but features shoulder-mounted wings and fixed-geometry lateral air inlets (with blow-in doors) for the pair of Rolls-Royce/Turboméca Adour afterburning turbofans, mounted side-by-side in the lower rear fuselage. All components of the tricycle landing gear retract into the fuselage. The instructor and pupil pilot are accommodated in tandem under separate canopy seats and are

provided with Daiseru-built Weber ES-7J zero-zero ejection seats. Wing and tailplane incorporate marked anhedral, and roll control is effected by differential spoilers forward of the wide-span trailing-edge flaps.

Fixed armament comprises an internal JM61 Vulcan 20-mm multi-barrelled cannon in the lower port side of the nose, and external stores can be mounted on one cen-

treline and four underwing hardpoints, while provision is made to mount AIM-9L Sidewinder AAMs on the wingtip stations. Avionics systems include Mitsubishi Electric J/AWG-11 search and ranging radar in the nose, Mitsubishi Electric (Thomson-CSF) head-up display, Mitsubishi Electric J/ARC-51 UHF, Nippon Electric J/ARN-53 TACAN, Tokyo Communication J/APX-101 SIF/IFF and Lear Siegler 501OBL AHRS.

The T-2 entered service in 1976 and joined the 4th Air Wing at Mitsushima, replacing North American F-86s, and has proved a popular and efficient aircraft, now obviously demonstrating the benefits of commonality with the F-1 fighter. One T-2 has been extensively modified for the Technical R&D Institute of the Japan Defence Agency as the **T-2CCV** control-configured vehicle (CCV). It features triplex digital fly-by-wire and computer control, vertical and horizontal canard surfaces, and is fitted with test equipment in the rear cockpit. The T-2CCV was first flown on 9 August 1983.

Total production orders amounted to 90 aircraft, of which 28 are T-2 advanced trainers and 62 are **T-2A** combat trainers, all of which have been completed. The Adour engines are licence-built by Ishikawajima-Harima under the designation TF40-IHI-801A. Ninety-four T-2s were built, including two which were converted to serve as F-1 development aircraft. Eighty-eight were delivered to 21 and 22 Hikotais of the 4th Kokudan at Hamamatsu, and six were later reallocated to the 'Blue Impulse' formation display team.

SPECIFICATION

Mitsubishi T-2
Wing: span 7.88 m (25 ft 10.25 in); aspect ratio 3.0; area 21.17 m² (227.88 sq ft)
Fuselage and tail: length 17.86 m (58 ft 7 in) including probe; height 4.39 m (14 ft 5 in); tailplane span 4.33 m (14 ft 2.5 in); wheel track 2.82 m (9 ft 3 in); wheel base 5.72 m (18 ft 9 in)
Powerplant: two Ishikawajima-Harima TF40-IHI-801A (Rolls-Royce/Turboméca Adour Mk 801A) turbofans each rated at 5,115 lb st (22.75 kN) dry and 7,305 lb st (32.49 kN) with afterburning
Weights: operating empty 6307 kg (13,905 lb); normal take-off 9805 kg (21,616 lb); maximum take-off

12800 kg (28,219 lb)
Fuel and load: internal fuel 3823 litres (1,010 US gal); external fuel up to three 821-litre (217-US gal) drop tanks; maximum ordnance about 2000 kg (4,409 lb)
Speed: maximum level speed 'clean' at 36,000 ft (10975 m) 917 kt (1,056 mph; 1700 km/h)
Range: ferry range 1,400 nm (1,611 miles; 2593 km)
Performance: maximum rate of climb at sea level 35,000 ft (10670 m) per minute; service ceiling

The Mitsubishi T-2 combat trainers of the 'Blue Impulse' aerobatic team have a secondary air defence war role. Here one of the team's aircraft is seen taking off with underwing fuel tanks and wingtip-mounted AIM-9 air-to-air missiles.

50,000 ft (15240 m); take-off run 2,000 ft (610 m) at normal take-off weight

Morane-Saulnier MS.760 Paris

Developed as one of the first light aircraft to use jet engine power, the **MS.760 Paris** first flew on 29 July 1954 and was built primarily as a communications/liaison aircraft and advanced trainer for military use. The Paris is a low-wing monoplane powered by a pair of Marboré turbojets mounted side-by-side in the fuselage and exhausting under the tail. The tricycle undercarriage uses relatively short components, facilitating access to the cabin door on the port side of the fuselage forward of the wing. The Paris seats four in two side-by-side pairs. The **Armée de l'Air** retains up to 50 in its inventory, the principal units flying the type being 41ᵉ and 43ᵉ Escadres de Transport et d'Entraînement and ET 2/65 'Rambouillet', all as part of CoTAM. The Aéronavale also retains eight MS.760s in 57ᵉ Escadrille at Landivisiau for continuation training, target simulation and liaison duties.

In **Argentina**, where FAMA assembled 48 Paris for the air force, about half that number remain in the hands of Escuadrónes II and III within IV Brigada Aérea at El Plumerillo, Mendoza, operating in the light strike/armed trainer role. Built as **MS.760A Paris I**s, with 3.91-kN (880-lb st) Turboméca Marboré IC turbojets, they have been upgraded to **MS.760B Paris II** standard with 4.71-kN (1,058-lb st) Marboré VIs. This version also introduced wingtip tanks.

SPECIFICATION

Morane-Saulnier MS.760B Paris II
Wing: span 10.15 m (33 ft 3.6 in); aspect ratio 5.72; area 18.00 m² (193.76 sq ft)
Fuselage and tail: length 10.24 m (33 ft 7.1 in);

This MS.760 Paris is used in the liaison role by Groupement d'Instruction 01/312 at Salon-de-Provence.

height 2.60 m (8 ft 6.4 in)
Powerplant: two Turboméca Marboré VI turbojets each rated at 4.71 kN (1,058 lb st) dry
Weights: empty equipped 2067 kg (4,557 lb); maximum take-off 3920 kg (8,642 lb)
Fuel and load: external fuel none; maximum ordnance 100 kg (220 lb)
Speed: maximum level speed 'clean' at 7620 m (25,000 ft) 695 km/h (375 kt; 432 mph)

Range: ferry range 1740 km (939 nm; 1,081 miles)
Performance: maximum rate of climb at sea level 750 m (2,461 ft) per minute; service ceiling 12000 m (39370 ft)

Argentina's ageing MS.760s continue to provide faithful service in the liaison, light strike and trainer roles.

Left: Escadrille de Servitude 57 uses a handful of MS.760s alongside Falcon 10MERs in the liaison and target roles.

Avions Mudry et Cie, Aérodrome de Bernay, BP 214, F-27300, Bernay, France

Mudry CAP 10/CAP 10B

A derivative of the **Piel Emeraude** light-plane, the **Mudry CAP 10** two-seat light elementary/aerobatic trainer was developed initially for the **Armée de l'Air**, which has received some 56 from total production of more than 250. The CAP 10 was first flown in August 1968. The **CAP 10B** version features a larger rudder and a ventral fin. CAP 10s and 10Bs serve at the Ecole de l'Air (GE 312) at Salon-de-Provence to give *ab initio* pilot training and at the Ecole de Formation Initiale du Personnel Navigant (307 EFIPN) at Avord for navigator selection training. The Aéronavale also has eight CAP 10s with Escadrille de Servitude 51 at Rochefort/Soubise for screening/grading multi-engine pilots. Twenty CAP 10s acquired by **Mexico** are used at the Colegio del Aire, Zapopan, for aerobatic training.

SPECIFICATION

Mudry CAP 10B
Wing: span 8.06 m (26 ft 5.25 in); aspect ratio 6.0; area 10.85 m² (116.79 sq ft)
Fuselage and tail: length 7.16 m (23 ft 6 in); height 2.55 m (8 ft 4.5 in); tailplane span 2.90 m (9 ft 6 in); wheel track 2.06 m (6 ft 9 in)
Powerplant: one Textron Lycoming AEIO-360-B2F flat-four air-cooled piston engine rated at 180 hp (134 kW)
Weights: empty equipped 550 kg (1,213 lb); normal take-off 760 kg (1,675 lb) for aerobatics; maximum take-off 830 kg (1,829 lb)
Fuel and load: internal fuel 108 kg (238 lb); external fuel none; maximum ordnance none
Speed: never exceed speed 340 km/h (183 kt; 211 mph); maximum level speed 'clean' at sea level

270 km/h (146 kt; 168 mph); maximum cruising speed at optimum altitude 250 km/h (135 kt; 155 mph)
Range: 1000 km (539 nm; 621 miles)
Performance: maximum rate of climb at sea level 480 m (1,575 ft) per minute; service ceiling 5000 m (16,405 ft); take-off run 350 m (1,149 ft) at maximum

take-off weight; take-off distance to 15 m (50 ft) 450 m (1,477 ft) at maximum take-off weight; landing distance from 15 m (50 ft) 600 m (1,968 ft) at normal landing weight; landing run 300 m (984 ft) at normal landing weight
***g* limits:** -4.5 to +6

The Mudry CAP 10s of Escadrille de Servitude 51 at Rochefort/Soubise are used for grading and screening potential Aéronavale pilot trainees.

Mudry CAP 230

After producing single-seat aerobatic versions of the CAP 10 as the **CAP 20** and **CAP 21**, Mudry received a 1984 order for the **CAP 230**, for use by the **Royal Moroccan air force's** 'Green March' aerobatic team. The CAP 230 was derived from the CAP 21 (also used by the 'Green March') but with a more powerful flat-six AEIO-540 engine, greater *g* limits and higher weight. The CAP 230 flew in prototype form on 8 October 1985. Four CAP 230s were supplied to the 'Green March' and four to the French 'Equipe de Voltige de **l'Armée de l'Air**', of GE 312, Salon-de-Provence (which previously flew the CAP 20). Two were built for civil use before production switched to the **CAP 231**.

SPECIFICATION

Mudry CAP 230
Wing: span 8.08 m (26 ft 6 in); aspect ratio 7.0; area 9.66 m² (103.98 sq ft)

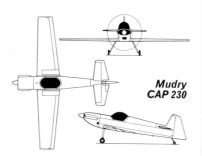

Mudry CAP 230

Fuselage and tail: length 6.75 m (22 ft 1.75 in); height 1.80 m (5 ft 11 in)
Powerplant: one Textron Lycoming AEIO-540-L1 flat-six air-cooled piston engine rated at 300 hp (224 kW)
Weights: empty 630 kg (1,389 lb); maximum take-off (aerobatic) 730 kg (1,609 lb); maximum take-off (normal) 820 kg (1,808 lb)
Fuel and load: external fuel none; ordnance none
Speed: never exceed speed 400 km/h (215 kt;

248 mph); maximum level speed 'clean' at sea level 340 km/h (183 kt; 211 mph); maximum cruising speed at optimum altitude and 75 per cent power 290 km/h (156 kt; 180 mph)
Range: 750 km (405 nm; 466 miles)
Performance: maximum rate of climb at sea level 1020 m (3,346 ft) per minute
***g* limits:** -10 to +10

The single-seat CAP 230 is used by the 'Equipe de Voltige' aerobatic team, the second display unit of the Equipes de Présentation de l'Armée de l'Air (the first being the 'Patrouille de France'), and for instructor's flying at the Ecole de l'Air at Salon-de-Provence.

Myasishchev M-4 'Bison'

Myasishchev Design Bureau, 140160 Zhukovskii, Moscow Region, Russia.

Designed as a long-range strategic bomber, the 'Bison' was always handicapped by its inability to meet a totally unrealistic requirement: that it be capable of attacking targets in North America, which was impossible using the Soviet technology of the time. Myasishchev himself believed that the requirement could only be met by using turboprop engines, or by building a 250-tonne bomber with eight AM-3 engines. Wisely, he produced a superb medium-range bomber with four of these engines, but the political leadership was unhappy with the aircraft (which couldn't reach the American homeland) and production was limited to about 200 aircraft (despite the fact that it was a better medium bomber than the contemporary Tu-16 'Badger', which was built in much larger numbers). One limiting factor was the size of the bomb bay, which was limited in extent because it lay between the main units of the bicycle undercarriage.

There were three basic sub-variants of the aircraft, most of which were quickly

This 'Bison-A' is one of those still based at Zhukhovskii, and is probably used by the OKB in support of the VM-T Atlant programme, and may even be a candidate for conversion.

converted as tankers or reconnaissance platforms. The basic **M-4 'Bison-A'** was a strategic nuclear bomber version powered by four 85.32-kN (19,180-lb) Mikulin AM-3D turbojets in the wingroots (the prototype having podded, underslung engines) and had a short glazed nose and dihedral tailplanes. It could carry its 9000-kg (19,840-lb) warload over a range of about 8100 km (4,384 nm/5,032 miles). An inflight-refuelling probe could be fitted above the nose, but was not normally carried. The relocation of the engines from underslung pods necessitated the addition of small wingtip pods for the undercarriage outriggers, which had previously been housed in the outer engine nacelles. Production aircraft had two overwing fences, located well outboard. A handful of M-4s remain in use, primarily for training and perhaps as tankers.

The **3M** (**'Bison-B'**) was powered by the more powerful 107.9-kN (24,250-lb) VD-7 turbojet and introduced an inflight-refuelling probe above the lengthened nose, which had a large radome covering much of the underside, in turn necessitating provision of an undernose visual bomb-aiming gondola. Dihedral was removed from the tailplanes and a third (more prominent) fence was added above the wing, which featured a slightly increased span (from 50.526 m/165 ft 9¼ in to 53.14 m/174 ft

4¼ in). Range was increased to 12000 km (7,457 miles), still some 1500 km (932 miles) less than the Tu-95, and 3000 km (1,864 miles) less than the Tu-95M. The final variant was the **3MD,** which was powered by 93.20-kN (20,944-lb st) VD-7B engines. This had a completely new nose profile, with a refuelling probe at the tip, and an undernose radome for the 'Puff Ball' radar. This was given the NATO reporting name **'Bison-C'**. A related record-breaking aircraft known as the **M-201** or **M-3M** was powered by 127.49-kN (28,660-lb) VD-15B turbojets.

'Bison' tankers bear the Russian designation **3MS-2** and are mainly converted **'Bison-B**s'. These are believed to have been re-engined with the 93.20-kN (20,944-

A tanker-configured 'Bison-B' clearly shows this variant's extended nose, undernose visual bomb-aiming gondola and non-dihedral tailplane.

lb st) RD-3M-500A turbojet. They refuel probe-equipped receiver aircraft using a centreline hose-drogue unit mounted in the former bomb bay. Carrying up to 40 tonnes of fuel, the 3MS-2 can transfer fuel at up to 2250 litres (495 Imp gal) per minute and has a maximum endurance of 12 hours and 15 minutes. Some sources suggested that the 'Bison' had been entirely withdrawn from Soviet/CIS service, and there was a massive, and heavily publicised, scrapping of air-

The VM-T Atlant can carry outsized loads above its fuselage. It is seen here carrying a space shuttle fuel tank, landing after a display at the Moscow Aeroshow.

craft during the late 1980s. Certainly some 40 'Bison-B' and 'Bison-C' airframes were dismantled as part of the superpower strategic arms reduction programme, but at least a handful of **Russian** tankers remained in use, notably with a regiment based at Engels, long after this. Others still fly from Zhukhovskii, and perhaps from Ryazan. Il-78M 'Mainstays' used during the Gulf War were reportedly refuelled by 'Bison' tankers, and pairs of the big Myasishchev bomber/tankers have flown at recent air displays in the Soviet Union.

Also still active is a pair of 'Bison-Bs' converted to serve as the carriers of outsize loads. Designated **VM-T** and known as **Atlant**, these aircraft carry their cargoes (mainly components from the Soviet space programme, including the Buran shuttle orbiter) on their backs. To correct airflow problems over the tail and subsequently improve stability when carrying outsized loads, the M-4's conventional single tailfin has been replaced by a pair of endplate fins on a new dihedral tailplane.

SPECIFICATION

Myasishchev 3MS-2 'Bison-B'
Wing: span 53.14 m (174 ft 4 in); estimated aspect ratio 7.96; estimated area 320.00 m² (3,444.56 sq ft)
Fuselage and tail: length 51.7 m (169 ft 7½ in);

estimated height 14.10 m (46 ft 3 in); estimated tailplane span 15.00 m (49 ft 2.5 in)
Powerplant: four MNPK 'Soyuz' (Mikulin) RD-3M-500A turbojets each rated at 93.20 kN (20,944 lb st)
Weights: empty 75740 kg (166,975 lb); normal take-off 192000 kg (423,280 lb)
Payload: 24000 kg (52,910 lb)
Speed: estimated maximum level speed 'clean' at 11000 m (36,090 ft) 998 km/h (538 kt; 620 mph)
Range: 12400 km (6,712 nm; 7,705 miles)
Performance: estimated service ceiling 13700 m (44,950 ft)

Myasishchev **M-17 Stratosfera and M-55 Geophysica 'Mystic'**

Little is known about the origins of the 'Mystic', which probably began as a military high-altitude reconnaissance platform, despite its much-publicised recent history as a simple record breaker and ecological protection/earth resources survey aircraft. It was probably intended as a direct replacement for the Yak-25 'Mandrake'. The aircraft first came to the attention of the West during 1982, when a satellite photographed one at Zhukhovskii, which the West still referred to as Ramenskoye after the nearby town. The provisional reporting name 'RAM-M' was allocated. Two of the original **M-17**s were built, each powered by a 68.6-kN (15,430-lb) Rybinsk RD-36-51V turbojet, reportedly developed from the Kuznetsov NK-144 engines of the Tu-144 'Charger' or the VD-7s of the M-50 'Bounder'. The first aircraft has been retired to the museum at Monino, while the second has made a series of flights monitoring pollution and examining the ozone layer. The M-17 is known as the **Stratosfera**.

A twin-engined derivative, the **M-55**, may have been developed because of shortcomings in the original M-17 design. The 'Mystic-B' has a slightly shorter-span wing than the original aircraft, and is powered by a pair of 49-kN (11,025-lb) Perm/Soloviev PS-30-V12 engines, derived from the powerplant of the MiG-31 'Foxhound'. The aircraft has a lengthened fuselage, accommodating a large sensor bay aft of the nosewheel bay. The M-55 Geophysica can carry a larger payload (up to 1500 kg/ 3,307 lb) and has a longer endurance (seven hours) than the M-17. The sensor package is believed to contain both optical and infra-red sensors (and possibly radar), including an A-84 camera, which covers an area 120 km (75 miles) wide from its operational height of 20000 m (65,600 ft). Development continues, reportedly under a Russian air force contract, and two pre-series aircraft are under construction.

Known mainly as a record-breaker and earth resources survey platform, the M-55 was almost certainly originally designed to meet a Soviet air forces requirement for a high-altitude reconnaissance aircraft, with U-2-type performance.

SPECIFICATION

Myasishchev M-17 Stratosfera 'Mystic-A'
Wing: span 40.70 m (133 ft 6.5 in)
Fuselage and tail: length 21.20 m (69 ft 6.5 in); height 5.25 m (17 ft 3 in); wheel track 6.65 m (21 ft 10 in); wheel base 5.60 m (18 ft 4.5 in)
Powerplant: one RKBM (Novikov) RD-36-51V turbojet rated at 68.65 kN (15,432 lb st)
Weights: maximum take-off 19950 kg (43,981 lb)
Fuel and load: external fuel none
Range: endurance 2 hours 30 minutes
Performance: service ceiling 20000 m (65,615 ft)

National Aerospace Laboratory (Kawasaki) **Asuka**

Using the airframe of the **Kawasaki C-1** transport (described separately), the Japanese National Aerospace Laboratory developed this highly-modified experimental STOL transport to explore the potential of upper surface blowing (USB) and other systems to achieve STOL performance. The C-1's two pylon-mounted JT8D engines were replaced by four indigenously-developed high-bypass ratio turbofans mounted in nacelles far ahead of the wing leading edges. The wings incorporate leading-edge and aileron BLC control systems. The fuselage and landing gear received structural strengthening, and a digital stability and control augmentation system was introduced. In this form, the **Asuka** first flew on 28 October 1985, and in its first STOL landing, on 23 March 1988, the prototype required a ground run of only 439 m (1,440 ft). The primary research programme was completed in 1989.

SPECIFICATION

NAL (Kawasaki) Asuka
Wing: span 30.60 m (100 ft 4.75 in); aspect ratio 7.8; area 120.50 m² (1,297.09 sq ft)
Fuselage and tail: length 33.154 m (108 ft 9.25 in); height 10.175 m (33 ft 4.5 in); tailplane span 11.30 m (37 ft 1 in); wheel track 4.40 m (14 ft 5.25 in); wheel base 9.33 m (30 ft 7.75 in)
Powerplant: four MITI/NAL FJR710/600S turbofans each rated at 10,582 lb st (47.07 kN)
Weights: normal take-off 38700 kg (85,320 lb) for short take-off; maximum take-off 45000 kg (99,210 lb) for conventional take-off
Fuel and load: internal fuel 12628 kg (27,840 lb); external fuel none

Speed: never exceed speed 320 kt (368 mph; 593 km/h); maximum cruising speed at optimum altitude 260 kt (299 mph; 482 km/h)
Range: range 720 nm (829 miles; 1334 km)

Performance: service ceiling 28,000 ft (8535 m); STOL take-off distance to 50 ft (15 m) 2,700 ft (853 m) at normal take-off weight; STOL landing distance from 50 ft (15 m) 2,800 ft (853 m) at normal landing weight

The Asuka is a Kawasaki C-1 with four turbofan engines and flap blowing over the upper surfaces.

NAMC YS-11

The Nihon Aeroplane Manufacturing Company (NAMC) was formed specifically to produce the YS-11 transport. As a collaborative project, it involved the following grouping of Japanese aerospace companies: Fuji, Kawasaki, Mitsubishi, Nippi, Shinmaywa and Showa

The only airliner of indigenous design to achieve production in Japan, the **NAMC YS-11** was conceived in 1957 as a medium-range transport. Development of the aircraft was carried out as a collaborative project involving Fuji, Kawasaki, Mitsubishi, Nippi, Shinmaywa and Showa – this grouping was eventually named the Nihon Aeroplane Manufacturing Company (NAMC). The first of two prototype YS-11s made its maiden flight on 30 August 1962.

Production batches of the commercial **YS-11A**, all with Dart 542 turboprops, fell into several series, starting with the **Series 100**. The **Series 200** had increased gross weight, the **Series 300** and **Series 400** were similar but for mixed traffic and all-cargo operation, respectively, and the **Series 500** and **600** were Series 200 and 100 equivalents with further gross weight increases. Passenger accommodation varied between 48 and 70. Production ended in 1974 after 182 aircraft, most being delivered to commercial operators.

Of the commercial examples, six **Series 220**s were acquired from Olympic Airways in 1980 by the **Hellenic air force**, and the surviving five aircraft are in service as personnel transports with 356 'Iraklis' Mira, a tactical transport unit within the 112ª Ptérix Mahis (Combat Wing) at Elefsina. One example is also used to calibrate radar and instrument landing systems.

A total of 23 YS-11s was procured by the **JMSDF** (13) and **JASDF** (10) in a number of sub-variants. The JASDF acquired two **Series 103**s and two **Series 105**s as **YS-11P** VIP personnel transports in 1965/66, a **Series 305** as **YS-11PC** personnel/cargo transport in 1968 and four **Series 402**s as **YS-11C** freighters in 1969/70.

The YS-11E is a dedicated ECM/EW training aircraft, festooned with antenna fairings and a huge chaff dispenser aft of the wingroot. Two are in service.

One of the latter was converted to the **YS-11NT** navigational trainer in 1977, and a **Series 213** was acquired in 1971 as **YS-11FC** for flight check duties; this is currently based at Iruma. Finally, three further Series 402s were acquired in 1971, of which two were heavily modified in 1976/79 as **YS-11E** ECM trainers and the other became the **YS-11E(EL)** in 1982 for Elint duty. Further modification programmes in the late 1980s were to result in one YS-11 receiving the ALQ-7 jamming system and being re-engined with T64 turboprops to carry the increased weight of avionics, a further two being fitted with Litton avionics for calibration duties, three serving as VIP transports, and another three undertaking Elint missions with J/ALR-2 systems. YS-11Es serve with the Electronic Warfare Training Unit at Iruma. Originally equipping three transport units, Support Command's reconfigured YS-11s currently serve with 402 Hikotai at Iruma and 403 Hikotai at Miho.

JMSDF operation of the YS-11 began in 1970 with a **Series 112** and a **Series 113** as **YS-11M** transports, joined in 1971/73 by two **Series 404**s **YS-11M-A**, all serving with 61st Kokutai at Atsugi. The mixed-complement transports feature accommodation for 48 personnel and incorporate a cargo compartment at the rear of the fuselage, with a freight loading door on the port side. Four **Series 206**s and two **Series 624**s, delivered 1970-74, serve

as **YS-11T-A** ASW crew trainers in 205th Kyoiku Kokutai of the Shimofusa Air Training Group. The YS-11Ts are equipped with a maritime search radar in a belly-mounted radome.

SPECIFICATION

NAMC YS-11A-300
Wing: span 32.00 m (104 ft 11.75 in); aspect ratio 10.8; area 94.80 m² (1,020.45 sq ft)
Fuselage and tail: length 26.30 m (86 ft 3.5 in); height 8.98 m (29 ft 5.5 in); tailplane span 12.00 m (38 ft 2.5 in); wheel track 8.60 m (28 ft 2.5 in); wheel base 9.52 m (31 ft 2.5 in)
Powerplant: two Rolls-Royce Dart RDa.10/1 Mk 542-10K turboprops each rated at 3,060 ehp (2282 ekW)

Weights: operating empty 15810 kg (34,854 lb); maximum take-off 24500 kg (54,012 lb)
Fuel and load: internal fuel 7270 litres (1,921 US gal); external fuel none; maximum payload 6190 kg (13,646 lb)
Speed: maximum cruising speed at 15,000 ft (4570 m) 253 kt (291 mph; 469 km/h); economical cruising speed at 20,000 ft (6095 m) 244 kt (281 mph; 452 km/h)
Range: 1,735 nm (1,998 miles; 3215 km) with maximum fuel or 588 nm (677 miles; 1090 km) with maximum payload
Performance: maximum rate of climb at sea level 1,220 ft (372 m) per minute; service ceiling 22,900 ft (6980 m); take-off distance to 35 ft (10.7 m) 3,650 ft (1113 m) at maximum take-off weight; landing distance from 50 ft (15 m) 2,170 ft (661 m) at maximum landing weight

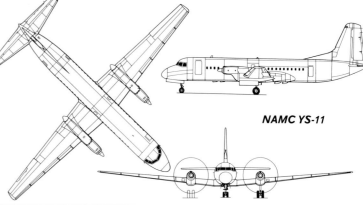

NAMC YS-11

The YS-11E(EL) dedicated Elint aircraft is of similar appearance to the YS-11E ECM trainer. The former aircraft wears a more warlike grey camouflage.

Nanchang (NAMC) CJ-6A

Serving the air force of the **People's Republic of China** as its standard basic trainer, the **CJ-6** piston-engined aircraft was developed at Shenyang in 1956-58 as a successor for the CJ-5 (itself a licence-built version of the Yak-18). Retaining the latter's overall configuration, it introduced a fully retractable undercarriage, with the main legs folding inwards into the wing centre-section and the nosewheel retracting aft into the forward fuselage. The outer wing panels introduced marked dihedral. The cockpit features tandem seating beneath a long 'glasshouse' canopy. The first prototype of the CJ-6, flown on 27 August 1958, was fitted with a 108-kW (145-hp) Mikulin M-11ER engine, with which it proved to be underpowered. The CJ-6 was later modified with an Ivchenko

Al-14R engine and first flew in this form on 18 July 1960. The **CJ-6A**, which became the standard production version from 1965, introduced an uprated HS6A engine. Ten armed **CJ-6B**s were built in 1964-66.

Production of the CJ-6A (the 'Westernised' designation of which is **PT-6A**) has totalled more than 1,800, and batches of the Nanchang trainer have been exported to several nations in the Chinese ambit including **Albania**, **Bangladesh**, **Cambodia**, **North Korea**, **Tanzania** and **Zambia**.

SPECIFICATION

Nanchang CJ-6A/PT-6A
Wing: span 10.18 m (33 ft 4.75 in)
Fuselage and tail: length 8.46 m (27 ft 9 in); height

3.25 m (10 ft 8 in)
Powerplant: one Zhuzhou (SMPMC) Huosai-6A (Ivchenko/Vedeneyev AI-14RF) nine-cylinder air-cooled radial engine rated at 213 kW (285 hp)
Weights: empty equipped 1172 kg (2,584 lb); maximum take-off 1419 kg (3,128 lb)
Fuel and load: internal fuel 110 kg (243 lb); external fuel none; ordnance none

Speed: maximum level speed 'clean' at optimum altitude 297 km/h (160 kt; 185 mph)
Range: endurance 3 hours 54 minutes
Performance: maximum rate of climb at sea level 380 m (1,248 ft) per minute; service ceiling 6250 m (20,500 ft); take-off run 280 m (920 ft) at maximum take-off weight; landing run 350 m (1,150 ft) at normal landing weight

The Chinese-built Nanchang BT-6 serves as the standard primary training aircraft of the Bangladesh air force, with No. 11 Squadron at Jessore. Twelve were delivered.

Nanchang Q-5/A-5 'Fantan'

The **Nanchang Q-5 'Fantan'** is a dedicated attack aircraft loosely based on the airframe of the Chinese-built MiG-19 or J-6. Development of the aircraft began in August 1958 to meet a **People's Liberation Army** requirement. The Nanchang Aircraft Factory had been established in

May 1951, and had been considerably rebuilt with Soviet assistance during the 1950s, but had always specialised in the production of propeller-driven aircraft. When development of the Q-5 attack aircraft was assigned to the factory, Nanchang therefore had much to learn. Shenyang helped with

initial design and mock-up construction, and the factory began licence-production of a small batch of MiG-19Ps and MiG-19PMs.

It would be easy to overstate the relationship of the Q-5 to the MiG-19, the new aircraft actually sharing only the rear fuselage and main undercarriage of the latter with a new, stretched fuselage, area-ruled to reduce transonic drag. The fuselage also accommodated a 4.00-m (13-ft) long internal weapons bay, with two adjacent fuselage

pylons. The new fuselage had a conical nose, giving an improved view forward and downward and providing a potential location for an attack radar (which never materialised). The Q-5 was also given wings of greater area and less sweep to give more lift and better turn performance. The tailplane was increased in size to improve longitudinal stability. This also necessitated the provision of lateral air intakes. The nosewheel was redesigned to rotate through 90°

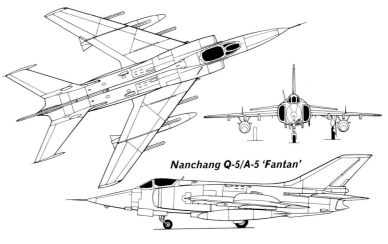

as it retracted, allowing it to lie flat in the underside of the fuselage.

Internal armament of the Q-5 comprises two 23-mm cannon (downgraded from the MiG-19's 30-mm NR-30 cannon) each with 100 rounds. Tandem pairs of pylons are each capable of carrying a 250-kg (551-lb) bomb. The inboard underwing pylons are used for carriage of lighter stores such as practice bombs and rocket pods. The central underwing pylons can carry 760-litre (201-US gal) fuel tanks or a 500-kg (1,102-lb) bomb. The outboard hardpoints can carry 400-litre (106-US gal) tanks or a variety of bombs or air-to-air missiles.

Prototype construction began in May 1960, but was abandoned during the political turmoil of the early 1960s and reinstated by stages, first as a 'spare time venture', then resumed full-time in 1963 because of the progress made. The prototype finally made its maiden flight on 4 June 1965, but extensive modifications proved necessary to solve problems encountered with the hydraulics, brakes, fuel and weapons systems. Two new prototypes flew in October 1969 and the type was ordered into production as the Q-5.

There is a dedicated nuclear weapons-carrier version of the Q-5, but little is known about this aircraft, which may retain its internal bomb bay. It carries a single 5- to 20-kT weapon. China's 13th nuclear test in 1970 was of a weapon lofted by a Q-5.

An extended-range variant, the **Q-5I**, was certificated in 1983. This had a fuel tank in place of the internal weapons bay, a modified landing gear and relocated brake chute fairing at the base of the fin. Two additional underfuselage hardpoints were provided. A new rocket-powered Type I ejection seat was fitted (allowing ejections above 260 m/850 ft and 348 km/h/188 kt), as was a new short-range SSB radio. The aircraft was powered by the new Series 6 Wopen WP6 engine. Together, these modifications brought about a 130-m (425-ft) reduction in landing run, a 500-kg (1,102-lb) increase in warload, and a 35 per cent increase in low-level radius of action (or a 26 per cent increase in normal range). Some Q-5Is were modified to serve as missile-carriers with the **PLA navy**, and some of these aircraft may have been fitted with Doppler-type nose radar. C-801 ASMs and torpedoes could also be carried.

The **Q-5IA**, certificated for production in 1985, was fitted with an additional underwing hardpoint and introduced pressure refuelling, a new gun/bomb sighting system and new defensive avionics. The **Q-5II** received a radar warning receiver but was otherwise similar. The **A-5C** was an export version of the Q-5IA for **Pakistan**, and actually entered production before the domestic variant. The Chinese designation **Q-5III** applies to this version. Avionics were substantially improved, and compatibility with various Western weapons (including the AIM-9 Sidewinder) was provided. The aircraft was also fitted with a Martin-Baker Mk 10L ejection seat.

Production of the Q-5 continues, and over 1,000 are believed to have been delivered. **North Korea** took delivery of 40 Q-5IAs, while Pakistan received 52 A-5Cs between January 1983 and January 1984. **Bangladesh** took delivery of a further 20 similar aircraft. Pakistan paid $2.6 million for each of its A-5Cs, this low purchase price being offset by low airframe (600 hours) and engine (200 hours) TBO figures. Pakistan now undertakes all of its own A-5C servicing and overhauls at Kamra's repair and overhaul facility. Recent reports suggest that RWRs are being fitted to these aircraft as they go through Kamra.

Before the Tiananmen Square massacre in June 1989, there were a number of programmes to upgrade Chinese combat aircraft with Western avionics and/or equip-ment, several of these involving the Q-5. Britain's Flight Refuelling Ltd was involved in a project to design inflight-refuelling probes for the aircraft, and two competing upgrades were designed to meet a Chinese requirement. The **A-5K Kong Yun** (Cloud) was designed in association with Thompson-CSF with a TMV630 laser rangefinder. Development began in June 1987, and yielded a flying prototype on 17 September 1988, but the project was abandoned in 1990. The **A-5M** programme was launched in August 1986, in association with Aeritalia, which added an AMX-style avionics system. This included a Pointer 2500 ranging radar, LN-39 INS, Alenia HUD 35, and new IFF and RWR equipment. An extra underwing pylon was added (bringing the total to four per side) and compatibility with the PL-5 AAM was also incorporated. The prototype was powered by 36.78-kN (8,267-lb st) Wopen WP-6A engines and made its maiden flight on 30 August 1988, but was written off on 17 October. A second prototype flew on 8 March 1989 and development was completed on 19 February 1991.

SPECIFICATION

Nanchang Q-5IA 'Fantan'
Wing: span 9.68 m (31 ft 9 in); aspect ratio 3.37; area 27.95 m2 (300.86 sq ft)
Fuselage and tail: length 15.65 m (51 ft 4.25 in) including probe; height 4.333 m (14 ft 2.75 in); wheel track 4.40 m (14 ft 5.25 in); wheel base 4.01 m (13 ft 2 in)
Powerplant: two Liming (LM) (previously Shenyang) Wopen-6A turbojets each rated at 29.42 kN (6,614 lb st) dry and 36.78 kN (8,267 lb st) with afterburning
Weights: empty 6375 kg (14,054 lb); normal take-off 9486 kg (20,913 lb); maximum take-off 11830 kg (26,080 lb)
Fuel and load: internal fuel 2827 kg (6,232 lb); external fuel up to 1178 kg (2,597 lb) in two 760- or 400-litre (201- or 106-US gal) drop tanks; maximum ordnance 2000 kg (4,409 lb)
Speed: maximum level speed at 11000 m (36,000 ft) Mach 1.12 (1190 km/h; 643 kt; 740 mph); maximum speed at sea level 1210 km/h (653 kt; 752 mph)
Range: combat radius with maximum external stores, afterburners off lo-lo-lo 400 km (216 nm; 248 miles), hi-lo-hi 600 km (324 nm; 373 miles); range at 11000 m (36,000 ft) with maximum internal/external fuel, afterburners off nearly 2000 km (1,080 nm; 1,243 miles)
Performance: maximum rate of climb at 5000 m (16,400 ft) 4980-6180 m (16,340-20,275 ft) per minute; service ceiling 15850 m (52,000 ft); take-off run 1250 m (4,100 ft); landing run 1060 m (3,480 ft)

Right: A pair of No. 8 Squadron, Bangladesh Defence Force Air Wing, Nanchang A-5s, armed with tiny Chinese rocket pods, executes a tidy break. A-5s also equip No. 21 Squadron at Dhaka.

Below: The A-5 equips three squadrons of the Pakistan air force, Nos 16 and 26 of No. 36 (Tactical Attack) Wing at Peshawar, and No. 7, the conversion unit, at Masroor.

Neico **Lancair 320**

Neico Aviation was based at Santa Paula in Cal;ifornia. Lancair aircraft are now produced by Lancair International, based at Redmond, Oregon. The Pacific Aeronautical Inc. is based at 25 First Avenue, Mactan Export Processing Zone, Lapu Lapu City 6015, Republic of the Philippines

The **Neico Lancair** family has been available to home-builders in kit form for some years, the side-by-side two-seater proving to be popular on account of its

modern looks and high performance, the latter thanks to streamlined design and retractable tricycle undercarriage. A single **Lancair 320** was supplied to **Bolivia** for

evaluation by the air force as a primary trainer, while Pacific Aeronautical Inc. (formerly Advanced Composite Technology) in the Philippines has developed the **ACT**

Apache I for use in a similar role. **Zaïre** reportedly ordered 30 for its air force training requirements, but the status of the Apache programme is in some doubt.

Neiva **C-42/L-42 Regente**

Sociedade Constructora Aeronautica Neiva Ltda. was established on October 1953. The company was acquired by EMBRAER in 1975, which took charge of the latter's light plane manufacturing programme

More than half of 120 Regentes built by Neiva between 1961 and 1971 remain in service with the **Brazilian air force**, distributed through a number of squadrons for communications duties, and equipping one of the squadrons of 8° Grupo de Aviaco at Santa Cruz. The **Neiva Regente 360C** prototype was first flown on 7 September 1961. The Regente is a four-seat high-wing monoplane with fixed tricycle undercarriage

and was the first of that company's light aircraft designs to feature all-metal construction. The single-spar wing incorporated semi-Fowler flaps and semi-Fowler ailerons.

For communications duties, the FAeB ordered 80 Regentes, initially with the des-

Having previously built copies of the Piper Cub, the U-42 Regente was Neiva's first original design.

ignation **U-42**, later changed to **C-42**. The first of these flew in 1965 and deliveries were completed in 1968. Seating four, the C-42 was powered by the 180-hp (156-kW) Lycoming O-360-A1D flat-four piston engine. To serve more specifically in the liaison and AOP role, the **L-42** was developed in 1967, differing from the C-42 in having only three seats, a cut-down rear fuselage to improve the all-round view (compensa-

tion for the reduced keel area being provided by a dorsal fin extension) and a more powerful IO-360 flat-six piston engine. Following the first flight of a **YL-42** prototype in October 1967, 40 were delivered from June 1969.

The three-seat L-42 Regente was a development of the U-42 which entered production in 1968.

NH Industries **NH 90**

NH Industries sarl, Le Quatuor, Batiment C, 42 Route de Galice F-13082 Aix en Provence France

In 1985 five European nations signed a Memorandum of Understanding covering a 'NATO helicopter for the '90s', designated **NH 90**. The United Kingdom dropped out of the programme in 1987, leaving France, Germany, Italy and the Netherlands in the project. Participating companies are Eurocopter France (43 per cent of the workshare), Agusta (26 per cent), Eurocopter Deutschland (24 per cent) and Fokker (seven per cent). Stated requirements were 220 for France, 214 for Italy, 272 for Germany and 20 for the Netherlands. A first flight is expected in 1995, with deliveries commencing in 1999.

Two versions are planned, the **NFH 90** (NATO Frigate Helicopter) with 360° search radar under the cabin and ASW equipment, and the **TTH 90** (Tactical Transport Helicopter) for assault transport, rescue, EW and VIP transport duties. The NH 90 exhibits a classic configuration, with a two-man flight deck and a cabin for either ASW equipment and one sensor operator or 20 fully-equipped troops. Power is to be provided by two of either the Rolls-Royce Turboméca/Piaggio/MTU RTM332 or General Electric/Alfa Romeo T700 turboshafts.

The first set of NH 90 rotor blades was handed over by NH Industries on 20 May

The NH 90 is planned in two versions. Seen in preliminary model form, they are (top) the NFH NATO Frigate Helicopter, and (below) the TTH Tactical Transport Helicopter. Estimated service requirements are for 192 NFHs and 554 TTHs. The first example is now heading towards roll-out in 1995.

1994, at La Corneuve. The blades mark the first use of new manufacturing techniques in such an item, as extensive use of CAD/CAM-originated resin components has been made, using the Catia 3-D design system.

SPECIFICATION

NH Industries NH 90 (provisional)
Rotor system: main rotor diameter 16.30 m (53 ft 5.5 in); tail rotor diameter 3.20 m (10 ft 6 in); main rotor disc area 213.82 m² (2,301.17 sq ft); tail rotor disc area 8.04 m² (86.57 sq ft)
Fuselage and tail: length overall, rotors turning 19.38 m (63 ft 7 in), fuselage 16.81 m (55 ft 1.75 in) and with main rotor blades and tail folded 13.50 m (44 ft 1.5 in); height overall 5.422 m (17 ft 9.5 in) with tail rotor turning, and 4.10 m (13 ft 5.5 in) with main rotor blades and tail folded; wheel track 3.20 m

(10 ft 6 in); wheel base 6.18 m (20 ft 3.25 in)
Powerplant: two Rolls-Royce/Turboméca/MTU (with Piaggio) RTM 322-01/02 turboshafts each rated at 1599.5 kW (2,145 shp) or two General Electric (with Alfa Romeo) T700-GE-401X turboshafts each rated at 2,400 shp (1789 kW)

Weights: empty 5700 kg (12,566 lb); maximum take-off 9100 kg (20,062 lb)
Fuel and load: internal fuel 1900 kg (4,189 lb); maximum payload more than 2000 kg (4,409 lb)
Range: operational radius 60 nm (69 miles; 111 km) for a 3-hour patrol; endurance 5 hours 30 minutes

Nord Aviation (Aérospatiale) **N 2501 Noratlas**

SNCAN (formed from a merger between Caudron and Amiot) later became Nord. The latter company itself merged with Sud Aviation to form Aérospatiale, in 1970.

Designed as a military transport for service with the Armée de l'Air, the **Nord N 2501 Noratlas** transport first flew with the intended Hercules engines on November 1950. It adopted the same configuration as the Fairchild C-82 Packet – namely a high wing, twin engines and twin tailbooms – and can accommodate 45 troops, 36 fully-equipped paratroops, or 18 stretchers and medical attendants. The Noratlas entered service with the Armée de l'Air in 1951 (in

N 2501F guise) and also served with the Luftwaffe, which received 186 **N 2501D**s. A few examples of this once widely-used tactical transport remain in service in some of the ex-French territories in Africa, having been supplied from surplus stocks after their retirement from both European air forces. Now nearing the end of their airframe lives, a total of 10 aircraft survives in service with the **Congo Republic**, **Djibouti**, **Niger** and **Rwanda**.

SPECIFICATION

Nord Aviation (Aérospatiale) N 2501 Noratlas
Wing: span 32.50 m (106 ft 7.5 in); aspect ratio 10.44; area 101.20 m² (1,089.34 sq ft)
Fuselage and tail: length 21.96 m (72 ft 0.6 in); height 6.00 m (19 ft 8.2 in)
Powerplant: two SNECMA-built Bristol Hercules Mk 738/739 14-cylinder air-cooled radial piston engines each rated at 2,040 hp (1521 kW)

Weights: empty equipped 13075 kg (28,825 lb); normal take-off 21000 kg (46,296 lb); maximum take-off 21700 kg (47,840 lb)
Load: maximum payload 7400 kg (16,314 lb)
Speed: maximum level speed 'clean' at 3050 m (10,000 ft) 440 km/h (237 kt; 273 mph); cruising speed at 1500 m (4,920 ft) 323 km/h (175 kt; 201 mph)
Range: 2500 km (1,349 nm; 1,553 miles) with a 4550-kg (10,031-lb) payload
Performance: maximum rate of climb at sea level 375 m (1,230 ft) per minute; service ceiling 7500 m (24,605 ft)

North American T-6 Texan

North American Aviation, founded in 1928, merged with the Rockwell-Standard Corporation, in 1967, becoming the North American Rockwell Corporation. This company became Rockwell International in 1973.

The **North American T-6** two-seat advanced trainer, officially named **Texan**, is better remembered by Commonwealth pilots as the **Harvard**. Similar to the USAAF's North American BC-1A basic combat trainer, the T-6 was introduced in 1938 and eventually replaced the BC-1A. Total T-6 production, which ended at the close of World War II, amounted to more than 16,000 in the US, while many more were manufactured under licence-production programmes throughout the Commonwealth.

The T-6 is an all-metal low-wing monoplane with retractable tailwheel landing gear. The pilot and instructor sat in tandem enclosed cockpits, the low sill of which gave an excellent view. Complete dual flight and engine controls are fitted in each cockpit. The powerful and reliable Pratt & Whitney Wasp air-cooled radial engine gave a sprightly performance, and the forgiving but responsive flying controls combined to make the T-6 an ideal training aircraft. Its distinctive rasping noise, not heard by the occupants, was caused by the high tip-speed of the direct-drive propeller.

The primary role of the T-6 as an armed trainer also made it suitable for light ground attack/COIN duties. Because of this, and its strong construction, reliability and ease of flying, the T-6 continued to be used for many years throughout the world.

Today the **South African Air Force** is the only major user, with over 100 Harvards

The South African Air Force was forced to retain substantial numbers of T-6 Harvards as its primary trainer well into the 1990s. Their replacement will come in the form of locally-assembled Pilatus PC-7 Mk IIs. While some aircraft have been disposed of, chiefly to civilian 'warbird' operators, the South Africans are being careful to dispose of their Harvards in a controlled fashion so as not to flood the market and depress the type's market value.

still flying with the Central Flying School at Langebaanweg. These were due for retirement in 1994, but their replacement has proceeded more slowly than expected. The Harvard's successor will be the Pilatus PC-7 Mk II, and small numbers of the SAAF's substantial T-6 fleet are being disposed of to civilian customers, but gradually, so as not to undermine their market value. Even when the type is finally replaced as the air force's primary trainer, 25 will reportedly be retained as a memorial to the wartime Empire flying programme, hosted by South Africa. Other military users include **Chile**, the **Dominican Republic**, **Portugal** and **Uruguay**, which each operates a pair of Texans. The **United Kingdom** has two Harvards at ETPS, Boscombe Down, as camera chase and training aircraft.

SPECIFICATION

North American T-6 Texan
Wing: span 42 ft 0.25 in (12.81 m); aspect ratio 6.96; area 253.70 sq ft (23.57 m²)
Fuselage and tail: length 29 ft 6 in (8.99 m); height 11 ft 9 in (3.58 m)
Powerplant: one Pratt & Whitney R-1340-AN-1 Wasp nine-cylinder air-cooled radial piston engine rated at 550 hp (410 kW)

Weights: empty equipped 4,158 lb (1886 kg); maximum take-off 5,300 lb (2404 kg)
Fuel and load: internal fuel 110 US gal (416 litres); external fuel none
Speed: maximum level speed 'clean' at 5,000 ft (1525 m) 178 kt (205 mph; 330 km/h); cruising speed at optimum altitude 148 kt (170 mph; 272 km/h)
Range: range 651 nm (750 miles; 1207 km)
Performance: maximum rate of climb at sea level 1,350 ft (411 m) per minute; service ceiling 21,500 ft (6555 m)

North American T-28 Trojan

Designed as a potential replacement for the successful T-6 Texan/Harvard family of trainers, the **T-28** was first flown on 26 September 1949 and entered production as a combined basic and primary trainer. The T-28 retained the T-6's basic trainer configuration, but introduced tricycle undercarriage and an 800-hp (597-kW) Wright R-1300-1A radial piston engine driving a two-bladed variable-pitch propeller. It was produced for the USAF (1,194 **T-28A**s) and the US Navy and Marine Corps, comprising 489 **T-28B Trojans** with more powerful 1,425-hp (1063-kW) Wright R-1820 engines driving three-bladed propellers, and 299 **T-28C**s with arrester hook and strengthened airframe to withstand carrier landings. Both these versions served until the 1970s. Production totalled 1,984 and numerous examples were delivered to foreign air forces through MAP and other arrangements.

In the early 1960s, subsequent conversion programmes produced the **T-28D** variant as a heavily-armed counter-insurgency aircraft. Several hundred surplus T-28As were modified by North American and Fairchild with R-1820 engines, three-bladed propellers, crew armour protection and six underwing stores hardpoints. T-28Ds served with US air commando squadrons as part of early American involvement in Vietnam, being fitted to carry podded 0.5-in (12.7-mm) machine-guns, 500-lb (227-kg) bombs, rockets and napalm weapons. Dissatisfaction with their performance led to transfer of 100 aircraft to the air forces of South Vietnam and the Philippines. A similar

programme in 1960-61 by Sud Aviation in France produced 245 **Fennec** conversions of the T-28A for the Armée de l'Air. These saw widespread service in the light-attack role in Algeria. Surplus Fennecs were sold to Morocco, Honduras and the Argentine navy (modified with arrester hooks).

T-28Ds remain in service as weapons/ COIN trainers in the **Dominican Republic** (six Trojans were withdrawn from service and two were subsequently restored to use by 1988) and the **Philippines**, which originally received 60 **AT-28D** aircraft up to the mid-1970s. Although frequently unserviceable, they participated in some ground-attack missions, including *coup* attempts in 1987 and 1989 (in which several were destroyed). Several examples remain in service with the 16 AS and 18 AS, 15th Strike Wing at Sangley Point. The **Uruguayan navy** operates four Fennecs that previously served with the **Argentine navy**, and that have been further modified in Uruguay to have 1,525-hp (1138-kW) Wright R-1820-82WA engines from S-2A Trackers.

T-28s were retired from Philippine air force service in the mid-1980s, only to return to duty on COIN missions (in 1985) until 1992. The aircraft below are armed with underwing guns, bombs and 81-mm cluster grenades.

SPECIFICATION

North American T-28D Trojan
Wing: span 40 ft 1 in (12.22 m); aspect ratio 6.0; area 268.00 sq ft (24.90 m²)
Fuselage and tail: length 33 ft 0 in (10.06 m); height 12 ft 8 in (3.86 m)
Powerplant: one Wright R-1820-86 Cyclone 14-cylinder air-cooled radial piston engine rated at 1,425 hp (1063 kW)

Weights: empty equipped 6,424 lb (2914 kg); maximum take-off 8,500 lb (3856 kg)
Fuel and load: external fuel none; maximum ordnance 1,200 lb (544 kg)
Speed: maximum level speed 'clean' at 10,000 ft

(3050 m) 298 kt (343 mph; 552 km/h)
Range: ferry range 921 nm (1,060 miles; 1706 km)
Performance: maximum rate of climb at sea level 3,540 ft (1079 m) per minute; service ceiling 35,500 ft (10820 m)

Northrop B-2 Spirit

Northrop Corporation, B-2 Division 8900 East Washington Boulevard, Pico Rivera California 90660-3737, USA

The **Northrop B-2** flying wing was developed in great secrecy as a stealthy, or radar-evading, strategic bomber for the Cold War mission of attacking Soviet strategic targets with nuclear bombs and stand-off weapons. The B-2 began as a 'black' programme, known in its infancy as **Project Senior C. J.** and later as the **ATB**

(Advanced Technology Bomber). In its early days, US Air Force leaders believed that the service's top priority was the B-1B bomber, and only a handful even knew of the B-2 project. To the latter group, the B-1B was an 'interim' weapon awaiting the B-2; at the height of the Cold War, the USAF expected to procure no fewer than 132.

Drawing heavily on its previous flying wing designs, Northrop was aided extensively by Boeing, Vought and General Electric, using a three-dimensional computer-aided design and manufacturing system to create the B-2's unique 'blended wing/double-W' shape. More than 100,000 radar cross-section images of B-2 models and

components were analysed to assess their stealth properties, followed by 550,000 hours of wind tunnel tests. Nine hundred new manufacturing processes had to be developed for the programme, including rugged, high-temperature composite materials, ultra-sonic cutting machinery, automated tooling via the 3D database and laser

Left: The B-2's blended wing design necessitates a unique control surface layout. From the wingtip moving inboard are a drag rudder/spoiler and then an elevon running along the same hingeline. Two more elevons are located on the next trailing edge section. These move in unison, but can function as separate units. Above and behind the articulated centrebody ('beaver tail') is an instrumentation drogue carried by all the test aircraft.

Below: As this aircraft rolls onto finals for runway 22 at Edwards AFB, its auxiliary intake doors above the engines are clearly visible. In the distance at the dry lakebed site can be seen the secret North Base facility. Even during the early stages of the test programme, the B-2 was rolled smoothly to an angle of 45°. With spoilers deployed it maintains a touch-down pitch angle of only 7°, and with only moderate braking can come to a stop within 4,000 ft (1220 m). The B-2 has 50 per cent better fuel efficiency than the B-1B, and it requires less than half the latter's refuelling support to carry out a strike mission.

sheraography inspection. Northrop is responsible for building the forward sections and the cockpit, and Boeing builds the aft centre and outboard sections, while Vought produces the mid-fuselage sections and aluminium, titanium and composite parts.

Graphite/epoxy composites are extensively used on the B-2, to provide a radar-absorbent honeycomb structure. To reduce infra-red signature, the four General Electric F118-GE-110 turbofans exhaust through V-shaped outlets set back and above the trailing edges to hide these heat sources from the ground. Chloro-flourosulphonic acid is injected into the exhaust plume to suppress the formation of contrails. The B-2's swept (33°) leading edge and saw-tooth trailing edge configuration trap radar energy. Further low-observables (LO) measures include 'S'-curved engine intakes and stealthy dielectric panels covering the AN/APQ-181 J-band radar that hides its antenna from reflecting hostile radar waves while allowing it to function normally. The cockpit is equipped for two, with upward-firing Douglas/Weber ACES II ejection seats, and there is room for a third crew member. The pilot has charge of the mission computer, which handles target tasking (or retasking in flight). Navigation and weapons delivery is the responsibility of the WSO, in the right-hand seat. The two primary positions have four multi-function, colour displays. The aircraft has a quadruply-redundant digital fly-by-wire system, actuating movable surfaces on the wing trailing edges, which combine aileron, elevator and flap functions and occupy 15 per cent of the wing area. A beaver tail acts as a pitch-axis trimming surface and, along with the elevons, helps in gust alleviation.

To verify targets at the last moment, the B-2 will briefly turn on its AN/APQ-181, spotlighting only a small area, and then attack. Since 1987 the unit has been under test in a specially modified USADF C-135 and, although radar is installed on some

of the prototype B-2s, all radar testing has been done on the C-135. The B-2 will be equipped with an electronic warfare system, comprising the IBM Federal Systems AN/APR-50 (ZSR-63) RWR and the secret ZSR-62 defensive aids system.

The B-2 was originally envisaged as a high-level penetrator but, by the time its design was frozen in 1983, a low-level role had been assumed. Modifications needed to adapt the original ATB design to this new role included moving the cockpit and engine inlets, adding inboard elevons (resulting in the distinctive 'double-W' planform), modifying the leading edge and making substantial internal changes, including new bulkheads. In a surprise move, the USAF released an artist's impression of the aircraft, which had previously been shrouded in total secrecy, in April 1988. Six prototypes (five for the USAF) were funded in 1982. The first (82-1066) was rolled out at USAF Plant 42, Palmdale, on 22 November 1988. Northrop carefully managed the ceremony to

hide details of the aircraft's wing design and the 500 assembled guests had only a limited front view of the B-2 from ground level. An enterprising photographer discovered that Northrop had not blocked off the airspace above the plant, and obtained the first complete photographs of the aircraft after a quick sortie in a Cessna.

The B-2's first flight took place on 17 July 1990 (originally planned for 1987), when this aircraft (also referred to as AV-1/Air Vehicle One) was delivered to the USAF at Edwards AFB, to begin the test programme. The final date had been delayed from 15 July by a fuel system malfunction, and had been preceded by a series of high-speed taxi runs on 13 July, when the nose wheel was lifted briefly. AV-1 was joined by 82-1067 on 19 October 1990. A test schedule of 3,600 hours was set out, commencing with 16 flights (67 hours) of airworthiness and handling trials. Completed in mid-June 1990, these flights also included the first air-to-air refuelling, with a KC-10A, on 8 November 1989. Block 2 testing began in October 1990, investigating the LO characteristics of the 'real thing'. These flights provided the first signs that all was not as advertised with the stealthy B-2, and subsequent flights were halted while modifications were carried out on 82-1066. Stealth testing continued into 1993, while 82-1067 was engaged on further performance and load trials. The

third aircraft (82-1068) made its maiden flight on 18 June 1991 and was the first to carry the full avionics mission fit, with the Hughes AN/APQ-181 LPI (low-probability of intercept) radar. The first weapons drop by a B-2 was made by the fourth aircraft (82-1069), which first took to the air on 17 April 1992. A single inert Mk 84 2,000-lb (908-kg) bomb was dropped by this aircraft on 4 September 1992. Earmarked for further weapons, LO and climatic testing, the fifth B-2 (82-1070) took to the air on 5 October 1992, followed by 82-1071 on 2 February 1993. By the end of 1993, the programme had chalked up 1,500 flying hours

In July 1991 deficiencies were revealed in the B-2's stealth profile. It has been admitted that the aircraft can be detected by some high-powered, land-based, early warning radars. Russian claims that the bomber is vulnerable to its new-generation SAM systems, such as the S-300PMU (SA-10/A 'Grumble') and S-300V-9M83/82 (SA-12A/B 'Gladiator'/'Giant'), have not been commented on. The USAF is implementing a 'set of treatments' to some leading edges and flying surfaces to reduce the aircraft's signature across a range of frequencies.

Problems with the B-2's performance have not aided it in the battle for funding on Capitol Hill. The original target was for a fleet of 133 airframes, including prototype, but by 1991 this had been cut back to 76 aircraft. After the original six aircraft, ordered in 1982, three more were funded while the B-2 was still a 'black' project. In 1989 money was allocated for a further three, followed by two in 1990 and two in 1991. Congress then froze acquisition at 16 (15

The 509th BW's first B-2, 'Spirit of Missouri', carries its 'tail markings' on the undercarriage doors, ACC badge on the starboard fuselage and wing insignia to port.

From the top of the B-2 facility at Edwards AFB, the aircraft's markings are visible: serials are on the centre fuselage, with a small star-and-bar on the starboard wing.

for the USAF). The USAF claims it cannot provide effective operational capability with less than 20 aircraft, and five more were subsequently approved by 1993. This approval came with the caveat that the type's LO problems must be rectified before any production occurs. Unit costs per aircraft (flyaway) have risen to $2,220 million. Original 1987 estimates for a 75-aircraft programme stood at $64,700 million (in total), although it is not beyond the bounds of possibility that some of the huge budget dedicated to the B-2 has been spent on other 'black' projects. The FY1995 budget included $793 million for support equipment and provision for the closure of the production line.

The first aircraft for the USAF (88-0329/ 'WM', 'Spirit of Missouri') was delivered to the 509th BW at Whiteman AFB, MO, on 17 December 1993, exactly 90 years to the day after the Wright Brothers' first flight. This was the eighth production B-2 (AV-8), the first aircraft to production standard, which preceded AV-7 into the air. AV-7 was still undergoing extensive electromagnetic and emission-control tests, but along with the other aircraft involved in the flight test programme it will be delivered to the USAF by 1997. AV-9 made its maiden flight on 24 January 1994. The 509th BW will be divided into two squadrons, the 393rd and 750th BS. Each will be operational with eight B-2s in 1996/97. Both AV-8 and AV-9 are Block 10 standard aircraft, incorporating many of the stealth improvements which resulted from the test programme. These will subsequently be modified to the definitive Block 30 standard (see Weapon Options, below), once the whole fleet is operational in 1997.

One of the less critical problems with the B-2 is the lack of vertical surfaces on which to apply 'tailcodes'. As a result, the main undercarriage doors now carry the base code, FY serial and, on 88-0329 at least, the legends 'Spirit of Missouri' and 'Follow Us'.

WEAPON OPTIONS

The B-2 is built around two large side-by-side weapons bays in its lower centrebody. In front of each bay are small spoiler panels which drop down to produce vortices, ensuring clean weapons release. Rotary launchers in both bomb bays can accommodate a theoretical bomb load of 75,000 lb (34020 kg) but, under the US national war fighting SIOP (Single Integrated Operational Plan), any nuclear load would be limited to 20,000 lb (9072 kg). While the B-2 can carry 80 Mk 82 500-lb (227-kg) bombs, it is too valuable to be used as a 'bomb truck'. Its strength, in a conventional role, will lie in its ability to deliver up to 16 smart weapons over a wide area, in a single pass, to 30-ft (10-m) accuracy. The five prototypes destined for the USAF, along with AV-7, -8 and -9, have been completed to Block 10 standard. This qualifies them to carry 16 B83 freefall nuclear bombs or 16 Mk 84 2,000-lb (908-kg) conventional bombs. For stand-off strategic missions, the B-2 can carry 16 AGM-69 SRAM II or AGM-129A cruise missiles. The intermediate production standard, Block 20, will add B61 nuclear capability (a maximum of 16) or up to 36 CBU-87, -89, -97 and -98 conventional munitions with a limited conventional PGM (precision-guided munitions) capability from 1997. This will entail adding two new weapons still under development. The first of these is the AGM-137 TSSAM (Tri-Service Stand-off Attack Missile), a stealthy, subsonic cruise missile with a range of 375 miles (600 km) and a payload of IR- and acoustically-guided sub-munitions. Eight AGM-137s would be carried, four on each rotary launcher. The second new weapon is the GPS-aided JDAM (Joint Direct Attack Munition). Fitted to a Mk 82, Mk 84 or BLU-109 weapon, JDAM will provide highly accurate targeting guidance through the aircraft's navigation system and an onboard INS.

Eventually it will be an all-weather, autonomous weapon with a programmable fuse. The two final production B-2s will be completed to full Block 30 standard. They will be fully PGM-capable, in addition to carrying 80 Mk 82 500-lb (227-kg), or 36 Mk 117 750-lb (340-kg) GP bombs or 80 Mk 62 aerial mines. Block 30 B-2s will boast fully operational offensive and operational avionics and an improved SAR.

SPECIFICATION

Northrop B-2A Spirit
Wing: span 172 ft 0 in (52.43 m); aspect ratio more than 5.92; area more than 5,000.00 sq ft (464.50 m²)
Fuselage and tail: length 69 ft 0 in (21.03 m); height 17 ft 0 in (5.18 m); wheel track 40 ft 0 in (12.20 m)
Powerplant: four General Electric F118-GE-110 non-afterburning turbofans each rated at 19,000 lb st (84.52 kN)
Weights: empty between 100,000 and 110,000 lb (45360 and 49900 kg); normal take-off 371,330 lb (168433 kg); maximum take-off 400,000 lb (181437 kg)
Fuel and load: internal fuel between 180,000 and 200,000 lb (81650 and 90720 kg); external fuel none; maximum ordnance 50,000 lb (22680 kg)
Speed: maximum level speed at high altitude about 416 kt (475 mph; 764 km/h)
Range: more than 10,000 nm (11,515 miles; 18532 km) with one flight refuelling; range with a 37,300-lb (169219-kg) warload comprising eight SRAMs and eight B83 bombs 6,300 nm (7,255 miles; 11675 km) with internal fuel on a hi-hi-hi mission or 4,400 nm (5,067 miles; 8154 km) on a hi-lo-hi mission with 1,000 nm (1,152 miles; 1853 km) at low level; range with a 24,000-lb (10886-kg) warload comprising eight SRAMs and eight B61 bombs 6,600 nm (7,600 miles; 12231 km) with internal fuel on a hi-hi-hi mission or 4,500 nm (5,182 miles; 8339 km) with internal fuel on a hi-lo-hi mission
Performance: service ceiling 50,000 ft (15240 m)

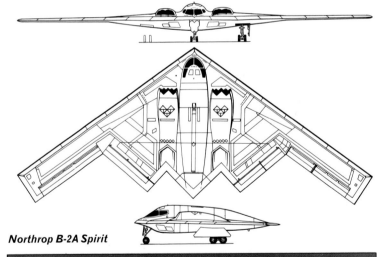

Northrop B-2A Spirit

The B-2's wingspan of 172 ft (52.43 m), is larger even than that of the KC-10A tanker. Its maximum internal fuel load of 200,000 lb (90720 kg) is sufficient for a mission of 7,500 miles (12000 km). With refuelling support, the Spirit's reach is global.

Northrop F-5 Freedom Fighter

Northrop Corporation, Aircraft Division
One Northrop Avenue, Hawthorne
California 90250, USA

In 1954 the US government initiated a study for a simple, lightweight fighter to be supplied to friendly nations via the Military Assistance Program. Northrop submitted its **N-156** proposal; in 1956 the USAF showed interest in a derivative supersonic trainer (the **T-38**, described separately) that was developed in parallel with the private-venture **N-156C**, which flew on 30 July 1959.

In April 1962 the US Secretary of Defense approved USAF selection of the N-156C as the required 'FX' fighter. This was designated **F-5**, and the **F-5A** prototype flew in May 1963. The two-seat **F-5B** fighter/trainer actually entered service ahead of the F-5A. Deliveries began on 30 April 1964 to the 4441st Combat Crew Training Squadron at Williams AFB. The first F-5As followed four months later, in August 1964.

The airframe incorporated new structural and aerodynamic features. These included leading-edge and trailing-edge flaps, area-ruled fuselage with two airbrakes on the undersurface, and in some versions manoeuvring flaps. Rocket-powered ejection seats were provided. The primary interception weapons comprised two nose-mounted 20-mm M39 guns, and two AIM-9 Sidewinder missiles on wingtip launchers. One underfuselage and four underwing pylons permitted the carriage of nearly 6,000 lb (2720 kg) of weapons, including a wide variety of bombs and rockets.

To evaluate the combat potential of the F-5A, 12 (later 18) aircraft were deployed to South East Asia in October 1965, under the codename Project Skoshi Tiger. The aircraft were diverted from the MAP and provided with a refuelling probe, armour, jettisonable pylons, additional avionics and camouflage.

In Canada, licence production was undertaken by Canadair for the **CF-5A/D** versions of the F-5A/B (Canadian Armed Forces designation **CF-116**) and for versions designated **NF-5A/B** for the Royal Netherlands air force. Both Canadian and Dutch versions are described separately. Some CF-5As can be fitted with a Vinten 70-mm camera nose and are then designated **CF-5A(R)**. The CF-5As can also be fitted with refuelling probes, but neither these nor the reconnaissance nose can be carried by the two-seat CF-5Ds. CASA-built Spanish versions are known in Spain's Ejercito del Aire as the **C.9** and **CE.9**, respectively, or as the **SF-5** and **SRF-5**. The **RF-5A** reconnaissance version is equipped with four KS-92A cameras mounted in the nose. Venezuela operates a mix of single- and two-seat F-5s known locally as **VF-5A** and **VF-5B**s.

Upgrades

The F-5, in all its versions, is a prime target for systems upgrades, and several companies are offering improvement packages. Simple system changes could include the addition of Westinghouse's AN/APG-66T multi-target track-while-scan radar (developed for the F-16A, now in trials for USN F-5s), or the General Electric AN/APG-67 multi-mode fire control radar (developed originally for the F-20 and now used by the AIDC Ching-Kuo), or Emerson's AN/APG-69 look-down/shoot-down radar.

Northrop invested heavily in the F-20 Tigershark (see F-5E entry) as an F-5 successor. When this project failed to attract sales, the manufacturer began to translate its F-20 experience into improved F-5 systems. As its chosen F-5 upgrade, Northrop offers APG-66 radar and an F-16-compatible cockpit with one or two Bendix multi-function, monochrome or colour displays (MFDs), Mason Electric HOTAS (Hands-On Throttle And Stick) controls, Honeywell laser-ring INS, Allied Signal air data and mission computer, Teac video recorder, new weapons control systems and a GEC Avionics wide-angle HUD. To fit new systems into the nose one M39 cannon has been removed, the bulkhead has been moved aft and the APG-66 antenna reduced in size. A new ejection seat, the Martin-Baker Mk 10LF, can also be fitted. Owing to the cost of the complete upgrade (approximately $4.5 million), prospective customers can choose which items they require from a list of options. While the F-5E is a more suitable recipient for upgrading, the **Turkish air force**'s F-5As are potential candidates (in a deal involving CASA and Allied Signal). A further option involves structural work, such as rewinging and fitting a new tail.

Thirteen **Canadian air force** CF-5As and 33 CF-5Ds (CF-116A/D) are being upgraded by **Bristol Aerospace**, to act as lead-in trainers for the CF-188 Hornet. New avionics items include a GEC Avionics HUD/WAC and air data computer, Litton ring-laser INS, AN/ARC-164 radios, Honeywell radar altimeter, Ferranti video camera and a remodelled HOTAS cockpit. The CF-5s are also having their wings and tails reskinned, a steel longeron fitted (replacing the original aluminium unit) and new landing gear. The first 'prototype' flew on 14 July 1991, upgraded CF-116s entered service with 419 Sqn in early 1992, and the programme is scheduled for completion in 1995. Bristol Aerospace was contracted in 1991 to overhaul 23 **Spanish air force** SF-5Bs, extending their useful lives as weapons trainers. They will also receive new IFF and RWR. So concerned was Northrop at Bristol Aerospace's gains in the upgrade market that they took the Canadian company to court, alleging 'infringement of their intellectual property' and specifically infringement of the Northrop licence to support the Canadian air force's F-5s. The two companies settled out of court in May 1994, with Bristol paying an undisclosed sum to Northrop. Furthermore, the two signed a teaming agreement for any further work on F-5E/Fs.

Bristol Aerospace has also now teamed with **Eidetics International** (USA) to offer the **Tiger 2000** F-5A/B upgrade. Having zero-timed the airframe, Bristol will add substantial LERXes and an automatic manoeuvre flap system to the wing. Eidetics will integrate a redesigned cockpit with two MFDs, TACAN, ILS and HSI, along with new RWR and chaff/flare dispensers.

A structural overhaul for the **Venezuelan air force**'s VF-5As and single VF-5B is being undertaken by **Singapore Aerospace**, which is also heavily involved in upgrading the Singapore air force's F-5E fleet. Venezuela withdrew its surviving 13 CF-5As and sole CF-5D (F-5B) in May 1990 due to fatigue problems. The first phase of a refurbishment programme commenced in May 1991, when one CF-5A (VF-5A) and one CF-5D (VF-5B) were dispatched to Singapore Aerospace, returning to service in May 1993. In the meantime, six former Netherlands air force F-5s (five NF-5As and one NF-5B) were acquired and refurbished, entering service in February 1992. The remaining Canadair-built aircraft are being rotated through Singapore Aerospace's facility at Paya Lebar.

Norway is another F-16 operator which relies on its F-5s as lead-in fighter trainers. **Vought Sierra Research Division** has been contracted to implement the **Tiger PAWS** (Programme for Avionics and Weapons Systems Improvements) for the Royal Norwegian air force. Beginning in late 1993, seven F-5As and eight F-5Bs were to be fitted with GEC Avionics HUD/WAC (compatible with Block 40 F-16C/Ds), MIL-STD-1553 digital databus, GEC Miniature Standard Air Data Computer, Litton AN-93 laser ring INS, new AoA sensors, colour video camera/recorder, and HOTAS controls. Norway was the first customer for a Sierra Industries upgrade, and the first aircraft was originally due to be handed over in May 1992. As the project grew in scope, the flight test programme stretched to hundreds of flights and, by November 1993, two of the first three F-5s were involved in weapons trials at Eglin AFB. All were handed over to the Norwegian air force the following month.

OPERATORS

Brazil: 80 CF-5A/Ds (including stored aircraft) – 14° GAvCa, 1° Esq 'Pampa', Canoas
Canada: 23 CF-5A (CF-116A), 14 CF-5D (CF-116D) – No. 419 Sqn, CFB Cold Lake
Greece: two squadrons of NF/F-5A and

Above: Surrounded by T-2D Buckeyes, this is one of the ex-KLu NF-5Bs refurbished for service with the Fuerza Aérea Venezolana. A small number of F-5A/Bs serve alongside Dassault Mirage III/5s (upgraded to Mirage 50EV standard), and F-16As.

Left: The Philippines has four AIM-9B-armed F-5As and a single F-5B operational. The 6th TFS moved to Mactan, from Basa, after the Mt Pinatubo eruption.

NF/F-5Bs, RF-5s reroled
 – 343 Mira, Thessaloniki; 349 Mira, Larissa
Morocco: 10 F-5A, two F-5B, one RF-5A
Norway: seven F-5A, eight F-5B – Skvadron 336, Rygge
Philippines: four F-5A, three F-5B
 – 6th TFS, 5th TFW, Mactan
Saudi Arabia: 15 F-5B – 3 Sqn, Taif; 16 Sqn, Tabuk
South Korea: F-5A, F-5B – 1st FW (OCU), Kwangju
Spain: 23 SF-5B– Esc 231/232, Ala 23, Talavera
Thailand: F-5A, F-5B
Turkey: three squadrons of CF/NF/F-5As,
 F-5Bs, RF-5A reroled
 – 133 Filo (3 Ana Jet Üs), Eskisehir
 – 151 and 152 Filos (5 Ana Jet Üs), Merzifon
Venezuela: 14 CF-5A, three CF-5D, six NF-5A
 – Escuadrón de Caza No. 36, Base
 Aérea Teniente Vicente Landaeta,
 Barquisimento
Yemen: four F-5B

SPECIFICATION

Northrop F-5A Freedom Fighter

Wing: span 25 ft 3 in (7.70 m) without tip tanks and 25 ft 10 in (7.87 m) with tip tanks; aspect ratio 6.35; area 170.00 sq ft (15.79 m²)
Fuselage and tail: length 47 ft 2 in (14.38 m); height 13 ft 2 in (4.01 m); tailplane span 14 ft 1 in (4.28 m); wheel track 11 ft 0 in (3.35 m); wheel base 15 ft 4 in (4.67 m)
Powerplant: two General Electric J85-GE-13 each turbojets rated at 2,720 lb st (12.10 kN) dry and 4,080 lb st (18.15 kN) with afterburning
Weights: empty equipped 8,085 lb (3667 kg); maximum take-off 20,677 lb (9379 kg)
Fuel and load: internal fuel 583 US gal (2207 litres) plus provision for 100 US gal (378.5 litres) in two tip tanks; external fuel up to three 150-US gal (568-litre) drop tanks; maximum ordnance 4,400 lb (1996 kg)
Speed: maximum level speed 'clean' at 36,000 ft

Turkey received huge numbers of F-5s. An original MAP consignment of 75 F-5As, 20 RF-5As and 13 F-5Bs was joined by 32 ex-Norwegian F/RF-5As, four ex-USAF and two former Taiwanese F-5Bs, and 60 former Dutch NF-5A/Bs. Upgraded aircraft will serve with three squadrons beyond the year 2000.

(10975 m) 802 kt (924 mph; 1487 km/h); cruising speed at 36,000 ft (10975 m) 556 kt (640 mph; 1030 km/h)
Range: ferry range 1,400 nm (1,612 miles; 2594 km); combat radius 485 nm (558 miles; 989 km) on a hi-lo-hi attack mission with two 530-lb (240-kg) bombs and maximum fuel, or 170 nm (196 miles; 315 km) on a hi-lo-hi attack mission with maximum warload
Performance: maximum rate of climb at sea level 28,700 ft (8748 m) per minute; service ceiling 50,500 ft (15390 m); take-off run 2,650 ft (808 m) at 13,677 lb (6203 kg) with two AIM-9 Sidewinder AAMs; take-off distance to 50 ft (15 m) 3,650 ft (1113 m) at 13,677 lb (6203 kg); landing distance from 50 ft (15 m) 3,900 ft (1189 m) at 9,843 lb (4464 kg) with brake chute

The aptly named Tiger PAWS (Programme for Weapons and Systems Improvements) upgrade currently being applied to all surviving Norwegian F-5As and F-5Bs (15 in total) ensures that the elderly aircraft will continue to have productive lives as lead-in trainers for the air force's F-16 fleet.

Northrop F-5E/F Tiger II

The **Northrop F-5E/F Tiger** is in widespread service around the world, having been developed from the manufacturer's earlier F-5A/B Freedom Fighter in response to a 1969 requirement for an International Fighter Aircraft to be sold to US allies. Selection of the Northrop design took place in November 1970. Development of the F-5E/F resulted from the August 1969 Nixon doctrine which called upon US allies to shoulder the burden of their defence, and provided the justification for 'Vietnamisation' of, and US withdrawal from, the South East Asia war. During the same period, the US was assisting the Shah of Iran in a massive modernisation of military forces. It was anticipated from the beginning that the first three customers for the IFA would be Iran, South Korea and South Vietnam.

A lightweight fighter with both air-to-air and air-to-ground capability, the single-seat **F-5E** is armed with two M39A2 20-mm cannon with 20-mm rounds, and typically carries two wingtip-mounted AIM-9 Sidewinder AAMs. The F-5E takes advantage of features developed for earlier F-5A/B aircraft, including two-position nosewheel gear which enables the aircraft to assume a higher angle of attack for take-off, as well as provision for JATO and an arrester hook. The **F-5F** tandem two-seat trainer had its fuselage lengthened by 3 ft 4 in (1.02 m) but retained the combat capabilities of the single-seater, although one cannon was deleted. First flight of an F-5F took place on 25 September 1974.

The first F-5E was flown on 11 August 1972. Initial deliveries of the F-5E were made to the US Air Force's 425th Tactical Fighter Squadron in early 1973, although the USAF's sole purpose at the time was to prepare the aircraft for foreign users. Some 1,300 F-5E/Fs were later supplied to 20 air forces. The F-5E was also assembled under licence in Taiwan and South Korea. The variant supplied to Saudi Arabia differed from other F-5Es in having a Litton LN-33 inertial navigation system which improved navigation and bombing accuracy. The **RF-5E** (described separately) was a proposed reconnaissance variant equipped with four KS-121A 70-mm framing cameras in a modified nose section.

Korean F-5s assembled by Korean Airlines, at Pusan, are referred to by the air force as Chegoong Ho (Air Master), while Taiwanese aircraft assembled by AIDC are known locally as Chung Cheng.

The considerably upgraded **F-20 Tigershark** (originally designated **F-5G**) was developed as an updated Tiger for service in the 1980s and 1990s, but was rendered superfluous by the availability of F-16As for export. Recently, existing F-5 customers have embarked on ambitious upgrade programmes to improve their aircraft, sometimes to the extent that the aircraft will become *de facto* F-20s.

Upgrades

The F-5 is a prime candidate for upgrading. Twelve **Chilean** F-5Es and two F-5Fs, for example, are being reworked by **IAI**'s Bedek division with HOTAS controls, monochrome MFDs, a new El-Op HUD, MIL-STD-

Chile's air defence-tasked F-5Es are undergoing a far-reaching upgrade in the hands of IAI and ENAER, becoming F-5E Plus Tigre IIIs. The tiger motif of Grupo 7 was adopted on aircraft fins in 1989, and the orange stripes signify an aggressor combat training F-5.

Northrop F-5E/F Tiger II

Switzerland's Sidewinder-armed F-5Es will lose their air defence role with the arrival of the air force's F/A-18 Hornets. Adopting a ground attack role, they will be armed with AGM-65 Maverick ASMs.

Left: Singapore's 10 F-5Fs supplement its F-5Es in the ground attack role, in addition to undertaking training duties with No. 144 Sqn, at RSAF Paya Lebar.

1553 digital databus and air data computer, a new INS and the Elta EL/M-2032B multi-mode radar originally developed for the Lavi. The aircraft will also have an integrated self-defence system with 360° RWR coverage, active jammers and chaff/flare dispensers. Two underwing Rafael Python III AAMs are available as a weapons option, complementing smaller wingtip AIM-9 Sidewinders. The first two **F-5E Plus Tiger III**s (or **Tigre III** in Chile) were converted in Israel, flying for the first time post-rebuild on 8 July 1993. The rest will undergo conversion in Chile by ENAER, with Israeli assistance. IAI expects to market its F-5 upgrades to several other customers, and can also offer add-on refuelling probes, helmet-mounted sights and new ejection seats. A further South American customer for an F-5E upgrade is **Brazil**, which plans to equip its aircraft with the indigenous Tecnasa/SMA SCP-01 radar and the OMI/Alenia HUD as fitted to its AMX fleet. Brazilian F-5s had already received upgrade kits from the US with refuelling probes for use with KC-130s.

More ambitiously, Taiwan is considering upgrading its Tigers to **F-5E-SX** configuration with a J101 engine (or the F125X used by the indigenous Ching-Kuo) and a new radar, possibly the APG-67-based Sky Dragon. AIM-120 missiles would be carried.

OPERATORS

The F-5E/F Tiger belatedly acquired a role in the US as an aggressor trainer and about 100 served in this role in the **US Air Force** until the late 1980s. The **US Navy**, which uses the term 'adversary' for this DACT mission, also acquired a small number of F-5E/Fs, the few remaining examples of which were concentrated by mid-1994 in just three US Navy and **US Marine** squadrons: VFA-127 'Cylons' at NAS Fallon, NV, VF-45 'Blackbirds' at NAS Key West, FL, and VMFT-401 'Snipers' at MCAS Yuma, AZ. All of these squadrons are in the process of adopting the F/A-18 Hornet. Non-US operators of the F-5E/F comprise:
Bahrain: eight F-5Es and four F-5Fs ordered by Bahrain Amiri Air Force in 1985. Delivered by 1987, these aircraft are now based at Sitra
Brazil: between 1975 and 1976, 36 F-5Es were

delivered (along with six F-5Bs) to the Força Aérea Brasiliera/Brazilian air force. Brazil then received 23 refurbished F-5Es from US stocks, along with three refurbished F-5Fs, between 1988 and 1989. All in service with 1° and 2° Esq, 1° GAvCa, at Santa Cruz and 1° Esq, 14° GAvCa, at Canoas
Chile: twelve (of 15 ordered) F-5Es and three F-5Fs, delivered to Fuerza Aérea de Chile/Chilean air force during 1976 despite arms embargo imposed that year. Offered for sale to Brazil in 1986, owing to low serviceability, but now undergoing Tigre III upgrade. In service with Grupo 7, Ala 1, 1Brigada, at Cerro Mereno, Antofagasta
Honduras: requested F-5E/Fs from 1982 to 1984. Ten refurbished F-5Es and two F-5Fs delivered to Fuerza Aérea Hondurena/Honduran air force between December 1987 and April 1989 to intercept 'arms flights to Nicaragua'. Operational with Escuadrilla de Caza, La Ceiba
Indonesia: by mid-1980, 12 F-5Es and four F-5Fs delivered to Tentara Nasional Indonesia – Angkatan Udara/Indonesian armed forces – air force. Surviving 10 F-5Es operational in air defence role (along with F-5Fs), at Madiun-Ishwayudi
Iran: Imperial Iranian Air Force acquired 166 F-5Es before fall of Shah, in February 1979. Small number of ex-Ethiopian F-5s believed obtained in 1986. Operational strength of Islamic Republic of Iran Air Force is estimated at 30-60 aircraft
Jordan: beginning 1975, 61 F-5Es and 12 F-5Fs delivered to Royal Jordanian Air Force. Operational with Nos 9 and 17 Sqns, air base H-5. Sought to acquire F-20 Tigershark as replacement in mid-1980s
Kenya: the '82 Air Force acquired 10 F-5Es and four F-5Fs between 1978 and 1982. Survivors remain operational at Nanyuki (Liakiapia)
Malaysia: between 1981 and 1985, 17 F-5Es delivered to Tentara Udara Diraja Malaysia/Royal Malaysian air force. Four ex-Thai F-5Fs acquired in 1982. Two RF-5E Tigereye delivered in 1983. Plans for 16 further F-5E/Fs abandoned in 1982. Aircraft

operational with Nos 11 'Cobra' and 12 'Tiger' Sqns, Butterworth
Mexico: between August and November 1984, 10 F-5Es and two F-5Fs delivered to Fuerza Aérea Mexicana/Mexican air force. All F-5Fs and nine F-5Es remain in service with Escuadrón de Defensa 401, 1 Grupo Aéreo, Santa Lucia
Morocco: Morocco's Force Royale Aérienne/Al Quwaat al Jawwiya al Malakiya received 16 F-5Es and four F-5Fs between 1981 and 1983. Followed by 10 ex-USAF F-5Es from October 1989, after overhaul in UK. Moroccan F-5s fitted with air-to-air refuelling probes, for use with KC-130s and converted 707 tanker. Several F-5s claimed shot down by Polisario guerrillas in operations over disputed Western Sahara. Aircraft believed based at Kenitra
Saudi Arabia: Royal Saudi Air Force/Al Quwaat al Jawwiya al Sa'udiya signed for 30 F-5Es in 1971, with a further 40 F-5Es and 20 F-5Fs ordered in 1974. Joined by four additional F-5Fs in 1976. Saudi Tigers armed with AGM-65 Maverick ASMs, AGM-45 Shrike ARMs, GBU-10/12 LGBs or Mk 20 CBUs. Aircraft also equipped with refuelling probes, Litton inertial navigation/attack systems, AN/ALQ-101/119/171 ECM pods, AN/ALE-46 RWR. Final F-5 deliveries, beginning in 1985, comprised 10 RF-5Es, plus attrition replacements in the form of four F-5Es and one F-5. Aircraft based at Taif, with Nos 3, 15 and 17 Sqns
Singapore: Republic of Singapore Air Force ordered 18 F-5s and three F-5Fs in 1979. Six F-5Es and three F-5Fs added in December 1987. Finally, five F-5Es assembled by Northrop from spares stock, after production line had closed, and delivered to Singapore in 1989. Six F-5Es upgraded to RF-5E standard by Singapore Aerospace with FLIR and IRLS. Aircraft in service with No. 144 'Lynx' Sqn, Paya Lebar and No. 149 'Shirkah' Sqn, Tengah
South Korea: some (up to 19) F-5E escapees from South Vietnam air force, in 1974 joined by 126 US-supplied F-5Es and 20 F-5Fs. Between 1982 and 1986, 48 locally-assembled F-5Es and 20 F-5Fs delivered to Hankook Kong Goon (Republic of Korea air force). Aircraft in service with 115, 122 and 123 FS of the 1st Fighter Wing at Kwangju, and 102, 103 and 111 FS of the 10th Fighter Wing at Suwon
Sudan: the Sudanese Air Force/Silkakh al Jawwiya as Sudaniya received two F-5Fs and two F-5Es (from an order for 10) underwritten by Saudi Arabia between 1982 and 1984. One F-5E lost one week after arrival and remainder of order cancelled due to lack of funding
Switzerland: Swiss Air Force and Anti-Aircraft Command/Kommando der Flieger- und Fliegerabwhertruppen took delivery of 66 F-5Es and six F-5Fs under Peace Alps programme beginning in

These F-5Es of the RoCAF's 455th TFW wear the markings of No. 23 'Tsi Ching' Squadron – 'Tsi Ching' meaning that the aircraft were paid for by the Taiwanese people.

1978. First 13 F-5Es and all F-5Fs completed by Northrop, while remainder assembled by FFA, at Emmen. FFA also received 50 per cent off-set for follow-on order of 32 F-5Es and six F-5Fs, ordered in 1981 and delivered by 1985. Aircraft fitted with Dalmo Victor RWR, but addition of conformaL AN/ALQ-171 ECM pods cancelled. Aircraft in service with Fliegerstaffel 1 and 11, Flugwaffen Brigade 31, at Dübendorf; Fliegerstaffel 1 and 6, Fliegerregiment 1, at Turtmann and Sion; Fliegerstaffel 8, 13 and 18, Fliegerregiment 2, at Meiringen and Payerne; Fliegerstaffel 11, 16 and 19, Fliegerregiment 3, at Alpnach and Stans/Buochs

Taiwan: from 1973, 162 F-5Es and 21 F-5Fs initially assembled by AIDC, for Republic of China air force/Chung-Kuo Kung Chuan, . Followed by 80 F-5Es and 35 F-5Fs delivered by 1986. Final batch of 30 F-5Es and 30 F-5Fs ordered in 1982. Aircraft later fitted with Litton ALR-46(V)3 RWR, Northrop AVQ-27 target designators, Tracor ALE-40(V)7 chaff/flare dispensers, with provision for AGM-65 ASMs and GBU-10 LGBs. Systems and radar upgrade now under consideration. Operational squadrons comprise 1,3, 9 Sqns (433rd TFW) at Tainan; 21,22, 23 Sqns (455th TFW) at Chia Yi; 17, 26, 27 Sqns (410st Tactical Combined Wing) at Taoyuan; 44, 45, 46 Sqns (737th TFW) at Taitung; and 14,15,16 Sqns (828th TFW) at Hualien

Thailand: first Tiger orders for the Royal Thai Air Force comprised 17 F-5Es and three F-5Fs in 1976. Beginning January 1981, second batch of 17 F-5Es and three F-5Fs delivered to form second squadron. Twenty aircraft upgraded from 1989 with Litton LN-39 INS, Texas Instruments AN/ALR-46 RWR, Tracor ALE-40 chaff/flare dispensers and GEC HUD/WAC. HUD and INS fitted to further 18 aircraft. GPU-5/A gun pods acquired for F-5s along with MATRA Durandal runway penetration bombs. Anti-shipping missile being sought. F-5 fleet augmented in late 1988 through addition of 10 ex-USAF F-5Es. Aircraft in service with No. 102 Sqn, No. 1 Wing, Korat and No. 403 Sqn, No. 4 Wing, Takhli

Tunisia: four F-5Fs delivered to Republic of Tunisia air force/Al Quwaat al Jawwiya al Jumhuriyah al Tunisiyah 1981. Followed by eight F-5Es between 1984 and 1985. Five ex-USAF F-5Fs added in 1989

Yemen: twelve F-5Es acquired, via Saudi Arabia, by Yemen Arab Republic air force (North Yemen) in 1979. Aircraft supported by Taiwanese technicians, and based at Sana'a. Current status unknown

SPECIFICATION

Northrop F-5E Tiger II

Wing: span 26 ft 8 in (8.13 m) without tip-mounted AAMs and 27 ft 11.875 in (8.53 m) with tip-mounted AAMs; aspect ratio 3.82; area 186.00 sq ft (17.28 m²)

Fuselage and tail: length 47 ft 4.75 in (14.45 m) including probe; height 13 ft 4.5 in (4.08 m); tailplane span 14 ft 1.5 in (4.31 m); wheel track 12 ft 5.5 in (3.80 m); wheel base 16 ft 11.5 in (5.17 m)

Powerplant: two General Electric J85-GE-21B turbojets each rated at 3,500 lb st (15.5 kN) dry and 5,000 lb (22.2 kN) with afterburning

Weights: empty 9,558 lb (4349 kg); maximum take-off 24,664 lb (11187 kg)

Fuel and load: internal fuel 677 US gal (2563 litres); external fuel up to three 275-US gal (1040-litre) drop tanks; maximum ordnance 7,000 lb (3175 kg)

Speed: maximum level speed 'clean' at 36,000 ft (10975 m) 917 kt (1,056 mph; 1700 km/h); cruising speed at 36,000 ft (10975 m) 562 kt (647 mph; 1041 km/h)

Range: ferry range 2,010 nm (2,314 miles; 3720 km) with empty tanks dropped or 1,715 nm (1,974 miles; 3175 km) with empty tanks retained; combat radius 760 nm (875 miles; 1405 km) with two AIM-9 AAMs

Performance: maximum rate of climb at sea level 34,300 ft (10455 m) per minute; service ceiling 51,800 ft (15590 m); take-off run 2,000 ft (610 m) at 15,745 lb (7142 kg); take-off distance to 50 ft (15 m) 2,800 ft (853 m) at 15,745 lb (7142 kg); landing distance from 50 ft (15 m) 3,900 ft (1189 m) at 11,340 lb (5143 kg); landing run 2,450 ft (747 m) at 11,340 lb (5143 kg) with brake parachute

COCKPIT
The most radical advance offfered by the upgrade concerns modifications made to the cockpit. Inside the F-5E Plus III, the pilot has one of the most up-to-date digital displays available. Two MFDs (either colour or monochrome) are provided, cued by HOTAS controls, and an El-Op HUD. Centralised computing allows data from all the aircraft's systems to be integrated and presented on a single tactical situation display, a feature which is available to very few pilots at present.

RAFAEL PYTHON MISSILE
The hard-hitting Python 3 entered service with the IDF/AF in time to see action over the Bekaa valley in 1982, where it was credited with many kills. With a launch weight of 264 lb (120 kg), the missile is 9 ft 10 in (3.0 m) long and has a body diameter of 6.3 in (0.16 m). The warhead is a 24-lb (11-kg) HE fragmentation unit, with active radar-homing. The Python 3 is primarily IR-guided, but can be radar-slaved in scan or boresight modes.

Northrop F-5E Plus Tiger III

Blessed with good performance and excellent agility, the Northrop F-5E serves in sufficient numbers to warrant substantial upgrade options. The IAI package does not alter the airframe or engines, as these were deemed to be adequate. However, avionics and armament have been greatly improved to include a new and far more capable radar, a much revised state-of-the-art cockpit layout (with two MFDs), new air-to-air missiles and provision for laser-guided weapons.

SIDEWINDER
The F-5 was designed around the lightweight AIM-9 Sidewinder, and this aircraft carries two late-model AIM-9Ps. The 'Papa' is 10 ft 1 in (3.07 m) long and, with a launch weight of 120 lb (82 kg), is substantially lighter than the 264-lb (120-kg) Python 3.

RADAR
A development of the EL/M-2035, the Elta EL/M-2032 multi-mode, pulse-Doppler fire control radar has a detection range of 20 miles (33 km) in the air-to-air mode. Its ultra-low sidelobe planar array was specially tailored to meet the narrow confines of the F-5's nose.

MARKINGS
The first F-5 Plus Tigre stayed in its basic FACh scheme (though without any national insignia) throughout the test programme, with various IAI-applied markings superimposed, principally for the type's appearance at the 1993 Paris air show.

CANNON
The F-5E is fitted with two M39A2 20-mm cannon, with 280 rounds. During the F-5E Plus test programme, the guns were removed and replaced with telemetry equipment.

RWR
The Chilean Tigre IIIs are fitted with a 360° radar warning receiver system (probably the ENAER Caiquen III), with antennas on either side of the nose and tail. This system displays its threat information on the cockpit MFDs.

Northrop **RF-5E Tigereye**

The F-5E, delivered from May 1973, has been a significant export success (with deliveries exceeding 1,000 aircraft) to a diverse range of nations. As a result of its universal appeal, on 31 March 1978 the US government approved the production of a specialised tactical reconnaissance version of the Tiger II, designated **Northrop RF-5E**. First flown in January 1979, the prototype of the **Tigereye** made its international debut at the Paris air show of the same year, following a flight from Edwards AFB, CA. Aircraft performance is barely affected by the additional weight of reconnaissance, navigation and communications equipment carried, and the Tigereye has essentially the same dimensions and characteristics as the F-5E, except for its weight, which is marginally increased.

The RF-5E is most easily distinguished from the conventional F-5E by its forward fuselage, which is modified to accommodate reconnaissance equipment: the nose is extended by 8 in (20.3 cm), and a KS-87D1 camera is fitted in a forward nose compartment. This camera is used in addition to either of two easily interchangeable pallets, each with a different set of reconnaissance cameras/sensors, to permit a greater degree of diversity in the use of the aircraft. Pallet 1 consists of KA-95B and KA-56E panoramic cameras and an RS-71 OE infrared linescanner, and Pallet 2 has KA-56E and KA-93B6 panoramic cameras. Under development is a third pallet carrying a KS-147A camera for LOROP missions; other pallet configurations are available.

The pilot of the RF-5E also has available a number of advanced navigation and communications systems and an ISCS to reduce workload and allow more time to operate and monitor reconnaissance and communications equipment. Otherwise, the Tigereye has basically the same capabilities (including the carriage of armament) as the F-5E.

Many of the nations currently employing the various versions of the F-5 have expressed an interest in the RF-5E since its debut. The first production aircraft flew in December 1982, and was one of two aircraft comprising the first export order, to the **Royal Malaysian air force** (serving with No. 11 'Cobra' Squadron). An additional 10 Tigereyes have been delivered to **Saudi Arabia** for No. 17 Squadron at Tabuk. In a three-year programme which began during 1990, six **Singapore air force** F-5Es were converted to RF-5E configuration by Singapore Aerospace, with assistance from Northrop.

SPECIFICATION

Northrop RF-5E Tigereye

Wing: span 26 ft 8 in (8.13 m) without tip-mounted AAMs and 27 ft 11.875 in (8.53 m) with tip-mounted AAMs; aspect ratio 3.82; area 186.0 sq ft (17.28 m²)
Fuselage and tail: length 48 ft 0.75 in (14.65 m); height 13 ft 4.5 in (4.08 m); tailplane span 14 ft 1.5 in (4.31 m); wheel track 12 ft 5.5 in (3.80 m); wheel base 16 ft 11.5 in (5.17 m)
Powerplant: two General Electric J85-GE-21B turbojets each rated at 3,500 lb st (15.5 kN) dry and

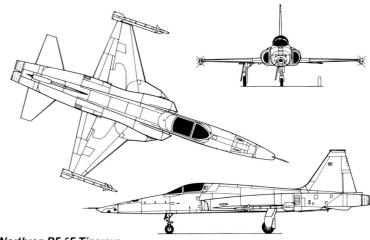

Northrop RF-5E Tigereye

5,000 lb (22.2 kN) with afterburning
Weights: empty 9,750 lb (4423 kg); maximum take-off 24,675 lb (11192 kg)
Fuel and load: internal fuel 677 US gal (2563 litres); external fuel up to three 275-US gal (1040-litre) drop tanks; maximum ordnance 7,000 lb (3175 kg), generally not carried
Speed: maximum level speed 'clean' at 36,000 ft (10975 m) 940 kt (1,082 mph; 1741 km/h)
Range: combat radius with one drop tank and two AIM-9 Sidewinder AAMs 250 nm (287 miles; 463 km) on a lo-lo-lo mission, or 410 nm (471 miles; 759 km) on a hi-lo-hi mission, or 365 nm (420 miles; 676 km) on a

hi-lo-lo-hi mission, or 495 nm (569 miles; 916 km) on a hi-hi-hi mission; combat radius with three drop tanks and two AIM-9 Sidewinder AAMs 365 nm (420 miles; 676 km) on a lo-lo-lo mission, or 560 nm (644 miles; 1037 km) on a hi-lo-hi mission, or 520 nm (598 miles; 963 km) on a hi-lo-lo-hi mission, or 630 nm (725 miles; 1166 km) on a hi-hi-hi mission

The reconnaissance-configured RF-5E is particular to Saudi Arabia, Malaysia and Singapore. This RMAF No. 11 Sqn RF-5E is seen in formation with two No. 11 Sqn F-5Es.

Northrop **T-38 Talon**

The **Northrop T-38 Talon** remains the USAF's standard advanced jet trainer. The first supersonic aircraft to be designed from the outset specifically as a trainer, the T-38 is of conventional design with two J85 engines mounted side-by-side, small span wings and a slender, area-ruled fuselage. The instructor sits behind and 10 in (25 cm) higher than the student.

Developed as the **N-156T** proposal, the first of three service-test **YT-38s** flew on 10 April 1959, powered by two non-afterburning YJ-85-GE-5 turbojets each rated at 2,100 lb st (9.41 kN). The first production T-38 was powered by two afterburning J85s each rated at 3,600 lb st (16.01 kN). The USAF ordered the T-38 into production in 1959 and the first **T-38A** became operational on 17 March 1961. Excluding prototype and pre-production aircraft, a total of 1,139 T-38s was manufactured, and although

In keeping with its other resident aircraft, the 9th Wing, at Beale AFB, have begun to repaint its T-38s in an overall black scheme.

the aircraft served primarily with the USAF, it was also sold to West Germany.

The first Talon went to the 3510th Flying Training Wing at Randolph AFB, TX, part of the USAF's Air Training Command. This organisation, which has been renamed Air Training and Education Command, remains the principal T-38A operator. In 1966, 46 T-38As were acquired by West Germany and they are still flown in standard USAF markings at Sheppard AFB, TX. NASA employs **T-38A(N)** variants as astronaut hacks; these differ in having heated intake lips and VHF radio. A small number of T-38As, **QT-38A** drones and **DT-38A** drone controllers served with the

US Navy. The USAF's 'Thunderbirds' flight demonstration team flew the T-38A during 1978-84. Several are used as chase aircraft at Air Force test establishments.

An early T-38A was fitted with hardpoints for ordnance to test the concept of a lead-in fighter trainer (LIFT) to provide a transition to high-performance warplanes such as the F-15 Eagle. A total of 132 aircraft was rebuilt

as **T-38B LIFT** aircraft, often referred to by the unofficial designation **AT-38B**. The AT-38B had a centreline station for an SUU-20/A rocket/practice bomb carrier, a practice bomb rack, or an SUU-11 7.62-mm Minigun pod. LIFT training was carried out by the 479th Tactical Training Wing at Holloman AFB, NM, before being replaced in 1989 by an abbreviated syllabus called basic

Left: With the arrival of the Força Aérea Portugesa's first F-16s, the days of its 'fighter' T-38s are finally at an end. The Talons will serve as pure trainers.

Turkey's advanced fast-jet training needs are fulfilled entirely by the survivors of 30 T-38s, and a new batch of 40 ex-USAF T-38s delivered in 1993.

fighter training (BFT), which has since been dispersed among other ATC Talon squadrons. Other early weapons-related applications included use as aggressor aircraft.

From 1961 to 1993, every USAF pilot, even those assigned to transport types, could boast of having flown at least one high-performance aircraft – the T-38A, as a result of universal pilot training (UPT). This contrasts with the US Navy, which funnels student aviators through 'pipelines' and uses fast jet trainers only for a few. The USAF is now changing this system, partly to prolong the service life of its T-38As. Under specialised undergraduate pilot training (SUPT), student pilots destined for multi-engine aircraft will forfeit any T-38A experience to fly the Beech T-1A Jayhawk. Only pilots destined for reconnaissance, attack and fighter types will continue to fly the T-38.

T-38s were assigned at SAC bases for several years to perform Accelerated Co-pilot Enrichment (ACE). This programme is now known as CPT (Companion Trainer Program). On 1 January 1993 the CPT detachments were transferred to the reconstituted host wings, joining either ACC or AMC and acquiring the colour scheme of the aircraft of the host wing. For example, CPT T-38s at ACC B-1 and B-52 bases have changed from white to bomber grey. With no suitable replacement in sight, the 700

T-38As remaining are scheduled to be retired between 2010 and 2015.

The T-38 was exported only to two countries, each receiving aircraft from surplus USAF stocks. Eight of Portugal's 12 T-38s were equipped with AIM-9 AAMS to fulfil the role of the Força Aérea Portugesa's primary interceptor, pending delivery of F-16s. Turkey's 30 T-38s are operated as part of Air Training Command.

Taiwan is leasing 40 from the USAF for three years to maintain supersonic pilot proficiency pending delivery of the first F-16s in 1997. The RoCAF previously operated 28 T-38s in the 1970s when F-5Es were urgently diverted to the South Vietnamese air force. At present, Taiwanese pilots undertake training on the T-38A with the 435th FS/49th FW at Holloman AFB, NM.

OPERATORS

Portugal: six T-38As delivered to Força Aérea Portugesa/Portuguese air force from late 1977 to supplement air defence F-86F Sabres. Equipped with AIM-9 Sidewinders and joined by another six aircraft in 1981. Eight T-38s now undertake 'Fighter Pilots' Complementary Instruction' and secondary air defence pending delivery of F-16s, with Esquadra 103, at Beja.
Taiwan: 40 aircraft to be leased from 1994-1997 to cover supersonic fighter availability shortfall

Turkey: 30 former USAF T-38As delivered to the Türk Hava Kuvvetleri/Turkish air force in 1979. A further batch of 40 was delivered in 1993, allowing retirement of T-33s from the training role. Aircraft operate as part of Häva Okullari Komuntanligi (Air Training Command), with 121 Filo, 2 Ana Üs, Cigli.

United States
Air Combat Command (ACC)
8th Air Force: 5th BW, Minot AFB, ND; 7th Wing Dyess AFB, TX; 28th BW, Ellsworth AFB, SD; 509th BW, Whiteman AFB, MO
9th Air Force: 4th Wing, Seymour Johnson AFB, NC
12th Air Force: 9th RW, Beale AFB, CA; 49th FW, Holloman AFB (433rd/435th FS), NM; 55th Wing, Offutt AFB, NE; 366th Wing, Mountain Home AFB, ID
Air Education and Training Command (AETC)
19th Air Force: 12th FTW, Randolph AFB, TX; 14th FTW, Columbus AFB, MI; 47th FTW, Laughlin AFB, TX; 64th FTW, Reese AFB, TX; 71st FTW Vance AFB, OK; 80th FTW, Sheppard AFB, TX; 82nd Training Wing, Sheppard AFB, TX (GT-38A and GAT-38B ground instructional airframes)
Air Mobility Command (AMC)
22nd ARW, McConnell AFB, KS; 43rd ARW, Malmstrom AFB, MT
Air Force Materiel Command (AFMC)
Air Force Flight Test Center/445th TS/412th TW, Edwards AFB, CA (includes Test Pilot School); Sacramento ALC/337th TS, McClellan AFB, CA; 586th TS/46th TG, Holloman AFB, NM

NASA: 31 T-38As are in service based at Ames, Langley, Dryden and Johnson Centers for astronaut proficiency and fast transport duties. Majority at Johnson (Ellington AFB)

SPECIFICATION

Northrop T-38A Talon
Wing: span 25 ft 3 in (7.70 m); aspect ratio 3.75; area 170.00 sq ft (15.79 m²)
Fuselage and tail: length 46 ft 4.5 in (14.14 m); height 12 ft 10.5 in (3.92 m); tailplane span 14 ft 1.5 in (4.31 m); wheel track 11 ft 0 in (3.35 m); wheel base 16 ft 11.5 in (5.17 m)
Powerplant: two General Electric J85-GE-5 turbojets each rated at 2,680 lb st (11.92 kN) dry and 3,850 lb st (17.13 kN) with afterburning
Weights: empty 7,174 lb (3254 kg); maximum take-off 12,050 lb (5465 kg)
Fuel and load: internal fuel 583 US gal (2206 litres); external fuel none; ordnance none
Speed: maximum level speed at 36,000 ft (10975 m) 745 kt (858 mph; 1381 km/h); maximum cruising speed at 40,000 ft (12190 m) 502 kt (578 mph; 930 km/h)
Range: ferry range 950 nm (1,094 miles; 1761 km); typical range 747 nm (860 miles; 1384 km)
Performance: maximum rate of climb at sea level 33,600 ft (10241 m) per minute; service ceiling 53,600 ft (16335 m); take-off run 2,500 ft (762 m) at maximum take-off weight; landing distance 3,000 ft (914 m) at maximum landing weight

Northrop (or Lockheed?) TR-3A

The existence of the **TR-3A** stealthy reconnaissance aircraft was first reported in mid-1991, at which time several were believed to be in USAF service alongside F-117A covert strike fighters. No official confirmation of the TR-3A's existence has been given. Of all-wing configuration, the single-seat TR-3A is believed to have a span of about 64 ft (19.50 m) and a length of 42 ft (12.80 m), with two engines in the 12,000-lb st (53.38-kN) class such as General Electric F404s. A somewhat smaller

prototype of similar construction was said to have flown in 1981 as the **Tactical High-Altitude Penetrator** (THAP), after Northrop had lost out to Lockheed in the Have Blue programme that produced the F-117A. The TR-3A is reportedly known as the **Black Manta**, and perhaps 20 to 30 may have been built for high-altitude reconnaissance as a stealthy replacement for the U-2R. The TR-3 was allegedly developed by Northrop alongside the F-117 at Groom Lake (Area 51, or simply 'the Box'). This team was

kept separate from Lockheed personnel at the same location and both designs were hidden from each other. Reportedly nicknamed 'Shamu' by its creators, aircraft answering the TR-3's description (slightly larger and faster than the Night Hawk) have been seen flying with F-117s near Tonopah, Edwards AFB and the Tehachapi Mountains.

Mention of the type was first made in a report by the Federation of American Scientists, and after Operation Desert Storm questions were raised regarding certain examples of target designation film supposedly taken through an F-117A's FLIR, which seemed to have come from a second orbiting aircraft.

The existence of a range of 'black' aircraft operating from Groom Lake and Papoose Lake, Nevada, has long been convincingly proposed, but little tangible evidence has appeared. What may be the first pictures of a TR-3 were taken during Operation Roving Sands 93 at Roswell, New Mexico. The aircraft was filmed in the air at dusk, revealing a flat-bottomed, V-shaped craft with a discontinuous trailing edge. It was also (perhaps) monitored arriving during the night at Holloman on 18 March 1993. At that time, an obviously sensitive aircraft that had made a precautionary landing (with another chase aircraft) was referred to over base radio as '806' and 'the STF'.

Pakistan Aeronautical Complex
Kamra, District Attock
Pakistan

PAC (AMF/Saab) Mushshak

After taking delivery from Sweden in 1974/75 of 28 **Saab MFI-17** light aircraft, Pakistan established an assembly line at Risalpur in an army workshop to build a further 92, delivered in kit form. Named **Mushshak** (Urdu for 'proficient'), the aircraft entered service with both the **Pakistan air force** and **army**, in training and liaison roles. The Aircraft Manufacturing Factory (AMF) was formed in 1983 to handle the Mushshak activity and transferred to Kamra, where more than 120 have since been built under licence, including 25 for the **Iranian air force** (Revolutionary Guards). The AMF developed an uprated version of the Mushshak, named **Shahbaz**, a prototype of which was first flown in July 1987 powered by a 210-hp (157-kW) Teledyne Continental TIO-360-MB turbo-supercharged engine. One further example was later completed.

SPECIFICATION

PAC (AMF) Mushshak
generally similar to the Saab MFI-17 Supporter except in the following particulars:
Fuel and load: maximum ordnance 300 kg (661 lb)
Speed: never exceed speed 365 km/h (197 kt; 227 mph); maximum level speed 'clean' at sea level 238 km/h (128 kt; 148 mph); cruising speed at sea level 210 km/h (113 kt; 130 mph)
Range: endurance 5 hours 10 minutes
Performance: maximum rate of climb at sea level 312 m (1,024 ft) per minute; climb to 1830 m (6,000 ft) in 7 minutes 30 seconds; service ceiling 4800 m (15,750 ft); take-off run 150 m (493 ft) at normal utility take-off weight; take-off distance to 15 m (50 ft) 305 m (1,000 ft) at normal utility take-off weight; landing distance from 15 m (50 ft) 350 m (1,149 ft) at normal utility landing weight; landing run 140 m (460 ft) at

normal utility landing weight
***g* limits:** -3 to +6 aerobatic, or -2.7 to +5.4 normal utility or -2.4 to +4.8 maximum take-off weight

Iran's Pasdaran (Revolutionary Guards) obtained 25 PAC Mushshaks to establish their first aviation unit in 1991.

Pacific Aerospace (Aerospace/NZAI) CT-4 Airtrainer

Pacific Aerospace Corporation
Private Bag HN 3027, Hamilton Airport
Hamilton, New Zealand

Serving the air forces of three nations in its design role of primary trainer, the **Airtrainer** can trace its origins back to a two-seat light aircraft designed in 1953 by Henry Millicer, then the chief aerodynamicist of the Australian Government Aircraft Factories. Winner of a competition organised by the Royal Aero Club in Britain, this design entered production in Australia as the **Victa Airtourer** for civil use. After the sale of design rights to AESL in New Zealand, the latter company was reorganised as NZAI and continued development and production of the Airtourer. Modifications to suit the same basic aircraft to the military training role were introduced, including a structure restressed for limits of +6/-3 g and aerobatic manoeuvres. Named the Airtrainer, the prototype of this **CT-4** version flew on 23 February 1972. Features included side-by-side seating for pupil and instructor, a one-piece canopy hinged at the rear to open upwards, and provision for 13-Imp gal (59-litre) wingtip fuel tanks.

Orders for Airtrainers were announced during 1972 by both the **Royal Australian Air Force** (for 37) and the **Royal Thai air force**. Australia eventually also received 14 embargoed **CT-4A**s built for the (illegal) Rhodesian regime, and 47 remained in service for primary training (nicknamed 'Plastic Parrots') at No. 1 FTS, Point Cook, until mid-1992. The Thai order totalled 24 aircraft, all for use at the Kamphaeng San Flying Training School. Eighteen of this original batch are currently being rewinged by the RTAF, with PAC assistance to extend their service life. An additional six aircraft were ordered

The RNZAF is the last major user of the CT-4 Airtrainer. The Airtrainers provide basic training for pilots who then progress to the Aermacchi M.B.339. The 'Red Checkers' display team (right) is made up from CFS instructors. Often flying simply as a synchronised pair, up to six CT-4s have displayed under the team's banner.

from Pacific Aerospace in 1992. The final Airtrainer purchase was by the **Royal New Zealand Air Force**, which operates 19 **CT-4B**s (with higher gross weight). The RNZAF also had four **AESL T6/24 Airtourer**s at the CFS until their retirement in 1993. The remaining 18 CT-4Bs serve with the Pilot Training School, North Island. One Victa Airtourer acquired secondhand formed the sole equipment of the **Tonga air force** (formed in 1986) in 1994. One further CT-4, which served with Bangladesh, has now been retired.

Ownership of design rights in Airtourer passed to Pacific Aerospace Corp. in 1982 and, on 21 January 1991, PAC flew a prototype **CT-4C Turbine Airtrainer** with a 420-shp (313-kW) Allison 250-B17D turboprop, this being a conversion of a damaged

RNZAF CT-4B airframe. A derivative of the CT-4C has been proposed with a retractable undercarriage as the **CT-4CR**, and PAC also unsuccessfully submitted a version of the original Airtourer for the USAF EFS requirement, as the **CT-4E**.

SPECIFICATION

Pacific Aerospace (Aerospace) Airtrainer CT-4A
Wing: span 26 ft 0 in (7.92 m); aspect ratio 5.25; area 129.00 sq ft (11.98 m²)
Fuselage and tail: length 23 ft 2 in (7.06 m); height 8 ft 6 in (2.59 m); tailplane span 11 ft 10 in (3.61 m); wheel track 9 ft 9 in (2.97 m); wheel base 5 ft 7.375 in (1.71 m)
Powerplant: one Rolls-Royce (Continental) IO-360-H flat-six air-cooled piston engine rated at 210 hp (157 kW)

Weights: basic empty 1,460 lb (662 kg); empty equipped 1,490 lb (675 kg); maximum take-off 2,400 lb (1089 kg)
Fuel and load: internal fuel 54 US gal (204.5 litres); external fuel none; ordnance none
Speed: never exceed speed 230 kt (265 mph; 426 km/h); maximum level speed 'clean' at 10,000 ft (3050 m) 142 kt (163 mph; 262 km/h) and at sea level 155 kt (178 mph; 286 km/h); cruising speed at 10,000 ft (3050 m) 125 kt (144 mph; 232 km/h)
Range: ferry range 708 nm (815 miles; 1311 km); typical range 596 nm (686 miles; 1104 km)
Performance: maximum rate of climb at sea level 1,350 ft (411 m) per minute; climb to 10,000 ft (3050 m) in 11 minutes 40 seconds; service ceiling 17,900 ft (5455 m); take-off run 733 ft (224 m) at MTOW; take-off distance to 50 ft (15 m) 1,237 ft (377 m) at MTOW; landing distance from 50 ft (15 m) 1,100 ft (335 m) at normal landing weight; landing run 510 ft (155 m)

Panavia Tornado IDS

As the most advanced tactical interdictor/strike (IDS) aircraft produced in Europe, the **Panavia Tornado** obviates NATO's lack of weapons standardisation by carrying almost every relevant air-launched armament in the inventory. It achieves this task at high subsonic speeds, masked from detection by automatic, all-weather terrain following, and protected from air and surface threats by a range of active and passive self-defence aids. Meeting a challenging specification issued in the late 1960s, the Tornado's intended roles were interdiction, counter-air operations against airfields,

battlefield interdiction, close air support, reconnaissance, maritime attack and point interception. An all-weather air superiority derivative, the **Tornado ADV** (described separately), was developed independently for UK requirements. Specific reconnaissance versions are also separately described. The three nations commissioning the Tornado are represented in prime contractor Panavia by their national aircraft industries, currently British Aerospace, DASA (Germany) and Alenia (Italy), which have programme shares of 42.5, 42.5 and 15 per cent, respectively. Assembly lines

have been established in all three countries, with manufacture for third parties being undertaken by the firm achieving the sale.

The Tornado is of modest overall dimensions and is powered by a pair of Turbo Union RB.199 reheated turbofans which are, like the majority of the avionics, a product of international collaboration. The shoulder-mounted, continuously variable-geometry wing incorporates full-span double-slotted flaperons, full-span leading-edge slats and upper surface spoilers/lift dumpers. A Krueger flap is located forward of each wing glove vane. The wing high-lift devices confer good field performance and, coupled with bucket-type thrust-reversers, allow the aircraft to land on short, perhaps damaged, lengths of runway and taxiway.

The Tornado's nav/attack system comprises a Texas Instruments multi-mode forward-looking, ground-mapping, terrain-following radar, Ferranti digital INS (DINS) and combined radar/map display, Decca 72 Doppler radar system, GEC Ferranti laser rangefinder and marked target seeker in an undernose fairing (RAF aircraft only) and Alenia radio/radar altimeter. The aircraft's flight control system primarily comprises a triply-redundant command stability augmen-

The JP 233 area denial weapon was first used by RAF Tornados against Iraqi airfields, with a warload of 30 57-lb (26-kg) SG357 cratering bomblets and 215 5.5-lb (2.5-kg) HB876 mines.

tation system (CSAS) using fly-by-wire and autostabilisation, and an autopilot/flight director (APFD). Coupled with the nav/ attack system, these allow the aircraft to fly with high stability and near-sonic speed at 200 ft (61 m) above ground level in all weathers. Over known flat surfaces, such as southern Iraq during the 1991 Gulf War, altitude can be further reduced by reliance on the radar altimeter alone. With a high wing loading to minimise low-altitude gust response, the aircraft is a stable weapons platform and is both fast and comparatively comfortable for its crew when flying through the dense, low-level air. The reliable DINS, updated by periodic radar fixes, makes possible a single-pass attack of pinpoint accuracy in all weathers. The Tornado was also the first combat aircraft designed with a fly-by-wire control system, but was preceded into service by the similarly-controlled Lockheed (GD) F-16 Fighting Falcon. Fixed armament comprises one 27-mm IWKA-Mauser cannon on each side of the lower fuselage with 180 rounds per gun. Weapons and other stores are carried on a total of seven hardpoints: one centreline pylon, two fuselage shoulder pylons and two swivelling pylons under each wing. The inboard wing pylons are fitted with mountings for self-defence missiles.

Tornado development

Design of the Tornado, initially known as the Multi-Role Combat Aircraft (**MRCA**), was initiated in 1968. The first of nine prototype and six pre-series Tornados flew on 14 August 1974, followed by the initial production aircraft on 10 July 1979. Six procurement batches covered by the original trinational agreement included 640 IDS aircraft, while a further 57 were added in Batch 7, as were four pre-series examples notionally refurbished to production standard. Aircraft of Batches 1-3 have 14,840-lb st (66.0-kN) RB.199 Mk 101 powerplants; the remainder have 16,075-lb st (71.5-kN) Mk 103s, although 100 RAF Mk 101 engines have been upgraded in service. RAF Tornados also have fin fuel tanks of 121-Imp gal (551-litre) capacity, augmenting a standard capacity of 1,285 Imp gal (5842 litres), and are cleared with the **F.Mk 3**'s 495-Imp gal (2250-litre) underwing drop tanks. Italy and Germany use only 220- or 330-Imp gal (1000- or 1500-litre) tanks, two

Right: Five Muharraq-based Tornados formate on a No. 55 Sqn Victor tanker.

Below: Operation Desert Storm marked the combat debut of the TIALD pod. Two prototype examples were rushed to the Gulf and were shared by at least six Tornados.

At the peak of its strength, the Luftwaffe had five Tornado strike wings. This JBG 38 aircraft, based at Jever, carries an MW-1 weapons dispenser, the German equivalent to JP 233. Underwing are a BOZ-101 chaff/flare pod (port) and a Cerebrus ECM pod (port). The Tornado wears the lizard scheme adopted from 1983.

of which can also be installed beneath the fuselage of all variants. All IDS operators have some fully combat-capable dual-control Tornados for conversion and continuation training. In RAF service these 'twin-stickers' are given the (little-used) designation **GR.Mk 1(T)**. Production batches 6 and 7 incorporate MIL-STD 1553B digital databus, upgraded radar warning equipment and active ECM, improved missile control unit and integration of AGM-88 HARM missile.

RAF **Tornado GR.Mk 1s** include those based at Cottesmore, where the Trinational Tornado Training Establishment uses aircraft from all three European nations for type conversion, weapons instruction being at individual units in each country. Deliveries to TTTE began in July 1980, followed by formation of the first operational squadron (No. IX) in June 1982. Orders have totalled 164 standard GR.Mk 1s, 50 (plus one refurbished pre-series) dual-control aircraft, and 14 new-build **GR.Mk 1A** reconnaissance aircraft (described separately), although 16 Batch 3/5 machines were retrofitted with Mk 103 engines and recce equipment under the same designation.

In 1993-94, two squadrons (Nos 12 and 617, at RAF Lossiemouth) began to receive a maritime attack tasking with BAe Sea Eagle anti-ship missiles and 'buddy' refuelling pods under the designation Tornado **GR.Mk 1B**, to replace the RAF's ageing Buccaneers. Ten aircraft (including seven twin-stickers) were modified to accept 15 Sargent-Fletcher 28-300 pods (purchased from the Marineflieger) during the Gulf War, and these may become the first GR.Mk 1Bs.

A mid-life update later in the 1990s will raise aircraft to Tornado **GR.Mk 4** standard. This was to have provided the Tornado with a GEC Spartan terrain-referenced navigation

Panavia Tornado IDS

Left: Initial Royal Saudi air force Tornado deliveries went to No. 7 Sqn, at Dhahran. The first four aircraft departed Warton on 26/27 March 1986. The aircraft seen here – 701 and 704 (a dual-control version) – were among a batch of 18 originally laid down for the RAF.

Below left: The Lynx badge of 156° Gruppo, Italy's second Tornado unit, is carried on the intake sides, which also have red intakes as a safety warning. 156° Gruppo is the AMI's anti-shipping squadron.

their combat debut in the 1991 Gulf War. One AMI and six RAF Tornados were lost in combat, the latter primarily due to AAA when employed on anti-airfield missions. The war also marked the operational debut of TIALD and ALARM. After closure of the German assembly line in January 1992, the UK remained the sole manufacturing source, delivering its last aircraft (an F.Mk 3) in 1993. Orders totalled 697 IDS, 35 ECR and 197 ADV interceptors. In mid-1994, the UK government was considering leasing GR.Mk 1s to the United Arab Emirates.

WEAPONS OPTIONS

The Tornado's fixed armament comprises a pair of 27-mm IWKA-Mauser cannon, with 180 rounds per gun. Most NATO standard weapons can be carried, on Sandall Mace ejector rails in the case of RAF aircraft and MWCS racks on German and Italian examples.

Weapons specific to RAF Tornados include the 950-lb (431-kg) WE177B nuclear bomb (remaining in the inventory until 2007), JP233 airfield-denial weapon, 1,000-lb (454-kg) freefall, retarded and Paveway II LGBs and (from 1991) BAe ALARM anti-radar missile and Marconi TIALD IR/laser designator pod. Defensive aids for the RAF include Bofors BOZ-107 chaff/flare dispenser pod, Marconi Sky Shadow jamming pod, two AIM-9L AAMs and internal Marconi RHWR radar warning receiver (replacing original Elettronica unit, which remains in Italian and German service). Aircraft tasked with replacing the Buccaneer in the maritime role will be equipped with the BAe Sea Eagle anti-shipping missile. Sea Eagle integration will be a two-stage process, with an interim fit providing for the carriage of two missiles and two underwing fuel tanks, or four underwing missiles. The full standard will provide for a further Sea Eagle-compatible station on the centreline, allowing five to be carried, or three missiles and two underwing tanks, or four missiles and a centreline fuel tank.

The GEC-Marconi Dynamics Lancelot PGM was offered in competition with the Paveway III in response to the Staff Requirement (Air) 1242 for a low-level stand-off bomb for the GR.Mks 1 and 4. Go-ahead for the purchase of Paveway III LGBs was approved in July 1994. Derived from the Al Hakim family of PGMs developed for the United Arab Emirates, the rocket-boosted 900-lb (408-kg) Lancelot can be fitted with mid-course guidance to provide a stand-off range of up to 10 miles (20 km) and carry a penetration or blast warhead. The first sightings of this class of weapon have been under an SAOEU Tornado GR.Mk 1. A variant known as Centaur is being offered for SR(A) 1236 for a conventional stand-off missile for the RAF.

suite (cancelled in early 1993), new Ferranti HUD, updated weapon control system, colour head-down display, improved electronic warfare suite and a FLIR (cancelled in 1993). P15 served as a GR.Mk 4 development aircraft, flying for the first time in its new configuration in late 1993. Further down-scaling of the upgrade was caused by constant Treasury opposition which threatened to cancel the project entirely, until the final decision to go ahead was announced under the 'Front Line First' study in July 1994. The resulting update will provide for a digital map display, GPS navigation, pilot's MFD, improved weapons systems, new HUD, video recorder and undernose FLIR. The GR.Mk 4 will be TIALD-capable. BAe will undertake the work on 80 aircraft between 1996 and 2000, with an option on a further 62 upgrades between 2000 and 2002. Service entry is slated for February 1998.

A peak of 11 squadrons was achieved in 1990 – eight in RAF Germany (II, IX, 14, XV, 16, 17, 20 and 31) and three in the UK (13, 27 and 617) – of which two were assigned to reconnaissance, but the 1994 position was to be eight: four in Germany (IX, 14, 17 and 31) and four in the UK, the latter comprising two recce (II and 13) and two maritime (12 and 617) squadrons.

In Germany, the Luftwaffe acquired 212 Tornado IDS, including two refurbished and 55 dual-control; the navy acquired 112, of which 12 are 'two-stick'. Luftwaffe aircraft were assigned to four fighter-bomber wings and one training wing, while the Marine-flieger fielded two maritime attack units. One of these naval squadrons (MFG 1) has been disbanded and its aircraft transferred to the Luftwaffe to re-equip reconnaissance units AkG 51 and 52, which were formerly RF-4E operators. Over the course of a year 40 aircraft were transferred to a new unit, AG 51, which has adopted the badge and traditions of AkG 52. Established in January 1994, AG 51 undertakes a Baltic reconnaissance role identical to that of MFG 1. These aircraft will be initially equipped with (only nine) MBB/Aeritalia pods housing two Zeiss cameras and a Texas Instruments RS-710 IRLS, inherited from the Marineflieger. This makes them less capable than the Phantoms which they replaced, but development of a new DASA system, to enter service in 1998, is underway. Nine remaining HARM-capable Marineflieger Tornados have joined MFG 2.

In association with Italy, Germany is pursuing a Mid-Life Improvement plan. A step-by-step programme, it will involve integrat-

ing a new main computer with software and weapons systems, with a view to adding a FLIR, GPS navigation and improved ECM capabilities in the future. The German-developed electronic combat reconnaissance variant is described separately.

Italy received 100 Tornado IDS, including one refurbished and 12 dual-control. Three squadrons formed in 1983-84 and a fourth converted in 1993. This latter unit (102° Gruppo) will have a dual reconnaissance/attack role using podded Martin-Marietta ATARS (Advanced Tactical Air Reconnaissance System), and 155° Gruppo is already equipped with an MBB/Aeritalia podded recce system. Maritime attack is the responsibility of the Kormoran-equipped 156° Grupo. Italian plans for an update programme are comparable to those of Germany.

The sole IDS export contract covers 48 (including 14 dual-control and six reconnaissance) delivered to Nos 7 (replacing F-5Es) and 66 Sqns of the Royal Saudi air force from 1986. The follow-on 1993 Al-Yamamah II contract covered an additional purchase of 48 IDS-configured aircraft. Originally to be split between IDS and ADV variants, this order, confirmed in June 1993, will comprise virtually all IDS Tornados, with a small number of reconnaissance-capable examples. The last six of the first batch were already completed to GR.Mk 1A standard.

RAF, Italian and Saudi Tornados received

Above: Still bearing traces of its Marineflieger past, this Tornado wears the panther badge of Luftwaffe reconnaissance unit AG 51 (formerly the badge of AkG 52).

Below: British Aerospace first flew their Tornado GR.Mk 4 demonstrator in May 1993, from the Warton factory. Note the new undernose sensor housings.

Panavia Tornado GR.Mk 1

Luftwaffe aircraft are armed with US-supplied B61 nuclear bombs, plus the MW-1 bomblet-dispensing system, AGM-65 and AGM-88 HARM. Self-defence is provided by Bofors BOZ-101 ECM pods, AIM-9Ls and Telefunken Systemtechnik Cerberus II, III or IV jamming pods. Under development is the Franco-German APACHE stand-off missile, intended for Eurofighter and the Tornado. Flight tests commenced in April 1994. APACHE could be offered to the RAF for SR(A) 1236. The Luftwaffe is also seeking to to add further PGM capability to the Tornado

Naval weapons are the MBB Kormoran anti-ship missile, backed by AGM-88 and the BL755 cluster-bomb, plus SFC 28-300 'buddy' pods. While all German aircraft are AGM-88-capable, only the Luftwaffe's ECR version would use it on an 'offensive' role. Marineflieger aircraft, in contrast, train with HARM as one of their main anti-shipping weapons.

Italian Tornado weapons and equipment are largely the same as for German aircraft: B61, MW-1, AGM-65, AGM-88, Kormoran, Bofors BOZ-102, AIM-9L and Cerberus. AMI Tornados can also carry JP233, 1,000-lb bombs, ALARM, AIM-9L and Sea Eagle, plus RAF-type defensive pods. The AMI also purchased 1,700 IAI Griffin LGB systems in November 1993.

OPERATORS

Royal Air Force
No. 2 Sqn: RAF Marham (GR.Mk 1A)

No. 9 Sqn: RAF Brüggen (tasked with ALARM)
No. 12 Sqn: RAF Lossiemouth (GR.Mk 1B)
No. 13 Sqn: RAF Marham (GR.Mk 1A)
No. 14 Sqn: RAF Brüggen (tasked with TIALD)
No. 15(R) Sqn: RAF Lossiemouth (TWU)
No. 17 Sqn: RAF Brüggen
No. 31 Sqn: RAF Brüggen
No. 617 Sqn: RAF Lossiemouth (GR.Mk 1B)
Strike/Attack Operational Evaluation Unit:
RAF Boscombe Down (GR.Mk 1/1A)
Tri-national Tornado Training Establishment:
RAF Cottesmore, comprising 'A', 'B' and 'C' Squadrons for conversion of RAF, Luftwaffe and AMI crews, and 'S' (Standards) Squadron for instructor training
Aircraft & Armament Evaluation Establishment:
RAF Boscombe Down (two GR.Mk 1 leased from BAe)
Defence Research Agency: RAF Boscombe Down (GR.Mk 1)

Luftwaffe
JBG 31 'Boelke': Norvenich
JBG 32 : Lechfeld (ECR)
JBG 33: Büchel
JBG 34: Memmingen
JBG 38 'Friesland': Jever
AG 51 'Immelmann': Schleswig/Jagel
Tslw 1: Kaufbeuren

Marineflieger
MFG 2: Schleswig/Jagel

Aeronautica Militare Italia
6⁰ Stormo: 102⁰ and 154⁰ Gruppi, Brescia-Ghedi
36⁰ Stormo: 156⁰ Stormo, Gioia de Colle
50⁰ Stormo: 155⁰ Stormo, Piacenza/San Damiano
Reparto Sperimentale di Volo: Pratica di Mare

Royal Saudi Air Force
No. 7 Sqn: Taif
No. 66 Sqn: Dhahran

SPECIFICATION

Panavia Tornado GR.Mk 1
Wing: span 45 ft 7.5 in (13.91 m) minimum sweep (25°) and 28 ft 2.5 in (8.60 m) maximum sweep (67°); aspect ratio 7.73 spread and 2.96 swept; area 286.33 sq ft (26.60 m²)
Fuselage and tail: length 54 ft 10.25 in (16.72 m); height 19 ft 6.25 in (5.95 m); tailplane span 22 ft 3.5 in (6.80 m); wheel track 10 ft 2 in (3.10 m); wheel base 20 ft 4 in (6.20 m)
Powerplant: two Turbo-Union RB.199-34R Mk 101 turbofans each rated at 8,475 lb st (37.70 kN) dry and 14,840 lb st (66.01 kN) with afterburning or, in later aircraft, Turbo-Union RB.199-34R Mk 103 turbofans each rated at 8,650 lb st (38.48 kN) dry and 16,075 lb st (71.50 kN) with afterburning
Weights: basic empty about 30,620 lb (13890 kg); operating empty 31,065 lb (14091 kg); normal take-off 45,000 lb (20411 kg); maximum take-off about

61,620 lb (27951 kg)
Fuel and load: internal fuel 11,221 lb (5090 kg); external fuel up to 13,200 lb (5988 kg) in two 2250-litre (396-US gal) and two 1500-litre (396-US gal) or four 1500-litre (396-US gal) drop tanks; nominal maximum ordnance more than 9000 kg (19,841 lb)
Speed: limiting Mach No. Mach 1.4 with LRMTS, M1.3 with intakes deactivated (all RAF aircraft); limiting IAS 1482 km/h (800 kt; 921 mph); maximum level speed 'clean' at 36,000 ft (10975 m) 1,262 kt (1,453 mph; 2338 km/h)
Range: ferry range about 2,100 nm (2,420 miles; 3890 km) with four drop tanks; combat radius 750 nm (863 miles; 1390 km) on a typical hi-lo-hi attack mission with a heavy warload
Performance: climb to 30,000 ft (9145 m) in less than 2 minutes 0 seconds from brakes-off; service ceiling more than 50,000 ft (15240 m); take-off run less than 900 m (2,953 ft) at maximum take-off weight; landing run 370 m (1,214 ft) at maximum landing weight
g limits: +7.5
Panavia Tornado IDS
generally similar to the Panavia Tornado GR.Mk 1 except in the following particulars:
Powerplant: two Turbo-Union RB.199-34R Mk 101 turbofans each rated at 8,700 lb st (38.70 kN) dry and 14,840 lb st (66.01 kN) with afterburning or, in later aircraft, Turbo-Union RB.199-34R Mk 103 each rated at 9,100 lb st (40.48 kN) dry and 16,075 lb st (71.50 kN) with afterburning
Fuel and load: internal fuel 10,251 lb (4650 kg)

Panavia **Tornado ADV**

Developed from the Tornado IDS interdictor for wholly British requirements, the **Tornado ADV (Air Defence Variant)** was optimised for long-range interception. The primary missions were the protection of NATO's northern and western approaches, and long-range air defence of UK maritime forces. As envisaged by Air Staff Requirement 395, the aircraft was to loiter for long periods far from base before undertaking a low-level dash in any weather to shoot down missile-launching Soviet bombers at beyond visual range. Having demonstrated 920 mph (1480 km/h) at 2,000 ft (610 m), the Tornado is faster than most potential adversaries, but reliance on turbofan engines leaves it deficient in speed at medium altitude. Agility and close-in fighting capability were not important considerations for destroying bombers at long range. However, the position changed in the mid-1980s when it became apparent that the manoeu-

vrable Sukhoi Su-27 'Flanker' long-range fighter might act as a bomber escort, and it shifted yet again with evaporation of the Soviet strategic threat in the early 1990s. Seen to be at a disadvantage for the limited or 'policing' type of warfare which the RAF now expects to be its future combatant role, the Tornado ADV is earmarked for early replacement by a more agile aircraft.

Design of the ADV was based around the carriage of four underfuselage BAe Sky Flash radar-homing AAMs, resulting in a 4-ft 5½-in (1.36-m) longer airframe which provides extra fuel space and increases internal capacity to 1,571 Imp gal (7143 litres). Only the port 27-mm cannon is retained, but the refuelling probe is housed internally, unlike the IDS's detachable bolt-on unit, and only inboard wing pylons are fitted. Each can carry a 495-Imp gal (2250-litre) drop tank and either one or two AIM-9L Sidewinder heat-seeking AAMs on additional launch

rails. Avionics differ considerably from the IDS, having little need for extremely accurate ground position, but a second GEC-Ferranti FIN1010 inertial platform is added in all except the first 18 aircraft.

The intercept radar is the GEC-Marconi AI.Mk 24 Foxhunter, a multi-mode, track-while-scan, pulse-Doppler unit. Requirements called for Tornado radar to be capable of detecting targets at more than 115 miles (185 km) and tracking 20 while continuing to scan. The subject of serious development problems, Foxhunter almost suf-

A former Phantom operator, No. 29 Sqn was the first RAF unit to receive the F.Mk 3 after the OCU. Assigned to SACLANT for maritime air defence, it is also tasked with an 'out of area' role.

During Operation Desert Storm, Royal Saudi air force Tornado F.Mk 3s maintained constant CAPs alongside their RAF counterparts. The only air-to-air kills scored by the air force fell to an F-15C.

Panavia Tornado ADV

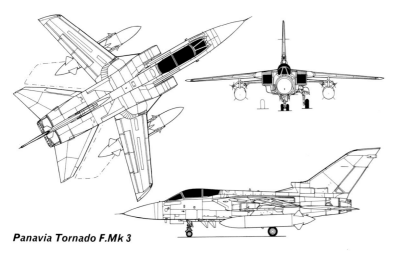

Panavia Tornado F.Mk 3

fered cancellation before being brought to a minimally acceptable standard (known as 'AA') early in 1989, this representing two-thirds of what was initially demanded. Further upgrading to 'AB' configuration, meeting the full specification, is due in the mid-1990s. Another delayed feature, automatic wing sweep, was developed to configure the aircraft optimally for any throttle setting, but is not employed at squadron level.

In 1976, it was revealed that 165 of the 385 Tornados earmarked for the UK would be ADVs. Of these, three emerged as non-operational prototypes and 18 as interim standard **Tornado F.Mk 2**s. The remainder are manufactured as Tornado **F.Mk 3**s, the current definitive production version. A

maiden flight by the first of the three ADV prototypes took place at BAe's Warton plant on 27 October 1979 and was followed by the first F.Mk 2 on 5 March 1984. Mk 2s, including eight with dual controls, were from Batch 4 and fitted with RB.199 Mk 103 powerplants of 16,075 lb st (38.5 kN), provision for only two Sidewinders, and a single FIN1010 INS. These early aircraft initially flew with ballast in place of delayed radars (the so-called 'Blue Circle' radar) and served only with No. 229 OCU at Coningsby for training. The last was replaced in January 1988. Plans for their conversion to near Mk 3 standard (apart from engines) as **F.Mk 2A**s have not been implemented and appear increasingly unlikely. One of the F.Mk 2s is currently operated by the DRA at Boscombe

Down as the **Tornado TIARA** (Tornado Integrated Avionics Research Aircraft). This is a testbed for next-generation fighter avionics including HOTAS controls, helmet-mounted sights and a holographic HUD.

The first Tornado F.Mk 3 flew on 20 November 1985, manufacture following of 144, including 38 with dual controls but fully combat-capable. A cancelled Omani order for eight was transferred to the RAF. Initial training was undertaken by No. 229 OCU, officially established at RAF Coningsby on 1 May 1985 (unofficially on 1 November 1984). This unit employed 16 F.Mk 2s, joined by its first F.Mk 3 on 28 July 1986. Delays in the training programme, and non-delivery of the radar, forced No. 229 OCU to declare itself to SACEUR as a combat-capable unit, and it adopted the identity of No. 65 (Reserve) Sqn as a result. This stayed the case until 1992, when the unit became No. 56(R) Sqn after the retirement of No. 56 Sqn's Phantoms. The first front-line unit was former Phantom-operator No. 29 Sqn, which became operational on 1 November 1987. It was followed by No. 5 Sqn (1 May 1988), No. 11 Sqn (1 November 1988), No. 23 Sqn (1 August 1989), No. 25 Sqn (1 January 1990), No. 43 Sqn (1 July 1990) and, finally, No. 111 Sqn (31 December 1990). Cut-backs in the 'Options for Change' defence review call for a reduction in the RAF's fighter force that saw No. 23 Sqn disband on 26 February 1994, to be followed by No. 25 Sqn.

F.Mk 3 improvements

The F.Mk 3 is fitted with an extended afterburner which increases the fuselage length by 14 in (36 cm). Other changes are provision for four, not two, Sidewinders, addition of a second INS, and incorporation of a spin prevention and incidence limitation system (SPILS) for 'carefree handling'. An upgrade, known as 'Stage 1+', was introduced on the production line early in 1989 and retrofitted throughout the fleet. Provisions include a new 'combat stick' with HOTAS controls, type AA Foxhunter radar, improvements to the Marconi Hermes radar homing and warning receiver, Have Quick UHF radios, radar-absorbent coating on the fin and wing leading edges, five per cent combat boost switch for engines, AIM-9M capability, and flare dispensers below the rear fuselage (briefly AN/ALE-40, but Vinten VICON 78 from 1991). The planned Stage 2, in the mid-1990s, will be concerned mainly with a further radar upgrade. JTIDS integration for the F.Mk 3 fleet is currently being undertaken by aircraft at RAF Coningsby.

Saudi Arabian Tornado ADVs were produced to RAF Stage 1 standard and, in fact, diverted from MoD contracts to speed delivery (the RAF gaining replacement machines built later). The total of 24 includes six with dual controls. Deliveries began to Nos 29 and 34 Squadrons in February 1989 and all had been received by early 1991, when RAF and RSAF Tornado interceptors participated in the Gulf War without seeing aerial combat.

A mix of No. 5 and No. 29 Sqn aircraft,

Left: The Tornado F.Mk 3 boasts a clean airframe and powerful engines, making it one of the best-performing fighters in the world.

Right: This Tornado bears the black eagle insignia of No. 11 Sqn. Based at Leeming, its aircraft are among those being fitted with JTIDS datalinks.

which were changing places for armament camp at Akrotiri, were dispatched from Cyprus to Dhahran on 29 August 1990, becoming No. 5 (Composite) Sqn. Six F.Mk 3s replaced the No. 29 Sqn examples in September 1990, establishing a new unit, No. 11(C) Sqn. A further six aircraft relieved the remaining No. 5 Sqn Tornados, and No. 11(C) Sqn was increased to war strength through the addition of six more F.Mk 3s on 22 September 1990. This Dhahran detachment was retitled No. 43(C) Sqn on 1 December 1990, until it flew its last operational sortie on 8 March 1991. The Tornados returned to the UK during the following week.

The drawdown in RAF strength has released sufficient airframes to equip a new Tornado F.Mk 3 operator. To act as a stopgap measure pending delivery of its Eurofighter EFA 2000s, the Italian air force is undertaking a five-year lease (with a five-year extension option) of 24 aircraft. After six months of negotiations, against rival US bids of secondhand F-15s and F-16s, an agreement was signed on 17 November 1993 for a no-cost lease to supplement the AMI's existing F-104S ASA Starfighters. The Tornado's Sky Flash missiles may be replaced by Selenia Aspide AAMs in Italian service, and the F.Mk 3s will be operated by 12º Grupo, 36º Stormo, at Gioia de Colle and 18º Stormo, 37º Stormo, at Trapani/Bergi. Acquisition of the F.Mk 3s was eased by Italy's existing Tornado maintenance capability and the relative ease with which its Foxhunter radar can be adapted to use the Aspide missile (as opposed to the F-15 or F-16). However, as the AMI has no trained backseaters available, the aircraft will be crewed by pilots in both seats. The first 12 aircraft will be delivered to Gioia de Colle in early 1995, followed by the second batch two years later. Initial training will be undertaken by No. 56(R) Sqn, at RAF Coningsby.

The final production ADV Tornado was an F.Mk 3, ZH559, delivered to No. 56(R) Squadron on 24 March 1993.

WEAPONS OPTIONS

The Tornado F.Mk 3 retains only one (port side) of the 27-mm IWKA-Mauser cannon fitted to the IDS/GR.Mk 1 version. Its main armament is four BAe Sky Flash semi-active radar-homing AAMs, carried semi-recessed under the fuselage on Frazer-Nash ejector rails. RAF weapons have an MSDS monopulse, continuous wave seeker head, operating in the J-band, a 66-lb (30-kg) HE warhead and an effective range of 29 miles (49 km). Backing up the Sky Flash are up to four AIM-9L Sidewinders, carried in pairs on shoulder pylons above the main inboard hardpoints. The F.Mk 3 has only one pair of wing hardpoints, unlike the IDS/GR.Mk 1. Self-defence capability is provided by a Bofors Phimat chaff dispenser (starboard outer Sidewinder pylon). Future weapons fits will include four AIM-120 AMRAAMs or BAe Active Sky Flash, along with up to four new-generation short-range AAMs.

OPERATORS

Royal Air Force
No. 5 Sqn: RAF Coningsby
No. 11 Sqn: RAF Leeming

No. 25 Sqn: RAF Leeming
No. 29 Sqn: RAF Coningsby
No. 43 Sqn: RAF Leuchers
No. 56(R) Sqn: RAF Coningsby
No. 111 Sqn: RAF Leuchers
No. 1435 Flt: RAF Mount Pleasant, Falkland Islands

Under Operation Grapple, a detachment of Tornado F.Mk 3s drawn from the Leeming wing is currently stationed at Gioia del Colle, Italy. The Tornados are tasked with air support of UN operations in Bosnia.

Tornado F.Mk 3 Operational Evaluation Unit:
RAF Coningsby

Aircraft & Armament Evaluation Establishment:
RAF Boscombe Down (F.Mk 2/3)
DRA Boscombe Down: (F.Mk 2 TIARA)

Royal Saudi Air Force
No. 29 Sqn: Dhahran
No. 34 Sqn: Dhahran

SPECIFICATION

Panavia Tornado F.Mk 3
Wing: span 45 ft 7.5 in (13.91 m) spread and 28 ft 2.5 in (8.60 m) swept; aspect ratio about 7.73 spread and 2.96 swept; area 286.33 sq ft (26.60 m²)
Fuselage and tail: length 61 ft 3.5 in (18.68 m); height 19 ft 6.25 in (5.95 m); tailplane span 22 ft 3.5 in (6.80 m); wheel track 10 ft 2 in (3.10 m)
Powerplant: two Turbo-Union RB.199-34R Mk 104 turbofans each rated at 9,100 lb (40.48 kN) dry and 16,520 lb st (73.48 kN) with afterburning
Weights: operating empty 31,970 lb (14502 kg); maximum take-off 61,700 lb (27986 kg)
Fuel and load: internal fuel 12,544 lb (5690 kg); external fuel up to 12,800 lb (5806 kg) in two 2250-litre (396-US gal) and two 1500-litre (396-US gal) or four 1500-litre (396-US gal) drop tanks; maximum ordnance 18,740 lb (8500 kg)

Speed: maximum level speed 'clean' at 36,000 ft (10975 m) 1,262 kt (1,453 mph; 2338 km/h)
Range: combat radius more than 300 nm (345 miles; 556 km) supersonic or more than 1,000 nm (1,151 miles; 1,852 km) subsonic; endurance 2 hours 0 minutes on a CAP at between 300- and 400-nm (345- and 460-mile; 555- and 740-km) radius
Performance: operational ceiling about 70,000 ft (21335 m); take-off run 2,500 ft (762 m) with normal fuel and weapon loads, or 5,000 ft (1524 m) in ferry configuration; take-off distance to 50 ft (15 m) less than 3,000 ft (915 m) at normal take-off weight; landing distance from 50 ft (15 m) about 2,000 ft (609 m) 1,215 ft (370 m) with thrust reversal

Panavia Tornado ECR and GR.Mk 1A

Although Marineflieger and (initially) AMI Tornado reconnaissance needs were met with a simple multi-sensor pod, the **Luftwaffe** and **RAF** have opted for more involved conversion. The German system is the more complex, as it includes a SEAD (Suppression of Enemy Air Defences) capability and so warrants the designation **Tornado ECR** (Electronic Combat and Reconnaissance). The first of two converted prototypes flew on 18 August 1988, while deliveries of 35 new-build ECRs from Batch 7 production began on 21 May 1990 and were completed on 28 January 1992. These were issued to two squadrons within two wings (JBGs 32 and 38), and are the only Tornados so far fitted with Mk 105 RB.199 turbofans.

Operational equipment includes a Texas Instruments ELS (Emitter Location System) with antennas in the wing glove and in the forward fuselage, and two underfuselage AGM-88 HARM missiles. Data is handled by a MIL STD 1553B databus and threat information is displayed on two dedicated screens in the WSO's cockpit. The pilot's standard combined electronic display and map can access the same information, as a back-up. The ELS allows the aircraft to plot and identify threat radars and, while it was designed for use against ground targets, it also has a limited capability against airborne radars (though without IFF). Its area coverage, unlike the USAF's F-4G's, is not 360°, and the ECR is blind to signals from the rear. Luftwaffe tactics call for two aircraft to operate in a racetrack pattern to overcome this deficiency. The ECR also relies on a pre-programmed library of radar signals, loaded on to the ELS prior to each sortie. The system is not reprogrammable in flight, or indeed on the flight line, and so is unable to respond to unexpected threats. The Luftwaffe claims that its (and NATO's) Sigint resource is more than adequate.

The crew can elect to attack a target independently or transmit target information to another aircraft via the ODIN (Operational Data INterface) datalink, carried in the forward fuselage. The ECR retains all the terrain-following capability of the standard IDS, so can carry out its mission at high speed, low level and in all weathers – unlike the medium-altitude F-4G. The ECR will release the Luftwaffe and other NATO air forces from reliance on USAF SEAD assets, such as the elderly 'Wild Weasel' F-4Gs, and can sweep an area or escort a strike as required.

Reconnaissance features are a Honeywell/Sondertechnik horizon-to-horizon IR linescan (or IIS – Imaging Infra-red System) in a blister under the forward fuselage, and Zeiss FLIR immediately ahead. The IIS is a film-based system that can relay a video image to the WSO, or transmit to a ground station via the ODIN link. Its information can be merged on the cockpit displays with data

from the ELS to produce a graphic image of an active threat area.

The ECR retains the Cerberus jamming pod, BOZ-101 chaff/flare dispenser and AIM-9L self-defence AAMs of the German Tornado IDS, but both internal cannon are deleted. Protracted delays with the emitter locater system led to the aircraft operating at a reduced level of capability, but production ELS sets began to be delivered from April 1993. After protracted indecision, Italy elected to produce 16 of its own ECRs by conversion of existing aircraft, which are to retain their original engines. The prototype **Tornado ITECR**, converted by Alenia at Turin, first flew in July 1992, the type being scheduled to achieve IOC in 1995. While the ECR provides a considerable reconnaissance asset for the Luftwaffe, the service is committed to acquiring 40 dedicated reconnaissance Tornados in a conversion programme of former Marineflieger aircraft announced in early 1994.

While ECR Tornados were originally delivered to two squadrons, the Luftwaffe has consolidated its SEAD force with one unit. On 1 July 1994, JBG 32, based at Lechfield, was declared operational as the sole ECR squadron. It operated a mix of ECR and IDS aircraft until October 1994, when all the ECRs delivered to JBG 38 were swapped for JBG 32's remaining IDS Tornados. JBG 38, based at Jever, then reverted to a standard Tornado IDS unit.

The surplus of German Tornados has opened the possibility of supplying 24 ECRs to the Republic of Korea. An MoU has been signed for the Korean requirement which had previously been for new-build aircraft. The current availability of airframes makes the deal far more likely.

RAF reconnaissance

RAF Tornado **GR.Mk 1A**s have no specific defence-suppression capability, but may revert to a secondary attack role with all weapons except WE177B nuclear bombs and internal cannon. They were the first reconnaissance aircraft to dispense completely with traditional film and rely entirely on video. A Vinten 4000 infra-red linescan is

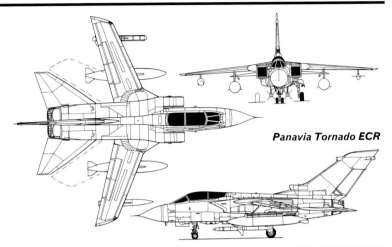

Panavia Tornado ECR

mounted in a blister fairing beneath the forward fuselage, giving 180° coverage. Since details near the horizon are indistinct on its wide-angle presentation, a BAe SLIR (Side-Looking IR) sensor with a 10° field is mounted in each side of the fuselage to cover this area. The system is optimised for ultra-low-level operations under cover of darkness, requires no illumination, and is self-stabilising up to an aircraft banking angle of 30°. The navigator is able to produce a tape of the most important aspects of the mission for immediate analysis after landing, but sensors are allowed to run during the whole time the aircraft is over hostile territory. The first of 16 conversions from GR.Mk 1 standard flew on 11 July 1985, while 14 new-build Mk 1As were delivered from 13 October 1989. Operating squadrons are Nos II and 13.

The housing for the Tornado GR.Mk 1A's Vinten 4000 IR linescan is visible behind the nose gear, under the fuselage, on this No. II Sqn example.

SPECIFICATION

Panavia Tornado ECR
generally similar to the Panavia Tornado GR.Mk 1 except in the following particulars:
Powerplant: two Turbo-Union RB.199-34R Mk 101 turbofans each rated at 8,700 lb st (38.70 kN) dry and 14,840 lb st (66.01 kN) with afterburning or, in later aircraft, Turbo-Union RB.199-34R Mk 103 turbofans each rated at 9,100 lb st (40.48 kN) dry and 16,075 lb st (71.50 kN) with afterburning
Fuel and load: internal fuel 10,251 lb (4650 kg)

JBG 32 is now the Luftwaffe's sole Tornado ECR unit, providing a powerful SEAD asset courtesy of its AGM-88-armed aircraft.

Piaggio **P.166**

Industrie Aeronautiche e Meccaniche Rinaldo Piaggio SpA
Via Cibrario 4, I-16154 Genova Sestri,
Genoa, Italy

First flown on 26 November 1957, the **Piaggio P.166** twin-engined utility transport was a direct evolution of the earlier, smaller P.136 amphibian that was of similar configuration and had flown for the first time on 29 August 1948. Features of the design were the high-mounted gull wing, pusher engines and wingtip fuel tanks. Powered by two 340-hp (254-kW) Lycoming GSO-480-B1C6 flat-six piston engines, the early production **P.166AL1**s were for commercial use, but were matched in most de-tails by the more numerous **P.166ML1**s, 51 of which were built by Piaggio for the **Italian air force**. With an additional cockpit door, stronger cabin floor, standard seating for eight passengers and larger main loading door, the **P.166M** was widely dispersed in the communications role, and about half continue to be so used by various of the 600-series Squadriglia Collegiamento (communication flights) attached to each major base.

On 3 July 1976, Piaggio flew the prototype of a turboprop version of the P.166, identified as the **P.166-DL3** and similar in most respects other than the powerplant to

the P.166M. Production of this version included four for **Somalia**, used in a quasi-military role by the Ministries of Defence and of Transport. Six P.166DL3s for the Italian air force are equipped with a vertically-mounted Zeiss camera in the cabin to serve in the aerial survey role with 303° Gruppo di Volo Autonomo at Guidonia, Rome, to supplement the **P.166M/APH** variant used previously for similar duties.

Between 1988 and 1990, delivery was made of variants for maritime and ecological patrols (Sorveglianza Ecologica e Marittima) flown by the **Italian navy** on behalf of the Ministry of Merchant Marine's Capitanerie di Porto (Coast Guard). These **P.166-DL3SEM**s carry Bendix RDR 1500 radar with a radome under the nose, FLIR, and have provision for two 177- or 284-litre (46.8- or 75-US gal) underwing fuel tanks, as the wingtip containers are used for sensors and equipment.

They equip four aircraft flights at Guidonia, Catania, Fontanarossa and Pescara. Ten similar P.166-DL3SEMs were purchased in 1991/92 by the Italian Guardia di Finanza (Customs Service).

Included in the fleet of 303° Gruppo, at Guidonia, are six 'sharp-nosed' P.166DL-3s, equipped for photo-survey duties with vertical Zeiss cameras in their fuselages.

SPECIFICATION

Piaggio P.166-DL3
Wing: span 13.51 m (44 ft 4 in) without tip tanks or 14.69 m (48 ft 2.5 in) with tip tanks; aspect ratio 7.3; area 26.56 m² (285.90 sq ft)
Fuselage and tail: length 11.88 m (39 ft 0 in); height 5.00 m (16 ft 5 in); tailplane span 5.10 m (16 ft 9 in)
Powerplant: two Textron Lycoming LTP101-700 turboprops each flat-rated at 600 shp (448 kW)
Weights: empty equipped 2650 kg (5,842 lb); maximum take-off 4300 kg (9,480 lb)

Fuel and load: internal fuel 1139 kg (2,511 lb); external fuel none; maximum payload 1073 kg (2,365 lb)
Speed: never exceed speed 220 kt (253 mph; 407 km/h); maximum level speed 'clean' at 10,000 ft (3050 m) 215 kt (248 mph; 400 km/h); economical cruising speed at 12,000 ft (3660 m) 162 kt mph; 300 km/h)
Range: 1,125 nm (1,295 miles; 2084 km) with max fuel or 750 nm (864 miles; 1390 km) with payload
Performance: maximum rate of climb at sea level 2,200 ft (671 m) per minute; service ceiling 28,000 ft (8535 m); take-off distance to 50 ft (15 m) 2,180 ft (665 m) at maximum take-off weight; landing distance from 50 ft (15 m) 1,500 ft (457 m) at maximum landing weight

---

Piaggio **P.180 Avanti**

At the 1983 NBAA convention in Dallas, Texas, Piaggio announced the birth of a new twin turboprop-powered business aircraft. Design work on the **P.180 Avanti** had begun at Piaggio's Genoa headquarters in 1979. Seating six to 10 passengers, it was a radical departure from anything the company had previously produced.

The major design feature of the aircraft is its use of three lifting surfaces. The main wing is fitted above the mid-set position in the fuselage, with the main spar running behind the passenger cabin. Its straight leading edge is broken only by the engine nacelle inlets and the wing has a slight dihedral of 2°. The T-tail and elevator act as the second lifting surface, in addition to being orthodox control surfaces. The foreplane, however, is not a simple canard, but provides a positive lift component in addition to that produced by the wing. This in turn allows the wing to be reduced in size, decreasing overall weight and drag. The engines specified were Pratt & Whitney Canada PT6A-66A turboprops, each driving a five-bladed Hartzell fully-feathering reversible-pitch propeller with spinner. The engines are mounted in composite-material nacelles. The Avanti makes considerable use of composites. Carbon-fibre and a graphite/epoxy mix represent about 10 per cent of the aircraft's weight. Wings and tail sections are produced by Piaggio at Genoa,

while the forward fuselage is the responsibility of Piaggio Aviation in Wichita. Final assembly is completed in Italy.

The cockpit is fitted with a Collins EFIS system, comprising three CRTs, and Collins navigation and weather radar systems are standard. The aircraft is certified for single-pilot operations. In 1983 Gates Learjet became a partner in the project, but withdrew for economic reasons in January 1986. All the tooling and the forward fuselages of the three pre-production Avantis which were on the line at Wichita were transferred to Italy. Assembly of the first P.180 began on Piaggio's Finale Ligne plant in 1986 and the first flight was made on 23 September 1986 (I-PJAV). The Avanti was certified in Italy in March 1990, and in May 1990 the first production aircraft was rolled out. The final hurdle of US certification was passed in October 1990 and the first customer delivery took place the following September. By early 1994, despite or perhaps because of its radical appearance and advanced design, only 27 Avantis had been built for its (intended) civilian market.

The Avanti has gained its only military order from the **Italian air force**, which ordered six aircraft for delivery in two batches. The first P.180s entered service, in 1993, with 313° Grupo Autonomo, at Guidonia, 636ª Squadriglia Collegamenti, at Gioia and 653ª Squadriglia Collegamenti, at

Cameri/Novara. The remaining three AMI Avantis will be delivered in 1994.

All of the Italian air force's intended complement of six Avantis had entered service by the end of 1994, a welcome addition to the type's halting sales.

SPECIFICATION

Piaggio P.180 Avanti
Wing: span 14.03 m (46 ft in); wing aspect ratio 12.30; foreplane aspect ratio 5.05; area, gross 16.00 m² (172.22 sq ft)
Fuselage and tail: length 14.41 m (47 ft 3½ in); height 3.94 m (12 ft 11 in); tailplane span 4.25 m (13 ft 11½ in); wheel track 2.84 m (9 ft 4 in)
Powerplant: two 1,485-shp (1107-kW) Pratt & Whitney PT6A-66 turboprops

Weights: empty, stripped 3384 kg (7,460 lb); maximum take-off 5080 kg (11,200 lb)
Speed: maximum operating Mach number Mach 0.67; maximum level speed 482 km/h (455 mph)
Range: at 11890 m (39,000ft), with reserves 3187 km (1,980 miles)
Performance: maximum rate of climb at sea level 875 m (2,870 ft) per minute; service ceiling 12500 m (41,000 ft); take-off to 15 m (50 ft) at sea level 864 m (2,835 ft)

Piaggio-Douglas **PD-808**

Originally known as the **Vespa-Jet**, the **PD-808** was essentially designed by Douglas Aircraft Co. in the US as the subject of a joint programme with Piaggio, the latter being responsible for marketing. Failing to attract orders in the corporate market at which it was aimed, the PD-808 was bought only by the **Italian air force**, which contracted for 22 in 1965. The prototype PD-808 flew on 29 August 1964 and production was in four versions: staff transport/communications with nine seats, VIP transport seating six, electronic warfare (guerra elettronica, **GE**) and airways/navaid checking (radiomisure, **RM**).

Almost all of the PD-808s remain in service, but most of the 12 transports are progressively being converted to the GE or RM mission. Five **PD-808TA** transports

are shared by 306° Gruppo TS and 92° Gruppo TS in 31° Stormo 'Carmelo Raiti' at Ciampini. The special-purpose aircraft are based at Pratica di Mare and flown by 14° Stormo 'Sergis Sartof', whose 8° Gruppo uses seven of the RM version, and 71° Gruppo which flies eight GE models.

SPECIFICATION

Piaggio-Douglas PD-808
Wing: span 37 ft 6 in (11.43 m) without tip tanks and 43 ft 3.5 in (13.20 m) with tip tanks; aspect ratio 6.25; area 225.00 sq ft (20.90 m²)
Fuselage and tail: length 42 ft 2 in (12.85 m); height 15 ft 9 in (4.80 m); tailplane span 17 ft 9.5 in (5.43 m); wheel track 12 ft 0.75 in (3.68 m); wheel base 14 ft 9 in (4.50 m)

14° Stormo, AMI, uses its ECM-configured PD-808GEs for NATO EW training. Its aircraft are now adopting an overall grey scheme.

Powerplant: two Piaggio (Rolls-Royce/Bristol Siddeley) Viper Mk 526 turbojets each rated at 3,350 lb st (14.90 kN)
Weights: empty equipped 4830 kg (10,648 lb); maximum take-off 8165 kg (18,000 lb)
Fuel and load: internal fuel 985 US gal (3727 litres); external fuel none; maximum payload 1,600 lb (726 kg)
Speed: maximum level speed 'clean' at 19,500 ft (5945 m) 460 kt (530 mph; 852 km/h); maximum cruising speed at 36,100 ft (11000 m) 432 kt (497 mph;

800 km/h); economical cruising speed at 41,000 ft (12500 m) 390 kt (449 mph; 722 km/h)
Range: 1,105 nm (1,272 miles; 2048 km)
Performance: maximum rate of climb at sea level 5,415 ft (1650 m) per minute; service ceiling 45,000 ft (13715 m); take-off run 2,905 ft (885 m) at maximum take-off weight; take-off distance to 50 ft (15 m) 3,350 ft (1020 m) at maximum take-off weight; landing distance from 50 ft (15 m) 3,800 ft (1158 m) at normal landing weight

Pilatus **P-3**

Pilatus Flugzeugwerke AG
CH-6370 Stans
Switzerland

Developed for the Swiss air force in the early 1950s as a replacement for the North American T-6, the **Pilatus P-3** has been in service as a primary trainer since 1955. Production totalled 72 for the **Swiss air force** and six for the **Brazilian navy**. The latter are no longer in service, but the Piloten Rekrutenschule 42 and 242 at Magadino retain a few, while others previously used for student pilot training are now distributed around operational bases for liaison and refresher flying tasks. The P-3 has been largely replaced in Swiss service by the Pilatus PC-7 Turbo Trainer.

SPECIFICATION

Pilatus P-3
Wing: span 10.40 m (34 ft 1.4 in); aspect ratio 6.56; area 16.50 m² (177.61 sq ft)
Fuselage and tail: length 8.75 m (28 ft 8.5 in); height 3.05 m (10 ft 0 in)
Powerplant: one Textron Lycoming GO-435-C2A piston engine rated at 260 hp (194 kW)
Weights: empty equipped 1110 kg (2,447 lb); maximum take-off 1500 kg (3,307 lb)
Fuel and load: external fuel none; maximum ordnance about 150 kg (331 lb)

Speed: maximum speed at 2000 m (6,560 ft) 167 kt (192 mph; 310 km/h); maximum cruising speed at optimum altitude 149 kt (171 mph; 275 km/h); economical cruising speed 137 kt (158 mph; 255 km/h)

Range: 405 nm (466 miles; 750 km)
Performance: maximum rate of climb at sea level 1,380 ft (421 m) per minute; service ceiling 18,000 ft (5485 m)

Sizeable numbers of P-3s remain in Swiss air force service as squadron and base liaison aircraft.

Pilatus **PC-6 Porter/Turbo Porter**

One of the most successful aircraft in its class, the **Pilatus PC-6 Porter** STOL utility transport has been produced in both piston-engined and turboprop versions. Design requirements were for a strong, reliable airframe, excellent STOL performance, good low-speed handling and excellent load-carrying capability. With seating for seven, the high-wing PC-6 first flew on 4 May 1959 with a supercharged Lycoming GSO-480-B1A6 piston engine rated at 253 kW (340 shp). A total of 50 or so Porters was built, before production changed to a turboprop-powered variant. With accommodation for up to nine passengers and a double loading door to facilitate cargo loading, the **PC-6/A-H1 Turbo Porter** first flew on 2 May 1961, powered by a 390-kW (523-shp) Turboméca Astazou IIE engine.

Subsequent production has encompassed several variants, mostly distinguished by versions of the Astazou engine (**PC-6/A**), Pratt & Whitney Canada PT6A (**PC-6/B**) or Garret TPE331 (**PC-6/C**) turboprops. A total of over 500 PC-6s of all versions has been built, including 90 manufactured under licence by Fairchild in the US (as **Heli-Porters**). Twenty-five armed PC-6/Cs were produced for COIN duties in Vietnam as the **Fairchild AU-23A Peacemaker** (described separately). The majority of the

considerable number of PC-6s sold for military use in the communications, liaison or reconnaissance roles have been the **B2-H2** version, with seating for 11 passengers. The current **PC-6/B2-H4** production variant features turned-up wingtips, enlarged dorsal fin, and minor structural and undercarriage improvements to increase payload by 570 kg (1,257 lb).

Principal users of the Turbo Porter include the **Australian army** (No. 173 GS Squadron) and **Switzerland**'s Leichtefliegerstaffel 7, a light transport squadron manned by the militia. Other operators include the military air arms in **Angola**, **Argentina** (navy), **Austria**, **Bolivia**, **Chad**, **Colombia** (operated by the para-military airline SATENA), **Dubai**, **Ecuador**, **Indonesia**, **Iran**, **Myanmar**, **Oman**, **Peru** (operated by the para-military airline TANS), **Sudan** and the former **Yugoslavia**. The **US Army** bought two Turbo Porters to operate in Berlin, with the designation **UV-20A** and name **Chiricahua**. The **French army** ordered five PC-6/B2-H4s in 1992 for use as transport/paradrop aircraft.

The PC-6 is ideally suited to operations in mountainous Austria, and some have even been modified for fire-fighting tasks.

SPECIFICATION

Pilatus PC-6/B2-H4 Turbo-Porter
Wing: span 15.87 m (52 ft 0.75 in); aspect ratio 8.4; area 30.15 m² (324.54 sq ft)
Fuselage and tail: length 11.00 m (36 ft 1 in); height 3.20 m (10 ft 6 in) tail down; elevator span 5.12 m (16 ft 9.5 in); wheel track 3.00 m (9 ft 10 in); wheel base 7.87 m (25 ft 10 in)
Powerplant: one 680-shp (507-kW) Pratt & Whitney Canada PT6A-27 turboprop flat-rated at 550 shp (410 kW)
Weights: empty equipped 1270 kg (2,800 lb); maximum take-off 2800 kg (6,173 lb) on wheels or 2699 kg (5,732 lb) on skis

Fuel and load: internal fuel 508 kg (1,120 lb); external fuel up to 392 kg (864 lb) in two 245-litre (65-US gal) underwing auxiliary tanks; maximum payload 1130 kg (2,491 lb) with reduced internal fuel, 1062 kg (2,341 lb) with maximum internal and 571 kg (1,259 lb) with maximum internal and external fuel
Speed: never exceed speed 151 kt (174 mph; 280 km/h); economical cruising speed at 10,000 ft (3050 m) 115 kt (132 mph; 213 km/h)
Range: ferry range 870 nm (1,002 miles; 1612 km) with auxiliary fuel; range 500 nm (576 miles; 926 km) with maximum internal fuel or 394 nm (453 miles; 730 km) with maximum payload
Performance: maximum rate of climb at sea level 941 ft (287 m) per minute; maximum operating altitude 25,000 ft (7620 m); take-off run 646 ft (197 m) at maximum take-off weight; landing run 417 ft (127 m) at normal landing weight
g limits: -1.5 to +3.72

Pilatus **PC-7 Turbo Trainer**

Although the **Pilatus PC-7** directly derives from the early 1950s piston-powered Pilatus P-3 (the prototype of which was re-engined with a 550-shp (410-kW) Pratt & Whitney Canada PT6A-20 turboprop to fly as HB-HON in April 1966), little of the original design is now retained in the definitive **Turbo Trainer**. After a forced landing through fuel mismanagement during initial flight development, the project was shelved until 1973, when one of SAFAAC's P-3 trainers (from 73 originally built) was bailed by Pilatus for similar modification with a 650-shp (484.9-kW) PT6A-25 flat-rated to 550 shp (410.3 kW). Registered HB-HOZ (later A-901 with SAFAAC), this first flew on 12 May 1975, but then underwent major structural changes to take full advantage of the extra power.

In conjunction with Dornier, Pilatus designed a completely new low-fatigue one-piece wing with leading-edge integral tanks ahead of the single mainspar, while retaining the P-3's original span, planform and 15-12 per cent NACA 64A laminar-flow section. Dornier also helped design an entirely new electrically-actuated undercarriage, replacing the P-3's oil-damped coil-spring shock absorbers with Do 27/28-type oleo-pneumatic legs, to meet a 57 per cent increase in maximum take-off weight. Flight development with these modifications in the second prototype also resulted in aerodynamic changes to the rear fuselage and tail, including

ing adding a tailcone and small ventral fin, and extending the fuselage aft of the tailplane, to which was added strakes on the inner leading edges for unlimited spin clearance. The tailplane was shortened, allowing its elevators to become externally horn-balanced.

These and other changes, including the clear-vision moulded bubble canopy for the non-pressurised cockpit, were all embodied in the first production PC-7 (HB-HAO), which made its initial flight on 18 August 1978 at Stans. First deliveries were to the **Myanmar air force**, as launch customer, following FAA civil certification in early 1979. With the Beech T-34C then its sole production competitor, the PC-7 achieved growing export success, supplemented in June 1981 after a year-long evaluation of two examples, plus the second prototype, by a **Swiss air force** order for 40 to equip the two *Fliegerschulen* at Magadino. For weapons training, six underwing hardpoints can accommodate external stores of up to 2,293 lb (1040 kg), and PC-7s are believed to have been used operationally by both sides in the Iran/Iraq war.

Between 1983 and 1984, 44 PC-7s replaced the Bulldog in Malaysian air force service. This is one of the nine aircraft flown by the 'Tamin Sari' ('Magic Sword') aerobatic display team, based at Alor Setar.

Pilatus PC-7 Turbo Trainer

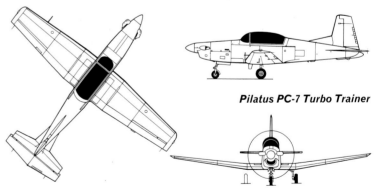

Pilatus PC-7 Turbo Trainer

The Swiss air force's Fliegerschule I Teil is based at Magadino, in the Ticino region near Italy. It flies PC-7s as basic and advanced instrument trainers.

France's civil/military Centre d'Essais en Vol (CEV) flight test establishment flies five PC-7s among a wide variety of jet, prop and rotary types for general trials duties.

In 1985, Pilatus offered an optional installation of twin Martin-Baker CH.Mk 15A ejection seats, to provide an escape envelope from ground level/60 kt to 32,000 ft (9753 m)/300 kt, with **Iran** as first retrofit customer. Nearly 500 PC-7s had been sold by early 1994 to mostly military customers, including **Abu Dhabi** (24), **Angola** (18), **Austria** (16), **Bolivia** (36), **Myanmar** (17), **Chad** (two), **Chile** (10), **France** CEV (five), **Guatemala** (12), **Iran** (35), **Iraq** (52), **Malaysia** (44), **Mexico** (75), **Netherlands** (10), **Nigeria** (seven), **Switzerland** (40), and **Surinam** (two). Planned orders for 60 **PC-7 Mk 2**s, equipped with a higher-powered flat-rated PT6A with a four-

bladed propeller and Martin-Baker ejection seats, were reported in late 1992 for the South African air force, for a total cost of some SwFr200 million. These were to be delivered from July 1994, with 55 per cent South African industrial participation, including local assembly, to replace the SAAF's veteran Harvard trainers. Interest in six PC-7s was also reported from Uruguay.

SPECIFICATION

Pilatus PC-7 Turbo Trainer
Wing: span 10.40 m (34 ft 1 in); aspect ratio 6.5; area 16.60 m² (178.69 sq ft)

Fuselage and tail: length 9.78 m (32 ft 1 in); height 3.21 m (10 ft 6 in); tailplane span 3.40 m (11 ft 2 in); wheel track 2.60 m (8 ft 6 in); wheel base 2.32 m (7 ft 7 in)
Powerplant: one 650-shp (485-kW) Pratt & Whitney Canada PT6A-25A turboprop flat-rated at 550 shp (410 kW)
Weights: basic empty 1330 kg (2,932 lb); normal take-off 1900 kg (4,188 lb) for aerobatics; maximum take-off 2700 kg (5,952 lb)
Fuel and load: internal fuel 474 litres (125 US gal); external fuel up to two 240- or 152-litre (63.5- or 40-US gal) drop tanks; maximum ordnance 1040 kg (2,293 lb)
Speed: never exceed speed 270 kt (311 mph; 500 km/h); maximum cruising speed at 20,000 ft (6095 m) 222 kt (256 mph; 412 km/h); economical

cruising speed at 20,000 ft (6095 m) 171 kt (197 mph; 317 km/h)
Range: ferry range 1,420 nm (1,634 miles; 2630 km) with drop tanks; range 647 nm (746 miles; 1200 km); endurance 4 hours 22 minutes
Performance: maximum rate of climb at sea level 2,150 ft (655 m) per minute; climb to 16,400 ft (5000 m) in 9 minutes 0 seconds; service ceiling 33,000 ft (10060 m); take-off run 780 m (2,560 ft) at maximum take-off weight; take-off distance to 50 ft (15 m) 1180 m (3,870 ft) at maximum take-off weight; landing distance from 50 ft (15 m) 800 m (2,625 ft) at maximum landing weight; landing run 505 m (1,655 ft) at maximum landing weight
g limits: -3 to +6 at normal take-off weight or -2.25 to +4.5 at maximum take-off weight

Pilatus **PC-9**

When rumours of a 'big brother' to the Pilatus PC-7 (described separately) began to circulate in 1983, it was thought to have a Garret engine, but when the prototype **Pilatus PC-9** made its first flight on 7 May 1984 it was powered by a Pratt & Whitney Canada PT6A-62. There is only 10 per cent commonality between the PC-7 and PC-9. The latter is similar, but recognisable by its larger canopy, stepped tandem cockpits with ejection seats, ventral airbrake and four-bladed prop. Development began in 1982, and flight testing of many features and components was carried out using a PC-7 testbed before the construction was initiated of two pre-production prototypes.

The PC-9 was one of four shortlisted contenders to meet the RAF's AST.412 requirement for a Jet Provost replacement, eventually losing to the Shorts-modified EMBRAER Tucano, amid some acrimony and accusations of a 'political' decision. By the time that the PC-9 was certificated on 19 September 1985 (three months ahead of schedule), the RAF competition had taken place, but Pilatus had retained its AST.412 marketing link with BAe. This was a strong factor in securing the initial PC-9 production order, announced only a week later, for 30 aircraft for the **Royal Saudi air force**.

Pilatus then switched its marketing effort to **Australia**, offering offset package deals on both the PC-7 and PC-9 to the Australian government as alternatives to the ailing Wamira programme for an RAAF trainer. The decision this time went in favour of the PC-9, which was co-produced by Hawker de Havilland in Australia under the designation **PC-9/A**. Australian PC-9s are equipped with Bendix EFIS, and PC-7-style low-pressure tyres. Two Swiss-built aircraft were delivered in 1987, and 17 more were supplied in kit form. The remaining 48 aircraft are being built by Hawker de Havilland.

A German target-towing version, designated **PC-9B**, is operated by Holstenair on behalf of the **Luftwaffe**. This is equipped with two Southwest RM-24 winches on inboard pylons, with the targets stowed aft of the winch, and sufficient fuel for a 3-hour 20-minute mission. Other PC-9 operators include the air forces of **Cyprus**, **Myanmar**, **Thailand** and **Switzerland**. Approximately 150 PC-9s had been sold by mid-1994.

The Royal Thai air force ordered 20 PC-9s in 1992, followed by a further 10, replacing RFB Fantrainers.

The announcement, in 1993, of a buy of 20 'TX-lo' trainers for the **Republic of Korea air force** was hit by controversy. The Korean PC-9s were to act as lead-in trainers for the BAe Hawk, but the air force wished them to be weapons-capable. Swiss law forbade such an 'arms' export and the deal stalled in a debate over whether Pilatus had ever confirmed the PC-9 could be fitted with hardpoints or not. In July 1994, South Korea shelved plans to acquire PC-9s after the contract expired, and chose instead to develop the rival Daewoo KTX-1 turboprop trainer. This, and other controversial deals, led Pilatus to announce that it was considering moving PC-7/-9 assembly to the Britten-Norman plant in the UK to circumvent current and pending Swiss legislation.

In conjunction with Beechcraft, Pilatus is offering the **PC-9 Mk 2** as a JPATS contender. This differs substantially from the PC-9, with a 70 per cent redesign, including a strengthened fuselage and pressurised cockpit. New digital avionics include GPS, MLS, collision avoidance system and provision for a HUD. An engineering testbed aircraft flew first, followed on 23 December 1992 by the first Beechcraft-assembled aircraft, at Wichita. After the final JPATS RFP was issued in May 1994, the first week-long flight tests of the PC-9 Mk II began in July 1994 at Wright-Patterson AFB, Ohio.

SPECIFICATION

Pilatus PC-9
Wing: span 10.124 m (33 ft 2.5 in); aspect ratio 6.3; area 16.29 m² (175.35 sq ft)
Fuselage and tail: length 10.175 m (33 ft 4.75 in); height 3.26 m (10 ft 8.33 in); wheel track 2.54 m (8 ft 4 in)
Powerplant: one 1,150-shp (857-kW) Pratt & Whitney Canada PT6A-62 turboprop flat-rated at 950 shp (708 kW)
Weights: basic empty 1685 kg (3,715 lb); normal take-off 2250 kg (4,960 lb) for aerobatics; maximum take-off 3200 kg (7,055 lb)
Fuel and load: internal fuel 535 litres (141.3 US gal); external fuel up to two 248- or 154-litre (65.5- or 40.7-US gal) drop tanks; maximum ordnance 1040 kg (2,293 lb)

This is the first Beech-built PC-9 Mk II. With the end of JPATS flight tests in October 1994, a final decision will be made in February 1995.

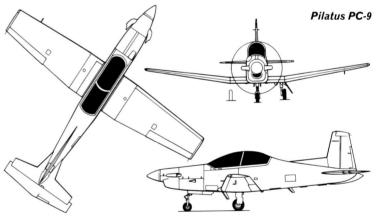

Pilatus PC-9

Speed: maximum level speed 'clean' at 20,000 ft (6095 m) 300 kt (345 mph; 556 km/h) and at sea level 270 kt (311 mph; 500 km/h)
Range: range 887 nm (1,020 miles; 1642 km); endurance two 1-hour missions
Performance: maximum rate of climb at sea level 4,090 ft (1247 m) per minute; service ceiling 38,000 ft

(11580 m); take-off run 227 m (745 ft) at normal take-off weight; take-off distance to 50 ft (15 m) 440 m (1,444 ft) at normal take-off weight; landing distance from 50 ft (15 m) 530 m (1,739 ft) at normal landing weight
g limits: -3.5 to +7 at normal take-off weight or -2.25 to +4.5 at maximum take-off weight

Pilatus Britten-Norman BN-2B Islander/Defender

Pilatus Britten-Norman Ltd
Bembridge, Isle of Wight PO35 5PR
United Kingdom

The **Britten-Norman Islander** was developed as a rugged and versatile twin-engined feederliner to replace aircraft like the de Havilland Rapide, but has confounded all expectations by becoming one of the most widely built aircraft of its class and a *de facto* Dakota replacement. By 1994, orders for all variants exceeded 1,200.

The prototype first flew on 13 June 1965, powered by 210-hp (157-kW) Rolls-Royce/Continental IO-360B engines. The production aircraft gained 4 ft (1.2 m) extra wingspan and Lycoming O-540 engines (both modifications being flown on the original prototype on 17 December 1965). The first production prototype was flown on 20 August 1966, and deliveries began one year later. By mid-1967 orders stood at over 200, and production was transferred to the British Hovercraft Corporation to meet the expanding order book. In addition, Islanders were built by Romania's IRMA, the first of an initial 215 such aircraft making its maiden flight on 4 August 1969. Romanian production continues, and has almost reached 500.

Despite its healthy order book, Britten-Norman ran into financial difficulties and was acquired by the Fairey Group on 31 August 1972. The company's lack of 'in-house' production capacity was eased by the establishment of a third production line at Fairey SA's factory at Gosselies, Belgium. In September 1979, Britten-Norman (Bembridge) Ltd and the production hardware at Gosselies was acquired by Pilatus. During 1974, production of the Islander began at the Philippines Aircraft Development Corporation, which eventually built 55, and assembled 67 from kits supplied by PBN.

The basic **BN-2** was succeeded on the production line by the improved **BN-2A** in June 1969, and then by the further improved **BN-2B**. Some improvements were introduced within the sub-variants, including an optional extended nose which gave 28 cu ft (0.79 m³) of baggage space, extended raked wingtips, and different engine options, from the 260-hp (194-kW) IO-540-E4C5 (with or without Rajay turbo-superchargers) to the 300-hp (224-kW) IO-540-K1B5 or the turbo-supercharged 300-hp (225-kW) TSIO-540E.

Unarmed Islanders have been delivered to several military customers, including **Ciskei**, **Haiti**, **Indonesia**, **Iraq**, **Israel**, **Qatar**, **Somalia**, **Turkey**, **Venezuela**, **Zaïre** and **Zimbabwe**, while a dedicated military derivative, named **Defender**, has been more widely exported. This has underwing hardpoints allowing the carriage of

Twenty-three PADC-assembled BN-2A Islanders were delivered to the Philippine air force between 1976 and 1981.

NATO pylons, stressed for loads of 450 kg (992 lb) (outboard) and 700 kg (1,543 lb) (inboard). These allow the aircraft to carry a variety of payloads, including 60-US gal (227-litre) external tanks and a variety of bombs, rockets, gun pods, wire-guided missiles, recce flares and anti-personnel mines. Defenders have been delivered to **Abu Dhabi**, **Belgium**, **Belize**, **Botswana**, **Ghana**, **Guyana**, **Hong Kong**, **Jamaica**, **Malagasy**, **Malawi**, **Mauritania**, **Mexico** (Presidential Flight), **Oman**, **Panama**, **Qatar**, **Rwanda**, **Seychelles** and **Surinam**.

The **Maritime Defender** is a dedicated naval variant, optimised for coastal patrol, fisheries protection, and search and rescue. A modified nose accommodates a Bendix-King RDR-1400 search radar, and the crew comprises two pilots, a radar operator and two observers. The aircraft is offered with a variety of enhanced avionics suites, and can carry loudspeakers, searchlights, FLIR, flares, dinghy packs or weapons on its underwing pylons. Maritime Defenders have been delivered to **Cyprus**, the **Indian Navy** (in addition to some non-radar Defenders), **Pakistan** and the **Philippines**.

PBN subsequently introduced a turbine-powered variant as the **BN-2T**. Powered by two Allison 250-B17C turboprops flat-rated at 320 shp (298 kW), the prototype first flew on 2 August 1980. The militarised equivalent of the BN-2T is named **Turbine Defender** and examples are operated by **Belgium** (Gendarmerie), **Botswana**, **Ghana**, and **Morocco**. A **Turbine Islander** with a sliding para-door is operated by the **British army**'s parachute association. The Turbine Islander has spawned a number of specialised military Pilatus Britten-Norman Ltd versions (described separately).

A maritime turbine derivative was the **ASW/ASV Islander**, flown in demonstrator form (G-OPBN) in time for the 1984 Hanover air show. A production version could have featured 360° radar, FLIR, sonobuoy processing and a MAD. Sea Skua missiles or Stingray torpedoes were offered as weapons options. The demonstrator was eventually purchased by the **Royal Navy** for underwater weapons trials.

An enhanced turbine derivative is the **BN-2T2 Defender 4000**, based on the long-span Trislander-winged and up-engined AEW Defender, enabling the aircraft to lift 1,500 lb (680 kg) greater weight and provide 50 per cent extra internal fuel capacity.

SPECIFICATION

Pilatus Britten-Norman BN-2B Defender

Wing: span 49 ft 0 in (14.94 m) with standard tips or 53 ft 0 in (16.15 m) with ferry tips; aspect ratio 7.39 with standard tips or 8.34 with ferry tips; area 325.00 sq ft (30.19 m²) with standard tips or 337.00 sq ft (31.31 m²) with ferry tips

Fuselage and tail: length 35 ft 7.75 in (10.86 m);

height 13 ft 8.75 in (4.18 m); tailplane span 15 ft 4 in (4.67 m); wheel track 11 ft 10 in (3.61 m); wheel base 13 ft 1.25 in (3.99 m)

Powerplant: two Textron Lycoming IO-540-K1B5 flat-six piston engines each rated at 300 hp (224 kW)

Weights: empty equipped 4,244 lb (1925 kg); maximum take-off 6,600 lb (2993 kg)

Fuel and load: internal fuel 780 lb (354 kg) plus 510 lb (231 kg) in optional ferry tips; external fuel up to two 50-US gal (227-litre) drop tanks; maximum ordnance 2,000 lb (907 kg)

Speed: never exceed speed 183 kt (211 mph; 339 km/h); maximum level speed 'clean' at sea level 151 kt (173 mph; 280 km/h); maximum cruising speed at 7,000 ft (2135 m) 142 kt (164 mph; 264 km/h); economical cruising speed at 12,000 ft (3660 m) 132 kt (152 mph; 245 km/h)

Range: ferry range 1,496 nm (1,723 miles; 2773 km) with auxiliary fuel; range 1,061 nm (1,221 miles; 1965 km) with optional fuel or 613 nm (706 miles; 1136 km) with standard fuel

Performance: maximum rate of climb at sea level 1,130 ft (344 m) per minute; service ceiling 17,200 ft (5240 m); take-off run 866 ft (264 m) at maximum take-off weight; take-off distance to 50 ft (15 m) 1,155 ft (352 m) at maximum take-off weight; landing distance from 50 ft (15 m) 980 ft (299 m)

Indian Naval Air Squadron 550 operates six radar-nosed Maritime Defenders that replaced de Havilland Doves as surveillance and training aircraft.

Pilatus Britten-Norman Turbine Islander/Defender special versions

The Islander/Defender's versatility and load-carrying capability has led to its adoption for a variety of roles. The first such specialised variant was the **CASTOR Islander** (later **ASTOR**). This was used as a testbed for the Corps Airborne Stand-Off Radar, developed to fulfil a UK Ministry of Defence requirement for a 'big picture' battlefield surveillance aircraft. Two separate competing platforms were evaluated, one based on a modified Thorn EMI Searchwater radar (CASTOR-C) carried by a Canberra, and the other based on a new Ferranti I-band radar (CASTOR-I). This was originally to have been helicopter-mounted, but was instead fitted on a Turbine Islander acquired for army evaluation. The Canberra began flight trials in 1982, but the Islander did not fly until 12 May 1984, and then only with a ballasted nose radome. This was flat-bot-

tomed and circular in plan view, and required a 12-in (30-cm) extension to the nosewheel leg and the fitting of Trislander mainwheel units. In 1988 the ASTOR Islander was fitted with a Thorn-EMI Skymaster radar in a bulbous spherical nose radome, continuing low-level ASTOR trials and evaluating interoperability with the Grumman E-8 J-STARS. At the end of the project definition stage, due to be completed in 1994, a development and initial production contract was to be awarded. The decision, made late in 1993, not to do so means that firms will be invited to tender on a revised specification, further setting back CASTOR's planned service date of 2003.

In association with Motorola and Thorn-EMI, PBN have further developed the **MASTOR** (Multi-role Airborne STand-off Radar) platform, which integrates the Thorn-

EMI Searchwater 2 radar with mobile ground stations based on those built by Motorola for the E-8 J-STARS. MASTOR's bulbous nose radome (similar to that of the MSSA) houses the MTI-capable radar, and the aircraft also has provision for a FLIR and LLLTV.

The Thorn-EMI Skymaster radar also formed the heart of the private-venture **AEW/MR Islander** demonstrator (G-TEMI), which could be used with pulse-Doppler processing to acquire and track airborne targets in the AEW role or, using a non-coherent, frequency-agile mode, could detect small surface targets, even in high sea states. A second radar operator's console (by comparison with the ASTOR aircraft) increased operational flexibility. A synthetic aperture mode was partly developed (aiming to give high-resolution video mapping) and the border surveillance role was

examined. The potential for fitting ESM, IFF and datalinks was also explored.

The AEW demonstrator was eventually converted to serve as the prototype **MSSA** (Multi-Sensor Surveillance Aircraft), being rolled out in its new guise at Baltimore on 10 September 1992. The MSSA is being developed in association with Westinghouse to provide a simple, low-cost, off-the-shelf surveillance, drug interdiction and border/fisheries patrol platform. The MSSA is equipped with an integrated sensor system which includes an AN/APG-66 radar with a 360° rotating antenna, WF-360 FLIR, GPS, LTN-92 ring-laser gyro INS and a real time video datalink. The demonstrator was leased to the **US Navy** for trials in 1992, and offered to the **British army** for use in Bosnia later that same year. **Turkey** has purchased one MSSA, with an option on

three, and the company hopes for an order for 12 from the US Air National Guard. In July 1993 the sale of three MSSAs was announced to an 'undisclosed Far Eastern nation', for delivery in 1994.

The **Internal Security Islander** has been supplied to the **Netherlands** and **Cyprus** police forces and is equipped with Bendix/King RDR 1400C radar, a Racal R-NAV2 navigation system, and underwing hardpoints for fuel tanks, weapons, camera pods, thermal imagers or FLIR sensors. The **British army**'s seven **Islander AL.Mk 1**s are similarly equipped, without radar, but with R-NAV2, Doppler 91, Mk 32 Decca navigator receiver and underwing hardpoints for a variety of sensors. They may be equipped to carry cameras and/or IRLS equipment in

When the CASTOR Islander first flew in May 1984, it was fitted with this flat-bottomed radome. It later received a lengthened undercarriage and a larger, bulbous radome.

the fuselage, which seems to have bulges (camera ports) in the belly. Even less is known about the **RAF**'s **Islander CC.Mk 2** and **CC.Mk 2A**, operated by RAF Northolt's Station Flight (not No. 32 Squadron), which are said to be equipped for mapping duties. The CC.Mk 2A aircraft (ZF573) was at one time a PBN demonstrator and retains the capability to fire torpedoes. Both aircraft are fully airways equipped and have Bendix/King weather radar in the nose.

The MSSA is based on the airframe of the AEW Islander and carries a Westinghouse APG-66SR radar with 360° coverage, FLIR and laser-ring gyro navigation system and INS.

SPECIFICATION

Pilatus Britten-Norman BN-2T Turbine Defender generally similar to the Pilatus Britten-Norman BN-2B Defender except in the following particulars:
Fuselage and tail: length 35 ft 7.75 in (10.86 m) with standard nose or 36 ft 3.75 in (11.07 m) with weather radar nose
Powerplant: two 400-shp (298-kW) Allison 250-B17C turboprops each flat-rated at 320 shp (238.5 kW)
Weights: empty equipped 4,220 lb (1914 kg);

maximum take-off 7,000 lb (3175 kg)
Fuel and load: internal fuel 1,191 lb (540 kg) plus 510 lb (231 kg) in optional ferry tips; external fuel up to two 50-Imp gal (60-US gal; 227-litre) drop tanks; maximum ordnance 2,000 lb (907 kg)
Speed: maximum cruising speed at 10,000 ft (3050 m) 170 kt (196 mph; 315 km/h); economical cruising speed at 5,000 ft (1525 m) 142 kt (164 mph; 263 km/h)
Range: 728 nm (838 miles; 1349 km)
Performance: maximum rate of climb at sea level 1,050 ft (320 m) per minute; service ceiling more than 25,000 ft (7620 m); take-off run 837 ft (255 m) at maximum take-off weight; take-off distance to 50 ft (15 m) 1,250 ft (381 m) at maximum take-off weight; landing distance from 50 ft (15 m) 1,115 ft (340 m) at normal landing weight; landing run 747 ft (228 m) at normal landing weight

Piper **PA-18 Super Cub**

Piper Aircraft Corporation
2926 Piper Drive, PO Box 1328, Vero Beach
Florida 32960, USA

Descended from the famed J-3C Cub and wartime L-4 Grasshopper, the **Piper PA-18 Super Cub** was the last of the Pipers to retain the classic high-wing, tailwheel configuration. Production against US government contracts totalled many hundreds for US Army and Mutual Defense Aid Programs under **L-18** and **L-21** designations. A handful now remain in service, with the final operators comprising the **Belgian air force**, providing five (of six originally supplied) **L-21B** glider tugs for the cadet force; the Israeli air force with over 15 for basic flying training; the **Uganda army air force**, which received 16 from Israel in the 1960s (although the serviceability of these aircraft is questionable); the **Uruguayan air force**, with two in its Escuadrilla de Enlaces (communications flight) at Durazno; and the **Uruguayan navy**, with a single example.

Uruguay is one of the very few military Super Cub operators remaining, with a handful in air force and navy service.

SPECIFICATION

Piper PA-18 Standard Super Cub 150
Wing: span 35 ft 2.5 in (10.73 m); aspect ratio 7.0; area 178.50 sq ft (16.58 m2)
Fuselage and tail: length 22 ft 7 in (6.88 m); height 6 ft 8.5 in (2.02 m); tailplane span 10 ft 6 in (3.20 m); wheel track 6 ft 0.5 in (1.84 m)
Powerplant: one Textron Lycoming (Continental) O-320 flat-four piston engine rated at 150 hp (112 kW)
Weights: empty equipped 946 lb (429 kg); maximum take-off 1,750 lb (794 kg)
Fuel and load: internal fuel 36 US gal (136 litres); external fuel none; maximum ordnance none
Speed: never exceed speed 133 kt (153 mph; 246 km/h);

maximum cruising speed 113 kt (130 mph; 208 km/h)
Range: 399 nm (460 miles; 735 km)
Performance: maximum rate of climb at sea level 960 ft (293 m) per minute; service ceiling 19,000 ft

(5795 m); take-off run 200 ft (61 m) at maximum take-off weight; take-off distance to 50 ft (15 m) 500 ft (153 m) at maximum take-off weight; landing distance from 50 ft (15 m) 725 ft (221 m) at normal landing weight

Piper **PA-23 Apache/Aztec**

Piper's first twin-engined aircraft, the **PA-23 Apache**, actually originated as the **Twin Stinson** prototype, flown before Piper acquired the Stinson division of Convair in November 1948. From 1953, Piper built 2,047 PA-23 Apache twins and 4,929 of the improved **PA-23 Aztec**, which was distinguished by a swept fin and rudder. Small numbers have reached military service over the years, mostly in the liaison/light transport role, and a few Aztecs are still used in this role. In particular, the **Spanish air force** has six (local designation **E.19**) used for refresher training by Esc 423 at Getafe. The PA-23 is also operated by the air arms of **Cameroon** (two), **Costa Rica** (one), **Madagascar** (one) and **Mexico** (one). Some examples may still be operated by **Uganda**. The US Navy acquired 20 Aztecs as **UO-1**s for logistic support; later redesignated **U-11A**s, these have been replaced by Beech UC-12s.

To the Ejercito del Aire Español, the Piper PA-23-250 Aztec is the E.19. The six Aztecs serve alongside Beech Barons, providing refresher flying training.

SPECIFICATION

Piper PA-23-250 Aztec D
Wing: span 37 ft 2.5 in (11.34 m); aspect ratio 6.67; area 207.56 sq ft (19.28 m2)
Fuselage and tail: length 30 ft 2.625 in (9.21 m); height 10 ft 4 in (3.15 m); tailplane span 12 ft 6 in (3.81 m); wheel track 11 ft 4 in (3.45 m); wheel base 7 ft 6 in (2.29 m)
Powerplant: two Textron Lycoming IO-540-C4B5 flat-six piston engines each rated at 250 hp (186 kW)
Weights: empty 2,933 lb (1330 kg); maximum take-off 5,200 lb (2359 kg)
Fuel and load: internal fuel 144 US gal (544 litres); external fuel none

Speed: maximum level speed 'clean' at optimum altitude 188 kt (216 mph; 348 km/h); normal cruising speed at 4,000 ft (1220 m) 182 kt (210 mph; 338 km/h); economical cruising speed at 6,400 ft (1950 m) 177 kt (204 mph; 328 km/h)
Range: 720 nm (830 miles; 1338 km) at maximum cruising speed or 1,050 nm (1,210 miles; 1947 km) at economical cruising speed

Performance: maximum rate of climb at sea level 1,490 ft (454 m) per minute; absolute ceiling 21,100 ft (6430 m); take-off run 820 ft (250 m) at maximum take-off weight; take-off distance to 50 ft (15 m) 1,250 ft (381 m) at maximum take-off weight; landing distance from 50 ft (15 m) 1,250 ft (381 m) at normal landing weight; landing run 850 ft (259 m) at normal landing weight

Piper **PA-28/-32 Cherokee/Arrow/Dakota/Cherokee Six**

First flown on 10 January 1960, the **PA-28 Cherokee** succeeded the high-wing Cub series as Piper's principal single-engined lightplane, production totalling 29,285 in a number of variants to which the names **Cruiser**, **Flite Liner**, **Cadet**, **Challenger**, **Archer**, **Charger**, **Pathfinder** and **Dakota** were progressively applied.

A number of PA-28 four-seat cabin monoplanes were sold to military operators. Remaining users include the **Chilean air force**, which has 16 **PA-28-236 Dakota**s (assembled by ENAER), used as instrument trainers and for SAR/liaison duties at various bases, and **Argentina**'s quasi-military

National Civil Aviation Institute, which has 10 Dakotas and four **PA-28-201 Arrow IV**s (assembled by Chincul) for training at Moron AFB. Four Arrow IVs are used by the KuljLv (Transport Squadron) of the **Finnish air force**, and five **Arrow II**s are distributed between the three operational squadrons Hav LLv 11, 21 and 31, the Air Academy and the HQ Flight. Five earlier **PA-28-140 Cherokee** trainers remain in service in **Tanzania**. Also in use are a few examples of the six-seat **PA-32 Cherokee Six**, flown for liaison and communications in the **Colombian air force**, **Costa Rican Police Security Air Section**, **Tanzanian air force** and **Turkish army**.

SPECIFICATION

Piper PA-28RT-201 Arrow IV

Wing: span 35 ft 5 in (10.80 m); aspect ratio 7.39; area 170.00 sq ft (15.79 m2)

Fuselage and tail: length 27 ft 0 in (8.23 m); height wheel track 10 ft 5.5 in (3.19 m); wheel base 7 ft 10.25 in (2.39 m)

Powerplant: one Textron Lycoming IO-360-C1C6 flat-four piston engine rated at 200 hp (149 kW)

Weights: empty 1,636 lb (742 kg); maximum take-off 2.750 ft (1247 kg)

Fuel and load: internal fuel 77 US gal (291 litres); external fuel none

Speed: never exceed speed 186 kt (214 mph; 344 km/h);

maximum level speed 'clean' at 14,000 ft (4625 m) 178 kt (205 mph; 330 km/h) and at sea level 149 kt (172 mph; 276 km/h); maximum cruising speed at optimum altitude 143 kt (165 mph; 265 km/h); economical cruising speed at optimum altitude 128 kt (147 mph; 237 km/h)

Range: 934 nm (1,076 miles; 1733 km)

Performance: maximum rate of climb at sea level 831 ft (253 m) per minute; service ceiling 16,200 ft (4940 m); take-off run 1,025 ft (312 m) at maximum take-off weight; take-off distance to 50 ft (15 m) 1,600 ft (488 m) at maximum take-off weight; landing distance from 50 ft (15 m) 1,625 ft (465 m) at normal landing weight; landing run 615 ft (187 m) at normal landing weight

The Finnish air force operates Piper PA-28R and T-tailed PA-28RT-201 Turbo Arrow IVs as primary training and liaison aircraft, based at Kauhava.

The long-nosed PA-32 Cherokee Six is a rare sight in military service, but the Colombian air force operates a single example, at Barranquilla.

Piper **PA-31/T Navajo/Navajo Chieftain/Cheyenne**

The six/eight-seat **Piper Navajo** was introduced in 1965, powered by 300-hp (224-kW) Lycoming IO-540-M engines. Developments introduced the **PA-31P Pressurised Navajo** with turbocharged engines, **PA-31-350 Navajo Chieftain** with a 2-ft (0.61-m) stretch and counter-rotating props, and the **PA-31T Cheyenne** with 500-shp (373-kW) Pratt & Whitney PT6A-11s. The principal military user is the **Aéronavale**, with 12 for transport (2S and 3S), crew ferrying (Escadrille de Réception et de Convoyage) and navigator/flight engineer training (56S). The **Finnish air force** operates seven Chieftains with transport

and communications flights, and Britain's **MoD (PE)** has four Navajo Chieftains to support A&AEE and Test & Evaluation Establishment operations. Two modified **Cheyenne II**s are operated by the **Mauritanian Islamic Republic Air Wing** for coastal patrols. One or two Navajo, Chieftain and Cheyenne twins are in service with the air arms of **Argentina**, **Bolivia**, **Chile**, **Colombia**, **Dominica**, **Honduras**, **Israel**, **Kenya**, **Nigeria**, **Panama**, **Peru**, **Spain** (designated **E.18** for the single PA-31P and **E.18B** for two PA-31Ts) and **Syria** (two Navajos operated for survey duties with civil registrations).

SPECIFICATION:

Piper PA-31-300 Navajo

Wing: span 40 ft 8 in (12.40 m); aspect ratio 7.23; area 229.00 sq ft (21.27 m2)

Fuselage and tail: length 32 ft 7.5 in (9.94 m); height 13 ft 0 in (3.96 m); tailplane span 18 ft 1.5 in (5.52 m); wheel track 13 ft 9 in (4.19 m)

Powerplant: two Textron Lycoming IO-540-M flat-six piston engines each rated at 300 hp (224 kW)

Weights: empty 3,744 lb (1698 kg); maximum take-off 6,200 lb (2812 kg)

Fuel and load: internal fuel 190 US gal (719 litres); external fuel none

Speed: maximum level speed 'clean' at sea level 197 kt (227 mph; 365 km/h); maximum cruising speed at 6,400 ft (1950 m) 185 kt (213 mph; 343 km/h); economical cruising speed at 14,600 ft (4450 m) 171 kt (197 mph; 317 km/h)

Range: range 1,107 kt (1,275 miles; 2052 km) at maximum cruising speed or 1,346 nm (1,550 miles; 2494 km) at economical cruising speed

Performance: maximum rate of climb 1,670 ft (509 m) per minute; service ceiling 16,600 ft (5060 m); take-off run 1,010 ft (308 m) at maximum take-off weight; take-off distance to 50 ft (15 m) 2,130 ft (646 m) at maximum take-off weight; landing distance from 50 ft (15 m) 2150 ft (655 m) at normal landing weight; landing run 1,725 ft (526 m) at normal landing weight

The Royal Air Force's quartet of PA-31-350 Navajo Chieftains is operated by the A&AEE at Boscombe Down, and T&TE at Llanbedr or West Freugh.

The more refined PA-31T Cheyenne is one of several types in service with Escuadrón de Transporte 214 of the Colombian air force.

Piper **PA-34 Seneca/PA-44 Seminole**

The six/seven-seat **PA-34 Seneca** was essentially a twin-engined PA-32. Piper then developed the **PA-34 Seneca II** with Continental TSIO-360-E engines, plus Bendix RDR-160 radar. Senecas have achieved limited military use and the major user is the **Brazilian air force**, which purchased 12 EMBRAER-manufactured **EMB-810C Seneca II**s (**U-7**s), followed by 20 **U-7A**s incorporating Robertson STOL modifications. Other operators of the Seneca are **Argentina**'s National Civil Aviation Institute with three (assembled by Chincul), **Colombia**, **Costa Rica** and **Pakistan** (No. 41 Sqn at Chaklala). **Colombia** also operates a single **PA-44 Seminole**, which is in effect a twin-engined T-tailed PA-28R and is generally similar to the Seneca.

SPECIFICATION

Piper PA-34 Seneca II

Wing: span 38 ft 10.75 in (11.85 m); aspect ratio 7.4; area 208.70 sq ft (19.39 m2)

Fuselage and tail: length 28 ft 7.5 in (8.73 m); height 9 ft 10.75 in (3.02 m); tailplane span 13 ft 6.75 in (4.14 m); wheel track 11 ft 1.25 in (3.38 m)

Powerplant: two Teledyne Continental TSIO-360-E flat-four turbocharged piston engines each rated at 200 hp (149 kW)

Weights: empty 2,857 lb (1296 kg); maximum take-off 4,570 lb (2073 kg)

Fuel and load: internal fuel 558 lb (253 kg) plus provision for 180 lb (82 kg) of auxiliary fuel in two 15-US gal (57-litre) wing tanks; external fuel none

Speed: maximum level speed 'clean' at 12,000 ft

(3660 m) 195 kt (225 mph; 361 km/h); maximum cruising speed at 20,000 ft (6100 m) and 75 per cent power 190 kt (219 mph; 352 km/h)

Range: with standard fuel and 45 minute reserves 546 nm (629 miles; 1012 km)

Performance: maximum rate of climb at sea level 1,340 ft (408 m) per minute; certificated ceiling 25,000 ft (7620 m); take-off run 900 ft (274 m) at maximum take-off weight; take-off run to 50 ft (15 m) 1,240 ft (378 m) at maximum take-off weight

This is a U-7A in service with 2ª ELO (naval co-operation squadron) of the Brazilian air force.

Piper PA-38-112 Tomahawk

Last of the primary trainers to bear the Piper name, the **PA-38-112 Tomahawk** was designed specifically for pilot training and was certified in December 1977. Production totalled 2,531 when the last Tomahawk was delivered in 1982. The Tomahawk is a cantilever low-wing monoplane with fixed, wide-track tricycle undercarriage, and a T-tail (the prototype originally flew in low-tailed configuration). The roomy cabin seats two, side-by side, with good all-round view and dual controls standard. Piper offered several Special Training Packages

with different instruments fit, and introduced the **Tomahawk II** in 1981 with minor equipment changes. The **Indonesian naval air arm** (TNI-AL) is the sole military customer, having acquired five Tomahawks to serve in Skwadron Udara 400 at Surabaya.

SPECIFICATION

Piper PA-38-112 Tomahawk II
Wing: span 34 ft 0 in (10.36 m); aspect ratio 9.27;

area 124.70 sq ft (11.59 m2)
Fuselage and tail: length 23 ft 1.25 in (7.04 m); height 9 ft 0.75 in (2.76 m); tailplane span 10 ft 6 in (3.20 m); wheel track 10 ft 0 in (3.05 m); wheel base 4 ft 9 in (1.45 m)
Powerplant: one Textron Lycoming O-235-L2C flat-four piston engine rated at 112 hp (83.5 kW)
Weights: empty 1,128 lb (512 kg); maximum take-off 1,670 lb (757 kg)
Fuel and load: internal fuel 32 US gal (121 litres); external fuel none; maximum ordnance none
Speed: never exceed speed 138 kt (159 mph; 256 km/h); maximum level speed 'clean' at sea level 109 kt

(126 mph; 202 km/h); maximum cruising speed at 7,100 ft (2165 m) 108 kt (124 mph; 200 km/h); economical cruising speed at 10,500 ft (3200 m) 100 kt (115 mph; 185 km/h)
Range: 468 nm (539 miles; 867 km)
Performance: maximum rate of climb at sea level 718 ft (219 m) per minute; service ceiling 13,000 ft (3960 m); take-off run 820 ft (250 m) at maximum take-off weight; take-off distance to 50 ft (15 m) 1,460 ft (445 m) at maximum take-off weight; landing distance from 50 ft (15 m) 1,544 ft (471 m) at normal landing weight; landing run 707 ft (215 m) at normal landing weight

---

Promavia SA
Chaussée de Fleurus 181, B-6041 Gosselies-Aéroport
Belgium

Promavia Jet Squalus F1300 NGT

Plans to launch production of the **Promavia Jet Squalus** in Portugal (by OGMA) to meet the needs of the Portuguese air force and other agencies were put into abeyance in 1991, leaving this basic jet trainer with no customers to date. Based on designs by Stelio Frati as an extension of his **F400 Cobra** prototype flown in Italy in 1960, the Jet Squalus (Shark) prototype was built by General Avia in Milan by arrangement with Promavia SA and with financial aid from the Belgian government, and first flew on 30 April 1987.

The Jet Squalus was designed to cover all stages of flying training, comprising *ab initio*, primary, basic and part of the advanced syllabus. The low-wing configuration features side-mounted intakes and side-by-side seating in Martin-Baker Mk 11 lightweight ejection seats, and design work has been completed to provide a pressurised cockpit if required. The prototype flew on 30 April 1987, powered by a TFE109-1 turbofan rated at 1,330 lb st (5.92 kN), and a second prototype was prepared for testing in 1991 with an uprated TFE109-3 and provision for external stores on four wing stations for weapons training or light tactical missions.

As part of its marketing effort, Promavia has proposed use of the Jet Squalus in an

AWS 'air ward system' in four versions: maritime surveillance/search and rescue (**AWS-MS/SAR**) with SLAR and VHF-FM com radio; photo-reconnaissance (**AWS-R**) with VLF/Omega R/Nav; weapons training and armed patrol (**AWS-W**); and target-towing (**AWS-TT**). The derived **ATTA 3000**, with an EFIS-cockpit and stepped tandem seats, was offered, unsuccessfully, to the US Air Force and US Navy as a JPATS contender. An agreement to transfer manufacturing to Saskatoon in Canada (pending its potential selection as a T-33 replacement for the Canadian air force) has been superseded by an agreement with Russian aerospace giant Mikoyan, despite the latter organisation already having several other trainer projects under development.

SPECIFICATION

Promavia Jet Squalus F1300 NGT
Wing: span 9.04 m (29 ft 8 in); aspect ratio 6.0; area 13.58 m2 (146.17 sq ft)
Fuselage and tail: length 9.36 m (30 ft 8.5 in); height 3.60 m (11 ft 9.75 in); tailplane span 3.80 m (12 ft 5.5 in); wheel track 3.59 m (11 ft 9.25 in); wheel base 3.58 m (11 ft 9 in)
Powerplant: one Garrett TFE109-3 turbofan rated at

1,600 lb st (7.12 kN)
Weights: empty equipped 1400 kg (3,086 lb); normal take-off 2100 kg (4,630 lb) for aerobatics; maximum take-off 2400 kg (5,291 lb)
Fuel and load: internal fuel 720 litres (190 US gal); external fuel none; maximum ordnance 600 kg (1,323 lb)
Speed: (with TFE109-1 engine) never exceed speed 345 kt (397 mph; 638 km/h); maximum level speed 'clean' at 14,000 ft (4265 m) 280 kt (322 mph; 519 km/h); cruising speed at optimum altitude 260 kt (299 mph; 482 km/h)
Range: (with TFE109-1 engine) ferry range 1,000 nm (1,152 miles; 1854 km)
Performance: (with TFE109-1 engine) maximum rate

Only two Jet Squalus have been completed since the first prototype flew in 1987. The design has competed for military and civil (airline) trainer orders, but so far to no avail.

of climb at sea level 2,500 ft (762 m) per minute; service ceiling 37,000 ft (11275 m); take-off run 1,100 ft (335 m); take-off distance to 50 ft (15 m) 1,300 ft (396 m); landing distance from 50 ft (15 m) 1,400 ft (427 m); landing run 1,200 ft (366 m)
g limits: -3.5 to +7 for aerobatics or +2.8 sustained at 10,000 ft (3050 m)

WSK-PZL Mielec
ul.Ludowego Wojska Polskiego 3
PL-39-300 Mielec, Poland

PZL Mielec M-18 Dromader

The **PZL Mielec M-18 Dromader** (Dromedary) was developed with the co-operation of Rockwell International and incorporates some components from the Thrush Commander S-2R. The M-18 is a low-wing, single-seat agricultural aircraft with fixed tailwheel undercarriage and is powered by a 746-kW (1,000-hp) PZL-Kalisz (licence-built Shvetsov) ASz-621R nine-cylinder supercharged air-cooled radial engine. In its original form, the M-18 first flew in Poland on 27 August 1976, and more than 600 have been built, including some developed as two-seat **M-18A** versions, primarily for export. Attrition of the fleet of Grumman Ag-Cats used for crop spraying by 359 Mira of the **Greek air force** led to the selection in 1983 of the

Dromader, a batch of 30 being ordered to augment the Ag-Cats. Based at Dekelia, and detached locally, the Dromaders are used also in the fire-fighting role, for which appropriate systems are available.

The PZL M-18 Dromader was chiefly built for export and is in widespread civil use, not only in Eastern Europe but also in such unlikely places as Chile, China, Morocco, Nicaragua, Swaziland and Venezuela. In military service, it is confined to the 30 aircraft purchased by the Greek air force, 29 of which are still active. This Elliniki Aeroporia (Greek air force) example displays the dromadary logo worn by most M-18s.

PZL I-22 Iryda

Just as it had preferred to procure its own trainer (the TS-11 Iskra) rather than take up the Czech L-29 adopted by every other Warsaw Pact nation, **Poland** opted to design an indigenous trainer rather than follow the overall Warsaw Pact line and adopt the L-29's successor, the L-39 Albatros.

The **PZL I-22 Iryda** (Iridium) was designed by Warsaw's Instytut Lotnictwa to succeed both the TS-11 and the LiM-6 (a Polish-built MiG-17 derivative used for advanced, tactical pilot training). About 50

are required to equip the Aviation Academy at Deblin, and the 45 LPSz-B at Babimost. Others will serve with front-line units as communications aircraft, for instrument and spin training and for standardisation. The I-22 will be able to train fast-jet pilots for air combat, ground attack and reconnaissance, and is designed to have a measure of night/all-weather capability.

Engineers from various research institutes formed a team under the leadership of Dr Eng Alfred Baron. The Warsaw team was responsible for initial design, and collaborated with WSK-Mielec for production and some flight test work. The prototype made its maiden flight on 5 March 1985,

but was lost in a crash on 31 January 1987. Four more prototypes were built and all were in flight test by late 1991, when an initial order for nine pre-production aircraft was announced at the Poznan air show.

Very similar in configuration to the Dassault-Breguet/Dornier Alpha Jet, the I-22 is a high-wing monoplane of typical light alloy construction. The wing, of laminar-flow aerofoil section, has 20° sweepback on the leading edge and incorporates conventional ailerons and single-slotted flaps at the trailing edge. The fuselage, of semi-monocoque construction, includes a door-type airbrake in each side of the upper rear surface, and has one non-afterburning turbojet engine

pod-mounted on each lower side of its central structure. The tandem-seat accommodation is pressurised and air conditioned, and the instructor's rear seat is elevated by 40 cm (15.75 in) to provide a good forward view. Both crew members have rocket-powered ejection seats that can be operated at zero altitude and at speeds exceeding 81 kt (150 km/h; 93 mph). Full blind-flying instrumentation is standard, and avionics can include VHF, UHF, ADF, marker beacon receiver, radar altimeter, radio compass and/or other equipment to individual customer requirements.

The main hydraulic system operates the undercarriage, flaps, airbrake, tailplane incidence, brake chute deployment and braking. Emergency undercarriage and flap extension is pneumatic, as is canopy opening. Engine bleed air is used for air conditioning, *g* suit operation, canopy demisting and de-icing of the engine intakes.

The I-22's light attack capability has been evaluated by the second prototype, which carries a 23-mm twin-barrelled cannon pod with 200 rounds on the underfuselage centreline. The aircraft's four underwing pylons are each stressed to a maximum loading of 500 kg (1,102 lb); in addition, the inboard pair is 'plumbed' for the optional carriage of 380-litre (83.6-Imp gal) drop tanks.

The Iryda can carry a maximum external stores load of 1200 kg (2,646 lb), and can also fulfil the light close-support task. The airframe is rugged and robust, and is designed to be quickly and easily repaired and resistant to battle damage. It is already stressed for the carriage of greater external loads, and for the fitting of more powerful engines than the PZL-5 (formerly SO-3W22) turbojets presently used.

The first two standard (PZL-5-powered) I-22s (serialled 103 and 105) were delivered to the air force on 24 October 1992, although problems with winterisation trials delayed full service clearance until November. These were followed by three further aircraft by early 1994, all of which are in service at the Deblin air academy. Four K-15-powered I-22M92s are due to be delivered by the end of 1994 and some reports suggest that at least one of these will be fitted with improved Sagem avionics. The PZL-5 engines are acknowledged as being inadequate for some roles, and Mielec is examining the possibilities of fitting a number of alternative powerplants, including the indigenous 17.69-kN (3,968-lb st) D-18A or K-15, and foreign engines. The first K-15-engined aircraft (SP-PWD, the fourth prototype), designated **I-22M92**, first flew on 22 December 1992. PZL next flew the 3,370-lb (15-kN) thrust Rolls-Royce Viper 545-powered **I-22M93V** (again SP-PWD) on 24 April 1994. The M93 is seen primarily as an export version, with new Sagem avionics (including INS, HUD, HOTAS and colour MFDs), and first flew with the new equip-

ment on 24 May 1994. K-15-powered upgraded aircraft are designated **I-22M93**.

Dedicated combat versions have also been proposed. The two-seat **M-95** reconnaissance/close-support version features a new supercritical wing, 30-mm integral cannon, reprofiled nose and tail, and eight underwing hardpoints. It would be fitted with foreign engines such as the Rolls-Royce Viper, General Electric J85 or Larzac 04P20. A similar single-seat fighter/attack version, fitted with wingtip missile rails, is designated **M-97S**. A second single-seat variant, the **M-97MS**, resembles the M-97S but is a simplified version, lacking a ventral gunpack and some avionics systems. It is likely that all these versions would be powered, at least initially, by 3,968-lb (17.65-kN) D-18A engines. Developed to compete with the now-defunct Skorpion, the **M-99 Orkan** single-seat battlefield support aircraft features a larger wing (with tip-mounted missile rails), larger engines and a forward fuselage section similar to that of the M-97MS.

SPECIFICATION

PZL I-22 Iryda

Wing: span 9.60 m (31 ft 6 in); aspect ratio 4.6; area 19.92 m^2 (214.42 sq ft)
Fuselage and tail: length 13.22 m (43 ft 4.5 in); height 4.30 m (14 ft 1.25 in); tailplane span 4.90 m (16 ft 1 in); wheel track 2.71 m (8 ft 10.75 in); wheel base 4.92 m (16 ft 1.75 in)
Powerplant: two PZL Rzeszow PZL-5 SO-3W22 turbojets each rated at 10.79 kN (2,425 lb st)
Weights: empty 4700 kg (10,361 lb); normal take-off 6650 kg (14,660 lb); maximum take-off 6900 kg (15,512 lb)
Fuel and load: internal fuel 1974 kg (4,352 lb); external fuel up to 600 kg (1,323 lb) in two 400-litre (106-US gal) drop tanks; maximum ordnance 1200 kg (2,646 lb)
Speed: maximum level speed 'clean' at 5000 m (16,405 ft) 840 km/h (453 kt; 522 mph); maximum cruising speed at 5000 m (16,405 ft) 720 km/h (389 kt; 447 mph); economical cruising speed at 5000 m (16,405 ft) 570 km/h (308 kt; 354 mph)
Range: ferry range 900 km (485 nm; 559 miles); range 420 km (226 nm; 261 miles) with maximum ordnance
Performance: maximum rate of climb at sea level 1500 m (4,921 ft) per minute; service ceiling 11000 m

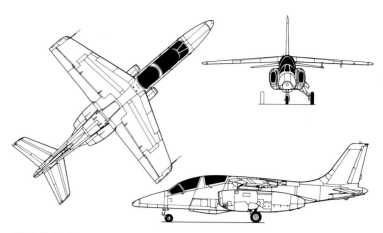

PZL I-22 Iryda

(36,090 ft); take-off run 785 m (2,575 ft) at normal take-off weight; take-off distance to 15 m (50 ft) 1260 m (4,135 ft) at normal take-off weight; landing distance from 15 m (50 ft) 1375 m (4,512 ft) at normal landing weight with brake chute; landing run 750 m (2,461 ft) at normal landing weight with brake chute
g limits: -4 to +8

While the Iryda has spent a long time under development, the first PZL-5-engined examples are now entering service at the Polish air force academy in Deblin. These will soon be joined by higher-powered I-22M92s.

PZL Mielec **TS-11 Iskra**

The **PZL Mielec TS-11 Iskra** (Spark) was designed to meet a Warsaw Pact specification for a jet-powered basic and advanced trainer. The prototype made its maiden flight on 5 February 1960. It lost an evaluation against the Czech Aero L-29, after which the latter aircraft was selected for production for the USSR and most of its clients. Poland, with its own aircraft industry to support, chose to develop the Iskra for its own use, and the aircraft entered quantity production in 1963. The first Iskra was formally handed over to the **Polish air force** in March 1963, and the type entered service in 1964.

A mid-wing monoplane of all-metal construction, the TS-11 has a pod-and-boom type fuselage structure, adopted to raise the tail unit well clear of the efflux of the turbojet engine, mounted within the fuselage aft of the cockpit. The instructor and pupil are in tandem on lightweight ejection seats, the instructor's (rear) seat being slightly raised, and both positions are enclosed by a one-piece canopy which is hinged at its rear edge and is jettisonable. The retractable tricycle landing gear has a pneumatic emergency extension system, and underwing hardpoints allow for the carriage of training weapons. Fully aerobatic, the Iskra is stressed to *g* limits of +8/-4.

The early production Iskra was powered initially by the Polish-designed H-10 turbojet

The Indian Air Force's Air Academy at Hakimpet (formerly the Fighter Training Wing) is the only TS-11 operator outside its native Poland. The oldest of these Iskras are approaching their 20th anniversary. Competition among Western manufacturers, particularly BAe and Dassault, to replace them is now hotting up.

of 7.65 kN (1,720 lb) thrust, pending availability of the intended 9.81-kN (2,205-lb) thrust SO-1 turbojet designed by the Instytut Lotnictwa and manufactured by WSK-PZL Rzeszow; from the late 1960s, the SO-1 was often replaced by the improved SO-3 of similar thrust rating.

There have been a confusing number of sub-variants, including the **Iskra-Bis A** with two underwing hardpoints and the **Iskra-Bis B** with four. A single-seat reconnaissance version was designated **Iskra-Bis C** and first flew in June 1972, but was not built in large numbers. At one time the single-seat prototype was known as the **Iskra 200**. The **Iskra-Bis D** or **Iskra 200SB** was a two-seat trainer able to carry a wider range of weapons, and 50 of these were exported to **India** between October 1975 and June 1976 for advanced flying training (unarmed) with the Air Force Academy at Hakimpet. At least five have been

lost in spinning and engine-related (flameout) accidents.

Production of the Iskra was halted in 1979, after about 500 Iskras had been built, then resumed in 1982. The only variant produced after 1982 was the **Iskra-Bis DF**. This was a dedicated reconnaissance trainer with an AFA-39 camera in each air intake fairing and one in the rear cockpit floor. The 23-mm cannon in the starboard forward fuselage was retained, along with its associated camera gun, and four underwing

pylons. Avionics include an RS6106 VHF, and ALR-1603 radio compass.

Six Iskra Bis DFs have been converted to **TS-11R** configuration with weather radar in a reshaped nose (and a display in the backseat) and three Russian AFA-39 cameras. These replaced ageing SBLim-2As (recceconfigured Polish-built MiG-15UTIs) with the navy's 7th Regiment at Siemirowice. Iskras remain in Polish air force service with 58 LPSz at Deblin, 60 LPSz at Radom and 66 LPSz at Tomaszow Mazowieckie.

PZL TS-11 Iskra

SPECIFICATION

PZL Mielec TS-11 Iskra-bis B
Wing: span 10.06 m (33 ft 0 in); aspect ratio 5.71; area 17.50 m² (188.37 sq ft)
Fuselage and tail: length 11.17 m (36 ft 7.75 in); height 3.50 m (11 ft 5.5 in); tailplane span 3.84 m (12 ft 7.25 in); wheel track 3.48 m (11 ft 5 in); wheel base 3.44 m (11 ft 3.5 in)
Powerplant: one IL SO-3 turbojet rated at 9.81 kN (2,205 lb st)
Weights: empty 2560 kg (5,644 lb); normal take-off

3800 kg (8,377 lb); maximum take-off 3840 kg (8,465 lb)
Fuel and load: internal fuel 1200 litres (317 US gal); external fuel none; maximum ordnance 400 kg (882 lb)
Speed: never exceed speed 750 km/h (405 kt; 466 mph); maximum level speed 'clean' at 5000 m (16,405 ft) 720 km/h (414 kt; 477 mph); cruising speed at optimum altitude 600 km/h (324 kt; 373 mph)
Range: standard range 1250 km (674 nm; 776 miles)
Performance: maximum rate of climb at sea level 888 m (2,913 ft) per minute; climb to 6000 m (19,685 ft) in 9 minutes 36 seconds; service ceiling 11000 m (36,090 ft); take-off run 700 m (2,296 ft) at normal take-off weight; take-off distance to 15 m (50 ft) 1190 m (3,904 ft) at normal take-off weight; landing distance from 15 m (50 ft) 1110 m (3.642 ft) at normal landing weight; landing run 650 m (2,132 ft) at normal landing weight
g limits: -4 to +8

PZL Mielec (Antonov) An-28 'Cash'

The **An-28** was derived from the Antonov An-14 (described separately) and was originally known as the **An-14M**. The prototype retained little more than the basic configuration of the An-14 and similar high-lift devices, double-slotted flaps and single-slotted ailerons. The An-14M prototype made its maiden flight in September 1969; it had a retractable undercarriage, but this was felt to impose an unacceptable cost and weight penalty and subsequent aircraft had simpler non-retractable levered undercarriage units. Changes were sufficient for a new designation of An-28 to be allocated. Development was protracted and production was assigned to PZL Mielec in 1978, the first Polish-built aircraft making its maiden flight on 22 July 1984.

The An-28 has double the capacity of the earlier aircraft, accommodating two pilots and up to 17 passengers, or a 2000-kg (4,409-lb) payload. The cabin is fitted with an internal cargo-handling hoist of 500-kg (1,102-lb) capacity. The aircraft incorporates several novel stall-protection devices, including tailplane slats which improve high angle-of-attack handling and also prevent ice from collecting on the tailplanes themselves if the normal anti-icing system fails. If an engine fails, a spoiler automatically opens in front of the opposite aileron, reducing wing drop.

Most production has been for civilian customers, although three **An-28B1R Bryza**s have been delivered to the Polish air force for SAR duties. These feature improved avionics, GPS, Doppler nav, ventral SRN-441XA search radar, flares, dinghy and stretchers. The air force has a requirement for eight, and also operates a small number of transport An-28s.

SPECIFICATION

PZL Mielec (Antonov) An-28 'Cash'
Wing: span 22.063 m (72 ft 4.5 in); aspect ratio 12.25; area 39.72 m² (427.56 sq ft)
Fuselage and tail: length 13.10 m (42 ft 11.75 in); height 4.90 m (16 ft 1 in); tailplane span 5.14 m (16 ft 10.25 in); wheel track 3.405 m (11 ft 2 in); wheel base 4.354 m (14 ft 3.5 in)
Powerplant: two WSK-PZL Rzeszów (Glushenkov) TWD-10B turboprops each rated at 716 kW (960 shp)
Weights: empty equipped 3900 kg (8,598 lb); maximum take-off 6500 kg (14,330 lb)
Fuel and load: internal fuel 1529 kg (3,371 lb); external fuel none; maximum payload 2000 kg (4,409 lb)

Speed: never exceed speed 390 km/h (210 kt; 242 mph); maximum level speed 'clean' and maximum cruising speed at 3000 m (9,845 ft) 350 km/h (188 kt; 217 mph); economical cruising speed at 3000 m (9,845 ft) 335 km/h (181 kt; 208 mph)
Range: range 1365 km (736 nm; 848 miles) with a 1000-kg (2,205-lb) payload and maximum fuel, or 560 km (302 nm; 348 miles) with maximum payload
Performance: maximum rate of climb at sea level 500 m (1,640 ft) per minute; service ceiling more than 6000 m (19,685 ft); take-off run 260 m (853 ft) at maximum take-off weight; take-off distance to 10.7 m (35 ft) 360 m (1,180 ft) at maximum take-off weight; landing distance from 10.7 m (35 ft) 315 m (1,035 ft) at normal landing weight; landing run 170 m (558 ft) at normal landing weight
g limits: +3

Alongside its naval SAR-configured 'Bryzas', the Polish air force operates a small number of standard transport An-28s.

PZL Swidnik (Mil) Mi-2 'Hoplite'

PZL Swidnik SA
ul.Przodowników Pracy 1,
21-045 Swidnik k/Lublina, Poland

The **PZL Swidnik Mi-2**, which has the NATO reporting name **'Hoplite'**, derives from the Soviet Mil Design Bureau, as indicated by the 'Mi-2' in its designation. At first intended as a replacement for the Mil Mi-1 and flown initially during September 1961, two prototypes were completed and flying before, in January 1964, an agreement was concluded with the Polish government under which PZL at Swidnik was given full responsibility for the development, manufacture and marketing of this helicopter. Following licence-production of 1,700 Mil-1 'Hare' Soviet helicopters built from 1955, the first Polish-built Mi-2 made its maiden flight on 4 November 1965, the first of over 5,000 built at the Swidnik factory.

Of conventional pod-and-boom configuration, with three-bladed main and two-bladed anti-torque tail rotors, the Mi-2 has twin-turbine powerplant mounted above the cabin, non-retractable tricycle landing gear, and a cabin that seats a pilot and up to eight passengers in an air-conditioned environment.

Seats are easily removable to permit the carriage of up to 700 kg (1,543 lb) of cargo and, in an ambulance role, the cabin can accommodate four stretchers and a medical attendant, or two stretchers and two seated casualties. For freight lifting, an external cargo hook of 800-kg (1,764-lb) capacity can be installed, this weight representing the Mi-2's maximum payload.

PZL not only licence-built the Mil Mi-2 but also embarked on an ambitious programme of development and modification to improve the basic helicopter and equip it for other roles. Dedicated air ambulance, agricultural, survey and TV relay versions were built, as well as a number of specific military variants.

Mil Mi-2Ts with dual controls serve as trainers, and **Mi-2R**s have a 120-kg (264-lb) capacity rescue winch, while more offensive variants include the **Mi-2US**, **Mi-2URN** and **Mi-2URP**. The Mi-2US sports a single NS-23KM cannon mounted on the port side of the cabin, below door and floor level, fed from an ammunition box in the cabin. This is aimed by the pilot, using a collimator-type PKV gunsight. It can also carry vestigial stub pylons for four 7.62-mm PK machine-guns.

Unarmed Mi-2s operate alongside Polish Mi-8/-17 units, while armed variants serve with the air force's two Mi-24 attack regiments.

Two more 7.62-mm machine-guns (each with 500 rounds) can be pintle-mounted in the rear windows.

The Mi-2URN was developed in 1973 and retains the NS-23 cannon, and carries two 57-mm Mars 2 rocket pods instead of the pylon-mounted machine-guns. The 1976-vintage Mi-2URP is similar, but carries up to four 9M14M Malyutka (AT-3 'Sagger') anti-tank missiles on its pylons. The **Mil Mi-2CH** is an unidentified military sub-type used by the Polish air force, while the **Mil Mi-2RM** is a naval variant. Improved **Mi-2B** versions are also available, with a revised electrical system and advanced navaids.

Some Warsaw Pact air forces may have used numerical designations for their Mi-2 sub-types. East Germany certainly used the designation **Variant 56** for one sub-type, **Variant 55** for the maritime version, and **Variant 51** for a reconnaissance sub-type. Designations for EW and artillery-spotting versions remain unknown.

In the late 1970s, PZL Swidnik, in conjunction with the Allison Division of General Motors in the USA, developed an export version of the Mil Mi-2 fitted with two Allison turboshaft engines. Given the names **Kania** or **Kitty Hawk**, they were generally similar to the PZL Swidnik Mi-2, being conversions of production airframes. The first (SP-PSA) was flown on 3 June 1979 and was intended, like the standard Mi-2, to fulfil a variety of roles. It could accommodate a pilot and a maximum of nine passengers or, alternatively, pilot and co-pilot plus eight passengers, and the cabin seats were removable to allow use in the agricultural or air ambulance roles. Reconfigured, it could carry up to 800 kg (1,764 lb) of cargo, some externally slung. The number ultimately converted (to the **Kania Model 1**) is believed

to have totalled four prototypes plus half a dozen definitive aircraft.

In August 1978, PZL Swidnik concluded an agreement with the Spitfire Helicopter Company of the US allowing them to market a modified version of the Kania as the **Spitfire Taurus**. This differed primarily from the Polish version by introducing up-rated Allison 250-C28 turboshafts, each with a take-off rating of 373 kW (500 shp)

fed by a large common intake, and having revised nose contours and a ventral fin. The company has since gone out of business.

More than 5,250 Mil Mi-2s had been built by the time production was suspended in 1991, pending PZL's 1992 privatisation. Mi-2s (but no Kanias) have been exported to a number of military customers, and remain in service in **Bulgaria** (14), **Cuba** (two for liaison), **Czech** and **Slovak Republics**

(38), **Hungary** (31), **Nicaragua** (two), **Poland** (113), **Romania** (six), **CIS** (about 750) and **Syria** (20).

Ethiopia, Iraq, Lesotho, Libya and North Korea have been quoted as Mi-2 operators, but none is believed to operate the aircraft now. East Germany took delivery of 44, and the surviving 36 were handed over to the Luftwaffe on reunification but were not taken into service.

PZL Swidnik **W-3 Sokól**

Although developed from the Mil Mi-2, the **W-3 Sokól** (Falcon) is a new design, retaining the configuration of the 'Hoplite' but with larger overall dimensions and extensive aerodynamic and structural changes. The first of five prototypes made its maiden flight on 16 November 1979, and the second, incorporating further changes, on 6 May 1982. Production began in 1985.

The aircraft has a new four-bladed fully-articulated main rotor, with tapered tips and a pendular Saloman-type vibration absorber. Bladder tanks below the floor give a combined capacity of 1700 litres (374 Imp gal) and there is provision for a 1100-litre (242-Imp gal) auxiliary tank. The cabin accommodates 12 in three-abreast rows, with access via sliding doors on each side of the cabin.

The first batch of 50 was completed in 1991, and another batch of 20 is under construction. Military customers include **Myanmar** (12) and **Poland**. Operating units com-

prise the navy (six), the 47th Helicopter Training Regiment at Nowe Miasto (six), the 36th Special Air Transport Regiment at Warsaw/Okecie (one), and the Straz (a paramilitary fire brigade) at Bemow (three).

Four of the Polish navy's aircraft are designated **W-3R Anakonda**, with six flotation bags and a rescue winch. They have an extra window in the lower half of each flight deck door, and have a sealed watertight cabin. The type was evaluated against the Mi-14PS in 1989, resulting in a 1992 order for 25 aircraft. Those delivered so far (two W-3s and the W-3Rs) serve with the 18 Eskandra. The **W-3U-1 Alligator** is a proposed ASW version. The unflown **W-3 Sokól-Long** has engines uprated to 1,000 shp (746 kW), and a stretched cabin seating 14 fully-equipped troops. Development was discontinued in early 1993, but plans for an EW variant remain.

At least one W-3 has been flown with a

GSh-23L cannon pack mounted along the port lower fuselage, and with an undernose EO package similar to that of the Mi-24V 'Hind-E'. The AT-6 ATGM command guidance radome is mounted in the nose. Outriggers carry two 10-round 80-mm rocket pods and four AT-6 'Spiral' missile launch tubes. In April 1993, PZL received an export order for a similar armed version, the **W-3 Huzar**, with an undernose 20-mm low-recoil cannon (in an AH-64-type mounting) and with a stabilised roof-mounted TV/IR sight for the laser-guided Grot missile. Provision is made for a laser rangefinder and a helmet-mounted sight. Alternative weapons can include the 16-round Mars-2 rocket pod, ZR-8 four-round rocket packs or 9M32M Strzala (SA-7 'Grail') AAMs.

In conjunction with Denel's guided weapons subsidiary, Kentron, PZL offered an export Huzar variant with a weapons system based largely on that of the CSH-2 Rooivalk attack helicopter. Armament included the ZT-3 laser-guided ATM, a turreted 20-mm cannon, and rocket pods. However, the agreement was terminated in

mid-1994, and PZL is continuing to examine both Western and Russian ATGMs, such as the 9M120 Vikhr missile.

SPECIFICATION

PZL Swidnik W-3 Sokól
Rotor System: rotor diameter 15.70m (51 ft 6 in); rotor disc area 193.6 m2 (2,083.8 sq ft)
Fuselage and tail: length, fuselage 14.21 m (46 ft 7½ in); height, to top of rotor head 4.12 m (13 ft 6¼ in); wheel track 3.40 m (1 ft 2 in)
Powerplant: two WSK-PZL Rzeszów TWD-10W turboshafts, rated at 671-kW (900-shp) for take-off
Weights: minimum basic empty 3300 kg (7,275 lb); normal take-off 6400 kg (14,110 lb)
Fuel and load: maximum payload 2100 kg (4,630 lb)
Speed: never exceed speed 145 kt (270km/h; 167 mph); maximum cruising speed 127 kt (235 km/h; 146 mph)
Range: with auxiliary fuel, no reserves 661 nm (1225 km/761 miles)
Performance: service ceiling 4650 m (15,250 ft); hovering ceiling, in ground effect 2500 m (8,200 ft), out of ground effect 660 m (2,165 ft); maximum rate of climb, at sea level 492 m (1,615 ft) per minute

Left: The W-3 Sokól entered service with the Straz unit of the Polish Ministry of the Interior, near Warsaw.

Right: The sole Bendix-King avionics-equipped W-3SP Anakonda Special began tests in mid-1993 at Bemowo.

PZL Warszawa-Okecie **PZL-104 Wilga**

PZL Warszawa-Okecie
Aleja Krakowska 110/114,
PL-00-971 Warsaw, Poland

The original **PZL 104 Wilga** (Thrush) prototype, powered by a 134-kW (180-hp) Narkiewicz WN-6 flat-six piston engine, first flew on 24 April 1962. It was intended to replace the Polish-built Yak-12 and its **PZL-101 Gawron** development. A cantilever high-wing monoplane with fixed tailwheel gear and an enclosed cabin, it was followed by the **Wilga 2P** and **Wilga CP**, powered by the 138-kW (185-hp) Narkiewicz WN-6RB2 and 168-kW (220-hp) Continental O-470-13A or O-470-L flat-six engines, respectively. The PZL 104 was offered initially in versions equipped for use as a four-seat passenger-carrying or liaison aircraft; for club flying, glider towing or parachuting; for agricultural use with a 500-litre (110-Imp gal) hopper for dust or liquid application; and as an air ambulance carrying pilot, doctor, two stretcher patients and medical equipment.

Following construction of a number of prototypes, the type entered production initially as the **Wilga 3A** club aircraft and the **Wilga 3S** air ambulance. In 1967 the design was revised with better cabin accommodation and improved landing gear, production beginning in 1968 of the **Wilga 35** which, powered by a 194-kW (260-hp) Ivchenko Al-14R engine, had flown for the

first time on 28 July 1967, and of the **Wilga 32** with a 172-kW (230-hp) Continental O-470-K flown on 12 September 1967. This last version was built under licence in Indonesia as the **Lipnur Gelatik 32** (Rice Bird), with a Continental O-470-R engine of similar output.

Developments of the Wilga 35 have included the multi-purpose Wilga 35M fitted with a 261-kW (360-hp) M-14P radial engine, flown in prototype form in 1990. A similar version, meeting US FAR Part 23 requirements, is designated the **Wilga 80**. The first of these flew on 30 May 1979. A more radical redesign, originally identified as the **Wilga 88**, has become the **PZL 105 Flamingo**. The Wilga 35 and revised 80 remained in production in 1993, by which time PZL had sold around 900 examples to countries around the world.

In an emergency, many civilian Wilgas would be impressed by the military and flown by reservists in the liaison, artillery-spotting, special forces insertion and even light attack roles. Some 15 Wilgas are also permanently on Polish air force charge, operating in the liaison role. Other military Wilgas serve in **Russia**, **Mongolia**, **Egypt** (10), and **Indonesia** (army and air force, totalling 24 Wilga 32s).

SPECIFICATION

PZL Warszawa PZL-104 Wilga 35
Wing: span 11.12 m (36 ft 5.75 in); aspect ratio 8.0; area 15.50 m2 (166.85 sq ft)
Fuselage and tail: length 8.10 m (26 ft 6.75 in); height 2.96 m (9 ft 8.5 in); tailplane span 3.70 m (12 ft 1.75 in); wheel track 2.75 m (9 ft 0.75 in)
Powerplant: one PZL (Ivchenko) Al-14RA flat-six piston engine rated at 260 hp (194 kW)
Weights: empty equipped 870 kg (1,918 lb); maximum take-off 1300 kg (2,866 lb)
Fuel and load: internal fuel 195 litres (51.5 US gal); external fuel none
Speed: never exceed speed 279 km/h (150 kt; 173

mph); maximum cruising speed at optimum altitude 157 km/h (84 kt; 97 mph)
Range: 510 km (275 nm; 317 miles)
Performance: maximum rate of climb at sea level 276 m (905 ft) per minute; climb to 1000 m (3,280 ft) in 3 minutes 0 seconds; service ceiling 4040 m (13,250 ft); take-off run 121 m (397 ft) at maximum take-off weight on a grass runway

PZL Warszawa PZL-104 Wilga 80
generally similar to the PZL Warszawa PZL-104 Wilga 35 except in the following particulars:
Wing: span 11.13 m (36 ft 6.25 in)
Fuselage and tail: length 8.03 m (26 ft 4.25 in)
Powerplant: one PZL (Ivchenko) Al-14RA-KAF rated at 260 hp (194 kW)

The PZL-104 became the first aircraft to be licence-built in Indonesia when 10 were initially assembled by Lipnur, as the Gelatik, for the army.

PZL Warszawa-Okecie PZL-130/T Orlik/Turbo Orlik

The **PZL-130 Orlik** (Spotted Eaglet) primary and basic trainer was designed as the airframe component of an overall training system which also included a simulator and an electronic diagnosis system. A team under Andrzej Frydrychewicz began detail design of this tandem two-seat trainer in the autumn of 1983.

Of all-metal construction, the **PZL-130 Orlik** was a low-wing monoplane, the wing incorporating single-slotted trailing-edge flaps and Frise-type ailerons; the tricycle landing gear is retracted and lowered pneumatically, and powerplant consisted of a Vedeneyev M-14Pm radial engine driving a constant-speed propeller. Both wing and tail unit leading edges had provision for the installation of an anti-icing system, if required. Access to the cockpit was via the sideways-hinged one-piece canopy (jettisonable in flight), the pupil being seated forward and the instructor aft on electrically adjustable seats, with the instructor's raised slightly. Full dual controls were standard, as was heating and ventilation for the cockpit.

The Orlik represents the airborne component of what is known as the 'System 130', which includes the PZL-130 Profesor flight simulator from which the student gains initial familiarisation before taking to the air in the Orlik. The remaining component of System 130 is the PZL-130 Inspektor, intended to ensure maximum utilisation of the Orlik fleet by providing automatic diagnosis of engine and system faults. One other advanced feature of the Orlik is the use of easily-changed modular displays and instruments in the cockpits; this feature is intended to allow use of the aircraft as a flying simulator for a variety of aircraft. The Orlik is intended to serve for the full spectrum of civil and military training, ranging from preselection to aerobatics, and including air combat, air gunnery, ground attack and reconnaissance.

Construction of four airframes – one for static testing plus three flying prototypes – began in 1982, and the first aircraft (SP-PCA) flew on 12 October 1983, followed quickly by the second. However, the third aircraft did not fly until January 1985, and the two pre-production machines which followed did not take to the air until February 1988, owing to serious delays in deliveries of the 246-kW (330-hp) Vedeneyev M14PM nine-cylinder Soviet powerplant. By that time PZL was seriously looking for another engine, and one contender was the company-produced but less powerful Kalisz K8-AA, which took the underpowered second pre-production aircraft ('006') into the air in March 1988. Although testing continued over the next two years, and included an evaluation by the Polish air force, the piston-engined Orlik was abandoned in 1990.

Turboprop power

In 1984, while still awaiting supplies of the Vedeneyev M14PM engine, PZL commenced development of a turboprop-powered Orlik. Accordingly, SP-PCC, the third airframe (of six original piston-engined aircraft, one a static test airframe) was re-engined with a Pratt & Whitney PT6A-25A engine and reregistered SP-RCC. It made its maiden flight in this configuration on 13 July 1986, but was lost in a crash in January 1987. A seventh Orlik was flown with a 750-shp (560-kW) Motorlet M601E as the **PZL-130TM**, and an eighth (SP-WCA) with a 550-shp (415-kW) PT6A-25A as the **PZL-130T**. The ninth was built with a PT6A-62 as the **PZL-130TP**, and two more aircraft were built during 1991 with M601E and PT6A engines.

The Polish air force production trainer, the **PZL-130TB**, was derived from the PZL-130TM, and is powered by an M601E engine, although the fully aerobatic M601T is also available as an option. The wing is increased in span and in incidence, lowering the nose in normal cruising flight. The ventral fin is redesigned, and double-slotted trailing-edge flaps are provided. The cockpit is closely related to that of the Su-22, and is covered by a canopy of revised shape. The prototype was rolled out in May 1991, and first flew on 18 September. The aircraft is fitted with East European avionics and indigenous LFK-K1 zero-70 (0 ft altitude, minimum 70 kt forward speed) ejection seats. Six underwing hardpoints are provided (inboard and centre stressed for loads of up to 160 kg/353 lb, outboard to 80 kg/176 lb) for bombs, Zeus 7.62-mm gun pods, 57-mm or 80-mm rocket pods, or even Strela IR-homing AAMs. Forty-eight have been ordered for the Polish air force.

Three similar versions are available for export, all equipped with Western avionics (to customer specification) and powered by Western engines. The **PZL-130TC** is the most potent, with a 950-shp (708-kW) Pratt & Whitney Canada PT6A-62 engine, Bendix King avionics and a Martin-Baker ejection seat, while the 750-shp (559-kW) PT6A-25C-powered **PZL-130TD** is equipped identically. The PZL-130TC first flew in early June 1993, after a delay reportedly due to the refusal of PZL test pilots to fly it on account of the new high-powered engine. The PZL-130TD followed in November of that year. The **PZL-130TE** is a proposed 'economy' export version, with no ejection seats, limited avionics and a 550-shp (410-kW) PT6A-25A engine. No export orders have yet been placed, although the aircraft has reportedly been evaluated by Israel and South Africa.

In late 1993, PZL applied for the Turbo-Orlik to be certified in the USA, and distributed by Illinois-based Cadmus (already PZL's general aviation distributor for North America). The PZL-130TC was the chosen version, but this variant was then grounded (in Poland) in October 1993, setting back the flight test programme significantly. At first this was believed to be the fault of the PT6A-62 engine, but PZL later admitted that financial constraints on the leased turboprops largely had forced them to halt flying.

By mid-1994, nine PZL-130TBs had been delivered to the Polish air force's 45 LED at Radom and 60 LPSz at Deblin. A further 15 aircraft are due to be delivered by the end of the year, and 15 pilots trained. Aircraft serial 009, the prototype PZL-130TB, has been converted to a version similar to the PZL-130TC with new avionics and ejection seats, designated **PZL-130TC1**, and it has been suggested that similar improved versions will comprise a portion of the air force's 48-aircraft order.

SPECIFICATION

PZL Warszawa PZL-130TB Turbo Orlik
Wing: span 9.00 m (29 ft 6¼ in); aspect ratio 6.23; area 13 m² (139.93 sq ft)
Fuselage and tail: length 9.00 m (29 ft 6¼ in); height 3.53 m (11 ft 7 in); tailplane span 3.50 m (11 ft 5¾ in); wheel track 3.10 m (10 ft 2 in); wheel base 2.90 m (9 ft 6 in)
Powerplant: one Motorlet M601E turboprop, rated at 750 kW (560 hp)
Weights: empty equipped 1600 kg (3, 527 lb); normal take-off 2000 kg (4,409 lb) for aerobatics; maximum take-off 2700 kg (5,952 lb)
Fuel and load: internal fuel 504 litres (142.7 US gal); external fuel 340 litres (90 US gal)
Speed: maximum level speed 'clean' at optimum altitude 501 km/h (270 kt; 311 mph)
Range: with maximum fuel 970 km (523 nm; 602 miles)
Performance: maximum rate of climb at sea level 798 m (2,620 ft) per minute; service ceiling, TC only 10,060 m (33,000 ft); take-off run 222 m (729 ft) at normal take-off weight
g limits: -3 to +6 at normal take-off weight or -1.76 to +4.4 at maximum take-off weight

Left: Initial production Orliks for the Polish air force are powered by the Motorlet M601E.

Right: The PZL-130TC has been re-engined with a PT6A-62. At first, test pilots refused to fly with this radically new engine.

PZL Warszawa-Okecie PZL-230F Skorpion

The **PZL-230F** was designed to meet a Polish air force requirement for a small, agile battlefield attack (SABA) aircraft. Development began in 1987, when the aircraft was envisaged as being powered by a pair of turbojet engines. These were soon replaced by twin pusher Pratt & Whitney Canada PT6A-67A turboprops, and then replaced again by unspecified turbofans (possibly two 5,225-lb st/23.24-kN Pratt & Whitney Canada PW305s) mounted further apart. This engine configuration was demonstrated in the full-scale mock-up that was rolled out on 23 December 1992.

The mock-up differed in many ways from previous artist's impressions of the aircraft, with a higher-set cockpit and canard foreplanes, and twin inward-canted tailfins in place of the original single fin. The basic philosophy behind the **Skorpion** was to produce a highly manoeuvrable but relatively slow (600-650 km/h; 350-400 mph) aircraft,

capable of evading SAMs and of carrying a 2000-kg (4,409-lb) warload on its eight underwing weapons pylons. A fixed gun was also envisaged, perhaps a 25-mm GAU-12. PZL planned for a first flight in 1996, with deliveries following in 2000.

Development of the Skorpion was terminated in June 1994. A more likely SABA candidate is a single-seat attack version of the I-22 Iryda (described separately), but in September 1993 PZL unveiled a second advanced contender in the form of the **PZL Kobra**, powered by a pair of thrust-vectoring Polish-built D-18 turbofan engines.

A full-size wooden mock-up of the PZL-230F Skorpion was unveiled at the Okecie plant in early 1993. The canard-equipped, double-delta design is intended to carry a podded GAU-8 30-mm cannon.

Reims Aviation-Cessna F406 Caravan II

Reims Aviation SA
Aérodrome de Reims Prunay, BP 1745
F-51062 Reims, France

Although Reims Aviation had built over 6,350 Cessna-designed aircraft by 1992, the US firm sold its 49 per cent interest in the French associate early in 1989. The sole aircraft in production at Reims in the early 1990s was the jointly-developed **F406 Caravan II** and its fisheries-protection counterpart with Ferranti Seaspray radar, the **Vigilant**. The aircraft is basically a turbine-powered **Cessna Titan**, itself derived from the **Cessna 402** twin-turbo-prop light business and 12/14-seat utility transport. Two **F406 Vigilant**s have been delivered to the Scottish Fisheries Protection Agency. Para-military users include the French customs service, which has four equipped with Crouzet Nadir navigation computer, and Bendix RDR 1500 radar with 360° scan in an underbelly radome.

Military operations are restricted to two target-towing aircraft operated by **French Army Light Aviation** (ALAT) for anti-aircraft artillery training, which were delivered

to the Peloton d'Avions (Aeroplane Platoon) of 3 Groupe d'Hélicoptères Légers (3 Light Helicopter Group) at Rennes in May/June 1987. The target gear, which includes 7 km (4.35 miles) of cable, may be quickly exchanged for nine passenger seats. Normally towing sleeve targets, the aircraft are regularly used over the ranges at Biscarosse and Toulon, and have also flown at Cherbourg, Veule-les-Roses, Mailly, Suippes, Canjuers and Baumholder (Germany).

Nearly 100 F406s have been built by Reims Aviation, which is 100 per cent French-owned. This is one of two target-tug versions operated by the ALAT.

SPECIFICATION

Reims-Cessna F 406 Caravan II
Wing: span 15.08 m (49 ft 5.75 in); aspect ratio 9.7; area 23.50 m² (252.96 sq ft)
Fuselage and tail: length 11.89 m (39 ft 0 in); height 4.01 m (13 ft 2 in); tailplane span 5.87 m (19 ft 3 in); wheel track 4.28 m (14 ft 0.5 in); wheel base 3.81 m (12 ft 5.875 in)
Powerplant: two Pratt & Whitney Canada PT6A-112

turboprops each rated at 500 shp (373 kW)
Weights: empty equipped 2460 kg (5,423 lb); maximum take-off 4468 kg (9,850 lb)
Fuel and load: internal fuel 1444 kg (3,183 lb); external fuel none; maximum payload 1563 kg (3,446 lb)
Speed: maximum operating speed 464 km/h (229 kt 263 mph); economical cruising speed at optimum altitude 370 km/h (200 kt; 230 mph)

Range: 2135 km (1,153 nm; 1,327 miles)
Performance: maximum rate of climb at sea level 564 m (1,850 ft) per minute; service ceiling 9145 m (30,000 ft); take-off run 526 m (1,725 ft) at maximum take-off weight; take-off distance to 15 m (50 ft) 803 m (2,635 ft) at maximum take-off weight; landing distance from 15 m (50 ft) 674 m (2,212 ft) at normal landing weight without propeller reversal

---

RFB Fantrainer and Ranger 2000

Rhein-Flugzeugbau Gmbh
Flugplatz (PO Box 408), D-4050 Mönchengladbach 1
Germany

The **RFB Fantrainer** is a two-seat primary and basic trainer and is a product of the Rhein Flugzeugbau company (which has successively been a subsidiary of VFW-Fokker, MBB and now ABS International). The configuration of the Fantrainer is unusual, with propulsion provided by an integral ducted fan, i.e. a small-diameter pusher propeller rotating in a shroud to provide thrust efficiently and allow for an aerodynamically clean airframe design. After this concept had been proved with the two-seat (side-by-side) **Fanliner** flown late in 1973, RFB obtained German Ministry of Defence backing for two prototypes of the **AWI-2 Fantrainer**. These featured tandem seating and the first, flown on 27 October 1977, was powered by two 150-hp (112-kW) Audi NSU EA 871-L Wankel rotary engines. A 420-shp (313-kW) Allison 250-C20B turboshaft was used in the second prototype, flown on 31 May 1978.

Production versions of the Fantrainer were of similar configurations to the prototypes, and were launched in August 1982 when the **Royal Thai air force** ordered 47. Thirty-one of these were to be **Fantrainer 400**s and 16 **Fantrainer 600**s, with one of each completed in Germany and the balance supplied in kit form for assembly in Thailand by the RTAF. Changes from the second prototype included a 15-cm (6-

in) fuselage stretch, an enlarged canopy for improved all-round vision, relocation of the air intakes above the wings and an improved fan reduction gearbox allowing full utilisation of engine thrust. The Fantrainer 600 is fitted with a 485-kW (650-shp) Allison 250-C30 turboshaft with consequent increases in weight and performance. In addition, metal wings were designed for manufacture in Thailand in place of the composite structure of the original aircraft.

The first Fantrainer 600 flew in Germany on 12 August 1984 and deliveries to Thailand began in October 1984. However, a setback in plans to fit the locally-assembled wings to German-supplied fuselage kits delayed until 1986 the roll-out of the first indigenously-assembled aircraft. Service use of the Fantrainer 600 began in January 1987 and all 16 serve with the Flying Training School/ No. 402 Sqn at Kamphong Son. Despite delivery of all German kits by late 1987, the programme has progressed only slowly. Assembly of the Fantrainer 400s was to be completed by the end of 1991. Thai air force dissatisfaction with the type has led to their rapid replacement with Aero L-39s, among others.

In association with Rockwell, RFB (under the auspices of DASA) has entered the **Rockwell/DASA Ranger 2000** for the USAF/USN JPATS competition. Launched in

May 1991, the first of two prototypes (D-FANA) flew from Manching on 15 January 1993. The Ranger 2000 is powered by a 3,190-lb (14.19-kN) Pratt & Whitney Canada JT15D-5C turbofan. Production aircraft will be assembled by Rockwell in the USA, while programme costs will be shared 50-50 between the two partners.

SPECIFICATION

RFB Fantrainer 400
Wing: span 9.74 m (31 ft 11.5 in); aspect ratio 6.8; area 14.00 m² (150.70 sq ft)
Fuselage and tail: length 9.48 m (31 ft 1.25 in) including probe and 9.20 m (30 ft 2.25 in) excluding probe; height 3.16 m (10 ft 4.5 in); tailplane span 3.59

m (11 ft 9.5 in); wheel track 1.94 m (6 ft 4.25 in); wheel base 3.89 m (12 ft 9 in)
Powerplant: one Allison 250-C20B turboshaft rated at 420 shp (313 kW)
Weights: empty equipped 1114 kg (2,456 lb); normal take-off 1600 kg (3,527 lb) for aerobatics; maximum take-off 1800 kg (3,968 lb)
Fuel and load: internal fuel 384 kg (847 lb); external fuel none; maximum ordnance none
Speed: never exceed speed 250 kt (288 mph; 463 km/h); maximum level speed 'clean' at 10,000 ft (3050 m) 200 kt (23 mph; 370 km/h); cruising speed at 10,000 ft (3050 m) 175 kt (201 mph; 325 km/h)
Range: 640 km (737 miles; 1186 km); endurance 4 hours 36 minutes
Performance: maximum rate of climb at sea level 1,550 ft (472 m) per minute; service ceiling 20,000 ft (6096 m)

The second prototype Ranger 2000 was lost in a crash, and a replacement is now under construction. German type approval was gained in June 1994, with the first prototype.

Robin HR.100

Avions Pierre Robin's first all-metal light-plane, the four/five-seat **HR.100** low-wing monoplane, made its maiden flight on 3 April 1969. In November 1972, Robin introduced the **HR.100/285**, which was the first model in the Robin range to feature retractable tricycle landing gear. A batch of 20 generally similar **R.100/250TR**s was acquired in 1975 for service in the liaison and communications roles with the **Centre**

d'Essais en Vol at Istres, where 13 remain. The HR-100 was also operated by the CEV on behalf of the **Aéronavale** for training duties at Brétigny. A further two HR-100 lightplanes are currently operated for communications tasks by the Direction des Constructions et Armes Navales, based at Hyères and Cuers.

SPECIFICATION

Robin HR 100/250TR
Wing: span 9.08 m (29 ft 2.5 in); aspect ratio 5.36;

area 15.20 m² (163.62 sq ft)
Fuselage and tail: length 7.59 m (24 ft 10.75 in); height 2.71 m (8 ft 10.75 in); tailplane span 3.20 m (10 ft 10 in); wheel track 3.225 m (10 ft 7 in); wheel base 2.16 m (7 ft 1 in)
Powerplant: one Textron Lycoming IO-540-C4B5 flat-six air-cooled piston engine rated at 250 hp (186 kW)
Weights: empty equipped 840 kg (1,852 lb); maximum take-off 1400 kg (3,086 lb)
Fuel and load: internal fuel 440 litres (116.25 US gal); external fuel none; maximum ordnance none
Speed: never exceed speed 360 km/h (194 kt; 223 mph); maximum level speed 'clean' at sea level 315 km/h (170 kt; 196 mph); maximum cruising speed at 2135 m

(7,005 ft) 297 km/h (161 kt; 185 mph); economical cruising speed at 3050 m (10,000 ft) 285 km/h (154 kt; 177 mph)
Range: ferry range 2344 km (1,264 nm; 1,456 miles); range 2130 km (1,149 nm; 1,323 miles)
Performance: maximum rate of climb at sea level 324 m (1,065 ft) per minute; service ceiling 5700 m (18,700 ft); take-off run about 325 m (1,066 ft) at maximum take-off weight; take-off distance to 15 m (50 ft) about 600 m (1,970 ft) at maximum take-off weight; landing distance from 15 m (50 ft) about 660 m (2,166 ft) at normal landing weight; landing run about 350 m (1.150 ft) at normal landing weight

---

Robinson R22

Robinson Helicopter Company
24747 Crenshaw Boulevard, Torrance
California 90505, USA

Development of the **Robinson R22** two-seat light helicopter began in 1973, with particular emphasis on efficiency, low noise and minimum maintenance. The R22 seats two side-by-side and is equipped with full dual controls. Since the first flight of the prototype on 28 August 1975, over 2,000 examples have been delivered, primarily for

commercial use. The improved **R22 Alpha** permitted a 31.5-kg (70-lb) increase in gross weight and was certificated in October 1983. From the 501st aircraft onwards, the standard production version has been the **R22 Beta**, which introduced various detail improvements. In March 1992, the **Turkish army** became the first military user of the

R22, when 10 Betas were acquired for service with the army's Aviation Training Centre in Ankara, where they operate alongside Enstrom TH-28s. A further 40 have been ordered by **Argentina**, including 10 **R22M Mariners**. These are equipped with floats and ground wheels, and are chiefly intended for the Buenos Aires Police.

SPECIFICATION

Robinson Model R22 Beta
Rotor system: main rotor diameter 25 ft 2 in (7.67 m); tail rotor diameter 3 ft 6 in (1.07 m); main rotor disc area 497.44 sq ft (46.21 m²); tail rotor disc area 9.63 sq ft (0.89 m²)

Robinson R-22

Fuselage and tail: length overall, rotors turning 28 ft 9 in (8.76 m) and fuselage 20 ft 8 in (6.30 m); height overall 8 ft 9 in (2.67 m) to top of rotor head; skid track 6 ft 4 in (1.93 m)
Powerplant: one 160-hp (119-kW) Textron Lycoming O-320-B2C flat-four piston engine derated to 131 hp (97.5 kW)
Weights: empty 824 lb (374 kg); maximum take-off 1,370 lb (621 kg)
Fuel and load: internal fuel 115 lb (52 kg) plus provision for 63 lb (28.6 kg) of auxiliary fuel; external fuel none

Speed: never exceed speed 102 kt (118 mph; 190 km/h); maximum level speed at optimum altitude 97 kt (112 mph; 180 km/h); normal cruising speed at 8,000 ft (2440 m) 96 kt (110 mph; 177 km/h); economical cruising speed at optimum altitude 82.5 kt (95 mph; 153 km/h)
Range: range 320 nm (368 miles; 592 km) with auxiliary fuel and maximum payload
Performance: maximum rate of climb at sea level 1,200 ft (366 m) per minute; service ceiling 14,000 ft (4265 m); hovering ceiling 6,970 ft (2125 m) in ground effect

Turkish Army Aviation has a large rotary-winged fleet, gathered from several sources. In 1992, 10 R22 Betas were obtained for training.

Rockwell **B-1 Lancer**

Rockwell International Corporation
2201 North Douglas Street, PO Box 4250
Seal Beach. California 90740-8350, USA

To provide an important component of the United States' 'Triad' nuclear deterrent, studies initiated in 1962 led, in 1965, to the **USAF**'s Advanced Manned Strategic Aircraft (AMSA) requirement for a low-altitude penetration bomber. Suffering a protracted gestation, today's **Rockwell B-1B Lancer** traces its origins via the AMSA back to the **B-1A**, the winning contender in a competition for a new strategic bomber involving North American, Rockwell, General Dynamics and Boeing. Selected for further development in June 1970, the first of four B-1A prototypes made its maiden flight from Palmdale, CA, on 23 December 1974.

At that time, SAC hoped for 250 to replace ageing B-52s. Congressional opposition and a new administration culminated in its downfall, President Carter announcing in June 1977 that testing of the four prototypes would continue only as a form of 'insurance'. At the same time, he confirmed that production would be shelved.

By 1981, the political climate (and the President) had changed again and the new

occupant of the White House took a much more hard-line attitude towards the Soviet Union. An immediate beneficiary was SAC, which was informed in September 1981 that it would at last receive the long-overdue new bomber, but in reduced numbers – exactly 100 derivative B-1Bs, outwardly generally similar to the fourth B-1A prototype.

The B-1B has a blended low-wing/body configuration with variable geometry on the outer panels. The structure utilises a mixture of aluminium and diffusion bonded titanium alloy construction, with some components manufactured from GRP. The fuselage structure is strengthened to resist nuclear blast overpressure. Aft of the titanium wing pivots are overwing fairings blended into the wing trailing edges and the engine nacelles. Four General Electric F101 turbofans are mounted in pairs beneath and aft of the fixed centre-section of the wing. The nacelles are close to the CoG for optimum stability in low-altitude turbulence. The wing itself incorporates full-span seven-segment leading-edge slats and six-segment, single-

slotted trailing-edge flaps. No ailerons are provided, roll control being effected by four-segment airbrakes/spoilers on each outer wing. All flying controls are operated by an electro-hydraulic system, with the exception of the two outboard spoilers on each wing, which are fly-by-wire. High-lift devices were incorporated to ensure that the B-1 could take-off more rapidly than the B-52, and to be able to deploy quickly in times of crisis to more austere forward operating bases. Small moveable composite vanes with 30° anhedral are located below and forward of the cockpit. These sense lateral and vertical motion in turbulent flight and provide both yaw and pitch damping. The B-1B is fitted with a nose-mounted refuelling receptacle.

B-1B modifications

The absolute performance of the B-1B has been downgraded compared to the B-1A, due primarily to reasons of cost. Major airframe improvements were introduced, including strengthened landing gear, a moveable bulkhead in the forward weapons bay to allow for the carriage of a diverse range of different-sized weapons, optional weapons bay fuel tanks for increased range, and external underfuselage stores stations for additional fuel or weapons. The reduction in the B-1A's high-level supersonic (Mach 2.5) dash capability led to the replacement of the variable engine inlets with those incorporating a fixed inlet geometry. The low-altitude, high-speed penetration role against sophisticated air defence systems was to be carried out using electronic jamming equipment, IR countermeasures, radar location and warning systems, and application of 'low observables' technology.

Careful attention to intake geometry resulted in the compressor face being hidden from radar, much use also being made of

RAM on key components. Perhaps the best evidence of success in reducing the electronic 'footprint' of the Lancer is provided by the fact that its radar cross-section is at least an order of magnitude smaller than that of a B-52, yet the B-1B is only marginally smaller and is of comparable weight.

The four-man crew of the B-1B consists of pilot, co-pilot, offensive systems operator (OSO) and defensive systems operator (DSO). The pilot and co-pilot are accommodated side by side, as are the OSO and DSO who occupy a compartment at the rear of the cockpit. All four crew are seated on Weber ACES II ejection seats with zero-zero capability. These replace the original B-1A's crew escape capsule. The FBW and electromechanical flight control systems are connected to the pilot and co-pilot, with common reversionary links in event of failure. The OSO functions mainly as a navigator, being tasked with guiding the B-1B to its target and ensuring that its weaponry is released at the optimum moment. All windows can be fitted with PLZT (zirconium titanate) radiation glare shields.

The offensive avionics systems was the main responsibility of Boeing. The primary system is the Westinghouse AN/APQ-164 multi-mode offensive radar system (derived from the F-16's AN/APG-66), which includes a low-observable phased-array antenna for low-altitude terrain following and accurate navigation. Other navigation systems include a high-accuracy INS and a Honeywell ASN-121 radar altimeter. The Honeywell offensive display sets comprise three MFDs with two for the OSO (one showing threats on alphanumeric labels and one for tabulated threat information) and one for the defensive systems operator.

The latter is concerned with countering external threats and monitors the much-troubled Eaton AN/ALQ-161 system, which forms the core of the Lancer's continuously upgradable defensive capability. The system comprises an AN/ALQ-161A radio frequency surveillance/ECM system, tail warning func-

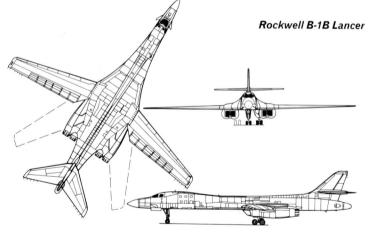

Rockwell B-1B Lancer

After a lengthy trials period, the B-1B is finally qualified to carry a maximum conventional load of 84 Mk 82 500-lb bombs.

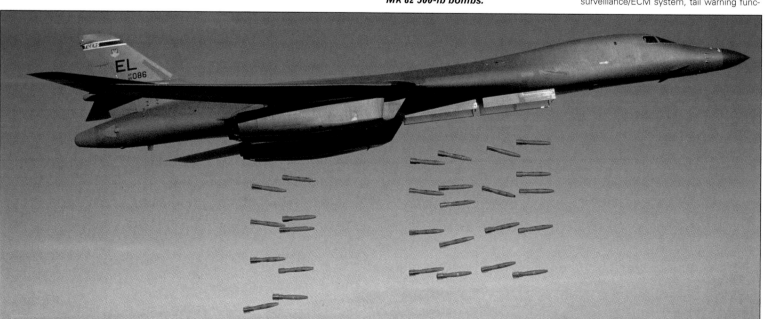

The B-1B fleet has adopted a new look, with tailcodes and an overall grey scheme. This 319th BW Lancer is based at Grand Forks.

tion, AN/ASQ-184 defensive management system and an expendable countermeasures system (chaff and flares). The system can detect, locate and classify signals from hostile emitters transmitting simultaneously via a number of receivers situated around the airframe in order to provide full 360° coverage. It is also able to establish priority in dealing with those threats and automatically initiates countermeasures via a large number of Northrop jamming transmitters and Raytheon phased array antennas.

The first production B-1B (82-0001) flew on 18 October 1984. Deliveries began on 27 July 1985 at Offutt AFB, Nebraska, with SAC achieving IOC exactly one year later, thereafter rapidly building up four bomb wings. The first 29 B-1Bs were assigned to the 96th BW at Dyess, Texas, excluding the ninth example, which was delivered to Edwards for test duties. Subsequent units to form comprised the 28th Wing at Ellsworth, SD, the 319th Wing at Grand Forks, ND, and the 384th Wing at McConnell, Kansas. 74-0160, a B-1A, is employed at Lowry, CO, as a ground instruction trainer.

Since then, the career of the B-1B has been coloured by controversy and interrupted by frequent lengthy grounding orders, and several highly-publicised losses. Problems were caused by false-alarms from the computerised self-diagnostic systems, non-functioning TFR, and repeated failure of the AN/ALQ-161 ECM system. Engine problems were also a significant factor in the type's grounding, and perhaps some of the losses. One of the more recent periods of enforced inactivity prevented the B-1B from playing any part in Desert Storm. However, the Lancer was still (nominally) fulfilling SAC's 'alert' nuclear role.

Under the FY1994 budget, $49 million has been allocated for R&D, while another $161 million has been set aside for modifications and components. So much money has been spent on the AN/ALQ-161 system that no funds have been released for FY1994.

Future plans for the fleet include the addition of GPS, a MIL-STD-1760 databus, ECM improvements and advanced weapons capability. A six-month operational readiness assessment began in June 1994, which the USAF hopes will break Congressional opposition to further funding. The USAF seeks to prove it can maintain a 75 per cent readiness level, in contrast to the current figure of only 55 per cent, which it blames on a poorly funded spares resource. The 28th Wing will be provided with a full complement of spares and crews to participate in deployments and exercises, thus further downgrading the 7th Wing and 384th BG. A report on the success of this endeavour is due to be presented by 1 March 1995. A positive result would ease release of the $2.7 billion required to upgrade the fleet's conventional capabilities, in addition to $830 million for full spares support.

WEAPON OPTIONS

Thus far, the Lancer has been primarily concerned with strategic applications. The B-1B is fitted with three internal weapons bays, comprising a 31-ft 3-in (9.53-m) long double bay forward of the wing carry-through structure and a single 15-ft (4.57-m) bay aft, with hydraulically actuated doors. Weapons include B61 and B83 thermonuclear bombs up to a maximum payload of 75,000 lb (34020 kg). Alternatively, the internal ordnance bays may contain three racks or SRAM launchers, for up to 24 AGM-69A short-range attack missiles (SRAM-As), 12 B-28 or 28 700-lb (318-kg) B-61, or 2,400-lb (1089-kg) B-83 freefall nuclear bombs. The B-1B also has the capacity to carry eight

AGM-86B ALCMs (with subsequent modifications to the forward double bomb bay using the moveable bulkhead) on a common strategic rotary launcher (CSRL), although cruise missiles have never been carried in routine operations.

Future strategic weapons options will include advanced PGMs, such as the AGM-129 Advanced Cruise Missile, AGM-137 Tri-service Stand-off Attack Missile (TSSAM), Joint Direct Attack Munition (JDAM), and Joint Stand-off Weapon (JSOW).

In the conventional role, the B-1B is potentially able to carry a maximum of 84 500-lb (227-kg) Mk 82 bombs or 500-lb (227-kg) Mk 36 mines internally. It is probably also compatible with the AGM-86C ALCM that is armed with a 1,000-lb (454-kg) blast-fragmentation warhead in place of the AGM-86B's nuclear warhead. The six underfuselage stores stations could carry an additional 12 ALCMs, or additional conventional stores for a maximum total load of 134,000 lb (60782 kg).

The B-1B's conventional weapons potential is being comprehensively upgraded, following the withdrawal of the B-52G. The Lancer will ultimately acquire the ability to utilise 'smart' PGMs such as the AGM-84 Harpoon anti-ship missile and, in time, the AGM-142 Popeye stand-off missile. This is a 3,300-lb (1497-kg) conventional stand-off missile developed by Rafael, and procured under the 'Have Nap' programme. Other missions might include interdiction of sea lanes through the use of air-delivered mines.

OPERATORS

Ninety-five B-1Bs remain in service with the USAF.
Air Combat Command (ACC)
7th Wing – Dyess AFB, TX ('DY')
28th Bomb Wing – Ellsworth AFB, SD ('EL')

319th Bomb Group – Grand Forks AFB, ND ('GF'), disbanding in 1994
366th Wing – Ellsworth AFB, SD ('MO')
384th Bomb Group – McConnell AFB ('OZ'), disbanding in late 1994. Aircraft assigned to the 184th Bomber Group of the Kansas ANG

Air Force Materiel Command (AFMC)
412th Test Wing – Edwards AFB, CA ('ED')

SPECIFICATION

Rockwell B-1B Lancer
Wing: span 136 ft 8.5 in (41.67 m) minimum sweep (15°) and 78 ft 2.5 in (23.84 m) maximum sweep (67° 30'); aspect ratio about 9.58 fully spread and 3.14 fully swept; area approximately 1,950.00 sq ft (181.16 m2)
Fuselage and tail: length 147 ft 0 in (44.81 m); height 34 ft 10 in (10.36 m); tailplane span 44 ft 10 in (13.67 m); wheel track 14 ft 6 in (4.42 m)
Powerplant: four General Electric F101-GE-102 turbofans each rated at 14,600 lb st (64.94 kN) dry and 30,780 lb st (136.92 kN) with afterburning
Weights: empty equipped 192,000 lb (87091 kg); maximum take-off 477,000 lb (216365 kg)
Fuel and load: internal fuel 195,000 lb (88450 kg); external fuel none; maximum ordnance 75,000 lb (34019 kg) carried internally and 59,000 lb (26762 kg) carried externally
Speed: maximum level speed 'clean' at high altitude about Mach 1.25 or 715 kt (823 mph; 1324 km/h); penetration speed at about 200 ft (61 m) more than 521 kt (600 mph; 965 km/h)
Range: range about 6,475 nm (7,455 miles; 12000 km) with standard fuel
Performance: service ceiling more than 50,000 ft (15240 m)

Rockwell International OV-10 Bronco

In the early 1960s, the **US Marine Corps** recognised its need for a purpose-built COIN aircraft and drew up the specification for what it identified as a LARA (Light Armed Reconnaissance Airplane) with additional observation and FAC roles. Procurement was initiated by a design competition, with North American's **NA-300** proposal being selected as the winner in August 1964. The initial contract covered seven

YOV-10A prototypes, the first flying on 16 July 1965 powered by two 492-kW (660-shp) Garrett T76 turboprops.

Testing revealed some shortcomings that were rectified by a 3.05-m (10-ft) increase in wingspan, and the introduction of an uprated version of the T76 engine in nacelles that were moved outboard slightly to reduce engine noise in the cabin. The increased span was premiered on a proto-

Rockwell OV-10A Bronco

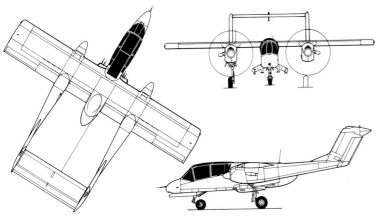

type first flown on 15 August 1966, and the seventh prototype was given alternative Pratt & Whitney Canada T74 engines (military designation for the PT6A turboprop) for comparative evaluation.

The resultant **Rockwell OV-10 Bronco** is of distinctive configuration with a shoulder-mounted constant-chord wing, and twin booms extending aft from the engine nacelles to terminate in vertical tail surfaces that are linked by a fixed-incidence

The Venezuelan air force received 18 surplus USAF OV-10As (seen here), which serve alongside 11 OV-10Es, from Maracaibo. The OV-10s are also detached to the Colombian border for COIN operations.

tailplane with inset elevator. A slender pod-type fuselage accommodates the crew of two in tandem under a large canopy with excellent all-round view. The fuselage pod could accommodate two stretchers and a medical attendant, or up to five paratroops.

The OV-10 was armed with four fixed 7.62-mm (0.3-in) M60C machine-guns (each with 500 rounds), comprising two in each sponson. Four 600-lb (272-kg) underwing hardpoints were located on sponsons projecting from the fuselage sides, with a 1,200-lb (544-kg) centreline hardpoint and two underwing stations. Weapons available for use included napalm, slick and retarded Mk 82 500-lb (227-kg) bombs, unguided 2.75-in or 5-in rockets, machine-gun and cannon pods, flares and smoke tanks.

Procurement of the initial **OV-10A** covered 114 aircraft for the US Marine Corps, the first of them flown on 6 August 1967. This service used the type for forward air

control and helicopter escort, in addition to the intended role of light armed reconnaissance. VMO-2 was the first unit to deploy, to Vietnam in July 1968, and the Bronco served with the Marines, Navy and Air Force. It soon demonstrated its superior performance against other FAC platforms. USMC OV-10As are fast disappearing, but continue to serve with HMT-303, VMO-1, VMO-2 and VMO-4. The USAF acquired 157 OV-10As, primarily for forward air control, but with a secondary limited ground support role in the absence of tactical fighters. USAF OV-10As have been retired, although some were transferred to the USMC.

Six generally similar **OV-10B** aircraft were supplied to West Germany for use as target tugs, followed by 12 higher-performance **OV-10B(Z)** aircraft with a 2,950-lb (13.12-kN) thrust General Electric J85-GE-4 turbojet pylon-mounted above the wing.

These aircraft are no longer in service.

Rockwell developed several production versions generally similar to the OV-10A. Thirty-two **OV-10C**s were delivered to the **Royal Thai air force** in 1971-74, of which 24 remain with No. 411 Squadron at Chiang Mai and No. 711 Squadron at Surat Thani. A further order for six was apparently not undertaken. The **OV-10E** (16 built – 11 remaining) serves with the **Venezuelan air force**. Venezuela also had taken delivery of 18 former USAF OV-10As by April 1991, and both versions serve with Escuadrón 151 'Geronimos', and 152 'Zorros', of Grupo 15, based at Base Aérea General En Jefe Rafael Urdaneta, Maracaibo, Zulia. The FAV undertakes detachments for COIN operations to the Colombian border (when they are usually armed with a single underwing rocket pod and flare pod). Three OV-10s were reported as shot down during

the attempted coup in late 1992. The **OV-10F** (16 built – 12 remaining) is currently operated at Baucau by Skwadron Udara 3 of the **Indonesian air force**. In 1981 the **Moroccan air force** took delivery of six refurbished, former USMC OV-10As for COIN operations. The (three) survivors are based at Ménara.

Additional deliveries of surplus USMC OV-10As include 24 to the **Philippine air force**. These were supplied to serve with the 15th Air Strike Wing at Sangley Point.

SPECIFICATION

Rockwell OV-10A Bronco
Wing: span 40 ft 0 in (12.19 m); aspect ratio 5.5; area 291.00 sq ft (27.03 m²)
Fuselage and tail: length 41 ft 7 in (12.67 m); height 15 ft 2 in (4.62 m); tailplane span 14 ft 7 in (4.45 m;

wheel track 14 ft 10 in (4.52 m)
Powerplant: two Garrett T76-G-416/417 turboprops each rated at 715 ehp (533 ekW)
Weights: empty equipped 6,969 lb (3161 kg); normal take-off 9,908 lb (4494 kg); maximum take-off 14,444 lb (6552 kg)
Fuel and load: internal fuel 578 US gal (976 litres); external fuel up to one 150-US gal (568-litre) drop tank; maximum ordnance 3,600 lb (1633 kg)
Speed: maximum level speed 'clean' at sea level 244 kt (281 mph; 452 km/h)
Range: ferry range 1,240 nm (1,428 miles; 2298 km) with drop tank; combat radius 198 nm (228 miles; 367 km) with maximum warload and no loiter
Performance: maximum rate of climb at sea level 2,650 ft (808 m) per minute; service ceiling 24,000 ft (7315 m); take-off run 740 ft (226 m) at normal take-off weight; take-off distance to 50 ft (15 m) 2,800 ft (853 m) at maximum take-off weight; landing distance from 50 ft (15 m) 1,220 ft (372 m) at normal landing weight; landing run 740 ft (226 m) at normal landing weight

Rockwell International OV-10D Bronco

SPECIFICATION

Rockwell OV-10D Bronco
generally similar to the OV-10A Bronco except in the following particulars:
Fuselage and tail: length 44 ft 0 in (13.41 m)
Powerplant: two Garrett T76-G-420/421 turboprops each rated at 1,040 ehp (776 kW)
Weights: empty equipped 6,893 lb (3127 kg)
Speed: maximum level speed 'clean' at sea level 250 kt (288 mph; 463 km/h)
Range: combat radius 265 nm (305 miles; 491 km) with maximum warload and no loiter
Performance: maximum rate of climb at sea level at 12,443 lb (5644 kg) 2,665 ft (812 m) per minute; service ceiling 30,000 ft (9145 m); take-off run 1,110 ft (338 m) at 13,284 lb (6025 kg); landing run 800 ft (244 m) at maximum landing weight

A suitably equipped OV-10 seemed ideal to fulfil a night FAC and strike designation role in the light of the **USAF**'s Vietnam experience. While the OV-10A was effective, it could not stop the infiltration of men and supplies at night. In the early 1970s, 15 OV-10As were modified under the USAF's Pave Nail programme. Specialised equipment given to these aircraft included a combined laser rangefinder/target illuminator, a LORAN receiver and a LORAN co-ordinate converter. After the withdrawal from Vietnam, these Pave Nail OV-10s reverted to standard configuration.

The **USN** had been slightly ahead of the USAF in considering the OV-10A for such a task, and in 1970 two Navy OV-10As were converted as **Rockwell YOV-10D NOGS** (Night Observation/Gunship System) prototypes with enhanced night and all-weather capability. They were equipped with an undernose turret in an extended nose carrying a FLIR and laser target designator, a rear underfuselage turret to mount a 20-mm can-

non, and two underwing pylons carrying extra stores. By the time evaluation was complete, the US had withdrawn its forces from Vietnam, but in 1974 the US Navy contracted Rockwell to establish and test an **OV-10D** production configuration. This resulted in 17 of the **USMC** OV-10As being converted as OV-10Ds for a **NOS** (Night Observation Surveillance) role, all of them being redelivered during 1979-80.

They are equipped with a Texas Instruments AN/AAS-37 pod that incorporates a FLIR sensor, laser target designator and automatic video tracker, and can be armed with an M197 20-mm three-barrelled cannon with 1,500 rounds (in place of the OV-10A's conventional armament), which can be directed by the AAS-37 system. These OV-10Ds also have uprated engines with IR-suppressing exhaust ducts, LW-3B zero-zero ejection seats, AN/APR-39 RWR and additional underwing pylons suitable for weapons (the OV-10D introduced AIM-9 capability) or auxiliary fuel. The OV-10D saw

active service during Operation Desert Storm, with two lost in combat. Fourteen survivors, plus 23 OV-10As, were to have been upgraded to a common **OV-10D+** standard, with structural strengthening to permit carrier operations plus upgraded avionics, navigation and weapons systems. The programme should have been completed by late 1993, but the final withdrawal of the type was brought forward to FY1994. VMO-1 and -2 disbanded on 20 May and 31 July 1993, respectively. VMO-4, the last (USMC Reserve) unit, followed in March 1994. It has been mooted that surplus aircraft will be passed on to South Korea.

Rockwell OV-10D Bronco

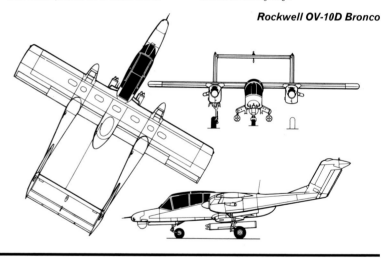

Formerly based at New River, alongside the FMFLant helicopter fleet, VMO-1 flew its OV-10Ds on observation and FAC missions.

Rockwell T-2 Buckeye

I n 1956 the **US Navy** identified a requirement for a jet trainer which would be suitable to take the pupil, after completion of the *ab initio* phase, through all the more advanced stages, including bombing, gunnery and fighter tactics, to the point of carrier qualification. Competitive procurement was contested by a number of US manufacturers but North American Aviation, which incorporated in its **NA-249** design proposal proven features from in-production aircraft (the FJ-1 Fury and T-28 Trojan), was selected and contracted in late 1946 to build six pre-production **YT2J-1** aircraft for evaluation; there was no prototype as such.

The first of the pre-production aircraft, flown initially on 31 January 1958, was of mid-wing configuration, accommodating pupil and instructor in tandem on LS-1 ejection seats. The instructor's seat, at the rear,

was raised to provide a good view forward. The design provided a robust landing gear, powered controls, large trailing-edge flaps, an airbrake on each side of the fuselage and a retractable sting-type arrester hook, all hydraulically actuated. The YT2J-1 and initial production **T2J-1** (designated **T-2A** from 1962) was powered by a single 3,400-lb (15.12-kN) thrust Westinghouse J34-WE-48 turbojet within the fuselage. Named **Buckeye** before entering service in July 1959, the T2J-1 initially equipped BTG-7, later named VT-7, based at NAS Meridian. T2J-1 (T-2A) production totalled 201 aircraft.

The first of two YT2J-2 test aircraft (T2J-1 conversions) was flown on 30 August 1962 with two 3,000-lb (13.34-kN) thrust Pratt & Whitney J60-P-6 turbojets. This version was selected to supersede the T-2A, the first of 97 production **T-2B** aircraft being

The US Navy trains 2,000 pilots and naval flight officers per year and, until the T-45 is fully in service, will continue to rely on the T-2Cs for most of its training needs. Unlike the USAF, it is only the prospective jet pilots who train on Buckeyes, such as these TW-6/VT-4 examples.

flown on 21 May 1965 and entering service with Training Squadron VT-4 at NAS Pensacola in December 1965. Following evaluation of a T-2B converted to **YT-2C** configuration with two General Electric J85-GE-4 engines, 231 aircraft designated **T-2C** were built for the US Navy Air Training Command, the first production example being flown initially on 10 December 1968. At a later date, small numbers of T-2B and T-2C aircraft were converted as drone directors under the respective designations **DT-2B** and **DT-2C**. In 1982, 17 US Navy T-2Bs were removed from storage and refurbished, 15 of them later entering service to supplement T-2Cs that currently remain active.

The US Navy also procured two T-2 trainer variants (basically similar to the T-2C) on behalf of the **Venezuelan** and **Greek** air forces. The FAV received 12 **T-2D** trainers in 1973, plus an additonal 12 weapons-capable aircraft in 1976. The 19 surviving aircraft comprise 10 weapons-capable T-2Ds and nine trainers, equipping the Grupo Aéreo de Entrenamiento, based at Boca Del Rio, Maracay. Some T-2Ds flew with rebel forces during the 1992 coup

attempt. The Greek air force relies for advanced training on the 36 surviving **T-2E**s of 362 'Nestor' Mira and 363 'Danaos' Mira, of 120 Ptérix, based at Kalamata.

The T-2C is the only current variant in service with the US Navy, flying with VT-4 and VT-26 at Pensacola, FL, VT-19 at Meridian, MS, VT-23 at Kingsville, TX, and VT-26 at Chase Field, TX, in the training role. A small number served with aggressor units VF-43 at Oceana, VA, and VF-126 at Miramar, CA, for spin-training, and the Naval Test Pilot's School at Patuxent River, MD.

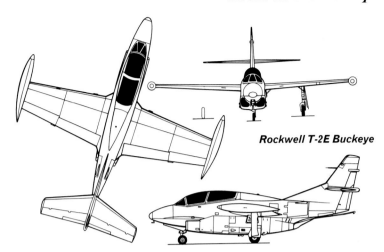

Rockwell T-2E Buckeye

SPECIFICATION

Rockwell T-2C Buckeye
Wing: span 38 ft 1.5 in (11.62 m) with tip tanks; aspect ratio 5.7; area 255.00 sq ft (23.69 m²)
Fuselage and tail: length 38 ft 3.5 in (11.67 m); height 14 ft 9.5 in (4.51 m); tailplane span 17 ft 11 in (5.46 m); wheel track 18 ft 6 in (5.64 m)
Powerplant: two General Electric J85-GE-4 turbojets each rated at 2,950 lb st (13.1 kN)
Weights: empty 8,115 lb (3680 kg); maximum take-off 13,179 lb (5977 kg)

Fuel and load: internal fuel 691 US gal (2616 litres); external fuel none; maximum ordnance 640 lb (290 kg)
Speed: maximum level speed 'clean' at 25,000 ft (7620 m) 469 kt (540 mph; 840 km/h)

Range: range 909 nm (1,047 miles; 1685 km)
Performance: maximum rate of climb at sea level 6,200 ft (1890 m) per minute; service ceiling 40,415 ft (12320 m)

Rockwell **Commander twins**

Shrike Commander was the final name used by Rockwell for the piston-engined light business twin originated in 1948 by Aero Design and Engineering (later Aero Commander). With engines of varying power, the aircraft were identified as **Aero Commander 500**, **Commander 560**, **Commander 680** and – with a lengthened fuselage – **Commander 680FL**. The name Shrike Commander applied to the seven-seat **Models 500V** and **500S**, built until 1979, and the 11-seat **Model 680FL** became the **Grand Commander**.

Commander twins have entered military service in the liaison and aerial survey roles. The **Argentinian** armed forces are the principal operators of the type, with a 12-strong fleet of **Model 500U**s used by the air force for medevac service and a single

Commander 560 for army transport duties. The **Mexican air force** uses 15 Model 500s for light transport and photographic reconnaissance. Other users of the Model 500 include the **Royal Bahamas Defence Force**, **Benin** armed forces and **Burkina Faso air force**. The long-fuselage Model 680FL serves with the armies of **Greece** and **Indonesia**, and a single Aero Commander 680 in **Dominica**.

SPECIFICATION

Rockwell Shrike Commander
Wing: span 49 ft 0.5 in (14.95 m); aspect ratio 9.45; area 255.00 sq ft (23.69 m²)
Fuselage and tail: length 36 ft 9.75 in (11.22 m); height 14 ft 6 in (4.42 m); tailplane span 16 ft 9 in

(5.10 m); wheel track 12 ft 11 in (3.95 m)
Powerplant: two Textron Lycoming IO-540-E1B5 flat-six piston engines each rated at 290 hp (216 kW)
Weights: empty equipped 4,608 lb (2090 kg); maximum take-off 6,750 lb (3062 kg)
Fuel and load: internal fuel 156 US gal (590 litres); external fuel none
Speed: maximum level speed 'clean' at sea level 187 kt

Thirteen of the 15 Aero Commander 500s that have been delivered to the air force of Argentina (SADEN) still serve in support of regional commands and HQs.

(215 mph; 346 km/h); maximum cruising speed at 9,000 ft (2745 m) 176 kt (203 mph; 326 km/h)
Range: range 936 nm (1,078 miles; 1735 km)
Performance: maximum rate of climb at sea level 1,340 ft (408 m) per minute; service ceiling 19,000 ft (5915 m); take-off distance to 50 ft (15 m) 1,915 ft (584 m) at maximum take-off weight; landing distance from 50 ft (15 m) 2,235 ft (681 m) at normal landing weight

Rockwell **Turbo Commander**

The early success of the Aero Commander 500/560 series had indicated a worthwhile market for a larger-capacity, higher-speed derivative. In its initial form, the Commander Model 680FL (Grand Commander) was first flown on 29 December 1962, incorporating a 1.88-m (6-ft 2-in) fuselage stretch to seat pilot and co-pilot on a separate flight deck, and from four to nine passengers according to cabin layout. A pressurised development with turboprops was flown by Aero Commander (then a division of Rockwell Standard) as the **Turbo Commander 690**, on 31 December 1964. Successive variants were built by Rockwell until February 1981, when the production line was sold to Gulfstream American and the name was changed to the **Gulfstream/Jetprop 840**, **900**, **980** or **1000**, depending on engine power and gross weight.

Military users of the Turbo Commander

in its various manifestations include the **Colombian air force** (one Turbo Commander 680V), the **Honduran air force** (one Gulfstream 1000), the **Iranian air force** (four Turbo Commander 681/Bs), **army** (five Turbo Commanders 690/As) and **navy** (four Turbo Commander 690/As), the **Mexican air force** (one Turbo Commander 690B, one Gulfstream 980, three Gulfstream 1000s) and **navy** (two Gulfstream 1000s), the **Pakistan army** (two Gulfstream 840s), the **Royal Thai air force** (one Turbo Commander 690A for survey duties), and the **Turkish air force** (one Turbo Commander 690A).

SPECIFICATION

Rockwell Turbo Commander 690B
Wing: span 46 ft 8 in (14.22 m); aspect ratio 8.19;

area 266.00 sq ft (24.71 m²)
Fuselage and tail: length 42 ft 11.75 in (13.10 m); height 14 ft 11.5 in (4.56 m); tailplane span 19 ft 9.25 in (6.03 m); wheel track 15 ft 5 in (4.70 m)
Powerplant: two Garrett TPE331-5-521K turboprops each rated at 700 ehp (522 ekW)
Weights: empty 5,910 lb (2681 kg); maximum take-off 10,250 lb (4649 kg)
Fuel and load: internal fuel 384 US gal (1453 litres); external fuel none
Speed: maximum level speed 'clean' at 12,000 ft

A sizeable number of Rockwell's sleek Turbo Commander family are in military service. This is one of the Pakistan army's two Gulfstream 840s.

(3660 m) 285 kt (328 mph; 528 km/h); economical cruising speed at 25,000 ft (7620 m) 231 kt (266 mph; 428 km/h)
Range: range 1,360 nm (1,567 miles; 2522 km) with maximum fuel and a 1,817-lb (824-kg) payload, or 701 nm (808 miles; 1300 km) with maximum payload
Performance: maximum rate of climb at sea level 2,849 ft (868 m) per minute; service ceiling 32,900 ft (10030 m); take-off run 1,434 ft (437 m) at maximum take-off weight; take-off distance to 50 ft (15 m) 2,216 ft (675 m) at maximum take-off weight

Rockwell/Deutsche Aerospace (MBB) **X-31A**

Flying under the programme title **EFM (Enhanced Fighter Maneuverability)**, the **X-31A** is an experimental aircraft intended to evaluate advanced aerodynamic and propulsive systems with the aim of increasing fighter agility, widening the flight

envelope and conferring an ability to point the nose 'off axis' to increase firing opportunities for boresighted or forward hemisphere weapons. The X-31A explores that area of the envelope which lies beyond the conventional 'stall barrier', and investigates

the tactical applications. The project will also help the development of requirements for future fighters, and will itself demonstrate and validate methods of producing low-cost prototypes. MBB has already proposed using flight control software devel-

oped for the X-31A as the basis of a new flight control system for the Eurofighter EFA, demonstrating the potential spin-offs from this remarkable programme. The use of advanced aerodynamics and flight control surfaces, combined with the use of engine thrust as a flight control in its own right, are the central key to avoiding departure and to manoeuvring successfully at very low airspeeds and very high angles of attack.

Rockwell/Deutsche Aerospace (MBB) X-31A

The X-31's sole purpose is to investigate low-speed, high angle-of-attack handling. From its current arrangement with thrust vectoring paddles, the aircraft will progress to a fully-tailless configuration in 1995. Already the X-31A has demonstrated a dramatic post-stall hammerhead called the 'Herbst manoeuvre'.

MBB began work in 1977 on the project, and was joined by Rockwell in 1983. Rockwell's HiMAT RPV and MBB's TKF-90 study (a progenitor of the Eurofighter) provided useful data for the X-31, development of which was covered by a joint US/German MoU in 1986. Funding for two prototypes was provided in August 1988. Rockwell was responsible for the configuration and aerodynamics of the X-31, and assembled the aircraft, the first of which (BuNo. 164584) made its maiden flight on 11 October 1990. The second (BuNo. 164585) followed on 19 January 1991. MBB built major sub-assemblies for the aircraft (including the wings), and designed the flight control system and thrust vectoring system. The programme is managed by DARPA (acting through the US Naval Air Systems Command) and the German Ministry of Defence.

The X-31 has a cranked delta wing incorporating twist, a single fin and powered canard foreplanes, all control surfaces being actuated by a fly-by-wire flight control system. Many sub-systems were taken from existing aircraft types to minimise costs. On 14 February 1991, the first aircraft flew with a three-paddle thrust vectoring system fitted, these units deflecting the exhaust by up to 10°. A four-phase 'pure research' programme has not prevented the aircraft from being used in simulated air combat against (for example) US Navy F/A-18s, in which its unique capabilities have enabled it to gain the upper hand.

SPECIFICATION

Rockwell/Deutsche Aerospace (MBB) X-31A
Wing: span 23 ft 10 in (7.26 m); aspect ratio 2.51; area 226.30 sq ft (21.02 m2); canard foreplane span 8 ft 8 in (2.64 m); aspect ratio 3.18; canard foreplane area 23.60 sq ft (2.19 m2)
Fuselage and tail: length 48 ft 8.5 in (14.85 m) including probe and 43 ft 4 in (13.21 m) excluding probe; height 14 ft 7 in (4.44 m)
Powerplant: one afterburning General Electric F404-GE-400 turbofan rated at 16,000 lb st (71.17 kN)
Weights: empty equipped 11,410 lb (5175 kg); normal take-off 14,600 lb (6622 kg); maximum take-off 15,935 lb (7228 kg)
Fuel and load: internal fuel 4,136 kg (1876 kg); external fuel none; ordnance none
Speed: never exceed speed and maximum level speed 'clean' between sea level and 28,000 ft (8535 m) 1,485 kt (1,710 mph; 2752 km/h) and between 28,000 and 40,000 ft (8535 and 12190 m) Mach 1.3
Performance: maximum rate of climb at sea level 43,000 ft (13106 m) per minute; maximum operating altitude 40,000 ft (12190 m); take-off run 1,500 ft (457 m) at maximum take-off weight; take-off distance to 50 ft (15 m) 2,700 ft (823 m) at maximum take-off weight; landing distance from 50 ft (15 m) 3,700 ft (1128 m) at maximum landing weight; landing run 2,700 ft (823 m) at maximum landing weight
g limits: -4 to +9

Rockwell (Lockheed) AC-130U Spectre

The **AC-130U** is a **Lockheed C-130H Hercules** converted by Rockwell into a third-generation **Spectre** gunship for the **US Air Force**'s Special Operations Command's 16th Special Operations Squadron at Hurlburt Field, FL. Painted gunship grey in service, the AC-130U is powered by four 4,900-shp (3655-ekW) Allison T56-A-15 turboprop engines and has a crew of 13. It has a performance that is generally similar to that of the C-130H transport.

To engage ground targets in a pylon turn, the AC-130U retains the single L-60 40-mm Bofors cannon and M102 105-mm howitzer of earlier Spectre gunships. A single 25-mm GAU-12 cannon with 3,000 rounds replaces the AC-130H's two M61 cannons. The new cannon is fitted on a trainable mount, with an autonomous ammunition-handling and feed system (firing rate 1,800 shots/minute) and a stand-off range of 12,000 ft (3657 m). The AC-130U's sensors include a Hughes AN/APQ-180 main fire control radar (a derivative of the APG-70 developed for the F-15E), Texas Instruments AAQ-117 FLIR, Ball Aerospace All-Active Low-Light-Level TV with laser target designator and rangefinder (mounted in a turret under the fuselage with a 360° field of view), and Rockwell ALQ-172 jammer and expendable countermeasures package. The four IBM IP-102 mission computers are linked by a 1553B databus. Navigation is greatly facilitated by a combined INS and GPS/Navstar. Fully all-weather capable, the AC-130U is able to engage two target simultaneously.

The first AC-130U, the sole full-scale development aircraft in the series (scheduled to become an operational aircraft at a later date), made its initial flight on 20 December 1990 and entered testing at Edwards AFB, CA, in September 1991. By January 1993, one FSD and five operational AC-130Us had been completed, and delivery of the first operational aircraft to Hurlburt Field was made, after further FSD work, in June 1994.

The USAF plans to acquire 13 AC-130U models, one of these being a replacement for an AC-130H lost in the Gulf War. The AC-130H Spectre will then be transferred to the Air Force Reserve, replacing its current, surviving elderly AC-130As.

Thirteen AC-130Us will be modified from standard C-130H Hercules, becoming the USAF Special Operations Command's next-generation gunship. While its armament may appear deficient when compared to the AC-130H or AC-130A, the new Spectre's targeting systems promise unrivalled accuracy. To carry out its designated fire support, interdiction, escort, armed surveillance or air base defence missions, the AC-130U also comes equipped with INS, GPS, pilot's HUD and Spectra ceramic armour. The eight AC-130Hs in service with the 16th SOS will be replaced by AC-130Us from 1994, and already its enthusiastic crews have dubbed their new mount the 'U-Boat'.

Rogerson Hiller VS-1100/M Hornet and UH-12E

Rogerson Hiller Corporation
2140 West 18th St, Port Angeles
Washington 98362, USA

Demonstrated in 1985, the **Rogerson RH-1100M** prototype is a multi-mission military derivative of the **Hiller RH-1100** five-seat utility helicopter. This was derived from the original **Hiller OH-5A** observation helicopter built to the US Army's LOH (Light Observation Helicopter) specification in 1963 but produced as a refined development only for commercial and foreign customers as the **Fairchild (Hiller) FH-1100**. These are described under the Fairchild-Hiller heading. Production totalled 246 and ended in 1974, with design rights subsequently acquired by Rogerson Aircraft. The **RH-1100M** offers a variety of armament options on fuselage-side pylons, including four TOW anti-armour missiles or a pair of rocket pods or machine-guns, and provision for autopilot, FLIR anti-missile warning systems, AAM system capability, and a chin- or roof-mounted sight.

Rogerson Hiller also resumed production, in the early 1990s, of the Hiller FH-1100 as the **RH-1100C** and seven-seat **RH-110S**. These proved unsuccessful in the civil market, and the company's attention turned to the US Army's NTH (New Training Helicopter) competition, for which a design based on the Hiller UH-12E was resurrected. Rogerson Hiller began building the civil **UH-12E Hauler** in 1992, and from it developed the Soloy/Allison 250-C20B-powered **UH-12ET** for the NTH requirement. The US Army selected Bell's Model 206 Jet Ranger derivative, the TH-57 Creek, as its NTH winner, as opposed to the archaic-looking UH-12ET. Thus far, customers for the basic UH-12E have been purely civilian, including crop-spraying aircraft ordered by the Indian government and several similar examples delivered to Taiwan and Hungary.

SPECIFICATION

Rogerson Hiller RH-1100M Hornet
Rotor system: main rotor diameter 35 ft 5 in (10.80 m); tail rotor diameter 6 ft 0 in (1.83 m); main rotor disc area 985.16 sq ft (91.52 m2); tail rotor disc area 28.27 sq ft (2.63 m2)
Fuselage and tail: length overall, rotors turning 41 ft 4 in (12.60 m) and fuselage 29 ft 9.5 in (9.08 m); height overall 9 ft 2 in (2.79 m) to top of rotor head; skid track 7 ft 2¾ in (2.20 m)
Powerplant: one Allison 250-C20R turboshaft rated at 450 shp (336 kW)
Weights: empty 1,710 lb (776 kg); maximum take-off 3,500 lb (1588 kg)
Fuel and load: internal fuel 459 lb (208 kg); external fuel none; maximum payload 1,500 lb (680 kg)
Speed: maximum level speed 'clean' at sea level 116 kt (134 mph; 216 km/h); maximum cruising speed at 5,000 ft (1525 m) 116 kt (134 mph; 216 km/h)
Range: range 341 nm (393 miles; 632 km)
Performance: maximum rate of climb at sea level 1,790 ft (546 m) per minute; service ceiling 19,000 ft (5790 m); hovering ceiling 11,000 ft (4990 m) in ground effect and 6,700 ft (2040 m) out of ground effect

Saab 32 Lansen

The transonic Avon-engined two-seat **Saab 32 Lansen** was operational with front-line squadrons of the **Flygvapen** (Swedish air force) until late 1979, when the last two S 32C squadrons disbanded in F11 (Recce). The Lansen was originally built from 1953-60 for attack (287 **A 32A**s), all-weather/night-fighting (120 **J 32B**s) and photo reconnaissance (45 **S 32C**s).

Lansens still operate in electronic warfare, aggressor and target-towing roles with F16M (Målflygdivision – MFD) detachment at Malmen, Linköping. This unit flies 25 Lansens, in three forms. Its chief equipment is 13 **J 32E** ECM-configured versions, which the squadron flies in its primary role as an EW aggressor training unit for the Swedish air force, army and naval units. In their ECM role, the Lansens can carry nose-mounted G24 jammers covering L-, S- and C- (NATO D-, E- & F- and G- & H-) bands for use against ground- and ship-based radars. Other integral equipment includes Mera VHF and UHF radio jammers and Ingeborg homing receivers. The J 32E can also carry Adrian S- and C- band, and Petrus X- (NATO I- and lower-J band) underwing jamming pods, in addition to two Bofors BOZ3 chaff dispensers.

The J 32E is a conversion of the two-seat J 32B all-weather fighter, which was replaced by the J35 Draken in 1969. MFD still retains three J 32Bs as crew trainers. The third Lansen variant remaining in use is the **J 32D** target tug. Five J 32Ds, with yellow Dayglo patches, are uses to tow VM-6 aerial targets and occasionally act as radar targets themselves. Some target tugs were operated by a civil contractor, Swedair, but these have now been reabsorbed by the Flygvapen. For approximately seven months of the year, two J 32Ds are based at Fällfors air base, in northern Sweden, supporting air-to-air gunnery training.

The Lansen was the first supersonic Swedish aircraft, and a prototype exceeded Mach 1 as early as 1952. This is one of F16M's remaining ECM J 32Es.

Saab 35 Draken

In 1949 the Swedish **Flygvapen** drew up an ambitious requirement for a new fighter to replace the Saab J 29, calling for a performance 50 per cent better than that of fighters then entering service with other nations. After extensive flight-testing on the seven-tenths scale **Saab 210**, three full-scale **Saab 35 Draken** prototypes with the distinctive double-delta wing followed. The first flew on 25 October 1955. The rest of the structure was largely conventional, apart from the wing configuration which was fitted with powered controls for each movable surface. These were operated by two tandem hydraulic jacks fed by separate hydraulic systems. Other novel features included a raked ejection seat (of indigenous design) which increased pilot tolerance to g forces. The prototypes were each powered by an imported Rolls-Royce Avon turbojet, but initial production **J 35A**s featured the licence-built Svenska Flygmotor (later Volvo Flygmotor) RM6B with a more efficient afterburner developed by the Swedes.

Air-defence J 35A Drakens first equipped Flygflottilj 13 (F13) at Norköping in March 1960. The subsequent air-defence **J 35B** variant had a lengthened rear fuselage and introduced twin retractable tailwheels intended primarily to permit more effective aerodynamic braking during the landing run; most J 35As were later modified to this configuration. The next air-defence version was the **J 35D**, featuring the more powerful RM6C engine plus more advanced radar and equipment. The final air-defence variant for the Flygvapen was the **J 35F**, developed from the J 35D. The J 35F introduced more capable radar and collision-course fire control, deleted one 30-mm cannon and introduced licence-built Hughes Falcon AAMs and, in the **J 35F-II**, a Hughes IR sensor. The J 35F also introduced a new, more bulged canopy, an improved autopilot and a ground-air datalink. Fuel capacity was increased to 880 Imp gal (400 litres), making the J 35F a much longer-ranged fighter than its precursors. A new afterburner further improved performance. One other variant for the Swedish air force was the reconnaissance **S 35E**, based on the J 35D, with the radar nose replaced by a pressurised nose section housing five cameras as standard.

All of these variants have now been retired, although 64 (or 66, according to some sources) J 35Fs were converted to **J 35J** standard. These continue to serve with the Flygvapen's F10 at Angelholm. The J 35J modification added extra armament capability in the form of two additional pylons under the engine intake ducts. The J 35J also gained improvements to the radar, IR sensor, IFF, cockpit and avionics.

A two-seat trainer version, designated **Sk 35C**, made its maiden flight on 30 December 1959. Initially a new-build development of the J 35A, but later including also J 35A conversions, the Sk 35C seated pupil and instructor in tandem in a modified forward fuselage that provided the additional rear position for the instructor without any increase in fuselage length. In Flygvapnet service, the Sk 35C initially equipped the Draken OCU that was based at Uppsala. A handful remain active today with F10 at Angelholm to provide training and standardisation for J 35J pilots.

In the mid-1960s, Saab began work on export versions of the Draken. The **J 35H** offered and demonstrated to Switzerland was stillborn, but more successful was a development of the J 35F that incorporated structural strengthening for the carriage of loads up to a maximum of 4500 kg (9,921 lb) and had increased internal and external fuel capacity. Designated **Saab 35X**, this soon proved of interest to the **Danish air force**, which ordered a total of 46 during 1968/69. This included the basic **A 35XD** fighter-bomber (Danish designation **F-35** – 20 built); a basically similar **RF-5** reconnaissance/fighter version that differs by having the camera nose of the S 35E Draken but retaining wing cannon (20 built); and **TF-35** (**Sk 35XD**) trainer similar to the Swedish Sk 35C but retaining one wing cannon. Denmark's Drakens were extensively modified during the mid-1980s, receiving a Lear-Siegler nav/attack computer, a Singer-Kearfott INS, a Marconi Series 900 HUD and a Ferranti LRMTS in a reprofiled nose. Esk 725 disbanded on 1 January 1992, passing on some of its F-35s to Esk. 729. This, the last Danish Draken unit, disbanded at Karup on 31 December 1993.

Finland was the second export customer, ordering 12 Saab 35Xs in 1970 for assembly by Valmet Oy. Six Swedish air force J 35Bs (designated **J 35S**, with radar removed) were first leased for training purposes and then purchased in 1975, becoming **J 35BS**. Finland has also procured 24 J 35Fs and Sk 35Cs from Sweden, the first five being redesignated **J 35FS** and the trainers becoming **J 35CS**. They currently equip Nos 11 and 21 squadrons, based at Rovaniemi and Tampere, repspectively.

The final Draken customer was **Austria**, whose air force was directed to purchase 24 surplus Swedish J 35Ds in 1985. The Swedish aircraft were selected instead of ex-Saudi Lightnings offered by BAe. The aircraft are fitted with J 35F-style bulged canopies, but apparently retained J 35D avionics and radar. Redesignated **J 35Ö**, the first Drakens were handed over in June 1987 and, after training in Sweden, the aircraft were ferried to Austria during 1988 and 1989. They equip No. 1 Staffel (Blau) and No. 2 Staffel (Rot), of the Fliegerregiment II's Überwachungsgeschwader, at Graz-Thalerhof. These aircraft have a podded reconnaissance system and acquired AIM-9P-3s in January 1994.

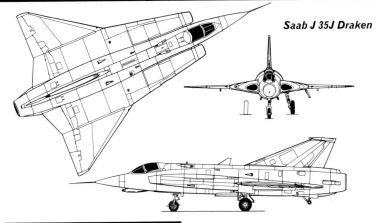

Saab J 35J Draken

SPECIFICATION

Saab J 35J Draken

Wing: span 9.40 m (30 ft 10 in); aspect ratio 1.77; area 49.20 m² (529.60 sq ft)

Fuselage and tail: length 15.35 m (50 ft 4 in); height 3.89 m (12 ft 9 in); wheel track 2.70 m (8 ft 10½ in)

Powerplant: one Volvo Flygmotor RM6C turbojet (licence-built Rolls-Royce Avon Series 300 turbojet fitted with a Swedish-designed afterburner) rated at 12,790 lb st (56.89 kN) dry and 17,650 lb st (78.51 kN) with afterburning

Weights: empty 8250 kg (18,188 lb); normal take-off 11400 kg (25,132 lb); maximum take-off 12270 kg (27,050 lb) interceptor. 15000 kg (33,069 lb) attack

Fuel and load: internal fuel 4000 litres (1,057 US gal); external fuel up to 5000 litres (1,321 US gal) in 1275-litre (280-US gal) and 500-litre (132-US gal) drop tanks; maximum ordnance 2900 kg (6,393 lb)

Speed: maximum level speed 'clean' at 36,000 ft (10975 m) more than 1,147 kt (1,321 mph; 2126 km/h) and at 300 ft (90 m) 793 kt (913 mph; 1469 km/h)

Range: ferry range 1,533 nm (1,765 miles; 2840 km); combat radius 304 nm (350 miles; 564 km) on a hi-lo-hi attack mission with internal fuel or 388 nm (477 miles; 720 km) on a hi-lo-hi attack mission with two 1,000-lb (454-kg) bombs and two drop tanks

Performance: maximum rate of climb at sea level 34,450 ft (10500 m) per minute with afterburning; service ceiling 65,600 ft (19995 m); take-off run 650 m (2,133 ft) at 11400 kg (25,132 lb) with afterburning; take-off distance to 50 ft (15 m) 960 m (3,150 ft) at normal take-off weight with afterburning or 1550 m (5,085 ft) at maximum attack mission take-off weight; landing run 530 m (1,739 ft) at 8800 kg (19,400 lb)

Above: Swedish J 35Js of F10 are adopting this two-tone grey scheme as they pass through overhaul.

Below: Austrian J 35Ös have been more active recently, owing to the nearby war in former Yugoslavia.

Saab AJ 37 Viggen

In the early 1960s, when seeking a multi-role J 32 replacement, Saab began studies of a relatively low-cost single-seat single-engined type capable of supersonic flight at low altitude and Mach 2 at height, but able to take off and land in 500 m (1,640 ft). This was necessary to operate from the SAF's STRIL 60 integrated air defence system and BASE 90 concept dispersed airstrips, comprising lengths of roadway 800 x 9 m (2,625 x 29.5 ft) in size. For good short-field performance, Saab pioneered the use of flap-equipped canard foreplanes with a delta-wing configuration in its new **System 37**, allowing over 50 per cent more lift than conventional delta types, in conjunction with an integral thrust-reverser for the RM8 turbofan.

For reliability, this powerplant was based on the 14,771-lb st (65.7-kN) commercial Pratt & Whitney JT8D-22 turbofan, developed and built by Svenska (later Volvo) Flygmotor for supersonic flight, and with a Swedish afterburner providing over 70 per cent thrust increase to around 26,014 lb (115.7 kN) for take-off. An autoland technique (again pioneered by Saab) for minimum approach speed control and selection of reverse thrust in a no-flare touchdown with compression of the 16.4 ft (5 m) per second oleos of the tandem mainwheels. The initial **AJ 37** attack aircraft, soon named **Viggen** (Thunderbolt), incorporated many other features novel for its time, including a Saab CK-37 miniaturised digital air data and nav/attack computer, SRA head-up display for primary flight data, and a Cutler-Hammer AIL microwave beam landing guidance system. A rocket-boosted Saab ejection seat provided zero-zero escape capabilities.

Built with extensive bonded alloy honeycomb structures, the first of seven prototypes made its initial flight on 8 February 1967, followed by the second aircraft on 21

September of the same year and the third on 29 March 1968. On 5 April 1968, the Swedish government authorised the air force to order 175 AJ/SF/SH 37s for delivery from 1971, and by April 1969 all six single-seat prototypes were flying, the last fully representative of the initial production attack variants. The first of these became airborne on 23 February 1971, deliveries starting soon afterwards in June to F7 at Satenas to replace A 32A Lansens; four attack squadrons became operational with AJ 37s by mid-1975. Seven of the Flyg-vapen's nine attack squadrons were scheduled to re-equip with AJ 37s, and the 109 aircraft built of this variant eventually equipped two squadrons each in F6, F7 and F15 at Karlsborg, Satenas and Söderhamn after F7's third squadron disbanded. The second unit at Söderhamn is the AJ 37 OCU, equipped jointly with two-seat Sk 37 Viggen trainers for type conversion. F6 disbanded at Karlsborg/Vastagota on 30 June 1994, while F15 will re-organise to declare two full AJ 37 squadrons (instead of the current 1½), using former F6 aircraft. AJ 37s are currently being upgraded to **AJS 37** standard (see separate entry), extending their useful life into the next century.

WEAPON OPTIONS

AJ 37 primary armament is the fire-and-forget Saab RB 15F anti-ship missile or Rb 75 TV-guided (AGM-65) Maverick ASMs on two to four underwing or three fuselage weapons pylons. Older weapons such as the the Saab Rb 04E anti-ship missile, and Rb 05A ASM are used largely for training. For their secondary interception role, the early Viggens carried licence-built Rb 27/28 Hughes AIM-4 Falcon or Rb 24 AIM-9B/J Sidewinder AAMs. Today Viggens are more likely to carry the AIM-9L version, designated Rb 74. With no built-in gun, the AJ 37 could carry underwing

pods containing 30-mm ADEN cannon as an alternative to four 2.95-in (7.5-cm) Bofors M57 or 5.3-in (13.5-cm) M70 six-round rocket pods, or up to five tonnes (11,023 lb) of conventional FFV 120-, 250-, 500- or 600-kg bombs or M71 Virgo retarded bombs. Fire control is via an Ericsson PS-37A X-band monopulse radar with a large-diameter cassegrain antenna.

OPERATORS

Flygvapnet (The Swedish air force)

Middle Air Command
F15 Soderhamn
1 Attackflygdivisionen (Olle röd)
2 Attackflygdivisionen (Olle blaü- OCU)

Southern Air Command
F10 Angelholm (forming one squadron with AJS 37)

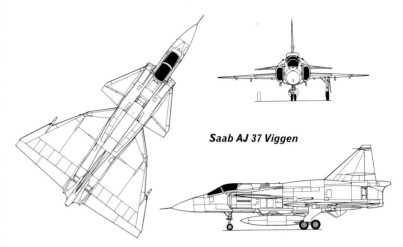

Saab AJ 37 Viggen

First Fighter Bomber Air Command
F7 Satenas/Skaraborgs (introducing JAS 39)
1 Attackflygdivisionen (Gustav röd)
2 Attackflygdivisionen (Gustav blaü)

SPECIFICATION

Saab AJ 37 Viggen
Wing: span 10.60 m (34 ft 9.25 in); aspect ratio 2.45; area 46.00 m² (495.16 sq ft); canard foreplane span 5.45 m (17 ft 10.5 in); canard foreplane area 6.20 m² (66.74 sq ft)
Fuselage and tail: length 16.30 m (53 ft 5.75 in) including probe; height 5.80 m (19 ft 0.25 in); wheel track 4.76 m (15 ft 7.5 in); wheel base 5.60 m (18 ft 4.5 in)
Powerplant: one Volvo Flygmotor RM8A turbofan (Pratt & Whitney JT8D-22 turbofan with Swedish-designed afterburner and thrust reverser) rated at 14,770 lb st (65.70 kN) dry and 26,015 lb st (115.72 kN) with afterburning
Weights: empty equipped about 11800 kg (26,014 lb); normal take-off 15000 kg (33,069 lb); maximum take-off 20500 kg (45,194 lb)
Fuel and load: internal fuel about 5700 litres (1,506 US gal); maximum ordnance 6000 kg (13,228 lb)
Speed: maximum level speed 'clean' at 11000 m (36,090 ft) more than 2125 km/h (1,146 kt; 1,320 mph)
Range: combat radius more than 1000 km (539 nm; 621 miles) on a hi-lo-hi attack mission, or more than 500 km (270 nm; 311 miles) on a lo-lo-lo attack mission
Performance: climb to 10000 m (32,810 ft) from brakes-off in less than 1 minute 40 seconds with afterburning; service ceiling about 18300 m (60,040 ft); take-off run about 400 m (1,312 ft); landing run about 500 m (1,640 ft) at normal landing weight

The AJ 37 'attack' Viggen is a potent weapon, made even more so by its wartime operation from concealed roadway strips hidden in Sweden's densely wooded landscape. The AJS 37 upgrade now underway will result in a truly multi-role Viggen.

Saab JA 37 Viggen

For its dedicated interception role, with a secondary ground-attack capability, Saab developed the **JA 37 Viggen**. Although little changed externally from the attack variant, the interceptor introduces more fundamental changes under the skin, with avionics, armament, engine and structural modifications. The JA 37's primary sensor is the Ericsson PS-46/A medium-PRF multi-mode X-band pulse-Doppler look-down/shoot-down radar, which has four air-to-air modes and a look-down range in excess of 48 km (30 miles). New avionics include an upgraded and higher-capacity Singer-Kearfott SKC-2037 central digital computer and KT-70L INS, Decca Doppler Type 72 nav

radar, Garrett AiResearch LD-5 digital air data computer, Saab-Honeywell SA07 digital AFCS, Svenska Radio integrated electronic display system, and an SRA HUD. The RM8B turbofan is uprated by Volvo to develop 16,600 lb (73.84 kN) maximum dry thrust and 28,109 lb (125 kN) with afterburning. This extra power allows the JA 37 to fly at Mach 1.2 at low altitude, and exceed Mach 2 at higher altitudes. Airframe changes include a wing restressed for a higher load factor, a fuselage stretch of 10 cm (4 in) ahead of the wing to accommodate the modified powerplant, a 10-cm (4-in) fin extension similar to that of the Sk 37 trainer, and four instead of three elevator actuators

under each wing. Radar trials, designed to intercept from east or west low-flying high-speed targets, such as cruise missiles, began in 1973 in a Lansen testbed aircraft that had made 87 test flights by late 1974.

Four AJ 37 prototypes were modified to JA 37 standard for the development programme, the first making its initial flight on 27 September 1974, a few days after SAF orders for the first 30 production Viggen interceptors. A fifth JA 37 prototype, which initially flew in 1975, was built to pre-production standards, the first series aircraft following on 4 November 1977.

In March 1980, the Swedish government authorised a third batch of 59 JA 37s, increasing overall production of this variant to 149 and the Viggen total to its final figure of 330. JA 37s were planned to replace Flyg-vapnet J 35 Drakens in the 1978-85 period

and to arm at least eight of the 10 Draken air defence squadrons at that time. Those re-equipped eventually comprised two divisionen (squadrons) each of F4, F16 and F21 at Ostersund, Uppsala and Lulea, and one divisionen each in F13 and F17 at Norköping and Ronneby. As part of the overall reduction in Swedish wings, F13 was disbanded on 30 June 1994, and the JA 37s of its single squadron, 2 Jaktflygdivisionen (Martin blä), were dispersed among other units.

A specially-equipped Viggen interceptor, the **Saab 37E Eurofighter**, was put forward as a possible alternative to the multinational European Fighter Group in 1975. Despite their many advanced features and excellent all-round performance, no Viggens have ever achieved any export sales, mostly because of Sweden's rigidly non-aligned political policies during the Cold War.

By mid-1994 most of Sweden's 'fighter' Viggen force had adopted this two-tone air superiority grey scheme, with high-visibility Dayglo orange codes on the tail and above the wings. These two-digit codes are usually (though not always) the last two numbers of the aircraft's full (five-digit) serial. Radio callsigns are allocated to the Flygvapen's four JA 37 Viggen wings (and all Swedish armed forces flying units) according to the wing number's position in the Swedish (phonetic) alphabet; thus, F21 uses the name 'Urban', F4 'David', and so forth. Each wing is divided into two or more squadrons (divisionen), always in the order red, blue and yellow.

WEAPON OPTIONS

The JA 37 introduces an integral high-velocity 30-mm Oerlikon KCA revolver cannon (offset to port) with 150 rounds mounted in a ventral pack, and aimed by a new radar-based weapons sight. JA 37 primary armament comprises up to six AAMs. Standard BVR weapon is the medium-range, semi-active radar-guided, all-weather BAeD Rb 71 Sky Flash. Rb 74 (AIM-9L) IR-homing Sidewinders are fielded for short-range work. Seven to nine weapons pylons similar to those on the AJ 37 accommodate up to 13,000 lb (5897 kg) of external stores. These include four pods each containing six Bofors 5.3-in (13.-5cm) rockets for air-to-surface use.

OPERATORS

Flygvapnet (The Swedish air force)
Northern Air Command
F4 Ostersund/Froson
1 Jaktflygdivisionen (David röd)
2 Jaktflygdivisionen (David blä)
F21 Luleå/Kallax
2 Jaktflygdivisionen (Urban blä)
3 Jaktflygdivisionen (Urban gul)

Middle Air Command
F16 Uppsala
1 Jaktflygdivisionen (Petter röd)
2 Jaktflygdivisionen (Petter blä)

Southern Air Command
F17 Ronneby/Belkinge
1 Jaktflygdivisionen (Quintus röd)
2 Jaktflygdivisionen (Quintus blä)

SPECIFICATION

Saab JA 37 Viggen
generally similar to the AJ 37 Viggen except for the following particulars:
Fuselage and tail: length 16.40 m (53 ft 9.75 in) including probe; height 5.90 m (19 ft 4.25 in); wheel base 5.69 m (18 ft 8 in)

Powerplant: one Volvo Flygmotor RM8B turbofan (Pratt & Whitney JT8D-22 with Swedish-designed afterburner and thrust reverser) rated at 16,200 lb st (72.06 kN) maximum military dry and 28,110 lb st (125.04 kN) with afterburning
Weights: normal take-off 15000 kg (33,069 lb); maximum take-off 17000 kg (37,478 lb) interceptor, or 20500 kg (45,194 lb) attack
Speed: maximum level speed 'clean' at 10975 m (36,000 ft) more than 2126 km/h (1,147 kt; 1,321 mph)
Performance: climb to 32,800 ft (10000 m) in less than 1 minute 40 seconds from brakes-off with afterburning; service ceiling about 60,000 ft (18290 m); take-off run about 400 m (1,312 ft) at typical take-off weight; landing run about 500 m (1,640 ft) at normal landing weight

Saab **SF 37/SH 37 Viggen**

Designed as an S 35E Draken replacement, the **SF 37** adaptation of the AJ 37 is equipped for all-weather day and night overland reconnaissance with low- and high-altitude film cameras giving complete horizon-to-horizon lateral coverage, plus a VKA 702 infra-red camera recording thermal images in place of the nose radar. Twin ventral pods also house night cameras and illumination equipment, the photoflash system operating with light just outside the visible wavelengths. A Red Baron IR line-scan system, with the standard active and passive underwing ECM pods, may also be carried, but the SF 37 has no attack capability and armament is normally confined only to defensive Rb 74 (AIM-9L) AAMs. All nine cameras have automatic exposure control and image motion compensation controlled by the aircraft's central computer.

First flight of the prototype SF 37 was on 21 May 1973, and deliveries began to the SAF in early 1977. The last of 28 SF 37s built was handed over for delivery to F21 at Lulea in northern Sweden on 7 February 1980, thereby ending AJ 37 series production. SF 37s also equip additional single reconnaissance squadrons in F13 at Norköping in the south-east and F17 at Ronneby in the south. In addition, they operate in conjunction with specially-equipped 'S 37 Intelligence Platoons', comprising mobile evaluation centres with briefing, processing, evaluation and interpretation facilities.

The **SH 37** was modified from the AJ 37 as a successor to the Saab S 32C Lansen for all-weather sea surveillance and patrol, with secondary maritime strike capability, and fitted with modified radar, plus ventral night reconnaissance and SKA 24D 600-mm lens long-range camera pods. Underwing ECM pods are also normally carried, as well as AAMs on the outboard wing stations. Both the SF and SH 37s normally operate with a ventral fuselage drop tank. F13 at Norköping formed the first SH 37 squadron in late 1976, and the 27 Viggens of this type built between 1977 and 1979 served alongside the SF 37s to equip the three mixed reconnaissance squadrons in F13, F17 and

F21. F13 disbanded on 30 June 1994, and F17 has also relinquished its reconnaissance role, though SF 37s remained at Ronneby in mid-1994. F10, and other units, are currently receiving the first AJS 37 Viggens, the combined attack/reconnaissance version (described seperately). Reconnaissance Viggens will benefit chiefly from improved (air-to-air) armament capability in the AJS 37 programme, and they are currently being distributed throughout the Flygvapen's AJ 37 units.

F13 was an SF 37 (Spanings Foto, or photo reconnaissance) operator until its 1994 disbandment. Some of its aircraft were transferred to F21, currently the sole SF/SH 37 unit.

Right: The SH 37 maritime radar-reconnaissance Viggen closely resembles the AJ 37. Only its podded cameras and LOROP betray its mission.

OPERATORS

SPECIFICATION

Saab SF 37 Viggen
generally similar to the Saab AJ 37 Viggen except in the following particulars
Weights: maximum take-off 17000 kg (37,478 lb)

Saab SF 37 Viggen

This SF 37 (Spanings Foto, photo reconnaissance) Viggen wears the markings of Bråvalla Flygflottilj F13, formerly based at Norköping, which disbanded in June 1994. The wing's first squadron (1 Spaning-flygdivisionen) flew both the SF and SH 37 (Spanings Havsövervakning, coastal surveillance) variants. With the advent of the AJS 37 programme, SF 37s (and SH 37s) are being allocated to the 'attack' Viggen units around Sweden.

WING
The wing incorporates hydraulically actuated two-section elevons on the trailing edge. The leading edge has compound sweep, and is extended forward on the outer sections, outboard of the prominent bullet fairings which accommodate an RWR antenna.

NOSE GEAR
The nose undercarriage unit incorporates twin, side-by-side nosewheels which retract forward. The Viggen is fitted with Dunlop anti-skid brakes, and the wheels' Goodyear tyres are inflated to 215 psi (15.11 kg/cm²) (main) and 155 psi (10.90 kg/cm²) (nose).

WINDSCREEN
The Viggen's hardened, wraparound single-piece windscreen provides not only excellent visibility, but also protection against birdstrikes.

UNIT MARKINGS
All camouflaged Flygvapnet aircraft carry their wing number in yellow on the forward fuselage, along with a two-digit individual identification code, in red, on the tailfin. In reconnaissance squadrons, even numbers were reserved for the SF 37s, while the SH 37s had odd numbers. Whenever possible, these two digits coincided with the last two of the aircraft's serial. Most Viggens now carry wing badges on the fin, while some carry individual squadron badges elsewhere.

CAMOUFLAGE
Apart from the majority of JA 37s, all Viggens wear a unique four-colour camouflage, often referred to as the 'splinter' scheme. The Flygvapen refers to it as the 'fields and meadows' camouflage, and it convincingly hides the aircraft at their forest dispersal bases and in their low-level operational environment. The undersides remain grey, but when seen from above the straight-edged pattern conceals the overall aircraft shape.

FOLDING TAILFIN
One of the Viggen's more unusual features is its folding fin. The aircraft's rudder is of metal-bonded honeycomb construction, and the entire unit folds to port to facilitate storage in underground and small hardened shelters.

MAIN UNDERCARRIAGE
The thinness of the wing dictated the use of tandem mainwheels, the incidental advantages of which include better energy absorption on landing and lower snow resistance when taxiing. The oleos are shortened during retraction. Built by Motala Verkstad, the undercarriage can withstand sink rates of up to 5 m (16 ft) per second, allowing steep approaches and no-flare landings.

CAMERA NOSE
The SF 37 dispenses with radar and instead carries a battery of cameras comprising three fanned 120-mm SKA 24C, one vertical VKA 702 infra-red and vertical SKA 24, two 600-mm SKA 31, and a 57-mm SKA 24 units.

Saab **Sk 37 Viggen**

With the Viggen fulfilling its role as the Flygvapen's primary combat aircraft system, there was a pressing need for a trainer version. The **Sk 37 Viggen** (Skol, or School) tandem two-seat trainer was developed simultaneously with the AJ 37. This variant is somewhat unusual in having two separate cockpits for pilot and instructor. The stepped rear instructor's cockpit is fitted with a bulged canopy and twin lateral periscopes, replacing some electronics and a forward fuel tank. Fuel capacity was partially restored by a permanently-mounted ventral fuel tank (although a centreline tank is also invariably carried). Other changes include a 10-cm (4-in) taller fin to restore stability after modification with the deeper forward fuselage. Because of its height, even the standard AJ 37 fin can be folded on the ground to allow clearance for the

SAF's cavern-based hangars. Despite its radome, the Sk 37 has no radar and, therefore, no radar navigation capability (and limited operational capability), having to rely on Doppler and DME. The first Sk 37 was the seventh Viggen prototype and initially flew on 2 July 1970. Sk 37 deliveries started to F7 in June 1972, and 15 of just 17 trainers built equip the Viggen OCU part of F15 at Söderhamn, alongside AJ 37s.

Hålsingge Flygflottilj F15 currently fields '1½' squadrons, as 2 Attackflygdivisionen/ Typingflyingskola (Olle blä) flies both AJ and Sk 37s. The wing's first squadron (1 Attackflygdivisionen, Olle röt) flies AJ 37s also, but the Sk 37s train Viggen pilots for all versions, even the JA 37. F15 is due to absorb some of the former F6 AJ 37s, and will ultimately possess two full attack squadrons, in addition to the OCU *divisionen*.

The small number of Sk 37s have been heavily utilised throughout their lives, restricting operations today to essential training only.

Saab **AJS 37 Viggen**

Modification of Viggens to **AJS 37** standard, plus approval for the Swedish government's proposals to disband one and a half Viggen squadrons, were among the Swedish Parliamentary Defence Committee recommendations adopted in June 1992. This SEK300 million ($50 million) upgrade proposed by Saab in mid-1991 involves 115 surviving AJ, SF and SH 37s, and will combine their various specialised systems, plus enhanced computer power from a multi-processor/databus, to produce the multi-role AJS 37 Viggen. This will use some of the JAS 39 Gripen's weapon systems, including the Saab Rb 15F anti-ship missile, BK/DWS sub-munitions dispenser, various advanced AAMs,

and the JAS 39's planned reconnaissance and ECM pods, for which Ericsson and MBB have been competing. Modified AJS 37s started to re-equip four Flygvapnet squadrons in 1993, being allocated to units on completion of conversion rather than forming dedicated AJS 37 units. All but the former SF 37s (which retain their camera nose) will be fitted with the SH 37's radar.

There will be no external differences to distinguish upgraded aircaft, which will in fact be completed to slightly differing standards depending on the original airframe (AJ, SF or SH 37). The SF and SH 37 will benefit chiefly from improved armament options, particularly the ability to carry additional air-to-air missiles.

The last production AJ 37 Viggen was also one of the first AJS 37 conversions to be completed. Older weapons, such as these Rb 05 ASMs, will be now be replaced by the JAS 39's Rb 15 ASMs and DWS 39 sub-munitions dispensers.

Saab **JAS 39 Gripen**

By early 1980, with Viggen deliveries continuing apace, it was clear that if Sweden was to maintain its status as a military airframe manufacturer, and its policy of operating only indigenous combat aircraft, work on a successor to the Saab Viggen would have to begin soon. Strict government control dictated an aircraft design that would cost only 60-65 per cent more than the Saab 37, and be only half the weight. Its primary role would be as a fighter interceptor, with an important, but secondary, attack mission. It was to be a fully multi-role aircraft, in marked contrast to the mission-specific Viggen family. It was also hoped that this new aircraft would provide a replacement for the ageing Sk 60 trainer fleet.

After IG JAS submitted its initial proposal in June 1981, over seven years passed before the prototype made its maiden flight.

The JAS Industry Group was formed by Saab, Volvo Flygmotor, Ericsson and FFV, and their bid to develop the new aircraft was accepted by the Swedish government. Following the cancellation of the Saab 38 (B3LA) light-attack/advanced trainer project in February 1979, Saab began development of preliminary designs for a single-seat, single-engined, fly-by-wire, delta-winged aircraft, with an all-flying canard. Thirty per cent of its eight-tonne final weight was to be of composite materials.

The proven General Electric F404J turbofan was chosen as the powerplant. Volvo Flygmotor would share assembly and testing of the engine, designated RM12, with the American manufacturer. The RM12 had a dry rating of 12,150 lb (54.05 kN), or 17,800 lb (79.18 kN) with a new Volvo/GE afterburner, to give the Gripen all-altitude supersonic performance with only fixed rectangular intakes.

Unlike the Viggen, the Gripen lacks a thrust reverser. It gains its short-field performance from its large, all-moving canard foreplanes, which can be rotated downwards through almost 90° to assist groundbraking in conjunction with the rear-fuselage lateral airbrakes. These are augmented by saw-toothed leading-edge flaps and linked with the four drooping elevon control surfaces through the full-authority triplex digital FBW system with an analog back-up. As a control-configured vehicle for extra agility, the Gripen is claimed by Saab to be the first inherently unstable canard production fighter and features 40 computers interlinked via three MIL STD 1553B databuses.

Ericsson was tasked with developing a new multi-mode, pulse-Doppler, X-band PS-046 (later PS-05) radar, while FFV developed the nav/attack systems. The HOTAS cockpit would have three Ericsson EP-17 multi-function cockpit displays and a wide-

angle holographic HUD, and it was planned to integrate a FLIR system with the radar and avionics. A Martin-Baker S10LS zerozero ejection seat replaces Saab systems used in all previous Flygvapnet combat jets.

Contracts between FMV (Defence Materiel Administration), the Swedish defence procurement agency and IG JAS for the newly designated **JAS 39** were signed in June 1982. These contracts (worth SEK11.5 billion, then $1.87 billion) covered the development of five prototypes and an initial production run of 30 aircraft. Options for a further 110 aircraft were also undertaken. In June 1984, the Riksdag (Swedish parliament) gave the go-ahead to this JAS (Jakt, Attak, Spanning: fighter,

The Gripen relies far more heavily on aerodynamic braking than its predecessors, using its all-moving canards for short stops.

Saab JAS 39 Gripen

The Gripen's initial task will be to replace the Flygvapen's 'first-generation' Viggens, the attack AJ 37s. The smaller JAS 39 will carry the same weapons, including the Rb 15F AShM and Rb 75 Maverick.

1991), and both air and ground tests proved encouraging, if time-consuming. A study for a projected two seat **JAS 39B** aircraft was begun in 1989, while the single-seat programme continued with the second aircraft (39-2) flying on 4 May 1990. This was followed by 39-4 (with the first full avionics fit) on 20 December 1990, 39-3 (the first with full radar and avionics fit) on 25 March 1991, and 39-5 on 23 October 1991.

Flight tests (costed at only $2,500 per hour) soon revealed that aerodynamic drag and induced drag, in clean configuration, were 10 per cent lower than expected. Any engine thrust anomalies had been ironed out, and airfield performance was above the specification. In freeflow, the canards are the primary brakes, deployed from a landing speed of 220 km/h (136 mph). Gripens have repeatedly demonstrated their ability to operate from a standard Base 90 runway, i.e. a hardened road-strip, typically 800 m x 9 m (2600 ft x 30 ft). The JAS 39 has been flown to a load of 9g and the static test airframe has been subjected to 230 per cent of the limit load before failure (design requirement was for 180 per cent only). In October 1991, Saab submitted its costing proposal for the **JAS 39B** operational trainer and the follow-on Batch 2 order for 110 single-seat aircraft. By January 1993 the flight test programme had reached 300 flights, and that year was joined by the first production aircraft (39-101) allocated after the crash of the prototype. Problems were encountered with the APU and the environmental control systems. A possible replacement APU has been mooted to overcome the current units high failure rate.

June 1992 saw the final go-ahead for the Batch 2 aircraft and the JAS 39B, for an adjusted cost of SEK18 billion ($3 billion). To be tasked primarily with conversion and tactical training, the JAS 39B operational trainer will have a performance equivalent to that of the single-seater but involves a 40 per cent change from that type, including a 65.5-cm (25.8-in) fuselage stretch. The rear cockpit is the same as the front, barring a HUD, but HUD imagery can be monitored on one of the displays. By mid-1994, the prototype (39-800) was taking shape at Linköping, along with 39-801 and a fatigue test airframe. Ejection seat sled tests commenced in the US in July 1993 and are progressing. First flight is planned for 1996, with deliveries in 1988.

A milestone in the test programme was reached on 21 April 1993, when the 1,000th test flight took place. The four prototypes were joined by the first production Gripen (39-101) on 4 March 1993, when it made its maiden flight, piloted by Lars Rådeström. The second production example (39-102) became the first to be handed over to the Flygvapen, at Linkoping on 8 June 1993, being delivered to F7 at Satenas the same day. On 18 August, 39-101 was lost in a dramatic crash during an air display over Stockholm, and the pilot (Lars Rådeström again) ejected. Saab later announced that the accident was caused by "the flight control system's high amplification of stick commands in combination with large, rapid stick movements by the pilot. This led to the stability margin being exceeded, and the aircraft entered a stall." A contributing fac-

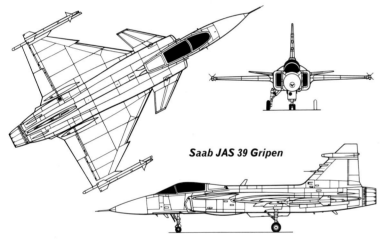

Saab JAS 39 Gripen

attack, reconnaissance) project as an affordable answer to the Flygvapen's need for a third-generation combat aircraft. New facilities were built by Saab at Linköping to cope with the demand. By now the name **Gripen** (Griffin) had been adopted. The projected requirement was for 350 aircraft, with the first in service by 1992, rather than 1990 as originally hoped .

Engine tests began in 1984, and five test rigs had accumulated over 800 running hours by June 1985. A full-size mock-up was completed by early 1986, differing from the initial conceptual drawings by being a more stocky and box-like design, while still retaining its small size. The first flight was planned for 1986, but problems with the software for the complex fly-by-wire system (developed by Lear-Siegler, now GEC Astronics) caused this date to be set back

progressively. The project was also troubled by rising costs, which threatened its cancellation by parliament. Finally, the aircraft was rolled out at Linköping on 26 April 1987 (Saab's 50th anniversary). The first JAS 39 (39-1) flew for a total of 51 minutes on 9 December 1988, in the hands of Stig Holmstrom. From then, the aircraft's performance helped it to survive a critical funding review in January of the following year, when the threat of an off-the-shelf purchase, instead of the Gripen, finally subsided.

A major set-back was suffered on the sixth flight, when a failure of the flight control system caused the crash of the first aircraft on 2 February 1989. The pilot, Lars Rådeström, was unhurt but for a broken arm. Major software corrections were undertaken in the United States by Calspan, with a modified T-33. This caused another 15 months' delay before the second prototype flew on 4 May 1990, putting the programme some three years behind schedule, though the JAS 39 returned to flying status in May. After two investigations, the FMV underlined its commitment to the JAS 39, and ultimately the government compensated Saab for its loss. Problems were also encountered with the RM12, which suffered from 'thrust-droop', and cracks in the compressor blades, but these, too, were soon rectified. The new PS-05/A radar was tested in a modified Viggen (until the end of

39-102, the second production Gripen, was formally handed over to the Swedish air force in June 1993 when it was escorted from Linköping to its future home of Satenas by a pair of F7 AJ 37s.

tor was the late display of the STYRSÄK (flight attitude) warning, giving the pilot too little time to react. Flying was suspended until 29 December 1993, after the fitting of updated flight control software.

By mid-1994, after nearly 1,300 flights, the remaining Gripens had completed 60 per cent of the total flight test programme, verifying 80 per cent of their contractual obligations. Weapons tests have included Rb 74 (AIM-9L) firings at 6*g*, Rb 75 (AGM-65) firings at 3*g* and successful separations from DWS 39, Rb 15 and external tanks. Flying was briefly suspended between 14 January and 15 February 1994, after Volvo identified blade failure in an RM12 low-pressure fan, caused by defective fuel injectors leading to uneven fuel flow and vibration. With deliveries resumed, 15 engines have so far been delivered.

By mid-1994, Gripens 39-105 to -113 are in check-out or final assembly. Saab expects to deliver 140 aircraft between 1993 and 2002, in addition to 14 JAS 39Bs. These aircraft will replace eight squadrons of AJ 37 Viggens, but there will then be a need to replace the younger JA 37 aircraft in the air defence role. A total Gripen purchase of 300 aircraft is likely, for an overall programme cost of SEK57.8 billion ($7.8 billion). Ten were planned to be delivered to the Flygvapen by the end of 1994 (though this is likely to be reduced to five, as so far only 39-104 and -105 have been handed over), and they will remain at Linköping, not Satenas. The first squadron (F7's 2 *divisionen*) will begin conversion by October 1995, and already Saab has a modification programme in hand to recall the initial 30 Batch 1 aircraft and update their software to Batch 2 standard. These will feature a PP12 processor for the EP17 MFDs, replacing the current EP1 and EP2 units which are twice the size and weight.

With a planned production rate of 20 to 30 aircraft a year, Saab is also working hard to sell the Gripen abroad, in a marked reversal of former policy. At Farnborough in 1992, Swedish Defence Minister Anders Bjoerck revealed SAF plans for a so-called upgraded 'Turbo Gripen', or **JAS 39C**, for a third production batch. This would have an uprated RM12 turbofan, Ericsson D80E computers and more weapons, for both potential export and for further Flygvapnet deliveries to replace the last of some 350 Viggens. Finland's fighter evaluation prior to its 1992 F/A-18 order included over 250 Gripen sorties by two Finnish test pilots, while in the same year Defence Minister Bjorck discussed possible **JAS 39X** (export) purchases.

WEAPON OPTIONS

Basic armament for all roles includes an integral 27-mm Mauser BK27 cannon under the port centre fuselage and two wingtip-mounted Rb 74 (AIM-9L) or other IR-homing AAMs, supplemented by four underwing and a ventral weapons pylons for external stores. These include medium-range active-radar AAMs, ASMs, Saab Rb 15F anti-ship missiles, DWS 39 or other cluster-bomb dispensers,

conventional or retarded bombs, air-to-surface rockets, fuel tanks or FLIR, reconnaissance and electronic warfare pods. In August 1994 the FMV announced a buy of 100 Hughes AIM-120 AMRAAMs to serve as an interim BVR missile for the JAS 39 force. This purchase, much smaller than the 500 expected, was made in favour of the MATRA Mica or BAe Active Sky Flash. However, it leaves the way open for the future acquisition of a more advanced long-range weapon, such as the S225X missile under development with BAe (already a close Saab partner), Thomson-CSF and GEC-Marconi.

SPECIFICATION

Saab JAS 39A Gripen
Wing: span 8.00 m (26 ft 3 in)
Fuselage and tail: length 14.10 m (46 ft 3 in); height 4.70 m (15 ft 5 in); wheel track 2.60 m (8 ft 6½ in); wheel base 5.30 m (17 ft 4¾ in)
Powerplant: one Volvo Flygmotor RM12 turbofan (General Electric F404-GE-400) rated at 12,140 lb st (54.00 kN) dry and 18,100 lb (80.51 kN) with afterburning
Weights: operating empty 6622 kg (14,599 lb); normal take-off about 8000 kg (17,637 lb); maximum take-off 12473 kg (27,498 lb)
Fuel and load: internal fuel 2268 kg (5,000 lb); maximum ordnance 6500 kg (14,330 lb)
Speed: maximum level speed 'clean' at 36,000 ft (10975 m) 1,147 kt (1,321 mph; 2126 km/h)
g limits: +9

Below: Gripen 39-101, the first production aircraft, joined the surviving four prototypes in the test programme after the loss of 39-1. 39-102 wears what will probably be the standard scheme for service aircraft, despite their attack role.

Above: In addition to Sidewinders, this Gripen (39-2) carries a dummy DWS 39 for separation tests. Two camera pods are carried, to starboard and on the centreline.

Below: The same aircraft is seen here with a less advanced, but equally effective, load of Bofors rocket pods. It, too, carries an all-aspect test camera pod.

Saab 105

Developed as a private venture, the **Saab 105** is a trainer and light ground-attack aircraft that is also capable of other roles, including reconnaissance, liaison and executive transport (for which the side-by-side ejection seats can be replaced by four fixed seats). The first of two prototypes flew on 29 June 1963, and the following year the Saab 105 was ordered into production for the Swedish air force, the first of 150 flying on 27 August 1965.

Designated **Sk 60**, the Saab 105 is powered by two Turboméca Aubisque turbofans and entered service in the spring of 1966 with F5, the Flygvapen Basic Flying Training School at Ljungbyhed, in southern Sweden. Most were later given armament hardpoints, gunsights and associated equipment. Variants include the **Sk 60B** with light attack capability, and the **Sk 60C**, which is equipped for photographic reconnaissance with a Fairchild KB-18 camera in the nose, yet retains a ground-attack capability. The Sk 60A and Sk 60B are virtually identical, though no Sk 60A ever carries underwing pylons. However, while all aircaft carry (F5)

codes on the nose, Sk 60B codes are higher to avoid a dielectric panel on the nosecone. The **Sk 60D** is a special crew trainer, while the **Sk 60E** is a four-seat liaison variant.

Over 100 Sk 60A/B/Cs remain in service, primarily in the training role, with four squadrons of F5 and with 5 *divisionen* (Petter Swarz) of F16, based at Uppsala. The latter unit also supports the Royal Air Cadet School. Every Sk 60 wears the unit identifier of F5, regardless of where it is based, as all aircraft are distributed from a central maintenance pool. All basic flying training is undertaken at the GFU (Basic Flying Training School) at Ljungbyhed, while weapons

qualification is the responsibility of the Uppsala-based GTU. This unit has a complement of 16-18 aircraft, and in time of war would act as an autonomous *Lätt Attackenheter* (Light Attack unit), along with a second unit drawn from F5 proper.

Three Sk 60Ds and 16 Sk 60Es remain in service, small numbers being assigned to the *Sambandsflygrupp* of each tactical wing. These aircraft are assigned to liaison and instrument check ride duties.

Between 1988 and 1991, the Sk 60 fleet underwent a programme of structural modifications that increased the aircrafts's *g* limits from 4.5 to 6 and added new ejection

Saab 105

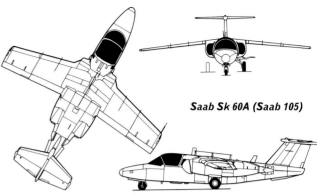

Saab Sk 60A (Saab 105)

Above: The Saab 105Ös of Austria's 1 Staffel, Jagdbombergeschwader, Fliegerregiment III, wear a fin badge depicting a cartoon tiger on a red '1', with a blue background encircled by a green laurel wreath.

Below: Designated Sk 60 in Flygvapnet service, the Saab 105 is fulfils a number of roles from light transport to light attack. It is also the mount of the national aerobatic team, 'Team 60', comprising six Sk 60s drawn from F5.

with 1,900-lb (8.45-kN) Williams Rolls FJ44 two-shaft turbofans. This will dramatically improve their overall and single-engine performance, in addition to appreciably reducing running costs, and aircaft noise. A first flight is planned for spring 1995, to be followed by nine conversions in 1996. From then, the bulk of the modifications will be carried out in the workshops of the Air Force Flight Academy, at Ljungbyhed, until their completion in 1998.

The **Saab 105XT** development, powered by J85 turbojets, first flew on 29 April 1967. Fuel capacity was increased to 2050 litres (451 Imp gal), two 500-litre (110-Imp gal) underwing drop tanks also being available. In addition to enhanced performance, the 105XT had improved avionics, and a strengthened wing allows the underwing load to be increased to 2000 kg (4,409 lb). This version can perform interception and target-towing roles. IR-guided missiles such as Sidewinder are carried for day interceptor duties. Forty aircraft designated **Saab 105Ö** were built for the **Austrian air force**. These aircraft were the country's only air defence assets for a period, pending delivery of Saab Drakens. Thirty survivors currently fly with Fliegerregiment III at Hörsching, employed on ground attack and reconnaissance duties. Two squadrons are identified by colour, 1 Staffel being 'gelb' and 2 Staffel 'grün'. The latter unit undertakes the reconnaissance mission with

large underwing camera pods, and provides aircraft for advanced and weapons training. A handful have had their ejection seats removed to be reconfigured as four-seat liaison aircraft.

seats and rewinging, therbey extending their working lives to 2000. In a programme costing SEK900 million, 115 aircraft (with an option on another 20) will be further upgraded from 1995 to extend their service

to 2010 and beyond. Two contracts cover design and modification of a single Sk 60, spares supply and engine maintenance for the first 10 years of operation. Chief among the improvements planned is re-engining

Saab **MFI-15 Safari and MFI-17 Supporter**

The remaining customer was the **Zambian air force**, which received 20 MFI-17s in 1977-78 for both COIN and training duties.

In 1967 Saab began the design of a two/three-seat lightplane for training and other utility duties, based largely on the **MFI-9 Minicom** two-seat lightplane. Six armed **MFI-9B**s (flown by mercenary pilots) were used by the Biafran air force during the four-year civil war. In 1968 construction began of a **Saab MFI-15** prototype (SE-301) that first flew on 11 July 1969. A monoplane of all-metal construction with a conventional tail unit, it had fixed tricycle (or optional tail-wheel) landing gear, a 119-kW (160-hp) Avco Lycoming IO-320-B2 flat-four piston engine, and a braced, shoulder-mounted wing incorporating unusual limited forward

sweep. Beneath an upward-hinged canopy were two side-by-side seats, with space behind them for baggage or an optional rear-facing third seat. Dual controls were standard, with provision for IFR instrumentation and a radio. Early tests led to the adoption of a T-tail layout (with an all-moving tailplane) reducing the risk of damage by debris and a new uprated Lycoming engine. The modified prototype resumed flying on 26 February 1971, entering production as the **Safari**. Most were sold for civil use, but some were delivered to military customers. The first two production examples were sold in 1973 to **Sierra Leone** for pilot train-

The Kongelige Danske Flyvevaaben's (Danish air force) Saab Supporters are still very active in their training and liasion roles. The Flyveskolen aircraft operate from Avnø, on the island of København, while others are attached to the transport unit, Esk 721 based at Vaerløse. Army MFI-17s fly from Kompagni, alongside Fennecs and Hughes 500s.

ing, and subsequently sold in 1978. **Norway** ordered an initial batch of 16 in 1981 for basic training as replacements for ageing Saab Safirs. Attrition replacements of three and four were received in 1982-83 and 1987, respectively. The 19 surviving MFI-15s are used for pilot screening at Vaernes.

In early 1972, the second Safari was modified with two hardpoints for up to 300 kg (661 lb) of ordnance including rockets, two twin-machine gun pods, or six Bantam wire-guided ATMs. First flown as the **MFI-17** on 6 July 1972, the type was named **Supporter** when offered for sale to air arms. When Saab ended manufacture in the late 1970s, the combined Safari/Supporter production total was approximately 250, including a small number for military use. **Denmark** received 32 Supporters (designated **T-17**) in 1976, primarily for pilot training. Nine were supplied to the army for artillery-spotting, observation and liaison, and the remainder went to the air force for pilot training at the Flyveskolen at Avnø (where they are also used to initially train army pilots) and for liaison duties. **Pakistan** received a substantial number of Supporters from 1974-75, the majority of which were manufactured locally under licence as the PAC Mushshak (described separately).

Saab 91 Safir

The **Saab-91 Safir** was a three-seat cabin monoplane of cantilever low-wing configuration which had retractable tricycle landing gear and was powered by a 130-hp (97-kW) de Havilland Gipsy Major 1C inline engine. Following the first flight of the prototype in 1945, successful testing led to the first production version, the **Saab-91A**, which differed by having the more powerful de Havilland Gipsy Major 10 engine. Interest in this aircraft by the **Swedish air force**

as a primary trainer led to a prototype powered by a 190-hp (142-kW) Avco Lycoming O-435-A flat-six engine, first flown on 18 January 1949. This was adopted by the Flygvapen as a standard trainer as the **Sk 50**, built by Saab with the same powerplant as the **Saab-91B**. It could be equipped to carry guns, practice bombs or rockets, and served also with the air forces of Ethiopia and Norway. For training, this version was also adopted by a number of European air-

lines. The **Saab-91C**, first flown in September 1953, differed from its predecessors by having four seats. The final production version was the **Saab-91D**, which introduced a number of improvements, including a new Avco Lycoming O-360-A1A engine, disc brakes and other advanced equipment that offered weight saving. Twenty-four Saab-91Ds were sold to the **Austrian air force**. When production ended, a total of 323 Safirs had been built.

Austria's last 15 Safirs served with the Ubungsstaffel of the Pilotenschule at Zeltweg, students then progressing to the PC-7. These veterans were retired in 1992. Safirs can still be found in Flygvapen markings, but the type is no longer on charge with the air force. Retired from their final role as liasion aircraft, Sk 50s have been disposed of to base flying club. Many retain full camouflage and markings with roundels, but are now civil registered.

Saab 340

The **Saab 340** 37-seat regional transport was originally developed in partnership with Fairchild and first flew on 25 January 1983. It has been a wholly Swedish programme since November 1985. By June 1994, 355 aircraft were in service. The original **340A** has been replaced by the **340B** featuring General Electric CT7-9B turboprops for improved 'hot-and-high' performance, higher weights, increased tailplane span and improved payload/range capability.

To date, only one example has been sold to a military customer. This aircraft is a Saab 340B (c/n 170) purchased for the Swedish air force. Delivered in February 1990 under the military designation **Tp 100** and serialled '10001', it is based at Stockholm-Tullinge with the Royal Flight. A current devlepoment of the Saab 340 holds the promise of significant future orders. In early 1993, Sweden chose the Saab 340B as an airborne early warning platform, carrying an Ericsson Erieye side-looking radar in a canoe fairing above the fuselage. Erieye is a long-range, S-band, pulse-Doppler radar which

The Flygvapen's Royal Flight operates a single VIP-configured Saab 340B, with the air force designation Tp 100.

uses a phased array antenna housed in a 9-m (29-ft 6-in) fairing and weighing some 900 kg (1,984 lb). The radar has a detection range of over 300 km (186 miles) against small airborne targets, from a cruising altitude of 8000 m (26,000 ft). The aircaft has been dubbed the Saab **340AEW&C**, as it also has a command and control role with one or more command consoles in the cabin, along with IFF/SSR interrogators, ESM capability, INS and GPS navigation systems and secure voice and datalinks. The prototype first flew, without the radar antenna, on 17 January 1994, and with the antenna on 1 July. It was fitted out by Hunting Ltd in the UK (as are all Saab 340s) before returning to Sweden for flight tests and delivery to the Flygvapen in early 1995. Several other nations have shown interest, including Australia.

This retouched picture illustrates the final configuration of the Swedish air force's Saab 340AEW&C.

Sabreliner Corp. (North American/Rockwell) Sabreliner/T-39 Sabre

Sabreliner Corportaion
6161 Aviation Drive, St Louis
Missouri 63134, USA

In 1956, when the **USAF** announced it sought a small jet transport and training aircraft on an off-the-shelf basis, North American Aviation (NAA) had such a design, which was renamed the **N.A.246 Sabreliner**. The prototype (N4060K) was rolled out at the manufacturer's Inglewood plant on 8 May 1956, and made its maiden flight on 16 September at Palmdale. As the only aircraft to actually fly (despite competition from eight other manufacturers), North American had presented the USAF with a *fait accompli*, and was notified that the Sabreliner had won the UTX competition.

The USAF placed an initial order for seven aircraft, designated **T-39A** (**N.A.265**). These were fitted with 13.35-kN (3,000-lb) Pratt & Whitney J60-P-3 engines. While the T-39As took shape, the USAF decided the type would make a suitable radar trainer for its F-105Ds. Consequently, the sixth T-39A was converted to **T-39B** (**N.A.265-20**) standard. On 15 January 1960 a follow-on order for 35 aircraft was placed, the first four of which would be T-39Bs. The first T-39A flew on 30 June 1960, operational deliveries commenced on 4 June 1962, and the last of 143 T-39As was delivered in late 1963. T-39Bs had slightly larger noses to house the F-105's R-14 radar and APN-131 Doppler. Lastly came three **T-39F** 'Teeny Weeny Weasels', which were As modified to train F-105G 'Wild Weasel' crews.

In 1961 the **US Navy** began to order the **T3J-1**, a navalised T-39B equipped with the Magnavox APQ-94 radar, to train pilots and RIOs for its Crusaders and Phantoms. In November 1962, before this version had actually flown, the USAF and USN designation system was brought into line and the T3J-1 became the **T-39D** (**N.A.265-30**). Forty-two were delivered to the Navy by

November 1964.

North American offered civil versions as the Pratt & Whitney JT12A-8-powered **Sabreliner 40**, and later stretched it to become the 10-seat **Sabreliner 60**. On 22 September 1967, NAA merged with the Rockwell-Standard Corporation to become the North American Rockwell Corp. and this later evolved into the Sabreliner Division of Rockwell International. The USN next ordered seven Sabreliner 40s in the form of **CT-39Es** (briefly **VT-39E**) in May 1967 for fleet support with TACAN and less-plush interiors. An order for the Sabreliner 60 was placed in September 1971. The first two were also designated **CT-39E**, until the **CT-39G** title was applied, and the Sabre 60 was acquired for the Navy and **Marine Corps**.

For the civil market, Rockwell later developed the enlarged **Sabreliner 70** in 1970 with 'stand-up cabin' (later renamed **Sabre 75**), the General Electric CF700D-2-powered **Sabre 80** in 1972 (later renamed **Sabre 75A**) and finally, in 1976, the Garrett TFE731-3-powered **Sabre 65**. The Sabre 65 featured a supercritical wing developed by the Reisbeck Corp. By the early 1980s the company's financial position was far from secure and only the Sabre 65 remained in production. On 1 January 1982 production at El Segundo ceased, and the plant's lease expired on that day. There followed a hiatus of over a year until July 1983, when Rockwell finally sold the production rights for the aircraft to the St Louis-based Sabreliner Corporation.

In 1987 Sabreliner was awarded a five-year contract to support USAF and USN T-39s, and also completed a SLEP on 10 USAF aircraft, delivered in 1988. Sabreliner's most recent activities include the Undergraduate Naval Flight Officer (UNFO) programme at NAS Pensacola. The UNFO con-

tract covers the training of of US Navy RIOs in 17 modified **T-39N** radar trainers, all converted by Sabreliner from civil Sabre 40s from 1991. With the exception of one **NT-39B** in service with the 412th TW, Edwards AFB, the T-39 is virtually out of service with the USAF. In addition to the UNFO aircraft, the USN operates two CT-39Es and five CT-39Gs (attached to VR-40, CFSLW and the Dept of the Navy). These serve alongside the USMC's six CT-39Gs

(attached to two Station Operations and Engineering Squadrons, and the HQ unit).

Other military users include **Argentina** (two Sabre 75As operated by the army and air force), **Ecuador** (two Sabreliner 40/As, two Sabre 60s and one Sabre 75 operated by the Ministerio de Defence Nacional), **Mexico** (two Sabre 60s operated by the army and navy) and **Sweden** (two Sabreliner 40s, operated as testbeds under the local designation **Tp 86**).

Above: Perhaps the last active Sabre in the USAF inventory is this NT-39B (seen here with underslung jamming pod) flown by the 453rd TS, 412th TW.

Right: Sweden also uses its two Sabreliner 40s (Tp 86s) as test aircraft. Recently they have been involved in the first successful tests of a synthetic airborne radar system that can detect buried objects.

Scaled Composites (Rutan Model 151) ARES

Scaled Composites Incorporated
Hangar 78, Mojave Airport, Mojave
California 93501, USA

The **Agile Response Effective Support (ARES)** aircraft was designed by Burt Rutan and built by his Scaled Composites company over the period 1985-1990. First flying on 19 February 1990, it closely matches a US Army proposal for a Low Cost Battlefield Attack Aircraft (LCBAA) drawn up in 1981, and is claimed to be of interest to developing countries as well as more advanced nations.

The prototype **Rutan Model 151** (N151SC) is essentially a proof-of-concept vehicle and features an unusual fuselage configuration, comprising an engine intake to port and a gun to starboard. The 25-mm five-barrelled GAU-12/U cannon is installed in a 'focused depression' in the lower forward fuselage to shield the cockpit canopy from the blast, and so that the gun blast impinges on the forward fuselage and counteracts recoil. The JT15D turbofan is offset 8° to port of the centreline and is served by a similarly offset circular intake to avoid ingesting gases from the gun; the jetpipe is curved to align the efflux along the fuselage axis. Both features contribute to low radar reflectivity by shielding the compressor and turbine. Twin booms carrying fins and rudders shield jet efflux from IR detection. For

agility, the wing layout uses compound sweep angles of 50° (inner wing) and 15° (outer panels), with canard foreplanes swept forward at 10° – with built-in aerodynamic AoA protection .The structure is primarily composite, comprising carbon-fibre/epoxy over foam/PVC. The pilot sits on an SIIS-3ER ejection seat. Provision is made for the carriage of two AIM-9L Sidewinder or four AIM-92 Stinger AAMs on external hardpoints. ARES completed live cannon firing tests in 1991, with USAF funding, and since then it has continued in flight test. A two-seat trainer variant is also planned.

SPECIFICATION

Scaled Composites (Rutan Model 151) ARES
Wing: span 35 ft 0 in (10.67 m); aspect ratio 6.5; area 188.30 sq ft (17.49 m2); canard foreplane span 19 ft 2 in (5.84 m) canard foreplane area 34.30 sq ft (3.19 m2)
Fuselage and tail: length 25 ft 5¼ in (8.97 m); height 9 ft 10 in (3.00 m)
Powerplant: one Pratt & Whitney JT15D-5 turbofan rated at 2,950 lb st (13.12 kN)
Weights: empty unarmed 2,884 lb (1308 kg); normal take-off unarmed 4,804 lb (2179 kg); maximum take-off 6,100 lb (2767 kg)

The Scaled Composites (Rutan) ARES has adopted a novel engine intake layout to avoid the problem of gun gas ingestion.

Fuel and load: internal fuel 1,700 lb (771 kg); external fuel none
Speed: never exceed speed Mach 0.65; maximum level speed 'clean' at 35,000 ft (10670 m) 375 kt (432 mph; 695 km/h); (demonstrated) up to 305 kts IAS (351 mph;

656 km/h) in level flight; 405 kts TAS (466 mph; 750 km/h) at 7620 m (25,000 ft)
Range: (demonstrated) more than 1,000 nm (1,150 miles;1850 km) flown on internal fuel at 7,620 m (25,000 ft)

Scheibe SF 25B/C Falke/Venture T.Mk

Schiebe Flugzeugbau Gmbh
August-Pfalz-Strasse 23, Postfach 1829
8060 Dachau, Germany

Examples of the **Scheibe SF 25B/C Falke** powered glider are operated by the air arms of **Singapore** and **Pakistan**, primarily for recreational and training duties. The Falke is a side-by-side two-seat motor glider, intended for training and with dual controls as standard. The two-piece cantilever wooden wing is fitted with airbrakes,

while the fuselage is fabric-covered welded steel tube. The undercarriage comprises a single main wheel, a steerable tailwheel and spring outrigger stabilising wheels under each wing. The Falke is powered by a 45-hp (33.6-kW) Stamo MS 1500 four-stroke horizontally-opposed engine. Five civil-registered **SF 25B**s equip the para-military

Junior Flying Club which the Singapore defence ministry operates at Seletar. This organisation has the 'shadow' designation of No. 151 Squadron in the RSAF.

The **SF 25C** is an improved version of the SF 25B, differing primarily by having a more powerful 60-hp (44.7-kW) Limbach SL 1700 EA modified Volkswagen automobile

engine. Four SF 25Cs provide for recreational flying at the Pakistan Air Force College at Sargodha. In 1970, the SF 25C was the basis for licence-production in the UK of 40 **Slingsby T.61E Venture T.Mk 2** trainers for the Air Cadet Force, replacement of which by the Grob G 109 Vigilant T.Mk 1 is now complete.

Schleicher Vanguard and Valiant T.Mk 1

Alexander Achleicher Segel-Flugzeugbau
6416 Poppenhausen/Wasserkuppe
Germany

Examples of the **Schleicher ASK-21** high-performance single-seat glider and of the **ASW-19** two-seat sailplane serve in the United Kingdom with the **Air Cadet**

Force, providing opportunities for more advanced flying by members of the Air Training Corps and Combined Cadet Force who have previously learned to fly on the

Grob Viking T.Mk 1. Five ASW-19 two-seaters were acquired and given the name **Valiant T.Mk 1**, while 10 ASK-21s became **Vanguard T.Mk 1**s. Both types

serve at the Air Cadet Central Gliding School at RAF Syerston, and Vanguards were also used to equip No. 618 Volunteer Gliding School at West Malling.

Schweizer (Hughes) Model 200/269/300

Schweizer Aircraft Corporation
PO Box 147, Elmira
New York 14902, USA

The Hughes Aircraft Company began specialising in helicopters in 1948, and its second design proved one of the most successful light helicopters ever. The first of two **Model 269** two-seat prototypes flew in October 1956 and, refined and re-engineered for production, became the **Model 269A**. Five were acquired by the **US Army** in 1958 for trials at Fort Rucker as observation helicopters, under the designation **YHO-2-HU**. The Model 269A had a

lightweight fuselage that accommodated its two crew members and the 180-hp (134-kW) Lycoming HIO-360-A1A powerplant. With a fully-articulated three-bladed main rotor, the Model 269A had a two-bladed anti-torque tail rotor (to port) and an upward-canted stabiliser to starboard. It was designated **Model 200** for civil customers.

Experience with the YHO-2-HU eventually led to an order in 1964 for a new primary trainer. A military version of the **Model**

269C was chosen, itself an improved version of the two-seat dual-control Model 269A, powered by a 180-hp (134-kW) Avco Lycoming HIO-360-B1A flat-four piston engine. An initial batch of 20 **TH-55A Osage**s was ordered, but total procurement eventually reached 792 by the time deliveries ceased in March 1969.

The TH-55A was supplied to **Spain** for training duties under the local designation HE.20 (17 delivered), and to **Sweden** as the **Hkp 5B** (16 delivered). Model 269As were supplied to **Brazil** (16), while TH-55s were delivered to **Nigeria** (15), **Algeria** (six), and **Haiti** (two). **Colombia** took eight Model 300Cs and six TH-55s. Thirty Model 300Cs were acquired by **Iraq** for crop-spraying, but were actually used for training military helicopter pilots. In **Japan**, Kawasaki assembled 38 of the **TH-55J** variant which was almost identical to the TH-55A. The **Model 269B** was a similar three-seater (designated **Model 300** for civilian customers), and the **Model 300C** is a further improved derivative, which first flew in August 1969 offering a 45 per cent

increase in payload. It is powered by a 225-hp (168-kW) HIO-360-D1A derated to 190 hp (142 kW). Hughes became a subsidiary of McDonnell Douglas on 6 January 1984, and was renamed McDonnell Douglas Helicopters on 27 August 1985, but production of the Model 300C had already been transferred to Schweizer in July 1983. The Model 300C was also built under licence by Breda Nardi in Italy as the **NH-300C**. Schweizer bought up the entire programme in November 1986, by which time Hughes production of all models had reached 2,800.

The first Schweizer-built helicopter, a Model 300C, flew in June 1984, followed by several new variants. These have included the **TH-300C** dual-control military trainer, with armoured seats and searchlight, and even the **Model 300QC** with a lengthened tailboom and a 75 per cent reduction in noise level.

Schweizer has delivered 30 Model 300Cs to the US Army (following a $4.9 million order in late 1985). Thirty TH-300Cs were delivered to **Turkey** during 1982/1983 and two batches (each of 24 TH-55Cs) went to the **Royal Thai army** in 1986, augmenting the survivors of 23 ex-US Army TH-55As. The type remains in service with Algeria (six Model 269), Colombia (six TH-55, seven Model 300C), **Greece** (26 **ND300C**),

In Spanish air force service the Hughes 269 is referred to as the HE.20 and serves in several different sub-types with basic traing unit Esc 782 of Ala 78, based at Granada.

Japan (33 TH-55J with the **JGSDF**), Nigeria (14 Model 300C), Sweden (26 with the army), Thailand (68), Turkey (30), the US Army and possibly Iraq.

SPECIFICATION

Schweizer (Hughes) Model 300C
Rotor system: main rotor diameter 26 ft 10 in (8.18 m); tail rotor diameter 4 ft 3 in (1.30 m); main rotor disc area 565.51 sq ft (52.54 m²); tail rotor disc area 14.19 sq ft (1.32 m²)
Fuselage and tail: length overall, rotors turning 30 ft 10 in (9.40 m); height overall 8 ft 8.675 in (2.66 m) to top of rotor head; skid track 6 ft 6.5 in (1.99 m)
Powerplant: one 225-hp (168-kW) Textron Lycoming HIO-360-D1A flat-four piston engine derated to 190 hp (142 kW)
Weights: empty 1,046 lb (474 kg);normal take-off 2,050 lb (930 kg); maximum take-off 2,150 lb (975 kg)
Fuel and load: internal fuel 49 US gal (185.5 litres); external fuel none
Speed: never exceed speed at sea level 91 kt (105 mph; 169 km/h); maximum cruising speed at optimum altitude 82.5 kt (95 mph; 153 km/h); economical

cruising speed at 4,000 ft (1220 m) 67 kt (77 mph; 124 km/h)
Range: 195 nm (224 miles; 360 km); endurance 3 hours 24 minutes
Performance: maximum rate of climb at sea level 750 ft (229 m) per minute; service ceiling 10,200 ft (3110 m); hovering ceiling 5,900 ft (1800 m) in ground effect and 2,750 ft (840 m) out of ground effect

The Schweizer/ Hughes 300 is the Turkish army's principal training helicopter, rival Enstrom TH-28s and Robinson R22s having proved surprisingly unpopular.

Schweizer **Model 330**

Aturboshaft-engined derivative of the Model 300 was flown by Schweizer during June 1988 as the **Model 330**. This was intended for commercial customers and to meet the US Army's NTH (New Training Helicopter) requirement. This allows the use of cheaper, more common turbine fuel (Avtur rather than Avgas) and gives much improved 'hot-and-high' performance. Increased power to the tail rotor also improves hover crosswind limits. The aircraft has three sets of flying controls and the student pilot seats can be moved to

allow one student to observe the other being given instruction. The tailplane is enlarged and features endplate fins, in addition to a large new dorsal fin. The Model 330 was unsuccessful in the NTH competition, losing out to the Bell 206 derivative.

As the TH-330, Schweizer offered its turbine-powered Model 330 for the US Army NTH competition, which was eventually won by the Bell TH-57 Creek. The 330 has chalked up some civilian sales, however.

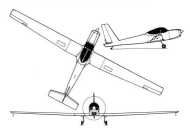

Schweizer **TG-7A (SGM 2-37)**

First flown on 21 September 1982, the **SGM 2-37** motorised glider was developed to meet a **USAF** requirement for such a craft to be used at the Air Force Academy for 'motivational' flight training on a voluntary basis up to solo standard. The Academy previously used sailplanes that required a a powered aircraft to tow them aloft. The SGM-2-37 is a low-wing glider which combines the wings of the Schweizer **SGS 1-36** single-seat sailplane with the rear of the earlier **SGS2-32** and the powerplant module of a Piper Tomahawk. Two side-by-side seats are provided beneath a sliding canopy and the SGM 2-37 has a fixed tailwheel-type undercarriage. Designated **TG-7A** in the DoD glider category,

the SGM 2-37 was first ordered with FY81 funds and a total of 12 has entered service with the 94th Air Training Squadron at the Academy at Colorado Springs. The TG-7A enables up to 1,200 cadets each year to make their first solo flights. The first aircraft was delivered in 1984, but early in its service life two were lost in crashes. To check the TG-7A's tendency to stall and 'depart', locally-designed leading-edge fillets (cuffs) were added after the second crash.

SPECIFICATION

Schweizer TG-7A
Wing: span 59 ft 6 in (18.14 m); aspect ratio 18.1;

area 195.71 sq ft (18.18 m²)
Fuselage and tail: length 27 ft 5 in (8.36 m); height 7 ft 9.5 in (2.37 m); wheel track 9 ft 2 in (2.79 m); wheel base 18 ft 10 in (5.74 m)
Powerplant: one Textron Lycoming O-235-L2C flat-four piston engine rated at 112 hp (83 kW)
Weights: empty 1,260 lb (572 kg); maximum take-off 1,850 lb (839 kg)
Fuel and load: internal fuel in port wing 15.5 US gal (59 litres) plus provision in starboard wing for 15.5 US gal (59 litres) of auxiliary fuel; external fuel none
Speed: maximum cruising speed at 7,500 ft (2285 m) 99 kt (114 mph; 183 km/h); economical cruising speed at optimum altitude 81 kt (95 mph; 153 km/h); maximum smooth-air gliding speed 116 kt (133 mph; 214 km/h); maximum rough-air gliding speed 88 kt (101 mph; 162 km/h)
Range: ferry range 520 nm (598 miles; 963 km) with auxiliary fuel; range 213 nm (246 miles; 396 km) with standard fuel
Performance: maximum rate of climb at sea level

Schweizer TG-7A

1,075 ft (328 m) per minute; service ceiling more than 24,000 ft (7315 m); best glide ratio 22; minimum gliding sink rate 3.7 ft (1.13 m) per second; take-off run 500 ft (152 m) at maximum take-off weight; landing distance from 50 ft (15 m) 1,266 ft (386 m) at normal landing weight; landing run 654 ft (200 m) at normal landing weight

Schweizer **RG-8A Condor (SA 2-37A)**

In continuation of the investigation into quiet surveillance and special missions aircraft begun with the Lockheed QT-I (a modified Schweizer SGS 2-32 sailplane), the **US Army** backed the development by Schweizer of a variant of the **TG-7A** (SGM 2-37) motorised glider (described separately). The **SA 2-37A** introduced increased wingspan with aerodynamic changes to improve stall characteristics, a bulged, upward-opening canopy for enhanced visibility and a 65-cu ft (1.84-m³) payload bay

behind the cockpit to carry various palletised sensors or cameras. The SA 2-37A featured a much more powerful engine, fitted with mufflers (a long exhaust on each side of the cowling) and driving an advanced McCauley three-bladed constant-speed low-noise propeller. The engine can be run at very low rpm, since only 52 hp (38.8 kW) is

required to maintain height, giving a very low acoustic signature. Internal fuel capacity was trebled, with mission duration reported to run as long as eight hours. To fit it for the covert surveillance role, the **RG-8A** is painted in low-visibility grey and can be equipped with a Hughes AN/AAQ-16 thermal imaging system, Texas Instruments

In stark contrast to their high-visibility red and white siblings, US Coast Guard RG-8As wear toned-down insignia over gunship grey.

Schweizer RG-8A Condor (SA 2-37A)

AAQ-15 FLIR, secure communications equipment, IR sensors, low-light TV and other payloads. The pilots' seats are armoured and the cockpit is NVG-compatible. Full IFR capability is provided, permitting operation around the clock, and other avionics equipment allegedly includes Litton INS as well as a Bendix/King avionics suite.

First flying in prototype form in 1986, an initial batch of two was procured by the US Army. Following the loss of one of the original pair, a replacement was obtained. The two survivors were subsequently passed to the **US Coast Guard** to be operated out of Opa Locka, FL, on long-endurance drug interdiction sorties. The RG-8As usually operating singly, flying a search pattern with a track of some 500 miles (805 km). One RG-8A has been used by the **CIA** as a data relay platform for reconnaissance drones flying over Bosnia.

SPECIFICATION

Schweizer RG-8A Condor

Wing: span 61 ft 6 in (18.745 m); aspect ratio 18.97; area 199.40 sq ft (18.52 m2)

Fuselage and tail: length, fuselage 27 ft 9 in (8.46 m); height 7 ft 9 in (2.36 m) tail down; wheel track 9 ft 2 in (2.79 m); wheel base 19 ft 8 in (5.99 m)

Powerplant: one Textron Lycoming IO-540-W3A5D flat-six piston engine rated at 235 hp (175 kW)

Weights: empty 2,025 lb (918 kg); maximum take-off 3,500 lb (1587 kg)

Fuel and load: internal fuel 52 US gal (196.8 litres) plus provision for 15 US gal (57 litres) of auxiliary fuel; external fuel none; maximum mission payload 750 lb (340 kg)

Speed: maximum cruising speed at 5,000 ft (1525 m) 138 kt (159 mph; 256 km/h); economical cruising speed at 5,000 ft (1525 m) 129 kt (148 mph; 239 km/h)

Range: endurance more than 8 hours

Performance: maximum rate of climb at sea level 960 ft (292 m) per minute; service ceiling 18,000 ft (5490 m); take-off run 1,270 ft (387 m) at maximum take-off weight from a paved runway or 1,750 ft (533 m) at maximum take-off weight from a grass runway; take-off distance to 50 ft (15 m) 2,010 ft (612 m) at maximum take-off weight from a paved runway or 2,490 ft (759 m) at maximum take-off weight from a grass runway; landing distance from 50 ft (15 m) 2,230 ft (680 m) at normal landing weight on a paved runway or 2,400 ft (732 m) at normal landing weight on a grass runway

g limits: -3.3 to +6.6

Schweizer **X-26A (SGS 2-32)**

A pair of two-seat SGS 2-32 sailplanes continues to serve with the **US Naval Test Pilot's School** at Patuxent River, MD. Five of these aircraft have been acquired since 1968, initially to give experience of yaw/roll coupling and other handling characteristics common to aircraft with high aspect ratio wings. Designated **X-26A**, they are essentially civilian gliders in military guise. Two 100-hp (74.6-kW) **X-26B**s were also delivered to the NTPS, these having been previously in US Army hands as **Lockheed QT-2PC (Quiet Thruster)** low-noise surveillance aircraft. Based on the SGS 2-32 airframe, there is modified seating for two in tandem. The X-26Bs were withdrawn from use during 1973.

SPECIFICATION

Schweizer X-26A

Wing: span 57 ft 1 in (17.40 m); aspect ratio 18.13; area 180.00 sq ft (16.70 m2)

Fuselage and tail: length 26 ft 9 in (8.15 m); height 9 ft 3 in (2.82 m); tailplane span 10 ft 6 in (3.20 m)

Weights: empty 857 lb (389 kg); maximum take-off 1,430 lb (649 kg)

Fuel and load: internal fuel none

Speed: maximum tow speed 96 kt (110 mph; 177 km/h); maximum gliding speed 137 kt (158 mph; 254 km/h)

Performance: service ceiling 18,500 ft (5640 m); best glide ratio 34:1 at 51 kt (59 mph; 95 km/h); minimum sinking speed 2.38 ft (0.72 m) per second at 43 kt (50 mph; 80 km/h)

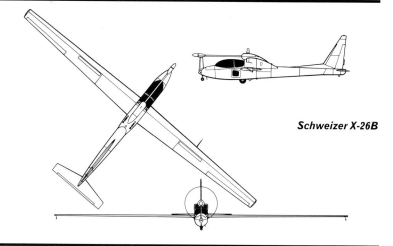

Schweizer X-26B

SEPECAT **Jaguar GR.Mk 1/T.Mk 2**

British Aerospace Defence Ltd
Warton Aerodrome, Preston
Lancashire PR4 1AX, UK

P roduced to meet a joint Anglo-French specification in 1965 for a dual-role aircraft (advanced/operational trainer and tactical support), the **SEPECAT Jaguar** was transformed into a potent fighter-bomber and gained some success in the export field, as described separately. Breguet (now part of Dassault) and the British Aircraft Corporation's Warton Division (later BAe Warton) were chosen to participate, the joint company being registered in France to reflect Breguet's design leadership. It was titled SEPECAT – Société Européenne de Production de l'Avion d'Ecole de Combat et d'Appui Tactique (European Production Company for the Combat Training and Tactical Support Aircraft) – and formed in May 1966. The Jaguar was the first Anglo-French combat aircraft and the first RAF aircraft designed completely in metric units. The RAF intended to use its aircraft exclusively as advanced trainers, whereas French interest lay in a ground-attack aircraft with STOL performance. Eventually, both the RAF and Armée de l'Air abandoned the combat training role and used the aircraft for strike and attack in single-seat form, merely retaining a handful of two-place machines for pilot conversion duties.

Designed from the outset for close support and daytime interdiction, the Jaguar has a configuration and wing loading optimised for ease of weapon-carrying and stability as a weapon platform at low altitude. Power is provided by two Rolls-Royce/Turboméca Adour reheated turbofans that were the subject of an associated joint development programme. Engine thrust originally lagged behind progressive increases in aircraft weight, leaving the Jaguar noticeably underpowered in hot climates, although this short-coming was eventually remedied in RAF and export aircraft. Low-speed handling is improved by double-slotted flaps along the entire wing trailing edge, ailerons being omitted in favour of outer wing spoilers.

The first of eight Jaguar prototypes was actually a French two-seat aircraft and made its maiden flight on 8 September 1968, the remaining aircraft of this batch soon displaying the significant differences between UK and French versions. Each air force agreed to buy 200 Jaguars, the RAF split being 165 single-seat and 35 two-seat machines, the former designated **Jaguar S** (for 'Strike') by the manufacturers and **GR.Mk 1** by the RAF. GR.Mk 1s are immediately recognisable by their chisel-shaped noses and fin-top pods, respectively housing a Ferranti ARI23231 LRMTS (Laser Ranger and Marked Target Seeker) and Marconi ARI18223 radar warning receiver. Internally, the GR.Mk 1 had a Marconi-GEC 920ATC NAVWASS (Navigation and Weapon-Aiming Sub-System) projecting relevant route and targeting information on the pilot's HUD and driving a look-down moving-map display. As built, RAF aircraft had an empty weight of 7390 kg (16,292 lb) and were powered by Mk 102 engines of 32.5 kN (7,305 lb st).

The first British aircraft was a single -seat Jaguar (the S-06 prototype XW560), which initially flew on 12 October 1969. Delivered between 1973 and 1978, RAF Jaguar GR.Mk 1s served four nuclear strike squadrons at Brüggen, Germany (Nos 14, 17, 20 and 31), a recce squadron (No. II) at Laarbruch, Germany, and the Coltishall Wing of Nos 6, 41 (recce) and 54 Squadrons, all three tasked with conventional support of NATO forces anywhere within Europe. Despite its lack of radar, a navigator and air defence capability,

The No. 6(C) Sqn Jaguars involved in Operation Grapple armed support flights over Bosnia have adopted this effective overall grey scheme.

the Jaguar marked a quantum improvement over the F-4 Phantoms it replaced, giving a genuine ability to find pinpoint targets and attack them with a hitherto unknown degree of accuracy. All-weather operation was not degraded, and the new aircraft proved much more difficult to intercept due to its high speed at very low level. The aircraft also introduced an oft-practised capability of operating from motorway strips, and an unpractised rough-field capability. The Jaguar is equipped with anti-skid Messier-Hispano undercarriage (each gear unit having twin low-pressure tyres) and a 5.5-m (18-ft 0.5-in) diameter brake parachute housed in the fuselage tailcone. Replacement a decade later by Panavia Tornados was comparatively rapid, but cast no aspersions on the Jaguar's capability in the conventional role. Reconnaissance aircraft carry a centreline pod containing a fan of five cameras, plus an infra-red linescan, although this was augmented in 1991 by a Vinten VICON 18 long-range optical pod.

The **Jaguar B** two-seat training variant features a 0.9-m (2-ft 11-in) fuselage stretch to accommodate a second seat, which is raised by 59.1 cm (15 in). The aircraft were built with the full navigation and attack avionics suite but have limited combat capability, since they lack lasers, inflight-refuelling probes or radar warning receivers, and have only the port cannon fitted. The first British Jaguar B flew as the B-08 prototype (XW566) on 30 August 1970. Britain assigned 35 Jaguar Bs to training duties. Designated **T.Mk 2**, they were delivered to No. 229 OCU at Lossiemouth for pilot conversion and to each squadron as continuation trainers. A total of 14 T.Mk 2s was upgraded with the more capable FIN1064 nav/attack unit, becoming **T.Mk 2A**s, and also gaining Mk 104 engines. In addition, three extra T.Mk 2s were bought for the Empire Test Pilots' School (two) and Royal Aircraft Establishment (now Defence Research Agency). All UK Jaguars are fitted with Martin-Baker Mk 10 zero-zero ejection seats.

Only the Coltishall Wing remains active. Its aircraft were upgraded in 1978-84 with 35.1-kN (7,900 lb-st) Adour Mk 104 engines, and raised further from December 1983 to **GR.Mk 1A** standard by replacement of NAVWASS with the considerably more accurate Ferranti FIN1064 inertial navigation system. Although FIN1064 is 50 kg (110 lb) lighter, aircraft weight increased through other modifications to 7700 kg (16,976 lb), against a take-off weight of 15500 kg (34,172 lb).

Further changes introduced from 1982 included addition of AN/ALE-40 flare dispensers in a scabbed fitting under the engine nacelles, Philips-MATRA Phimat flare pods and Westinghouse AN/ALQ-101(V)-10 jamming pods. Both Phimat and ALQ-101 are interchangeable with AIM-9G (later -9L) Sidewinder AAMs.

For the 1991 Gulf War, radar warners were uprated to Sky Guardian 200 standard, and CBU-87 medium-altitude releasable cluster bombs and CRV-7 rockets were added to the usual armoury of BL755 low-level CBUs, 540-lb (245-kg) and 1,000-lb (454-kg) bombs carried on a fuselage centreline and four underwing hardpoints. Self-defence was improved by the addition of overwing Sidewinder pylons, obviating the previous 'either/or' situation. Another Jaguar upgrade with higher-powered engines and night-vision systems has been abandoned for reasons of cost, despite the aircraft being destined to serve into the 21st century. Mk 1A conversions total 75, of which most remain.

Twelve Coltishall-based Jaguars were among the first British forces deployed in October 1990 for Operation Granby. The aircraft were based at Thumrait, Oman, and Muharraq, Bahrain, and were assigned battlefield air interdiction missions on tactical targets, mainly in Kuwait. They flew a total

The RAF's Jaguar record in the Gulf was outstanding, with several aircraft chalking up over 40 missions. Twelve aircraft flown by 22 pilots operated the 'JagDet' from Muharraq, Bahrain. Initially armed with BL755 cluster bombs, the Jaguars later adopted CRV-7 rocket pods.

of 618 sorties, including 31 reconnaissance missions, and incurred no combat losses. After the Gulf War, Jaguars flew Operation Warden missions over northern Iraq until their replacement by Harrier GR.Mk 7s in April 1993. In mid-1994, a detachment of up to 12 aircraft is based at Gioia del Colle for Operation Grapple, supporting the UN mission in Bosnia.

OPERATORS

Royal Air Force

No. 6 Sqn: (GR.Mk 1A/T.Mk 2A) – RAF Coltishall
No. 41 Sqn: (GR.Mk 1A/T.Mk 2A) – RAF Coltishall
No. 54 Sqn: (GR.Mk 1A/T.Mk 2A) – RAF Coltishall
No. 16(R) Sqn: (GR.Mk 1A/T.Mk 2A)
– Operational Conversion Unit, RAF Lossiemouth

Operation Grapple, Jaguar Detachment
No. 6 (Composite) Sqn: Gioia de Colle, Italy

Strike/Attack Operational Evaluation Unit
– A&AEE, RAF Boscombe Down (T.Mk 2A)
Aircraft & Armament Evaluation Establishment
– RAF Boscombe Down (GR.Mk 1A)
Empire Test Pilots' School
– RAF Boscombe Down (T.Mk 2A)
Defence Research Agency
– RAF Boscombe Down (GR.Mk 1A/T.Mk 2)

SPECIFICATION

SEPECAT Jaguar S (Jaguar GR.Mk 1A)
Wing: span 8.69 m (28 ft 6 in); aspect ratio 3.13; area 24.18 m² (260.27 sq ft)
Fuselage and tail: length 16.83 m (55 ft 2.5 in) including probe and 15.52 m (50 ft 11 in) excluding probe; height 4.89 m (16 ft 0.5 in); wheel track 2.41 m (7 ft 11 in); wheel base 5.69 m (18 ft 8 in)
Powerplant: two Rolls-Royce/Turboméca Adour Mk 104 turbofans each rated at 5,320 lb st (23.66 kN) dry and 8,040 lb st (35.75 kN) with afterburning
Weights: empty equipped 7700 kg (16,975 lb); normal take-off 10954 kg (24,149 lb); maximum take-off 15700 kg (34,612 lb)
Fuel and load: internal fuel 3337 kg (7,357 lb); external fuel up to 2844 kg (6,270 lb) in three 1200-litre (317-US gal) drop tanks; maximum ordnance 4,536 kg (10,000lb)
Speed: maximum level speed 'clean' at 36,000 ft (10975 m) 917 kt (1,056 mph; 1699 km/h) and at sea level 729 kt (840 mph; 1350 km/h)
Range: ferry range 1,902 nm (2,190 miles; 3524 km) with drop tanks; combat radius 460 nm (530 miles; 852 km) on a hi-lo-hi attack mission with internal fuel, or 290 nm (334 miles; 537 km) on a lo-lo-lo attack mission with internal fuel, or 760 nm (875 miles;

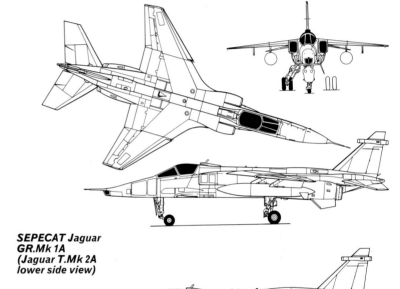

SEPECAT Jaguar GR.Mk 1A (Jaguar T.Mk 2A lower side view)

1408 km) on a hi-lo-hi attack mission with drop tanks, or 495 nm (570 miles; 917 km) on a lo-lo-lo attack mission with drop tanks
Performance: climb to 9145 m (30,000ft) in 1 minute 30 seconds; service ceiling 14000 m (45,930 ft); take-off run 565 m (1,854 ft) 'clean' or 880 m (2,887 ft) with four 1,000-lb (454-kg) bombs, or 1,250 m (4,101 ft) with eight 1,000-lb (454-kg) bombs; take-off distance to 50 ft (15 m) 940 m (3,084 ft) at typical take-off weight; landing distance from 50 ft (15 m) 785 m (2,575 ft) at typical landing weight; landing run 470 m (1,542 ft) at typical landing weight with brake chute
g limit: +8.6 at typical weight or +12 ultimate

No. 41 Sqn is one of two Jaguar recce units, with a wartime ACE NATO Mobile Force base at Tromsø in Norway. This aircraft carries an EMI optical/IRLS pod.

SEPECAT Jaguar B (Jaguar T.Mk 2A)
generally similar to the SEPECAT Jaguar S (Jaguar GR.Mk 1A) except in the following particulars:
Fuselage and tail: length 17.53 m (57 ft 6¼ in) including probe and 16.42 m (53 ft 10½ in) excluding probe; wheel track 2.40 m (7 ft 10½ in); wheel base 5.67 m (18 ft 7¼ in)

SEPECAT Jaguar A/E

France elected to procure 200 Jaguars for the **Armée de l'Air**, eventually purchasing 160 single-seat and 40 two-seat aircraft. Compared with their British equivalent, French single-seat **Jaguar A**s (for 'Appui', or attack) have a generally less capable standard of avionics fit, but remain effective strike aircraft. Like RAF GR.Mk 1s, they have a retractable refuelling probe and two internal 30-mm cannon (DEFA 553 in place of ADEN). The off-the-shelf avionics include a CSF31 weapon-aiming computer, SFIM 250-1 twin-gyro platform, Decca RDN72 Doppler and a Crouzet 90 navigation computer. There has been no avionics upgrade, although the second half of aircraft procured have a Thomson-CSF TAV-38 laser ranger under the nose and an improved version of CFTH RWR, and the last 30 are able to carry a nose-mounted Thomson-CSF ATLIS laser designator, introduced in 1980. An OMERA 40 panoramic camera was installed beneath the nose of the 113th and subsequent Jaguar As and retrofitted, while a few carry an RP36 drop tank fitted with a fan of three cameras. With the temporary exception of the first 10 production aircraft, Armée de l'Air Jaguars were fitted with and retain Mk 102 engines.

France's 40 tandem-seat **Jaguar E**s (for 'Ecole', or school) are issued only at squadron level, rather than to a single OCU. They lack a full nav/attack avionics fit, but those from No. 27 were fitted on the production line with a fixed refuelling probe to provide limited tanker training (the A's retractable probe being in a different position). Some 25 Es remain in service.

The first Jaguar to fly was a French Jaguar E prototype, E-01, on 8 September 1968, and was followed on 23 March 1969 by the first flight of the prototype Jaguar A (A-03). The **Jaguar M** carrier-based strike fighter was flown in prototype form (M-05) on 14 November 1969. This retained the original short fin configuration and intake splitter plates, but had a much-modifed

undercarriage comprising single-wheel main units and twin-nosewheels on an extended leg, a 5.5g arrester hook (as opposed to the land-based variant's 2g) and laser range-finder as standard. The promising Jaguar M completed deck landing trials before falling victim to escalating costs and hostility from Dassault (which was marketing its Super Etendard). It was subsequently cancelled.

Initial deliveries of the Jaguar A were made to the Armée de l'Air from January 1972, and EC 1/7 'Provence' became the first unit to equip with the type, at St Dizier in June 1973. With deliveries completed in December 1981, Jaguars went on to equip nine squadrons, four each in 7 and 11 Escadres (Wings) and one element of 3E. Two nuclear-strike squadrons of 7E were tasked with delivering AN52 25-kT nuclear bombs (these bombs were withdrawn in September 1991), the others concentrating on tactical attack in Europe and in those African countries that have defence agreements with France.

The range of French Jaguar weapons is considerable and includes the laser-guided BGL 1,000-lb (454-kg) bomb and AS30L laser-guided missile; Aérospatiale AS37 Martel anti-radar missiles; 125-, 250- and 400-kg (275-, 551- and 882-lb) bombs; MATRA Belouga cluster-bombs; MATRA F1 (36 x 68 mm) and R3 (4 x 100 mm) rocket pods; Thomson-Brandt BAP-100 anti-runway and BAT-120 area-denial bomblets; and MATRA Magic infra-red AAMs. Thirty Jaguars have been fitted with an ATLIS (Automatic Tracking and Laser Illumination System) comprising a Martin-Marietta pod on the fuselage centreline, to give self-designation capability for the BGLs and AS30L missiles. System integration was the responsibility of Thomson-CSF. In the offensive jamming role, the Thomson-CSF CT51J pod can be used as an alternative to the Thomson-CSF Barracuda or Dassault Barax. Chaff/flare pods are either the Philips-MATRA Phimat or Bofors BOZ-103,

although an 18-shot Lacroix flare unit may be fitted in the braking parachute housing. The Jaguar may also be fitted with an Alkan LL 5020 conformal pod which contains chaff and flare dispensers under the wingroot.

Armée de l'Air Jaguars have seen action in Mauritania, Chad and the Gulf. During the latter conflict, a total of 28 Jaguars flew 615 sorties (three fewer than the RAF's 12 Jaguars). By mid-1994, France was operating some 85 Jaguar As within five squadrons.

OPERATORS

SPECIFICATION

SEPECAT Jaguar A
Wing: span 8.69 m (28 ft 6 in); aspect ratio 3.13; area 24.18 m2 (260.27 sq ft)
Fuselage and tail: length 16.83 m (55 ft 2½ in) including probe and 15.52 m (50 ft 11 in) excluding probe; height 4.89 m (16 ft 0½ in); wheel track 2.41 m (7 ft 11 in); wheel base 5.69 m (18 ft 8 in)
Powerplant: two Rolls-Royce/Turboméca Adour Mk 102 turbofans each rated at 5,115 lb st (22.75 kN) dry and 7,305 lb st (32.49 kN) with afterburning
Weights: empty equipped 7000 kg (15,432 lb); normal take-off 10954 kg (24,149 lb); maximum take-off 15700 kg (34,612 lb)
Fuel and load: internal fuel 3337 kg (7,357 lb); external fuel up to 2844 kg (6,270 lb) in three 1200-litre (317-US gal) drop tanks; maximum ordnance 4536 kg (10,000 lb)
Speed: maximum level speed 'clean' at 36,000 ft (10975 m) 917 kt (1,056 mph; 1699 km/h) and at sea level 729 kt (840 mph; 1350 km/h)
Range: ferry range 1,902 nm (2,190 miles; 3524 km) with drop tanks; combat radius 460 nm (530 miles; 852 km) on a hi-lo-hi attack mission with internal fuel, or 290 nm (334 miles; 537 km) on a lo-lo-lo attack mission with internal fuel, or 760 nm (875 miles; 1408 km) on a hi-lo-hi attack mission with drop tanks, or 495 nm (570 miles; 917 km) on a lo-lo-lo attack mission with drop tanks
Performance: climb to 9145 m (30,000ft) in 1 minute 30 seconds; service ceiling 14000 m (45,930 ft); take-off run 565 m (1,854 ft) 'clean' or 880 m (2,887 ft) with four 1,000-lb (454-kg) bombs, or 1,250 m (4,101 ft) with eight 1,000-lb (454-kg) bombs; take-off distance to 50 ft (15 m) 940 m (3,084 ft) at typical take-off weight; landing distance from 50 ft (15 m) 785 m (2,575 ft) at typical landing weight; landing run 470 m (1,542 ft) at typical landing weight with brake chute
g limit: +8.6 at typical weight or +12 ultimate

SEPECAT Jaguar E
generally similar to the SEPECAT Jaguar A except in the following particulars:
Fuselage and tail: length 17.53 m (57 ft 6¼ in) including probe and 16.42 m (53 ft 10½ in) excluding probe; wheel track 2.40 m (7 ft 10.5 in); wheel base 5.67 m (18 ft 7¼ in)

SEPECAT Jaguar A
(Jaguar E upper side view)

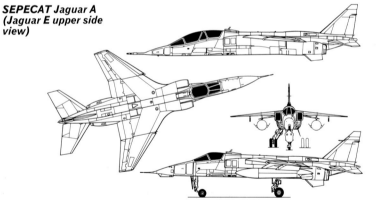

Above: French aircraft wearing desert camouflage carry small, toned-down markings. Serials are prefixed 'E' for two-seat, and 'A' for single-seat Jaguars.

Left: During Operation Daguet, the French codename for operations during the Gulf War, a force of 28 Jaguars, drawn from EC 11 (with pilots from that unit and EC 7), was based at Al Ahsa, in Saudi Arabia. Missions were flown from 17 January 1991 to 27 February. This aircraft carries laser-guided AS30L ASMs with an ATLIS designation pod on the centreline.

SEPECAT Jaguar International

All export Jaguars have been based on the Jaguar B/S airframe, and all orders have been secured by BAC or BAe, since Dassault has always preferred to market wholly French types, where an order results in 100 per cent of the work. Thus, the Jaguar has frequently competed against the Mirage.

Serious marketing of the Jaguar began in 1974, when BAC revealed details of export orders from undisclosed customers (Ecuador and Oman). Several days later an RAF aircraft (actually the first production S) appeared at the Farnborough show with **Jaguar International** titles and a mocked-up radar nose, surrounded by weaponry appropriate to an export aircraft. This aircraft was subsequently fitted with Adour Mk 104 RT-172-26 engines with 27 per cent higher thrust than the original Mk 102s, effectively becoming the prototype Jaguar International.

The designation **Jaguar K** had originally been reserved for export variants based on the **Jaguar S** and **Jaguar B**, but this was never used, each export customer receiving its own specific two-letter designator. The first production Jaguar International was an Ecuadorean two-seater, correctly known as a **Jaguar EB**, and it first flew on 19 August 1976. The Ecuadorean single-seat variant is designated **Jaguar ES**. Ecuador's 12 aircraft (including two EBs) were delivered during 1977, replacing Meteor FR.Mk 9s, and the seven survivors (including one EB) were augmented by three refurbished RAF aircraft during 1991.

Oman began to receive its Jaguar Internationals during March 1977, taking delivery of an initial batch of 12 aircraft (10 **Jaguar OS** and two **Jaguar OB** trainers), these wearing national markings in red and white. A second batch, of similar composition but with blue markings, was delivered during 1983. The two-seaters in the second batch are unique in having fin-mounted antennas for ARI18223 RWR and French-style, nose-mounted, fixed inflight-refuelling probes. All of the second-batch aircraft were powered by 8,400-lb st (37-kN) RT-172-58 Adour Mk 811 turbofans. Oman's original 24 aircraft were augmented by an ex-RAF T.Mk 2 previously loaned to India, and an ex-RAF single-seater. These were delivered in 1982 and 1986, respectively. Originally using overwing Magic AAMs, Oman's Jaguars switched to AIM-9P4 Sidewinders carried

on the outboard underwing pylons. Between 1986 and 1989, the 21 survivors were upgraded with FIN1064 nav/attack systems in place of their original GEC 920ATC NAVWASS computers, bringing them up to RAF GR.Mk 1A standard.

The biggest Jaguar operator today is India, which took delivery of an eventual 116, plus 18 on loan from the RAF (returned by 1984). These equip five squadrons, with one more unit being due to form. The loaned RAF aircraft were used for training and to form the first squadron, No. 14, while the second batch of aircraft, comprising 35 **Jaguar IS** and five **Jaguar IT** trainers, was undergoing assembly by HAL, from BAe kits. These aircraft were powered by 8,040-lb (35.75-kN) Adour 804s and were fitted with NAVWASS.

India's third batch consisted of 35 Jaguar ISs and 10 Jaguar ITs, assembled by HAL from kits which contained progressively fewer large UK-built sub-assemblies under Phases II-VI. These aircraft were fitted with a locally integrated DARIN (Display Attack and Ranging Inertial Navigation) system, with a Sea Harrier-type GEC Type 1301 HUDWAS, a GEC Ferranti COMED 2054 combined map and electronic display, as used on the F/A-18, and a SAGEM ULISS 82 INS. These aircraft were also powered by the more powerful Adour Mk 811.

Artist's impressions of radar-equipped Jaguar Internationals were released by BAe during the 1970s, and the Agave radar was actually flown in the nose of a modified fuel tank, slung beneath a French two-seat Jaguar. This was intended both for air-to-surface and air-to-air use and would probably have been adopted by the Aéronavale's carrierborne Jaguar M had it entered production. For anti-shipping duties with the Indian Air Force, BAe designed and HAL built the **Jaguar IM** with the same Agave radar (as used in the Super Etendard) replacing the nose-mounted LRMTS. The prototype made its maiden flight during November 1985. Eight were delivered to equip No. 6 Squadron's A Flight at Poona, and are armed with the BAe Sea Eagle missile, operating alongside Canberras in the anti-shipping role.

These aircraft were drawn from Batch Three and Batch Four. The latter had originally been intended to cover full licence-production of 56 Jaguars, and then to fulfil the

remainder of the original IAF requirement for 160 aircraft. In the end, it covered the assembly of 31 more Jaguar ISs supplied in kit form. From Batch Three, all Indian Jaguars have indigenously-designed IFF, ADF, radar, V/UHF radios and HF SSB, and locally built Martin-Baker I9B ejection seats, RWRs, hydraulic and fuel systems. Indian Jaguars have provision for the distinctive Jaguar International overwing launch rails which are used to carry MATRA Magic AAMs. Armament can include BL755 cluster bombs, MATRA Durandal runway-cratering weapons and MATRA F4 rocket pods.

The final export customer was Nigeria, which took delivery of 13 **Jaguar SN**s and five two-seat **Jaguar BN**s during 1984. The 10 surviving SNs and four BNs face retirement as an economy measure. BAE is attempting during 1994 to acquire them for possible resale to Oman.

OPERATORS

Ecuador – Fuerza Aérea Ecuatoriana
Escuadrón de Combate 2111
Grupo 211, Ala de Combate 21, Base Aérea Militar Taura, Guayaquil

India – Indian Air Force
No. 5 Sqn 'Tuskers': Ambala
No. 6 Sqn (A Flight) 'Dragons': Poona (Jaguar M)
No. 14 Sqn 'Bulls': Poona
No.16 Sqn 'Cobras': Gorakhpur
Aircraft and Systems Testing Establishment
Bangalore

Nigeria – Nigerian Air Force
One Squadron, Makurdi

Oman – Royal Air Force of Oman
No. 8 Sqn: Masirah
No. 20 Sqn: Masirah

SPECIFICATION

SEPECAT Jaguar International
Wing: span 8.69 m (28 ft 6 in); aspect ratio 3.13; area 24.18 m² (260.27 sq ft)
Fuselage and tail: length 16.83 m (55 ft 2½ in) including probe and 15.52 m (50 ft 11 in) excluding probe; height 4.89 m (16 ft 0.5 in); wheel track 2.41 m (7 ft 11 in); wheel base 5.69 m (18 ft 8 in)
Powerplant: two Rolls-Royce/Turboméca Adour Mk 804 turbofans each rated at 5,320 lb st (23.66 kN) dry and 8,040 lb st (35.75 kN) with afterburning, or Adour Mk 811 turbofans each rated at 5,520 lb st (24.55 kN) dry and 8,400 lb st (37.36 kN) with afterburning
Weights: empty equipped 7700 kg (16,975 lb); normal take-off 10954 kg (24,149 lb); maximum take-off 15700 kg (34,612 lb)
Fuel and load: internal fuel 3337 kg (7,357 lb); external fuel up to 2844 kg (6,270 lb) in three 1200-litre (317-US gal) drop tanks; maximum ordnance 4763 kg (10,500lb)
Speed: maximum level speed 'clean' at 36,000 ft (10975 m) 917 kt (1,056 mph; 1699 km/h) and at sea level 729 kt (840 mph; 1350 km/h)
Range: ferry range 1,902 nm (2,190 miles; 3524 km) with drop tanks; combat radius 460 nm (530 miles; 852 km) on a hi-lo-hi attack mission with internal fuel, or 290 nm (334 miles; 537 km) on a lo-lo-lo attack mission with internal fuel, or 760 nm (875 miles; 1408 km) on a hi-lo-hi attack mission with drop tanks, or 495 nm (570 miles; 917 km) on a lo-lo-lo attack mission with drop tanks
Performance: climb to 9145 m (30,000ft) in 1 minute 30 seconds; service ceiling 14000 m (45,930 ft); take-off run 565 m (1,854 ft) 'clean' or 880 m (2,887 ft) with four 1,000-lb (454-kg) bombs, or 1,250 m (4,101 ft) with eight 1,000-lb (454-kg) bombs; take-off distance to 50 ft (15 m) 940 m (3,084 ft) at typical take-off weight; landing distance from 50 ft (15 m) 785 m (2,575 ft) at typical landing weight; landing run 470 m (1,542 ft) at typical landing weight with brake chute
***g* limit:** +8.6 at typical weight or +12 ultimate

Below: India has eight distinctive Jaguar IMs for maritime strike. These aircraft are equipped with Agave radar and Sea Eagle AShMs.

Right: All Jaguar International operators fly two-seat aircraft. This Omani example has a refuelling probe and a fintop ARI18223 RWR.

Seyedo Shohada **Zafar 300**

Defence Industries, Seyedo Shohada Project
Km 5, Qom Road, Kashan
Iran

The **Zafar 300** is a locally-developed conversion of a Bell 206A JetRanger engineered in **Iran** by Akbar Akhundzadeh as the **Seyedo Shohada** project of the Defence Industries. For use as a two-seat light attack helicopter but also applicable to agricultural duties, the Zafar 300 retains the main and tail rotor systems of the Jet-Ranger, with some changes to the control system. The forward fuselage has a modified profile with flat side windows, tandem seating for two with individual doors, and

incorporates an outer shell of reinforced glass-fibre. The front seat is occupied by the gunner, who controls a multi-barrelled cannon located under the nose, and a seven-round rocket launcher on each side of the fuselage to the rear of the pilot's position.

Design began in March 1987 and the Zafar 300 prototype was first flown on 31 January 1989. It is equipped for VFR/VMC flights only. More comprehensive avionics and instrumentation may be fitted to any future conversions of JetRangers, of which

the Islamic Republic of Iran army aviation force has a substantial number remaining from 184 AB 206B-1s purchased from the Agusta licence-production line in Italy.

SPECIFICATION

Seyedo Shohada Zafar 300
Rotor system: main rotor diameter 35 ft 4 in (10.77 m); tail rotor diameter 5 ft 2 in (1.575 m); main rotor disc area 980.51 sq ft (91.09 m2); tail rotor disc area

20.97 sq ft (1.95 m2)
Fuselage and tail: length overall, rotors turning 39 ft 7.5 in (12.075 m); height overall 9 ft 6.75 in (2.915 m)
Powerplant: one Allison 250-C18 turboshaft rated at 317 shp (236 kW)
Weights: empty 758 kg (1,671 lb); maximum take-off 1300 kg (2,866 lb)
Fuel and load: internal fuel 270 litres (71.3 US gal); external fuel none
Speed: never exceed speed at sea level 130 kt (149 mph; 240 km/h)
Range: endurance 3 hours with 20 minute reserves

Shaanxi **Y-8/Y-8MPA**

Shaanxi Aircraft Company
PO Box 34, Chengdu, Shaanxi 723213
People's Republic of China

The **Yunshuji 8** (Transport aircraft number 8) is a reverse-engineered unlicensed copy of the **Antonov An-12 'Cub'** (described separately). The task of designing and developing the aircraft was initially given to the Xian Aircraft Company, which built and subsequently flew the first prototype on 25 December 1974. Production was transferred to the Shaanxi Aircraft Company in 1972, and their first aircraft flew on 29 December 1975. From the start, the Chinese-built 'Cub' could be distinguished by its longer nose glazing, which is similar to that fitted to the Chinese-built 'Badger'. The prototypes and initial aircraft were simply designated **Y-8** and were quickly replaced on the production line by a number of specialised types.

The **Y-8A** is a dedicated helicopter-carrier, optimised for transporting **China**'s Sikorsky S-70 Black Hawks to more remote areas. Internal cabin height was increased by deleting the internal gantry and travelling cranes/hoists. A civilian passenger/freighter version is designated **Y-8B**, while a fully pressurised version (all other versions are, like An-12s, only partly pressurised), the **Y-8C**, was developed in collaboration with Lockheed. Intended for civil and military customers, the aircraft has a redesigned cargo door, a longer hold (with no fuselage stretch), and various new systems. Two prototypes are flying.

The **Y-8D** is a dedicated military export version, one pair of which was bought by both **Sri Lanka** and **Sudan**; **Myanmar**

has also ordered the type. Sri Lankan aircraft have reportedly been converted for use as bombers, but one Y-8 was lost soon after delivery. The **Y-8E** is a drone-carrier, developed to replace elderly Tupolev Tu-4 'Bulls' used in the same role. The forward pressurised cabin accommodates a drone-controller's console, and two drones can be carried on trapezes under the wings. The **Y-8F** is a uniquely Chinese aircraft, a dedicated livestock carrier with cages for 350 goats or sheep.

Other versions are under development, including an inflight-refuelling tanker and an AEW platform (GEC Marconi are collaborating on the latter programme). A prototype of the **Y-8X** (previously known as the **Y-8MPA**) is flying. This has a Litton (Canada) AN/APS-504(V)3 search radar under the nose, in a new, deepened drum-like radome, and Western INS, ADF, DME, and other avionics. The aircraft also carries optical and infra-red cameras, an IR detection system and sonobuoys.

SPECIFICATION

Shaanxi Y-8C
Wing: span 38.00 m (124 ft 8 in); aspect ratio 11.85; area 121.86 m2 (1,311.73 sq ft)
Fuselage and tail: length 34.02 m (111 ft 7.5 in); height 11.16 m (36 ft 7.5 in); tailplane span 12.196 m (40 ft 0.25 in); wheel track 4.92 m (16 ft 1.75 in); wheel base 9.58 m (31 ft 5 in)
Powerplant: four Zhuzhou (SMPMC) Wojiang-6

(Ivchyenko AI-20K) turboprops each rated at 3,169 ekW (4,250 ehp)
Weights: empty equipped 35500 kg (78,263 lb); maximum take-off 61000 kg (134,480 lb)
Fuel and load: internal fuel 22909 kg (50,505 lb); external fuel none; maximum payload 20000 kg (44,092 lb)
Speed: maximum level speed 'clean' at 7000 m (22,965 ft) 662 km/h (357 kt; 411 mph); maximum cruising speed at 8000 m (26,250 ft) 550 km/h (297 kt; 342 mph); economical cruising speed at 8000 m (26,250 ft) 530 km/h (286 kt; 329 mph)
Range: 5615 km (3,030 nm; 3,489 miles) with maximum fuel or 1273 km (687 nm; 791 miles) with maximum payload; endurance 11 hours 7 minutes

The Y-8 is an unlicensed copy of the An-12. Whereas Antonov has rolled out the An-70, no such Chinese developments have occurred, and Shaanxi continues to produce 40-year old technology.

Performance: maximum rate of climb at sea level 473 m (1,552 ft) per minute; service ceiling 34,120 ft (10400 m); take-off run 1,230 m (4,035 ft) at maximum take-off weight; take-off distance to 50 ft (15 m) 3,007 m (9,866 ft) at maximum take-off weight; landing distance from 50 ft (15 m) 2174 m (7,133 ft) at normal landing weight; landing run 1100 m (3,609 ft) at normal landing weight

---

Shenyang **J-5/F-5**

Shenyang Aircraft Corporation
PO Box 328, Shenyang, Liaoning 110034
People's Republic of China

The **Shenyang J-5** was **China**'s first indigenously-built fighter, 'J-2' having been a Western designation erroneously applied to Soviet-built MiG-15, and the J-4 designation being wrongly applied to MiG-17s from the same source. It has often been reported that China built the MiG-15 and MiG-15UTI, but this was never the case. The J-5 was the real Chinese designation for a Chinese-built copy of the MiG-17F. Unlike later 'Chinese MiG copies'

the J-5 was produced with close Soviet collaboration. The Shaanxi Aircraft Company itself was largely designed and constructed by the Soviets, and J-5 production followed a carefully planned, four-phase programme under which local workers learned each major production process, starting with mere assembly of Soviet-built sub-assemblies and ending with manufacture of about 48 per cent of each aircraft.

The first J-5 made its maiden flight on 19

July 1956, and in September was cleared for mass production. Seventeen were completed in 1956, with 142 following in 1957, 429 in 1958 and 179 in 1959, bringing the total to 767. Production then switched to the J-6 (MiG-19). The introduction of the aircraft was a tremendous morale booster to industry and air force alike, and allowed the Chinese to shoot down a number of Taiwanese 'intruders', including two F-84Gs, six F-86s and an F-100 in 1958, an RB-57 in 1957, and an F-4 in 1967. J-5s are believed to remain in service with the People's Liberation Air Force. The type was exported, under the designation F-5, to **Albania** (where about 11 remain in service), and to **North Korea**, **Sudan** and **Tanzania**, where handfuls may remain active.

Later derivatives of the MiG-17F were developed and constructed by Chengdu (described separately under the **JJ-5/FT-5** heading).

While in its day it was an impressive fighter, the Chinese J-5 MiG-17 copy (export designation F-5) is now little more than a museum piece. However, circumstances have forced the Albanian air force to retain its services.

SPECIFICATION

Shenyang J-5/F-5 'Fresco'
Wing: span 9.63 m (31 ft 7 in); aspect ratio 4.1; area 22.60 m2 (243.27 sq ft)
Fuselage and tail: length 11.36 m (37 ft 3.25 in); height 3.80 m (12 ft 5.5 in
Powerplant: one Liming (LM) Wopen-5 (Klimov VK-1F) turbojet rated at 29.50 kN (5,732 lb st) dry and 33.14 kN (7,451 lb st) with afterburning
Weights: maximum take-off 6075 kg (13,393 lb)
Fuel and load: internal fuel 1155 kg (2,546 lb); external fuel up to 655 kg (1,444 lb) in two 400- or 240-litre (106- or 63-US gal) drop tanks; maximum ordnance 500 kg (1,102 lb)
Speed: maximum level speed 'clean' at 3000 m (9,845 ft) 1145 km/h (617 kt; 711 mph) or at 10000 m (32,810 ft) 1071 km/h (578 kt; 666 mph)
Range: ferry range 1980 km (1,068 nm; 1,230 miles) with drop tanks; combat radius 700 km (378 nm; 435 miles) on a hi-lo-hi attack mission with two 250-kg (551-lb) bombs and two drop tanks
Performance: maximum rate of climb at sea level 3900 m (12,795 ft) per minute; climb to 5000 m (16,405 ft) in 2 minutes 36 seconds at dry thrust or 1 minute 48 seconds at afterburning thrust; service ceiling 15000 m (49,215 ft) at dry thrust and 16600 m (54,460 ft) at afterburning thrust; take-off run 590 m (1,936 ft) at normal take-off weight; landing run 850 m (2,789 ft) at normal landing weight

Shenyang J-6/F-6

China began assessment of the supersonic MiG-19 during the late 1950s. It was selected for production under the second Five Year Plan. Design drawings were supplied to the Shenyang Aircraft Factory, which produced their own production tooling and design documentation for a copy of the basic **MiG-19P** all-weather interceptor under the designation **J-6**. The first Chinese-assembled aircraft made its maiden flight on 17 December 1958, and the first Chinese-built aircraft followed on 30 September 1959.

Licence-production of the MiG-19 and **MiG-19PM** was also assigned to the Nanchang Aircraft Factory, laying the foundations for later production of the **Q-5** (described separately). Seven MiG-19Ps were built, the first flying on 28 September 1959. Five MiG-19PMs were assembled from Soviet kits, and another 19 were built at the factory, these apparently being designated **J-6B**. Unfortunately, the turbulence of the 'Great Leap Forward' destroyed the carefully built-up quality control procedures instituted during the first Five Year Plan, and between 1958 and 1960 not one J-6 from Shenyang or Nanchang was accepted by the **PLA air force**. Many were scrapped after failing post-production inspections, and others had to be rebuilt before delivery.

The programme to build the MiG-19 began again in 1961 using Soviet-supplied drawings and technical documents, after having completely rebuilt the production tooling. Production was of the basic **MiG-19S 'Farmer-C'** day fighter, rather than the radar-equipped MiG-19P, although small numbers of the latter, and the MiG-19PM, may also have been constructed. The first 'second batch' J-6 flew in December 1961.

The aircraft was recertificated in December 1963, and began to enter service in significant numbers in 1964-65. The period between 1963 and 1966 was one of relative stability, and high morale, high quality, sensible production targets and a logical engineering approach prevailed. All this was swept away in the Cultural Revolution, in which political dogma replaced planning, and a period turbulence once more affected the industry. The effect on the J-6 programme was devastating, and provoked a restoration of investment, proper inspection, quality control and workers' education.

By 1973, the prevailing situation had improved sufficiently for the development of new variants. The most important of these was the **JJ-6** trainer, but this was accompanied by the **JZ-6**. Handfuls of J-6s had been built for medium-level and low-level recce duties from 1967, under the JZ-6 designation, and three more were modified for high-altitude reconnaissance between 1971 and 1975. A requirement for an entirely new JZ-6 was issued in January 1976, and construction of a prototype/demonstrator began in April. This used optical and infra-red sensors.

Frequently misidentified as the **J-6Xin**, and attributed to have an indigenous all-weather radar in a 'needle-nose radome' intake centrebody, the **J-6III** was actually a high-speed day fighter whose sharp, conical, needle nose served as a variable shock-cone. Development of the new variant began in 1969, and a prototype flew on 6 August 1969. The J-6III was a very different looking aircraft, with short-span, cropped wings and increased-chord ailerons and flaps. The aircraft was powered by uprated WP6A turbojets. The J-6III proved to be faster, faster climbing and tighter turning than the basic J-6, but was plagued by handling and quality control problems. 'Hundreds' had to be returned to the factory and rebuilt during a four-year programme.

The more modest **J-6C** was more successful, differing from the basic J-6/MiG-19S in having a relocated brake-chute fairing at the base of the trailing edge of the tailfin, below the rudder.

Guizhou was responsible for the final variant, the all-weather **J-6A**, which may also have been designated **J-6IV**. This was based on the J-6C airframe, but introduced all-weather radar and compatibility with the PL-2 missile. By comparison with the original all-weather J-6s (based on the MiG-19P and MiG-19PM), the J-6A/J-6IV had slightly recontoured radomes, with a larger and more bulbous 'upper lip' and a more pointed and conical centrebody. It is unknown whether the aircraft retains cannon in the wingroots or under the fuselage.

The 1950s-vintage J-6 was produced into the 1980s, by which time approximately 3,000 had been built. It was exported in substantial quantities to **Albania, Bangladesh, Egypt, Iran, Iraq, North Korea, Pakistan, Somalia, Tanzania, Vietnam** and **Zambia**, most of which continue to operate the type in small numbers. It remains in service in larger numbers with the Air Force of the People's Liberation Army, with which service it is numerically the most important type, fulfilling both attack and fighter roles.

Pakistan purchased two batches of 60 F-6s after the 1971 conflict with India, and even in late 1994 the type remained in service with No. 15 Sqn at Kamra, No. 19 (OCU) Sqn at Mianwali and Nos 17 and 23 Sqns at Samungli. The massive overhaul facility at Kamra kept the aircraft viable through frequent overhauls and by incorporating many modifications, including AIM-9 Sidewinder compatibility, Martin-Baker ejection seats and various new avionics systems, probably including most of those fitted to upgraded Nanchang A-5s (though not the RWRs). Pakistani F-6s are also configured to carry a huge semi-conformal bathtub external fuel tank below the belly. Some aircraft were passed to Bangladesh, where the type remains in use with No. 25 (OCU) Sqn as an advanced/tactical trainer.

SPECIFICATION

Shenyang J-6/F-6 'Farmer'
Wing: span 9.20 m (30 ft 2¼ in); aspect ratio 3.24; area 25.00 m² (269.11 sq ft)
Fuselage and tail: length 14.90 m (48 ft 10½ in) including probe and 12.60 m (41 ft 4 in) excluding probe; height 3.88 m (12 ft 8¾ in); tailplane span 5.00 m (16 ft 4¾ in); wheel track 4.15 m (13 ft 7½ in)
Powerplant: two Liming (LM) Wopen-6 (Tumanskii R-9BF-811) turbojets each rated at 5,730 lb st (25.49 kN) dry and 7,165 lb st (31.87 kN) with afterburning
Weights: nominal empty 5760 kg (12,698 lb); normal take-off 7545 kg (16,634 lb); maximum take-off about 10000 kg (22,046 lb)
Fuel and load: internal fuel 1687 kg (3,719 lb); external fuel up to two 1140-litre (301-US gal) or 760-litre (201-US gal) drop tanks; maximum ordnance 500 kg (1,102 lb)
Speed: never exceed speed at 35,000 ft (10670 m) 1700 km/h (917 kt; 1,056 mph); maximum level speed 'clean' at 36,000 ft (10975 m) 1540 km/h (831 kt; 957 mph); cruising speed at optimum altitude 950 km/h (512 kt; 590 mph)
Range: ferry range 2200 km (1,187 nm; 1,366 miles) with two 760-litre (201-US gal) drop tanks; normal range at 46,000 ft (14020 m) 1390 km (750 nm; 863 miles); combat radius 685 km (370 nm; 426 miles) with two 760-litre (201-US gal) drop tanks
Performance: maximum rate of climb at sea level more than 9145 m (30,000 ft) per minute; service ceiling 58,725 ft (17900 m); take-off run about 670 m (2,198 ft) with afterburning; take-off distance to 80 ft (25 m) 1525 m (5,003 ft) with afterburning; landing distance from 80 ft (25 m) 1980 m (6,496 ft) without brake chute; landing run 600 m (1,969 ft) with brake chute

Shenyang J-6/F-6 'Farmer'

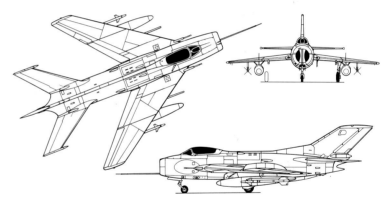

Above: Still the AFPLA's most numerically important type, this J-6 is one of several Communist aircraft to defect to Taiwan over the years.

Below: Pakistan operates J-6s in two-tone grey and natural metal schemes, but this No. 19 Sqn example wears an all-white finish.

Right: The Bangladesh Defence Force Air Wing has now only a single J-6 (F-6) unit: No. 25 Sqn (OCU) 'The Trendsetters', based at Jessore.

Below: While deficient in range, the J-6 remains a useful ground attack aircraft. This Pakistan Fiza'ya aircraft carries a pair of rocket pods.

Shenyang JJ-6

Another manifestation of the restoration of stability for the aircraft industry was the production by Shenyang of the **JJ-6** two-seat trainer, which first flew on 6 November 1970, but the certification of which was delayed until December 1973. A two-seat MiG-19UTI was built in small numbers by Mikoyan, but the type never entered service, conversion from the MiG-15UTI not being judged to be a problem. By the 1970s, however, flight safety considerations had assumed greater importance, and China felt that a trainer with handling characteristics similar to the J-6 was essential. This view was reinforced by significant export orders.

The Chinese two-seat trainer owes little to the Russian original. The fuselage is stretched by some 84 cm (33 in) ahead of the wing, and the wingroot-mounted NR-23 cannon are deleted to make room for extra fuel, restoring fuel capacity to within 150 litres (33 Imp gal) of the single-seater. A single cannon is usually retained below the fuselage. Two ventral fins are added below the rear fuselage to maintain stability.

The JJ-6 is based on the airframe of the later J-6C with the relocated brake-chute fairing, tubeless tyres, and disc brakes on the main undercarriage units. The type also has nosewheel braking, and various new avionics systems.

Production of the JJ-6 totalled 634 examples, and many were exported under the designation **FT-6** to serve as conversion and continuation trainers for the F-6 and A-5. In **Pakistan**, surviving FT-6s have been extensively upgraded (to the same standards as that nation's F-6 fighters) with Martin-Baker Mk 10L rocket-powered ejection seats. The zero-zero capability offered by this seat is a quantum leap from the 260 m (853 ft)/350 km/h (218 mph) minima of the original Shenyang seat. Using the 'lower-slung' Martin-Baker seat, pilots whose height exceeds 1.73 m (5 ft 8 in) can at last wear a proper flying helmet. JJ-6 trainers also remain in service in **Bangladesh**, **China** and **North Korea**.

SPECIFICATION

Shenyang/Tianjin JJ-6/FT-6
Wing: span 9.20 m (30 ft 2.25 in); aspect ratio 3.24; area 25.00 m² (269.11 sq ft)
Fuselage and tail: length 13.44 m (44 ft 1 in) excluding probe; height 3.88 m (12 ft 8¾ in); tailplane span 5.00 m (16 ft 4¾ in); wheel track 4.15 m (13 ft 7½ in)
Powerplant: two Liming (LM) Wopen-6 (Tumanskii R-9BF-811) turbojets each rated at 25.50 kN (5,732 lb st) dry and 31.88 kN (7,167 lb st) with afterburning
Fuel and load: internal fuel about 2000 litres (528 US gal); external fuel up to two 1140- or 760-litre (301- or 201-US gal) drop tanks; maximum ordnance 500 kg (1,102 lb)
Speed: never exceed speed at 10670 m (35,000 ft) 1700 km/h (917 kt; 1,056 mph); maximum level speed 'clean' at 11000 m (36,090 ft) 1540 km/h (831 kt; 957 mph) and at sea level 1340 km/h (723 kt; 832 mph); cruising speed at optimum altitude 950 km/h (512 kt; 590 mph)
Range: ferry range 2200 km (1,186 nm; 1,366 miles); standard range 1390 km (749 nm; 863 miles); combat radius 685 km (370 nm; 426 miles) on a typical hi-lo-hi mission with two drop tanks
Performance: maximum rate of climb at sea level more than 9145 m (30,000 ft) per minute with afterburning; service ceiling 17900 m (58,725 ft); take-off run about 670 m (2,200 ft) at maximum take-off weight with afterburning; take-off distance to 25 m (82 ft) 1525 m (5,000 ft) at maximum take-off weight with afterburning; landing distance from 25 m (82 ft) 1700 m (5,580 ft) at normal landing weight with brake chute; landing run 600 m (1,970 ft) at normal landing weight with brake chute
g limit: +8

With the MiG-19-derived J-6 as China's most significant warplane, the JJ-6 conversion trainer fulfils an important function.

Shenyang J-8 and J-8I 'Finback-A'

The **J-8** originated from a **PLA** requirement for a fighter with performance and combat capability superior to that of the MiG-21. Shenyang's decision to use twin engines, and the company's long association with the 'tailed delta' MiG-21-type configuration, ensured that the new aircraft looked like a scaled-up MiG-21; as such, it bore an astonishing resemblance to Mikoyan's Ye-152A 'Flipper'. The requirement was proposed in 1964, and development was in full swing by 1965.

The two prototypes were completed in July 1968, at the height of the Cultural Revolution but, remarkably, the flight test programme went ahead, albeit at a slow pace. The first J-8 made its maiden flight on 5 July 1969, and certification followed 10 years later. Engine shutdowns, high temperatures in the rear fuselage and transonic vibration were the only problems. These were quickly solved, and the 10-year gap before certification was almost entirely due to political interference and disruption to the factory by the repression of many of its key workers.

The original J-8 had a small ranging radar in the intake centrebody, and retained the single-piece forward-hinging canopy of the original J-7. The aircraft was armed with a single 30-mm cannon and up to four underwing PL-2 air-to-air missiles. Any production was very limited.

The **J-8I** was designed as an all-weather fighter derivative of the basic J-8, and featured a new Type 204 Sichuan SR-4 radar in an enlarged intake centrebody. The 30-mm cannon was replaced by a twin-barrelled 23-mm 23-III cannon, and provision was made for four rocket pods as an optional alternative to the PL-2 missiles. The J-8I retained the same 59-kN (13,450-lb st) WP-7B engines as the basic J-8 (also used in the Chengdu F-7M) but introduced some aerodynamic refinements, with small fences above the wing, revised wingtips and relocated airbrakes. The aircraft also introduced a two-piece canopy, with an upward-hinging rear transparency and a fixed windscreen. This marked the replacement of the highly unpopular Type I ejection seat with the Type II, which was more reliable and which could be used at ground level at speeds in excess of 140 kt (160 mph; 259 km/h).

Prototype assembly was completed in May 1980, but the aircraft burned out during its first engine run after a fuel or hydraulic pipe fractured due to resonance. The second prototype was hurriedly completed and made the type's maiden flight on 24 April 1981. Certification was granted in July 1985. J-8 and J-8I production totalled about 100 aircraft, and some of the original J-8s are said to have been converted to the later standard.

SPECIFICATION

Shenyang J-8 I 'Finback-A'
generally similar to the Shenyang J-8 II 'Finback-B' except in the following particulars:
Powerplant: two Liyang (LMC) Wopen-7B turbojets each rated at 43.15 kN (9,700 lb st) and 59.82 kN (13,448 lb st) with afterburning
Range: combat radius 800 km (497 miles)
Performance: maximum rate of climb at sea level 12000 m (39,370 ft) per minute; service ceiling 18000 m (59,050 ft)

Above: This line-up probably shows most of the original J-8Is, believed to have been used only for trials duties.

Left: The J-8I carries an air intercept radar in its conical intake centrebody.

Shenyang J-8II 'Finback-B'

Although the J-8I marked a great improvement over the original 'Finback', there was clearly scope for a more radical redesign. This led to the development of the **J-8II 'Finback-B'**, which was given the go-ahead in May 1981. The new variant had relocated lateral air intakes to feed its 69-kN (15,430-lb st) WP-13B turbojets, leaving the nose free for a radar antenna of the largest possible diameter. The engine intakes bear a striking similarity to those of the MiG-23 'Flogger', which should come as no surprise, since some of Egypt's MiG-23s were shipped to **China** in exchange for J-7 deliveries. The original aircraft's twin ventral strakes were replaced by a MiG-23-style folding fin. Seventy per cent of the airframe was changed by comparison with the original J-8, as were 30 per cent of the contractor-supplied parts.

The operational requirement for the new variant was approved in September 1980. The extensive use of CAD/CAM reduced design and development time to the minimum, the first of four prototypes flying on 12 June 1984. There has been small-scale batch production of the J-8II, but the type may not have entered service. An export version, designated **F-8B**, is powered by a pair of WP-13B turbojets and introduces a pulse-Doppler look-down radar and digital avionics, with a HUD and two HDDs.

On 5 August 1987 Grumman received a $501.8 million contract to design, develop and test an avionics upgrade for the J-8II under the Foreign Military Sales Program. Sponsored by the USAF's Aeronautical Systems Division, the contract covered installation of the new avionics package in two J-8II airframes supplied by China, and the provision of 50 shipsets for local installation, with development to be completed by February 1991 and delivery of the modification kits to be completed by January 1995. The new avionics package included a modified Westinghouse AN/APG-66 radar, with a constant wave illuminator to give compatibility with semi-active radar homing missiles like the AIM-7 Sparrow. The aircraft would also receive a modern HUD, a US ejection seat and a Litton LN39 INS, plus a bubble canopy and frameless wraparound windscreen. The massacre in Tiananmen Square in June 1989 led to an immediate halt on work on the project, and the expulsion of many of the Chinese engineers. Development restarted, but flight test and kit delivery would have required a change in State Department policy; with deliveries unlikely, China pulled out of the project, leading to its cancellation.

The cancellation of the Peace Pearl upgrade may have killed off the J-8. The PLAAF has taken delivery of Su-27 'Flankers', and seems more likely to purchase further examples, and perhaps MiG-29s, than to procure an indigenous alternative lacking sophisticated modern avionics and which represents an 'F-4-generation' aircraft.

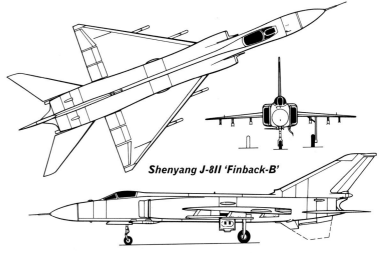

Shenyang J-8II 'Finback-B'

SPECIFICATION

Shenyang J-8 II/F-8B 'Finback-B'
Wing: span 9.34 m (30 ft 7.875 in); aspect ratio 2.1; area 42.20 m² (454.25 sq ft)
Fuselage and tail: length 21.59 m (70 ft 10 in) including probe; height 5.41 m (17 ft 9 in); wheel track 3.74 m (12 ft 3¼ in); wheel base 7.34 m (24 ft 0¾ in)
Powerplant: two Liyang (LMC) Wopen-13A II turbojets each rated at 9,590 lb st (42.66 kN) dry and 14,815 lb st (65.90 kN) with afterburning
Weights: empty 9820 kg (21,649 lb); normal take-off 14300 kg (31,526 lb); maximum take-off 17800 kg (39,242 lb)
Fuel and load: internal fuel about 5400 litres (1,426 US gal); external fuel up to three drop tanks
Speed: maximum level speed 'clean' at 36,000 ft (10975 m) 2338 km/h (1,262 kt; 1,453 mph)
Range: ferry range 2200 km (1,187 nm; 1,367 miles) with drop tanks; combat radius 800 km (432 kt; 497 miles)
Performance: maximum rate of climb at sea level 12000 m (39,370 ft) per minute; service ceiling 20200 m (66,275 ft); take-off run 670 m (2,198 ft) at maximum take-off weight with afterburning; landing run 1000 m (3,280 ft) with brake chute
g **limits:** +4.83 in a sustained turn at Mach 0.9 at 16,400 ft (5000 m)

Development of the J-8 was halted by the Tiananmen Square massacre, which left development aircraft embargoed in the USA. Since then, China has opted to buy Su-27 'Flankers' from Russia.

Shijiazhuang (SAP) Y-5

Shijiazhuang Aircraft Plant
PO Box 164, Shijiazhuang, Hebei 050062
People's Republic of China

Manufactured under Soviet licence, the Antonov An-2 general-purpose biplane was built in China for 30 years for both civil and military tasks. The first Chinese-produced An-2 was flown on 7 December 1957 as the **Y-5**, a total of 727 aircraft of this type being built at Nanchang, of which 384 were either for military use or for export. Production terminated at Nanchang in 1968, but was resumed in 1970 at Shijiazhuang (SAP), where an additional 221 were built before manufacture ended in 1986.

Extensively employed for utility tasks by the Chinese armed forces, the Y-5 was widely exported. A major recipient was the **Korean People's Army Air Force**, this North Korean service having received in excess of 160 aircraft of this type from Nanchang and Shijiazhuang production. For a number of years, the North Korean Y-5s were used for nocturnal missions over South Korea, flying at extremely low altitudes and sometimes depositing agents and saboteurs.

In 1989 the type again entered production as the **Y-5B**, a specially modified agricultural version.

SPECIFICATION

Shijiazhuang Y-5N
generally similar to the PZL Mielec (Antonov) An-2T Antek 'Colt' except in the following particulars:
Powerplant: one SMPMC (Zhuzhou) Huosai-5 (Shvetsov ASh-62IR) radial piston engine rated at 986 hp (735.5 kW)

ShinMaywa Industries US-1 (SS-2A)

ShinMaywa Industries Ltd
Nippon Building, 6-2, Otemachi 2-chome, Chiyoda-ku
Tokyo 100, Japan

Following the 1989 retirement of PS-1 patrol aircraft, the related **US-1** remains in military service in **Japan**. Fourteen were procured to serve with the 71st Kokutai of the **JMSDF** at Iwakuni and Atsugi, in the SAR role. The US-1 first flew on 16 October 1974 (from water) and on 3 December 1974 (from land). With a crew of nine, the US-1 has provision for 20 seated survivors or 12 stretchers. Experiments have also been made with one aircraft converted for the fire-fighting role by means of a tank system developed by Comair in Canada. All remaining aircraft have been converted to **US-1A** standard with the replacement of original T64-IHI-10 engines by more powerful -10J versions.

In 1992 Shin Meiwa (known as Kawanishi until 1949) was renamed ShinMaywa Industries and the US-1 production line was surprisingly reopened to meet an order for a 14th aircraft for the JMSDF. Another US-1A was approved in the FY 1993 budget, and more examples may yet follow.

SPECIFICATION

ShinMaywa Industries US-1A
Wing: span 108 ft 9 in (33.15 m); aspect ratio 8.1; area 1,462.00 sq ft (135.82 m²)
Fuselage and tail: length 109 ft 9¼ in (33.46 m); height 32 ft 7¾ in (9.95 m); tailplane span 40 ft 8½ in (12.36 m); wheel track 11 ft 8¼ in (3.56 m); wheel base 27 ft 4 in (8.33 m)
Powerplant: four Ishikawajima-built General Electric T64-IHI-10J turboprops each rated at 3,493 ehp (2605 ekW) and, powering the boundary layer control system, one Ishikawajima-built General Electric T58-IHI-10-M2 turboshaft rated at 1,360 shp (1014 kW)
Weights: manufacturer's empty 23300 kg (51,367 lb); empty equipped 25500 kg (56,217 lb); normal take-off 43000 kg (94,797 lb) from water; maximum take-off 45000 kg (99,206 lb) from land
Fuel and load: internal fuel 22489 litres (5,941 US gal); external fuel none
Speed: maximum level speed at 10,000 ft (3050 m) 282 kt (325 mph; 522 km/h); cruising speed at 1,000 ft (3050 m) 230 kt (265 mph; 426 km/h)
Range: 2,060 nm (2,372 miles; 3817 km)
Performance: maximum rate of climb at sea level 1,600 ft (488 m) per minute; service ceiling 23,600 ft (7195 m); take-off run 1,820 ft (555 m) at normal take-off weight on water; take-off distance to 50 ft (15 m) 2,150 ft (655 m) at maximum take-off weight on land; landing distance from 50 ft (15 m) 2,655 ft (809 m) at normal landing weight on land with propeller reversal; landing run 720 ft (219 m) at normal landing weight on water without propeller reversal

In a surprising move, the US-1 re-entered production in 1992, and further deliveries are pending.

ShinMaywa Industries (Learjet) U-36A

Four **Learjet 36A** twin-jets were converted by Shin Meiwa (renamed in 1992 as ShinMaywa) to serve as fleet training support aircraft for the JMSDF, with the designation **U-36A**. Extensive modifications allow these aircraft to tow targets and fly anti-ship missile simulation and ECM missions. Large wingtip pods house an HWQ-1T missile seeker simulator, AN/ALQ-6 jammer and cameras. A long-range ocean surveillance radar is fitted, with a large underbelly radome housing the scanning aerial, and the U-36A also carries AN/ALE-43 chaff dis-

penser and a high-speed sleeve target with scoring equipment. The U-36A operates at higher weights than the Learjet 36A, and has expanded underwing stores capability.

SPECIFICATION

ShinMaywa Industries (Learjet) U-36A
generally similar to the Learjet 35A except in the following particulars:
Fuel and load: internal fuel 1,110 US gal (4202 litres); external fuel none

The JASDF's U-36s are flown by the 81st Kokutai at Iwakuni, and in addition to ECM duties are used as target tugs – hence the orange colour scheme.

Shorts SC-7 Skyvan

Short Brothers PLC
PO Box 241, Airport Road, Belfast BT3 9DZ
Northern Ireland

Of notably utilitarian appearance, the **Shorts Skyvan** began life in piston-engined form (first flown 17 January 1963, with Continental engines) but acquired Astazou II turboprops (flown 2 October 1963) before production began for both military and civil use. The principal military variant is the **Skyvan 3M**, flown early in 1970 and subsequently purchased by about 20 air forces. In military guise, the Skyvan 3M can accommodate 22 equipped troops, 16 paratroops (dropped through the rear loading ramp), 12 stretchers or a variety of cargo.

Among the first, and still the largest, military user is the **Royal Air Force of Oman** (formerly the Sultan of Oman Air Force), which bought 16 for operation by No. 2 Squadron. **Ghana** and **Singapore** each bought six, used for both transport and SAR/coastal patrol duties by, respectively, No. 1 Squadron at Takoradi and No. 121 Squadron at Changi. Other users, mostly with two aircraft each, are **Austria**, **Botsawana**, **Ciskei**, **Guyana**, **Mauritania**, **Mexico**, **Nepal**, and **(North) Yemen**.

SPECIFICATION

Shorts SC.7 Skyvan Series 3M
Wing: span 64 ft 11 in (19.79 m); aspect ratio 11.0; area 373.00 sq ft (34.65 m2)
Fuselage and tail: length 40 ft 1 in (12.21 m) with standard nose or 41 ft 4 in (12.60 m) with weather radar nose; height 15 ft 1 in (4.60 m); tailplane span 17 ft 4 in (5.28 m); wheel track 13 ft 10 in (4.21 m); wheel base 14 ft 10 in (4.52 m)
Powerplant: two Garrett TPE331-2-201A turboprops each rated at 715 shp (533 kW)
Weights: operating empty 7,400 lb (3356 kg) in utility configuration, or 7,620 lb (3456 kg) in freighter configuration, or 8,330 lb (3778 kg) in trooping configuration; normal take-off 13,700 lb (6214 kg); maximum take-off 14,500 lb (6577 kg)
Fuel and load: internal fuel 2,320 lb (1052 kg) plus provision for 800 lb (363 kg) of auxiliary fuel; external fuel none; maximum payload 5,200 lb (2358 kg) standard or 6,000 lb (2722 kg) overload
Speed: never exceed speed 217 kt (250 mph; 402 km/h); maximum cruising speed at 10,000 ft (3050 m) 175 kt (202 mph; 324 km/h); economical cruising speed at

The Royal Nepalese Army Air Corps (which gained autonomy from the air force in 1979) operates a mix of fixed- and rotary-winged types that includes three Shorts Skyvan 3s, based at Tribhuvan.

10,000 ft (3050 m) 150 kt (173 mph; 278 km/h)
Range: 582 nm (670 miles; 1075 km) with maximum fuel or 208 nm (240 miles; 386 km) with a 5,000-lb (2268-kg) payload
Performance: maximum rate of climb at sea level 1,530 ft (466 m) per minute; service ceiling 22,000 ft

(6705 m); take-off run 780 ft (238 m) at maximum take-off weight; take-off distance to 50 ft (15 m) 1,260 ft (384 m) at maximum take-off weight; landing distance from 50 ft (15 m) 1,395 ft (425 m) at maximum landing weight; landing run 695 ft (212 m) at maximum landing weight

---

Shorts 330/C-23 Sherpa

Developed from the Skyvan light transport, the **Shorts 330** was a regional airliner which could also be reconfigured for transport tasks. Its box-like fuselage offered exceptional load-carrying capacity for the aircraft's size, and the high-lift wing and powerful engines provided good STOL performance. Cargo versions were configured with a full-width rear loading ramp. The **Thai army** operates two aircraft designated **Shorts 330UTT** in the transport role.

The major military customer was the **US Air Force**, which bought 18 **C-23As** for its EDSA (European Distribution System Aircraft) requirement, these being used to shuttle spare parts between the USAFE maintenance and distribution centres and the front-line bases. Based with the 10th MAS at Zweibrücken AB, Germany, the C-23As served from November 1984 until 31 October 1990, when the EDSA programme was ended.

Four C-23As remained in USAF hands at Edwards AFB, where they served the 6510th Test Wing (now 412th TW) for the USAF Test Pilots' School. Eight were diverted to the US Forestry Service, and six were transferred to the **Army National**

This Connecticut AVCRAD C-23B (note the cabin windows) is a US Army-operated Sherpa and sports Desert Storm nose art.

Guard, which also ordered 10 more new-build **C-23B**s, distinguished by their cabin windows.

It is believed that four 330s are in Army service. The Army fleet flies utility transport missions on behalf of the Army's maintenance organisation, single aircraft being assigned to the STARCs (State Area Commands) of Alabama, California, Connecticut, Mississippi, Oregon, Puerto Rico and Utah. At least three are assigned to the Missouri AVCRAD, and six more were delivered during 1992. At least one of the Army C-23s is reputed to have a special mission, perhaps involving electronic reconnaissance, and was seen on service during the Gulf War.

Under the designation **C-23B+**, 20 modified **Shorts 360** commuter airliners (with an option on 10) are to be acquired by the US Army National Guard. These aircraft, bought back by Shorts, will be converted to (twin-tailed) C-23 standard through the addition of new tail sections, along with new

avionics, in a programme to be undertaken at the West Virginia Air Center. The first conversion began in January 1994, and deliveries are due to be completed by 1996.

SPECIFICATION

Shorts C-23A Sherpa
Wing: span 74 ft 8 in (22.76 m); aspect ratio 12.2; area 453.00 sq ft (42.08 m2)
Fuselage and tail: length 58 ft 0½ in (17.69 m); height 16 ft 3 in (4.95 m); tailplane span 18 ft 7¾ in (5.68 m)
Powerplant: two Pratt & Whitney Canada T101-CP-100 (PT6A-45R) turboprops each rated at 1,198 shp (893 kW)
Weights: empty equipped 14,727 lb (6680 kg);

maximum take-off 25,500 lb (11566 kg)
Fuel and load: internal fuel 4,480 lb (2032 kg); external fuel none; maximum payload 7,100 lb (3221 kg)
Speed: maximum cruising speed at 10,000 ft (3050 m) at 21,000 lb (9526 kg) 190 kt (218 mph; 352 km/h); economical cruising speed at 10,000 ft (3050 m) at 21,000 lb (9526 kg) 157 kt (181 mph; 291 km/h)
Range: 669 nm (770 miles; 1239 km) with 5,000-lb (2268-kg) payload or 195 nm (225 miles; 362 km) with 7,000-lb (3,175-kg) payload
Performance: maximum rate of climb at sea level 1,180 ft (360 m) per minute; service ceiling 20,000 ft (6095 m); take-off distance 1,840 ft (561 m) at maximum take-off weight; take-off distance to 50 ft (15 m) 2,610 ft (796 m) at maximum take-off weight; landing distance from 50 ft (15 m) 1,900 ft (579 m) at maximum landing weight

---

Shorts Tucano

In 1985 the **RAF** selected the **Tucano** as its new *ab initio* trainer following an international competition that had involved the Pilatus PC-9, the Hunting Turbo-Firecracker and the AAC/Westland A 20. Based on an original design by EMBRAER of Brazil, the turboprop-powered Tucano offered by

Shorts promised economy and a performance not far short of that of the Jet Provost T.Mk 5, the main type it would replace in RAF service. As the first tandem-seat non-jet trainer to be ordered for the RAF since the Chipmunk, the Tucano reflects a current trend back to a more 'traditional' seating arrangement for pupil and instructor.

Considerable modification was undertaken to tailor the basic airframe to British

requirements, including substituting a Garrett turboprop in place of the original Pratt & Whitney PT6A – which significantly improved the rate of climb – and reprofiling the cockpit to provide commonality with the BAe Hawk. EMBRAER flew a Garrett-engined prototype in Brazil in February 1986 and delivered this to Shorts in Belfast as a pattern aircraft, the first **Tucano T.Mk 1** making its maiden flight on 30 December that year. The total RAF production order

covered 130 aircraft, first delivery to the Central Flying School at Scampton taking place in June 1988. The balance of the RAF order was completed in 1993. Tucanos equip No. 1 FTS at Linton-on-Ouse, No. 3 FTS at Cranwell, and No. 6 FTS at Finningley, with others at Scampton with the CFS.

By opting to train embryo fast-jet pilots on a turboprop aircraft, the RAF gained considerably. Economically a better proposition than a jet type, the Tucano is less demanding from the viewpoint of student pilots in the earliest stages of flight training. To extend the Tucano's capability in both military training and counter-insurgency roles, Shorts conducted a series of Tucano weapon trials in the spring of 1991 using twin FNNH machine-gun pods, the FNNH heavy MG and rocket launcher and the LAIJ32 seven-round rocket launcher, plus bombs up to 250 kg (551 lb). Customers for the armed export Tucano have been **Kuwait** (**T.Mk 52**), which took delivery of the last of 16 aircraft in 1991 (though they remained in the UK pending reformation of the KAF and formation of their operating unit, No. 19 Sqn), and **Kenya** (**T.Mk 51**), which received the last of 12 in June 1991.

SPECIFICATION

Shorts Tucano T.Mk 1
Wing: span 37 ft 0 in (11.28 m); aspect ratio 6.58; area 208.00 sq ft (19.33 m2)
Fuselage and tail: length 32 ft 4¼ in (9.86 m); height

This Tucano T.Mk 1 wears the blue band of No. 3 FTS, at Cranwell. The modified (frameless) canopy was one of the design changes specified by the RAF.

11 ft 1¾ in (3.40 m); tailplane span 13 ft 3½ in (4.66 m); wheel track 12 ft 4 in (3.76 m); wheel base 19 ft 4½ in (3.16 m)
Powerplant: one Garrett TPE331-12B turboprop rated at 1,100 shp (820 kW)
Weights: basic empty 4,872 lb (2210 kg); normal take-off 5,952 lb (2700 kg) for aerobatics; maximum take-off 6,470 lb (2935 kg)
Fuel and load: internal fuel 1,202 lb (545 kg); external fuel up to two 71-Imp gal (85.3-US gal; 323-litre) drop tanks; ordnance none
Speed: never exceed speed 330 kt (380 mph; 611 km/h); maximum level speed 'clean' and maximum cruising speed at 10,000 ft (3050 m) 277 kt (319 mph; 513 km/h) and at sea level 269 kt (310 mph; 498 km/h); economical cruising speed at 20,000 ft (6095 m) 220 kt (253 mph; 407 km/h)
Range: ferry range 1,790 nm (2,061 miles; 3317 km) with drop tanks; range 954 nm (1,099 miles; 1767 km)

with internal fuel; endurance 5 hours 12 minutes
Performance: maximum rate of climb at sea level 3,270 ft (997 m) per minute; service ceiling 34,000 ft (10365 m); take-off run 1,190 ft (363 m) at normal take-off weight; take-off distance to 50 ft (15 m) 1,930 ft

(590 m) at normal take-off weight; landing distance from 50 ft (15 m) 2,050 ft (625 m) at normal landing weight; landing run 1,180 ft (360 m) at normal landing weight
g limits: -3.3 to +6.5

SIAI-Marchetti **S.208M**

Agusta SpA Rome Works (Siai-Marchetti)
Via della Vasca Navale 79/81
I-00146 Rome, Italy

Based on the S.205 four-seat touring aircraft, the first post-war production aircraft of SIAI-Marchetti, the **S.208** was developed in 1967 with more power, retractable gear and five seats. The **Italian air force** acquired 45 in the **S.208M** version (with jettisonable cabin door) and these continue to be used for liaison duties and as glider tugs. A couple of the Italian aircraft

were passed to the **Tunisian air force** to serve in the communications role.

SPECIFICATION

SIAI-Marchetti S.208M
Wing: span 10.86 m (35 ft 7.5 in); aspect ratio 7.33; area 16.09 m2 (173.20 sq ft)

Fuselage and tail: length 8.00 m (26 ft 3 in); height 2.89 m (9 ft 5¾ in); tailplane span 3.42 m (11 ft 2½ in); wheel track 3.55 m (11 ft 8 in); wheel base 1.90 m (6 ft 2¾ in)
Powerplant: one Textron Lycoming O-540-E4A5 flat-six piston engine rated at 260 hp (194 kW)
Weights: empty equipped 780 kg (1,720 lb); maximum take-off 1350 kg (2,976 lb)
Fuel and load: internal fuel 215 litres (56.8 US gal)

plus provision for 231 litres (61 US gal) of auxiliary fuel in two wingtip tanks; external fuel none
Speed: maximum level speed 'clean' at sea level 320 km/h (173 kt; 199 mph); cruising speed at optimum altitude 300 km/h (162 kt; 187 mph)
Range: ferry range 2000 km (1,079 nm; 1,243 miles) with optional fuel; range 1200 km (648 nm; 746 miles) with internal fuel
Performance: service ceiling 5400 m (17,715 ft)

SIAI-Marchetti **SF.260/TP**

Designed by Stello Frati, the three-seat **SF.260** was put into production by SIAI Marchetti after prototypes had been built and flown by Aviamilano (as the **F.250** and **F.260**). The SF.260 was soon marketed in military guise as the **SF.260M** and **SF.260W**, the latter named **Warrior** and having a strengthened airframe and underwing hardpoints for the ground attack role. Production has totalled well over 850, including dedicated variants for the civil market (**SF.260A, B, C** and **D**).

The SF.260M was first flown on 10 October 1970 and is equipped to provide basic and instrument flying. First flown in May 1972, the SF.260W has two or four pylons with a combined capacity for 300 kg (661 lb), and is suitable for light COIN duty and armament training. A turboprop version of the SF.260M/W, the **TP** model, first flew in July 1980, the prototype being a converted airframe. Apart from changes ahead of the firewall to accommodate the Allison 250-B17D turboprop, differences from the piston-engined version were limited to the fuel feed system and a changed rudder trim tab. Production of the SF.260TP is reported to exceed 60.

OPERATORS

Specific customer variants of the SF.260 are identified by a letter suffix added to the basic 'M' or 'W' designation. Among these are the **SF.260 MB**, Burma; **MP**, Philippines; **MS**, Singapore; **MT**, Thailand; **MC**, Zaïre; and **MZ**, Zambia. Warrior designations included **SF.260 WD**, Dubai; **WE**, Ireland (Eire); **WL**, Libya; **WP**, Philippines; **WS**, Somalia; **WT**, Tunisia; and **WC**, Zimbabwe (local name is **Genet**). Aircraft for the Italian air force are designated **SF.260AM** and a batch ordered by the Turkish air force in 1989 for co-production and local assembly are **SF.260D**s (a civil designation); 39 remain active. Small numbers of SF.260WLs were transferred to Chad and to Nicaragua by Libya, where a local assembly/production centre was established with Italian help to supplement 110 aircraft delivered from Italy. Other users of SF.260Ms include Belgium, Brunei, Burkino-Faso and Burundi.

Customers for the SF.260TP include the Burundi army aviation, Dubai air wing, Ethiopian air force, Haitian air corps and Sri Lanka air force. Ethiopian and Sri Lankan aircraft have seen service in the armed light COIN role but are often used, like the others, for basic training. In addition, the air force of Zimbabwe has 10 SF.260TP that were, uniquely, locally converted from piston-engined SF.260WC Genet armed trainers

for use by No. 2 Squadron at Gwelo. In 1994-1995 the Philippine air force will take delivery of 19 SF.260TPs to replace existing SF.260Ms.

SPECIFICATION

SIAI-Marchetti SF.260W Warrior
Wing: span 8.35 m (27 ft 4¾ in) over tip tanks; aspect ratio 6.3; area 10.10 m2 (108.72 sq ft)
Fuselage and tail: length 7.10 m (23 ft 3½ in); height 2.41 m (7 ft 11 in); elevator span 3.01 m (9 ft 10½ in); wheel track 2.27 m (7 ft 5½ in); wheel base 1.66 m (5 ft 5¼ in)
Powerplant: one Textron Lycoming O-540-E4A5 flat-six piston engine rated at 260 hp (194 kW)
Weights: empty equipped 830 kg (1,830 lb); normal take-off about 1140 kg (2,513 lb); maximum take-off

1300 kg (2,866 lb)
Fuel and load: internal fuel 169 kg (372.5 lb); external fuel up to 114 kg (251.5 lb) in two 80-litre (21-US gal) drop tanks; maximum ordnance 300 kg (661 lb)
Speed: maximum level speed 'clean' at sea level 165 kt (190 mph; 305 km/h); cruising speed at 5,000 ft (1525 m) 152 kt (175 mph; 281 km/h)
Range: ferry range 925 nm (1,066 miles; 1716 km); combat radius 300 nm (345 miles; 556 km) on a single-seat hi-lo-hi attack mission, or 250 nm (287 miles; 463 km) on a single-seat attack mission with two 5-minute loiters over separate en-route target areas
Performance: maximum rate of climb at sea level 1,250 ft (381 m) per minute; climb to 7,550 ft (2300 m) in 10 minutes 20 seconds; service ceiling 14,700 ft (4480 m); take-off distance to 50 ft (15 m) 825 m (2,707 ft) at maximum take-off weight
g limits: -2.2 to +4.4 without external stores

The Sri Lankan air force has a single SF.260 unit, No. 1 Flying Training Wing at Anuradhapur. This is one of its eight SF.260TPs, with rockets.

SIAI-Marchetti **SM 1019**

Eighty of these FAC and liaison aircraft were built for the **Italian army** between 1972 and 1979, after SIAI-Marchetti had fitted turboprop engines in two remanufactured Cessna O-1s to serve as prototypes; these were first flown on 24 May 1969 and on 18 February 1971 as **SM 1019** and **SM 1019A**. The production **SM 1019E1** was largely redesigned in Italy but retained the O-1's basic configuration. Seating two in tandem, the SM 1019 introduced hardpoints for external loads of up to 227 kg (500 lb) that could include gun pods, rockets and bombs. Most remain in service, including some with the **air force**, which handles *ab initio* training of army pilots.

SPECIFICATION

SIAI-Marchetti SM.1019EI
Wing: span 10.97 m (36 ft 0 in); aspect ratio 7.44;

area 16.16 m2 (173.95 sq ft)
Fuselage and tail: length 8.52 m (27 ft 11½ in) tail up; height 2.86 m (9 ft 4½ in) tail down; tailplane span 3.42 m (11 ft 2¾ in); wheel track 2.29 m (7 ft 7¼ in); wheel base 6.23 m (20 ft 5¼ in)
Powerplant: one Allison 250-B17 turboprop rated at 400 shp (298 kW)
Weights: empty equipped 690 kg (1,521 lb); operating empty 730 kg (1,609 lb); normal take-off 1300 kg (2,866 lb); maximum take-off 1450 kg (3,196 lb)
Fuel and load: internal fuel 320 litres (84 US gal); external fuel none; ordnance none
Speed: never exceed speed 169 kt (194 mph; 313 km/h); maximum cruising speed at 8,200 ft (2500 m) 162 kt (186 mph; 300 km/h); economical cruising speed at

8,200 ft (2500 m) 152 kt (175 mph;281 km/h)
Range: ferry range 730 nm (840 miles; 1352 km) with auxiliary fuel; range 610 nm (702 miles; 1130 km) with standard fuel; endurance 8 hours 45 minutes with auxiliary fuel or 7 hours 20 minutes with standard fuel
Performance: maximum rate of climb at sea level 1,810 ft (551 m) per minute; service ceiling 25,000 ft (7620 m); take-off run 218 ft (716 m) at maximum take-off weight; take-off distance to 50 ft (15 m) 1,185 ft (361 m) at maximum take-off weight; landing distance from 50 ft (15 m) 992 ft (281 m) at maximum landing weight; landing run 443 ft (135 m) at maximum landing weight

Sikorsky (Orlando Helicopter Airways) S-55/H-19

In 1964 Orlando Helicopter Airways Inc., (OHA) of Florida, was founded to support and, in some cases, restart production of Sikorsky helicopters no longer built by the parent company. In addition to a huge spares resource, Orlando Helicopters held the FAA type certificates for all **Sikorsky H-19** and civilian **S-55** models, until the company stopped trading in 1993. Several S-55 versions were developed by the firm. The majority of these were aimed at the civil market for applications including VIP transport, aerial advertising, crop spraying and logging or construction work.

Seeking to obtain drone helicopters simulating the Mil Mi-24P 'Hind-F' assault helicopter, the US Army Missile Command in Huntsville, Alabama, latched on to a proposal from OHA to modify H-19/S-55s into realistic 'Hind' Look-Alike drones with similar size, appearance, radar return and infra-red emissions.

When flown by a live pilot, the H-19 'Hind' is flown from the original cockpit, behind the simulated 'intakes' for the Isotov turboshafts.

OHA designed a new nose section, with simulated cockpits for the weapons operator in front and the pilot aft and above, and added stub wings with external store pylons. The simulated cockpits were empty (except, if desired, for the addition of mannequins to give a more realistic appearance), the 'Hind' Look-Alike being flown by a pilot in a cockpit hidden above and behind the simulated twin intakes for the absent Isotov TV3-117 turboshaft engines. All aircraft retained the 597-kW (800-hp) Lycoming-built Wright R-1300-30 radial. The first two aircraft retained the original three-bladed rotor of the S-55/H-19. However, like subsequent drones, they were later fitted with a new five-bladed main rotor.

To simulate more realistically the operating characteristics of the 'Hind', the Look-Alikes were fitted, after completion of initial trials, with infra-red equipment, duplicating the exhaust of the Mi-24s, and with IR and RF jammers having capabilities similar to those in Russian service. Two of the 'Hind' Look-Alike helicopters have been retained as trainers, whereas the other 13 have been fitted by Sperry Defense Systems with full radio controls. Still man-rated, the 13 drones are being expended in missile trials at the White Sands Missile Range.

A second, more aggressive military version was marketed by OHA as the armed **OHA-AT-55 Defender**, design of which began in 1990. Re-engined with a Garrett TPE331-3 turboshaft or a Wright R-1330-3 radial, the Defender also features a stub wing with pylons capable of carrying up to 500 kg (227 lb) of weapons, and a five-bladed rotor. Capable of carrying up to 10 fully-equipped troops, the Defender could also be fitted out to accommodate six stretchers and two attendants.

Sikorsky S-58/H-34 Choctaw

Sikorsky Aircraft, Division of United Technologies Corporation, 6900 Main Street, Stratford, Connecticut 06601-1381, USA

Developed initially for the US Navy in the anti-submarine role, the **S-58** first flew on 20 September 1954 and was produced in military and civil versions as a general transport helicopter, carrying up to 18 troops in military **CH-34 Choctaw** configuration. In its original form with an R-1820-84 piston engine it is now out of service, but small numbers of the twin-turbine **S-58T** conversion remain in use.

Sikorsky flew the first re-engined S-58T on 19 August 1970, powered by the 1,800-shp (1343-kW) Pratt & Whitney PT6T-3 Twin Pac paired turboshaft. The manufacturer produced nearly 150 conversions or kits for local programmes before selling S-58T rights to California Helicopters International in 1981.

Twelve S-58Ts are used by No. 201 Squadron of the **Royal Thai air force** at Lop Buri, and a similar number are flown by Logistics Command of the **Indonesian air force** (TNI-AU). Two are maintained by the Presidential Aircraft Squadron in Argentina, but three supplied to South Korea have been retired. The **Uruguayan navy** exchanged two of its **CH-34J**s for three refurbished **Westland Wessex 60s** (described separately). The latter were overhauled by Hi-Lift Helicopters International, Florida. The company began to develop the S-58 design by converting an ex-RTAF S-58T with a new cockpit and forward fuselage section, similar in profile to the Sikorsky S-76. This **Viking** project had been temporarily shelved in July 1994.

SPECIFICATION

Sikorsky S-58 (CH-34A Choctaw)
Rotor system: main rotor diameter 56 ft 0 in (17.07 m); tail rotor diameter 9 ft 6 in (2.90 m); main rotor disc area 2,463.01 sq ft (228.81 m²); tail rotor disc area 70.88 sq ft (6.58 m²)
Fuselage and tail: length overall, rotors turning 56 ft 8.25 in (17.27 m) and fuselage 46 ft 9 in (14.25 m); height overall 15 ft 11 in (4.85 m) and 14 ft 3.5 in (4.36 m) to top of rotor head; wheel track 14 ft 0 in (4.27 m); wheel base 28 ft 3 in (8.75 m)
Powerplant: one Wright R-1820-84B/D Cyclone radial piston engine rated at 1,525 hp (1137 kW)
Weights: empty equipped 7,750 lb (3515 kg); normal take-off 13,000 lb (5897 kg); maximum take-off 14,000 lb (6350 kg)
Fuel and load: internal fuel 306.5 US gal (1159 litres) plus provision for 150 US gal (568 litres) of auxiliary fuel in an external tank; external fuel none
Speed: maximum level speed at sea level 106 kt (122 mph; 196 km/h); maximum cruising speed at optimum altitude 84 kt (97 mph; 156 km/h)
Range: 215 nm (247 miles; 397 km) with standard fuel
Performance: maximum rate of climb at sea level 1,100 ft (335 m) per minute; service ceiling 9,500 ft (2895 m); hovering ceiling 4,900 ft (1490 m) in ground effect and 2,400 ft (730 m) out of ground effect

The Royal Thai air force flies 18 S-58Ts converted from CH-34C Choctaws. They are operated by No. 201 Sqn at Lop Buri on heli-support duties.

Sikorsky S-61/SH-3 Sea King

US Navy experience with the Sikorsky S-58 highlighted the shortcomings of operating hunter/killer pairs of helicopters in the anti-submarine role, so in 1957 Sikorsky was awarded a contract to combine the two functions in a single airframe. The resulting S-61 prototype, designated **YHSS-2 Sea King**, made its first flight on 11 March 1959. Production aircraft were known as the **HSS-2** until 1962, when redesignation resulted in the Sea King becoming the **SH-3A**.

The new helicopter featured two General Electric T58 turboshafts above the main cabin, driving a five-bladed rotor. The rugged fuselage had a two-man cockpit, a cabin with two sensor operators and their ASW equipment, a boat hull for amphibious operations (rarely practised) and outrigger floats which also housed the main undercarriage. As a 'hunter', the SH-3A's primary sensors were a Bendix AQS-10 dipping sonar and a Ryan APN-130 search radar; in the 'killer' role, it could carry a pair of torpedoes or depth charges. Mounted over the sliding starboard-side cabin door was a SAR rescue winch.

Two hundred and forty-five SH-3As were built, followed by a prototype and 73 production **SH-3D**s, these introducing uprated T58-GE-10 engines, AQS-13A sonar and APN-182 radar. One hundred and three SH-3As and two SH-3Ds were converted to **SH-3G** standard to act as general-purpose rescue platforms and transports. The modification involved removing the ASW equipment and installing 15 canvas seats and long-range fuel tanks.

A decision to retire dedicated ASW carriers in the early 1970s dictated the next Sea King version, the **SH-3H**. These had to perform not only the inner-zone ASW mission, but also plane-guard, surface surveillance and surface targeting missions within the all-purpose carrier air wing. One hundred and sixteen of the earlier three variants were converted to the new standard. This comprised installation of AQS-13B sonar, Canadian Marconi LN66HP radar, chaff dispensers and ASQ-81 towed MAD bird, the latter housed in the starboard undercarriage sponson. Subsequently, ESM equipment and the radar were deleted, the weight saved being expended on a modern tactical navigation suite and improved sonobuoy and sonar processing capability.

In US Navy service, the SH-3H was deployed in six-aircraft squadron detachments on each carrier. It has now largely been replaced by the Sikorsky SH-60F Ocean Hawk, and by mid-1994 it served only with HS-1, 11 and 75 at NAS Jacksonville, FL, for Atlantic Fleet support, and with HS-12 (NAS Atsugi, Japan), and HS-85 (NAS Alameda, CA) with the Pacific Fleet. Others are spread around disparate test and utility units. The remaining SH-3Gs are primarily operated by HC-1 at North Island and HC-2 at NAS Norfolk, VA (with detachments at Naples and Bahrain), and with a few composite units, base flights, etc. The **UH-3A** and **VH-3A** were utility transport conversions of the SH-3A, and some examples remain in Navy service, while the **HH-3A** was a SAR conversion. The US Marine Corps continues to operate the **VH-3D** with the executive transport flight of HMX-1 at MCAS Quantico, these fulfilling Presidential transport duties.

OPERATORS

Sikorsky licensed the Sea King to a number of companies. Agusta in **Italy** and Westland in the **United Kingdom** both developed the aircraft further, and their variants are described separately. In Japan,

Left: The veteran SH-3H has carried out the vital ASW task for many years from US Navy carriers. The type's retirement is long overdue and it is now giving way to the more capable SH-60F. However, a few SH-3Hs remain in service.

Right: The Spanish navy took delivery of former US Navy SH-3Ds. Some have been progressively upgraded to SH-3G and, finally, SH-3H standard. The ASW variants will receive further modernisation in the form of new sonar and radar.

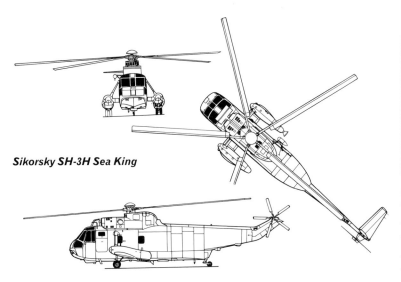

Sikorsky SH-3H Sea King

Mitsubishi built the S-61 for the **Japanese Maritime Self-Defence Force**, producing 55 **HSS-2**s (SH-3A – now all withdrawn), 29 **HSS-2A**s (SH-3D) and 83 **HSS-2B**s (SH-3H). These serve with 101, 121 and 122 Kokutai at Tateyama, 123 and 124 Kokutai at Ohmura, the Ohmura and Ominato base squadrons and 211 Kokutai at Kanoya for training. Sikorsky-built **S-61A**, **S-61A-1** and **S-61AH** helicopters serve with the JMSDF for SAR duties.

United Aircraft of Canada assembled 37 **CHSS-2**s, after the supply of four US-built aircraft for the Canadian forces. Most were upgraded to **CH-124A** standard. Eight CH-124As subsequently received a package of modifications for service in 1990/91 during Operation Friction. The ASW gear was removed and a 'Gulf Mods' package was installed. This included a FLIR turret, chaff and flare dispensers, and provision for a machine-gun in the door. The

modified aircraft were initially designated **CH-124C**, but later reverted to the CH-124A designator. Many of the modifications have been retained (now known as 'surveillance mods') and are used during anti-smuggling patrols. The **CH-124B** designation was to have been assigned to six modified Sea Kings which were to have served as lead-in trainers to the cancelled EH.101. These were equipped with HELTAS (Helicopter Towed Array Support) and updated mission systems.

Further export orders were received from **Argentina** (which bought five **S-61D-4**s, similar to the SH-3D, supplemented by Agusta-built ASH-3Hs), **Brazil** (six SH-3Ds purchased for 1° Esquadrão de Helicopteros Anti-Submarinos) and **Denmark** (eight remaining of nine **S-61A-5**s bought for long-range SAR work without ASW equipment with Eskadrille 722 at Vaerløse). **Malaysia** purchased 40 **S-61A-4**

Nuri transports for the air force. Thirty-four survivors have been upgraded by LAS and Aerospace Industries of Malaysia with new radar and Doppler; these serve with No. 3 Sqn at Butterworth, No. 5 Sqn at Labuan, No. 10 Sqn at Subang and 2 FTS at Keluang. A total of 18 SH-3A/D/Gs was transferred from the US Navy to **Spain**'s Arma Aérea de la Armada. Eight of these have been progressively upgraded to SH-3H standard for ASW work with Escuadrilla 005 at Rota. Three SH-3Ds were converted under a 1984 contract with Thorn-EMI Searchwater radar to perform the AEW role. Preliminary plans have been approved for the purchase of six Sea Kings by the **Royal Thai navy**. These are to be operated from its new aircraft-carrier under construction in Spain, and are to be joined by an additional eight SH-3s.

SPECIFICATION

Sikorsky S-61 (SH-3H Sea King)
Rotor system: main rotor diameter 62 ft 0 in (18.90 m); tail rotor diameter 10 ft 7 in (3.23 m); main rotor disc area 3,019.0 sq ft (280.47 m²); tail rotor disc area 87.97 sq ft (8.17 m²)
Fuselage and tail: length overall, rotors turning 72 ft 8 in (22.15 m), fuselage 54 ft 9 in (16.69 m), and with

The Brazilian navy received six SH-3Ds from 1970 for coastal patrol, marines support and carrier-based ASW duties. The Sea Kings fly with HS-1 from São Pedro de Aldeia. This example is armed with an AM39 Exocet anti-ship missile.

tail pylon folded 47 ft 3 in (14.40 m); height overall 16 ft 10 in (5.13 m) and to top of rotor head 15 ft 6 in (4.72 m); wheel track 13 ft 0 in (3.96 m); wheel base 23 ft 1.5 in (7.18 m)
Powerplant: two General Electric T58-GE-10 turboshafts each rated at 1,400 shp (1044 kW)
Weights: empty 12,350 lb (5601 kg); maximum take-off 21,000 lb (9526 kg)
Fuel and load: internal fuel 840 US gal (3180 litres); external fuel none; maximum ordnance 840 lb (381 kg)
Speed: maximum level speed 'clean' at optimum altitude 144 kt (166 mph; 267 km/h); economical cruising speed 118 kt (136 mph; 219 km/h)
Range: 542 nm (625 miles; 1005 km)
Performance: maximum rate of climb at sea level 2,200 ft (670 m) per minute; service ceiling 14,700 ft (4480 m); hovering ceiling 10,500 ft (3200 m) in ground effect and 8,200 ft (2500 m) out of ground effect

Sikorsky **S-61/HH-3 Pelican**

US Air Force interest in the S-61 as a transport resulted in several airframes being used to support the East Coast 'Texas Tower' radar platforms. In turn, this led to a specific requirement for a long-range tactical transport, which was answered by a reworked Sea King known as the **S-61R**, or **CH-3C**. This was a radically revised variant, retaining the boat hull but with a redesigned rear fuselage incorporating a rear loading ramp. The undercarriage floats gave way to sponsons and the tailwheel was replaced by a nosewheel.

Sikorsky built 75 CH-3Cs, most of which were re-engined with T58-GE-5 engines to become **CH-3E**s, this variant also accounting for 45 new-build airframes. Several CH-3C/Es joined six new-build aircraft

as **HH-3E** rescue platforms with IFR probes as the renowned 'Jolly Green Giants' of Vietnam fame. These are virtually out of service, and many been replaced on rescue and SOF units by the HH/MH-60G Pave Hawk. Until as late as the end of 1992, HH-3Es could be found with the 33rd Rescue Squadron at Kadena, Japan.

Another US S-61R operator is the Coast Guard, which bought 40 **HH-3F Pelican**s from 1968 for SAR duties. Essentially similar to the HH-3E, they lack armour protection and other combat-related equipment, but have a search radar in a nose radome offset to port, and are internally configured for the carriage of up to 15 stretchers. The Coast Guard also purchased at least nine surplus CH-3Es and HH-3Es to augment its

MRR (medium-range recovery) fleet. Some were used as spares for the flying fleet and five were brought up to HH-3F standard.

Sikorsky HH-60J Jayhawks have now entirely supplanted the HH-3F in the MRR role, although the Pelicans' amphibious landing capability, endurance and sheer lifting ability will be missed. The type is scheduled

to be retired from the Coast Guard inventory by late 1994 and, as of February 1994, only five airframes remained in service. All operate from CGAS Clearwater, FL, and are employed for OPBAT (Operations in the Bahamas, Turks and Caicos Islands) drug patrols.

Five HH-3Fs remain in service with the US Coast Guard. This example is fitted with a FLIR turret and a powerful searchlight for anti-drug patrols.

Sikorsky **S-65 Sea Stallion/CH-53**

Answering a US Marine Corps requirement to replace its Sikorsky CH-37 heavylift helicopters, the prototype **S-65** was first flown on 14 October 1964, entering service in September 1965. One hundred and forty-one of the first production model, the **CH-53A**, were built but none remains in US service. The last examples served with USMC training and reserve units, but were retired in July 1993.

Powered by two T64 engines mounted either side of the upper fuselage, driving the transmission proven by the CH-54 Tarhe, the CH-53 featured a large box-like cabin with a rear loading ramp and forward side doors. The main undercarriage retracted into sponsons slung low on the fuselage sides, and in most respects the helicopter was conventional. It was big,

however, and on delivery to the war zone in Vietnam quickly established a reputation for carrying outstanding loads either internally or from its cargo hook. Known as the **Sea Stallion**, the CH-53A was to become the USMC's principal heavylift helicopter, a position it has held ever since through updated variants.

The major current variant of the first-generation Stallions is the **CH-53D**, of which 124 were built with uprated engines, automatic blade folding and revised interior for more troop accommodation. Many of these are still in Marine service, flying with the following Marine Air Groups (MAGs): MAG 26 at New River, NC (HMM-362, HMT-204); MAG 16 at Tustin, CA (HMH-363, HMH-462); MAG 24 at Kanehoe Bay, HI (HMH-463); and the USMC reserve unit MAG 41

at NAS Dallas, TX (HMH-777). Two **VH-53D** aircraft are assigned to VIP transportation unit HMX-1 at Quantico.

Sea Stallions have been involved in many

The USMC remains the principal user of twin-engined CH-53s. This war-weary CH-53D was deployed to Saudia Arabia for Desert Storm operations by HMH-462.

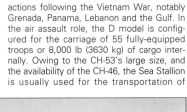

actions following the Vietnam War, notably Grenada, Panama, Lebanon and the Gulf. In the air assault role, the D model is configured for the carriage of 55 fully-equipped troops or 8,000 lb (3630 kg) of cargo internally. Owing to the CH-53's large size, and the availability of the CH-46, the Sea Stallion is usually used for the transportation of

supplies and equipment rather than personnel. However, for rapid evacuation duties, the CH-53 is ideal, its internal volume being able to accommodate large numbers of evacuees in an emergency, and its good range reducing the time spent on refuelling between trips. For ferry purposes, the CH-53D can be fitted with up to five auxiliary tanks in the cabin.

Although the Marine Corps is the main user of the first-generation CH-53s, there have been others. A small number of ex-USMC CH-53As were transferred to the

US Air Force as **TH-53A**s, used by the 1550th FTS at Kirtland AFB, NM, for aircrew training for the MH-53 fleet. These replaced CH-53As borrowed from the USMC. US Air Force interest in the early variants led to purchase of the **HH-53B** and **HH-53C** rescue platforms, which introduced a refuelling probe and external tanks fitted to the undercarriage sponsons. The similar **CH-53C** lacked the probe, and was used for training, general transport duties and for the support of ground-based forward air control teams. Survivors

of the CH/HH-53B/C fleet were upgraded to **MH-53J** standard in the 1980s, and are described in a separate entry.

OPERATORS

Exports were restricted to **Austria**, **West Germany** and **Israel**. The Austrians purchased two **S-65C-2**s, also known as the **S-65O** and similar to the USAF's CH-53C. Ordered in March 1969 and delivered in 1970, the pair of heavylifters was purchased to assist relief agencies during disasters. Despite their suitability for role, the pair proved expensive to operate, and was sold to Israel in May 1981.

Israel received 33 **S-65C-3**s from 1969. These are fitted with a refuelling probe and are similar to the USAF's HH-53C. They have proved extremely useful in a variety of roles, including combat rescue and heavylift and, together with the two S-65C-2s from Austria, continue to provide the IDF/AF with its only heavylift capability. After the 1991 Gulf War, Israel was supplied with an additional 10 ex-USMC CH-53As. The Mata Helicopter Division of IAI is

The major S-65 export customer was the Heeresflieger (German army), which received licence-built CH-53Gs. This aircraft demonstrates its precise handling during a competition.

responsible for a major structural and systems upgrade programme, known as **CH-53 2000**, or **Yas'ur 2000** (Albatros 2000) to keep the aircraft serviceable into the next century. This will provide a new Elisra EW system, two multi-function cockpit displays, a new autopilot and a new mission computer. Seventy-two systems are upgraded, 42 are replaced and 24 are completely new. The first prototype made its maiden flight in May 1992 and was returned to service in early 1993.

West Germany was the major foreign user of the type, choosing the CH-53 to replace Piasecki H-21s and Sikorsky H-34s on army assault units. Beating off the CH-47 in competition, the **CH-53G** was first ordered in June 1968. Two Sikorsky-built aircraft were supplied, similar to the CH-53D. These were followed by 20 assembled from kits by a VFW-Fokker-led consortium, and then 90 built in Germany with a gradually decreasing number of US-made parts. Dornier supplied the rotor blades.

First flight of a German-assembled CH-53G occurred at Speyer on 11 October 1971, and the first example was put into operational service in March 1973 with Heeresfliegerregiment 15 at Mendig. This unit was joined by HFR 15 at Rheine/Bentlage, HFR 25 at Laupheim and the Heeresfliegerwaffenschule at Bückeberg. In 1993, 107 CH-53Gs were still in service with the Heeresflieger.

SPECIFICATION

Sikorsky S-65 (CH-53A Sea Stallion)
generally similar to the Sikorsky S-65 (RH-53D Sea Stallion) except in the following particulars:
Powerplant: two General Electric T64-GE-16 turboshafts each rated at 3,435 shp (2562 kW)
Weights: normal take-off 35,000 lb (15876 kg)
Fuel and load: internal fuel 630 US gal (2384 litres); maximum payload 8,000 lb (3629 kg) as an internal load or 13,000 lb (5897 kg) as an external load
Speed: maximum level speed 'clean' at sea level 169 kt (195 mph; 314 km/h); cruising speed at sea level 149 kt (172 mph; 277 km/h)
Range: 223 nm (257 miles; 413 km); endurance more than 4 hours
Performance: maximum rate of climb at sea level 2,240 ft (683 m) per minute; service ceiling 18,550 ft (5655 m)

Sikorsky **S-65/HH-53 and MH-53**

Development of the H-53 as a combat rescue/special operations helicopter in USAF service began with the loan of two CH-53As from the USMC in late 1966. These were followed by eight **HH-53B**s and 44 **HH-53C**s tailored to the rescue role with extra external tanks and a refuelling probe, and 20 **CH-53C**s used for general transport work. In late 1969, the Pave Low I LLLTV system was applied to one HH-53 to provide some measure of night capability.

A single HH-53B was converted to **YHH-53H Pave Low II** standard, which added a terrain-following radar in a nose radome, offset to port, and other night/adverse-weather equipment. Subsequently, eight HH-53s and two CH-53Cs were upgraded to **HH-53H Pave Low III** standard, featuring an AN/APQ-158 TF radar, Marconi Doppler navigation, Litton INS, AAQ-10 FLIR in a turret under the nose fairing, map display system and numerous countermeasures. When a Spe-

cial Forces role was added under the Constant Green programme, the designation changed to **MH-53H**, one major change being the adoption of an NVG-compatible cockpit.

Under a programme beginning in 1986 and running for four years, 39 HH-53B/C/H and CH-53C airframes were all upgraded to the current **MH-53J Pave Low III Enhanced** standard. This features the full range of upgrades, including TFR, FLIR,

NVG, armour plating, mounts for 0.50-in (12.7-mm) machine-guns and/or 7.62-mm Miniguns, AN/ALQ-162 continuous-wave radar missile jammers, ALE-40 chaff/flare dispensers, ALQ-157 IR missile jammers, ALR-69 missile warning receivers, GPS, projected map display, IFR probe, external tanks, secure communications, undernose searchlight, starboard-side heavy-duty hoist with jungle penetrator or litter attachments, and 1,000 lb (454 kg) of titanium armour. Power is provided by the uprated T64-GE-415. Not all MH-53Js are identical, as those converted from the HH-53B retain strut bracing for the sponson tanks.

A UK-based 21st SOS MH-53J demonstrates some of its special operations/rescue equipment. The winch has a tree penetrator attached, with the winch litter beside it. Note the IRCM turret on the sponsons. A Block 1 upgrade programme adds a rotor fold facility, improved EW systems and a 45 per cent increase in payload capability.

Sikorsky MH-53J Pave Low III Enhanced

MH-53J deliveries commenced in 1987. Three tasks are assigned, the major one being support of Special Forces. Using inflight refuelling to increase range, the Pave Low uses its comprehensive avionics to penetrate hostile airspace covertly at very low level in all weathers to infiltrate or extract Special Forces teams and their equipment. Secondly, the aircraft flies the combat rescue mission to retrieve downed airmen from hostile territory, either alone at night or under the cover of support aircraft during the daytime. Lastly, the MH-53Js are made available to civilian rescue agencies during peacetime. The crew consists of two pilots and two pararescuemen (PJs), the latter acting as loadmasters, winchmen, medics and gunners, for the MH-53J has provision for three 7.62-mm Miniguns in the door/rear ramp positions.

MH-53Js inserted SEAL commandos during the invasion of Panama, and were heavily used in Desert Storm, notably in the 'Special Forces theme park' of the western Iraqi desert, where teams used sand rovers to locate 'Scud' missiles, sabotage air defence installations and other SOF activities.

Three units fly the MH-53J: the 20th SOS/16th SOW at Hurlburt Field, FL, 21st SOS/352nd SOG at RAF Alconbury, England, and the 31st SOS/353rd SOG at Osan AB, RoK. Additionally, the 16th SOW at Hurlburt Field may be supported by two **NCH-53**s for test duties. The 58th SOW (formerly the 542nd CTW) of Air Training and Education Command at Kirtland AFB, NM, trains aircrew for the active fleet using four MH-53Js and four **TH-53A**s. These are ex-USMC CH-53As which have been modified with T64-GE-416 engines, an IFR probe and some USAF systems, for use as basic qualification trainers. Another two CH-53As are scheduled for conversion.

The USAF has undertaken a series of upgrades, known collectively as the **Block 1** modifications, which it is envisaged will keep its MH-53J fleet viable until 2008-10. Most aircraft have already undergone a service life extension programme (SLEP), which is applied at the Navy's aviation depot at Pensacola, Florida. The SLEP modernises the basic airframe structure, hydraulics and wiring. The structural modifications increase gross weight by 8,000 lb (3629 kg) to give an effective increase of 45 per cent in payload capability. In operational terms, the MH-53J can carry an additional 3,970 lb (1800 kg) of fuel, which can extend time between refuellings from three hours to five hours.

A further modification known as Shipboard Operations (SBO) was funded in light of the abortive rescue attempt in Iran in 1980, and aims to improve shipboard stowage by adding fully-automatic rotor blade and tail pylon folding. An additional benefit of this modification is that it greatly reduces the time taken to prepare the MH-53J for transport aboard a C-5 Galaxy. Thirty-three MH-53Js have been cycled through the SLEP, and it is expected that the remaining eight aircraft will have received this update by July 1995.

Further upgrades

A contract was awarded to IBM/Loral in November 1993 to integrate and test new avionics and systems on two MH-53Js. These include an Integrated Defensive Avionics System via a Mil Std 1553 databus (incorporating the AAR-47 missile plume detector and the ALQ-136 missile jammer) and a Multi-Mission Advanced Tactical Terminal (IDAS/MATT). The latter adds a receiver which can downlink threat information from a classified database known as Constant Source, and display this data on a cockpit digital map system.

The USAF will decide to apply IDAS/MATT to the remaining 39 MH-53Js once flight testing has been accomplished.

A 20th Special Operations Squadron MH-53J cruises just above the trees during a training mission. The installed avionics allow it to perform similar profiles at night, vital for covert infil/exfil missions into hostile territory.

SPECIFICATION

Sikorsky S-65 (MH-53J Pave Low III Enhanced)
Rotor system: main rotor diameter 72 ft 3 in (22.02 m); tail rotor diameter 16 ft 0 in (4.88 m); main rotor disc area 4,099.82 sq ft (380.87 m2); tail rotor disc area 201.06 sq ft (18.68 m2)
Fuselage and tail: length overall, rotors turning 88 ft 3 in (26.90 m) and fuselage 67 ft 2 in (20.47 m) excluding IFR probe; height overall 24 ft 11 in (7.60 m) and to top of rotor head 17 ft 1.5 in (5.22 m); wheel track 13 ft 0 in (3.96 m); wheel base 27 ft 0 in (8.23 m)
Powerplant: two General Electric T64-GE-7A turboshafts each rated at 3,936 shp (2935 kW)
Weights: empty 23,569 lb (10691 kg); mission take-off 38,238 lb (17344 kg); maximum take-off 42,000 lb (19051 kg)
Fuel and load: internal fuel 630 US gal (2384 litres); external fuel up to two 450-US gal (1703-litre) drop tanks; maximum payload 20,000 lb (9072 kg)
Speed: maximum level speed 'clean' at sea level 170 kt (196 mph; 315 km/h); cruising speed at optimum altitude 150 kt (173 mph; 278 km/h)
Range: 468 nm (540 miles; 868 km)
Performance: maximum rate of climb at sea level 2,070 ft (631 m) per minute; service ceiling 20,400 ft (6220 m); hovering ceiling 11,700 ft (3565 m) in ground effect and 6,500 ft (1980 m) out of ground effect

Sikorsky **S-65/RH-53D**

From the 34th aircraft, all CH-53s were fitted with hardpoints for the towing of mine countermeasures equipment. However, the use of such equipment required a greater level of power than was generally available. Consequently, the US Navy re-engined 15 aircraft with the T64-GE-413 powerplant, and added rear-view mirrors on tube mounts either side of the nose. Designated **RH-53A**, these served with HM-12, but were subsequently demodified back to CH-53A status. Some Marine CH-53Ds have been used in the mine-hunting role.

Aiding this application was the adoption of the definitive **RH-53D** variant, which introduced T64-GE-415 engines of greater power and the option to mount a refuelling probe and sponson tanks. The mine countermeasures equipment is towed behind the aircraft from a heavy trapeze attached to the rear ramp and rear fuselage. Optional equipment includes various floating sleds to handle contact, acoustic and magentic mines. The SPU-1 Magnetic Orange Pipe system is used against shallow-water mines. Mines brought to the surface by the system are detonated by using a pair of door-mounted 0.50-in machine-guns. In addition to its primary role, the RH-53D can also be employed in the transport role.

RH-53Ds are being phased out of service as the more capable MH-53E (described separately) is introduced. Two US Navy Reserve squadrons, HM-18 at Norfolk and HM-19 at Alameda, continue to fly the type, as do USMCR units HMH-769 and HMH-772 Det A. The former unit was reactivated at NAS Alameda, CA, in April 1993. The latter unit deployed some aircraft during the Gulf War. Unfortunately, the best-remembered use of the RH-53D was during the disastrous Eagle Claw operation to rescue US hostages from Iran. Eight helicopters set off but three dropped out and, of the five that arrived at the Desert One refuelling stop, one struck a Hercules and was destroyed. The remainder were left in the desert.

This proved to be fortuitous for **Iran**, which is the only foreign operator of the type. Six were delivered to an MCM unit at Kharg Island, but the US embargo following the taking of the hostages severely affected their serviceability. The Desert One debacle provided a source of spares for the Iranian fleet, but it is thought that only two are now in a serviceable state.

RH-53Ds were deployed to the Persian Gulf for mine-sweeping operations in 1987, and in 1991. During Desert Storm, a six-aircraft detachment from USMCR squadron HMH-772 operated from Al Jubail. RH-53Ds are now used for exercise support as aggressors.

SPECIFICATION

Sikorsky S-65 (RH-53D) Sea Stallion
Rotor system: main rotor diameter 72 ft 3 in (22.02 m); tail rotor diameter 16 ft 0 in (4.88 m); main rotor disc area 4,099.82 sq ft (380.87 m2); tail rotor disc area 201.06 sq ft (18.68 m2)
Fuselage and tail: length overall, rotors turning 88 ft 3 in (26.90 m) and fuselage 67 ft 2 in (20.47 m) without probe; height overall, rotors turning 24 ft 11 in (7.60 m) and to top of rotor head 17 ft 1.5 in (5.22 m); wheel track 13 ft 0 in (3.96 m); wheel base 27 ft 0 in (8.23 m)
Powerplant: two General Electric T64-GE-415 turboshafts each rated at 4,380 shp (3266 kW)
Weights: empty 22,444 lb (10180 kg); normal take-off 42,000 lb (19050 kg); maximum take-off 50,000 lb (22680 kg)
Fuel and load: internal fuel 622 US gal (2354 litres); external fuel up to two 550-US gal (2082-litre) drop tanks; ordnance none
Speed: maximum level speed 'clean' at sea level 170 kt (196 mph; 315 km/h); cruising speed at sea level 150 kt (173 mph; 278 km/h)
Range: 223 nm (257 miles; 413 km); endurance more than 4 hours
Performance: maximum rate of climb at sea level 2,100 ft (664 m) per minute; service ceiling 21,000 ft (6400 m); hovering ceiling 13,400 ft (4080 m) in ground effect and 6,500 ft (1980 m) out of ground effect

Sikorsky **S-70A/UH-60 Black Hawk**

As early as 1965, the US Army began to look for a replacement for the Bell UH-1 assault helicopter, but the needs of the Vietnam War continually delayed any serious attempts to provide a successor. The request for proposals for what became known as the UTTAS (utility tactical transport aircraft system) were not issued until January 1972. These called for a helicopter to carry the same squad-sized unit as the UH-1H, but with far better performance and crashworthiness. Sikorsky submitted its **S-70** design, designated **YUH-60A**, which first flew on 17 October 1974.

In configuration, the YUH-60A featured a broad, squat cabin with rearward-sliding doors, and had a two-pilot flight deck. The four-bladed rotor was driven by two T700-GE-700s mounted above the cabin, and the aircraft featured immensely strong undercarriage. The all-round survivability of the aircraft was exceptional, and in December 1976 Sikorsky was announced the winner of the competition after a long evaluation against Boeing Vertol's competing YUH-61 submission. The first production **UH-60A Black Hawk** flew on 17 October 1978, and the type entered service with the 101st Airborne Division in June 1979.

At once the Black Hawk demonstrated considerable advances over the Huey. The nominal load was two pilots, one crew chief/door gunner and 11 troops, but the cabin could take up to 20 if required. Heavy external loads could be carried from a cargo hook, and overall performance, notably under 'hot-and-high' conditions, was dramatically improved. Manoeuvrability and crashworthiness were also improved considerably.

Production UH-60As incorporated bulletproof fuel tanks and folding tails, the latter so that the helicopter could be air-transportable in Lockheed C-5s. Over the years several modifications have been introduced to the fleet, including the ESSS shoulder-mounted wings with four pylons for fuel or weapons, an optional medevac kit, winterisation kit, rescue hoist, pintle-mounted M134 Miniguns or 7.62-mm M60 machine-guns,

wire strike protection, HIRSS to cool the exhaust and reduce vulnerability to heat-seeking missiles, and improved avionics and defensive countermeasures.

The US Army naturally took the major share of UH-60As, these being distributed (apart from the 101st) mainly to theatre forces in Europe and Korea before the re-equipment of CONUS units began. Under the Foreign Military Sales programme, one UH-60A was delivered to Bahrain and 10 to the Colombian air force, the latter for anti-drug operations. This role is also undertaken by 16 aircraft transferred to the US Customs Service. Equipped with large searchlights, they are informally known as 'Pot Hawks'. Two UH-60As were handed to the US Navy Test Pilot's School at Patuxent River, while another was transferred to the Philippine air force. Saudi Arabia received eight during Desert Shield. The US Army also uses **GUH-60A** ground instructional airframes and **JUH-60A** test machines.

Improved L model

As more equipment was added to the UH-60, so the weight grew and power margins were reduced. Accordingly, uprated versions were discussed, including the cancelled **UH-60M**. Sikorsky introduced the cheaper **UH-60L** on the production line, this featuring the uprated T700-GE-701C engine that restored the performance and allowed the helicopter to lift an HMMWV with TOW anti-tank installation. The first UH-60L flew on 22 March 1988; deliveries began in October 1989 and continue at a high rate today. The US Army expects to procure a total of at least 1,400 UH-60A/Ls, compared to the initial requirement for 2,262. Two UH-60Ls were transferred to Bahrain in 1991, and 100 essentially similar aircraft, designated **UH-60P**, are being supplied to the Republic of Korea army. The first was handed over by Sikorsky on 10 December 1990, the next 19 being assembled by Korean Air from kits. Subsequent production is handled in Korea.

For the medical evacuation role, the US Army is to acquire the **UH-60Q** to replace medevac-configured UH-60A/Ls in the 'Dustoff' role. Among the changes is the adoption of an external hoist rather than the swing-out, internally-stowed unit currently fitted, and an entirely new aero-medical interior. It will also have weather radar, FLIR and comprehensive defensive systems, plus a digital avionics suite similar to that of HH/MH-60 variants. A single proof-of-concept prototype was converted from a UH-60A and first flown in January 1993. It was delivered to the Tennessee Army National Guard in March 1993, and will be used to conduct a test and evaluation programme to determine what equipment and modifications will be selected for the definitive 'production' UH-60Q.

Based closely on late-model UH-60As are the **VH-60N** 'Presidential Hawks' used by the Marine Corps' HMX-1 based at MCAS Quantico, VA. Nine were supplied in November 1988, originally known as **VH-60A**s but redesignated a year later. They differ from late-production UH-60As by having SH-60B flight control system, cabin radio operator position, soundproofed VIP-configured cabin, avionics upgrades and hardening against the effects of electro-magnetic pulse. Their primary task is trans-

The UH-60A Black Hawk was the initial production variant of the US Army's main assault helicopter. This example has ESSS pylons and wears the overall desert camouflage scheme applied for participation in Operation Desert Storm.

port of the President (with callsign 'Marine One') and his staff, both at home and on overseas trips.

OPERATORS

In addition to the aircraft under UH-60 designations mentioned above, there have been many exports under the **S-70A** designation. The **S-70A-1 Desert Hawk** was sold to **Saudi Arabia**, the purchase comprising 12 in utility transport configuration for the **Royal Saudi land forces**, one with a VIP interior and eight dedicated **S-70A-1L** medevac aircraft. Two **S-70A-5**s were supplied to the **Philippines**, and one **S-70A-9** to **Australia**. This preceded 38 more aircraft built locally by Hawker de Havilland. At first assigned to the **RAAF**, they were subsequently turned over to the **Australian army**. Further exports comprise three **S-70A-11**s to **Jordan** and one **S-70A-12** to **Japan**. This SAR-dedicated variant is fitted with a rescue winch, nose search radar and FLIR. Following the delivery of the first aircraft, Mitsubishi assembled two from kits and then built eight for the **JASDF** and 18 for the **JMSDF** under the designation **UH-60J**. This variant is described in greater detail in a separate entry. A single **S-70A-14** was supplied to **Brunei**, one **S-70A-16** to **Rolls-Royce** for use as a testbed for the Rolls-Royce/Turboméca RTM 332 engine, and 12 **S-70A-17**s to **Turkey** for the police and para-military police forces. The **S-70A-19** designation covered one aircraft assembled by **Westland** as the **WS-70** prior to potential UK production. Further exports have been made to **Egypt** (two **S-70A-21**s), **Mexico** (two **S-70A-24**s), **Morocco** (two **S-70A-26**s), and **Hong Kong** (two **S-70A-27**s). The latest customer is **Israel**, which received 10 surplus Black Hawks in July 1994 free of charge from the US drawdown inventory.

The **S-70C** designation ostensibly covers the civil versions of the Black Hawk, but 24 **S-70C-2** utility helicopters were delivered to the **People's Republic of China**, while the **Republic of China (Taiwan)** received 14 **S-70C**s for rescue duties with external hoist. **Brunei** has also received one S-70C.

SPECIFICATION

Sikorsky S-70A (UH-60A Black Hawk)
Powerplant: two General Electric T700-GE-700 turboshafts each rated at 1,560 shp (1151 kW) or, in export helicopters, two General Electric T700-GE-701A turboshafts each rated at 1,723 shp (1285 kW)
Rotor system: main rotor diameter 53 ft 8 in (16.36 m)

The UH-60L superseded the A model on the production line. It introduces more powerful engines, uprated transmissions and a refined gearbox to give much improved performance, especially in 'hot-and-high' conditions or with external loads. The HIRSS exhaust suppression system is fitted as standard.

Australia took delivery of both US-built S-70A-9s and Hawker de Havilland-manufactured examples. The Black Hawks served originally with the Royal Australian Air Force but were subsequently transferred in 1990 to the army.

tail rotor diameter 11 ft 0 in (3.35 m); main rotor disc area 2,262.03 sq ft (210.14 m²); tail rotor disc area 95.03 sq ft (8.83 m²)

Fuselage and tail: length overall, rotors turning 64 ft 10 in (19.76 m), fuselage 50 ft 0.75 in (15.26 m) and with rotors and tail pylon folded 41 ft 4 in (12.60 m); height overall 16 ft 10 in (5.13 m) with tail rotor turning, to top of rotor head 12 ft 4 in (3.76 m) and in air-transportable configuration 8 ft 9 in (2.67 m); stabiliser span 14 ft 4.5 in (4.38 m); wheel track 8 ft 10.5 in (2.705 m); wheel base 28 ft 11.75 in (8.83 m)

Weights: empty 11,284 lb (5118 kg); normal take-off 16,994 lb (7708 kg); maximum take-off 20,250 lb (9185 kg)

Fuel and load: internal fuel 360 US gal (1361 litres) plus provision for 370 US gal (1400 litres) of auxiliary fuel in two fuselage tanks; external fuel up to two 230-US gal (870-litre) and/or two 450-US gal (1703-litre) tanks; maximum payload 2,640 lb (1197 kg) carried internally or 8,000 lb (3629 kg) carried externally

Speed: maximum level speed 'clean' at sea level 160 kt (184 mph; 296 km/h); maximum cruising speed at 4,000 ft (1220 m) 145 kt (167 mph; 268 km/h); economical (single-engine) cruising speed at 4,000 ft (1220 m) 105 kt (121 mph; 195 km/h)

Range: ferry range 1,200 nm (1,382 miles; 2224 km) with four external auxiliary tanks; range 319 nm (368 miles; 592 km) with standard fuel; endurance 2 hours 18 minutes

Performance: maximum vertical rate of climb at 4,000 ft (1220 m) 411 ft (125 m) per minute; service ceiling 19,000 ft (5790 m); hovering ceiling 9,500 ft (2895 m) in ground effect and 10,400 ft (3170 m) out of ground effect

The Royal Saudi Land Forces initially received 13 S-70A-1 Desert Hawks (illustrated) configured for a variety of duties. These were later supplemented by eight US Army UH-60As transferred during the Gulf War, and eight S-70A-1L dedicated medevac helicopters.

Sikorsky **S-70A/EH-60**

As an ongoing part of its SEMA (special electronics mission aircraft) programme, the **US Army** fitted several Bell UH-1Hs with the ALQ-151 Quick Fix II direction-finding, intercept and communications jamming equipment, the resultant conversions being known as EH-1Xs. The volume and weight of the ALQ-151 installation – approximately 1,800 lb (815 kg) – proved too heavy for the Huey, so in 1980 Electronic Systems Laboratories was awarded a contract to fit improved Quick

Fix IIB equipment into a UH-60A. The resultant **YEH-60A** proved effective in trials of the battlefield jamming system, and the Army progressed to acquiring production examples. The Sikorsky/ESL team lost out to Tracor, which undertook the conversions at its Flight Systems division at Mojave, CA. The first **EH-60A** was delivered in July 1987. The model designation was subsequently changed to **EH-60C**.

EH-60Cs are readily identified by the two dipole antennas on either side of the tail-

boom, and the retractable whip aerial under the fuselage. One aircraft has been noted with revised tailboom antennas with a square, tubular aerial whose 'uprights' are located in approximately the same location as the normal vertical dipoles. A two-man operator station is in the main cabin, and the EH-60C has datalinks to downlink

information to ground units, or to interface with other SEMA aircraft. Originally 138 EH-60Cs were planned, but in the event only 66 were funded. The US Army is, however, seeking the necessary finance for a command and control version equipped with the ASC-15B(V)1 communications suite.

This close-up view of an EH-60C clearly shows the forward-hemisphere radar warning receiver antennas, the prominent dipole antennas mounted on the tailboom and the massive HIRSS engine exhausts.

The fuselage-mounted antennas immediately identify this Black Hawk as a Quick Fix EH-60C. Its retractable ventral whip antenna is fully deployed.

Sikorsky **S-70A/HH-60G and MH-60G Pave Hawk**

Procured as a replacement for the Sikorsky HH-3E, the H-60 underwent a confusing birth in USAF service. The original requirement was for the superbly-equipped **HH-60D Night Hawk** and, of 10 UH-60As bought by the USAF to support this programme, one aircraft was converted to serve as the prototype but without mission avionics. This plan was too

costly and was leavened by the adoption of a mix of D models with the **HH-60E**, which dispensed with many night/adverse-weather avionics. The HH-60D/E plan was then cancelled in favour of the **HH-60A** 'Rescue Hawk', which was pitched closer to the HH-60E in terms of fit. The HH-60D was redesignated to serve as a flying prototype, but this, too, was unable to find

funding, and the USAF adopted a three-phase procurement process.

Phase One consisted of upgrading the 10 existing USAF Black Hawks, plus nine more, to **UH-60A Credible Hawk** standard. These featured an inflight-refuelling probe, options for external tank pylons and additional cabin tanks. Pintle-mounted 0.50-in (12.7-mm) machine-guns were fit-

ted. The next two phases involve upgrading the existing Credible Hawks and new-build UH-60As to one of two standards, although both were initially designated **MH-60G Pave Hawk**.

Sikorsky delivers the UH-60As with only some Air Force equipment installed, consisting of folding stabilator, HIRSS, winterisation and wire-strike kits, rescue

Sikorsky S-70A/HH-60G and MH-60G Pave Hawk

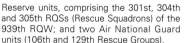

The USAF's MH-60G was developed as a dedicated combat rescue and SOF support helicopter. This 1st SOW example wears desert camouflage and white recognition stripes for Desert Storm, where the type saw active service.

hoist and NVG-compatible cockpit. Next, Sikorsky Support Services at Troy fits a refuelling probe, auxiliary cabin tanks and hardpoints for external tank carriage, and finally the mission avionics are installed at the Naval Air Depot at Pensacola, FL.

A total of 98 HH/MH-60 aircraft had been funded up to FY 1991, with a further five in the FY1992 budget. Sixteen aircraft are dedicated to the special operations role; 10 serve with the 16th SOW at Hurlburt Field/Eglin AFB, FL, and the remainder are operated by the 58th SOW at Kirtland, NM. All retain the MH-60G designation, and are fitted with a Bendix-King 1400C colour radar in a port-side nose radome, global positioning, Carousel INS, map display, Doppler, secure communications equipment and full countermeasures. Further SOF-dedicated equipment includes AAQ-16 FLIR under the

nose, pilot head-up display that projects on to one of the lenses of the NVG system, and numerous other improvements.

Eighty-two aircraft have been designated **HH-60G** since October 1991 to reinforce the combat rescue role they undertake. These aircraft have the basic Phase Two avionics, but funding for their updating with the Phase Three equipment (FLIR, HUD etc.) has not yet been forthcoming. HH-60Gs are usually seen with M60 or Minigun door weapons in place of the MH-60G's usual 0.50-in (12.7-mm) guns.

HH-60Gs are operated by three Air Combat Command wings: the 49th FW at Holloman, NM, the 57 Wing at Nellis (including the Combat Rescue School), NV, and the 35th Wing at NAS Keflavik, Iceland; and PACAF's 18th Wing at Kadena, Japan. They are also assigned to three Air Force

Reserve units, comprising the 301st, 304th and 305th RQSs (Rescue Squadrons) of the 939th RQW; and two Air National Guard units (106th and 129th Rescue Groups).

SPECIFICATION

Sikorsky S-70A (MH-60G Pave Hawk)

Rotor system: main rotor diameter 53 ft 8 in (16.36 m); tail rotor diameter 11 ft 0 in (3.35 m); main rotor disc area 2,262.03 sq ft (210.05 m²); tail rotor disc area 95.03 sq ft (8.83 m²)

Fuselage and tail: length overall, rotors turning 64 ft 10 in (19.76 m) and fuselage including retracted flight refuelling probe 57 ft 0.25 in (17.38 m); height overall, rotors turning 16 ft 10 in (5.13 m) and to top of rotor head 12 ft 4 in (3.76 m); stabiliser span 14 ft 4.5 in (4.38 m); wheel track 8 ft 10.5 in (2.705 m); wheel base 29 ft 0 in (8.84 m)

Powerplant: two General Electric T700-GE-700 turboshafts each rated at 1,622 shp (1210 kW)

Weights: maximum take-off 22,000 lb (9979 kg)

Fuel and load: internal fuel 360 US gal (1361 litres) plus provision for 117 US gal (443 litres) of auxiliary fuel; external fuel up to two 450- or 230-US gal (1703- or 871-litre) drop tanks; maximum payload 8,000 lb (3629 kg)

Speed: maximum level speed 'clean' at sea level about 160 kt (184 mph; 296 km/h); cruising speed at 4,000 ft (1220 m) 145 kt (167 mph; 268 km/h)

Range: ferry range about 1,200 nm (1,380 miles; 2220 km); operational radius about 520 nm (599 miles; 964 km) with two 450-US gal (1703-litre) drop tanks or about 347 nm (400 miles; 644 km) with two 230-US gal (871-litre) drop tanks; endurance 4 hours 51 minutes with maximum fuel

Performance: maximum vertical rate of climb at sea level more than 450 ft (137 m) per minute; service ceiling 19,000 ft (5790 m)

Sikorsky S-70A/MH-60K

Looking to expand its ability to support special operations forces, the US Army modified 30 UH-60A Black Hawks to **MH-60A** standard, with some special

equipment fitted, such as FLIR, extra nav/comms, auxiliary fuel tanks and Miniguns, intended for the covert infil/exfil mission. As much of the equipment was

fitted at unit level more by ingenuity than design, the aircraft are colloquially known as 'Velcro Hawks'. Initially serving with the 160th Special Operations Aviation Regiment at Fort Campbell, KY, the MH-60As now serve with the Oklahoma Army National Guard. Their place with the 160th SOAR was taken by a similar number of **MH-60L** 'Velcro Hawks', which are fitted with the same systems but are based on the more powerful UH-60L.

These are themselves to be replaced by the definitive US Army SOA variant, the **MH-60K**, which features a comprehensive range of night/adverse-weather low-level avionics, including APQ-174 terrain-following radar in a nose radome, AAQ-16B FLIR underneath, night vision imaging system

Compared to the USAF's MH-60G, the US Army's special operations MH-60K is equipped from the outset with dedicated mission equipment and systems. Note the nose-mounted sensors (FLIR turret and radome for TFR), IFR probe and external tanks.

and moving map display. Other features are pintle-mounted 0.50-in machine-guns, stub wings for external fuel tanks, retractable refuelling probe, HIRSS exhaust suppressors, comprehensive communications and navigation gear, and an impressive array of defensive warning receivers and countermeasures. The aircraft can launch AIM-92A Stinger air-to-air missiles. The FLIR is being reworked under the AESOP (Airborne Electro-Optical Special Operational Payload) programme to allow it to act as a thermal-imaging sight for the launch of Hellfire missiles.

The first prototype MH-60K flew from the Stratford, Connecticut, plant on 10 August 1990 and was followed on 26 February 1992 by the first of 22 currently-funded production MH-60Ks. Deliveries began to the 1st Battalion of the 160th SOAR in June 1992. Thirty-eight additional MH-60Ks are believed to be included in a multi-year contract awarded in April 1992, and will eventually equip the 1/245th Avn, a special operations unit of the Oklahoma Army National Guard, plus an Army reserve special operations battalion.

Sikorsky S-70B/SH-60B Seahawk

Navalising of the H-60 was performed by Sikorsky in response to the LAMPS (light airborne multi-purpose system) III requirement, which specified a helicopter to be used for providing an over-the-horizon search and strike capability for the latest

ASW frigates and destroyers, partnering the Kaman SH-2 Seasprite which served on earlier vessels. Sikorsky was awarded the development contract on the basis of its mock-up and proposal based on the Black Hawk in September 1977. Indeed, the

Army's decision to adopt the UH-60 was seen as a major factor in influencing the Navy to choose the **S-70B Seahawk**.

The first **YSH-60B** flew on 12 December 1979 to initiate a successful flight test programme. The first production **SH-60B** flew on 11 February 1983. Retaining some 83 per cent commonality with the UH-60A, the Seahawk nevertheless introduced some important features, including anti-corrosion treatment on airframe and T700-GE-401 engines, and RAST (recovery assist secure and traverse) gear for use during landing on

Although the Royal Australian Navy's initial S-70B-2s were received directly from Sikorsky, the third and subsequent Seahawks were locally assembled. Their mission-specific equipment includes a new MEL Super Searcher radar.

small platforms in heavy seas. Mission equipment consisted of an APS-124 360° search radar housed under the forward fuselage, a 25-tube sonobuoy launcher in the port side of the cabin, ASQ-81(V)2 towed MAD mounted on a pylon on the starboard rear fuselage, ALQ-142 ESM antennas in four box-like fairings, datalinks, secure communications and various onboard computers and processing units. A hoist is fitted for a secondary SAR role and the aircraft can be employed on utility transport missions.

A crew of three consists of a pilot, an airborne tactical officer/co-pilot and a sensor operator. The basic functions of the search are handled remotely by the parent vessel's combat information centre, although the final localisation of submarines using MAD and the prosecution of attacks is handled autonomously by the SH-60B crew. The standard weapon is the Mk 46 torpedo, of which two can be carried under stub pylons attached to the fuselage sides. Anti-ship capability is being added in the form of the

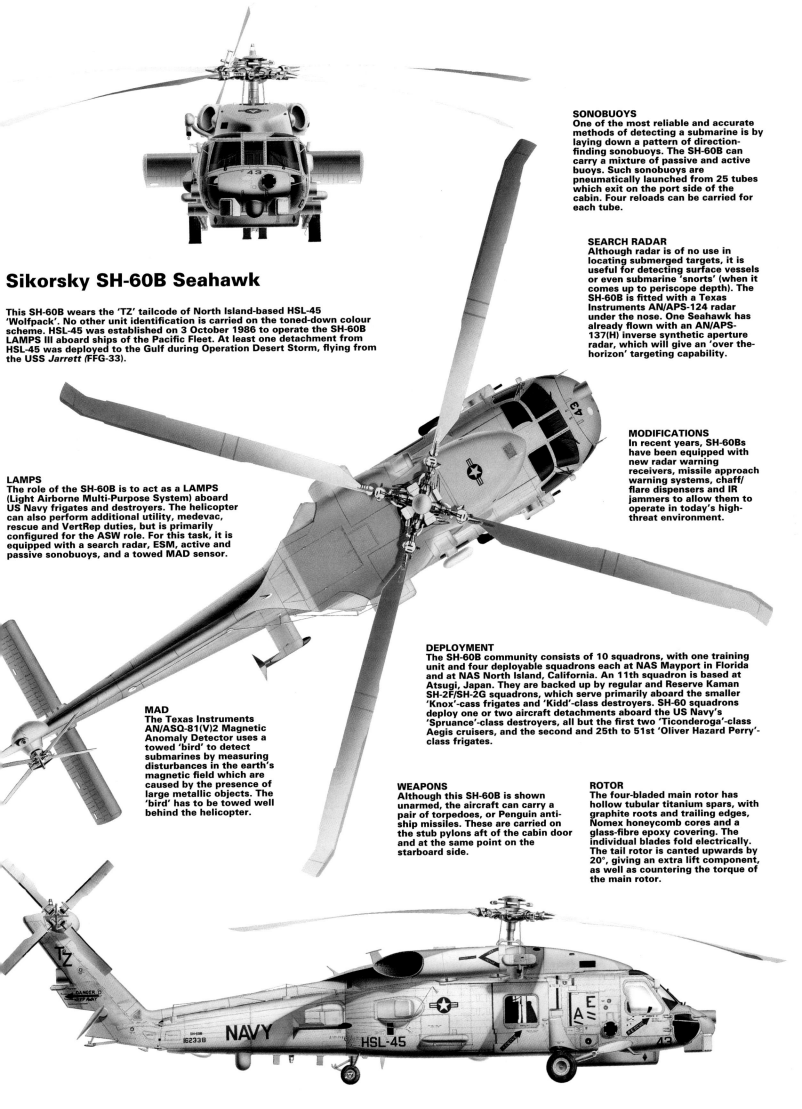

Sikorsky SH-60B Seahawk

This SH-60B wears the 'TZ' tailcode of North Island-based HSL-45 'Wolfpack'. No other unit identification is carried on the toned-down colour scheme. HSL-45 was established on 3 October 1986 to operate the SH-60B LAMPS III aboard ships of the Pacific Fleet. At least one detachment from HSL-45 was deployed to the Gulf during Operation Desert Storm, flying from the USS *Jarrett* (FFG-33).

SONOBUOYS
One of the most reliable and accurate methods of detecting a submarine is by laying down a pattern of direction-finding sonobuoys. The SH-60B can carry a mixture of passive and active buoys. Such sonobuoys are pneumatically launched from 25 tubes which exit on the port side of the cabin. Four reloads can be carried for each tube.

SEARCH RADAR
Although radar is of no use in locating submerged targets, it is useful for detecting surface vessels or even submarine 'snorts' (when it comes up to periscope depth). The SH-60B is fitted with a Texas Instruments AN/APS-124 radar under the nose. One Seahawk has already flown with an AN/APS-137(H) inverse synthetic aperture radar, which will give an 'over the-horizon' targeting capability.

MODIFICATIONS
In recent years, SH-60Bs have been equipped with new radar warning receivers, missile approach warning systems, chaff/flare dispensers and IR jammers to allow them to operate in today's high-threat environment.

LAMPS
The role of the SH-60B is to act as a LAMPS (Light Airborne Multi-Purpose System) aboard US Navy frigates and destroyers. The helicopter can also perform additional utility, medevac, rescue and VertRep duties, but is primarily configured for the ASW role. For this task, it is equipped with a search radar, ESM, active and passive sonobuoys, and a towed MAD sensor.

DEPLOYMENT
The SH-60B community consists of 10 squadrons, with one training unit and four deployable squadrons each at NAS Mayport in Florida and at NAS North Island, California. An 11th squadron is based at Atsugi, Japan. They are backed up by regular and Reserve Kaman SH-2F/SH-2G squadrons, which serve primarily aboard the smaller 'Knox'-cass frigates and 'Kidd'-class destroyers. SH-60 squadrons deploy one or two aircraft detachments aboard the US Navy's 'Spruance'-class destroyers, all but the first two 'Ticonderoga'-class Aegis cruisers, and the second and 25th to 51st 'Oliver Hazard Perry'-class frigates.

MAD
The Texas Instruments AN/ASQ-81(V)2 Magnetic Anomaly Detector uses a towed 'bird' to detect submarines by measuring disturbances in the earth's magnetic field which is caused by the presence of large metallic objects. The 'bird' has to be towed well behind the helicopter.

WEAPONS
Although this SH-60B is shown unarmed, the aircraft can carry a pair of torpedoes, or Penguin anti-ship missiles. These are carried on the stub pylons aft of the cabin door and at the same point on the starboard side.

ROTOR
The four-bladed main rotor has hollow tubular titanium spars, with graphite roots and trailing edges, Nomex honeycomb cores and a glass-fibre epoxy covering. The individual blades fold electrically. The tail rotor is canted upwards by 20°, giving an extra lift component, as well as countering the torque of the main rotor.

393

The SH-60B is the US Navy's primary embarked H-60 variant, fulfilling the vital ASW role from frigates and destroyers. In a typical operational scene, a Seahawk of HSL-46 winds up to full power in anticipation of getting airborne from the USS Doyle, somewhere in the Indian Ocean.

AGM-119B Mod 7 Penguin missile, and pintle-mounted 0.50-in machine-guns are becoming increasingly common. One SH-60B has flown with Rolls-Royce Turboméca RTM 322 engines (this is described separately under the heading Westland WS-70), and another has been fitted with a GEC Sea Owl passive IR detection system.

During operations in the Gulf from 1987, 25 SH-60Bs received AN/ALQ-144 IR jammers, chaff/flare dispensers, AN/AAR-47 MAWS and a Texas Instruments AN/TAS-6A thermal imager. Seven aircraft were equipped with a Ford AN/AAS-38 FLIR pod.

US Navy requirements for the SH-60B are stated to be 260, of which about 150 have been delivered. These serve with US Navy squadrons HSL-40, 41, 42, 43, 44, 45, 46, 47, 48 and 49, homeported at NAS Mayport, FL, for Atlantic Fleet units, and NAS North Island, CA, for Pacific units. HSL-51 is forward-based at NAS Atsugi, Japan.

In the mid- to late 1990s, plans call for surviving SH-60Bs and SH-60Fs to be brought up to a common standard, known as **SH-60R**, which will give increased armaments options, improved defences and the combined sensor options of both variants.

OPERATORS

Export orders have come from **Spain**, which has bought 12 Seahawks under the designation **HS.23**. These differ from the SH-60B by having Bendix Oceanics AQS-13F dipping sonar. They are operated from the main Armada air base at Rota, although deployments are made aboard 'Santa Maria'-class guided missile frigates. **Australia**'s **S-70B-2** aircraft combine features of both SH-60B and SH-60F (described separately) with RAN-specified equipment. This includes MEL Super Searcher X-band search radar in a new, smaller radome, CAE Electronics AQS-504 internally-mounted MAD system and other sonar processing equipment. The S-70B-2 also carries 25 SSQ-801 Barra sonobuoys and may later have provision for Sea Skua and Penguin Mk 2 Mod 7 anti-ship missiles. Eight were built by Sikorsky, and a further eight completed by ASTA in Australia from US-supplied kits. RAN S-70B-2s deployed to the Gulf were equipped with AN/AAQ-16 FLIR and AN/AAR-47 MAWS. **Japan** is procuring the indigenously-assembled **S-70B-3** for its Maritime Self-Defence Force to replace ageing Sikorsky HSS-2s. These are designated **SH-60J** in service and are described more fully in a separate entry. Two were supplied by Sikorsky, and fitted out by Mitsubishi with indigenous equipment as **YSH-60Js**. Subsequent aircraft, of which 47 have been funded from a requirement of 80,

are built by Mitsubishi. **Greece** has purchased five **S-70B-6** aircraft for operation from its MEKO 200 frigates. These are SH-60B/F hybrids with Eaton AN/APS-143 (V)3 radar, Bendix AN/ASQ-18 (V)3 dipping sonar and Penguin missile capability. Deliveries are scheduled to start in 1995.

SPECIFICATION

Sikorsky S-70B (SH-60B Seahawk)
Rotor system: main rotor diameter 53 ft 8 in (16.36 m); tail rotor diameter 11 ft 0 in (3.35 m); main rotor disc area 2,262.03 sq ft (210.05 m); tail rotor disc area 95.03 sq ft (8.83 m²)
Fuselage and tail: length overall, rotors turning 64 ft 10 in (19.76 m), fuselage 50 ft 0.75 in (15.26 m), and with rotor and tail pylon folded 40 ft 11 in (12.47 m); height overall, rotors turning 17 ft 0 in (5.18 m), to top of rotor head 11 ft 11 in (3.63 m), and with tail pylon folded 13 ft 3.25 in (4.04 m); stabiliser span 14 ft 4.5 in (4.38 m); wheel track 9 ft 2 in (2.79 m); wheel base 15 ft 10 in (4.83 m)
Powerplant: two General Electric T700-GE-401 turboshafts each rated at 1,690 shp (1260 kW) or, in helicopters delivered from 1988, two General Electric T700-GE-401C turboshafts each rated at 1,900 shp (1417 kW)
Weights: empty 13,648 lb (6191 kg) for the ASW mission; mission take-off 20,244 lb (9182 kg) for the ASW mission or 18,373 lb (8334 kg) for the ASST mission; maximum take-off 21,884 lb (9926 kg) for the utility mission
Fuel and load: internal fuel 590 US gal (2233 litres); external fuel up to 120-US gal (455-litre) drop tanks; maximum payload 8,000 lb (3629 kg)
Speed: dash speed at 5,000 ft (1525 m) 126 kt (145 mph; 234 km/h)
Range: operational radius 50 nm (57.5 miles; 92.5 km) for a 3-hour loiter, or 150 nm (173 miles; 278 km/h) for a 1-hour loiter
Performance: maximum vertical rate of climb at sea level 700 ft (213 m) per minute

Sikorsky S-70B/SH-60F Ocean Hawk

Anti-submarine work is also performed by the **SH-60F Ocean Hawk**, but this differs significantly from the SH-60B. Obtained to replace the elderly SH-3H on aircraft-carrier decks, the SH-60F performs the **US Navy**'s CVW Inner Zone ASW mission, known informally as 'CV-helo'. In addition, it is required to have secondary missions of plane-guard rescue and general utility transport.

The SH-60F is designed for inner-zone ASW protection of the carrier battle group, using its sonar to detect enemy submarines, which it may then engage or leave to other assets. A cousin of the SH-60B, it differs in having a cleaner appearance, with the deletion of external ESM and MAD bird.

Although the airframe of the Ocean Hawk is similar to that of the Seahawk, the latter's LAMPS III system is completely removed, along with small vessel-related items such as the RAST. Instead, the mission equipment centres around the Bendix AQS-13F dipping sonar and improved detection systems such as FLIR and ESM. An extra weapon station on the port side allows the carriage of three torpedoes, usually the Mk 50 weapon. Its performance is generally similar to that of the SH-60B, although maximum take-off weight is now increased to 23,500 lb (10659 kg).

The first flight of an aircraft in SH-60F configuration took place on 19 March 1987, and its initial fleet deployment was made aboard USS *Nimitz* in 1991. The variant now serves with squadrons HS-2, 3, 6, 8, 9, 10 and 15, these being shore-based at NAS North Island, CA, or NAS Jacksonville, FL. Options remain for fitting other sensors such as MAD and search radar, and increasing armament options. Along with SH-60Bs, this will bring surviving SH-60Fs up to a common **SH-60R** standard.

Taiwan has bought 10 similar aircraft designated **S-70C(M)-1 Thunderhawk**. Based closely on the SH-60F, they are fitted with Telephonics AN/APS-128C pulse compression radar, Bendix AN/AQS-18(V) dipping radar, and with fixed searchlights in the old ESM fairings, and new antennas for the Litton AN/ALR-606(V)2 ESM. They are being deployed aboard six 'Kwang Hua I'-class ('Oliver Hazard Perry'-class) guided missile frigates. The pseudo-civilian designation is in fact a political expedient to smooth relations between the US and the two Chinese republics.

Sikorsky S-70B/HH-60H Rescue Hawk

Closely based on the SH-60F Ocean Hawk, the **HH-60H Rescue Hawk** is the **US Navy**'s strike rescue/covert operations platform. Procurement of 45 examples is continuing, the first 18 being acquired for two Reserve squadrons, HCS-4 at NAS Norfolk, VA, and HCS-5 at NAS Point Mugu, CA. The remainder are distributed among SH-60F-operating HS units at NAS North Island, CA, and NAS Jacksonville, FL, each unit sending a mix of four Ocean Hawks and two Rescue Hawks as part of each carrier air wing.

The HH-60H is tailored to its primary role of recovery of downed aircrew. Whereas the Navy had previously undertaken the role it called combat rescue, a reactive mission to retrieve crew, the HH-60H's role of strike rescue is intended as a proactive mission, with the Rescue Hawk an integral part of any mission planning. A requirement to recover a four-man crew 250 nm (287 miles; 463 km) from base was the primary goal behind the initial requirement. The sec-

During Desert Storm, Minigun-armed HH-60Hs were based at Al Jouf, from where they were used for covert operations. Navy operations placed a greater emphasis on combat rescue and anti-terrorist support than the USAF's SOF helicopters.

Sikorsky HH-60H Rescue Hawk

ondary role of covert operations largely centres around the infil/exfil of SEAL commando teams. For this tasking the HH-60H has RAST gear to allow it to operate from vessels other than its parent aircraft-carrier.

The Rescue Hawk features a wide array of equipment suitable to its tasks. All avionics are concerned with self-protection and accurate navigation. HIRSS can be fitted to reduce the infra-red signature. The Rescue is fitted with door guns, initially 0.30-in (7.62-mm) M60s, but they are being replaced by GECAL 0.50-in (12.7-mm) machine-guns.

The first HH-60H flew on 17 August 1988 and deliveries to the first unit, HCS-5, com-

menced on 8 July 1989. The first fleet unit (HS-2) took HH-60Hs aboard USS *Nimitz* on 25 February 1991. HCS-4 and HCS-5 each sent two-aircraft detachments to Al Jouf for operations in Desert Storm. From their experience, the HH-60H is being upgraded with a turreted AAQ-16 FLIR, lengthened sponsons to house more defensive systems, and forward-firing armament, probably 2.75-in rocket pods and 0.50-in guns. Early aircraft are being retrofitted, while new aircraft will have the modifications fitted during production. At a later date, it is intended to fit provision for launching Maverick, Sidewinder or Sidearm missiles. Plans

exist to fit a Texas Instruments AN/APS-137(H) inverse synthetic aperture radar, if funds can be obtained.

SPECIFICATION

Sikorsky HH-60H Rescue Hawk
Rotor system: main rotor diameter 53 ft 8 in (16.36 m); tail rotor diameter 11 ft 0 in (3.35 m); main rotor disc area 2,262.03 sq ft (210.05 m2); tail rotor disc area 95.03 sq ft (8.83 m2)
Fuselage and tail: length overall, rotors turning 64 ft 10 in (19.76 m), fuselage 50 ft 0.75 in (15.26 m), and with rotor and tail pylon folded 41 ft 0.625 in (12.51 m); height overall with rotors turning 17 ft 0 in

(5.18 m), to top of rotor head 11 ft 11 in (3.63 m), and with tail pylon folded 13 ft 3.25 in (4.04 m); stabiliser span 14 ft 4.5 in (4.38 m); wheel track 9 ft 2 in (2.79 m); wheel base 15 ft 10 in (4.83 m)
Powerplant: two General Electric T700-GE-401C turboshafts each rated at 1,900 shp (1417 kW)
Weights: empty 13,480 lb (6114 kg)
Fuel and load: internal fuel 590 US gal (2233 litres); external fuel up to two 120-US gal (455-litre) drop tanks; maximum payload 8,000 lb (3629 kg)
Speed: dash speed at 5,000 ft (1525 m) 126 kt (145 mph; 234 km/h)
Range: operational radius 250 nm (288 miles; 463 km) on a SAR mission or 200 nm (230 miles; 370 km) on a a SEAL insertion/extraction mission

---

Sikorsky **S-70B/HH-60J Jayhawk**

Procured to replace HH-3Fs in US Coast Guard service, the **HH-60J Jayhawk** is essentially similar to the US Navy's HH-60H Rescue Hawk, but dispenses with combat equipment such as HIRSS and defensive avionics in favour of dedicated search equipment. Chief among these is a thimble radome on the nose housing a Bendix/King RDR-1300 search/weather radar, supported by a direction finder and ILS/VOR receiver. A 30-million candlepower searchlight can be fitted to the port fuel tank pylon, and the cockpit is NVG-compatible. Funding for a thermal imager is being sought. Whereas the HH-60H routinely carries two external fuel tanks, the HH-60J can carry an additional tank on the port pylon to meet Coast Guard range requirements, the asymmetric arrangement being dictated by the need to provide clearance for the rescue hoist on the starboard side. RAST gear can be fitted for operations

from Coast Guard cutters in the 'Hamilton' and 'Bear' classes.

A crew of four flies the Jayhawk, comprising two pilots, flight engineer/hoist operator and a rescue swimmer. With all three external tanks, the HH-60J can fly to 300 nm (345 miles/555 km) from base, remain on scene for 45 minutes and return with six survivors with a safe fuel margin. There is no emergency capability of alighting on the water, one retrograde step compared to its predecessor.

The first HH-60J flew on 8 August 1990, and Jayhawks were soon delivered to the USCG Aviation Technical Training Center at Elizabeth City, NC, and the Air Training Center at Mobile, AL. Jayhawks are now operational with Coast Guard Air Stations at Cape Cod, MA, Elizabeth City, NC, Clearwater, FL, Mobile, AL, Traverse City, MI, San Francisco, CA, Kodiak, AK, and Sitka, AK. The USCG is investigating the feasibility of

deploying Jayhawks regularly aboard surface vessels, and trials have been conducted aboard various medium- and heavy-

endurance USCG cutters. A total of 42 has been ordered, of which 37 aircraft had been delivered by February 1994. The US Coast Guard has a requirement for a further 33 to reinforce the numbers operating in the secondary role of the Jayhawk, namely that of drug interdiction.

The HH-60J is the US Coast Guard's standard MRR (medium-range recovery) platform, operating from shore bases. Plans exist to increase the Jayhawks' flexibility by regular deployments aboard USCG vessels.

Sikorsky **S-76/H-76 Eagle**

The eight/12-passenger **S-76** was developed by Sikorsky as a general-purpose twin-turbine helicopter. It first flew on 13 March 1977, powered by 650-shp (485-kW) Allison 250-C30 turboshafts, and was followed by the improved **S-76 Mark II**. The **S-76 Utility** is a more basic version of the S-76 Mk II and is of greater interest to military customers. The **AUH-76** armed utility derivative incorporates optional sliding doors, armour protection, defensive avionics and a wide range of weapon options, including gun and rocket pods, anti-armour missiles and associated targeting equipment. First flying on 22 June 1984, the current **S-76B** production variant features two 981-shp (732-kW) Pratt & Whitney PT6B-36A turboshafts. The **S-76A** and **S-76C**, flown on 18 May 1990, became available with 732-shp (539-kW) Turboméca Arriel 1S1 engines. A more specifically militarised S-76B variant is the **H-76 Eagle**, which offers a similar range of options to the AUH-76. Other features include door-mounted weapons, an uprated transmission and strengthened structural items.

OPERATORS

The **Philippine air force** was an early military user. Its order for 17 S-76 Utility aircraft comprises 12 AUH-76s for COIN, troop/logistic support and medevac duties and five S-76 Mk IIs – two for SAR and three passenger transports. The AUH-76s are armed with FN Herstal HMP 0.50-in (12.7-mm) machine-gun pods and other light weapons. The **Royal Jordanian air force** bought 18, of which four were for medevac duty in paramilitary service and 12 for SAR/general transport duty, with two others (later replaced by S-76Bs) for VIP use. Jordan transferred two of its S-76s to **Iraq** and four are reported to have gone to **Guatemala**. It has disposed of the remaining S-76s. In the VIP role, single examples are used by the **Chilean army**, the **Dubai air wing** and the **Honduras air force**. The **Royal Hong Kong Auxiliary Air Force** has six S-76As, of which three have an advanced equipment fit (including FLIR) for all-weather SAR and patrol, plus two S-76Cs for VIP transport. Eight **Spanish air force** S-76Cs are for IFR training, provided by Esc 783 at Granada, and **Japan** is to acquire up to 20 S-76Cs for SAR duty. More than 150 H-76 Eagles are to be produced locally for the **South Korean army**.

SPECIFICATION

Sikorsky H-76 Eagle
Rotor system: main rotor diameter 44 ft 0 in (13.41 m); tail rotor diameter 8 ft 0 in (2.44 m); main rotor disc area 1,520.53 sq ft (141.26 m2)
Fuselage and tail: length overall, rotors turning 52 ft 6 in (16.00 m) and fuselage 43 ft 4.5 in (13.22 m); height overall 14 ft 9.25 in (4.52 m) with tail rotor turning; stabiliser span 10 ft 4 in (3.15 m)
Powerplant: two Pratt & Whitney Canada PT6B-36 turboshafts rated at 960 shp (716 kW) for take-off and 870 shp (649 kW) for continuous running
Weights: basic empty 5,610 lb (2545 kg); empty equipped

6,680 lb (3030 kg); maximum take-off 11,400 lb (5171 kg)
Fuel and load: internal fuel 262 US gal (993 litres)
Speed: never exceed speed 155 kt (178 mph; 287 km/h); maximum cruising speed at optimum altitude 145 kt (167 mph; 269 km/h); economical cruising speed at optimum altitude 131 kt (151 mph; 243 km/h)
Range: about 312 nm (359 miles; 578 km)
Performance: maximum rate of climb at sea level 1,500 ft (457 m) per minute; service ceiling 15,000 ft (4570 m); hovering ceiling 5,400 ft (1645 m) out of ground effect

The Spanish air force's eight S-76Cs (local designation HE.24) are used for rotary wing training by Esc 783.

Sikorsky S-80/CH-53E Super Stallion

Early generations of CH-53 had proved their ability to recover downed aircraft, but the process was marginal at best. This prompted the **USMC** to issue a specification for a heavylift helicopter with 1.8 times the lifting capacity of the CH-53A, but still small enough to operate from its amphibious assault vessels. Sikorsky, meanwhile, had been working to a similar goal, and came up with the elegant solution of adding a third T64 engine to the basic design. This

is mounted behind the rotor mast and is fed by an intake on the port side.

The new variant was assigned the company model number **S-80**, and the first **YCH-53E** prototype flew from Stratford on 1 March 1974, initially with a large tailfin and low-set tailplane. Power was provided by three T64-GE-415s driving a seven-bladed main rotor, via an uprated transmission. Twin-engined CH-53s have six rotor blades. The airframe itself was longer than

earlier CH-53s, enabling it to carry 55 troops and light vehicles easily, while the fuselage sponsons were lengthened to house more fuel, and external tank capability was provided from the outset. Following the destruction of the first prototype in a ground run, the second prototype resumed flying with a revised tail, the upright fin being canted 20° to port and fitted with a gull-wing tailplane cantilevered to starboard.

First of the pre-production **CH-53E**s flew on 8 December 1975, but it was not until February 1981 that the first USMC unit, HMH-464 (now HMM-464), achieved initial operating capability at MCAS New River, NC. Five more units have been equipped with the type (HMM-461 at New River, HMH-361, 465 and 466 at Tustin, CA, and HMT-302 at Tustin for training). The CH-53E is now a vital part of USMC amphibious operations, partnering the smaller CH-46 on assault missions. Thanks to its lifting capability, the CH-53E is primarily used to move materiel as opposed to personnel. In a typical composite squadron aboard an assault ship, four CH-53Es are assigned. The type was used widely in the Desert Storm conflict.

US Navy interest in the Sea Stallion lay in its use for supplying vessels from shore bases, the combination of lifting ability and range proving ideal for the task. Small numbers fly with HC-1 at NAS North Island, CA, HC-2 at NAS Norfolk, VA, and HC-4 at NAS Sigonella, Sicily, respectively supporting the Pacific, Atlantic and Mediterranean Fleets.

No foreign sales of the **S-80E** export

model have yet been made, and current US Navy and Marine Corps acquisitions stand at 142, although eventual requirements are for 177, with production ending in 1995.

Sikorsky S-80 (CH-53E Super Stallion)
Rotor system: main rotor diameter 79 ft 0 in (24.08 m); tail rotor diameter 20 ft 0 in (6.10 m); main rotor disc area 4,901.67 sq ft (455.38 m²); tail rotor disc area 314.16 sq ft (29.19 m²)
Fuselage and tail: length overall, rotors turning 99 ft 0.5 in (30.19 m), fuselage 73 ft 4 in (22.35 m), and overall with rotor and tail pylon folded 60 ft 6 in (18.44 m); height overall, rotors turning 29 ft 5 in (8.97 m), to top of rotor head 17 ft 5.5 in (5.32 m), and overall with rotor and tail pylon folded 18 ft 7 in (5.66 m); wheel track 13 ft 0 in (3.96 m); wheel base 27 ft 3 in (8.31 m)
Powerplant: three General Electric T64-GE-416 turboshafts each rated at 4,380 shp (3266 kW) for 10 minutes, 4,145 shp (3091 kW) for 30 minutes and 3,696 shp (2756 kW) for continuous running
Weights: empty 33,338 lb (15072 kg); maximum take-off 69,750 lb (31640 kg) with an internal payload or 73,500 lb (33340 kg) with an external payload
Fuel and load: internal fuel 1,017 US gal (3849 litres); external fuel up to two 650-US gal (2461-litre) drop tanks; maximum payload 36,000 lb (16330 kg), or 30,000 lb (13607 kg) carried internally over a 100-nm (115-mile; 185-km) radius or 32,000 lb (14515 kg) carried externally over a 50-nm (57-mile; 92.5-km) radius
Speed: maximum level speed 'clean' at sea level 170 kt (196 mph; 315 km/h); cruising speed at sea level 150 kt (173 mph; 278 km/h)
Range: ferry range 1,120 nm (1,290 miles; 2075 km) without flight refuelling; operational radius 500 nm (575 miles; 925 km) with 20,000-lb (9072-kg) external payload or 50 nm (57.5 miles; 92.5 km) with 32,000-lb (14515-kg) external payload
Performance: maximum rate of climb at sea level with 25,000-lb (11340-kg) payload 2,500 ft (762 m) per minute; service ceiling 18,500 ft (5640 m); hovering ceiling 11,550 ft (3520 m) in ground effect and 9,500 ft (2895 m) out of ground effect

The US Navy's CH-53Es provide heavylift and vertical delivery support of the Mediterranean, Pacific and Atlantic Fleets. HC-4 covers the European/Middle East theatre and is based at Sigonella, Italy.

Above: The addition of a third powerplant dramatically improved the CH-53's lifting abilities. It is the USMC's primary heavylift type and is used by five operational units. Early problems during trials were rectified by a canted fin and a gull-wing tail.

Sikorsky S-80M/MH-53E Sea Dragon

Just as the CH-53E dramatically improved the assault capabilities of the Stallion, so the **MH-53E Sea Dragon** has increased the ability of the AMCM (airborne mine countermeasures) force. Utilising the basic airframe of the CH-53E, the MH-53E differs by having grossly enlarged fuselage sponsons housing fuel which allows the type to mine-sweep for four hours while operating 30 minutes from base. The refuelling probe can further extend time on station, and ferry tanks can be fitted internally. Mine-hunting equipment remains essentially that devel-

oped for the RH-53D, but with additional items such as the ALQ-160 acoustic countermeasures system, ALQ-166 magnetic mine hydrofoil sled and the Northrop ALARMS (airborne laser radar mine sensor), the latter housed in a 35-ft (10-m) internal container. The MH-53E also retains a secondary transport role, but this is little used due to the Navy's adoption of the CH-53E.

The first pre-production machine took to the air on 1 September 1983, following trials of a **YMH-53E** that initially lacked the enlarged sponsons. Deliveries began to the

US Navy in June 1986 and in April 1987 the type joined HM-14 at NAS Norfolk, VA, followed by HM-12 at the same base and HM-15 at NAS Alameda, CA. The total US Navy requirement is for 56 airframes and the formation of a fourth squadron.

One export customer has been found for the Sea Dragon, this being the **Japanese Maritime Self-Defence Force**, which has purchased 11 **S-80M-1** aircraft, essentially similar to the MH-53E but lacking the refuelling probe. After trials with 51 Kokutai at Atsugi, the S-80M entered service with

31 Kokutai at Iwakuni to replace KV-107-IIs in the AMCM role.

Sikorsky S-80 (MH-53E Sea Dragon)
generally similar to the Sikorsky S-80 (CH-53E Super Stallion) except in the following particulars:
Weights: empty 36,336 lb (16482 kg); maximum take-off 69,750 lb (31640 kg) with an internal payload or 73,500 lb (33340 kg) with an external payload
Fuel and load: internal fuel 3,200 US gal (12113 litres) plus provision for 2,100 US gal (7949 litres) of auxiliary fuel in up to seven internal tanks; useful load for influence sweep mission 26,000 lb (11793 kg)

The latest mine-countermeasures S-80 variant offers greatly improved capability through its increased power and advanced avionics. Huge external sponsons and rear-view mirrors identify this mine-hunter as a Japanese S-80M-1. It lacks the refuelling probe associated with the US Navy's MH-53E.

Sikorsky MH-53E Sea Dragon

Sikorsky S-92

In 1992 Sikorsky unveiled a mock-up of its **S-92 'Helibus'**, a growth derivative of the S-70 series aimed primarily at the civilian market. As currently marketed, the civil **S-92C** will combine a new conventional structure fuselage of increased dimensions, with a 6 ft x 6 ft (1.83 m x 1.83 m) cross-section, a cabin length of 19 ft 4 in (5.89 m), and accommodation for up to 22 passengers. It will also feature the SH-60B's 3,350-shp (2500-kW) transmission, a modified UH-60L main rotor head, and an improved main rotor

with graphite blade spar, broader-chord blades and anhedral blade tips. Power is to be provided by two 2,200-shp (1640-kW) General Electric CT-7 or Rolls-Royce Turboméca RTM 322 turboshafts. Crash-resistant fuel tanks will be incorporated in enlarged sponsons on the fuselage sides, and an optional loading ramp at the rear of the cabin will be available.

A military **S-92M** derivative is also being marketed, with refuelling probe, aft-loading ramp, automatic main rotor blade-fold and

tail-fold. Capable of carrying 18 to 24 troops, or 16 litter patients, on 200-nm (230-mile; 370-km) missions, the S-92M is initially aimed at satisfying anticipated USMC/USN requirements for medium-lift helicopters to replace Boeing CH-46E/UH-46Ds in the combat assault/vertical replenishment roles respectively. In the combat SAR role, the S-92M is being promoted as an alternative to the V-22 Osprey and is being proposed to replace Sikorsky MH-53Js in service with the USAF's AFSOC.

Powered by uprated General Electric T701-GE 401X engines, the S-92M will have a full range of 400 nm (460 miles; 740 km) and a cruising speed of 150 kt (173 mph; 278 km/h). Maximum take-off weight will be 22,000 lb (9980 kg) in the land assault mission, and 23,000 lb (10435 kg) in the amphibious assault role.

Development of the S-92 was delayed in 1993 due to the economic downturn. Sikorsky is currently looking for further international partners to launch the programme.

Singapore Aerospace A-4SU Super Skyhawk

Singapore Aerospace Ltd
540 Airport Road,
Paya Lebar, Singapore 1953

The A-4 Skyhawk first entered service with the **Republic of Singapore Air Force** in 1974. Some 40 former US Navy A-4Bs were removed from storage following a mid-1972 order from the RSAF. The first eight were refurbished by Lockheed to **A-4S** standard with over 100 modifications. These included installation of 8,400-lb st (37.36-kN) J65-W-20 turbojets, twin 30-mm ADEN cannon, new instrumentation and a Ferranti lightweight lead-computing weapon aiming system. The aircraft also featured unique overwing spoilers, and a brake parachute below the rear fuselage. The remaining 32 aircraft were refurbished in Singapore by January 1976. The upgraded aircraft entered service with Nos 142 'Gryphon' and 143 'Phoenix' Sqns, along with seven Skyhawks modified to **TA-4S** trainers with unique, separate tandem cockpits.

Singapore purchased 70 additional A-4Cs in 1980 and 16 more A-4Bs in 1983 from the same source, cannibalising many of them to provide spares, and converting 40 to **A-4S-1** and 10 to **TA-4S-1** configuration with spoilers, minor avionics modifications, rewiring and higher-rated wing hardpoints. The additional procurement allowed the formation of No. 145 'Hor-

net' Squadron. By 1984 the Singaporean government decided not to procure a new-generation fighter (for reasons of affordability), and elected instead to upgrade these modestly-equipped, elderly aircraft to **A-4SU Super Skyhawk** standard. An additional benefit of upgrading the aircraft indigenously was the boost it would give to Singapore's developing aerospace industry.

Phase One of this effort involved the replacement of the J65 turbojet with a non-afterburning variant of the General Electric F404-GE-100D turbofan that develops a maximum of 10,800 lb st (48.04 kN). The package also involved the associated structural hardening, modification of the engine intakes, redesigned mounts and installation of new engine ancillary systems. The work was carried out by SAe and was supervised by Grumman. The 27 per cent increase in thrust is claimed to provide a 15 per cent increase in maximum dash speed, 35 per cent faster climb rate, 40 per cent increase in level acceleration, a better sustained turn performance than the A-4M and substantial improvement in take-off performance and agility. The 34 per cent heavier F404 also features significantly improved specific fuel consumption and maintainability.

One prototype each of the single-seat A-4S and two-seat TA-4S was re-engined, the first of these taking to the air for the initially on 19 September 1986. Production-conversions of 40 A-4S-1s and eight TA-4S-1s were completed during 1989, with No. 143 squadron the first to achieve IOC (on 1 March 1989), followed by Nos 145 and 142. In 1990 six re-engined A-4S Skyhawks were displayed as the 'Black Knights' aerobatic team.

Delphi avionics upgrade

The completely separate Phase Two of the programme involved a comprehensive avionics modernisation developed by Ferranti Defence Systems of the UK (now part of GEC-Marconi). Named Delphi, it was applied by a joint RSAF/SAe team at the company's facility at RSAF Paya Lebar. It comprises a GEC-Ferranti Type 4510 raster/stroke HUD and MED 2067 head-down MFD; a Litton LN-93 ring-laser gyro INS; Bendix flight data recorder; and a mission computer complete with data transfer module for computerised mission planning. The aircraft have been rewired with the standard MIL 1553B databus. One of the factors governing the choice of Ferranti's

package was a refusal by the US government to allow American contractors to release computer system software codes to Singapore. All aspects of software development for the avionics package were reportedly developed indigenously.

Singapore declared its first A-4SU Super Skyhawk fighter unit, No. 145 Squadron, fully operational on 24 February 1992. Two further Super Skyhawk squadrons, Nos 142 and 143, are receiving aircraft as they are recycled through the modification package. The entire RSAF Skyhawk fleet is based at RASAF Tengah. The A-4SUs are fitted with LAU-10 and Alkan triple ejector racks, and can carry a wide range of ordnance including AGM-65B/E Maverick ASMs, Mk 82 bombs, CRV-7 rocket pods, AIM-9J AAMs, SUU-40/A flare dispensers, SNEB 68-mm rockets and SUU-23 20-mm gun pods.

Further modifications are being planned. These include the provision of 20 GEC Avionics Atlantic FLIR pods for all-weather navigation and weapons targeting, as well as laser rangefinders for air-to-ground ranging and targeting. The RSAF already has about 30 Martin-Marietta AN/AAS-35 Pave Penny laser spot tracker pods which may be installed on the A-4SUs.

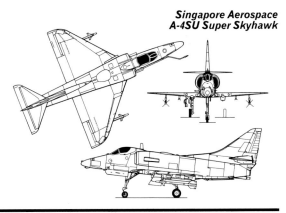

Singapore Aerospace A-4SU Super Skyhawk

Arguably the most advanced A-4s in service anywhere today, the RSAF's A-4SU Super Skyhawks were declared operational with No. 145 Squadron in early 1992. These were the first to feature the Delphi avionics modernisation package, as well as F404 turbofan powerplants.

Slingsby T67 Firefly

Slingsby Aviation Limited,
Ings Lane, Kirbymoorside,
North Yorkshire YO6 6EZ, United Kingdom.

After acquiring a licence for production in the UK of the **Fournier RF-6B** motorised glider (as the **T67A Firefly**), Slingsby developed an all-composite airframe for the **T67B** and subsequent vari-

ants of this two-seat, side-by-side aerobatic, training and sporting aircraft. Intended primarily for military use, the **T67M** featured an AEIO-320-D1B engine and, in its **Mk II** version, a one-piece upward-opening

canopy. The **T67M200** was first flown on 16 May 1985 and introduced a 200-hp

(149-kW) AEIO-360-A1E engine and three-bladed propeller.

Slingsby T67 Firefly

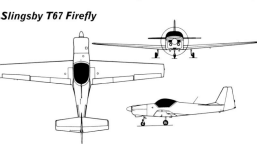

The T-3A is steadily replacing ageing Cessna T-41A/C Mescaleros with the 557th FTS at the Air Force Academy in Colorado, and with AETC's 1st FTS at Hondo, Texas. This T-3A is shown at the roll-out ceremony at Kirbymoorside in late 1993.

In 1991, Slingsby developed the more powerful **T67M260** with a 260-hp (195-kW) AETO-540-D4A5 flat-six engine to meet the USAF requirement for an Enhanced Flight Screener. The service will acquire 113 of these Fireflies with the designation **T-3A**. Hunting Aircraft Ltd has been contracted to provide elementary flying training (effectively for screening inexperienced trainee pilots) using **T67M-II**s. These will replace ageing de Havilland Chipmunks and Scottish Aviation Bulldogs presently used by the EFTS at RAF Swinderby and by the RNEFTS at Topcliffe.

Four T67s are operated by the **Royal Hong Kong AAF**. Twelve similar **T67C3**s are used by Canadair to train pilots for the **Canadian Forces** at Portage la Prairie. Other users include civil schools in **Turkey**, the **Netherlands** and **Norway** that have some responsibilities for preliminary training and grading of military pilots. The **USAF**'s T-3As are replacing T-41A/Cs with the Air Force Academy, Colorado, and with a training squadron in Texas.

SPECIFICATION

Slingsby T67M Mk II Firefly
Wing: span 34 ft 9 in (10.59 m); aspect ratio 8.88; area 136.00 sq ft (12.63 m²)
Fuselage and tail: length 24 ft 0.25 in (7.32 m); height 7 ft 9 in (2.36 m); tailplane span 11 ft 1.75 in (3.40 m)
Powerplant: one Textron Lycoming AEIO-320-D1B four cylinder horizontally-opposed piston engine rated at 160 hp (119 kW)
Weights: empty equipped 1,450 lb (658 kg); maximum take-off 2,100 lb (952 kg)

Fuel and load: internal fuel 252 lb (114 kg)
Speed: maximum level speed 'clean' at sea level 136 kt (157 mph; 252 km/h); maximum cruising speed at 8,000 ft (2440 m) 127 kt (146 mph; 235 km/h)
Range: 529 nm (608 miles; 980 km) at maximum cruising speed; endurance 5 hours 5 minutes at economical cruising speed
Performance: maximum rate of climb at sea level 1,100 ft (335 m) per minute; service ceiling 15,000 ft (4570 m); take-off distance to 50 ft (15 m) 1,319 ft (402 m) at MTOW; landing distance from 50 ft (15 m) 1,750 ft (533 m) at normal landing weight
g limits: -3 to +6

SOCATA (Aérospatiale) **Rallye/Guerrier**

SOCATA,
12 Rue Pasteur,
F-92150 Suresnes, France

In 1966 the SOCATA subsidiary of Aérospatiale took over production of the **Rallye** lightplane, which was first flown on 10 June 1959 as a Morane-Saulnier product. SOCATA also developed the **Rallye 235G Guerrier** for light attack, army support and weapons training. Based on the four-seat **Rallye 235GT Gabier**, it features a two-seat cabin with dual controls, provision for two further seats behind the pilots and a tailwheel undercarriage. It introduces four underwing hardpoints for twin 7.62-mm (0.3-in) gun pods, MATRA F22 rocket launchers each with six 68-mm (2.68-in) rockets, 50-kg (110-lb) bombs or battlefield illumination, surveillance or SAR equipment. It can also carry a stretcher or an underwing TV reconnaissance pod.

The major user is the French **Aéronavale**. Four Rallyes of 50S at Lanvéoc-Poulmic provide informal flying instruction to students of the Ecole Navale (Naval College). 51S at Rochefort/Soubise has 11 Rallyes to grade NCO students. Other Rallye operators include the Royal air force of **Morocco** (10), the **Moroccan Gendarmerie** (two) and **Libya** (eight). Single examples serve in **Chad**, **Djibouti**, the **Dominican Republic** and the **Seychelles**. Two Guerriers went to the **Rwandese army air corps** and four to the air force of **Senegambia**, which also bought four Rallyes as trainers.

The Aéronavale's Rallye lightplanes are used primarily to grade prospective students, and for general instruction for non-aircrew. Two variants are operated, the two-seat spinnable Rallye Club 100S and the three/four-seat Rallye Club 100ST.

SPECIFICATION

SOCATA Rallye 235 Guerrier
Wing: span 9.74 m (31 ft 11 in); aspect ratio 7.57; area 12.28 m² (132.19 sq ft)
Fuselage and tail: length 7.25 m (23 ft 9.5 in); height 2.80 m (9 ft 2.25 in); tailplane span 3.67 m (12 ft 0.5 in); wheel track 2.01 m (6 ft 6.5 in); wheel base 1.71 m (5 ft 7.25 in)

Powerplant: one Textron Lycoming O-540-B4B5 six-cylinder horizontally-opposed piston engine rated at 235 hp (175 kW)
Weights: empty 710 kg (1,565 lb); normal take-off 1200 kg (2,646 lb); maximum take-off 1350 kg (2,976 lb)
Fuel and load: internal fuel 282 litres (74.5 US gall); external fuel none; maximum ordnance 300 kg (661 lb)
Speed: maximum level speed 'clean' at sea level 275 km/h (148 kt; 171 mph); cruising speed at 1500 m (4,925 ft) 245 km/h (132 kt; 152 mph)
Range: ferry range 1300 km (701 nm; 807 miles); combat radius 515 km (278 nm; 320 miles) on an armed reconnaissance mission with two machine-gun pods, or 265 km (143 nm; 165 miles) on an armed reconnaissance mission with four rocket launchers
Performance: maximum rate of climb at sea level 300 m (984 ft) per minute; service ceiling 4500 m (14,760 ft); take-off run 150 m (492 ft) at maximum take-off weight; take-off distance to 15 m (50 ft) 305 m (1,000 ft) at maximum take-off weight; landing run 130m (427 ft) at normal landing weight

SOCATA (Aérospatiale) **TBM700**

First flown on 14 July 1988, the **SOCATA TBM700** was at first a joint project between Aérospatiale subsidiary SOCATA and Mooney in the US, but it is now an all-French programme. The **Armée de l'Air** became the first military user of the TBM700 when it took delivery in May 1992 of two of these seven-seat single-engined 'mini-airliners', from an unannounced order for six aircraft. The TBM700s have been acquired to serve with the Groupe Aérien d'Entraînement et de Liaison (GAEL) at Villacoublay, replacing veteran twin-jet MS 760 Paris communications aircraft in Escadron de Transport 2/65 'Rambouillet'. The Armée de l'Air has a requirement for up to 35 TBM700s for use in the vital, if unsung, liaison and light utility roles.

SPECIFICATION

SOCATA (Aérospatiale) TBM700
Wing: span 12.16 m (39 ft 10.75 in); aspect ratio 8.21; area 18.00 m² (193.75 sq ft)
Fuselage and tail: length 10.43 m (34 ft 2.5 in); height 3.99 m (13 ft 1 in)
Powerplant: one Pratt & Whitney Canada PT6A -64 turboprop rated at 522 kW (700 shp)
Weights: empty equipped 1826 kg (4,025 lb); maximum take-off and landing 2991 kg (6,595 lb)

The Armée de l'Air is currently the sole military operator of SOCATA TBM700 business aircraft. They are based at Villacoublay, near Paris, and are used for liaison duties.

Fuel and load: useable fuel 866 kg (1,910 lb); total baggage load 80 kg (176 lb)
Speed: maximum cruising speed at 7925 m (26,000 ft) 555 km/h (300 kt; 345 mph)
Range: at maximum speed with maximum payload and 45 min reserves 1,001 nm (1855 km; 1,152 miles); at long-range cruising speed with maximum fuel and no reserves 1,611 nm (2985 km; 1,855 miles)
Performance: maximum rate of climb at sea level and at all-up weight of 2500 kg (5,511 lb) 702 m (2,303 ft) per minute, certificated ceiling 9150 m (30,000 ft)

SOKO **G-2A Galeb**

First flown in May 1961, the **G-2A Galeb** (Seagull) was the first indigenous Yugoslav jet design to enter production. The Galeb is a conventional low-wing monoplane. The wing has strong points for two 100-kg (220-lb) bombs and up to six 57-mm rockets. Two 12.7-mm machine-guns are fitted in the nose. A version of the trainer flew on 19 August 1970 with an uprated Viper 532 engine as the **Galeb 3**, this being in effect the prototype for the two-seat **TJ-1 Jastreb** (described separately). The Galeb entered service with the **Yugoslav air force** (JRV) in 1965, production of more than 120 being needed to meet the requirements of the Air Academy and the fighter and fighter ground-attack schools. In post-civil war Yugoslavia, Galebs were flying exclusively with the **Serbian air force**, equipping the 105th Fighter-Bomber Regiment at Kovin. The other major customer was **Libya**, which received 120 in two batches before production ended in 1985; six others went to **Zambia**.

SPECIFICATION

SOKO G-2A Galeb
Wing: span 11.62 m (38 ft 1.5 in) with tip tanks; aspect ratio 5.55; area 19.43 m² (209.15 sq ft)
Fuselage and tail: length 10.34 m (33 ft 11 in); height 3.28 m (10 ft 9 in); tailplane span 4.27 m (14 ft 0 in)
Powerplant: one licence-built Rolls-Royce (Bristol Siddeley) Viper 11 Mk 22-6 turbojet rated at 2,500 lb st (11.12 kN) dry
Weights: empty equipped 2620 kg (5,776 lb); normal take-off typically 3828 kg (8,439 lb) with tip tanks; maximum take-off 4300 kg (9,480 lb)
Fuel and load: internal fuel 780 kg (1,720 lb); external fuel up to 340 kg (750 lb) in two jettisonable tip tanks; maximum ordnance 300 kg (661 lb)
Speed: maximum level speed 'clean' at 6200 m (20,340 ft) 812 km/h (439 kt; 505 mph) and at sea level 756 km/h (408 kt; 470 mph); maximum cruising speed at 6000 m (19,685 ft) 730 km/h (393 kt; 453 mph)
Range: ferry range 670 nm (772 miles; 1242 km) with tip tanks; endurance 2 hours 30 minutes
Performance: maximum rate of climb at sea level 1370 m (4,495 ft) per minute; climb to 6000 m (19,685 ft) in 5 minutes 30 seconds; service ceiling 12000 m (39,370 ft); take-off distance to 15 m (50 ft) 640 m (2,100 ft) at MTOW; landing distance from 15 m (50 ft) 710 m (2,329 ft) at normal landing weight
g limits: -4 to +8

The largest export recipient of the SOKO Jastreb was the Libyan air force. About 30 G-2As remain in service for counter-insurgency and training duties.

SOKO **G-4 Super Galeb**

First flown on 17 July 1978, the **SOKO G-4 Super Galeb** is a two-seat advanced and tactical trainer of similar configuration to the BAe Hawk. The G-4 was developed during the 1970s as a replacement for the G-2A Galeb and T-33. Pre-production aircraft followed from late 1980 and full service use began in 1985, with G-4s replacing G-2As at the advanced flying training school at Titograd. Further deliveries allowed G-4s to supplant the earlier model at the **JRV**'s Air Academy at Zadar and a second training school at Pula. At least 30 Super Galebs now fly at each unit, from production of more than 136. Pilots are streamed following 60 hours in G-4s at Zadar. Ground-attack pilots go to Titograd and interceptor pilots go to Pula for a further 120 hours. The air academy has an aerobatic team (the 'Flying Stars'/'Letece Zvezde') equipped with six G-4s. Super Galebs also equip the 105th LBAP at Kovin, the 172nd LBAP at Golubovci, Macedonia, and the 252nd LBAE at Batajnica. Export sales are limited to six G-4s for the **Myanmar air force**.

When the Mostar factory was abandoned in May 1992, some G-4 airframes were left uncompleted. The production jigs were transferred to UTVA, although no evidence exists that production has restarted. An enhanced ground-attack capability is offered in the **G-4M**, which appeared in 1991 and can carry 1680 kg (3,704 lb) of ordnance. It features a new avionics system and new nav/attack equipment including HUD, INS, electronic sight and MFDs. Capable of covering the continuation phase of training for which two-seat versions of operational aircraft are frequently used, the

In an attempt to upgrade its forces in the face of stiffening guerrilla resistance, and in the face of international sanctions which have hindered arms procurement, the Myanmar air force became the first export customer for the Super Galeb, acquiring a quantity of these light attack aircraft/jet trainers from 1990.

G-4M is being used to replace Jastrebs in some ground-attack units.

WEAPON OPTIONS

For the ground attack role, the G-4 can carry a ventral 23-mm GSh-23L gun pod with 200 rounds and up to 1280 kg (2,822 lb) of ordnance on four hardpoints. These include a wide range of indigenously-developed weapons such as S-8-16 cluster bombs, KPT-150 expendable containers with anti-tank or anti-personnel bomblets, L-57-16MD 57-mm rocket pods, SN-3 carriers for 50-kg (110-lb) and 100-kg (221-lb) bombs, and 12.7-mm gun pods. The G-4M can carry both AGM-65B Maverick and AS-7 'Kerry' ASMs, KMGU cluster bombs and BL755 bombs. There is provision for wingtip missile rails that can mount K-13 (AA-2 'Atoll') or R-60 (AA-8 'Aphid') AAMs for self-defence and for a secondary point defence role.

SPECIFICATION

SOKO G-4 Super Galeb
Wing: span 9.88 m (32 ft 5 in); aspect ratio 5.0; area 19.50 m2 (209.90 sq ft)
Fuselage and tail: length 12.25 m (40 ft 2.25 in) including probe; height 4.30 m (14 ft 1.25 in); tailplane span 3.97 m (13 ft 0.25 in); wheel track 3.49 m (11 ft 5.5 in); wheel base 4.15 m (13 ft 7.5 in)
Powerplant: one ORAO (Rolls-Royce/Bristol Siddeley) Viper Mk 632-46 turbojet rated at 4,000 lb st (17.79 kN)
Weights: empty equipped 3172 kg (6,993 lb); normal take-off 4708 kg (10,379 lb) as a trainer; maximum take-off 6300 kg (13,889 lb)
Fuel and load: internal fuel 1307 kg (2,881 lb); external fuel up to 575 kg (1,268 lb) in two 368.5-litre (97.3-US gal) drop tanks; maximum ordnance 1280 kg (2,822 lb)
Speed: maximum level speed 'clean' at 6000 m (19,685 ft) 920 km/h (491 kt; 565 mph); maximum

cruising speed at 6000 m (19,685 ft) 845 km/h (456 kt; 525 mph)
Range: ferry range 1,349 nm (1,553 miles; 2500 km) with drop tanks; range 1,025 nm (1,180 miles, 1900 km) with internal fuel or 701 nm (807 miles; 1300 km) with cannon pack and four BL755 cluster bombs; combat radius 210 nm (242 miles; 389 km) on a lo-lo-lo attack with cannon pack and four BL755 cluster bombs, or 438 nm (504 miles; 812 km) on a hi-lo-hi attack with two BL755 cluster bombs and two drop tanks
Performance: maximum rate of climb at sea level 1860 m (6,100 ft) per minute; climb to 8000 m (26,245 ft) in 6 minutes; service ceiling 12850 m (42,160 ft); take-off run 572 m (1,877 ft) at normal take-off weight; landing distance from 15 m (50 ft) 1065 m (3,494 ft) at normal landing weight without brake chute or 690 m (2,264 ft) at normal landing weight with brake chute; landing run 815 m (2,674 ft) at normal landing weight
g limits: -4.2 to +8

SOKO **J-1 Jastreb**

Entering production in 1970, the single-seat **J-1 Jastreb** (Hawk) eventually equipped five wings of the **Yugoslav air force** (JRV) for ground-attack duties, for which it was armed with three 12.7-mm machine-guns in the nose and bombs or rocket pods on four wing hardpoints. Although the single-seat J-I (**J-21** in the JRV) has been progressively replaced by the Orao, about 40 J-21s remained in service as late as 1992, including a few for continuation training of reservist officers. In mid-1994, J-21s equipped the 92nd AB at Banja Luka, the 98th AB at Petrovac, and the 252nd LBAE at Batjnica.

Production of the Jastreb totalled 250-300, of which 30 were the **RJ-1** (**IJ-21** in the JRV) reconnaissance model with wingtip camera pods. A handful survive in service with the **Serbian air force**.

The production total also included 15 **JT-1** (**TJ-21**) two-seat training variants that closely resembled the Galeb basic jet trainer from which the Jastreb was origi-

Derived from the G-2 Galeb trainer, the single-seat J-1 (J-21 in Yugoslav service) Jastreb light attack aircraft has been used extensively during Yugoslavia's protracted civil war.

nally developed. The sole export customer was the **Zambian air force**, which received 20 **J-1E/RJ-1E** aircraft in 1971, about half of which may currently remain operational.

SPECIFICATION

SOKO J-1 Jastreb
Wing: span 10.56 m (34 ft 8 in) with tip tanks; aspect ratio 5.74; area 19.43 m2 (209.14 sq ft)
Fuselage and tail: length 10.88 m (35 ft 8.5 in); height 3.64 m (11 ft 11.5 in); tailplane span 4.27 m (14 ft 0 in); wheel track 3.89 m (12 ft 9 in); wheel base 3.61 m (11 ft 10 in)

Powerplant: one licence-built Rolls-Royce (Bristol Siddeley) Viper Mk 531 turbojet rated at 3,000 lb st (13.32 kN)
Weights: empty equipped 2820 kg (6,217 lb); normal take-off 4666 kg (10,287 lb); maximum take-off 5100 kg (11,243 lb)
Fuel and load: internal fuel 440 kg (970 lb); external fuel up to two 275-litre (72.6-US gal) drop tanks; maximum ordnance 800 kg (1,764 lb)
Speed: maximum level speed 'clean' at 6000 m

(19,685 ft) 820 km/h (442 kt; 510 mph); maximum cruising speed at 5000 m (16,405 ft) 740 km/h (399 kt; 460 mph)
Range: ferry range 820 nm (1520 km; 945 miles) with drop tanks
Performance: maximum rate of climb at sea level 1260 m (4,134 ft) per minute; service ceiling 12000 m (39,370 ft); take-off run 700 m (2,297 ft) at 3968 kg (8,748 lb); landing run 600 m (1,969 ft) at normal landing weight

---

SOKO **J-20 Kraguj**

After a 20-year period of service, SOKO's **J-20 Kraguj** lightweight close support aircraft was retired by the Yugoslav air force in 1990, a few survivors being then passed to the Slovenian national guard. These were, however, repossessed by the JRV before Slovenia broke away, in June 1991, from the former Yugoslavian confederation.

The single-seat Kraguj has a built-in armament of two 7.7-mm machine-guns and six wing hardpoints for bombs, rocket pods or other light weapon loads. Bosnian Serb militia have used the Kraguj in the civil war against the Moslem and Croat forces.

SPECIFICATION

SOKO J-20 Kraguj
Wing: span 10.64 m (34 ft 11 in); aspect ratio 6.66; area 17.00 m2 (182.99 sq ft)
Fuselage and tail: length 7.93 m (26 ft 0.25 in); height 3.00 m (9 ft 10 in); tailplane span 3.04 m (10 ft 0 in)
Powerplant: one Textron Lycoming GSO-480-B1A6 piston engine rated at 340 hp (253.3 kW)
Weights: empty equipped 1130 kg (2,491 lb); maximum take-off 1624 kg (3,580 lb)
Fuel and load: internal fuel 240 litres (63.4 US gal)
Speed: maximum level speed 'clean' at 1500 m (4,920 ft) 295 km/h (159 kt; 183 mph); maximum cruising speed at 1500 m (4,920 ft) 280 km/h

This J-20 Kraguj displays some of the stores available for its close support role. The type remains in limited service with Bosnian Serb militia forces in 1994.

(151 kt; 174 mph)
Range: 432 nm (497 miles; 800 km)
Performance: maximum rate of climb at sea level

480 m (1,575 ft) per minute; take-off run 110 m (361 ft) at normal take-off weight; landing run 120 m (394 ft) at maximum landing weight

SOKO (Eurocopter) SA 342 Gazelle/Partizan

After taking delivery of 21 **SA 341H** Gazelles from Aérospatiale in 1972/1973, Yugoslavia obtained a licence for Gazelle production by SOKO at Mostar. Production of 132 SA 341Hs was followed by approximately the same number of **SA 342L**s, which is a military variant with higher weights. Known as **Partizan** in Yugoslavia, the Gazelles served principally with the **Yugoslav air force** (JRV) and in small numbers with the navy and army.

SOKO developed the armed **GAMA** model of the Gazelle for anti-tank duties. This can carry four AT-3 Maljutka missiles on twin rail assemblies on the pylons on either side of the fuselage, aimed by a roof-mounted sight. Between each pair of 'Saggers' can be carried an SA 7 Strela 2M AAM for anti-helicopter work. The anti-tank Gazelles are supplemented by the **HERA** version, which serves in the observation role. Typically, operational squadrons of Partizans fly four each of the GAMA, HERA and liaison versions.

Gazelles of the JRV participated in the various conflicts that followed the break-up of the Yugoslav federation. As a consequence of these activities, one SA 341H became the nucleus in June 1991 of the **Slovenian Territorial Defence Force**, and at least one was in the hands of the newly-formed **Croatian air force**. Most are concentrated with **Serb**ian forces.

SPECIFICATION

SOKO (Aérospatiale) SA 342L-1 GAMA
generally similar to the Aérospatiale SA 341L-1 Gazelle

SOKO assembled more than 250 Gazelles and has developed two distinct variants to serve in anti-tank (GAMA) and observation (HERA) duties.

SOKO/IAv Craiova J-22 Orao/IAR-93

The **SOKO/IAv Craiova J-22 Orao/ IAR-93** is the product of an unlikely collaborative agreement between Yugoslavia and Romania. Both nations had a requirement for a lightweight but robust transonic close-support/ground-attack aircraft with secondary interceptor and reconnaissance capabilities, to enter service around 1977. Construction was allocated to two companies: Romania's CNIAR (now IAv Craiova) and SOKO in Yugoslavia.

The aircraft emerged with a configuration reminiscent of the larger SEPECAT Jaguar. It features a shoulder-mounted wing of similar planform and a similar sturdy undercarriage. SOKO had gained experience of building the Rolls-Royce Viper turbojet under licence for other military aircraft, and selected non-afterburning Turboméecanica/ ORAO Viper Mk 632-41Rs as powerplants. These are mounted side-by-side in the rear fuselage and are each rated at 17.79 kN (4,000 lb st). Reheat was considered a desirable option for production aircraft, however.

Single-seat and two-seat prototypes were constructed in each country, and these made simultaneous first flights on 31 October 1974 and 29 January 1977 (two-seaters). Manufacture of pre-production batches of 15 aircraft then began in both countries, and the first of these made their maiden flights in late 1978.

Series production of the Romanian **IAR-93** followed in 1979, and of the Yugoslavian **J-22 Orao** (Eagle) in 1980. Continued non-availability of afterburners meant that the first 20 production aircraft in each country were delivered without reheat.

The first Romanian version of the aircraft was the non-afterburning **IAR-93A**, which made its maiden flight in 1981. CNIAR built 26 single-seaters and 10 two-seat trainers with an extended forward fuselage and sideways-opening canopies. The following **IAR-93B** variant first flew in 1985 and introduced afterburning Viper Mk 633-41 turbojets. It also featured wing leading-edge root extensions but lacked inboard wing fences. IAR-93Bs, and two-seat IAR-93As, lack ventral fins. Interestingly, single-seat IAR-93Bs feature a manually operated sideways-opening canopy, whereas all other single-seaters have an upward-hinging, electrically actuated canopy. Romania ordered 165 Oraos, including two-seaters.

Production variants

In Yugoslavia, the first production variant was the **Orao 1**, powered (like the IAR-93A and pre-series aircraft) by non-afterburning Vipers, as a result of the continuing problems with developing an afterburner. The lack of performance of these early production aircraft was such that they were allocated to the tactical reconnaissance role under the designation **IJ-22**. A handful of the batch of 20 aircraft appeared as two-seat trainers designated **NJ-22**. These aircraft still equip a photo reconnaissance *eskadrilla* based near Zagreb.

The Orao 1 was followed by the single-seat **Orao 2** or **J-22(M)**, with enlarged integral wing fuel tanks, and with increased capacity in two fuselage tanks. Afterburning Viper 633-41 engines made possible a small increase in payload. The Orao 2 also has a Thomson-CSF HUD. The prototype flew for the first time on 20 October 1983 and the new variant entered production in late 1984, but by mid-1985 there were 16 complete aircraft awaiting reheated engines. These eventually arrived and the aircraft began to enter service in 1986.

The two-seat Orao 1 proved to be somewhat underpowered and short-legged, and SOKO therefore designed a new two-seat trainer incorporating the more powerful engines and the increased-capacity wing tanks of the Orao 2. The first example of the new **Orao 2D**, or **NJ-22(M)**, made its maiden flight on 18 July 1986, and production 2Ds have been augmented by a conversion programme bringing all surviving Orao 1 two-seaters up to the same standard. Like the Orao 2, the 2D has the same wing LERXes as are fitted to the IAR-93B.

By 1994, the Orao 2 was operated by the following **Serbian air force** units: the 92nd Aviation Brigade (AB) at Banja Luka, the 98th AB at Petrovac and the 172 Fighter-Attack Squadron at Batajnica. In **Romania**, the IAR-93B was in service with the 67th Regiment at Craiova.

WEAPON OPTIONS

The IAR-93/Orao is equipped with two GSh-23L twin-barrelled 23-mm cannon mounted in the forward fuselage. The Orao 1 has five weapons pylons, one under the fuselage and two under the inner wings stressed to carry up to 500 kg (1,102 lb), and two outboard pylons for stores of up to 300 kg (660 lb).

The outboard pylons of the Orao 2 are stressed for loads of up to 500 kg (1,102 lb), while the fuselage pylon on this variant can carry up to 800 kg (1,763 lb). Oraos can carry a range of stores including AGM-65 Maverick and Grom (an indigenous version of the AS-7 'Kerry') ASMs and Durandal penetration bombs.

SPECIFICATION

SOKO/CNIAR (now SOKO/Avioane) J-22 Orao
Wing: span 9.30 m (30 ft 6.25 in); aspect ratio 3.33; area 26.00 m2 (279.87 sq ft)
Fuselage and tail: length 14.90 m (48 ft 10.625 in) including probe; height 4.52 m (14 ft 10 in); tailplane span 4.59 m (15 ft 0.75 in); wheel track 2.50 m (8 ft 2.5 in); wheel base 5.40 m (17 ft 8.5 in)
Powerplant: two Turboméecanica/ORAO-built Rolls-Royce Viper Mk 632-41R turbojets each rated at 4,000 lb st (17.79 kN) dry or, in most aircraft, two Turboméecanica/ORAO-built Rolls-Royce Viper Mk 633-41 each rated at 4,000 lb st (17.79 kN) dry and 5,000 lb st (22.24 kN) with afterburning
Weights: empty equipped 5500 kg (12,125 lb); normal take-off 8170 kg (18,012 lb); maximum take-off 11080 kg (24,427 lb)
Fuel and load: internal fuel 2430 kg (5,357 lb); external fuel up to 1500 kg (3,307 lb) in three 500-litre (132-US gal) drop tanks; maximum ordnance 2800 kg (6,173 lb)
Speed: maximum level speed 'clean' at 11000 m (36,090 ft) 1020 km/h (551 kt; 634 mph) and at sea level 1130 km/h (610 kt; 702 mph); maximum cruising speed at 11000 m (36,090 ft) 743 km/h (401 kt; 462 mph)
Range: ferry range 712 nm (820 miles; 1320 km) with two drop tanks; combat radius 282 km (324 nm; 522 miles) on a hi-lo-hi attack mission with four cluster bombs and one drop tank, or 248 nm (286 miles; 460 km) on a hi-lo-hi attack mission with four 500-kg (1,102-lb) air mines and one drop tank, or 200 nm (230 miles; 370 km) on a hi-lo-hi attack mission with eight 250-kg (551-lb) bombs and one drop tank
Performance: maximum rate of climb at sea level 5340 m (17,520 ft) per minute; climb to 6000 m (19,685 ft) in 1 minute 20 seconds; service ceiling 15000 m (49,210 ft); take-off run 880 m (2,888 ft) with four cluster bombs; take-off distance to 15 m (50 ft) 1255 m (4,118 ft) at normal take-off weight; landing distance from 15 m (50 ft) 1295 m (4,249 ft) at normal landing weight; landing run 755 m (2,477 ft) at normal landing weight without brake chute or 530 m (1,739 ft) at normal landing weight with brake chute
g limits: -4.2 to +8

This early IAR-93A (note wing fences and ventral fins) wears the original Romanian air force insignia. The IAR-93As were virtually identical to early J-22 Oraos, differing only in minor avionics items.

One of the 20 J-22 Orao 1s taxis in after a sortie, still trailing its brake chute. These aircraft were powered by non-afterburning Viper engines and have been relegated to reconnaissance duties with an eskadrilla *near Zagreb. They are equipped with a centreline camera pod, as seen here.*

The range and power shortcomings of the two-seat Orao 1 were rectified by the improved Orao 2 trainer. This Orao 1 two-seater has been brought up to Orao 2D standards with the extended leading edges of the Orao 2, and afterburning engines, but retaining the original four-fence outer wing.

Sperry/North American QF-86 Sabre

North American Aviation Inc., established in 1928, merged with the Rockwell-Standard Corporation in September 1967 to form the North American Rockwell Corporation

Undeniably one of the great warplanes of history, the **North American F-86 Sabre** is now used primarily as a drone by the **US Navy**. Surplus USAF/ANG **F-86H** aircraft provided the initial basis for conversion, but the only version in current use is the **QF-86F**, primarily ex-JASDF and -RoKAF aircraft converted to drone status under a programme managed by Sperry. Although Sabres are expended during live missile tests, the US Navy maintains sufficient stocks to keep the type in service for some years yet. The two operating units are at Point Mugu and China Lake in California, both part of the Naval Air Warfare Center/Weapons Division.

Elsewhere, Sabres are used as civilian 'warbirds' on the air show circuit, but a handful continue in use for military duties. **Corporate Jets Inc.** operates a pair of Orenda 14-engined Canadair-assembled

Sabre Mk 6s as target tugs from Decimomannu, Sardinia, operating occasionally from other NATO air bases. Grupo Aéreo de Caza 32 of the **Fuerza Aérea Boliviana** at Santa Cruz retains the F-86E, but these are seldom flown, pilots instead using the T-33 to maintain currency.

SPECIFICATION

Sperry (North American) QF-86F Sabre
Wing: span 38 ft 9.5 in (11.82 m); aspect ratio 4.8; area 313.40 sq ft (29.12 m2)
Fuselage and tail: length 37 ft 6 in (11.43 m); height 14 ft 8.75 in (4.49 m)
Powerplant: one General Electric J47-GE-27 turbojet rated at 5,970 lb st (26.56 kN) dry
Weights: empty 11,125 lb (5046 kg); normal take-off 15,198 lb (6893 kg)
Speed: maximum level speed 'clean' at sea level

589 kt (678 mph; 1091 km/h)
Performance: maximum rate of climb at sea level 9,800 ft (2987 m) per minute

A Corporate Jets Canadair-manufactured Sabre Mk 6 taxies out for a gunnery training hop, carrying an underwing target winch.

Sperry/Tracor/North American QF-100 Super Sabre

The **F-100** was a stalwart of the USAF for many years. A total of 340 was earmarked for conversion to drone status for use in air defence exercises and missile tests. The first 100 were **QF-100D**s converted by Sperry, but subsequent conversions, including some two-seat **QF-100F** aircraft, have been undertaken by **Tracor Flight Systems** at Mojave, CA. This total included ex-Turkish and ex-USAF aircraft.

QF-100s can be flown in piloted or pilotless ('nolo' – no live operator) mode, and many have been expended by the two **USAF** operating units (the 6585th TG at Holloman AFB, NM, and the 82nd Tactical Aerial Targets Squadron of the 475th Weapons Evaluation Group at Tyndall AFB). QF-106 and QF-4 drones are replacing the QF-100s.

SPECIFICATION

Sperry (North American) QF-100 Super Sabre
Wing: span 38 ft 9.5 in (11.82 m); aspect ratio 3.91; area 385.00 sq ft (35.77 m2)
Fuselage and tail: length excluding probe 47 ft

1.25 in (14.357 m); height 16 ft 2.67 in (4.945 m)
Powerplant: one Pratt & Whitney J57-P-21A turbojet rated at 11,700 lb st (52.04 kN) dry and 16,950 lb st (75.4 kN) with afterburning

Weights: mission take-off 31,000 lb (14062 kg)
Fuel and load: internal fuel 770 US gal (2915 litres); external fuel two 450-US gal (1703-litre) drop tanks
Speed: maximum level speed 'clean' at 36,000 ft

(10975 m) 750 kt (864 mph; 1390 km/h) and at sea level 669 kt (770 mph; 1239 km/h)
Range: typical range 521 nm (600 miles; 966 km); operational radius 120 nm (138 miles; 222 km) under radar control; endurance between 40 and 55 minutes
Performance: maximum rate of climb at sea level 16,550 ft (5045 m) per minute; service ceiling 50,000 ft (15240 m); minimum operating height 200 ft (60 m)

The 475th WEG at Tyndall 'flies' target drones on behalf of the AWDC, and in support of William Tell gunnery/missile competitions. QF-100s wear high-visibility orange wingtips, noses, tailfins and tailplanes, and are fitted with underwing pylons for chaff/flare dispensers and propane burners to increase IR signature.

Sukhoi Su-7 'Fitter-A/B'

Sukhoi Design Bureau Aviation Scientific-Industrial Complex, 23A Polikarpov Street, Moscow 125284, Russia

From December 1949, the Sukhoi OKB was closed on the orders of Stalin to punish Sukhoi for the failure of a jet fighter prototype. Sukhoi and his team transferred to Tupolev, where they worked on their own projects until the death of Stalin, when permission was given to reopen the bureau. During his time at Tupolev, Sukhoi had worked on two configurations which he dubbed S (swept wing, 60-62° sweep) and T (delta wing, 57-60° sweep). All subsequent prototypes were numerically designated with an S- or T- prefix.

The first product of the reopened bureau was the **S-1**, prototype of the **Su-7**. This was designed as an air-to-air fighter, but the existence of the smaller, more agile MiG-21 prompted a redesign for the ground attack role. The resulting **S-2** was followed by a series of pre-production aircraft, culminating in the **S-22** which formed the basis of the production **Su-7B** (Bombardirovschkik, or fighter-bomber). Powered by a Lyul'ka AL-7 turbojet and with a variable shock cone in the pitot intake, the Su-7 was capable of speeds of up to Mach 1.6, but fuel consumption was excessive, and even with two underfuselage fuel tanks radius of action was unimpressive.

The Su-7B was armed with a pair of Nudelmann Richter NR-30 cannon in the wingroots, and had a retractable box con-

taining 32 spin-stabilised rockets in the belly. UV-8-32 rocket pods could be carried under each wing. The rocket box was deleted in the **Su-7BM** which followed, and which introduced the more powerful 99.12-kN (22,282-lb st) Lyul'ka AL-7F-1 engine. Underwing pylons were restressed for loads of up to 500 kg (1,102 lb) and were plumbed for the carriage of fuel tanks. The avionics were improved, and a pair of side-by-side cable ducts was added above the fuselage. The pitot probe gained yaw vanes and was moved from the top of the intake to a '10 o'clock' position. The designation

Su-7BMK was applied to an export version.

In order to improve rough-field capability, Sukhoi developed the **Su-7BKL**, which became the standard version in **VVS** service. This introduced provision for SPRD-110 assisted take-off rockets, a new brake chute fairing at the base of the tailfin which housed new twin brake parachutes, and also featured redesigned trailing-edge flaps. The undercarriage was redesigned, with a new low-pressure nosewheel which necessitated the provision of bulged nosewheel doors, and the addition of small skis on shock struts outboard of each mainwheel. These could

be extended to bear almost the full weight of the aircraft on soft ground, or retracted when operating from a hard surface.

Two-seat trainer versions were designated **Su-7U** and **Su-7UM** (based on the BM airframe) and received the NATO reporting name **'Moujik'**. Su-7BMs and Su-7Us remain in service in **Algeria** and perhaps in **Iraq**, and Su-7BKLs may serve in **North Korea**. In early 1994, the **Czech** and **Slovak Republics** still had a handful of Su-7s on charge, probably as ground instructional airframes.

In the former Soviet Union, a handful of Su-7s remain in service for test duties. This Su-7U was used as an ejection seat test aircraft, with the test seat (and an instrumented dummy) in the rear cockpit.

Sukhoi Su-7 'Fitter-A/B'

SPECIFICATION

Sukhoi Su-7BMK 'Fitter-A'
Wing: span 8.93 m (29 ft 3.5 in); aspect ratio 2.89; area 27.60 m² (297.09 sq ft)
Fuselage and tail: length 17.37 m (57 ft 0 in)

including probe; height 4.57 m (15 ft 0 in)
Powerplant: one NPO Saturn (Lyul'ka) AL-7F-1 turbojet rated at 68.65 kN (15,432 lb st) dry and 99.12 kN (22,282 lb st) with afterburning
Weights: empty equipped 8620 kg (19,004 lb); normal take-off 12000 kg (26,455 lb); maximum take-off 13500 kg (29,762 lb)

Fuel and load: internal fuel 2350 kg (5,181 lb); external fuel up to two 600-litre (158.5-US gal) and two 1800- or 900-litre (457.5- or 237.75-US gal) drop tanks; maximum ordnance 2500 kg (5,511 lb)
Speed: maximum level speed 'clean' at 11000 m (36,090 ft) 1700 km/h (916 kt; 1,055 mph) and at sea level 1350 km/h (729 kt; 840 mph)

Range: ferry range 1450 km (782 nm; 901 miles) with drop tanks; combat radius 345 km (186 nm; 214 miles) on a hi-lo-hi attack mission with a 1000-kg (2,205-lb) warload and two drop tanks
Performance: maximum rate of climb at sea level about 9120 m (29,920 ft) per minute; service ceiling 15150 m (49,705 ft); take-off run 880 m (2,887 ft)

Sukhoi Su-15 'Flagon'

The career of the **Sukhoi Su-15 'Flagon'** is drawing to a close, with only a handful of **PVO** regiments remaining active in Ukraine, Siberia and other remote regions. The type has been replaced by more modern interceptors, including the Su-27 and the MiG-31.

The Su-15 was of enormous importance, serving as the standard PVO interceptor at bases across the length and breadth of the former USSR. When the Korean Airlines Boeing 747 (Flight KE007) was shot down in September 1983, after overflying the Kamchatka Peninsula, it was no surprise that the fighter involved was an Su-15.

Of similar configuration to the earlier Su-9 and Su-11, the Su-15 was a larger aircraft, powered by twin R-25 engines and

Sukhoi Su-15TM 'Flagon-F'

This Sukhoi Su-15UM 'Flagon-G' is one of those used by the LII Gromov Flight Research Centre at Zhukhovskii for test and trials work. A handful of two-seat 'Flagons' also remain in use to support the dwindling number of PVO Su-15 interceptors.

with a large search radar occupying the nose, necessitating the use of separate lateral air intakes on each side of the fuselage.

The prototype, designated **T-58**, first flew in 1961 in the hands of Vladimir Ilyushin, and was followed by a pre-production batch of similar aircraft, designated **Su-15** and allocated the reporting name **'Flagon-A'** by NATO. The reporting name **'Flagon-B'** was allocated to the **T-58VD**, a one-off STOL research aircraft with a redesigned wing having reduced span on the outer panels, and with three RD-36-35 lift jets in the fuselage. This made its maiden flight during 1966 and was demonstrated at Domodyedovo in July 1967. The **Su-15U** was a tandem two-seat trainer version of the basic fighter, with the instructor's cockpit in place of the No. 1 fuselage fuel tank and with separate upward-hinging canopies over the cockpits. This trainer variant was dubbed **'Flagon-C'** by NATO.

The first 'second-generation' Su-15 was the **Su-15M**, which introduced a new wing based on that of the T-58VD with extended ailerons, and a tailplane with reduced anhedral. This was called **'Flagon-D'** by NATO.

'Flagon-E', introduced in 1973, superseded the earlier variant. This was powered by a pair of R-13F-300 engines, and featured increased internal fuel capacity. To cope with the increased weight, the undercarriage was strengthened, and a new twin-wheel nose gear was introduced, with bulged doors. Extra underwing pylons allowed the carriage of up to four R-60s (AA-8 'Aphids') in addition to the K-8 (AA-3 'Anab') missiles on the outboard pylons. Alternatively, each underfuselage pylon was stressed for the UPK-23-250 cannon pod or

an external fuel tank.

The **Su-15TM 'Flagon-F'** introduced the Taifun radar, which required a shorter ogival radome in place of the conical radome fitted to earlier variants. It was powered by a pair of R-13F2-300 engines and entered service during 1974. The two-seat trainer version with Taifun radar and the new wing is designated **Su-15UM**, and has the reporting name **'Flagon-G'**.

Western speculation that the designation **Su-21** was applied to the later 'Flagons' has since proved incorrect.

In 1994 a confirmed Su-15 user is **Ukraine**, which has two units operational. These are the 62nd Fighter Aviation Regiment at Bel'bek and the 636th Fighter Aviation Regiment at Kramatorsk.

SPECIFICATION

Sukhoi Su-15TM 'Flagon-F'
Wing: span 10.53 m (34 ft 6.6 in); aspect ratio 3.08; wing area 36.00 m² (387.51 sq ft)
Fuselage and tail: length 20.50 m (67 ft 3.1 in); height 5.00 m (16 ft 5 in); tailplane span 6.10 m (20 ft 0.2 in)
Powerplant: two MNPK 'Soyuz' (Tumanskii) R-13F2-300 turbojets each rated at 40.21 kN (9,039 lb st) dry and 69.63 kN (15,653 lb st) with afterburning
Weights: empty 12250 kg (27,006 lb); normal take-off 18000 kg (39,683 lb); maximum take-off 20000 kg (44,092 lb)
Speed: maximum level speed 'clean' at 11000 m (36,090 ft) 2655 km/h (1,433 kt; 1,650 mph)
Range: ferry range 2250 km (1,214 nm; 1,398 miles) with drop tanks; combat radius 745 km (371 nm; 450 miles) on a hi-hi-hi interception mission
Performance: maximum rate of climb at sea level 13700 m (44,948 ft) per minute; service ceiling 20000 m (65,615 ft); take-off run about 460 m (1,509 ft) at MTOW

Sukhoi Su-17/-20 'Fitter-C'

While the original Su-7 'Fitter' was highly prized for its handling, robust and rugged airframe and outright performance, it proved deficient in range and short take-off/landing capability. It was decided to produce an improved version with a variable-geometry wing. Sukhoi used the same TSAGI-developed VG wing configuration as Tupolev used for the Tu-22M, with pivots outboard. This allowed the existing wing-mounted main undercarriage to be retained and minimised shifting of the centre of lift as the wing swept. Vladimir Ilyushin flew the **S-22I** (also known as the **Su-7IG**) for the first time on 2 August 1966, and it was publicly displayed at Domodyedovo in July 1967. The Su-7IG was assumed by many

Western observers to be a mere VG research aircraft, and not the effective prototype for a new swing-wing fighter-bomber, although it was allocated the NATO reporting name **'Fitter-B'**.

The Su-7IG (a converted Su-7BMK) was followed by two squadrons worth of pre-production **Su-17**s (with the OKB designation **S-32**). These had a longer forward fuselage based on that of the Su-7U and a large, bulged fuselage spine like the definitive **'Fitter-C'**, but retained the external cable ducts of the Su-7BM and BMK/BKL, and probably retained the same AL-7F-1 engine rated at 68.64 kN (15,432 lb st). The first series production variant was designated **Su-17M** (OKB designation **S-32M**)

and shared the same NATO reporting name of 'Fitter-C'. The Su-17M differed primarily in that it featured the 20 per cent more powerful (and more fuel efficient) AL-21F-3 engine rated at 110.32 kN (24,802 lb st), and introduced a new nav/attack system, which received inputs from twin nose-mounted pitot booms.

An AoA vane (located on the port side of the cockpit) helps the 'Fitter-C' to land some 62 mph (100 km/h) slower than the Su-7BMK, reducing the requirement for very heavy braking and allowing a single brake chute to replace the original Su-7's twin chutes. Nine hardpoints are provided: one on the centreline, tandem pairs on the fuselage 'shoulders' and pairs under the fixed inboard wing sections.

A handful of 'Fitter-Cs' were built for reconnaissance duties, with provision for mounting a variety of multi-sensor reconnaissance pods, under the designation **Su-17R** or **Su-20R**.

OPERATORS

'Fitter-Cs' remain in front-line service in Poland and, under the export designation **Su-20** (OKB designation **S-32MK**), were delivered to Afghanistan, Algeria, Angola, Egypt, Iraq, North Korea, Syria and Vietnam.

Initial deliveries to Poland of the variable-geometry 'Fitter' were of the Su-20 'Fitter-C' version, powered by the Lyul'ka AL-21 turbojet. Su-20s remain in service with a regiment based at Pila, in north-west Poland.

Two ex-Egyptian Su-20s were delivered to Germany in 1985 for evaluation. Soviet Su-17 'Fitter-Cs' have probably been retired.

SPECIFICATION

Sukhoi Su-17M 'Fitter-C'
Wing: span 13.80 m (45 ft 3 in) spread and 10.00 m (32 ft 10 in) swept; aspect ratio 4.8 spread and 2.7 swept; area 40.00 m² (430.57 sq ft) and about 37.00 m² (398.28 sq ft) swept
Fuselage and tail: length 18.75 m (61 ft 6.25 in) including probes; height 5.00 m (16 ft 5 in)
Powerplant: one NPO Saturn (Lyul'ka) AL-21F-3 turbojet rated at 76.49 kN (17,196 lb st) dry and 110.32 kN (24,802 lb st) with afterburning, plus provision for two RATO units
Weights: normal take-off 16400 kg (36,155 lb); maximum take-off 19500 kg (42,989 lb)
Fuel and load: internal fuel 4550 litres (1,202 US gal); external fuel up to four 800-litre (211-US gal) drop tanks; maximum ordnance 4250 kg (9,369 lb) theoretical and 1000 kg (2,205 lb) practical when drop tanks are carried
Speed: maximum level speed 'clean' at 11000 m (36,090 ft) 2220 km/h (1,198 kt; 1,379 mph) and at sea level 1285 km/h (693 kt; 798 mph)
Range: 2300 km (1,240 nm; 1,430 miles) at high altitude or 1400 km (755 nm; 870 miles) at low altitude; combat radius 685 km (370 nm; 426 miles) on a hi-lo-hi attack mission with a 2000-kg (4,409-lb) warload, or 445 km (241 nm; 277 miles) on a lo-lo-lo attack mission with a 2000-kg (4,409-lb) warload
Performance: maximum rate of climb at sea level 13800 m (45,276 ft) per minute; service ceiling 15200 m (49,870 ft); take-off run 900 m (2,953 ft) at maximum take-off weight; landing run 950 m (3,117 ft) at normal landing weight

Sukhoi Su–17M–2/–3/–22M–3 'Fitter-D/-F-/H/-J'

Known to the OKB as the **S-32M2**, the **Su-17M-2D 'Fitter-D'** entered production in 1974. Based on the airframe of the 'Fitter-C', it introduced a slightly lengthened, slightly drooping nose and a revised avionics suite. The Su-7's SRD-5M ranging radar was finally abandoned, and the intake centrebody was fixed in one position instead of being able to move in and out. This had little effect except on absolute Mach number attainable at high level. The conical centrebody now served as the location of a Klem laser rangefinder (which probably also functions as a marked target seeker). A fairing was added below the nose to accommodate the new Doppler and, according to some reports, a terrain-avoidance radar. The latter seems unlikely.

A slightly sanitised version, with a new dorsal fin fillet and possibly without a laser rangefinder, was built for export under the designation **Su-17M-2K** (or **S-32M-2K**). The **'Fitter-F'** was powered by a Tumanskii/Khatchaturov R-29BS-300 engine (as fitted to some MiG-23 variants) and thus required a slightly bulged, slightly shortened rear fuselage. Operators have included **Angola**, **Libya** and **Peru**.

The S-32M-2 was soon replaced by the **Su-22M-3**, which was based on the airframe of the two-seat **'Fitter-G'** trainer (described separately). The Su-22M-3 featured the same deepened forward fuselage and tall, squared-off tailfin and removable

Tyres stream clouds of smoke as an Su-22M-3 'Fitter-H' lands at Taszar, making a characteristically heavy, no-flare arrival. Hungarian 'Fitter-Hs' serve with the 3rd ('Bumble Bee') squadron of the Kapos wing.

ventral fin, but with two wingroot cannon and only a single cockpit. The deeper fuselage allowed the Doppler to be fitted internally, behind a flush dielectric panel, and the undernose fairing of the S-32M-2 was deleted. To improve self-defence capability, a dedicated AAM launch rail is added beneath each inner wing, between the two existing pylons, and this carries an R-60 (AA-8 'Aphid') or K-13 (AA-2 'Atoll') IR-homing AAM. Internal fuel capacity is considerably increased, and can be augmented by up to four external fuel tanks.

Designated **Su-17M-3** in service (NATO reporting name **'Fitter-H'**), the aircraft was delivered only to **Frontal Aviation**. The very similar **Su-22M-3K** (mostly fitted with the R-29BS engine) was exported to **Angola**, **Hungary**, **Libya**, **Peru** and both **Yemen** republics.

SPECIFICATION

Sukhoi Su-17M-2 'Fitter-D'
generally similar to the Sukhoi Su-17M 'Fitter-C' except in the following particulars:
Fuselage and tail: length 19.13 m (62 ft 9.2 in) including probes
Performance: take-off run 900 m (2,953 ft) at maximum take-off weight

Variable-geometry wings enable the Su-17's field performance to be kept within acceptable limits. Hungary's 12 'Fitter-Hs' replaced the earlier Su-7.

Sukhoi Su–17UM–2 'Fitter-E' and Su–17/–22UM–3 'Fitter-G'

The first two-seat 'Fitter' trainer was the **Su-17UM-2D** (bureau designation **U-32**), given the reporting name **'Fitter-E'** by NATO. This was based on the airframe of the Su-17M-2D but with no increase in fuselage length. The fuselage was deepened and 'drooped' and the windscreen was moved forward, giving a better view forward and down. This location of the forward cockpit was to be retained on all subsequent single-seat variants. The port cannon was not fitted, but all avionics, including the laser rangefinder, were retained. The Su-17UM-2D was powered by the Lyul'ka AL-21F-3 engine, while export aircraft, designated **Su-17UM-2K**, used the R-29BS-300, as used in various 'Flogger' variants. The latter type was exported to **Afghanistan**, **Algeria**, **Angola**, **Iraq**, **Libya**, **Peru**, **Vietnam** and both **Yemen** republics.

The next two-seater (given the OKB designation **S-52**) was based on the tall-tailed airframe of the Su-17M-3. The **'Fitter-G'** did not retain full operational capability, having had some avionics items deleted, but is by far the fastest Su-17, being capable of reaching Mach 2.1, while single-seaters are limited to Mach 1.7. The instructor has a sophisticated system for simulating the workings of the weapons delivery system, and generating synthetic emergen-

This Sukhoi Su-17UM 'Fitter-G' was one of those based at Kunmanderas, east of Budapest, which housed a Soviet reconnaissance/EW regiment equipped with Su-24MR 'Fencer-Es' and Su-17M-4 'Fitter-Ks'. Like most single-seat 'Fitter' units, it had a handful of two-seaters on charge for conversion, continuation and instrument training. This aircraft carries ECM pods on its inboard underwing pylons, perhaps indicating an Elint or 'Wild Weasel' role. Long-range fuel tanks are carried outboard.

cies. Those for export customers were all designated **Su-22UM-3K**, those for Afghanistan, Czechoslovakia, East Germany, Hungary, and Poland retaining Lyul'ka engines, the others having the bulged rear fuselage and Tumanskii/Khatchaturov engines. Su-22UM-3Ks were exported to all 'Fitter-H', 'Fitter-J' and 'Fitter-K' operators including **Afghanistan**, **Angola**, **Czechoslovakia**, **East Germany**, **Hungary**, **Libya**, **Peru**, **Poland**, **Syria** and the **Yemen** republics.

Sukhoi Su–17M–4 and Su–22M–4 'Fitter-K'

Under the OKB designation **S-54**, a new 'Fitter' variant, with new avionics and compatibility with an even wider range of weapons, was developed for the Soviet air forces and for export. The **Su-22M-4 'Fitter-K'** is externally identifiable by a prominent ram-air inlet projecting forward from the finroot. This increases cooling airflow to the afterburner. Ram air inlets on the sides of the rear fuselage were enlarged and repositioned at the same time.

Since the aircraft was optimised for high speed at low level, with no requirement for high-level performance, the intake centrebody is fixed, and a removable ventral fin is fitted below the rear fuselage. (The latter feature has been retrofitted to some earlier 'Fitter-Hs' and 'Fitter-Js'.)

New avionics included a new CVM 20-22 mission computer and PrNK-54 navigation system (using the LORAN-equivalent RSDN and the TACAN-equivalent A-312), which reduced pilot workload and improved navigational and weapons delivery accuracy. Other avionics include a DISS-7 Doppler, a Klem-45 laser rangefinder, an ASP-17BC gunsight, an IKV-8 inertial platform, an ARK-22 radio compass, an SRO-2 IFF system, an SO-69 transponder and an SPO-15LE (Sirena) RWR.

WEAPON OPTIONS

In its primary ground attack role, the Su-22M-4 can carry a wide range of freefall bombs and podded and unpodded unguided rocket projectiles ranging in calibre from 57 mm to 330 mm. For precision attacks from stand-off range, the aircraft can carry a variety of air-to-surface missiles, including the radio command-guided or laser-homing, or anti-radiation Kh-25 (AS-10 'Karen' and AS-12 'Kegler') and Kh-29, and the Kh-58E (AS-11 'Kilter') anti-radar missile. When the latter is used, a box-like BA-58 Vjuga emission location system pod is carried on the centreline. Later Su-22M-4s have a TV display to allow the use of TV-guided missiles, and this can be retrofitted to earlier aircraft.

The new variant has the auxiliary underwing AAM pylon also seen on some 'Fitter-Hs', located between the two normal underwing pylons. This is normally used to carry an R-60 (AA-8 'Aphid') IR-homing air-to-air missile, but can also take a K-13 (AA-2 'Atoll'). To further improve self-defence capability, four 32-round upward-firing ASO chaff/flare dispensers can be scabbed on to either side of the tailfin, augmenting

Sukhoi Su-17M-4 and Su-22M-4 'Fitter-K'

Afghanistan received a number of Su-22M-4s which were probably directly transferred from the Soviet Union. A disaffected pilot flew this 'Fitter-K' to Pakistan.

This sharkmouthed 20th Guards Fighter-Bomber Regiment Su-17M-4 was based at Templin in the former East Germany until May 1994. It departed for Taganrog on the Black Sea and may possibly be reallocated to the AV-MF.

the two six-tube KDS-23 dispensers mounted flush with the dorsal spine.

For strafe attacks, the Su-22M-4's wingroot-mounted NR-30 30-mm cannon (each with 80 rounds) can be augmented by gun pods carried under the wings or fuselage. These can include the SPPU-22-01 (with 260 rounds), whose twin 23-mm barrels can be depressed, and which can be mounted facing forward or aft. The 'Fitter-K' can be used in the tactical reconnaissance role, carrying the same KKR

reconnaissance pod as has been applied to the 'Fitter-C' and 'Fitter-H'. This contains three optical cameras, flares and Elint modules, and is usually carried in association with the SPS ECM pod.

SPECIFICATION

Sukhoi Su-17M-4 'Fitter-K'
generally similar to the Sukhoi Su-17M 'Fitter-C' except in the following particulars:
Speed: maximum level speed 'clean' at sea level 1400 km/h (756 nm; 870 mph)
Range: combat radius 1150 km (621 nm; 715 miles) on a hi-lo-hi attack mission with a 2000-kg (4,409-lb) warload, or 700 km (378 nm; 435 miles) on a lo-lo-lo attack mission with a 2000-kg (4,409-lb) warload
Performance: service ceiling 15200 m (49,870 ft)

OPERATORS
'Fitter-Ks' are in widespread service with a number of air forces in the former Soviet Union. In Ukraine, about 130 serve with regiments at Ovruch and Limanskoye. Less than five aircraft each are operational with Azerbaijan and Byelorussia. More 'Fitter-Ks' are in service with Turkmenistan. The Su-22M-4 was exported to Poland, Czechoslovakia, the former East Germany and Afghanistan.

CAMOUFLAGE
Polish air force Su-22M-4s wear an effective green and brown colour scheme.

Sukhoi Su-22M-4 'Fitter-K'

This 'Fitter-K' wears the colourful markings of the Polskie Wojska Lotnicze (Polish air force). The 'Fitter-K' is the latest and most advanced 'Fitter', with much improved avionics and equipment. The aircraft appears to be fitted with the new K-36D seat, as used by the MiG-29 and Su-27.

DEFENSIVE ARMAMENT
Although its twin 30-mm cannon are primarily intended for strafing ground targets, they can be used against airborne targets ranging from enemy helicopters to opposing fighters. Additionally, the aircraft has the extra AAM pylons originally fitted to the Su-22M-3, carrying K-13 (AA 2 'Atoll'), R-60 (AA-8 'Aphid') and perhaps R-73 (AA-11 'Archer') IR homing AAMs.

SWING WINGS
Sukhoi adopted an outboard pivoting VG configuration (with a large wing glove and relatively small wing panels) to minimise the shift in aerodynamic centre as the wings sweep. It also allows fixed hardpoints to be mounted below the wing, and gives a suitably wide-track undercarriage.

WEAPON OPTIONS
The 'Fitter-K' retains eight dedicated weapons pylons, and these are used to carry a variety of stores, including the Type S-24 240-mm rocket, GSh-23L 23-mm cannon pods, UV-32-57 rocket pods, chemical weapons and the full range of 100-, 200-, 500- and even 1000-kg (220-, 440-, 1,102- or 2,204-lb) bombs, cluster, anti-runway, slick, retarded, incendiary or even tanks full of FAE or nuclear weapons.

ENGINE INSTALLATION
The 'Fitter-K' is powered by a Lyul'ka AL-21F-3 turbojet, but this is given increased cooling through a number of vents and intakes, most noticeably at the base of the fin.

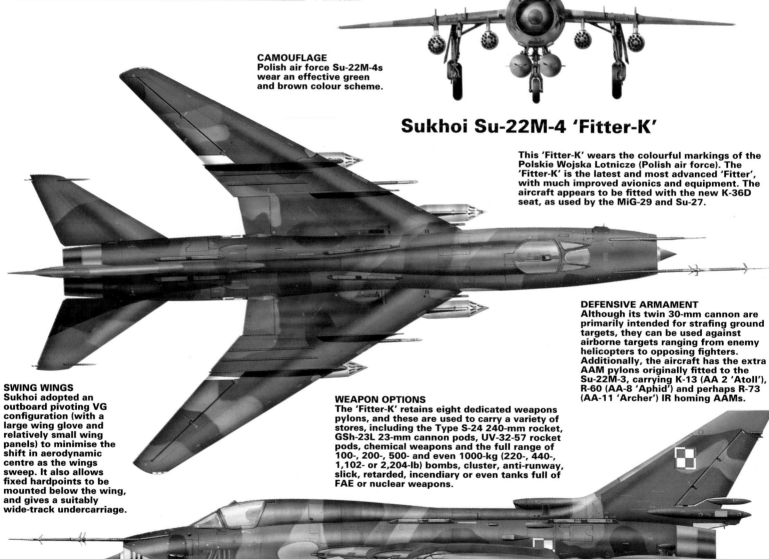

Sukhoi Su-24 'Fencer-A/-B/-C'

The increasing efficiency of SAMs and interceptors led aircraft designers all over the world to the same conclusion. To penetrate enemy defences one would have to fly 'under the radar' at very low altitude, using terrain masking to hide from probing radars. The Sukhoi OKB was entrusted with the task of developing such a bomber as a replacement for the Ilyushin Il-28 and Yak-28 in Soviet service.

The requirement was extremely ambitious, calling for an aircraft with supersonic performance (even at low level), capable of day and night/adverse weather operation, and able to find and attack fixed and mobile targets with pinpoint accuracy using manual and automatic control modes. Furthermore, the aircraft was expected to be able to undertake a secondary photographic reconnaissance role, and to destroy enemy transport, liaison and observation aircraft using IR-homing AAMs or its built-in cannon. Mindful of the vulnerability of long fixed runways, the requirement also specified that the aircraft should be able to operate from unpaved airstrips of limited size.

The latter part of the requirement led Sukhoi to develop a delta-winged VTOL bomber, with separate cruise and lift engines. This was built as the **T-6-1** and first flew in June 1967. The wing was of compound leading-edge sweep, and was based on the planform used by the T-58VD. This aircraft proved unsuccessful, and planned participation at Domodyedovo was cancelled because of the aircraft's atrocious handling characteristics. The aircraft was later converted to STOL configuration, with the lift jets removed, and with downturned wingtips, prominent ventral fins and enormous new slotted flaps. The vertical tailfin was also shortened, cut off immediately above the top of the rudder. In its later configuration the aircraft proved more practical, and bore some resemblance to the British BAC TSR.Mk 2, but the large size of the wing gave a poor low-level ride. "It was like being dragged across a washboard," complained one Sukhoi test pilot.

The success of the S-22I (Su-17) and Mikoyan 23-11 pointed the way forward, which was to adopt a variable-geometry wing. This was applied to a second T-6 prototype (the **T-6-2IG**), retaining the same basic fuselage and equipment. The vertical fin was restored to its original height, and the main undercarriage doors were modified to serve as airbrakes. The removal of the heavy lift jets from the centre fuselage left space for extra fuel or weapons. The wing, like that of the broadly contemporary F-111, incorporated similar full-span leading-edge slats and double-slotted flaps. Ailerons are not fitted, the Su-24 being controlled in roll by the all-moving tailerons. The wing can be swept forward to 16° for take-off

and landing, giving an approach speed of 124 kt (230 km/h; 143 mph) and consequent good STOL capability. At the other extreme the wing can be swept fully back to 69° (compared to the F-111's 72½°), with intermediate settings of 35° and 45°. The aircraft made its maiden flight during May 1970 and may have been powered by a pair of AL-7F-1 turbojets. It was given the cover designation **Su-15M**, and mistranslation of this led to initial Western reports erroneously referring to the aircraft as the **Su-19**.

The production **Su-24 'Fencer-A'** was powered by a pair of Perm/Soloviev AL-21F-3 turbofans. These were originally fed by intakes with variable ramps, which allowed Mach 2.18 performance at high level. Because the Su-24 spends its entire life at low level, where such Mach numbers are impossible, the actuators have since been removed to save weight and reduce maintenance requirements. This disables the variable intakes and restricts top speed to about Mach 1.35, but has virtually no effect on low-level performance.

The Su-24 was designed around the Soviet Union's first integrated avionics system, with a bombsight, weapons control system and navigation complex linked by computer. This made possible major weight savings, but required huge advances in processing speed and capacity. The total system allowed fully automatic terrain-following flight and facilitated automatic attacks. The Su-24 was also the first Soviet aircraft to be equipped with the zero-zero Severin K-36D ejection seat, and also featured a command ejection system which could be actuated by either crew member. This

allowed the minimum time separation between ejections while still ensuring that seat collisions could not occur.

Relatively minor changes in equipment fit resulted in the allocation of new NATO reporting names, although the Soviet designation remained the same, and NATO's different variants were probably regarded in the USSR as a single sub-type, albeit with minor differences in equipment. The **'Fencer-B'** had a rear fuselage more closely following the jet pipes, by comparison with the 'boxed-in', slab-sided rear fuselage of the prototypes and 'Fencer-A'. It also introduced a cylindrical brake chute fairing below the base of the rudder.

'Fencer-C'

The **'Fencer-C'** is similar to the 'Fencer-B', and is distinguishable only by the triangular RWR fairings (similar to those fitted to the Su-24M 'Fencer-D') on the sides of the fin tip and on the engine intakes extending ahead of the wing leading edge. 'Fencer-Cs' were first noted in 1981. Contrary to early Western reports, apart from a handful of early '-As' all three sub-types have a small air intake at the base of the fin leading edge and the same kink in the tailfin leading edge higher up, which is level with the top of the rudder.

Because a control column can easily be fitted in front of the WSO, no dedicated dual-controlled trainer variant of the Su-24 has ever been developed.

It is believed that the Su-24 entered squadron service during 1974, and began to be deployed outside the USSR in 1979 when a regiment of 'Fencer-Bs' deployed to

Templin in East Germany for operational evaluation. In 1984 a regiment began operations over Afghanistan (flying from airfields in the USSR), participating in air strikes against rebel targets in the Panjshir Valley with freefall bombs and precision-guided missiles. During the 1980s, Su-24 bomber regiments were based in Germany (at Grossenhain, Templin and Brand), in Poland (at Zagan, Szprotawa and Krzywa), and in Hungary, with more regiments in the Western part of the USSR.

'Fencer-Bs' and 'Fencer-Cs' remain in widespread front-line use with the **Russian air force**, and with the air arms of a number of former Soviet states. One of three front-line Su-24 bomber regiments withdrawn from Poland in 1992 was equipped solely with these 'early models', for example.

WEAPON OPTIONS

The early 'Fencers' were armed with a single GSh-6-23M cannon in the starboard side of the lower fuselage, with the muzzle covered by an eyelid shutter. Ammunition was housed in a port underfuselage fairing. There are hardpoints for a centreline and two underfuselage pylons, with further pylons under the fixed inboard sections of the wing, and with swivelling pylons under the outboard panels. The aircraft could carry the freefall TN-1000 and TN-1200 nuclear bombs, and a variety of conventional freefall bombs and guided ASMs.

This Osla-based 'Fencer-B' Su-24 appears to have a non-standard nose sensor, with side-by-side pitots below the curved 'hockey stick'. It also seems to have an extra projection on the undernose sensor.

Three Su-24 regiments were based in Poland until they were withdrawn in 1992/93. This Osla-based 'Fencer-B' carries white two-digit tactical codes.

Sukhoi Su-24 'Fencer-A/-B/-C'

Sukhoi Su-24 'Fencer-C'

An underside view of a Poland-based 'Fencer-C' (note the intake-mounted triangular RWR fairing) shows no provision for built-in cameras or other optical or electro-optical sensors. There may, of course, be a SLAR in the forward fuselage, with an overpainted radome, or podded reconnaissance equipment may be carried. Alternatively, these aircraft may serve as the attack half of a 'Foxbat-F'/ 'Fencer-C' hunter/killer 'Wild Weasel' team.

SPECIFICATION

Sukhoi Su-24 'Fencer-C'

Wing: span 17.63 m (57 ft 10 in) spread and 10.36 m (34 ft 0 in) swept; estimated area 42.00 m² (452.10 sq ft)
Fuselage and tail: length 24.53 m (80 ft 5.75 in)

including probe; wheel track 3.70 m (12 ft 1.5 in)
Powerplant: two NPO Saturn (Lyul'ka) AL-21F-3A turbojets each rated at 76.49 kN (17,196 lb st) dry and 110.32 kN (24,802 lb st) with afterburning thrust
Weights: estimated empty equipped 19000 kg (41,887 lb); normal take-off 36000 kg (79,365 lb); maximum take-off 39700 kg (87,522 lb)
Fuel and load: estimated internal fuel about 13000

litres (3,434 US gal); external fuel up to four 1250-litre (330-US gal) drop tanks; maximum ordnance 8000 kg (17,637 lb)
Speed: maximum level speed 'clean' at 11000 m (36,090 ft) 2320 km/h (1,251 kt; 1,441 mph) and at sea level 1470 km/h (793 kt; 913 mph)
Range: combat radius 1050 km (565 nm; 650 miles) on a hi-lo-hi attack mission with a 3000-kg (6,614-lb)

warload and two drop tanks, or 950 km (512 nm; 590 miles) on a lo-lo-hi attack mission with a 2500-kg (5,511-lb) warload, or more than 322 km (174 nm; 200 miles) on a lo-lo-lo attack mission with an 8000-kg (17,637-lb) warload
Performance: service ceiling 17500 m (57,415 ft); take-off run 1300 m (4,265 ft) at maximum take-off weight

Sukhoi **Su-24M and Su-24MK** 'Fencer-D'

Work on improving the Su-24's combat effectiveness began in 1975 (and continues today), eventually resulting in the **Su-24M 'Fencer-D'** which entered service in 1986. This introduced a retractable IFR probe above the nose, on the centreline immediately ahead of the windscreen, and the ability to carry a UPAZ-A buddy refuelling pod on the centreline. These modifications were intended to allow the Su-24 to carry a greater weapons load by taking off with partial fuel and topping up after take-off. The avionics suite was upgraded to allow the aircraft to carry a new generation of TV- and laser-guided weapons, to improve navigational and bombing accuracy, and to enhance survivability.

Most noticeably, the Su-24M received a new radar which is housed in a shortened, reshaped radome and tipped by a single simple pitot in place of the multiple fittings of the earlier variants. The Orion-A forward-looking attack radar is partnered by a Relief terrain-following radar. The latter is coupled to the SAU-6M1 AFCS, which allows fully

automatic terrain-following flight. Other elements of the PNS-24M sighting and navigation complex include the pilot's PPV HUD, the Kaira 24 laser and TV sighting system, the MIS-P/II inertial platform and the TsVU-10-058K digital computer.

The Kaira laser and TV designator/tracker gives compatibility with the newest Soviet ASMs, and is housed behind a glazed fairing on the centreline ahead of the gun and ammunition fairings. The Su-24M can also carry all of the weapons carried by the earlier 'Fencers'. Survivability is enhanced by the improved defensive aids, which include an SPO-15S RHAWS, an LO-82 missile launch warning system, an SPS-161 active ECM, and an APP-50 chaff/flare dispenser. SRZO IFF interrogator and SO-69 transponder are also incorporated.

Many 'Fencer-Ds' lack the large combined fences/underwing pylons which act as mountings for the chaff/flare dispensers, and such aircraft sometimes have chaff/flare launchers scabbed on above the rear fuselage, on each side of the tailfin. A hand-

ful of Su-24Ms in Soviet colours have been seen in this configuration, along with some (but definitely not all) export aircraft. Aircraft with these fences may qualify for the revised reporting name **'Fencer-D (Mod)'**. Export Su-24 'Fencer-Ds' are designated **Su-24MK**, and presumably have a downgraded avionics system, although reports that some Su-24MKs lack inflight-refuelling capability are believed to be erroneous.

OPERATORS

Su-24s were produced for Frontal Aviation and were assigned directly to Strategic Air Armies, and to Tactical Air Forces supporting fronts and regions. The break-up of the Soviet Union did not lead to a proliferation of new users, however, since Russia was careful to ensure that these advanced strike aircraft returned to Russia wherever possible. Current

operators of all 'Fencer' variants are as follows:
Russia: The Russian republic has some 480 bomber and 90 reconnaissance-tasked Su-24s. The 3rd BAP at Krzywa in Poland returned to Russia with its Su-24s, while the Su-24Ms of the 42nd Guards BAP at Zagan and the 89th BAP at Szprotawa returned to bases in the Eastern MD and near Kuban, respectively. East Germany-based Su-24s returned to Starokonstantinov in Ukraine and to a base in Russia (an unidentified unit formerly at Brand). In May 1992, Su-24MRs of the 164th Guards RAP moved from Kryzwa (Poland) to Staelewo near Smolensk. Germany-based 'Fencer-Es' of the 11 'Vitebski' RAP from Neu Welzow returned to Marinovka in Russia. Russia also has four Su-24MPs which were formerly with the 11th RAP.
Ukraine: The largest non-Russian operator is Ukraine, which has gained a large number (over 175) of attack-dedicated Su-24s. Units comprise the following BAPs: 7th BAP at Starokonstantinov (formerly at Grossenhain in East Germany), 727th BAP at Kanatovo, 69th BAP at Ovruch South-West, 806th BAP at Lutsk and 947th BAP at Dubno. Su-24MR units are the 511th RAP at Blagoyevo and the 48th RAP at Kolomyya. Eight Su-24MPs of the former 11th RAP are based with the 118th RAP at Chortkov

An Su-24M 'Fencer-D' takes off from Szprotawa in Poland. The manner in which the main gear doors can also act as airbrakes can be clearly seen. It carries a single rocket pod and a FAB-250 fragmentation bomb.

Sukhoi Su-24M 'Fencer-D'

An Su-24M rests on the flight line. The retractable inflight-refuelling probe is visible above the nose, immediately below the windscreen, and the Kaira laser and TV designator can be seen below the forward fuselage.

Azerbaijan: The Azeri republic also seized some 11 Su-24s when the USSR disintegrated. These are not believed to be in an airworthy condition.

Kazakhstan: Attack-tasked Su-24s serve with the 149th BAP at Nikolaevka, while reconnaissance Su-24s serve with the 39th RAP at Balkesh.

Export customers: Su-24MKs have been delivered to **Libya** (between six and 15 of the 18 ordered before relations cooled) and to **Iran** and **Iraq** (all 24 of the latter being absorbed into the Iranian air force after fleeing to Iran during Desert Storm), and 42 are believed to have been delivered to **Syria**. Both bomber and reconnaissance versions of the aircraft are being actively marketed.

SPECIFICATION

Sukhoi Su-24M 'Fencer-D'

Wing: span 17.63 m (57 ft 10 in) at 16° sweep and 10.36 m (34 ft 0 in) at 69° sweep; area 55.16 m² (593.75 sq ft) at 16° sweep and 51.00 m² (548.95 sq ft) at 69° sweep

Fuselage and tail: length 24.53 m (80 ft 5.75 in) including inflight-refuelling probe; height 6.19 m (20 ft 3 in);

Powerplant: two Perm/Soloviev (Lyul'ka) AL-21F-3A turbojets each rated at 109.83 kN (24,691 lb st) with afterburning thrust

Weights: empty equipped 22320 kg (49,206 lb); normal take-off 36000 kg ((79365 lb); maximum take-off 39700 kg (87,522 lb)

Fuel and load: internal fuel 11,700 litres (2574 Imp gal); maximum combat load 8000 kg (17,637 lb); normal combat load 3000 kg (6614 lb)

Speed: maximum level speed 'clean' at 11000 m (36,089 ft) Mach 1.35 and at low-level 1320 km/h (712 kt; 820 mph); maximum level speed at low-level with six FAB-500 bombs 1200 km/h (648 kt; 746 mph)

Range: ferry range 2500 km (1349 nm; 1553 miles) with maximum internal and external fuel and 4270 km (2304 nm; 2653 miles) with one in-flight refuelling; lo-lo-lo radius with six FAB-500 bombs 410 km (221 nm; 255 miles) without external fuel and 560 km (302 nm; 348 miles)

Performance: service ceiling 11000 m (36090 ft); take-off run between 1300-1400 m 4265-4593 ft); landing distance 950 m (3117 ft) with brake parachute

Sukhoi **Su-24MR** 'Fencer-E' and **Su-24MP** 'Fencer-F'

The Su-24 airframe was a natural choice when it came to looking for a replacement for the Yak-28 'Brewer' in the tactical and maritime reconnaissance and tactical electronic warfare roles, since it combined long range and excellent performance with the ability to carry a reasonable payload. The resulting **Su-24MR** was designed for the primary role of tactical reconnaissance using internal and podded sensors of various types, able to transmit reconnaissance data from some sensors to a ground station in real time. The aircraft also has secondary civilian roles of ecological, environmental, agricultural and forestry monitoring, and can be used in emergency situations.

The 30-mm cannon and Kaira laser/TV system are deleted, allowing the installation of an AP-402 panoramic camera in the

The Su-24MP has an undernose fairing and 'hockey-stick' aerials under the intakes, and is assigned the reporting name 'Fencer-F'. Only a handful (about a dozen) of these EW aircraft were built.

underside of the nose and an A-100 forward/oblique camera mounted in the floor of the port air intake duct. Working on the AP-402 is remarkably easy, since it can be dropped down on cables, complete with its hatch and window, giving all-round access. The AP-402 camera has a 90.5-mm lens and produces an 80-mm x 250-mm frame, with a linear resolution of 0.2 m at a height of 400 m (1,312 ft). The camera can be used at altitudes from 150 - 2000 m (492 - 6,562 ft) and at speeds of 600 - 1320 km/h (373 - 820 mph). Coverage is equivalent to 10x altitude. At the cost of limited film capacity, the Kadr (picture) device can be used, which allows a cassette of processed film to be parachuted to the ground. The A-100 camera has a 100-mm lens and can be used at altitudes down to 50 m (164 ft), producing a 75-mm frame.

Located immediately behind the AP-402 is an Aist-M (Stork-M) TV reconnaissance camera, covering a swath of ground equivalent to 9x aircraft height. This can transmit pictures back to the ground station using the VPS-1 broadband radio channel. The air-

craft is also fitted with an RDS BO Shtik (Bayonet) synthetic aperture side-looking radar which has a moving target indicator mode and a high resolution (5-m) mapping mode. Radar maps thus produced can be recorded on film. The radar can cover an area 4 - 28 km (2.5 - 17 miles) out from the aircraft and has two large flush antennas,

one on each side of the nose, immediately ahead of the windscreen. Another onboard sensor is the Zima (Winter) IR reconnaissance system. This can detect temperature differences as low as 0.3°C (1.8°F) and scans a strip equivalent to 3.4x aircraft height. It can downlink directly to ground stations (which must be within line-of-sight

The Su-24MR is a dedicated tactical reconnaissance model of the 'Fencer'. Emerging from overhaul at Novosibirsk, and still in primer finish, is this 'Fencer-E', complete with new fuselage chaff/flare dispensers.

Sukhoi Su-24MR 'Fencer-E'

One of the 11th Independent Reconnaissance Aviation Regiment's Su-24MR 'Fencer-Es' is seen leaving its base at Welzow in East Germany for its new home at Marinovka. The flush dielectric panels on the sides of the nose are clearly visible. Internal sensors are augmented by various pods.

range) using the VPS-1, or can record on film, using up to seven shades of grey. It is located in the starboard air intake duct.

Other reconnaissance sensors carried by the Su-24MR are podded, carried underwing or on the centreline. The largest of these is the 6-m (19.7-ft) long Shpil-2M (Needle-2M) laser reconnaissance pod which scans an area equivalent to 4x aircraft height. This can be used by day or night in VMC conditions, and offers outstanding resolution (0.25 m/0.82 ft). Data can be downlinked or recorded on film, which can be processed in flight. Alternatively the slab-sided Tanghazh Elint pod can be carried on the centreline. The final type of pod carried is the Efir-1M radiation detector, which contains two sensors, each with a 120° scanning angle. This can plot the extent of radioactive contamination on the

ground from an altitude of 500 m 1,640 ft), recording this on tape and transmitting data to ground stations. This much smaller pod (some 3 m/9.8 ft long) is normally carried on the starboard outboard underwing pylon, with a pair of R-60 AA-8 'Aphid' AAMs to port, and external 3000-litre (660-Imp gal) fuel tanks inboard.

Those sensors which can directly transmit data to a ground station feed the incredible Posrednik-1 data reception, processing and decoding complex, based in 12 lorries. Two of these are generator trucks and another is believed to be used for aircraft tracking. Data is transmitted via the VPS-1 broadband radio link to the receiver truck, which in turn feeds three processing laboratories for the TV, IR and laser sensors. Photographic films and radar/Elint tapes unloaded from the aircraft after it lands are

processed in three more trucks. Data from all six processing trucks are printed and copied in two more trucks for interpretation and distribution to the tasking authorities. The complex can decode and process data from a one-target mission in an average of 20 minutes from landing, and can process up to 18000 m (59,055 ft) of film and print up to 2000 photos in a 24-hour period.

The Su-24MR is fitted with a Relief terrain-avoidance radar, a radio altimeter, a DISS-7 Doppler, an MIS-P inertial platform, and an SBU Orbita-10-058R digital computer, as well as an RSBN-6S Shoran/ILS, an ARK-15M radio compass and other navaids. The Karpati integrated defence system includes SRO-15 Bereza RWRs, a MAK-UL missile launch warning receiver, Gerani-F active jammers (controlled by a Neon-F control unit) and Automat-F chaff/flare dispensers.

'Fencer-Es' have been seen with and without the distinctive combined fences/ underwing pylons, and aft of the windscreen are externally almost indistinguishable from the 'Fencer-D' bomber. The most obvious external change is the provision of a larger-capacity, bulged heat exchanger to give increased cooling for the reconnaissance aircraft's many new black boxes.

Ukraine has two recce 'Fencer' units. These comprise the 511th RAP at Buyalik (Blagoyevo) with 24 aircraft and the 48th RAP at Kolomyya with 12 Su-24MRs. In **Russia**, two Su-24 reconnaissance regiments have been confirmed. In May 1992, Poland-based Su-24MRs of the 164th

Guards RAP moved from Kryzwa to Staelewo near Smolensk. Germany-based 'Fencer-Es' of the 11 'Vitebski' RAP from Neu Welzow returned to Marinovka. **Kazakhstan** operates some reccconaissance-tasked 'Fencers' with the 39th RAP at Balkesh.

The **Su-24MP** (Modification Pastan-ovchik – Modification to Direct) is a similar-looking aircraft, and like the Su-24MR often has its nose painted white to resemble a standard Su-24M bomber. It can be distinguished from the earlier aircraft by a prominent fairing below the nose, behind the radome, and by the provision of swept-back 'hockey stick' antennas outboard of long shallow strakes on the bottom corners of the intakes, immediately ahead of the main-wheel bays. The pattern of flush dielectric antennas on the sides of the nose is also different, and the smaller 'Fencer-C/-D' heat exchanger is mounted above the fuselage.

The Su-24MP is designated **'Fencer-F'** by NATO, and is believed to have a primary electronic intelligence-gathering role. Before the demolition of the Berlin Wall, recce 'Fencer' units in Poland and Germany included both Su-24MRs and Su-24MPs, but the Su-24MPs were rapidly withdrawn, perhaps to avoid the attentions of spotters' cameras. It is believed that only 12 of these aircraft were built, and eight were retained by **Ukraine** after their withdrawal from Germany. The 11 RAP's MPs ended up at Chortkov with the 118th Independent Aviation Regiment, leaving **Russia** with only four aircraft and a need to retain its exhausted Yak-28 'Brewer-Es'.

Sukhoi Su-24MR 'Fencer-E'
generally similar to the Sukhoi Su-24 'Fencer-D' except in the following particulars:
Weights: normal take-off 33325 kg (73,468 lb); maximum take-off 39700 kg (87,522 lb)
Speed: maximum low-level speed with reconnaissance pods and two R-60 AAMs 1200 km/h (648 kt; 746 mph)
Range: ferry range with one iflight refuelling 4360 km 2353 nm; 2709 miles); operating radius on a lo-lo-lo mission 410 km (221 nm; 255 miles) without fuel tanks and 560 km 302 km; 348 miles) with external fuel tanks
Performance: take-off run 1100-1200 m (3609-3937 ft)
g limits: +6.5

Sukhoi **Su-25 'Frogfoot-A'**

Development of the **Su-25 'Frogfoot'** began during the late 1960s, when the Sukhoi OKB commenced studies of a jet *Shturmovik*, parallelling the US studies which resulted in the AX competition and the ensuing Northrop YA-9 and Fairchild YA-10 prototypes. Sukhoi, like the American firms, was heavily influenced by USAF experience in the Vietnam War, but all three firms reached different conclusions. Sukhoi believed that high speed was essential to ensure survivability over the battle-

field, and chose to use turbojet engines and relatively little armour, while the US designs were turbofan-powered, emphasising very high agility and heavy armour.

The design team, which was successively led by Oleg Samolovich, Yuri Ivas-hechkin and Vladimir Babak, eventually won the support of General A. N. Yefimov, air force Deputy C-in-C and himself a former Il-2 *Shturmovik* pilot, who in turn won the support of the ground forces commander, General Pavlovsky. In this unorthodox man-

ner (by Soviet standards), Sukhoi eventually received funding for a prototype, designated **T-8**. This made its first flight at Zhukhovskii in the hands of Vladimir Ilyushin, Sukhoi's chief test pilot, on 22 February 1975. A second prototype followed, introducing a two-piece rudder, revised wing fences, wingtip pods and a taller tailfin. The **T-8-2** was also the first aircraft with a titanium-armoured cockpit, the first prototype having used steel of equivalent weight. Like the first aircraft, it had an SPPU-22-01 23-mm cannon pod in a gondola fairing below the starboard lower fuselage, and was powered by a pair of Tumanskii RD-9B turbojets, as used by the MiG-19. However, the after-

burners were removed, giving 27 kN (6,070 lb st) of thrust. The aircraft was spotted by a passing US satellite soon after its first flight, and was allocated the provisional reporting name '**Ram-J**', indicating that it was the 10th new type spotted at what the West still called Ramenskoye.

The two T-8 prototypes were equipped with the weapons system of the Su-17M2 'Fitter-D', with ASP-PF gunsight, PBK-3 bombsight and Fone laser rangefinder. The second was re-engined with the R-95Sh (receiving the new designation **T-8-2D**) in March 1976, and the **T-8-1** was re-engined in 1978. The R-95Sh was a non-afterburning modified version of the MiG-21's R-13-300 turbojet and was capable of running on a variety of fuels. Weapons trials at Akhtubinsk had shown that the aircraft was underpowered and prone to compressor stalls when firing cannon or rockets. It was also felt that production could not be authorised while the aircraft used a powerplant which was out of production.

The new powerplant necessitated some changes, including the angling down of the engine nozzles and the incorporation of 5° dihedral on the tailplane, instead of the original 5° anhedral. With the new engine fitted, the two prototypes began state acceptance trials.

Further prototypes were built at Tbilisi, these having the production armament

Czechoslovak Su-25s equipped the 30th Close Air Support Regiment at Pardubice, whose aircraft wear the white horse badge of the city crest. This Su-25K also carries a fearsome sharkmouth on the nose.

of an AO-17 twin-barrelled 30-mm cannon and the weapons system of the Su-17M-3 'Fitter-H' with ASP-17 gunsight, and a Klen laser rangefinder. Series production was finally authorised, and the first and third prototypes were sent to Afghanistan for a combined series of operational and state acceptance trials (Operation Rhombus), alongside a handful of Yak-38 'Forgers' flying from Shindand. The trials lasted from 16 April to 5 June 1980, the two aircraft flying 30 state acceptance and 70 combat sorties. The first pre-production Su-25 introduced a number of changes, including modified tailplanes, enlarged air intakes, heavier, thicker cockpit armour and increased armour around critical components, including the oil tank. The fuel tanks were filled with reticulated foam and the control rods were formed from 40-mm diameter titanium rods, capable of withstanding a direct hit from a 12.7-mm shell. One prototype even tested a radar-absorbing material coating on the forward fuselage and leading edges, but this was not adopted.

Afghan deployment

Some sources suggest that the initial batch of aircraft retained the T-8 designation even in service, and that the designation Su-25 was applied to series production aircraft, whose main recognition feature was a small ram-air intake at the base of the tailfin leading edge. Whatever the designation, the early batch aircraft saw extensive service in Afghanistan, where the first 12 aircraft served with the 200th Guards Independent Attack Squadron at Shindand, pilots including the former Russian Federation Vice-President, then-Colonel Alexander Rutskoi, who became the most highly decorated pilot of the war. The 200th formed at Sital-Chai in Azerbaijan on 4 February 1981, receiving their Su-25s from April, and moving to Shindand on 18 June. This unit gave the Su-25 its *grach* (rook) nickname, and began the tradition of painting a rook onto the intake. The unit was later expanded to full regimental strength, as the 60th Independent Attack Regiment, and maintained a squadron-sized rotational deployment in Afghanistan. The Su-25 eventually flew some 60,000 combat sorties in Afghanistan, and 23 were lost.

Experience in Afghanistan led to a number of modifications, including bolt-on ASO-2V chaff/flare dispensers, an exhaust IR signature reduction system, a freon gas fire-extinguishing system, and a titanium plate between the engines, designed to prevent debris or fire from a damaged engine from damaging its neighbour. Other improve-

ments adopted during the course of production included refinements to the wingtip speed-brakes, with two extra separately controlled forward-folding segments being added. Wingtip pods were also fitted with plate-like fins designed to prevent the pop-down landing lights from dazzling the pilot. Larger twin braking parachutes were also adopted.

During 1987, production aircraft were fitted with the more powerful R-195 engine, which was also fitted to all production 'Frogfoot' two-seaters. The new engine further improves the Su-25's ability to operate from austere forward airfields, and to support such operations a special set of support equipment has been developed which can be carried by the aircraft itself in four underwing pods. These contain test equipment, an electrical generator and starter unit, a fuel pump and protective covers and maintenance equipment. The engines can run on kerosene, diesel and petrol, if required.

Su-25 production at Tbilisi ended in 1989, after some 330 aircraft had been delivered. A handful of Su-25s have been modified to serve as target tugs, with gun removed and gun port faired over, with the laser removed and faired over, and with a TO-70 target winch and Kometa target mounted under the port inboard underwing pylon. These aircraft are designated **Su-25BM** (Buksir Misheni, or target tug).

WEAPON OPTIONS

Ten underwing hardpoints are provided, the outermost pair being smaller and more lightly stressed and used almost exclusively to carry R-60 (AA-8 'Aphid') AAMs for self-defence. External fuel tanks can be carried on the inboard pylons, and a second pair can be carried on the next-but-one pylon further outboard.

The Su-25 is equipped with an internal 30-mm AO-17A cannon in the port lower fuselage, with 250 rounds of ammunition. The nosewheel is offset about 11.5 cm (4½ in) to the right of the centreline to give greater clearance for the gun. The aircraft can carry a wide range of ordnance underwing, including unguided rockets ranging in calibre from 57 mm to 330 mm. ASMs include the Kh-23 (AS-7 'Kerry'), Kh-25 (AS-10 'Karen') and Kh-29 (AS-14 'Kedge').

When laser-guided weapons are carried, the Su-25 must carry an underwing laser illuminator since the onboard laser in the nose is insufficiently powerful to illuminate a target for long-range missiles, but is adequate for guiding laser-guided bombs. Various freefall and laser-guided bombs, cluster bombs, dispenser weapons and incendiary weapons can also be carried, along with a variety of cannon pods, including the SPPU-22, whose 23-mm cannon has barrels which can be depressed for strafing ground targets.

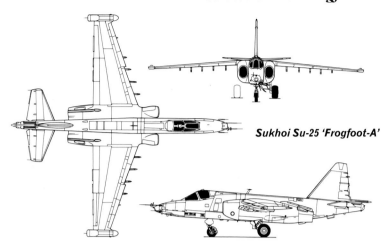

Sukhoi Su-25 'Frogfoot-A'

OPERATORS

The **Soviet air forces** had a peak strength of about 270 Su-25s. Known Su-25 operators were the 200th Guards OShAP in Afghanistan, and one squadron of the 234th Guards at Kubinka (which parents the 'Sky Hussars' aerobatic team) with other regiments in Turkmenistan and Byelorussia. Su-25s deployed to the Group of Soviet Forces in Germany operated in two direct-reporting units as part of the 16th Air Army. The break-up of the former Soviet Union has led to the Su-25 gaining new users.

The 357th OShAP was based at Brandis and returned to **Russia** in 1992. The 368th OShAP formerly at Demmin-Tutow is now based at Budyennovsk. At least three regiments in Georgia remain under Russian control, including the two units from the 16th Air Army. Some Su-25s (mainly UTGs and UBs) serve with naval units. **Ukraine** has a total of 35 Su-25s . The 452nd OShAP, based at Chorkov, has become part of that republic's air arm. Further 'Frogfoots' are based at Ovruch and at Saki, including some of the navalised Su-25UTGs. **Byelorussia** has 100 Su-25s based at Luninets. Su-25s from the 80th OShAP at Sital-Zhay defected to **Azerbaijan** and have been absorbed into the Azeri air force. Three have been shot down by Armenian forces, but five remain in service. **Georgia**, which is home to the Tbilisi plant which manufactures single-seat Su-25s, has less than five 'Frogfoots' on strength. More were lost in action to Abkhasian forces.

Export 'Frogfoots' are designated **Su-25K**. Thirty-six were delivered to **Czechoslovakia**, the first export customer, to equip the 34th Fighter-Bomber Division's 30th 'Ostravsky' Close Air Support Regiment . Some remained with the Czech Republic (still with the 30th at Pardubice) after division, 13 others going to Slovakia's 2 ZDLP at Piestany. **Bulgaria** took delivery of a further 36, these equipping a regiment at Bezmier. **Iraq** received 30

Su-25Ks, 20 of which were extant at the start of Operation Desert Storm. Several were destroyed on the ground or in air combat, and seven survivors fled to Iran. The last overseas customer was **North Korea**, which also received 36 aircraft. Czech and Bulgarian examples differ little from standard Russian Su-25s, but Iraqi and Korean aircraft may have downgraded avionics. Plans to transfer Su-25 production to **Poland** during 1977 were cancelled when the Polish air force rejected the aircraft. Some reports suggest that Su-25s were also exported to **Afghanistan** and **Angola**, and there have been recent reported sightings in both countries.

SPECIFICATION

Sukhoi Su-25K 'Frogfoot-A'
Wing: span 14.36 m (47 ft 1.4 in); aspect ratio 6.12; area 30.10 m² (324.00 sq ft)
Fuselage and tail: length 15.53 m (50 ft 11.5 in); height 4.80 m (15 ft 9 in)
Powerplant: two MNPK 'Soyuz' (Tumanskii) R-195 turbojets each rated at 44.13 kN (9,921 lb st) dry
Weights: empty equipped 9800 kg (21,605 lb); normal take-off 14600 kg (32,187 lb); maximum take-off 18600 kg (41,005 lb)
Fuel and load: internal fuel about 5000 kg (11,023 lb); maximum ordnance 4000 kg (8,818 lb)
Speed: maximum level speed 'clean' at sea level 950 km/h (513 kt; 590 mph)
Range: combat radius 495 km (267 nm; 308 miles) on a hi-lo-hi attack mission with a 4000-kg (8,818-lb) warload and two drop tanks
Performance: service ceiling 7000 m (22,965 ft); take-off run 600 m (1,969 ft) typical at maximum take-off weight or less than 1200 m (3,937 ft) at maximum take-off weight from an unpaved runway; landing run 600 m (1,969 ft) at normal landing weight without brake chutes or 400 m (1,312 ft) at normal landing weight with brake chutes

Regarded as a latter-day successor to the legendary Il-2 Shturmovik, the Su-25 saw use in Afghanistan. Still wearing the distinctive desert-type camouflage applied for operations in Afghanistan, this Su-25 served with the Soviet 16th Air Army in Germany. The success of the aircraft has been limited, many potential operators preferring to buy supersonic fighters with a nominal ground attack capability.

Sukhoi **Su-25UB/UT/UTG 'Frogfoot-B'**

Development of a two-seat trainer version of the Su-25 was not accorded a high priority, since the basic single-seater was simple to fly, with benign handling characteristics. **VVS** Su-25 regiments therefore used Czech Aero L-39s for training and standardisation, and also for FAC duties. These aircraft have still not been entirely replaced by two-seat Su-25Us.

Two prototype trainers were converted from unfinished Su-25s at Tbilisi, under the designations **T-8-UB1** and **T-8-UB2**, making their maiden flights during 1985. After acceptance trials, the first prototype was flown to Ulan Ude to serve as a pattern aircraft. Production of the definitive **Su-25UB 'Frogfoot-B'** began in 1987, all aircraft produced there being decorated with the factory's bear badge.

The Su-25UB has forward fuselage slightly lengthened to accommodate the new stepped cockpits. These are covered by separate canopies and are divided by a sealed, armoured windscreen which prevents both cockpits depressurising if only one loses its integrity. The instructor is provided with a retractable periscope to improve his view directly forward on approach or on the ground. The tailfin is increased in height to compensate for the greater 'keel' area forward. The trainer retains all operational equipment and is fully combat-capable, although the weight and drag of the second cockpit, and the slight reduction in fuel capacity, have an impact on performance.

Production of the Su-25UB ended in December 1991, after five Soviet Su-25 regiments had received their aircraft. Production also included about 16 **Su-25UBK** trainers for **Bulgaria**, **Czechoslovakia**, **Iraq** and **North Korea**. These aircraft lacked chaff/flare dispensers and were fitted with downgraded avionics.

The Su-25UB has also formed the basis of three more Su-25 sub-variants. The first of these was the **Su-25UT**, later redesignated **Su-28**. The prototype was a converted Su-25UB, with all armament and weapons systems removed, and it made its maiden flight on 6 August 1985. The aircraft was intended as a successor to the Czech Aero L-29 and L-39 in the pilot training role in both air force and DOSAAF service. It retained only two underwing hardpoints, to carry fuel tanks.

One prototype was painted in DOSAAF colours and participated in the 1988 DOSAAF aerobatic competition, pilot Yevgeni Frolov gaining a creditable third place. Although it offered some advantages over the L-39 (whose airframe life is already running out) the aircraft was unable to attract an order.

The basic Su-25 two-seater also served as the basis for the **Su-25UTG**, a dedicated carrier training aircraft (the G in the suffix stands for Gak, or hook) for pilots destined to serve aboard the *Kuznetsov* (formerly *Tbilisi*). Development work began in 1987, and the prototype made its maiden flight in that same year. The airframe and undercarriage were considerably strengthened, and a heavy-duty arrester hook was mounted below the tailcone.

At one stage it was reported that a pre-production batch of 10 aircraft had been ordered, and these were constructed at Ulan Ude during 1989-90. Only the first was used for trials aboard the *Kuznetsov* flown

The Su-28 is a dedicated advanced trainer version of the Su-25UB. Whereas the heavier machine is fully armed and armoured and is used for conversion training, the Su-28's main role is intended to be advanced pilot training.

by Igor V. Botintsev and Alexander V. Krutov. It was also used for training test pilots involved in the Su-27K programme. One of the remainder crashed, and five were left at Saki (to be integrated into the **Ukrainian** forces), leaving four to be transferred to Severomorsk on the Kola Peninsula. This location has taken over from Saki as the **AV-MF**'s development centre. In March 1993, Sukhoi claimed that 10 Su-25UBs were being converted to a similar standard under the designation **Su-25UBP** (P for Palubnyi, or shipborne).

Finally, the Su-25UB served as the basis for the **Su-25T**, described separately.

SPECIFICATION

Sukhoi Su-25UB 'Frogfoot-B'
generally similar to the Sukhoi Su-25K 'Frogfoot-A' except in the following particulars:
Fuselage and tail: height 5.20 m (17 ft 0.75 in)

Left: The hook-equipped Su-25UTG is a dedicated carrier training variant of the two-seat 'Frogfoot'. Ten were built for trials (this one almost certainly the first) and have been augmented by a batch of similar Su-25UBPs. The aircraft may be converted to have a secondary attack role now that the MiG-29K seems unlikely to be procured for the carrier Kuznetsov.

Below: Many Su-25UBs carry a bear badge on the nose. This is the emblem of the Ulan Ude factory which produced all two-seat Su-25s. This particular aircraft is armed with S-8 20-round 80-mm rocket pods. Plates on the wingtip fairings shield the pilot from the glare of the pop-down landing lights.

Sukhoi **Su-25T** (no reporting name allocated)

The **Su-34** is an extensively upgraded and modernised derivative of the Su-25 'Frogfoot' and was originally designated **Su-25T**, the designation being changed to differentiate it from the older aircraft and thereby attract funding on the basis of being a 'new' project. The Su-34 designation is being reused to denote an advanced attack derivative of the Su-27 'Flanker'. The Su-25T designation is now used again by this advanced 'Frogfoot'.

Work on the new aircraft began in 1984, as Su-25 combat losses in Afghanistan were beginning to cause concern. The basic 'Frogfoot' was subjected to a host of modifications to improve survivability, but other problems, including lack of all-weather and night capability and insufficient range/ endurance also needed to be addressed, and it was decided to design a new variant. The basic single-seat Su-25 lacked internal space, so the new variant was based on the airframe of the Su-25UB, using the rear cockpit and former gun and ammunition bay to house new avionics and extra fuel tanks. To camouflage the aircraft's true role, a dummy second cockpit was painted onto the prototypes. Three **T-8M** prototypes were converted from Su-25UB airframes, the first making its maiden flight on 17 August 1984 at Ulan Ude. The T-8Ms differed from Su-25UBs in having a GSL-30-6 30-mm cannon mounted below the centre fuselage, and some sources suggest that the new variant also had a slightly lengthened nose. The radar warning receiver

'spike' at the base of the fin was also deleted.

A pre-production batch of 10 aircraft was built under the designation **Su-25T**, the T standing for Tankovyi, or anti-tank. These aircraft were not all built to a completely common standard, but all feature a large (192-round) chaff/flare dispenser in a cylindrical fairing below the trailing edge of the rudder. The nose gear is offset to port and a variety of externally-mounted cannon have been fitted beside it, to starboard. The GSL-30-6 seems to have been abandoned and has been replaced by the Su-25's original twin-barrelled AO-17A 30-mm cannon, or by a single-barrelled weapon on some aircraft.

To give true night capability, the aircraft has a new avionics system, with a new Voskhod INAS and two digital computers. The nose is widened to accommodate an improved Schkval EO package, containing a new TV camera and laser designator, spot tracker and rangefinder. This can give a 23X magnification image of the target area. A variety of equipment pods can be carried under the belly, including a Mercury LLLTV/ FLIR system or a low-light-level navigation system. An onboard electronic reconnaissance system allows hostile emissions to be detected, identified and located, increasing survivability and allowing the aircraft to undertake defence suppression missions. The aircraft has been offered for export under the designation **Su-25TK**, with Abu Dhabi targeted as one potential customer.

In March 1993, when it seemed as

One of three Su-25T prototypes converted from UB airframes. The second cockpit and gun/ammunition bays are used to house extra avionics and fuel tankage. An AO-17 cannon is scabbed on below the fuselage.

though the MiG-29K had not been selected for production, Sukhoi claimed to have received funding to develop a maritime strike aircraft based on the Su-25T, for service aboard the *Kuznetsov*. Designated **Su-25TP**, it reportedly combines the features of the Su-25UTG with the weapons system of the Su-25T. A prototype is reportedly under construction. During the same month, Sukhoi also announced a production order for a land-based Su-25T variant, redesignated **Su-25TM**, with Kinzhal podded MMW radar and a Khod FLIR targeting device (the latter replacing the original Mercury unit).

SPECIFICATION

Sukhoi Su-25TK
generally similar to the Su-25K 'Frogfoot' except in the following particulars:
Wing: span 14.52 m (47 ft 7.5 in)
Fuselage and tail: length 15.33 m (50 ft 3.5 in); height 5.20 m (13 ft 2.5 in)
Weights: maximum take-off 18600 kg (41,005 lb) Fuel and load: internal fuel 3840 kg (8,466 lb)
Range: combat radius with 2000-kg (4,409-lb) warload and two external fuel tanks 400 km (216 nm; 249 miles) on a lo-lo-lo profile, and 700 km (378 nm; 435 miles) on a hi-lo-hi profile

Sukhoi **Su-27 'Flanker'**

The **Su-27 'Flanker'** represents one of the jewels in the Soviet aerospace industry's crown. A modified version of the aircraft shattered 27 world records (taking most from a similarly modified example of its Western equivalent, the F-15 Eagle), and in countless displays the aircraft has demonstrated manoeuvres which no Western fighter can emulate, and has done so reliably and safely, at air show altitudes. The aircraft's reputation is nonetheless tarnished by doubts about its avionics, by doubts about its agility at operational weight, and by an early history of problems severe enough to require a total redesign.

Work on the **T-10** design began in 1969, when the Sukhoi OKB began work on a new interceptor for the IA-PVO, working closely with TSAGI, the MM Saturn engine design bureau and a number of research establishments. The design team was led by Yevgeny Ivanov, although Sukhoi himself took a close interest in the aircraft until his death in 1975. The requirement was for a highly manoeuvrable fighter with very long range, heavy armament and modern sensors. It was to be capable of intercepting low-flying NATO attack aircraft and high-level bombers, and to be able to meet agile fighters like the F-15 on equal terms.

In many ways, the Su-27 could be regarded as a scaled-up MiG-29, although Mikoyan and Sukhoi arrived at similar configurations because they were designing similar highly-agile fighters which were to be able to explore hitherto impossible parts of the flight envelope, and were relying on input from the same research institutes. The aircraft was thus designed around a highly-blended forebody and high-lift wing, with ogival leading-edge root extensions.

To maximise manoeuvrability, the T-10 was designed from the outset to be unstable, and therefore required a computer-controlled fly-by-wire control system at least in pitch. The OKB was able to draw on the experience it had accumulated during the T-4/Su-100 Mach 3 bomber programme, for which a FBW control system had been

designed. The first prototype T-10, powered by a pair of AL-21F-3 turbojets, made its maiden flight on 20 May 1977 in the hands of chief test pilot Vladimir Ilyushin. The provisional reporting name **'Ram-J'** allocated then was eventually replaced by the appellation **'Flanker-A'**. The first four prototypes (**T-10-1/-4**) were constructed at the bureau's own experimental shop in Moscow, and five more (**T-10-5, -6, -9, -10** and **-11**) were built at Komsomolsk-na-

Early production Su-27s had simple strakes on either side of the tail sting, rather than the box-like fairings which on later aircraft house chaff/flare dispensers. They also retain small anti-flutter weights on the leading edge of each tailfin.

Above: This Lipetsk-based Su-27 is fitted with wingtip Sorbitsiya ESM pods. 'Red 10' is seen diving on a ground target during a strafe attack, demonstrating the aircraft's secondary attack role. It sports a gaudy sharkmouth on each engine intake and carries a five-round 130-mm rocket pod under the starboard wing.

Below: Ukraine has about 60 Su-27s in service with at least two regiments: the 62nd IBAP at Bel'bek, as part of the new Air Defence Force's Southern Region, and the 831st IBAP at Mirgorod, which is part of the tactical air arm.

Above: This late-production Su-27 carries an individual aircraft excellence award on the nose, together with a series of small red stars. It is seen on approach to Chojna, once home to the 582nd IBAP and one of two Frontal Aviation 'Flanker' bases in Poland. The two-tone radome is noteworthy, the lighter colour denoting the extent of the Su-27's twist cassegrain antenna.

Amur. From **T-10-3** the aircraft were powered by Saturn (Lyul'ka) AL-31F turbofans, which gave about 12 per cent more thrust and much better specific fuel consumption.

The early flight development programme revealed serious problems. The second prototype was lost in a fatal crash, the aircraft weight escalated and fuel consumption proved higher than expected. Furthermore, the F-15 entered service, and it became clear that the T-10 as it was would be an inferior aircraft. Accordingly, the new designer general, Mikhail P. Simonov, supervised a total redesign. The **T-10-7** was completed as the first prototype of the new design, under the new designation **T-10S-1**, making its maiden flight on 20 April 1981. This was effectively a completely new aircraft, with a redesigned wing which had a straight, slatted leading edge and cropped wingtips incorporating missile launch rails. The latter also doubled as antiflutter weights.

Ailerons were deleted, to be replaced by flaperons and differential tailerons, while the entire fuselage was redesigned, with a deeper spine and shallower nose. The mainwheel door airbrakes were replaced by a spine-mounted airbrake and the undercarriage was redesigned and repositioned. The nosewheel was moved aft to improve taxiing characteristics and to minimise foreign object ingestion on take-off or landing. The tailfins were moved outboard from the tops of the engine nacelles to booms which lay alongside them. These changes were sufficient to prompt NATO to allocate a new reporting name of **'Flanker-B'**.

The original T-10s were used in the flight test programme alongside the T-10S-1, and preparations were put in hand for series production. Before production could begin,

more problems had to be solved, the most serious being a wing fault which killed one pilot and nearly destroyed a second aircraft. Reducing the area of the leading-edge slats proved to be the answer.

The Su-27 finally began to enter operational service during the mid-1980s, although deliveries were at one stage held up by delays with the aircraft's advanced new radar. This led to completed but radarless Su-27s being stockpiled outside the Komsomolsk factory for several months. The earliest Su-27s delivered had a frameless rear canopy section and square-topped tailfins, but later aircraft added a frame behind the pilot's ejection seat headrest and cropped off the rear top corners of the fintips. Later still, prominent spikes on the fin leading edges (thought to be anti-flutter devices) were removed.

One interesting Su-27 sub-variant was the **P-42**. This had its radar and radome removed and replaced by ballast and a metal nosecone, and had ventral fins, fincaps and paint removed. The aircraft was powered by uprated AI-31F engines (designated R-32) and was used to set a series of time-to-height and other records, in the hands of Victor Pugachev, Nikolai Sadovnikov, Oleg Tsoi and Yevgeni Frolov. Because the lightened aircraft's brakes could not hold it against the full thrust of the more powerful R-32 engines, it had to be tethered to an armoured vehicle while it ran up to full power, before being released using an electronic locking device.

The standard Su-27 fighter is now in service with the Russian and Ukrainian air forces, and serves with Frontal Aviation as well as the old PVO air defence force. It is used primarily in the air-to-air role, although it can carry a range of freefall bombs and unguided rockets underwing, and the air-to-

ground role has been practised by some Su-27 units. Even in Frontal Aviation, however, the Su-27 is primarily used as an interceptor or escort fighter and not as a ground attack aircraft.

The Su-27 is equipped with an advanced pulse-Doppler radar, whose large antenna gives a long range, although poor signal processing means that only one target can be engaged at a time. The radar is backed up by a sophisticated EO complex which includes an IRST system and a collimated laser rangefinder. This allows the Su-27 to detect, track and engage a target without using radar. The Su-27 is also compatible with a helmet-mounted target designation system, facilitating the pilot's engagement of off-axis targets by cueing sensors or missile tracker heads onto a target which has not been boresighted.

WEAPON OPTIONS

The Su-27 has a total of 10 hardpoints that allow it to carry up to six R-27 (AA-10 'Alamo') and four AA-11 'Archer' air-to-air missiles, giving a remarkable degree of combat persistence. Missiles are backed up by a 30-mm GSh-30-1 cannon in the starboard wingroot, with 150 rounds of ammunition. In either the air-to-air or air-to-ground roles, the wingtip missile launch rails can be replaced by ECM pods.

OPERATORS

Su-27s were originally delivered to the integrated armed forces of the **former USSR**, but most have now been absorbed into **Russia**'s armed forces, the CIS having failed to keep central control of unified forces. The aircraft were originally ordered for the IA-PVO air defence force, but were also delivered to Frontal Aviation units. In 1994, approximately 200 serve with the **IA-PVO**, while a further 150 are in service with **Frontal Aviation**. Known users include the 234th 'Proskurovskii' Guards IAP at Kubinka, the 159th 'Novorossiisk' Guards IAP at Biesowice (formerly at Kluczewo, Poland), the 831st IAP at Mirogorod (Carpathian Military District), 54th IAP at Vainodo and 689th IAP at Nivenskoye (both Leningrad/St Petersburg MD). The 582nd IAP at Chojna, Poland, moved to Smolensk and disbanded at the end of 1992. Perhaps the best known Su-27s are the aircraft of the 234 'Proskurovskii' Guards Fighter Regiment based at Kubinka, near Moscow, which provides the 'Russian Knights' aerobatic team.

The break-up of the USSR left some Su-27 regiments on non-Russian territory, most such units then being absorbed by the new air arms of the states involved. The 62nd IAP at Bel'bek became part of the **Ukrainian air force**, and other Ukrainian Su-27

The sole export customer to date has been China, whose People's Liberation Army Air Force has taken delivery of 24 or 26 'Flankers'. They were delivered in a new medium grey scheme with an unusual 'cut-out' in the lower part of the radome.

regiments were based at Zhitomir and Sevastopol. In 1994 Ukraine fielded a further Su-27 regiment at Mirgorod. Formerly assigned to the 24th Air Army, the 831st IAP now forms part of the 5th Air Army's tactical assets and retains its previous role of long-range fighter escort for Ukraine's Su-24 'Fencers'. In **Byelorussia**, Su-27s may serve with the former 61st IAP at Baranovidu. Since all Su-27 production is centered in Russia, spares support for these aircraft may be difficult, and many may be replaced by types which are easier to support locally.

The first true export customer for the Su-27 was **China**, ordering 24 aircraft which were delivered from August 1991, following a March 1991 contract signature. The aircraft were initially based on Hainan Island, but were then moved back to the mainland. A second similar batch is reportedly sought by China.

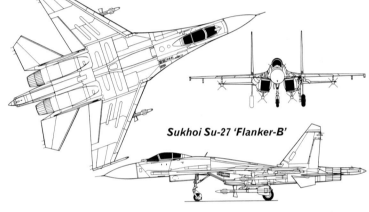

Sukhoi Su-27 'Flanker-B'

SPECIFICATION

Sukhoi Su-27 'Flanker-B'
Wing: span 14.70 m (48 ft 2.75 in); aspect ratio 5.6; wing area 46.50 m² (500.54 sq ft)
Fuselage and tail: length 21.90 m (71 ft 10 in) excluding probe; height 5.90 m (19 ft 4 in); tailplane

span 9.90 m (32 ft 6 in); wheel track 4.33 m (14 ft 2½ in); wheel base 5.88 m (19 ft 3.5 in)
Powerplant: two NPO Saturn (Lyul'ka) AL-31F turbofans each rated at 79.43 kN (17,857 lb) dry and 122.58 kN (27,557 lb st) with afterburning
Weights: empty 17700 kg (39,021 lb); normal take-off 23250 kg (51,257 lb); maximum take-off 33000 kg (72751 lb)
Fuel and load: normal internal fuel about 527 (11,618 lb); maximum internal fuel 9400 kg (20,723 lb); maximum ordnance 6000 kg (13,228 lb)
Speed: limiting Mach No. 2.35; maximum level speed

'clean' at 11000 m (36,090 ft) 2280 km/h (1230 kt; 1417 mph) and at sea level 1370 km/h (739 kt; 851 mph)
Range: at high-altitude 3680 km (1,986 nm; 2,287 miles); range at low-altitude 1370 km (739 nm; 851 miles)
Performance: maximum rate of climb at sea level 19800 m (64,960 ft) per minute; service ceiling 17700 m (58,071 ft); take-off run 450 m (1,476 ft) at maximum take-off weight; landing run 700 m (2,297 ft) at normal landing weight
g limits: +8

Sukhoi **Su-27UB** 'Flanker-C'

I t is believed that no two-seat Su-27s based on the early 'Flanker-A' were produced, and that the prototype **Su-27UB**, designated **T-10U-1**, was based on the definitive production Su-27 'Flanker-B'. This aircraft reportedly made its maiden flight on 7 March 1985, piloted by Nikolai Sadovnikov. Series production of the Su-27UB began at Irkutsk in 1986, and deliveries began in 1987. Before the type became available in large numbers, Su-27 regiments used MiG-23UB 'Flogger', Su-17U 'Fitter' and MiG-29UB 'Fulcrum' two-seaters for conversion and continuation training.

The Su-27UB differs from the single-seater in having a lengthened forward fuselage with stepped tandem cockpits under a single canopy. The tailfins are increased in height and area, as is the airbrake. Due to a 740-kg (1,631-lb) increase in normal take-off weight and the increased drag caused by the new canopy, maximum speed is reduced by about 70 km/h (38 kt; 43 mph) at low level and 160 km/h (86 kt; 99 mph) at

height, while low-level range is reduced by 100 km (54 nm; 62 miles) and high-level range by 680 km (367 nm; 423 miles). Turn radius, rate of climb and take-off/landing distances are less affected.

Su-27UBs have also been used for a number of experimental programmes. Two-seat Su-27s conducted buddy refuelling trials using a centreline UPAZ refuelling pod, and made a number of extremely long distance flights, including a marathon 15-hour 42-minute, 13440-km (7,253-nm; 8,351-miles) sortie in 1987 flown by Sadovnikov and I. Votintsev. Other Su-27UBs have been used as airborne laboratories to support the

This Su-27UB 'Flanker-C' of the 234th 'Proskurovskii' Guards Fighter Regiment at Kubinka wears the striking colour scheme of the 'Russian Knights' aerobatic demonstration team. The front cockpit has been fitted with rails for an instrument flying training hood.

Gulfstream/Sukhoi SSBJ programme, and to test the vectoring nozzles under development for advanced versions of the Su-27.

SPECIFICATION

Sukhoi Su-27UB 'Flanker-C'
generally similar to the Sukhoi Su-27 'Flanker-B' except in the following particulars:

Fuselage and tail: height 6.36 m (20 ft 10.25 in)
Weights: normal take-off 23990 kg (52,888 lb)
Range: range at high altitude 3000 km (1,619 nm; 1,864 miles); range at low altitude 1270 km (685 nm; 789 miles)
Performance: maximum rate of climb at sea level 16200 m (53,150 ft) per minute; service ceilin 16700 m (54,790 ft); take-off run 580 m (1,903 ft) at maximum take-off weight; landing run 650 m (2,133 ft) at normal landing weight

Sukhoi **Su-27K/Su-33**

Development of the **Su-27K** was in-tended to produce a shipborne long-range interceptor to complement MiG-29Ks in air wings that would equip the Soviet Union's four new conventional aircraft-carriers. One carrier was never started, another (*Ulyanovsk*) was scrapped on the slipway, and *Varyag* (formerly *Riga*) remains incomplete and unlikely to enter Russian/CIS service, leaving only *Kuznetsov* in service with the **Russian navy**. This makes the provision of one dedicated carrierborne fighter (let alone two) an extremely expensive proposition, killing the original plan of having a navalised Su-27 as a kind of F-14-equivalent long-range interceptor plus a navalised MiG-29 as an F/A-18-equivalent shorter-range multi-role fighter. Although the logical decision would be to procure only the multi-role aircraft (especially since its intercept capability is identical, except in terms of range), the Su-27K still has a chance of snatching any order since the Sukhoi OKB appears to enjoy much greater political influence than its competitor.

Like the Su-27M/-35 (which is described separately), the Su-27K can trace its ancestry back to the **T-10-24**, the first Su-27 to be flown with canard foreplanes, which the Sukhoi OKB studied as a means of improving take-off performance and of reducing approach speed, as well as for improving agility. Navalising the Su-27 was a major task, and resulted in a host of modifications, most of which were applied to a series of at least seven prototypes.

The first of these, perhaps designated **T-10-37**, or perhaps **Su-27K-1**, (plus all subsequent Su-27Ks) was fitted with canard foreplanes and an arrester hook, and also had a retractable inflight-refuelling probe and the associated offset IRST. The prototype made its first flight on 17 August 1987, piloted by Victor G. Pugachev. The wing was initially unmodified, but eventually received a new, two-section double-slotted trailing-edge flap and drooping ailerons. No other Su-27 variant has ailerons, which confer better roll control on approach. Later prototypes had folding wings and even folding tailplanes, and were used in trials on land and aboard the *Tbilisi*, later renamed *Kuznetsov*. Victor Pugachev made the first arrested carrier shipboard landing in Soviet naval history in Su-27K '39', on 1 November 1989.

The Su-27K is based upon the airframe and weapons system of the basic Su-27, with the same radar and a virtually unchanged cockpit. It thus has minimal air-to-ground capability, unlike the competing MiG-29K, which is closely based on the airframe and systems of the multi-role MiG-29M. The Su-27K can carry a maximum ordnance load of 6500 kg (14,330 lb) and maximum take-off weight is reduced to 32000 kg (70,546 lb). Various air-to-surface weapons have been displayed under or beside statically displayed Su-27Ks, including the massive 250-km (135-nm; 155-mile) range Kh-41 Moskito ASM, the anti-radar Kh-31 and the smaller Zvezda Kh-35 ('Har-

Sukhoi Su-27K

This heavily armed Su-27K carrying a centreline Kh-41 Moskito ASM and a full load of AAMs sits at Zhukovskii, with wings and tailplanes folded.

poonski') ASM. The Su-27K is also the first 'Flanker' sub-type plumbed for the carriage of external fuel – in this case, a 1500-litre (396-US gal) centreline tank. It was widely believed that if an Su-27K were to be selected for production, it would be a hybrid aircraft more closely based upon the Su-35, and probably with vectoring nozzles. Such supposition was denied at Le Bourget in June 1993, when it was stated that the 20 **Su-33**s under construction at Komsomolsk on Amur were merely navalised ver-

sions of the basic interceptor Su-27, without multi-role capability or the flight control and weapons system improvements of the Su-35. 'Flanker' production at Komsomolsk was halted temporarily in early 1994, and there are reports that the more versatile MiG-29K may be put into production.

An Su-27K and a MiG-29K are seen together on the deck of the carrier **Kuznetsov**. *The Su-27K is optimised as an interceptor.*

Sukhoi **Su-27P/PU/Su-30**

The basic Su-27 interceptor and Su-27UB trainer produced a rash of derivatives which were publicly unveiled during the early 1990s. One such derivative was the **Su-27PU**, which at first glance seemed to differ very little from the Su-27UB trainer. Apart from provision of a retractable inflight-refuelling probe (also fitted to the Su-27K, Su-27KU/IB and Su-27M/Su-35), and with its IRST 'ball' offset to starboard to compensate, the aircraft is externally almost identical. Some analysts hypothesise that the radome is of different profile (perhaps the same as that fitted to the Su-27M/-35), suggesting that a new radar has been fitted. This was denied at the 1993 Paris Air Salon, where the aircraft's designer, Igor Emelianov, confirmed that the Su-30 retains the same

radar as the baseline Su-27 interceptor.

The aircraft was designed to meet a PVO requirement for a long-range, high-endurance interceptor that could secure Russia's enormous borders and provide air cover for naval forces. The requirement included a 10-hour endurance stipulation, necessitating provision for inflight refuelling, systems proved for 10 hour's continuous operation and identical twin cockpits housing two pilots, either of whom can assume command at any stage of the mission. Range of the aircraft is given as 3000 km (1,620 nm; 1,864 miles) with internal fuel, and 5200 km (2,808 nm; 3,231 miles) with inflight refuelling. Development funding was ensured by changing the designation to **Su-30** (existing aircraft projects being starved

of resources). The Su-30 has a new miniaturised navigation system, based on that fitted to Aeroflot's international airliners with a GPS and Loran, Omega and Mars navigation equipment. The prototype made its maiden flight on 30 December 1989 at Irkutsk, in the hands of Yevgeni Revunov. Since then, a small number of production Su-30s have been built, including a pair which was specially constructed to meet an order from the 'Test Pilots' aerobatic team. The latter aircraft were fitted with the IFR probe and navigation system, but lacked all combat equipment and military systems.

The aircraft is reportedly fully combat-capable and, with the addition of extra equipment in the rear cockpit, is also able to operate as a mini-AWACS and command post, operating in conjunction with up to four other single-seat fighters (other Su-30s, Su-27 single-seat fighters, or Su-27Ps), directing or even automatically controlling them to the

most suitable target, and transferring information within the formation by datalink to build up the best possible tactical situation display. This is the same concept that has been pioneered by the MiG-31 'Foxhound'. In this role, the Su-30 carries a dedicated fighter controller in the back seat.

The single-seat **Su-27P** is a less well known aircraft. It is believed to have the same navigation system and increased endurance systems as the Su-30, but its single cockpit would make such capability difficult to exploit operationally. A number of stripped aircraft are operated by the 'Test Pilots' team, but the aircraft's service status is uncertain, and any redesignation must remain a matter of speculation.

The **Su-30MK** is an export Su-30 derivative for multi-role use with added ground-attack capability. The aircraft remains primarily a long-range interceptor, however, and comparisons with the F-15E have been

Above: One of the Su-30 prototypes refuels the T-10-37, a canard- and hook-equipped forerunner of the Su-27K that lacked folding wings, outboard ailerons and double-slotted flaps.

Right: This heavily armed aircraft is one of the demonstrators and development aircraft for the Su-30MK, the export version of the multi-role version of the original Su-30 interceptor. India has been mooted as a potential customer for the aircraft.

rejected. The Sukhoi OKB is eager to export the Su-30MK, whose flight test programme was reportedly completed in the early summer of 1993.

Sukhoi **Su-27IB/KU/Su-34**

A great deal of confusion exists even as to the proper designation of this two-seat Su-27 derivative. When the aircraft was displayed at Minsk-Maschulische (its first official unveiling) in a closed display for CIS leaders, an information board bore the designation **Su-27IB**. However, until the 1993 Paris air show this designation was consistently denied and the alternative designation **Su-27KU** was used instead.

This muddle over designation is more significant than being mere semantics, since the two designations represent two very different roles. The first sight of the aircraft was afforded in a TASS photo released in August 1991, showing it on approach to the carrier *Tbilisi*, although it seemed to lack arrester hook and folding wings (as was later confirmed). Side-by-side seating, giving pilot and instructor the same approach picture, is of obvious benefit for a carrier training aircraft, as is the strengthened undercarriage with twin nosewheels, and the newly revealed designation KU (Korabelnii Uchebno or, literally, shipborne trainer) would seem to support such a role, although the lack of arrester hook, wing and tailplane folding and the longer wheelbase would mitigate against naval use.

The IB designation (Istrebitel Bombardirovshchik or, literally, fighter-bomber) used at Minsk was supported by the aircraft's retractable inflight-refuelling probe (internal fuel would surely be adequate for carrier training) and (admittedly unlikely) load of bombs and air-to-surface missiles. With suitable sensors, the Su-27, with its excellent range and endurance, would make a commendable strike aircraft, and recent articles in the Russian press claim a titanium armoured cockpit, armoured glass and CRT displays. The intakes are also said to have been redesigned for higher speed at low

level and the aircraft is reportedly optimised for 'contour-hugging' flight.

It seems likely that the aircraft was originally developed as a two-seat carrier trainer but that changed circumstances have led to its consideration as a potential basis for an Su-24 replacement, and its use as a demonstrator for such an aircraft. This would explain the aircraft's lack of radar, IRST and sensors. The original KU designation may have been resurrected for political reasons.

Whatever the confusion over designation, the nickname 'Platypus' is universally recognised, leading from the flattened, slightly-upturned nose shape, whose chines make it reminiscent of the SR-71 nose. The Su-27IB might form the basis of EW and recce variants of the Su-27. The production version, designated **Su-34**, is of similar configuration but has tandem twin main-

wheels and an extended, raised and enlarged tail sting.

SPECIFICATION

Sukhoi Su-27IB
generally similar to the Sukhoi Su-27 'Flanker-B' except in the following particulars:

The Su-27IB was probably developed as a carrier-based training aircraft, but the design has since been revised slightly to meet the Russian air forces' requirement for an Su-24 replacement in the interdiction and strike roles. The production version will be the Su-34.

Powerplant: Two NPO Saturn (Lyul'ka, AL-31FM turbofans, each rated at 130.42 kN (29,320 lb st) with afterburning)
Weights: maximum take off 44,360 kg (97,795 lb)
Fuel and load: maximum ordnance 8,000 kg (17,636 lb)
Performance: service ceiling 17,000 m (55,755 ft)

Sukhoi Su-27IB/Su-34

Sukhoi Su-27M/Su-35

In an atmosphere in which funding for existing aircraft projects was impossible, the Sukhoi OKB ensured continuing financial support for its advanced Su-27 derivative, initially designated **Su-27M**, by the simple expedient of redesignating it as **Su-35**. In contrast to Mikoyan's openness about its advanced MiG-29 derivatives, Sukhoi has remained remarkably tight-lipped about its Su-35 project. At Farnborough in September 1992, OKB designer general Simonov and project chief Nikolai Nikitin contradicted one another on several key questions when separately interviewed about the Su-35.

As far as can be ascertained, the project to develop an advanced version of the Su-27 was launched during the early 1980s, before the initial variant had entered service, with the primary aim of producing an aircraft with better dogfighting characteristics. A proof-of-concept aircraft with moving canard foreplanes, the **T-10-24**, first flew during 1982, and was the first of a confusing array of converted production aircraft used as testbeds, and newly built Su-27M 'prototypes'. Better agility (including higher Alpha limits and improved handling at high angles of attack) has reportedly been achieved through use of the canards, and through provision of heavy internal fuel tanks in the tailfins.

The aircraft is equipped with a completely new flight control system, with four longitudinal channels and three transverse. The channel for the canard foreplane also functions as a redundant channel. To compensate for the canards, the tailfin area has also been increased on some Su-35 prototypes, and the new, square-topped tailfin will reportedly be incorporated on any production Su-35.

In addition to the aerodynamic and control system improvements, Sukhoi has been working on vectoring engine nozzles and on various avionics improvements. Simple two-dimensional vectoring nozzles (similar to those flown on the F-15 S/MTD) have been tested on at least one Zhukhovskii-based Su-27UB, and are intended to be incorporated on any production Su-35 (if funding permits). Such nozzles could be retrofitted at a later date. A number of avionics improvements will definitely be incorporated in any production Su-35.

A new radar has been installed. Perhaps designated N-011, and probably similar in concept to the N-010 of the MiG-29M, it reportedly has a range of up to 400 km (248 miles) (or 200 km/124 miles against ground targets) and can simultaneously track more than 15 targets, and engage up to six. The aircraft also has advanced datalink equipment allowing the kind of group operation practised by the MiG-31, whereby a formation leader can directly and automatically control his wingmen's aircraft, receiving radar and sensor inputs from (and automatically redistributing to) all formation aircraft, ground stations and AWACS aircraft.

A cryptic reference to 'radar tracking of multiple targets in free air or on the surface, at both forward or rear hemisphere' is believed to allude to the function of a dielectric radome in the tailcone, which is believed to house the antenna for a rear-facing search radar. In February 1993, at an international conference, Major General Vassily Alexandrov, head of the Russian Federation air force's Central Scientific and Research Institute, revealed that a rearward-facing air intercept radar was under development for the Su-35 to allow 'over-the-shoulder' missile shots.

In service, the Su-35 will be able to carry up to seven examples of the new Novator KS-172 AAM-L ultra-long-range missile. Originally revealed with a range of 300 km (186 miles), this has a new solid-propellant booster section (which adds 1.4 m/4.6 ft to the 6-m/19.7-ft long missile), increasing effective range to 400 km (248 miles). Fitted with an active radar seeker, the missile also has inertial mid-course guidance and correction, and can be used at altitudes of up to 30000 m (98,425 ft)

The cockpit of the Su-35 features three large CRT MFD screens, each surrounded by 20 surprisingly crude input buttons, with a separate navigation display. No attempt seems to have been made to control these by HOTAS buttons, as in the MiG-29M. A sidestick controller was flown by a NIIAKM Su-27, but has not yet been incorporated in the Su-35. The new avionics give much better air-to-surface capability, conferring compatibility with a range of laser- (and perhaps TV-) guided air-to-ground weapons. Automatic terrain following is also possible. A retractable inflight-refuelling probe makes possible a further increase in the Su-27's already impressive radius of action.

Nikitin claims that the first of six Su-27M/Su-35 prototypes made its maiden flight on 28 June 1988, in the hands of Oleg Tsoi. In February 1993, Major General Alexander Yonov, director of operations and deputy chief of the Russian Federation air staff, stated that flight testing was complete and that production aircraft would enter operational service in the near future.

The Su-35 is being aggressively marketed by the Sukhoi OKB, and prototypes have been painted in several eye-catching camouflage schemes.

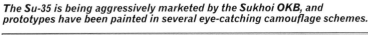

SPECIFICATION

Sukhoi Su-35
generally similar to the Sukhoi Su-27 'Flanker-B' except in the following particulars:
Wing: span 15.16 m (49 ft 8.75 in) over ESM pods
Fuselage and tail: length 22.183 m (72 ft 9 in) height 6.84 m (22 ft 5 in)
Powerplant: two NPO Saturn (Lyul'ka) AL-31FM turbofans, each rated at 130.42 kN (29,321 lb st) with afterburning
Weights: empty (40,564 lb); normal take-off 26000 kg (57,319 lb); maximum take-off 34000 kg (74,956 lb)
Load: maximum external load 8000 kg (17,637 lb)
Speed: maximum level speed 'clean' at 11000 m (36,089 ft) 2500 km/h (1,349 kt; 1,553 mph), and at sea level 1400 km/h (756 kt; 870 mph)
Range: at high-altitude with four AAMs 3500 km (1,889 nm; 2,175 miles); range at low-altitude with four AAMs 1450 km/h (783 nm; 901 miles); ferry range 4200 km (2,267 nm; 2,610 miles); range with inflight refuelling in excess of 6800 km (3,670 nm; 4,225 miles)

Below: The Su-35 differs from the basic 'Flanker' in having a new radar, flight control system and airframe improvements. It also has tall square-topped fins.

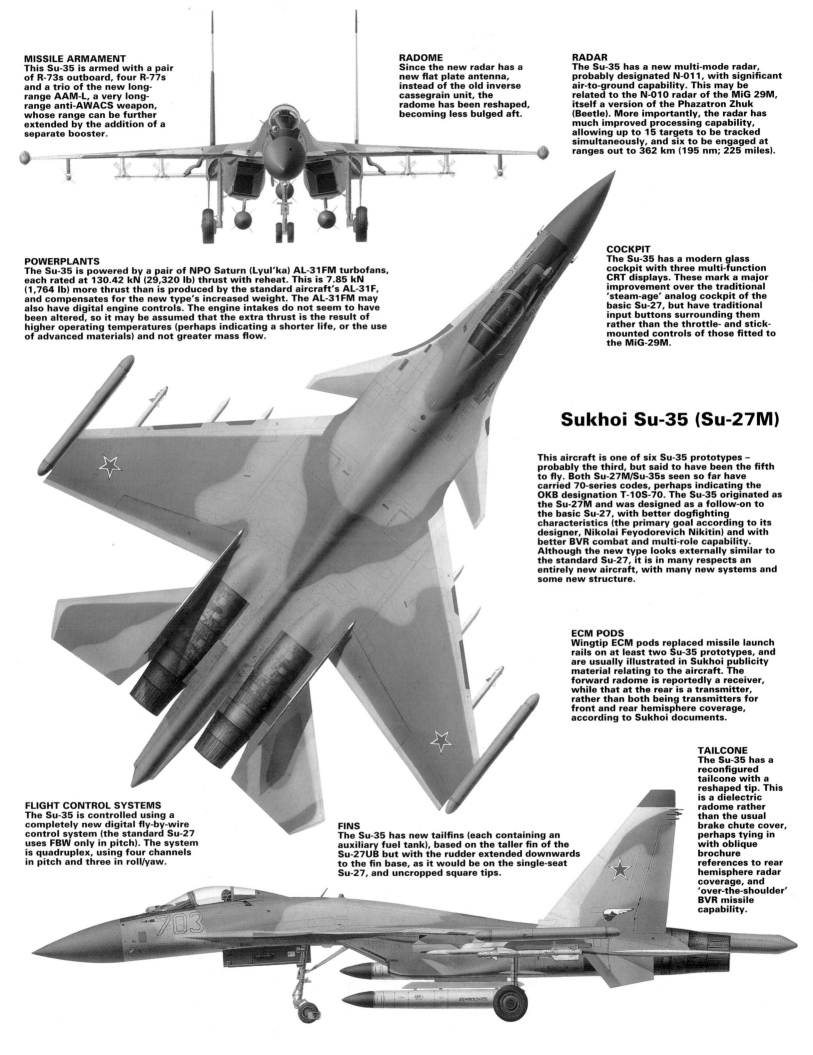

MISSILE ARMAMENT
This Su-35 is armed with a pair of R-73s outboard, four R-77s and a trio of the new long-range AAM-L, a very long-range anti-AWACS weapon, whose range can be further extended by the addition of a separate booster.

RADOME
Since the new radar has a new flat plate antenna, instead of the old inverse cassegrain unit, the radome has been reshaped, becoming less bulged aft.

RADAR
The Su-35 has a new multi-mode radar, probably designated N-011, with significant air-to-ground capability. This may be related to the N-010 radar of the MiG 29M, itself a version of the Phazatron Zhuk (Beetle). More importantly, the radar has much improved processing capability, allowing up to 15 targets to be tracked simultaneously, and six to be engaged at ranges out to 362 km (195 nm; 225 miles).

POWERPLANTS
The Su-35 is powered by a pair of NPO Saturn (Lyul'ka) AL-31FM turbofans, each rated at 130.42 kN (29,320 lb) thrust with reheat. This is 7.85 kN (1,764 lb) more thrust than is produced by the standard aircraft's AL-31F, and compensates for the new type's increased weight. The AL-31FM may also have digital engine controls. The engine intakes do not seem to have been altered, so it may be assumed that the extra thrust is the result of higher operating temperatures (perhaps indicating a shorter life, or the use of advanced materials) and not greater mass flow.

COCKPIT
The Su-35 has a modern glass cockpit with three multi-function CRT displays. These mark a major improvement over the traditional 'steam-age' analog cockpit of the basic Su-27, but have traditional input buttons surrounding them rather than the throttle- and stick-mounted controls of those fitted to the MiG-29M.

Sukhoi Su-35 (Su-27M)

This aircraft is one of six Su-35 prototypes – probably the third, but said to have been the fifth to fly. Both Su-27M/Su-35s seen so far have carried 70-series codes, perhaps indicating the OKB designation T-10S-70. The Su-35 originated as the Su-27M and was designed as a follow-on to the basic Su-27, with better dogfighting characteristics (the primary goal according to its designer, Nikolai Feyodorevich Nikitin) and with better BVR combat and multi-role capability. Although the new type looks externally similar to the standard Su-27, it is in many respects an entirely new aircraft, with many new systems and some new structure.

ECM PODS
Wingtip ECM pods replaced missile launch rails on at least two Su-35 prototypes, and are usually illustrated in Sukhoi publicity material relating to the aircraft. The forward radome is reportedly a receiver, while that at the rear is a transmitter, rather than both being transmitters for front and rear hemisphere coverage, according to Sukhoi documents.

TAILCONE
The Su-35 has a reconfigured tailcone with a reshaped tip. This is a dielectric radome rather than the usual brake chute cover, perhaps tying in with oblique brochure references to rear hemisphere radar coverage, and 'over-the-shoulder' BVR missile capability.

FLIGHT CONTROL SYSTEMS
The Su-35 is controlled using a completely new digital fly-by-wire control system (the standard Su-27 uses FBW only in pitch). The system is quadruplex, using four channels in pitch and three in roll/yaw.

FINS
The Su-35 has new tailfins (each containing an auxiliary fuel tank), based on the taller fin of the Su-27UB but with the rudder extended downwards to the fin base, as it would be on the single-seat Su-27, and uncropped square tips.

Sukhoi Su-37

The **Su-37** was developed as a private-venture replacement for aircraft like the Su-25 'Frogfoot'. A single-seat fighter-bomber, the aircraft represented a major shift away from the dedicated ground attack concept embodied by the Su-25, perhaps reacting to the school of thought in the USSR which wanted to move towards greater use of multi-role aircraft and whose most prominent statesman was Colonel General Yevgeni Shaposhnikov, C-in-C of the Russian air forces and former MiG-21 pilot. The Su-37 is therefore fitted with an advanced multi-mode radar (probably the Zhuk, or the MiG-29M's similar N-010) and is compatible with the full range of Soviet air-to-air missiles. This radar reportedly gives automatic terrain-following capability and is augmented by an electro-optical complex which includes a laser rangefinder, an IRST and guidance for TV- and laser-guided missiles.

Details of the Su-37 first emerged during 1991, when the Yugoslav magazine *Aerosvet* published an artist's impression of the aircraft, illustrating a detailed but largely speculative article, which nevertheless revealed a great deal about the new design. Similar in configuration to the Dassault Rafale or Saab Gripen, with no tailplanes, a cropped delta wing and close-coupled canard foreplanes, the Su-37 combines excellent performance with some stealth characteristics and exceptional agility. Eighteen hardpoints are provided for up to 6000 kg (13,227 lb) of weapons, and a 30-mm cannon is reported to be buried in the starboard wingroot, although this has not been shown on models of the aircraft. Wing folding is provided to allow stowage in a restricted space.

A model of the aircraft was displayed at Dubai in 1992, and a model of the two-seat version was revealed in Moscow during the same year. Marketing of the aircraft has been at best sporadic, however. Enquiries about the aircraft at Farnborough in 1992 were met with feigned incomprehension or an old-style Soviet 'that is not interesting' type of answer. Interestingly, a handful of leaflets about the aircraft were accidentally released to the press. The break-up of Sukhoi and emergence of a new Sukhoi Attack Aircraft Division might lead to increased efforts to launch the aircraft, although a Russian/CIS order seems unlikely and progress is probably dependent on finding an overseas partner. The Sukhoi OKB has hinted at plans to fit a vectoring nozzle to further enhance manoeuvrability.

Swearingen (Fairchild) Merlin IIIA

Fairchild Aircraft Incorporated
PO Box 790490, San Antonio
TX 78279-0490, USA

In 1966 Swearingen began production of its Merlin II series of pressurised twin-turboprop executive transports. This continued from 1970 with the Merlin III that introduced revised tail surfaces, among other improvements. The **Merlin IIIA** introduced additional cabin windows and major system and flight deck improvements. Seating eight to 11 passengers, this version appealed to the **Belgian air force**, which purchased six in 1976, and the **Argentine army**, which acquired four the following year. Five of the Belgian aircraft are still in use with 21 Sm/Esc, while three of the Argentine aircraft remain.

In January 1981 Swearingen products were retitled under the Fairchild Swearingen banner, and subsequent developments, the stretched Merlin IV and Metro, are described under that manufacturer.

SPECIFICATION

Swearingen Merlin IIIA
Wing: span 46 ft 3 in (14.10 m); aspect ratio 7.71; area 277.5 sq ft (25.78 m2)
Fuselage and tail: length 42 ft 2 in (12.85 m); height 16 ft 9.5 in (5.12 m); tailplane span 15 ft 1.5 in (4.61 m); wheel track 15 ft 0 in (4.57 m); wheelbase 10 ft 7 in (3.23 m
Powerplant: two Garrett AiResearch TPE331-3U-303G turboprops, each rated at 840 shp (626.5 kW)
Weights: empty equipped 7,400 lb (3356 kg);

Belgium's five Merlin IIIAs are used by 21 Smaldeel/Escadrille on staff transport duties.

maximum take-off 12,500 lb (5670 kg)
Fuel and load: internal fuel capacity 648 US gal (2452 litres)
Speed: maximum cruising speed at 16,000 ft (4875 m) 282 kt (325 mph; 523 km/h); economical cruising speed 250 kt (288 mph; 463 km/h)
Range: at maximum cruising speed 1,709 nm (1,968 miles; 3167 km); ferry range at economical cruising speed 2,483 nm (2,860 miles; 4,602 km)

Performance: maximum rate of climb at sea level 2,530 ft (770 m) per minute; service ceiling 28,900 ft (8810 m); take-off run 2,150 ft (655 m)

Transall C.160

*Original Transport Allianz group consisted of Nord, VFW and HFB.
Transall now responsibility of Aérospatiale (France) and
DASA (Germany)*

Originally conceived as a replacement for the Nord Noratlas, which equipped transport units of France's **Armée de l'Air** and West Germany's **Luftwaffe**, the C.160 was one of the first successful joint European aerospace ventures, being produced by a consortium of companies which was collectively known as the Transport Allianz group. Indeed, the name and designation chosen for the resulting machine reflected the origins of the project, for the initial quantity to be acquired was set at 160, comprising 50 **C.160F**s for France and 110 **C.160D**s for West Germany. Another possible explanation may be that the aircraft's wing area is 160 m2. The **Transall** name was merely a contraction of Transport Allianz. Members of the original production group included Nord-Aviation, Hamburger Flugzeugbau (HFB) and Vereinigte Flugtechnische Werke (VFW), these joining forces at the beginning of 1959.

Three prototypes were built in all, one by each of the three major partners in this venture, and the first of these made a successful maiden flight on 25 February 1963. They were followed by six pre-production examples from May 1965, while production-configured C.160s began to emerge in the spring of 1967, deliveries getting under way soon afterwards; by the time manufacture ceased in 1972, a total of 169 had been built. In addition to the 160 supplied to the two principal partners, nine **C.160Z**s were sold to **South Africa**. The only other air arm to operate the original type is **Turkey**, which took delivery of 20 **C.160T** aircraft (former Luftwaffe examples) in the early 1970s.

Subsequently, at the end of the 1970s, it was decided to reopen the production line in France, that country's air force ordering 25 more examples under the designation **C.160NG** (Nouvelle Génération) which differ from their predecessors by virtue of additional fuel capacity and improved avionics. Range limitations have been partly resolved by the extra centre-section fuel tank, but the newest C.160s also feature inflight-refuelling capability in the form of a probe above the cockpit. Maximum payload

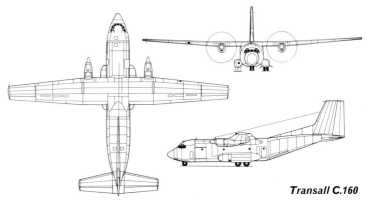

Transall C.160

is 16000 kg (35,275 lb), while 93 troops or 88 paratroops can be accommodated.

Four more C.160NGs were added in 1982, and production ended in 1985. Ten aircraft were completed with a hose-drum unit in the port undercarriage sponson for refuelling tactical aircraft, and five more have provision for the fitment of this feature so that they can be rapidly reconfigured as tankers. In 1994 the Transall fleet was engaged in an upgrade programme which adds defences against missile attacks and other improvements.

French Transalls serve in the transport role with ET 1/61 'Touraine' and ET 3/61 'Poitou' at Orléans, ET 1/64 'Béarn' and ET 2/64 'Anjou' at Evreux, CIET 340 at Toulouse, GAM 56 at Evreux, ETOM 58 'Guadeloupe' at Pointe-à-Pître, ETOM 52 'La Tontouta' at Tontouta, New Caledonia, ETOM 55 'Ouessant' at Dakar, Senegal, ETOM 88 at Djibouti and ETOM 50 'Réunion' at St Denis. Luftwaffe units are LTG 61 at Landsberg, LTG 62 at Wunsdorf and LTG 63 at Hohn. Turkish Transalls are based at Erkilet with 221 Filo, and the C.160Zs of South Africa have been recently retired.

In addition to the two original manufacturing nations, the Transall is flown by Turkey (right). Germany operates three wings as its principal transport type.

SPECIFICATION

Transall C.160 (first generation)
Wing: span 40.00 m (131 ft 3 in); aspect ratio 10.0; area 160.10 m² (1,723.36 sq ft)
Fuselage and tail: length 32.40 m (106 ft 3.5 in); height 11.65 m (38 ft 5 in); tailplane span 14.50 m (47 ft 7 in); wheel track 5.10 m (16 ft 9 in); wheel base 10.48 m (34 ft 4.5 in)
Powerplant: two Rolls-Royce Tyne RTy.20 Mk 22 turboprops each rated at 6,100 ehp (4548 ekW)
Weights: empty equipped 28758 kg (63,400 lb); normal take-off 44200 kg (97,443 lb); maximum take-off 49100 kg (108,245 lb)
Fuel and load: internal fuel 16500 litres (4,359 US gal); external fuel none; maximum payload 16000 kg (35,273 lb)
Speed: maximum level speed 'clean' at 4500 m

(14,765 ft) 536 km/h (289 kt; 333 mph); maximum cruising speed at 5500 m (18,045 ft) 513 km/h (27 kt; 319 mph) and at 8000 m (26,245 ft) 495 km/h (267 kt; 308 mph)
Range: 4500 km (2,428 nm; 2,796 miles) with an 8000-kg (17,637-lb) payload or 1182 km (637 nm; 734 miles) with a 16000-kg (35,273-lb) payload
Performance: maximum rate of climb at sea level 440 m (1,444 ft) per minute; service ceiling 8500 m (27,885 ft); take-off run 795 m (2,608 ft) at maximum take-off weight; take-off distance to 35 ft (10.7 m) 1100 m (3,609 ft) at maximum take-off weight; landing distance from 50 ft (15 m) 640 m (2,100 ft) at normal landing weight; landing run 360 m (1,181 ft) at normal landing weight

The C.160NG is easily identified by the refuelling probe. It also features additional internal fuel capacity.

Transall **C.160 GABRIEL/ASTARTE**

The French air force Transport Command fleet of 77 C.160s (in 1994) includes six second-generation aircraft assigned to two forms of special duties. All were built as transports but underwent protracted conversion and testing before delivery. As replacements for eight Elint and jamming Nord N.2501 GABRIEL Noratlas variants, two aircraft were converted to **C.160 GABRIEL** (C.160G) and entered service with 11ᵉ Escadrille of 54ᵉ Escadron Electronique Tactique 'Dunkerque' at Metz in December 1988. Features include wingtip pods with UHF/DF blade antennas, a group of five large blade antennas on top of the forward fuselage, a blister fairing on each side of the rear fuselage, and a retractable dome, produced by Thomson-CSF, under the forward fuselage. Both have refuelling probes and a hose-drum unit in the port undercarriage pannier. In the lead-up to the

1991 Gulf War, missions were flown against Iraq by a C.160G based at Al Ahsa, Saudi Arabia. The aircraft flew another four sorties during hostilities.

Another electronic surveillance version, the **C.160SE**, was offered by the manufacturers in the early 1980s but received no orders. It was similar in concept to the C.160G, with equipment that included a retractable radome with 360° scan.

C.160H is the version of Transall adapted to carry Rockwell Collins TACAMO VLF radio transmission equipment, as also used by the US Navy's Boeing E-6A Hermes. This takes the form of a long trailing aerial that enables the aircraft to communicate with missile-armed nuclear submarines of the Force Océanique Stratégique without the need for them to surface. The aerial platform is known as **ASTARTE** (Avion STAtion Relais de Transmissions Excep-

Mounting a plethora of antennas, the GABRIEL is a Sigint-gathering platform used by EET 54.

tionnelles – aircraft relay station for special transmissions) and is part of the overall RAMSES system (Réseau Amont Maillé Stratégique et de Survie – overhead strategic and survival link service). A new squadron, 59ᵉ Escadron Electronique 'Astarte', formed at Evreux on 1 January 1988 to operate the C.160Hs, the

first of which had arrived a month or so previously. All four aircraft have refuelling probes and hoses.

Tupolev **Tu-4 'Bull'**

For an unlicensed copy of the wartime B-29 to appear in this book is remarkable, but it is the case that a handful may remain in occasional use in **China** as drone carriers and testbeds. Re-engined some years ago, with the same Zhuzhou WJ-6 turboprops as the Shaanxi Y-8, **Tupolev**

Tu-4s in the Chinese air force museum are reportedly regularly put back into service for particular trials.

Remarkably, a few Chinese Tu-4s are believed to serve still on military test duties. Note the turboprops.

Tupolev **Tu-16/A/N/T 'Badger-A'**

Aviation Scientific-Technical Complex named after A.N. Tupolev
17 Naberejnaia Akademika Tupoleva
Moscow 11250, Russia

Originally designated **'Aircraft N'** or **Tu-88**, the **'Badger'** was developed as a twin-jet medium bomber to complement the strategic Myasishchev M-4 and Tupolev Tu-95. The bomb bay was sized to accommodate the Soviet Union's largest bomb, the 9000-kg (20,000-lb) FAB-9000. This allowed the use of a fuselage shortened from, but closely based on, that of the Tu-85 (itself derived from the Tu-4/B-29). The central part of the fuselage was waisted to minimise cross-sectional area where the engines joined the fuselage, reducing drag considerably. The swept wing was based on that of the Tu-82, and incorporated huge integral fuel tanks. The wing proved too thin to accommodate the bogie

Illustrating the unique wingtip-to-wingtip method of refuelling other 'Badgers', a Tu-16N 'Badger-A' (background) passes fuel to a reconnaissance 'Badger-L'. Some 'Badger-A' tankers differ by having a fuselage HDU for refuelling other aircraft types.

undercarriage, which retracted into streamlined pods projecting from the trailing edge instead. Such pods became something of a Tupolev Design Bureau trademark.

The Tu-88 prototype made its maiden flight on 27 April 1952, powered by AM-3A engines, while the second AM-3M-engined prototype flew later the same year. Evalua-

tion against Ilyushin's conservative Il-46 only served to underline the Tu-88's remarkable performance, and it was ordered into production as the Tu-16. Nine were available for the 1954 May Day flypast, while 54 were in the 1955 Aviation Day flypast 15 months later. About 2,000 were built before production ceased, excluding manufacture

in China, where the aircraft is designated **Xian H-6** (described separately).

The production Tu-16 bomber dispensed with the pressurised tunnel between cockpit and rear gunner's compartment, necessitating the provision of separate entry hatches for the rear fuselage. The under-nose radome for the Argon nav/bombing

Tupolev Tu-16/A/N/T 'Badger-A'

Virtually all surviving 'Badger-As' have been converted for special duties or as tankers. The Tu-16N is the dedicated refueller for the Tu-16 force.

radar was deepened slightly and the over-wing fences were lengthened. Several versions of the basic bomber were produced, including the **Tu-16A** nuclear bomber, and the navy's **Tu-16T**, which was equipped to carry four RAT-52 torpedoes or AMD-1000 mines, or up to 12 AMD-500 mines. The **Tu-16K Korvet** was equipped for SAR duties, with a radio-controlled lifeboat carried under the fuselage. None of these specialised variants remains in service, unlike the **Tu-16N**.

The Tu-16N was developed as a tanker for other Tu-16s, using a modernised ver-sion of the wingtip-to-wingtip refuelling system used on the Tu-4 'Bull'. The tanker can be recognised externally by a wingtip extension, outboard of a pipe-like tube which projects aft from the trailing edge. It has a total transferable fuel load of 19000 kg (42,000 lb). A large white panel is often painted on the rear fuselage of the Tu-16N to help the pilot of the receiver aircraft keep station.

In addition to the Tu-16N, some 'Badger-As' have been converted as tankers for probe-equipped aircraft like the Tu-22 'Blinder', Tu-95 'Bear-G' and Tu-95MS 'Bear-H'. These aircraft have a hose/drogue unit installed inside the former bomb bay, but may not be converted from Tu-16Ns and may not retain the wingtip-to-wingtip equipment needed to refuel other Tu-16s. The probe-and-drogue tankers have a total transferable fuel load of only 15000 kg (33,000 lb) because the HDU takes up room in the bomb bay usually occupied by fuel tanks. About 20 remain in **Russian air force** service, and another six are believed to remain in use with the former **AV-MF**.

Many redundant 'Badger-A' freefall bombers were also converted to serve as missile carriers, recce platforms or EW aircraft (described separately), and many examples of these remain in service. Other Tu-16 variants that retain the 'Badger-A' reporting name include the **Tu-16LL**, a dedicated engine testbed able to carry a variety of test engines on a semi-retractable cradle under the fuselage. About five may remain in use at Zhukhovskii. The 'Badger-A' reporting name also applies to a pair of slightly modified aircraft referred to as **Aircraft No. 14** and **Aircraft No. 16**. These set a number of world payload-to-height (rate of climb with payload) and speed with payload records during February-October 1991. Aeroflot's **Tu-16G** crew trainers reverted to standard bomber configuration many years ago.

SPECIFICATION

Tupolev Tu-16 'Badger-A'
Wing: span 32.93 m (108 ft 0.5 in); aspect ratio 6.59; area 164.65 m² (1,772.34 sq ft)
Fuselage and tail: length 36.25 m (118 ft 11.25 in); height 14.00 m (45 ft 11.25 in); tailplane span 11.75 m (38 ft 6.5 in); wheel track 9.77 m (32 ft 0.75 in); wheel base 10.57 m (34 ft 8 in)
Powerplant: two MNPK 'Soyuz' (Mikulin) AM-3A turbojets each rated at 85.22 kN (19,158 lb st) dry or, in later aircraft, MNPK 'Soyuz' (Mikulin) AM-3M-500 each rated at 93.16 kN (20,944 lb st) dry
Weights: empty equipped 37200 kg (82,012 lb); normal take-off 75000 kg (165,347 lb); maximum take-off 75800 kg (167,110 lb)
Fuel and load: internal fuel 36600 kg (80,688 lb) plus provision for fuel in two underwing auxiliary tanks; maximum ordnance 9000 kg (19,841 lb)
Speed: maximum level speed 'clean' at 6000 m (19,685 ft) 992 km/h (535 kt; 616 mph); cruising speed at optimum altitude 850 km/h (460 kt; 530 mph)
Range: 5925 km (3,198 nm; 3,682 miles) with 3800-kg (8,377-lb) warload; combat radius 3150 km (1,700 nm; 1,957 miles)

Tupolev **Tu-16K/KS 'Badger-B/C/G'**

The first missile-carrying 'Badger' was the **Tu-16KS-1** (NATO **'Badger-B'**). This was little more than a 'Badger-A' airframe with a retractable missile guidance radome in the rear of the former bomb bay, and underwing pylons for the carriage of two KS-1 Komet III (NATO AS-1 'Kennel') I-band radar-guided anti-ship missiles with mid-course guidance provided by the Kobalt radar of the Tu-4K. None remains in use in their original configuration, although some may have been converted as 'Badger-Gs'.

The **Tu-16K-10 'Badger-C'** was immediately recognisable by its broad, flat nose radome. This serves an I-band 'Puff Ball' radar associated with the K-10S (NATO AS-2 'Kipper') missile that the aircraft carried semi-recessed under the belly. About 100 aircraft (approximately 15 of which remain in service) were produced, and supplied to the Baltic, Black Sea, Northern and Pacific Fleets of the **AV-MF**. About 15 are

Left: Egypt still operates about eight Tu-16K 'Badger-Gs' from Cairo-West. These are primarily used for anti-shipping duties, using the 'Kelt' missile.

in service. 'Kipper' is now obsolete, and all 'Badger-Cs' have been converted to later standards or scrapped. Some were converted to carry the K-26 (AS-6 'Kingfish') missile underwing (retaining the capability to carry a centreline K-10) under the revised reporting name **'Badger-C Mod'** (possible Soviet designation **Tu-16K-10-26** or **Tu-16KM**). Normally only a single K-26 is carried, below the port wing. Some 'Badger-C Mods' may remain in use.

It has often been suggested that the **Tu-16K-11-16 'Badger-G'** was produced by conversion of redundant 'Badger-Bs', but this seems unlikely, since the normal bomb bay is available, with no sign of the earlier aircraft's retractable guidance radome. Whatever its origins, the original 'Badger-G' was developed as a launch vehicle for the K-11/K-16 (AS-5 'Kelt') rocket-powered air-to-surface missile, entering service in 1968. Carried underwing, the 'Kelt' carried a 1000-kg (2,200-lb) warhead and had a range in excess of 320 km (200 miles) and a maximum speed of Mach 1.2. The missile followed a pre-programmed course, using its autopilot, but could accept course corrections from the launch aircraft before the active terminal homing phase.

To ensure the correct nose-up launch attitude, the 'Badger-G' is fitted with a simple sighting device on the nose glazing. This looks like an inverted 'T'. The original under-nose Argon navigation and bombing radar of earlier Tu-16s is believed to have been replaced by the J-band target acquisition radar known to NATO as 'Short Horn'. This was housed in a slightly more bulged radome and had a range in excess of 200 km (125 miles). The Tu-16/'Short Horn'/'Kelt' combination proved devastatingly effective, and 'Badger-Gs' were exported to **Egypt** and **Iraq**, where about eight remain in service with each country, Iraq's force having been augmented by Chinese-built B-6Ds. Some Soviet 'Badger-Gs' were adapted as the **Tu-16K-26** to carry the AS-6 'Kingfish', usually (but not always) with 'Short Horn' removed and a new radar under the fuselage, adjacent to the air intakes. The NATO reporting name **'Badger-G Mod'** is applied to aircraft in this configuration. AS-6-equipped 'Badger-Gs' were first identified in 1977. About 30 remain in **VVS** service, with more in the **Ukraine**.

SPECIFICATION

Tupolev Tu-16 'Badger-G'
generally similar to the Tupolev Tu-16 'Badger-A' except in the following particulars
Wing: span 32.99 m (108 ft 3 in); aspect ratio 6.61
Fuselage and tail: length 36.80 m (118 ft 11.25 in); height 10.36 m (34 ft 0 in); wheel base 10.91 m (35 ft 9.5 in)
Powerplant: two MNPK 'Soyuz' (Mikulin) AM-3M-500 turbojets each rated at 93.16 kN (20,944 lb st)
Fuel and load: internal fuel 34360 kg (75,750 lb)
Speed: maximum level speed 'clean' at 6000 m (19,685 ft) 1050 km/h (566 kt; 652 mph)
Range: 7200 km (3,885 nm; 4,474 miles) with 3000-kg (6,614-lb) warload
Performance: service ceiling 15000 m (49,215 ft)

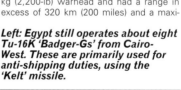

A few Tu-16K-10-26s remain in Russian navy service, equipped with the massive KSR-5/K-26 missile. This is available with either a large conventional charge or a tactical nuclear warhead.

GUN ARMAMENT
Because of the large radome, the 'Badger-C' does not have a fixed nose cannon, but retains dorsal, ventral and tail turrets, each equipped with two 23-mm cannon.

K-26 MISSILE
Probably a product of the Raduga NPO, the K-26/KSR-5 (NATO AS-6 'Kingfish') measures 34 ft 8 in (10.56 m) in length, has a body diameter of 3 ft (0.92 m) and a wing span of 8 ft 6 in (2.6 m). The launch weight is about 9,920 lb (4500 kg). With a range of about 185 miles (300 km), the K-26 has inertial mid-course guidance after a high-altitude launch, followed by one of three terminal modes. For nuclear attack, with a 350-kT yield warhead, guidance remains inertial to a pre-programmed point, but for pinpoint attacks with a 1000-kg (2,200-lb) HE warhead an active radar guidance function is available (for anti-ship attacks), as is a passive anti-radar mode.

This underview of a Tu-16K-10-26 shows not only the AS-6 missile, but also the cutaway bomb bay recess for the earlier AS-2 'Kipper'.

BLISTERS
The large teardrop observation blisters on the sides of the rear fuselage are used by the tail gunner for controlling the ventral gun. The dorsal gun is aimed from a small blister behind the cockpit.

POWERPLANT
Early Tu-16s had the Mikulin AM-3, but current aircraft are powered by the Tumanskii RD-3M-500 offering 20,920 lb (93 kN) thrust.

Tupolev Tu-16K-10-26 'Badger-C Mod'

'Badger-C Mod' is one of two major missile-carrying versions left in service. The primary weapon is the K-26 missile, usually carried singly under the port wing, but the aircraft does retain the ability to launch the elderly K-10 missile from the weapon bay recess. In addition to those serving with the Russian navy, a fair number also serve with the Ukraine, both nations using the type on anti-shipping duties.

With the designation Tu-16K-26, the 'Badger-G Mod' is a dedicated AS-6 carrier, equipped with a new ventral radar in place of the undernose unit. The excrescence on the nose ensures correct launch attitude.

WINGS
The wing features 3° of anhedral, and 41° of leading-edge sweep changing to 35° on the outer panels. It has two spars and has two large fences to prevent spanwise migration of the sluggish boundary layer.

RADAR
The massive radome houses the 'Puff Ball' I-band radar, which provides search, mapping and targeting functions. Its range is in the order of 90 miles (145 km).

Tupolev Tu-16PP/RM/KRM 'Badger-H/J'

An unknown number of 'Badgers' were converted to serve as ECM escorts under the designation **Tu-16PP**, code-named **'Badger-H'** by NATO, carrying a chaff cutter and dispenser in the former bomb bay, dispensing chaff through three slightly swept chutes along the centreline. The aircraft carries up to 9000 kg (19,800 lb) of chaff in special containers in the bomb bay. Passive receivers detect hostile emissions, analyse threat priorities and cut strips of chaff to an appropriate length according to the frequency of the enemy signal. 'Badger-Hs' have a variety of antenna configurations, but most have a large hemispherical radome on the centreline, immediately aft of the former bomb bay.

The **Tu-16RM** sub-type is known to

The Tu-16RM 'Badger-J' is readily identified by the large canoe fairing under the belly. Surrounding the fairing are intakes and exhausts for the heat exchangers needed to cool the extensive amount of electronic equipment in the aircraft's former bomb bay.

Tupolev Tu-16PP/RM/KRM 'Badger-H' and 'Badger-J'

the black boxes in the former bomb bay. The aircraft also has unique flat plate antennas on each wingtip.

An additional 'Badger-J' variant is the **Tu-16KRM**, which acts as a drone director for PVO targets. 'Badger-H' and 'Badger-J' serve with both the **Russian air force** and the former **AV-MF**.

SPECIFICATION

Tupolev Tu-16PP 'Badger-J'
generally similar to the Tupolev Tu-16 'Badger-A' except in the following particulars:
Powerplant: two MNPK 'Soyuz' (Mikulin) AM-3M-500 each rated at 93.16 kN (20,944 lb st)
Range: 5925 km (3,198 nm; 3,682 miles)

NATO as the **'Badger-J'**. An active ECM jammer, the 'Badger-J' has a distinctive ventral canoe fairing, housing radomes for the noise, spot, click and barrage jammers and covering the A- to I-bands. Ram air inlets alongside the canoe provide cooling air for

---

Tupolev **Tu-16 'Badger-D/E/F/K/L'**

Several recon Tu-16s display considerable differences from the standard variants. This aircraft appears to be a 'Badger-E', yet has the forward camera window of the 'K' or 'L'.

The first dedicated reconnaissance Tu-16 identified by NATO was the **Tu-16Ye 'Badger-D'**, an Elint conversion based on redundant 'Badger-C' airframes which retained that aircraft's distinctive broad, flattened nose radome. The chin radome was replaced by a slightly larger item, and three passive antenna blisters were added along the centreline, one large and two small. Crew complement was increased to eight or nine by equipment operators.

The **Tu-16R 'Badger-E'** was produced by converting redundant 'Badger-A' bombers, and is a dedicated reconnaissance aircraft with provision for a camera/sensor pallet inside the former bomb bay, and with two widely spaced passive receiver antennas under the fuselage. The **Tu-16P 'Badger-F'** is similar in appearance, but carries large equipment pods on its underwing pylons and sometimes has prominent blade antennas above and below the fuselage. The 'Badger-F' has been seen with a wide

variety of aerial and antenna configurations and is believed to be a dedicated maritime Elint platform. The Elint-tasked **Tu-16P 'Badger-K'** can be identified by its less widely spaced underfuselage teardrop fairings, which are also of equal size. The rearmost antenna is located just inside the area of the former bomb bay, leaving a long gap between it and the ventral gun turret. The aircraft has a row of tiny protuberances in the former bomb doors and usually has a camera window ahead of the port intake.

The **Tu-16P 'Badger-L'** reporting name is reserved for an updated maritime Elint or EW platform of configuration similar to the 'Badger-F', with underwing pylons carrying a variety of pods (including some similar to those carried by the 'Badger-F') and with the same unevenly-sized, widely-spaced underfuselage antennas as are carried by 'Badger-E' and '-F'. Differences include a thimble radome mounted in the transparent nosecone (designation becomes **Tu-16PM**)

Below: The giant radome for the 'Puff Ball' radar and ventral antenna radomes are the main identification features of the 'Badger-D'.

The 'Badger-F' was an early electronic reconnaissance variant, featuring wing pods.

WING PODS
Differing from those fitted to earlier Tu-16Ps, the wing pods carried by the Tu-16PM have cooling air inlets in the nose.

Tupolev Tu-16PM

Known to NATO as 'Badger-L', the Tu-16PM is the latest variant in a long line of electronic intelligence gatherers, but introduces a lengthened tailcone with EW equipment and a thimble radome on the nose. Only a handful of these conversions were undertaken, and the fleet exhibits several variations of antenna fit.

EQUIPMENT BAY
The weapon bay of the original 'Badger' was designed to accommodate huge bombs, and is the key to the aircraft's versatility. Large amounts of electronic equipment can be housed inside.

and an extended tailcone that replaces the rear gun turret, and is similar to the extended tailcone of the 'Bear-G'. This may house ECM equipment, or a trailing wire VLF antenna. About 80 reconnaissance and ECM Tu-16s are estimated to remain in former **AV-MF** service, alongside some 70 Tu-16N tankers and a handful of missile-carriers. The **Russian air force** operates only 15 Tu-16Rs (probably 'Badger-Fs' and '-Ls'); 15 Tu-16s also serve with **Byelorussia**, and 53 in **Ukraine** with the 260 HBAP at Stryy and the 251 HBAP at Belaya Tserkov.

SPECIFICATION

Tupolev Tu-16R 'Badger-D'
generally similar to the Tupolev Tu-16 'Badger-A' except in the following particulars:
Powerplant: two MNPK 'Soyuz' (Mikulin) AM-3M-500 turbojets each rated at 93.16 kN (20,944 lb st)
Range: 5925 km (3,198 nm; 3,682 miles)

Tupolev Tu-16R 'Badger-F'
generally similar to the Tupolev Tu-16 'Badger-A' except in the following particulars:

Powerplant: two MNPK 'Soyuz' (Mikulin) AM-3M-500 turbojets each rated at 93.16 kN (20,944 lb st)
Range: 5925 km (3,198 nm; 3,682 miles)

'Badger-K' is yet another Elint variant, identified by the equal size of its ventral radomes.

Tupolev **Tu-22 'Blinder'**

A Russian aviation journalist recently bemoaned the fact that while information on modern aircraft types like the MiG-29 and Tu-160 has been released for publication, many more elderly types are still top secret, and no information can be released. He referred specifically to the **Tu-22**, where "the number remaining in service is almost exceeded by examples in museums or raised on pedestals as gate guards."

Thus, any assessment of the Tu-22, and other same-generation Soviet aircraft, must rest partly on conjecture and informed guesswork. The original Tu-22 was developed to fly the missions of the Tu-16 'Badger', but with supersonic capability to give better penetration of sophisticated defences.

The Tupolev Design Bureau began working on high-speed supersonic bombers even before the Tu-16 'Badger' and Tu-95 'Bear' had flown, producing various designs, including the Tu-98 'Backfin'. The Tu-102 of 1957 shared a similar configuration, and was originally intended to be a multi-role aircraft, although it entered service only in its Tu-128/Tu-28 interceptor form.

The Tu-22 began life with the Bureau designation **'Aircraft Yu'** (the penultimate letter of the Cyrillic alphabet), and bore striking structural similarities to the Tu-98 and Tu-102, which in turn traced back their lineage to the Tu-16, the Tu-4 and the Boeing B-29. The Bureau designation **Tu-105** was later allocated, and the type was ordered into production under the Soviet military designation Tu-22. To add to the confusing profusion of designations and names, NATO's original reporting name of **'Beauty'** was judged 'too complimentary', and the less laudatory **'Blinder'** replaced it.

The first Tu-105 prototype is believed to have made its maiden flight during 1959, probably with Mikulin AM-3M engines, since the production Koliesov VD-7F engines were not ready. Little is known about the early flight test programme, beyond the

fact that it was conducted from Kazan. To reduce transonic drag, the Tu-22 conforms quite strictly to area-rule principles, with a waisted fuselage, engines mounted in pods above the rear fuselage, and the undercarriage carried in trailing-edge pods. The lip of each air intake forms a ring, which can be powered forward on take-off to expose an annular slot that functions as an auxiliary air intake. With little clearance between tail and runway on take-off and landing, a retractable tailskid is provided and, because of the likelihood of a tailscrape at high angles of attack, the consequent relatively high landing speed is compensated for by two massive braking parachutes. The three crew members sit in tandem, two using downward-firing ejection seats, with only the pilot in an upward-firing seat.

The first production version of the Tu-22 was disappointing, capable of about Mach 1.5, but with poor endurance and range capabilities. Basically a freefall bomber like the Tu-16 'Badger-A', its supersonic dash capability could not outweigh its inadequate radius of action. It was once believed that only a pre-production batch of **'Blinder-As'** was completed, but it now seems that the basic freefall bomber was procured in larger numbers, some still surviving as trainers and others probably having been converted to **Tu-22K 'Blinder-B'** standards, or as reconnaissance platforms or trainers.

The type made its public debut in July 1961, at the Tushino aviation display, when nine 'Blinder-As' and a single 'Blinder-B' made a flypast. By comparison with the earlier variant, the missile-carrying 'Blinder-B' had an enlarged undernose radome housing a 'Down Beat' missile guidance radar. Another feature is an overnose fairing housing a semi-retractable inflight-refuelling probe. This incorporates a triangular 'guard' on the lower surface, to prevent the refuelling drogue from damaging the nosecone. The same refuelling probe was probably

Tupolev Tu-22R 'Blinder-C'

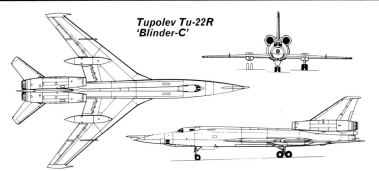

retrofitted to surviving 'Blinder-As'. The weapons bay doors were cut away to allow the AS-4 'Kitchen' ASM to be carried semi-recessed on the centreline, and improved defensive equipment and avionics were fitted in the landing gear pods and wingtip fairings. The AS-4 gave a measure of stand-off capability, and proved so successful that the missile was later adapted to the Tu-95

The Tu-22UB 'Blinder-D' trainer variant features a raised second cockpit aft of the normal flight deck.

'Bear'. When 22 Tu-22s flew over Moscow on Aviation Day (16 August) 1967, most were 'Blinder-Bs' with missiles and refuelling probes.

Two more variants of the original Tu-22

A pair of Tu-22K 'Blinder-Bs' demonstrates the carriage of the Kh-27 (AS-4 'Kitchen') missile, which nestles in a recess in the lower fuselage, formerly the bomb bay. The refuelling probe has a nosecone guard attached.

Tupolev Tu-22 'Blinder'

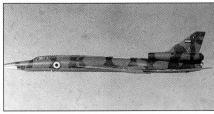

Above: Tu-22s were supplied to Iraq and Libya, the latter country operating this example. Libyan 'Blinders' saw action over Chad.

The Russian navy's main variant is the Tu-22R 'Blinder-C', used for maritime reconnaissance.

have been identified, both with the original 'Blinder-A'-type nose radome. The first of these is a dedicated reconnaissance version (possibly designated **Tu-22R**) with camera windows and dielectric panels in the nose and lower fuselage (**'Blinder-C'**), and the second is the **Tu-22UB** trainer (**'Blinder-D'**) with a raised cockpit for the instructor aft of the normal flight deck. There may be more than one version of the 'Blinder-C' operational, since different aircraft have different

camera and radome configurations, including an Elint-configured sub-variant sometimes reported as **Tu-22P 'Blinder-E'**. This has no optical sensors at all, and seems to be used purely in the electronic reconnaissance role. More recently, small numbers of Tu-22Rs have been seen with an unidentified pod below the nose, perhaps housing some kind of test equipment.

About 65 Tu-22s remain operational with **Russia**'s Long-Range Aviation, some 12 of these equipping one small regiment of the training centre at Ryazan, and about six reconnaissance-tasked Tu-22Rs are understood to equip one naval aviation regiment.

Fifty-five 'Blinders' serve with **Ukraine**, and 55 with **Byelorussia**. Tu-22s were also delivered to **Libya** (12) and **Iraq**. A handful remain operational in Libya, one of which bombed Tanzania during Libyan operations in support of Uganda. Another mounted a solo attack against N'Djamena airport, Chad, in February 1986, in retaliation for a French raid on Ouadi Doum: the 'Blinder' dropped four bombs from 16,500 ft (5030 m) at near supersonic speed, all hitting their target. Used during the long war with Iran, few of the Iraqi 'Blinders' are likely to have survived coalition attacks during Operation Desert Storm in 1991.

SPECIFICATION

Tupolev Tu-22 'Blinder-A'
Wing: span 23.75 m (77 ft 11 in)
Fuselage and tail: length 40.53 m (132 ft 11.7 in) excluding flight refuelling probe; height 10.67 m (35 ft 0 in); wheel track 8.72 m (28 ft 7.3 in); wheel base 13.73 m (45 ft 0 in)
Powerplant: two RKBM (Koliesov) VD-7M each turbojets rated at 156.90 kN (35,273 lb st) with afterburning
Weights: basic empty about 40000 kg (88,183 lb); maximum take-off about 83900 kg (184,965 lb)
Fuel and load: internal fuel about 36000 kg (79,365 lb); external fuel none; maximum ordnance 10000 kg (22,046 lb)
Speed: maximum level speed 'clean' at 12000 m (39,370 ft) 1480 km/h (800 kt; 920 mph) and at sea level 890 km/h (480 kt; 553 mph)
Range: ferry range 6500 km (3,508 nm; 4,039 miles); combat radius 3100 km (1,673 nm; 1,926 miles)
Performance: service ceiling 18300 m (60,040 ft); take-off run 2500 m (8,202 ft) at MTOW; landing run 1600 m (5,249 ft) at normal landing weight

Tupolev **Tu-22M 'Backfire'**

Initially known in the West as the Tu-26, it now seems that all 'Backfires' were actually known as **Tu-22M**s in Soviet service, and that the Tu-22M designation was not (as had once been thought) applied only to the initial 'converted' 'Blinders' ('Backfire-As'), and used by Brezhnev during the SALT-2 talks to confuse the West as to the

nature of what was called 'Backfire-B'.

It seems likely that the Tu-22M programme was launched at roughly the same time that the Su-7 was given a VG wing to become the Su-7IG (and later the Su-17). The two aircraft shared a very similar wing planform before conversion, and adopted a similar variable-geometry wing, with pivots

in roughly the same place, indicating that the same TsAGI-designed wing was used by both types. Some Western analysts have suggested that the Su-7IG was originally intended purely as an aerodynamic test vehicle for a scaled-down version of the Tu-22M wing, and that a VG wing was considered for an Su-7 derivative only as a result of these tests.

Whatever the truth, it seems that a decision was taken to fly the new wing at full scale, apparently using a radically converted

Tu-22 'Blinder' airframe (or possibly a batch of 14 'Blinder' airframes). Such reports as there are suggest that the initial **Tu-22M-1 'Backfire-A'** featured two new, larger engines in a bigger, box-section fuselage without area-ruling. These were fed by side-

A Tu-22M-3 taxis out in front of Il-76 command posts and a Tu-142LL testbed at Zhukhovskii. A set of auxiliary intakes supplements the main inlets at low speeds.

Right: The Tu-22M-2 featured simple intakes and a side-by-side twin-gun installation. The standard load was one 'Kitchen' under the belly.

Below: A large array of flaps, slats and spoilers combines with the sweeping wing to provide the Tu-22M-3 with excellent low-speed flying qualities.

on the centreline, semi-recessed, but today a more usual load seems to be two of these potent missiles on underwing pylons. External stores racks for other types of weapon are often seen under the engine intake trunks. The 'Backfire' also has capacious internal bomb bays, capable of carrying an estimated 12000 kg (26,450 lb) of bombs.

In the later **Tu-22M-3 'Backfire-C'**, these bays can accommodate the rotary launchers for the RKV-500B (AS-16 'Kickback') SRAM, used mainly for defence suppression, with two more of these missiles under each wing. Defensive armament is reduced to a single GSh-23 twin-barrelled 23-mm tail cannon.

The new variant is distinguished by new wedge-type intakes similar to those fitted to the MiG-25, and has a recontoured, upturned nose. This may accommodate a new attack radar and TFR. The variant reportedly introduces new KKBM NK-25 turbofans that increase thrust by approximately 25 per cent. There is no external evidence of a refuelling probe, although this might merely mean that a low-drag fully-retractable probe has been fitted. The aircraft is believed to have entered service with the air force of the Black Sea Fleet during 1985, and has replaced the earlier 'Backfire-B' in production.

About 220 'Backfires' of different types are in service with **Russia**, 165 of them (and possibly more, following recent large-scale transfers of equipment from the air force to avoid infringing CSE limits) with the naval air forces.

Others Tu-22Ms serve with various Long-Range Aviation strategic regiments. Many of these are now concentrated within the Smolensk and Irkutsk air armies, having been withdrawn from the area west of the Urals to avoid being included in CSE-limited forces. Further 'Backfires' serve in **Byelorussia** (52) and in **Ukraine**, where 29 serve with the 185 HBAP at Poltava and the 260

mounted intakes forward of the wingroot, which were reminiscent of those fitted to the F-4 Phantom, with prominent variable intake ramps that doubled as splitter plates. The forward fuselage was unchanged, and the wings were given swinging outer panels. The latter were located outboard of the undercarriage pods, which seem to have been retained.

The very existence of any 'converted' 'Blinders' has been called into question recently, since an aircraft (coded '33') at Monino has been described as the prototype for the Tu-22M, and this has the standard 'Backfire-B' nose, undercarriage and intakes. It differs mainly in having a huge (brake-chute?) fairing on the trailing edge of the tailfin, displacing the gun turret and tail warning radar, and in having a large spike fairing projecting forward from the fintip. Soviet sources refer to an in-house Design Bureau designation of **Tu-126**, perhaps

explaining why the aircraft has been known as the **Tu-26**. There may still have been interim aircraft between the standard Tu-22 'Blinder' and this aircraft, of course.

It is believed that development began in about 1965, but no date or details are known concerning the first flight or flight test programme. NATO announced the existence of a variable-geometry Soviet bomber in 1969, and one was spotted on the ground at Kazan in July 1970. The production **Tu-22M-2 'Backfire-B'** is believed to have made its first flight in about 1975, and has always been said to have introduced a longer-span wing, a redesigned forward fuselage (with pilot and co-pilot sitting side-by-side, and with an extra crew member bringing the complement to four) and a revised undercarriage. This now retracts inboard, so that the six-wheeled undercarriage bogies fold inward to lie in the lower fuselage. These 'changes' are

thrown into doubt by the aircraft at Monino, although others are not.

Tail armament, for example, is increased by comparison with the older Tu-22, the single remotely-controlled GSh-23 twin 23-mm cannon in the tail being replaced by a pair of these weapons. The guidance/ranging radar for these weapons has been replaced by 'Fan Tail' equipment, since the original ogival radome has been replaced by a larger diameter 'drum'.

SALT limitations

During the abortive SALT-2 arms limitation talks, 'Backfire-Bs' had their nose-mounted refuelling probes removed to back up Brezhnev's contention that the aircraft was a medium bomber with no intercontinental capability, and were thus exempt from limitations proposed under the still-born treaty. Initially, Tu-22Ms were usually seen carrying a single AS-4 'Kitchen' ASM

With wings swept back, the Tu-22M-3 is capable of supersonic dashes during the attack phase of its mission. This aircraft carries racks for conventional bombs under the engine intakes.

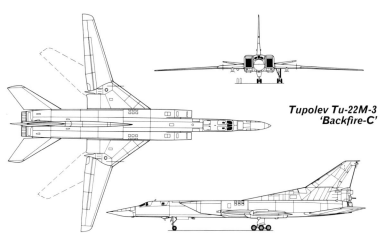

Tupolev Tu-22M-3 'Backfire-C'

Tupolev Tu-22M 'Backfire'

HBAP at Stryy. The exact locations of bomber regiments are unknown but, during 1989/90, the Tu-22Ms were said to be based at Machulische, Zhitomir, Neshun, Gomel and Baranovichi. Some carried unit insignia (a Tu-22M-3 wore a winged missile on its nose, for example) and some even carried Cyrillic characters spelling out BBC CCCP (VVS SSSR, or air forces of the USSR) on their intakes. Production is believed to continue at a rate of 30 per year, and may allow the final retirement of older aircraft (especially the Tu-22 and surviving Tu-16 bombers) in the near future.

A fully operational 'Backfire' is an extremely potent aircraft. With a substantial warload, which includes some of the latest and most lethal Soviet weapons, the Tu-22M can attack targets with deadly accuracy and an extremely heavy punch. Defensive systems are generously provided, with the 23-mm cannon providing a useful deterrent to enemy fighter pilots approaching within gun range, and extensive batteries of flares and chaff cartridges to 'spoof' enemy missiles. ECM and ECCM systems are also fitted, and some reports suggest that decoy

drones can be carried. With its wings fully swept back (to 65°), the Tu-22M is capable of a Mach 2 dash at high altitude, and of speeds up to Mach 0.9 at low level. The unrefuelled combat radius of the Tu-22M-2 'Backfire-B' is quoted as 4000 km (2,485 miles), and the radius of action of 'Backfire-C' may be even better. The recent termination of 'Blackjack' production has served to increase the importance of the 'Backfire' fleet. With only two squadrons of Tu-160s in service, the former Soviet air forces have only the Tu-95 'Bear' for long-range duties, and for penetration missions must rely on the Tu-22M to back up the handful of Tu-160s.

Severe spares shortages, reliability problems, and more recent problems in retaining trained air and ground crews render this significant bomber fleet much less effective than the overall number of airframes would suggest. Not only are engine failures and other major unserviceabilities common but, when an aircraft has been grounded for technical reasons, it will often stay grounded for up to six months. Training has deteriorated in both quality and quantity, with pilots 'chasing' an ever-dwindling number of

aircraft, and with severe fuel shortages severely rationing operational flying. Many problems have been laid squarely at the door of industry, where quality control is said to have declined markedly in recent years. Problems aside, the Tu-22M continues to play a vital role in the defence of the former Soviet Union, albeit now as part of the strategic forces nominally under the central control of the Commonwealth of Independent States. About 220 remain in service (and another 160 with the former AV-MF) and low-rate production may continue. The Tu-22M-3 has also been offered for export and may have been purchased by **Iran**.

WEAPON OPTIONS

Defensive armament of two (Tu-22M-2) or one (Tu-22M-3) GSh-23 23-mm cannon in remotely-operated tail turret. Two wing pylons and fuselage recess for the carriage of up to three Kh-22 (AS-4 'Kitchen') nuclear or conventional stand-off missiles. Alternative missile armament for Tu-22M-3 consists of six Kh-15P (AS-16 'Kickback') short-range nuclear missiles on internal rotary launcher with another four on two wing

pylons, or a combination of internal Kh-15P and external Kh-27. Conventional bomb load maximum of 24000 kg (52,910 lb), although 12000 kg (26,455 lb) more usual. Bombs of up to 3000 kg (6,614 lb) can be carried. Bomb racks under the intakes augment internal and wing pylon carriage.

SPECIFICATION

Tupolev Tu-22M-2 'Backfire-B'
Wing: span 34.30 m (112 ft 6.5 in) spread and 23.40 m (76 ft 9.25 in) swept; aspect ratio 6.92 spread; area 170.00 m² (1,829.92 sq ft) spread
Fuselage and tail: length 39.60 m (129 ft 11 in); height 10.80 m (35 ft 5.25 in)
Powerplant: probably two KKBM (Kuznetsov) NK-144 turbofans each rated at 196.13 kN (44,092 lb st) with afterburning
Weights: basic empty 54000 kg (119,048 lb); normal take-off 122000 kg (268,959 lb); maximum take-off 130000 kg (286,596 lb)
Fuel and load: internal fuel 57000 kg (125,661 lb); maximum ordnance 12000 kg (26,455 lb)
Speed: maximum level speed 'clean' at 11000 m (36,090 ft) 2125 km/h (1,146 kt; 1,320 mph) and at sea level 1100 km (594 kt; 684 mph)
Range: ferry range 12000 km (6,476 nm; 7,457 miles); combat radius 4000 km (2,159 nm; 2,486 miles)
Performance: service ceiling 18000 m (59,055 ft)

Tupolev Tu-22M-3 'Backfire-C'
generally similar to the Tupolev Tu-22M-2 'Backfire-B' except in the following particulars:
Powerplant: two KKBM (Kuznetsov) NK-25 turbofans each rated at 245.2 kN (55,115 lb st) with afterburning
Weights: maximum take-off 130000 kg (286,596 lb)
Fuel and load: external fuel none; maximum ordnance 12000 kg (26,455 lb)

Tupolev **Tu-95/95M 'Bear-A'**

Derived from the Tu-4 'Bull' and its enlarged and refined derivatives, the Tu-80 and Tu-85, the **Tu-95 'Bear'** was designed around the 12,000-shp (8952-kW) Kuznetsov NK-12M turboprop and slow-turning contra-rotating AV-60N airscrew, although the first aircraft flew on 12 November 1952 powered by four pusher-tractor tandem pairs of TV-2 turboprops. The immensely powerful NK-12M allowed jet-like speeds to be achieved (thus the need for swept wings and tailplane) but with much greater fuel economy, giving a genuine intercontinental range. In fact, the original 'Bear-A' is now estimated as having a range of 9,200 miles (14805 km) without inflight refuelling and while carrying a 25,000-lb (11340-kg) bomb load, with a cruising speed of Mach 0.67 (442 mph; 711 km/h). The maximum speed is Mach 0.82 (570 mph; 917 km/h) at 25,000 ft (7620 m) or Mach 0.78 (520 mph; 835 km/h) at 40,000 ft (12192 m). Later variants, with more powerful engines and cleaner airframes, can achieve higher speeds.

The basic **Tu-95M 'Bear-A'** was intro-

The 'Bear-A' was originally procured for the freefall nuclear bomber role, but the deterrent largely passed to missile-based systems many years ago. The bombers were mostly converted for other duties, although a handful remain in their original configuration for training purposes, some with sealed bomb bays.

duced into air force service in April 1956, as a freefall nuclear bomber with the air force designation **Tu-20**, featuring reverse pitch in place of a brake parachute. It relied on its speed and high-altitude capability to slip through enemy defences, with insurance provided in the form of five powered gun turrets in the tail and above and below the fuselage, operated by four gunners. The bomb bay was 14.2 m (46.6 ft) long. The dawn of the missile age brought with it an unacceptable degree of vulnerability, and an end to freefall bombing. Most 'Bear-As' were converted for other duties, mostly as missile-carrying 'Bear-Bs' and 'Bear-Cs'. The remainder were relegated to training duties.

To avoid being counted under START's limitations on strategic bombers, about a dozen surviving 'Bear-As' were converted to **Tu-95U** configuration, with sealed bomb bays and a broad red band painted around the rear fuselage. Most served with the Long-Range Aviation training centre at Ryazan. The unofficial reporting name **'Bear-T'** has been applied to these aircraft, most of which were withdrawn from use during 1991 and 1992 with the availability of other variants for training.

SPECIFICATION

Tupolev Tu-95 'Bear-A'
Wing: span 51.10 m (167 ft 7.75 in); aspect ratio 8.41; area 310.50 m² (3,342.30 sq ft)
Fuselage and tail: length 47.50 m (155 ft 10 in)

excluding flight refuelling probe and 49.50 m (162 ft 4.8 in) including flight refuelling probe; height 12.12 m (39 ft 9.2 in); tailplane span 14.90 m (48 ft 10.6 in); wheel track 12.95 m (42 ft 5.8 in); wheel base 15.85 m (52 ft 0 in)
Powerplant: four KKBM (Kuznetsov) NK-12MV turboprops each rated at 11033 ekW (14,795 ehp)
Weights: empty equipped 86000 kg (189,594 lb); normal take-off 154200 kg (339,947 lb); maximum take-off 188000 kg (414,469 lb)
Fuel and load: internal fuel 58500 kg (128,968 lb); external fuel none; maximum ordnance 20000 kg (44,092 lb)
Speed: maximum level speed 'clean' at 7600 m (24,935 ft) 925 km/h (500 kt; 575 mph); cruising speed at optimum altitude 708 km (382 kt; 440 mph)
Range: 14800 km (7,987 nm; 9,197 miles) with 11340-kg (25,000-lb) payload
Performance: climb to 5000 m (16,405 ft) in 13 minutes; service ceiling 13500 m (44,290 ft)

Tupolev Tu-95K 'Bear-B/C/G'

Improvements in SAM and interceptor technology during the late 1950s rendered traditional Soviet strategic bomber tactics unworkable. The use of freefall bombs was replaced by the use of stand-off missiles, and the 'Bear' was hastily modified to launch such weapons.

The first missile-carrying 'Bear' was the **Tu-95K-20 'Bear-B'**. Most Tu-95K-20s were produced by conversion of Tu-95Ms, and featured a broad, flat-bottomed radome under the nose and a dielectric panel following the normal nose contours above. The glazed nose was entirely faired over. The large undernose radome housed a 130-in (3.3-m) wide scanning antenna for the low I-band A-336Z 'Crown Drum' missile guidance radar. This was used in association with the Mikoyan-developed Kh-20 (AS-3 'Kangaroo') missile.

The Kh-20 was a turbojet-engined swept-wing missile weighing almost 25,000 lb (11340 kg) and carrying a 5,100-lb (2313-kg) 800-kT warhead. Launched from high altitude, the missile had a range estimated at about 400 miles (643 km) and had no terminal guidance. Once it was out of range of the launch aircraft (which could then turn away), the missile's autopilot simply flew a pre-programmed course to the target area. Some 'Bear-Bs' later received nose-mounted inflight-refuelling probes (**Tu-95KD**) and some may have been fitted with an Elint antenna on the starboard rear fuselage. Others may have been further upgraded to 'Bear-G' standards.

Some 'Bear-Bs' replaced by later missile carriers were relegated to training duties, and now serve with the former Long-Range Aviation's training centre at Ryazan. These aircraft do not have IFR probes fitted and the sides of the rear fuselage lack Elint antennas and other protuberances. They are now powered by 14,795-ehp (11037-kW) NK-12MV turboprops.

The **Tu-95KM 'Bear-C'** is believed to have been a new-build aircraft, and not a conversion from the 'Bear-A'. Intended as a missile carrier with a secondary multi-role capability, the aircraft was almost identical

Above: Most Tu-95KMs have since been modified or retired, although a few may remain on patrol duties.

Right: The Tu-95K-22 serves as a stand-off missile carrier. The wing pods are a notable feature, as is the solid ECM tailcone carried by most examples.

to late-series Tu-95K-20s in appearance, but had Elint antennas on each side of the rear fuselage, together with other reconnaissance sensors and equipment not normally fitted to 'Bear-Bs'. Many Tu-95KMs were upgraded to 'Bear-G' standards and it is unlikely that any remain operational in their original configuration.

The **Tu-95K-22 'Bear-G'** has a strong resemblance to the 'Bear-B' and 'Bear-C', although its broad flat nose radome differs in detail and accommodates an antenna for the 'Down Beat' radar associated with the Kh-22 (NATO AS-4 'Kitchen') missile. It was probably produced only by conversion of 'Bear-B' and 'Bear-C' airframes. The Tu-95K-22's AS-4 missiles are carried under the wingroots on pylons instead of semi-recessed under the belly. The rocket-powered AS-4 weighs about 13,000 lb (5897 kg) and is some 37 ft (11.3 m) long. It can be fit-

ted with a nuclear warhead of up to 350 kT or a smaller warhead and active radar terminal homing. Ranges vary from 270 miles (435 km) at high altitude to 190 miles (305 km) at low level.

The 'Bear-G' has a comprehensive defensive avionics suite, marked by the provision of a plethora of radomes and fairings. A thimble radome on the nose, between the undernose radome and the inflight-refuelling probe, is believed to be for a TFR, and small pylon-mounted pod-like ECM antennas are mounted below the lower fuselage in front of and behind the wing. Elint antennas are installed on the sides of the rear fuselage, and the aircraft has an extended tailcone,

with a distinctive external cable duct along the lower right rear fuselage running aft from below the Elint blister. The extended tailcone replaces the tail turret, and the dorsal turret is also removed, leaving only a single ventral gun turret for self-defence.

Most 'Bear-Gs' also carry an unidentified pod under each outer wing panel. These have a distinctive conical nose and may be ECM jamming pods, air sampling pods or chaff/flare dispensers. Forty-six serve with the Irkutsk Air Army at Ukrainka, perhaps alongside 15 earlier missile carriers. Three more are in storage at Belaya Tserkov, and there are more among the seven kept at Zhukhovskii for test duties.

Tupolev Tu-95MS 'Bear-H'

The production line at Taganrog reopened in 1983 to manufacture the 'Bear-F' and the **Tu-95MS 'Bear-H'**. The 'Bear-H' is a new strategic bomber version incorporating many features of the maritime Tu-142 airframe, and the latter aircraft's more powerful NK-12MV engines. Thus the Tu-95MS has the redesigned cockpit and slightly longer nose of the Tu-142M, and the same undercarriage (with its associated bulged undercarriage doors) and extended-chord rudder. Like the Tu-142M, the Tu-95MS lacks dorsal and ventral gun turrets, allowing the sighting blisters under the tailplanes to be removed. It does not have the 70-in (178-cm) forward fuselage plug of the maritime 'Bears', however, and retains the shorter fin and horizontal, undrooped refuelling probe of other bomber 'Bears'.

At first glance the nose of the Tu-95MS appears similar to that of the 'Bear-C' and 'Bear-G', but the resemblance is superficial. The deeper, shorter radome houses an unknown radar and has cable ducts running back from it on both sides of the fuselage. To port, this runs back almost to the tailfin,

An immaculate Tu-95MS 'Bear-H' tucks up its undercarriage after take-off. Something of a Tupolev trademark, the main bogies somersault through 90° as the gear retracts backwards, so that they lie flat in the rear of the extended engine nacelle.

and to starboard almost to the wing leading edge. Under the extreme rear fuselage the aircraft has a sensor/antenna package similar to that fitted to the 'Bear-F Mod IV'.

The Tu-95MS was developed specifically to carry the new RK-55 (AS-15 'Kent') cruise missile that also equips the Tu-160 'Blackjack'. Details of the RK-55 became available as a result of the INF treaty talks, from which it was learned that the missile is a turbofan-engined weapon with terrain comparison and inertial guidance. Weighing about 3,750 lb (1700 kg), the 26-ft (8-m) long weapon has a spread wingspan of

nearly 11 ft (3.3 m) and a range in excess of 2,175 miles (3500 km).

The 'Bear-H's' 7.5-m (24.6-ft) long weapons bay accommodates a rotary launcher for six of these missiles, and early aircraft, without underwing pylons, are designated **Tu-95MS-6 'Bear-H6'**. Three underwing pylons are fitted under each inner wing panel of later aircraft, the outboard pair

carrying three missiles and the other two single missiles. This brings the total number of missiles to 16 RK-55s, and changes the designation to **Tu-95MS-16 ('Bear-H16')**. For self-defence the Tu-95MS has only its rear gun turret. This is of entirely new design, with a single twin-barrelled GSh-23L cannon in place of a pair of single-barrelled NR-23s.

The 'Bear-H' has now ceased production, but there are five examples at Belaya Tserkov in storage, and another two at the Kubyshev factory, in addition to those in service at Mozdok (22 MS16s), Uzin (under the command of **Ukraine**) and Semipalatinsk (Kazakhstan). The 40 aircraft (13 MS16s and 27 MS6s) at the latter base remain under control of **Russia**.

Escorted by a Massachusetts ANG F-15A, a Tu-95MS probes US air defences. The variant is designed to launch cruise missile attacks from outside hostile air space.

Tupolev **Tu-95RT/MR 'Bear-D/E'**

Tupolev Tu-95RT 'Bear-D'

The **Tu-95RT 'Bear-D'** was first identified in 1967, and was a dedicated naval version converted from surplus Tu-95M 'Bear-As'. The new variant featured a new enlarged chin radome, and a much larger I-band search radar ('Big Bulge') in place of the former weapons bay. Another much smaller radome is located further aft. There are Elint blisters and other antennas on the fuselage. A handful of 'Bear-Ds' had their tail turrets removed and were fitted with a solid t. cone like that fitted to the 'Bear-G' or Tu-126 'Moss'. There are also streamlined pods on the tips of the tailplanes, serving an unknown purpose. Some reports suggest that these accommodate a magnetic anomaly detector of some sort, but this would seem unlikely since the aircraft has no other ASW sensors or weapons.

It is believed that the Tu-95RT was developed as a mid-course missile guidance platform, acquiring targets for ship-, submarine- and air-launched missiles and sending guidance information to them before onboard terminal guidance cou⁴ take over. It also has an important secondary maritime radar reconnaissance role, and often serves as an Elint and reconnaissance platform.

To extend range and endurance, the 'Bear-D' is fitted with a fixed inflight-refuelling probe above the nose. In April 1970 a

Tu-95RT took off from a base in the Kola Peninsula to participate in a Soviet naval exercise in the Iceland-Faroes gap, and then flew on south to Cuba. This marked the beginning of a 22-year cycle of deployments to Cuba by 'Bears', often with the big Tupolevs rumbling down the Eastern seaboard of the USA under escort by US fighters. Naval aviation 'Bears' have operated from a number of bases outside the USSR, including San Antonio de los Banos in Cuba, Conakry in Guinea, Belas in Angola, Okba ben Nafi in Libya and Cam Ranh Bay in Vietnam, as well as bases in Ethiopia and Mozambique.

Thirty-seven Tu-95RTs remaining in service were excluded from the 19 START negotiations on the basis that they were based at naval airfields and performed a purely naval role. About 15 were believed to remain in service with the **AV-MF** in 1994, fulfilling a maritime reconnaissance function now that most ship-launched missiles do not need mid-course guidance.

The **Tu-95MR 'Bear-E'** was also produced for the AV-MF by conversion of redundant Tu-95Ms, although a much

Right: A close-up reveals the reconnaissance camera pack in the weapons bay of the Tu-95MR.

smaller number (about 12) was produced. The aircraft is fitted with a slightly bulged removable reconnaissance pallet in the former bomb bay. This has seven camera windows set into it, three side-by-side pairs of windows forward with a single window further aft to starboard. It retains the 'Bear-A's' chin teardrop radome on the centreline just ahead of the wingroots. Elint blisters and what look like faired-over camera ports are mounted on the sides of the rear fuselage, and the aircraft is usually fitted with an inflight-refuelling probe. Some surviving Tu-95Rs have

been transferred to the air force and serve with the former Long-Range Aviation Training Centre at Ryazan. Red bands are painted around the rear fuselage for arms treaty verification purposes.

Above: The Tu-95RT was the most widely encountered 'Bear' variant due to its maritime reconnaissance brief. It was also used for missile guidance.

Below: Only a few Tu-95MRs were produced, these undertaking a long-range naval photo-reconnaissance role. Some Elint capability is incorporated.

Tupolev **Tu-128 'Fiddler'**

The career of the world's largest interceptor is virtually at its end. A mere handful (if any) remain airworthy, having been replaced by MiG-31 'Foxhounds' and Su-27 'Flankers' in their primary role. Derived from the unsuccessful Tu-98 'Backfin' supersonic medium bomber prototype, the **Tu-128** (some reports suggest an alternative OKB designation of **Tu-102**) was developed into a long-range interceptor, flying in its new guise during 1959.

Developed to meet the threat posed by long-range stand-off missiles, the Tu-128 was armed with the enormous AA-5 'Ash' missile, and had a huge radar antenna in the nose. Two prototypes (**'Fiddler-A'**), with ventral fins, a large ventral fairing and two underwing missiles, made their public debut at Tushino in 1961. The production aircraft, without ventral bulge or fins, had four underwing missiles, and was designated **'Fiddler-B'**. It made its debut at Domodedovo in 1967.

A dedicated trainer variant, with an extra cockpit in the nose, ahead of the usual cockpit, was reportedly designated **Tu-128M**.

The Tu-128 protected the frozen wastes of the Soviet Arctic. It is believed to be out of front-line service.

Tupolev **Tu-134 'Crusty'**

The **Tu-134 'Crusty'** was developed directly from the earlier Tu-124 'Cookpot', retaining the basic wing and fuselage, undercarriage and high-lift devices, but adopting a T-tail and rear-mounted engines, as well as incorporating slight increases in wingspan and fuselage length and an underfuselage airbrake to allow steeper approaches to be flown. It was originally designated **Tu-124A**, but was redesignated before the first flight in 1962. Production started in 1964 and the new 72-seater entered Aeroflot service in 1967. In 1970 the **Tu-134A** replaced the original aircraft on the production line. The new variant had a 2.1-m (6-ft 10-in) fuselage stretch and was fitted with an APU. The aircraft was re-engined with Soloviev D-30 Series II turbofans, and most Tu-134As also had a radar nose in place of the original variant's glazed navigator's position.

Primarily delivered to civilian customers, the Tu-134A serves with the air forces of **Angola**, **Czechoslovakia**, **Poland** and **Russia**, while Tu-134s serve with **Bulgaria** and Russia, mainly in the VIP transport role. Two aircraft previously based at Sperenburg in Germany carried extra communications antennas in their role as transports for the GSFG commander. Russia also has a handful of Tu-134s converted for bomber crew training duties. The **Tu-134BSh** is

There have been several special variants of the Tu-134, used for equipment tests or bomber training purposes. Fitted for the latter with Tu-160 radar is this Tu-134UBL.

a dedicated bombardier trainer, and has a Tu-22M radar in the nose, with underwing pylons for the carriage of practice bombs. Consoles and radar bombsights for 12 students are provided in the cabin. These are used by fourth year students at the Higher Military School at Tambov. The **Tu-134UBL** (Uchebno-boevoi dla lotchikov, or trainer for pilots) has a similar external appearance, but is designed as a Tu-160 'Blackjack' crew trainer, with Tu-160 radar and avionics. It is primarily designed to train 'Blackjack' pilots, and simulates the bomber's handling characteristics (especially in the circuit and on take-off and landing) particularly well. Two entered service with the 184th Bomber Regiment at Priluki during early 1991.

SPECIFICATION

Tupolev Tu-134A 'Crusty'
Wing: span 29.00 m (95 ft 1.75 in); aspect ratio 6.6; area 127.30 m² (1,370.29 sq ft)
Fuselage and tail: length 37.10 m (121 ft 8.75 in); height 9.02 m (29 ft 7 in); tailplane span 9.20 m (30 ft 2 in); wheel track 9.45 m (31 ft 0 in); wheel base 13.93 m (45 ft 8.5 in)
Powerplant: two PNP 'Aviadvigatel' (Soloviev) D-30 II turbofans each rated at 66.68 kN (14,991 lb st)
Weights: operating empty 29000 kg (63,933 lb); maximum take-off 47000 kg (103,616 lb)
Fuel and load: internal fuel 16500 litres (4,359 US gal); external fuel none; maximum payload 8165 kg (18,000 lb)
Speed: maximum cruising speed at 8500 m (27,885 ft) 900 km/h (485 kt; 559 mph) or at 11000 m (36,090 ft) 870 km/h (470 kt; 541 mph); normal cruising speed at 11000 m (36,090 ft) 750 km/h (405 kt; 466 mph)

Range: 3500 km (1,889 nm; 2,175 miles) with a 4000-kg (8,818-lb) payload or 2000 km (1,079 nm; 1,243 miles) with an 8215-kg (18,111-lb) payload
Performance: service ceiling 11900 m (39,040 ft); balanced field length 2400 m (7,874 ft) at maximum take-off weight; balanced landing field length 2200 m (7,218 ft) at maximum landing weight; landing run 780 m (2,559 ft) at maximum landing weight

Tupolev Tu-134 'Crusty'

Tupolev **Tu-142 'Bear-F'**

The plentiful availability of 'Bear' airframes quickly led to the type's adoption by the **AV-MF** in the shape of the 'Bear-D' and 'Bear-E', which impressed their new operators with their performance, capacity and long range. The navy felt that it had only scratched the potential of the aircraft, and only ordered Tupolev to develop a dedicated maritime reconnaissance and ASW variant, retaining the basic airframe but incorporating every necessary structural, aerodynamic and systems improvement. The wing is believed to have undergone a major redesign, although references to increased camber are believed to indicate the provision of new double-slotted flaps rather than a new wing section.

The wing is also strengthened for operation at higher all-up weights. The undercarriage is redesigned with larger tyres and more powerful brakes, and this necessitated the provision of bulged nosewheel doors and enlarged trailing edge fairings for the main undercarriage. A 70-in (178-cm) section was added to the fuselage ahead of the wing, and the rear pressure bulkhead

The Tu-142M3 'Bear-F Mod 4' is the current standard version of ASW aircraft, complete with antenna arrays under the nose and tail.

was moved aft to make possible major improvements to the crew accommodation and galley. To compensate for the increased forward fuselage length the trailing edge of the rudder was extended aft.

The weapons bays were completely redesigned, with a new rear bay for sonobuoys replacing the ventral turret, and with the main bay being divided into front and rear halves, covered by separate pairs of doors. These probably have a maximum capacity similar to the Tu-95's 25,000 lb

(11340 kg) and are configured to carry antisubmarine torpedoes, depth charges, sonobuoys and SAR equipment, and possibly auxiliary fuel tanks. The 'Bear-F' also introduced a new ventral radome, slightly smaller than that fitted to 'Bear-D' and located further forward. The new radar operates at a higher frequency than 'Bear-D's' 'Big Bulge' (in J-band at about 21 gHz) and is optimised for overwater operation.

A second radome was mounted under the nose, in a longer and narrower radome than that fitted to the 'Bear-A', 'Bear-D' and 'Bear-E'. The aircraft had a remarkably clean fuselage, with tandem twin ADF blade antennas, but with no Elint blisters on the

rear fuselage. It reintroduced streamlined pods on the tailplane tips similar to those seen on the Tu-95RT 'Bear-D'. If these fairings do accommodate a magnetic anomaly detector, it is probable that there is a galvanometer in each, their right/left symmetry cancelling out the magnetic influences of the airframe itself.

The resulting aircraft was given the designation **Tu-142** by the design bureau, emphasising the radical changes from the original air force Tu-95s. NATO allocated the reporting name **'Bear-F'**. Fifteen examples were built from 1970 before production changed to the modified **Tu-142A 'Bear-F Mod 1'**. Apart from minor changes to

Tupolev Tu-142 'Bear-F'

antennas and airscoops, the new aircraft had the undernose radome removed, and most also reverted to the smaller, standard trailing edge undercarriage fairings.

The basic Tu-142 was replaced on the production line by the **Tu-142M** that introduced major airframe changes. The forward fuselage was extended by a further 9 in (23 cm), and the cockpit was completely redesigned. Instead of sloping down to the windscreen, the roof of the flight deck continues straight forward, giving an extra 14 in (36 cm) of headroom at the front. This gives the pilots a better working environment and improves the view forward, which is also enhanced by the IFR probe being drooped downwards by 4°. The first Tu-142M sub-variant was given the reporting name

'Bear-F Mod 2' by NATO, and retained the same basic ASW systems as earlier 'Bear-Fs', with a small hemispherical thimble radome (perhaps for satellite communications) being the only notable addition to the antenna fit.

The addition of a new MAD in a spike-like fairing projecting aft from the tail, and an increased-length sonobuoy bay, resulted in the **Tu-142M2 'Bear-F Mod 3'** which entered service in about 1982. The latest sub-type is the **Tu-142M3 'Bear-F Mod 4'** which was identified in 1986. This was similar to the 'Bear-F Mod 3' but introduced a new undernose sensor package (probably including FLIR) and a new equipment package under the tail. The old gunner's sighting blisters below the tail were removed, and replaced by small blister fairings. There is a large cable duct or similar fairing running along the lower part of the port fuselage, from the cockpit almost back to the tailplane. A tiny 'pimple' radome on the nose may serve a TFR, or may have an ECM or EW function.

At least one converted 'Bear-F' has served as an engine testbed, under the designation **Tu-142LL**, with the test engine slung in a semi-retractable cradle under the centre-section. This aircraft is currently

From below, a 'Bear-F Mod 3' displays its tail-mounted MAD.

in open storage at Zhukhovskii. Between March and October 1988, eight Tu-142Ms were delivered to No. 312 Squadron of the **Indian Navy** at Dabolim. Often reported to be rebuilt or upgraded 'Bear-Fs', the Indian aircraft are to 'Bear-F Mod 3' standard, with the longer fuselage and taller cockpit of the Tu-142M, so this seems unlikely. India was the first, and so far the only, export customer for the 'Bear', but the 'Bear-F Mod 4' remains in low volume production, and further orders could follow.

India's eight Tu-142Ms serve with INAS 312 'Albatross'. The aircraft are to 'Bear-F Mod 3' standard.

SPECIFICATION

Tupolev Tu-142M 'Bear-F Mod 3'
Wing: span 51.10 m (167 ft 8 in); aspect ratio 8.39; area 311.10 m² (3,348.76 sq ft)
Fuselage and tail: length 49.50 m (162 ft 5 in); height 12.12 m (39 ft 9 in); tailplane span 14.90 m (48 ft 10.6 in); wheel track 12.95 m (42 ft 5.8 in); wheel base 15.85 m (52 ft 0 in)
Powerplant: four KKBM (Kuznetsov) NK-12MV turboprops each rated at 11033 ekW (14,795 ehp)
Weights: maximum take-off 185000 kg (407,848 lb)
Fuel and load: internal fuel 87000 kg (191,799 lb); external fuel none; maximum ordnance 11340 kg (25,000 lb)
Speed: maximum level speed 'clean' at 7620 m (25,000 ft) 925 km/h (500 kt; 575 mph); cruising speed at optimum altitude 711 km/h (384 kt; 442 mph)
Range: operational radius 6400 km (3,454 nm; 3,977 miles)

Tupolev **Tu-142MR 'Bear-J'**

The latest 'Bear' variant is known to NATO as **'Bear-J'** and was first identified in 1986. It is believed to be designated **Tu-142MR** and fulfils an airborne communications relay role, allowing national command authorities and strategic missile-carrying submarines to communicate with one another, like the Lockheed EC-130Q or Boeing E-6A. To fulfil this task the aircraft is equipped with an underfuselage winch pod for a trailing wire antenna (several kilome-

tres long) and is liberally bedecked with blade and whip aerials. The underfuselage

The Tu-142MR is obviously based on the 'Bear-F Mod 4', and is often seen with an ASW aircraft. However, it has a completely different mission equipment fit consisting of a varied array of communications antennas, including a bullet fairing projecting forward from the fin. Not visible in this view is the large ventral trailing wire aerial housing.

search radar has been removed. The aircraft also has an unidentified blister above the centre fuselage, and an unidentified spike projecting forward from the fintip. Coincidentally, the latter is similar in size and shape to the MAD that projects aft from

the fintip of the 'Bear-F Mod 3' and 'Bear-F Mod 4'. Otherwise the aircraft is identical to the 'Bear-F Mod 4' and may have been produced by conversion. It is believed that the small number of conversions all serve with the **AV-MF**.

Tupolev **Tu-154 'Careless'**

The **Tu-154** tri-jet airliner was designed as a replacement for the Ilyushin Il-18 and Tu-104, and was required to couple good cruise performance and economy with 'hot-and-high' and short airstrip capability. Tupolev's response to the Aeroflot requirement was recognisably a scaled-up Tu-134, but had hydraulically-actuated leading-edge slats, triple-slotted trailing-edge slats, powered ailerons and four-section spoilers that augment the ailerons for roll control and act as lift dumpers and airbrakes. The fuselage was lengthened, and increased in diameter to allow six-abreast seating, allowing a maximum capacity of 167 passengers (128-158 is more normal). The third engine was located in the extreme rear fuselage, with an intake in the leading edge of the fin.

The prototype made its maiden flight on 4 October 1968 and the type entered service in February 1972. In 1975, the improved **Tu-154A** introduced a revised seating arrangement, additional emergency exits, increased fuel capacity and uprated engines,

together with improved avionics. In 1977 the Tu-154A was superseded in production by the improved **Tu-154B**, and then by the **Tu-154B-2**. The **Tu-154S** is a dedicated freighter, with a freight door forward of the wing, and roller tracks inside the cabin. The aircraft is offered primarily as a conversion of existing Tu-154Bs, and it is not known whether any have been ordered or delivered.

Flight testing of the more radically modified **Tu-154M** began in 1982. This aircraft introduced new Kuznetsov D-30KU-154-II turbofans. Those mounted on the sides of the rear fuselage were in redesigned nacelles, similar to those fitted to the Il-62M, with similar clamshell thrust reversers. The APU had to be relocated to accommodate the centre engine. Other modifications included a redesigned tailplane, reduced size slats, enlarged spoilers and seating for up to 180 passengers (11 more than the standard aircraft).

Three Tu-154B-2s serve with the **Czech**

Republic air force and three more with **North Korea**'s air force, and Tu-154Ms serve with **Poland** (two), and **Russia**.

SPECIFICATION

Tupolev Tu-154M 'Careless'
Wing: span 37.55 m (123 ft 2.5 in); aspect ratio 7.0; area 201.45 m² (2,168.46 sq ft)
Fuselage and tail: length 47.90 m (157 ft 1.75 in); height 11.40 m (37 ft 4.75 in); tailplane span 13.40 m (43 ft 11.5 in); wheel track 11.50 m (37 ft 9 in); wheel base 18.92 m (62 ft 1 in)
Powerplant: three PNPP 'Aviadvigatel' (Soloviev) turbofans D-30KU-154-II each rated at 103.95 kN (23,369 lb st)
Weights: operating empty 55300 kg (121,914 lb); maximum take-off 100000 kg (220,459 lb)
Fuel and load: internal fuel 39750 kg (87,632 lb); external fuel none; maximum payload 18000 kg (39,683 lb)
Speed: maximum cruising speed at 11900 m (39,040 ft) 950 km/h (389 kt; 590 mph)
Range: 6600 km (3,561 nm; 4,101 miles) with maximum fuel and a 5450-kg (12,015-lb) payload or 3740 km (2,018 nm; 2,324 miles) with maximum payload
Performance: take-off balanced field length 2500 m (8,202 ft) at maximum take-off weight; landing balanced field length 2500 m (8,202 ft) at normal landing weight

The Czech air force operates three Tu-154B-2s with its transport unit.

Tupolev Tu-160 'Blackjack'

The **Tu-160 'Blackjack'** is the largest bomber in the world, dwarfing the similar-looking American B-1B, and is the heaviest combat aircraft ever built. The Soviet bomber was heavily influenced by the original Rockwell B-1A, which first flew on 23 December 1974, but which was cancelled by President Carter in 1977. Originally designated **Product 70**, the Tu-160 made its maiden flight on 19 December 1981 at Zhukhovskii, in the hands of Boris Veremei. Spotted by an orbiting US spy satellite three weeks before its first flight, on 25 November 1981, the new aircraft received the reporting name **'Ram-P'** before being re-designated 'Blackjack'. Parked between a pair of Tu-144 'Chargers' the aircraft revealed many features in common with the American B-1, although comparison with the Tu-144 showed the Soviet aircraft to be very much bigger.

The B-1A was designed to penetrate enemy air defences at high level, relying on performance and a highly sophisticated ECM suite to get through. When the project was reborn as the cheaper, less complex B-1B, all thoughts of high-level penetration had been abandoned, and the less sophisticated aircraft was expected to use low-level flight (where it is limited to subsonic speeds) and a reduced radar cross-section to penetrate enemy defences. Back in the USSR there was no such cost-cutting exercise, and the Tu-160 remains committed to both low-level penetration (at transonic speeds) and high-level penetration at speeds of about Mach 1.9.

Variable geometry and full-span leading-edge slats and trailing-edge double-slotted flaps confer a useful combination of benign low-speed handling and high supersonic speed. Wing sweep is manually selected, with three settings: 20° for take-off and landing, 35° for cruise, and 65° for high-speed flight. The trailing edge of the inboard section of the flaps (immobilised when the wings are swept back) has no fuselage slot to retract into when the wing is swept, so instead folds upwards to be aligned with the aircraft centreline and thereby act as a fence. Some aircraft have a 'double-jointed' folding section which can fold up to be a fence at either 35° or 65°.

The Tu-160 has a crew of four, sitting in side-by-side pairs on Zvezda K-36D ejection seats. The crew enter the cockpit via a ladder in the rear part of the nose gear bay.

This unpainted Tu-160 is from the test base at Zhukhovskii. Visible under the nose is the camera fairing for visual aiming of weapons.

The pilot and co-pilot are provided with fighter-type control columns and, although the aircraft has a fly-by-wire control system, all cockpit displays are conventional analog instruments, with no MFDs, CRTs and no HUD. In front of the cockpit is the long pointed radome for the terrain-following and attack radar, with a fairing below it for the forward-looking TV camera used for visual weapon aiming. Intercontinental range is assured by the provision of a fully retractable inflight-refuelling probe.

The 'Blackjack's' offensive warload is carried in two tandem weapons bays in the belly. These are each normally equipped with a rotary carousel which can carry either six RK-55 (AS-15 'Kent') cruise missiles or 12 AS-16 'Kickback' 'SRAMskis'. The RK-55 has a range in excess of 3000 km (1,864 miles) and has a 200-kT nuclear warhead.

The development programme of the Tu-160 was extremely protracted, and at least one prototype is believed to have been lost. Series production was at Kazan and continued until January 1992, when President Yeltsin announced that no further strategic bombers would be built. In fact, it now seems that limited production will be reinstated, not least to replace aircraft lost to the Ukraine. Even after the aircraft entered service, problems continued to severely restrict operations. A shortage of basic flying equipment was a major irritation to aircrew, while a lack of ear defenders and anti-vibration boots for ground crew caused deafness in some men. Problems with the aircraft's ejection seats led to a situation in which seats could not be adjusted to individual crew members, and reliability of the aircraft, its engines and systems bordered on the unacceptable. Operations were supported by teams from the Kazan factory and the Tupolev OKB, which continued delivering aircraft before a common standard and configuration was agreed. Thus, wingspans, equipment fit, and intake configuration differs from aircraft to aircraft.

Eighteen of the 'Blackjacks' completed were delivered to the two squadrons of the 184th Heavy Bomber Regiment at Priluki beginning in May 1987. These were left at the Ukrainian base under Ukrainian command after the USSR split asunder, but are now reportedly to retransfer to **Russia** at an unspecified later date. The four newest aircraft, however, were delivered to Engels in the Saratov region of Russia, which was always intended to be the first 'Blackjack' base, Priluki being a temporary base pending the completion of construction work at Engels. At least six Tu-160s are at Zhukhovskii, in various states of repair, and these

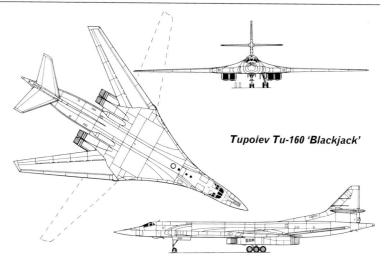

Tupolev Tu-160 'Blackjack'

include at least two 'flyers', one unpainted. These probably include the prototypes, and are used for trials and perhaps spares recovery. Plans exist to use the Tu-160 as a carrier for the Burlak space vehicle, in the same way that the United States' 'Pegasus' is launched by an L-1011 TriStar.

SPECIFICATION

Tupolev Tu-160 'Blackjack-A'

Wing: span 55.70 m (182 ft 9 in) spread and 35.60 m (116 ft 9.75 in) swept; aspect ratio 8.56 spread and swept; area 360.00 m² (3,875.13 sq ft)

Fuselage and tail: length 54.10 m (177 ft 6 in); height 13.10 m (43 ft 0 in); tailplane span 13.25 m (43 ft 5.75 in); wheel track 5.40 m (17 ft 8.5 in); wheel base 17.88 m (58 ft 8 in)

Powerplant: four SSPE Trud (Kuznetsov) NK-321 turbofans each rated at 137.20 kN (30,843 lb st) dry and 245.16 kN (55,115 lb st) with afterburning

Weights: empty equipped 118000 kg (260,140 lb); normal take-off 267600 kg (589,947 lb); maximum take-off 275000 kg (606,261 lb)

Fuel and load: external fuel none; maximum ordnance about 16330 kg (36,000 lb)

Speed: maximum level speed 'clean' at 11000 m (36,090 ft) 2000 km/h (1,079 kt; 1,243 mph); long-range cruising speed at optimum altitude 850 km/h (460 kt; 528 mph)

Range: 14000 km (7,555 nm; 8,699 miles)

The Tu-160 is similar in configuration to the Rockwell B-1B, but is significantly larger. The main weapons are housed in a large bay on a rotary launcher.

431

UTVA-66

UTVA-SOUR Metalne Industrije, RO Fabrika Aviona
Jabucki Put bb
YU-26000 Pancevo, Serbia

A four-seater of classic high-wing, single-engined configuration, the **UTVA-66** is a descendant of the UTVA-56 which first appeared in 1959. After experience had been gained with the UTVA-60 in **Yugoslav air force** service, the improved -66 was flown in 1966 and introduced fixed leading-edge slats, a larger tail unit and strengthened undercarriage. Variants included the **UTVA-66H** floatplane, the **UTVA-66V** with underwing armament options, and the **UTVA-66AM** to carry two stretcher casualties. The remnants of the Yugoslav air force continue to fly some 25 of the 90 UTVA-66s originally received, for communications and 'hack' duties.

SPECIFICATION

UTVA-66
Wing: span 11.40 m (37 ft 5 in); aspect ratio 7.19; area 18.08 m² (194.50 sq ft)
Fuselage and tail: length 8.38 m (27 ft 6 in); height 3.20 m (10 ft 6 in); tailplane span 4.08 m (13 ft 4.5 in); wheel track 2.55 m (8 ft 4.25 in)
Powerplant: one Textron Lycoming GSO-480-B1J6 flat-six piston engine rated at 270 hp (201 kW)
Weights: empty equipped 1250 kg (2,756 lb); maximum take-off 1814 kg (4,000 lb)
Fuel and load: internal fuel 250 litres (66 US gal) plus provision for 200 litres (52.8 US gal) of auxiliary fuel in two wing tanks; external fuel none
Speed: maximum level speed 'clean' at optimum altitude 250 km/h (135 kt; 155 mph) or at sea level 230 km/h (124 kt; 143 mph); maximum cruising speed at optimum altitude 230 km/h (124 kt; 143 mph)
Range: 750 km (404 nm; 466 miles)
Performance: maximum rate of climb at sea level 270 m (885 ft) per minute; service ceiling 6700 m (21,980 ft); take-off run 187 m (614 ft) at maximum take-off weight; take-off distance to 15 m (50 ft) 352 m (1,155 ft) at maximum take-off weight; landing distance from 15 m (50 ft) 274 m (899 ft) at maximum landing weight; landing run 181 m (594 ft) at maximum landing weight

UTVA-75

The **UTVA-75** side-by-side two-seat conventional lightplane has been produced for civilian club and **JRV** use. First flown on 19 May 1976, the UTVA-75 has two wing fittings for the carriage of light weapon loads. At least 50 were delivered to serve at the Air Force College (VVG) at Mostar and the co-located Primary Flying Centre. Courses in both Air Force Academy establishments included 10 hours on the UTVA-75 for all pilots entering the air force.

Since the break-up of Yugoslavia, UTVA-75s have served with various air arms, including the **Croatian air force** and the **Bosnian republic**, the latter using the type as a light attack platform. The Serb-controlled **Yugoslav Air Force and Defence Force** operates UTVA-75s as aptitude trainers for prospective pilots with the 172nd Aviation Regiment at Podgorica.

SPECIFICATION

UTVA-75
Wing: span 9.73 m (31 ft 11 in); aspect ratio 6.5; area 14.63 m² (157.48 sq ft)
Fuselage and tail: length 7.11 m (23 ft 4 in); height 3.15 m (10 ft 4 in); tailplane span 3.80 m (12 ft 5.5 in); wheel track 2.58 m (8 ft 5.5 in); wheel base 1.93 m (6 ft 4 in)
Powerplant: one Textron Lycoming IO-360-B1F flat-four piston engine rated at 180 hp (134 kW)
Weights: empty equipped 685 kg (1,510 lb); maximum take-off 960 kg (2,116 lb)
Fuel and load: internal fuel 103 kg (227 lb); external fuel up to 153 kg (337 lb) in two 100-litre (26.4-US gal) drop tanks; maximum ordnance 200 kg (441 lb)
Speed: maximum level speed 'clean' at optimum altitude 215 km/h (116 kt; 133 mph); maximum cruising speed at optimum altitude 185 km/h (100 kt; 115 mph); economical cruising speed at optimum altitude 165 km/h (89 kt; 102 mph)
Range: ferry range 1,079 nm (1,242 miles; 2000 km); standard range 432 nm (497 miles; 800 km)
Performance: maximum rate of climb at sea level 270 m (886 ft) per minute; service ceiling 4000 m

This Bosnian republic UTVA-75 is fitted with light bomb racks.

(13,125 ft); take-off run 125 m (410 ft) at MTOW; take-off distance to 15 m (50 ft) 250 m (821 ft) at MTOW; landing distance from 15 m (50 ft) 340 m (1,115 ft) at normal landing weight
g limits: -3 to +6

Valmet L-70 Miltrainer/Vinka

Valmet Aviation Industries
Kuninkaankatu 30 (PO Box 11)
SF-33201 Tampere, Finland

The **Finnish air force** is the sole operator of the **Valmet L-70 Miltrainer**, to which it gives the name **Vinka** (Blast). A conventional low-wing lightplane of metal construction, the Vinka first flew on 1 July 1975, the prototype being designated **L-70X**. With two seats side-by-side under a large one-piece canopy, the L-70 was designed to be able to accommodate two additional seats behind the pilots, if required, for the liaison role. The name Miltrainer, proposed by the manufacturer, was appropriate, as provision was made on four wing hardpoints for up to 300 kg (660 lb) of weaponry such as gun pods, rockets or bombs. As a replacement for Saab Safirs in the training role, the L-70 was ordered by Suomen Ilmavoimat in 1978 and the first of the 30-aircraft batch flew in December 1979. Deliveries began on 13 October 1980 and were completed during 1982. The Vinkas serve primarily in the Kou1LLv training squadron at the Air Academy, Kauhava, to provide the initial 40 hours of primary flying for student pilots. One aircraft each is attached to the three fighter squadrons (HavLLv 11, 21 and 31) for liaison, and the type also serves at the Koelentue flight test unit at Kuorevesi.

SPECIFICATION

Valmet L-70 Miltrainer
Wing: span 9.63 m (31 ft 7.25 in); aspect ratio 6.62; area 14.00 m² (150.70 sq ft)
Fuselage and tail: length 7.50 m (24 ft 7.25 in); height 3.31 m (10 ft 10.25 in); wheel track 2.30 m (7 ft 6.5 in); wheel base 1.61 m (5 ft 3.5 in)
Powerplant: one Textron Lycoming AEIO-360-A1B6 flat-four piston engine rated at 200 hp (149 kW)
Weights: operating empty 767 kg (1,691 lb); normal take-off 1040 kg (2,293 lb) for aerobatic use or 1050 kg (2,315 lb) for utility use; maximum take-off 1250 kg (2,756 lb)
Fuel and load: internal fuel 170 litres (45 US gal); external fuel none; maximum ordnance 300 kg (661 lb)
Speed: never exceed speed 360 km/h (194 kt; 223 mph); maximum level speed 'clean' at sea level 235 km/h (127 kt; 146 mph); cruising speed at 1525 m (5,000 ft) 222 km/h (120 kt; 138 mph)
Range: standard range 950 km (512 nm; 590 miles)
Performance: maximum rate of climb at sea level 342 m (1,120 ft) per minute; service ceiling 5000 m (16,405 ft); take-off run 230 m (755 ft) at normal take-off weight; landing run 175 m (575 ft) at normal landing weight

g limits: -3 to +6 at aerobatic weight, -2.02 to +4.4 at utility take-off weight, and -1.8 to +3.3 at maximum take-off weight

Vinkas serve with the Finnish air force academy at Kauhava, and in pairs with liaison flights attached to front-line units.

Valmet L-90TP Redigo

After flying a prototype **L-80TP** as a slightly enlarged and turboprop-powered derivative of the L-70 Vinka, Valmet further developed the basic design to produce the **L-90TP Redigo**. As well as having an Allison 250 turboprop engine, this differed from the L-70 in having a retractable undercarriage and a revised wing. Prototype testing began on 1 July 1986, and a second prototype followed in 1987 with a Turboméca TP319 engine. Modifications to the tail unit were made before production was launched against an order placed by the **Finnish air force** in January 1989. Delivered in 1991/92, the Redigos supplement L-70 Vinkas in the training role with the air force academy at Kauhava. The Redigo has also been sold to **Mexico**.

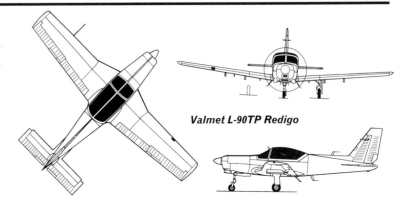

Valmet L-90TP Redigo

SPECIFICATION

Valmet L-90TP Redigo
Wing: span 10.60m (34 ft 9.25 in); aspect ratio 7.62; area 14.748 m² (158.75 sq ft)
Fuselage and tail: length 8.53 m (27 ft 11.75 in); height 3.20 m (10 ft 6 in); elevator span 3.684 m (12 ft 1 in); wheel track 3.367 m (11 ft 0.5 in); wheel base 2.112 m (6 ft 11.25 in)
Powerplant: one 500-shp (373-kW) Allison 250-B17F turboprop flat-rated at 420 shp (313 kW)
Weights: empty equipped 950 kg (2,094 lb); normal take-off 1350 kg (2,976 lb) for aerobatic use, or 1470 kg (3,241 lb) for utility use or 1600 kg (3,527 lb) for normal use; maximum take-off 1900 kg (4,189 lb)
Fuel and load: internal fuel 303 kg (668 lb); external fuel none; maximum ordnance 800 kg (1,764 lb)
Speed: never exceed speed 465 km/h (251 kt; 289 mph); maximum level speed 'clean' at optimum altitude 415 km/h (224 kt; 258 mph); maximum cruising speed at 2400 m (7,875 ft) 352 km/h (190 kt; 219 mph); economical cruising speed at 2400 m (7,875 ft) 312 km/h (168 kt; 194 mph)
Range: 1400 km (755 nm; 870 miles); endurance 6 hours 20 minutes
Performance: maximum rate of climb at sea level 540 m (1,771 ft) per minute; climb to 3000 m (9,845 ft) in 5 minutes and to 5000 m (16,405 ft) in 11 minutes; service ceiling 7620 m (25,000 ft); take-off run 240 m (788 ft) at normal take-off weight; take-off distance to 15 m (50 ft) 340 m (1,116 ft) at normal take-off weight; landing distance from 15 m (50 ft) 410 m (1,345 ft) at normal landing weight; landing run 240 m (788 ft) at normal landing weight without propeller reversal

VFW-Fokker **VFW-614**

VFW was merger of Focke-Wulf, Weser and Heinkel. It became equal trading partner with Fokker on 1 January 1969 although two divisions functioned separately. VFW 's activities now grouped under the DASA banner.

The **Luftwaffe** was one of four customers for the uniquely configured **VFW-Fokker VFW-614**, designed as a short-haul airliner for the commercial market. Powered by two overwing-mounted turbofans, the VFW-614 first flew on 14 July 1971 and production ended in 1978 after 12 had been built. The Luftwaffe took delivery of its three aircraft in 1977/78 and put them into service with its special air missions squadron for VIP transportation (the Flugbereitschaftsstaffel), with which they have remained based at Köln/Bonn.

The VFW-614 is remarkable for its unique layout. Three survive with the Luftwaffe's VIP unit.

SPECIFICATION

VFW-Fokker VFW-614
Wing: span 21.50 m (70 ft 6½ in); aspect ratio 7.22; area 64.00 m² (688.89 sq ft)
Fuselage and tail: length 20.60 m (67 ft 7 in); height 7.84 m (25 ft 8 in); tailplane span 9.00 m (29 ft 6¼ in); wheel track 3.90 m (12 ft 9½ in); wheelbase 7.02 m (23 ft 0¼ in)
Powerplant: two Rolls-Royce/SNECMA M45H Mk 501 turbofans each rated at 32.4 kN (7,280 lb) thrust
Weights: operating empty 12180 kg (26,850lb); maximum take-off 19950 kg (43,980 lb)
Fuel and load: internal fuel 6200 litres (1,363 Imp gal); standard seating for 40 plus two flight crew
Speed: maximum level speed 735 km/h (457 mph); never-exceed speed Mach 0.74; cruising speed at 7620 m (25,000 ft) 722 km/h (449 mph)
Range: with maximum fuel 2010 km (1,250 miles); with 40 passengers 1205 km (748 miles)
Performance: maximum rate of climb at sea level 945 m (3,100 ft) per minute; service ceiling 7620 m (25,000 ft); take-off distance to 10.7 m (35 ft) 956 m (3,135 ft); landing distance from 15 m (50 ft) 658 m (2,160 ft)

Vickers **Viscount**

The aircraft of 224 Filo, Turkish air force, based at Erkilet, are believed to be the last military Viscounts. Three aircraft were transferred from the national airline, and two are still in service.

Several air forces found a use for the **Vickers Viscount** as a staff/VIP transport, mostly using aircraft acquired secondhand from the airlines. Such use is now dwindling, but the **Turkish air force** still has two **Series 700**s in 224 Filo (squadron) as part of the Etimesgut-based Transport Wing .Turkey's **Vickers Viscount 794s** were acquired from the national airline and are powered by 1,740-shp (1299-kW) Rolls-Royce Dart 510 turboprops. One civil-registered **Viscount 781D** used by Zwartkop-based No. 44 Sqn of the South African Air Force was sold in late 1991, and one or two ex-civil **Series 810**s may still fly in military guise in the People's Republic of China. The last Viscount in UK DRA service at RAE Bedford was retired in 1993.

Vought **F-8E(FN) Crusader**

At the time of its entry into service, the **Vought F-8 Crusader** offered the US Navy an excellent fighter that was more than equal to its land-based counterparts. Successes in both Navy and Marine Corps hands during the Vietnam War enhanced its reputation. Out of service for some years with US forces (and with the Philippines, where a handful of F-8Hs were used for fighter duties), the Crusader continues to provide the French **Aéronavale** with its only dedicated fighter assets.

Designated **F-8E(FN)**, 42 were built for France, the (FN) differing from the standard multi-role **F-8E** by having blown flaps and other high-lift devices in order to operate from the small French carriers *Clémenceau* and *Foch*. Retaining the four Colt-Browning 20-mm cannon, the French Crusaders regularly carry MATRA Magic or R.530 air-to-air missiles in place of the Sidewinders previously carried by US aircraft. The multi-role capability is not practised, F-8E(FN)s being dedicated to the air defence of the carrier and its strike aircraft. The standard air wing has seven Crusaders.

The 19 survivors fly with Flottille 12F, shore-based at Landivisiau. Crusaders are expected to serve until replacement by the naval Rafale M in 1998. To keep the veterans relatively current, they are undergoing a minor upgrade programme which improves the navigation system and includes the addition of a missile warning system. In 1993 the first two upgraded machines were returned to the Aéronavale, with 15 to follow through the improvement programme. This adds little to the combat capability of the type, which is woefully insufficient to protect the carrier group in the current climate. The lack of look-down radar, all-round visibility and lack of a true BVR missile are the main deficiencies, but on the Crusader's side is good manoeuvrability and the affection and loyalty of its pilots. In the US, Thunderbird Aviation and Rockwell use **F-8K**s and **RF-8G**s as test/chase aircraft.

SPECIFICATION

Vought F-8E(FN) Crusader
Wing: span 35 ft 8 in (10.87 m); width folded 22 ft 6 in (6.86 m); aspect ratio 3.63; area 350.00 sq ft (32.515 m²)
Fuselage and tail: length 54 ft 6 in (16.61 m); height 15 ft 9 in (4.80 m); tailplane span 19 ft 3.5 in (5.88 m); wheel track 9 ft 8 in (2.94 m)
Powerplant: one Pratt & Whitney J57-P-20A turbojet rated at 10,700 lb st (47.60 kN) dry and 18,000 lb st (80.07 kN) with afterburning
Weights: empty 19,925 lb (9038 kg); normal take-off 28,000 lb (12701 kg); maximum take-off 34,000 lb (15420 kg)
Fuel and load: internal fuel 1,400 US gal (5300 litres); external fuel none; maximum ordnance 5,000 lb (2268 kg)
Speed: maximum level speed 'clean' at 36,000 ft (10975 m) 986 kt (1,135 mph; 1827 km/h); cruising speed at 40,000 ft (12190 m) 486 kt (560 mph; 901 km/h)
Range: ferry range 1,216 nm (1,400 miles; 2253 km); combat radius 521 nm (600 miles; 966 km)
Performance: maximum rate of climb at sea level about 21,000 ft (6400 m) per minute; service ceiling 58,000 ft (17680 m)

The Crusader features a novel variable-incidence wing to lower the nose on approach.

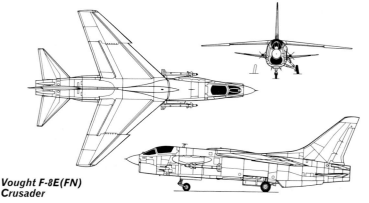

Vought F-8E(FN) Crusader

Westland (Aérospatiale) Gazelle

Westland Helicopters Ltd
Yeovil, Somerset, BA20 2YB
United Kingdom

In the mid-1960s, Sud Aviation began development of the **SA 340** to replace the Alouette II. The prototype **Gazelle** first flew on 7 April 1967 and retained a Turboméca Astazou IIN turboshaft and transmission similar to the SA 318C. In the renamed Aérospatiale group, the Gazelle sold well in civil and military markets. It was also developed and co-produced by Westland, with the SA 330 Puma and WG.13 Lynx, within the 1967 Anglo-French collaborative helicopter agreement. French-built Gazelles are described under Eurocopter.

In the **United Kingdom**, apart from a few civil sales, Gazelle military orders eventually totalled 282, comprising 212 **Army Air Corps AH.Mk 1**s (including at least 15 for the **Royal Marines**), 40 **Royal Navy HT.Mk 2**s and 30 **Royal Air Force HT.Mk 3**s. SA 341B Gazelle AH.Mk 1s entered AAC service with No. 660 Sqn at Soest, in the FRG, in July 1974, the last being delivered in March 1984. From 1977, 67 were upgraded to **SA 342** standard with 895-shp (668-kW) Astazou IIIN2 turboshafts and larger fenestron tail rotors, plus new radios, a tactical Doppler navigation system

and roof-mounted Ferranti AF532 gyro-stabilised periscopic sight, later with a bore-sighted laser-targeting system, for Lynx pathfinder/designation support. About 180 Gazelle AH.Mk 1s now serve alongside Lynxes with 16 UK AAC squadrons, and in flights in Belize, Berlin, Brüggen, Dhekelia, Nicosia in Cyprus, and Suffield in Canada. Some 29 RN **SA 341C** HT.Mk 2s are still operated, mainly for helicopter training by No. 705 Sqn at Culdrose. Approximately 20 Royal Marine AH.Mk 1s have been on establishment since December 1974 with 3 Commando Brigade Air Sqn at Yeovilton. The RAF operates some 20 **SA 341D**

Left: 3 Commando Brigade Air Squadron flies Gazelle AH.Mk 1s and Lynx to provide support for the Royal Marines. They are based at Yeovilton.

Right: A Gazelle from No. 670 Sqn, AAC.

HT.Mk 3 trainers with No. 2 FTS at Shawbury, plus four for VIP use with No. 32 Sqn from Northolt. A handful were briefly used by RAF Chinook squadrons as route-finders.

Nine Gazelle AH.Mk 1s of 3 CBAS and six initially unarmed Gazelles from No. 656 AAC Sqn underwent their operational baptism in the Falklands in April and May 1982 in support of their associated ground forces. The 3 CBAS Gazelles were hurriedly fitted with twin outrigger pods each containing six 68-mm (2.67-in) MATRA/SNEB air-to-ground rockets, and a beam-mounted 7.62-mm (0.3-in) GP machine-gun.

SPECIFICATION

Westland (Aérospatiale) SA 341B Gazelle AH.Mk 1
generally similar to the Eurocopter SA 341F Gazelle except in the following particulars:
Powerplant: one Turboméca Astazou IIIN rated at 441 kW (592 shp)

Westland Lynx (Army versions)

Launched as part of the Anglo-French helicopter agreement of February 1967, the **Westland Lynx** is an extremely versatile machine. Its design is wholly of Westland origin, but the production of the type is shared in the ratio of 70/30 between the UK and France, in the form of the nationalised Aérospatiale (now Eurocopter) concern. One of the primary French responsibilities is the forged titanium hub, a one-piece structure for the four-bladed semi-rigid main rotor which is one of the most important features of the design.

All versions of the Lynx have advanced digital flight controls plus all-weather avionics, and no previous helicopter can equal the type for agility and all-weather single-crew operation. The origins of the design lie with the **WG.13** proposal, which was schemed in general-purpose naval and civilian applications. So versatile did the design appear that the concept was expanded to land-based tactical operations, in which the type's agility and performance would prove a very considerable asset. The first prototype of the Lynx flew on 21 March 1971, and the six prototypes were used exhaus-

The Lynx AH.Mk 7 is the British army's standard battlefield helicopter, equipped with TOW missiles, a roof-mounted sight and infra-red exhaust suppressors.

tively for all aspects of the certification programme, for trials and for record-breaking.

The second production model (following the naval HAS.Mk 2, which is described separately) was the **Lynx AH.Mk 1** battlefield helicopter for the **British army**. This first flew on 11 February 1977, and the type was cleared for service introduction at the end of 1977. Since that time, the Lynx has built up an enviable reputation as a versatile battlefield helicopter, being able to carry up to 12 troops in addition to a crew of two, or 907 kg (2,000 lb) of internal freight, or a slung load of 1361 kg (3,000 lb), or a wide assortment of weapons including eight TOW anti-tank missiles aimed with a stabilised sight mounted in the flight deck roof. The chief distinguishing feature of the land-based Lynx is its skid landing gear, the naval Lynx having wheeled tricycle landing gear.

A total of 113 Lynx AH.Mk 1s was built, and more than 100 are still in service with the Army Air Corps and Royal Marines. Nine Lynx **AH.Mk 5** aircraft were ordered, but only one example flew as such before the remainder of the order was switched to **Lynx AH.Mk 7** standard. This has the direction of rotation of the tail rotor reversed, uprated Gem 41 engines and a box-like IR shroud on the exhaust, in addition to improved electronics. Earlier AH.Mk 1s are being upgraded to this standard, or an interim **AH.Mk 1GT** standard without new

electronics, by RNAY Fleetlands. Eight AH.Mk 1s have also been converted to **AH.Mk 9** standard (described separately). The only overseas customer for the army Lynx was **Qatar**, which bought three for use with the police wing. These are now retired from service.

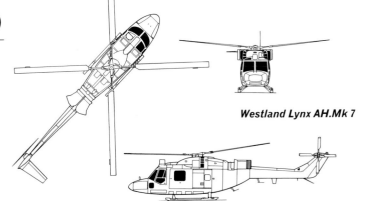

Westland Lynx AH.Mk 7

SPECIFICATION

Westland Lynx AH.Mk 1
Rotor system: main rotor diameter 42 ft 0 in (12.80 m); tail rotor diameter 7 ft 3 in (2.21 m); main rotor disc area 1,385.44 sq ft (128.71 m²); tail rotor disc area 41.28 sq ft (3.835 m²)
Fuselage and tail: length overall, rotors turning 49 ft 9 in (15.163 m) and fuselage 39 ft 6.75 in (12.06 m);
height overall 11 ft 6 in (3.504 m) with both rotors stationary, stabiliser span 5 ft 10 in (1.78 m); skid track 6 ft 8 in (2.032 m)
Powerplant: two Rolls-Royce Gem 2 turboshafts each rated at 900 shp (671 kW) or, in later helicopters, two Rolls-Royce Gem 41-2 each rated at 1,120 shp (835 kW); from 1987 the engines were upgraded to Gem 42-1 standard rated at 1,135 shp (846 kW)
Weights: manufacturer's empty 5,683 lb (2578 kg); manufacturer's basic 5,860 lb (2658 kg); operating empty 6,144 lb (2787 kg) in the troop transport role, or 6,772 lb (3072 kg) in the anti-tank role, or 6,532 lb (2963 kg) in the three-crew SAR role; maximum take-off 9,600 lb (4354 kg)
Fuel and load: internal fuel 214 Imp gal (257 US gal; 973 litres) plus provision for 47 Imp gal (56.4 US gal; 214 litres) of auxiliary fuel in a fuselage tank replaceable by 192 Imp gal (230.6 US gal; 873 litres) of ferry fuel in two fuselage tanks; external fuel none
Speed: maximum continuous cruising speed at optimum altitude 140 kt (161 mph; 259 km/h); economical cruising speed at optimum altitude 70 kt (81 mph; 130 km/h)
Range: 340 nm (392 miles; 630 km) with standard fuel; ferry range 724 nm (835 miles; 1342 km) with auxiliary fuel; typical range 292 nm (336 miles; 540 km) on a troop-carrying mission; endurance 3 hours
Performance: maximum rate of climb at sea level 2,480 ft (756 m) per minute; hovering ceiling 10,600 ft (3230 m) out of ground effect

Westland Lynx AH.Mk 7
generally similar to the Westland Lynx AH.Mk 1 except in the following particulars:
Fuselage and tail: height overall 12 ft 0 in (3.66 m) with rotors stationary
Powerplant: two Rolls-Royce Gem 41-1 turboshafts each rated at 1,120 shp (835 kW); from 1987 the engines were upgraded to Gem 42-1 standard rated at 1,135 shp (846 kW)
Weights: maximum take-off 10,750 lb (4876 kg)
Fuel and load: maximum ordnance about 1,210 lb (549 kg)

Westland **Lynx AH.Mk 9**

Features of the **Army Air Corps'** upgraded **Lynx AH.Mk 9**, including a nosewheel undercarriage instead of skids, and exhaust diffusers, were first shown by Westland at the 1988 Farnborough air show on the company demonstrator G-LYNX. The AAC is taking delivery of 24 AH.Mk 9s, including eight Lynx AH.Mk 7 conversions, the first new-build example (ZG884) of which flew on 20 July 1990 and was delivered by the year's end. Westland flew the 16th new-build AH.Mk 9 on 21 June 1992, and is continuing the Lynx AH.Mk 7 conversion programme.

The AH.Mk 9 consolidates all the AH.Mk 7 modifications incorporated in 107 AAC AH.Mk 1 conversions, comprising reversed-direction tail rotor, BERP main rotor blades and uprated gearbox, plus an 11,300-lb (5125-kg) maximum gross weight, secure speech transmission equipment, TACAN and improved IFF. Defence economies precluded the provision of TOW ATM capability, although this may follow if funds permit, using a modified weapons pylon made necessary by the new undercarriage.

In this form, the AH.Mk 9 is similar to Westland's **Battlefield Lynx** export project, apart from an extra fuel tank below the rear bench seat which increases total capacity by 375 lb (170 kg) to 2,088 lb (930 kg), and optional exhaust diffusion. Armament options can include GIAT 20-mm cannon pods, FN Herstal 7.62-mm machine-gun pods, rocket pods, and HOT or Hellfire ATGMs in place of the AH.Mk 9's TOW installation. Current production and Lynx conversions utilise Rolls-Royce Gem 42-1 turboshafts uprated to 1,135 shp (846 kW), although one aircraft was tested with the LHTEC 800 as the **Battlefield Lynx 800**.

No. 9 Regiment at Dishforth began Lynx AH.Mk 9 conversion in late 1991, No. 672

Squadron being the first operational AAC unit to re-equip (with 12 examples), followed by No. 664 Squadron, which began to replace its Lynx AH.Mk 1s in 1992. No. 673 Squadron received Lynx AH.Mk 9s in 1993. Some 150 Lynxes, including the 16 new-build AH.Mk 9s, remain in service in 1994 with the AAC, Royal Marines, MoD(PE) and Westland.

SPECIFICATION

Westland Lynx AH.Mk 9
generally similar to the Westland Lynx AH.Mk 1 except in the following particulars:
Rotor system: tail rotor diameter 7 ft 9 in (2.36 m); tail rotor disc area 47.17 sq ft (4.38 m²)
Fuselage and tail: length overall, rotors turning 50 ft 0 in (15.24 m) and with rotors folded 43 ft 5.25 in (13.24 m); height overall 12 ft 3 in (3.73 m) with tail rotor turning; stabiliser span 4 ft 4 in (1.32 m); wheel track 9 ft 2.25 in (2.80 m); wheel base 9 ft 11 in (3.02 m)

Powerplant: two Rolls-Royce Gem 42-1 turboshafts each rated at 1,135 shp (846 kW)
Weights: basic empty 7,006 lb (3178 kg); operating empty 8,707 lb (3949 kg) in the anti-tank role with TOW missiles, or 7,592 lb (3444 kg) in the reconnaissance role, or 7,707 lb (3496 kg) in the troop transport; maximum take-off 11,300 lb (5126 kg)
Fuel and load: maximum payload 3,000 lb (1361 kg)
Speed: maximum continuous cruising speed at optimum altitude 138 kt (159 mph; 256 km/h)

Range: typical range 370 nm (426 miles; 685 km) on a tactical transport mission; combat radius 25 nm (29 miles; 46 km) for a 2-hour patrol on an anti-tank mission

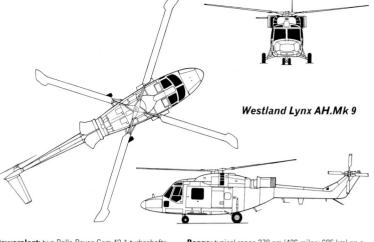

Westland Lynx AH.Mk 9

The wheeled undercarriage is the most notable AH.Mk 9 feature. Of greater significance is the BERP rotor with paddle tips, which improves high-speed performance.

Westland **Lynx** (Navy versions)

On technical grounds, the Westland Lynx is one of the foremost medium shipboard helicopters in the world, and from the original WG.13 concept (which formed part of the Anglo-French helicopter agreement of 1967) has come a series of uprated versions which not only bring in additional missions but also greatly enhanced capabilities. The original **Lynx HAS.Mk 2** for the Royal Navy was actually the first production variant to fly, in February 1976. Powered by two 559-kW (750-shp) Gem 2 engines, this has a gross weight of 4309 kg (9,500 lb), yet carries a crew of two (three in the ASW or SAR roles) plus all equipment for a wide range of shipboard missions including ASW, SAR, ASV (anti-surface vessel) search and strike, reconnaissance, troop transport (typi-

cally 10 troops), fire support, communication and fleet liaison, and VertRep duties.

Equipment of all these models includes a search radar, which in the 60 Lynx HAS.Mk 2s of the RN was the Ferranti Seaspray; the equivalent machines of the French Aéronavale have the OMERA-Segid ORB 31W. In the ASW search role other sensors can include Bendix or Alcatel dipping sonars or a Texas Instruments MAD. The basic Lynx has one of the world's most advanced flight control systems which, in conjunction with comprehensive navaids, makes possible precision flying in even the worst weather, as was amply proved during over 3,000 hours of combat operations off the Falklands in 1982. The campaign saw the operational combat debut of the new Sea Skua

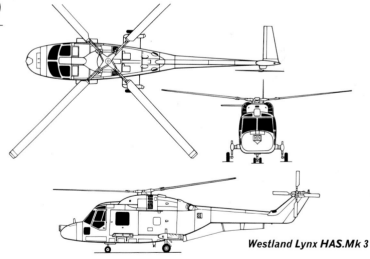

Westland Lynx HAS.Mk 3

anti-ship missile. Although other missiles can be carried, the Sea Skua is the most effective in the world for this mission, and up to four can be fired and guided automatically by radar homing.

The Royal Navy received the first of 23 upgraded **HAS.Mk 3**s in March 1982, and converted its HAS.Mk 2s to this standard. Among the improved systems were Gem 41-1 engines. The **HAS.Mk 3ICE** designation covers a few aircraft with downgraded systems for utility work on the Antarctic patrol vessel HMS *Endurance*. Subsequently, seven HAS.Mk 3s were procured

with secure speech facility and other upgrades (**HAS.Mk 3S**). Eighteen aircraft were upgraded to **HAS.Mk 3GM (Gulf Mod)** standard with improved cooling, and during Desert Storm were seen with infrared jammers and ALQ-167 ECM pods. The final Royal Navy version is that which adds a central tactical system and a flotation bag (**HAS.Mk 3CTS**). The definitive upgraded aircraft is the Lynx HAS.Mk 8/Super Lynx (described separately).

WEAPON OPTIONS

External pylons for the carriage of two torpedoes (Mk 44, 46 or Sting Ray), two Mk 11 depth charges or four Sea Skua anti-ship missiles. French aircraft have AS12 wire-guided missiles. Royal Navy aircraft can carry an FN HMP 0.50-in machine-gun for self-protection. ALQ-167 ECM pod also carried.

The current standard RN version is the HAS.Mk 3, seen here armed with Sea Skua. There are several current mod states, the most recent being the Mk 3CTS with a RAMS 4000 central tactical system.

Westland Lynx (Navy versions)

Left: France bought a total of 40 Lynx for the Aéronavale, split between HAS.Mk 2(FN) and HAS.Mk 4(FN) models. They serve with Flottilles 31F and 34F, and with Escadrille 20S.

Right: German navy Lynx Mk 88s deploy aboard frigates to provide ASW coverage. They are shore-based at Nordholz.

SPECIFICATION

Westland Lynx HAS.Mk 2
Rotor system: main rotor diameter 42 ft 0 in (12.80 m); tail rotor diameter 7 ft 3 in (2.21 m); main rotor disc area 1,385.44 sq ft (128.71 m²); tail rotor disc area 41.28 sq ft (3.835 m²)
Fuselage and tail: length overall, rotors turning 49 ft 9 in (15.163 m), fuselage 39 ft 1.3 in (11.92 m), and with main rotor blades and tail folded 34 ft 10 in (10.618 m); height overall 11 ft 5 in (3.48 m) with rotors stationary; stabiliser span 5 ft 10 in (1.78 m); wheel track 9 ft 1.4 in (2.778 m); wheel base 9 ft 7.75 in (2.94 m)
Powerplant: two Rolls-Royce Gem 2 turboshafts each rated at 900 shp (671 kW) or, in later helicopters, two Rolls-Royce Gem 41-2 each rated at 1,120 shp (835 kW); from 1987 the engines were upgraded to Gem 42-1 standard rated at 1,135 shp (846 kW)

Weights: manufacturer's empty 6,040 lb (2740 kg); manufacturer's basic 6,680 lb (3030 kg); operating empty 7,370 lb (3343 kg) in the ASW role, or 7,224 lb (3277 kg) in the two-crew reconnaissance role, or 7,654 lb (3472 kg) in ASW classification and attack role, or 7,526 lb (3414 kg) in the ASV search and attack role with two crew and four Sea Skua missiles, or 7,531 lb (3416 kg) in the three-crew SAR role; maximum take-off 10,500 lb (4763 kg)
Fuel and load: internal fuel 214 Imp gal (257 US gal; 973 litres) plus provision for 47 Imp gal (56.4 US gal; 214 litres) of auxiliary fuel in a fuselage tank replaceable by 192 Imp gal (230.6 US gal; 873 litres) of ferry fuel in two fuselage tanks; external fuel none; maximum payload 3,000 lb (1361 kg)
Speed: maximum continuous cruising speed at optimum altitude 125 kt (144 mph; 232 km/h); economical cruising speed at optimum altitude 70 kt (81 mph; 130 km/h)
Range: ferry range 565 nm (651 miles; 1047 km) with

auxiliary fuel; range 320 nm (368 miles; 593 km) with standard fuel; combat radius 96 nm (111 miles; 178 km) on a SAR mission with 11 survivors, or 50 nm (58 miles; 93 km) for a 65-minute ASW dunking sonar search and attack loiter, or for a 96-minute ASV loiter, or for a 120-minute ASW classification and attack loiter with two torpedoes, or for a 149-minute ASW anti-submarine strike loiter endurance 2.8 hours
Performance: maximum rate of climb at sea level 2,170 ft (661 m) per minute; hovering ceiling 8,450 ft (2575 m) out of ground effect

OPERATORS

All naval variants:
Argentina: two Mk 23s now sold, the remainder of the order embargoed after the Falklands War
Brazil: seven remaining of nine Mk 21s
Denmark: eight new Mk 80s, two Mk 23s from the

embargoed Argentine order and one direct from Argentina. One new Mk 90. Remainder upgraded
France: 24 HAS.Mk 2(FN) and 13 HAS.Mk 4(FN), the latter with Gem 41 engines. 40 were delivered
Germany: 19 Mk 88s flying with MFG 3
Netherlands: purchased six utility Mk 25/**UH-14A**, 10 sonar-equipped Mk 27/**SH-14B** and eight MAD-equipped Mk 81/**SH-14C** Lynxes, the 22 survivors being converted to a common **SH-14D** standard with full ASW kit, RWRs, FLIR, GPS and uprated Gem Mk 42 engines, following the interim conversion of the SH-14Cs to SH-14B configuration
Nigeria: two remaining of three Mk 89s
Norway: five remaining of six Mk 86s
Portugal: three Mk 95 Super Lynx
South Korea: 12 Mk 99 Super Lynx
United Kingdom: purchased 60 HAS.Mk 2 and 31 HAS.Mk 3 for Royal Navy. 53 surviving Mk 2s upgraded to Mk 3 status. 65 Mk 3s being converted to HAS.Mk 8 standard

Westland **Lynx HAS.Mk 8**/Super Lynx

SPECIFICATION

Most of the 219 Westland WG.13 Lynx helicopters built for the Army Air Corps (128 AH.Mks 1-7) and the **Royal Navy** (91 HAS.Mks 2/3), excluding 11 prototypes, plus survivors of 26 French naval HAS.Mk 2(FN)s, are receiving new high-efficiency composite rotor blades through a £25 million MoD contract awarded to Westland in April 1991. This funds over 800 blades from Westland Engineering Composites with the RAE's record-breaking anhedralled and swept high-speed tips developed through the British Experimental Rotor Programme (BERP), plus over 100 similar blades for the Dutch navy's 22 SH-14s. These provide greater performance, speed and lift, as well as a higher fatigue life, and

A complete revision of the Royal Navy's existing Lynx fleet has resulted in the HAS.Mk 8, with BERP blades, GEC Sensors Sea Owl thermal imager and a repositioned GEC Ferranti Sea Spray radar. The onboard electronic suite is considerably revised.

are among the main upgrades for 65 RN Lynx HAS.Mk 3 to **HAS.Mk 8** standard.

This £200 million three-stage upgrade which followed the 1982 Falklands War parallels the AAC's AH.Mk 9, starting with installation of GEC Marconi AD3400 secure speech communications equipment. Second-stage integration is following in six trials Lynx HAS.Mk 3s of Racal's RAMS 4000-based automated and computerised central tactical management system.

Apart from the new BERP main rotor and reverse-direction tail rotor to improve yaw control at higher take-off weights of 11,300 lb (5125 kg) from the original 10,750 lb (4876 kg), third-stage Mk 8 changes include a nose-mounted GEC Sensors Sea Owl passive identification thermal imager turret, a rear-mounted CAE magnetic anomaly detector, INS and GPS satellite nav systems, Racal MIR-2 Orange Crop ESM and a Whittaker Yellow Veil ECM jamming pod. Defence cuts having deleted the 360° Ferranti Seaspray Mk 3 radar planned by the RN for its Mk 8s, the original 180° Seaspray Mk 1 being retained in a chin radome. As

well as detecting surface targets, Seaspray provides guidance for the Lynx's BAeD Sea Skua anti-ship missiles, as used in the 1991 Gulf War, or over-the-horizon targeting for the RN's frigate-launched MDC RGM-84D Block 1C Harpoon anti-ship missiles.

Originally equipped with three Lynx HAS.Mk 3CTS aircraft (ZF557, ZF563 and ZF558), with first- and second-stage upgrade equipment, No. 700L Squadron, the Lynx Operational Flight Trials Unit at Portland, received its first fully-equipped HAS.Mk 8s in mid-1992 when it combined with No. 815 Squadron.

Many Lynx Mk 8 features are incorporated in the export **Super Lynx**, which has been chosen by Portugal (five **Mk 95**s) and **South Korea** (12 **Mk 99**s). The Portuguese aircraft have 360° Allied Signal RDR 1500 search radar for service aboard 'Vasco da Gama'-class frigates, while the Korean aircraft are equipped with Sea Spray Mk 3 radar and Bendix AQS-18 dipping sonar for service aboard 'Sumner'- and 'Gearing'-class frigates. Neither has Sea Owl thermal imagers.

Westland Lynx HAS.Mk 8
generally similar to the Westland Lynx HAS.Mk 2 except in the following particulars:
Rotor system: tail rotor diameter 7 ft 9 in (2.36 m); tail rotor disc area 47.17 sq ft (4.38 m²)
Fuselage and tail: length overall, rotors turning 50 ft 0 in (15.24 m) and with main rotor blades and tail folded 35 ft 7.25 in (10.85 m); height overall 12 ft 0½ in (3.67 m) with tail rotor turning, and with main rotor blades and tail folded 10 ft 8 in (3.25 m); stabiliser span 4 ft 4 in (1.32 m); wheel track 9 ft 2¼ in (2.80 m); wheel base 9 ft 11 in (3.02 m)
Powerplant: two Rolls-Royce Gem 42-1 turboshafts each rated at 1,135 shp (846 kW)
Weights: basic empty 7,255 lb (3291 kg); operating empty 9,276 lb (4207 kg) in the ASW role, or 7,929 lb (3597 kg) in the surveillance and targeting role, or 9,373 lb (4252 kg) in ASV role with four Sea Skua missiles, or 8,064 lb (3658 kg) in the SAR role; maximum take-off 11,300 lb (5126 kg)
Range: combat radius 20 nm (23 miles; 37 km) for a 140-minute anti-submarine patrol with dunking sonar and one torpedo, or 148 nm (170 miles; 274 km) for an anti-ship point attack with four Sea Skua missiles, or 75 nm (86 miles; 139 km) for a 246-minute surveillance patrol

Above: Korea's 12 Super Lynx Mk 99s are in service with No. 627 Sqn. They are characterised by the lack of Sea Owl thermal imaging devices, but do have a dipping sonar, visible in the centre of the fuselage underside.

Westland Scout

In 1956 Saunders-Roe initiated design of a new light helicopter identified as the **P.531**, and began cutting metal on two prototypes in early 1958; both were flown that year, the first (G-APNU) on 20 July and the second (G-APNV) on 30 September. Following the acquisition of Saunders-Roe by Westland, it was this latter company which continued development, winning an order from the **Army Air Corps** for a pre-production batch of **P.531-2 Mk 1** aircraft. Evaluation, from August 1960, led to an initial production order in September 1960 for the **Westland Scout AH.Mk 1**, the first of these five-seat helicopters entering service in early 1963.

Scout AH.Mk 1 production for the UK Army Air Corps totalled 150, the last 30 or so survivors being retired in 1994. One aircraft was then still serving with the **Empire Test Pilot School** at Boscombe Down, and one with the AAC Historic Flight at Middle Wallop.

The Scout served the AAC faithfully until 1994, leaving this example with the ETPS at Boscombe as the only one in military service.

SPECIFICATION

Westland Scout AH.Mk 1
Rotor system: main rotor diameter 32 ft 3 in (9.83 m); tail rotor diameter 7 ft 6 in (2.29 m); main rotor disc area 816.86 sq ft (75.89 m²); tail rotor disc area 44.18 sq ft (4.10 m²)
Fuselage and tail: length overall, rotors turning 40 ft 4 in (12.29 m) and fuselage 30 ft 4 in (9.24 m); height overall 11 ft 8 in (3.56 m) with tail rotor turning, and 8 ft 11 in (2.72 m) to top of rotor head; skid track 8 ft 6 in (2.59 m)
Powerplant: one 1,050-shp (783-kW) Rolls-Royce (Bristol Siddeley) Nimbus Mk 101 or Mk 102 turboshaft derated to 685 shp (511 kW)
Weights: operating empty 3,232 lb (1465 kg); maximum take-off 5,300 lb (2404 kg)
Fuel and load: internal fuel 1,240 lb (562 kg); external fuel none; maximum ordnance 540 lb (245 kg) or maximum payload 1,500 lb (680 kg)
Speed: maximum level speed 'clean' at sea level 114 kt (131 mph; 211 km/h); maximum and economical cruising speed at optimum altitude 106 kt (122 mph; 196 km/h)
Range: 273 nm (314 miles; 505 km) with four passengers
Performance: maximum rate of climb at sea level 1,670 ft (510 m) per minute; service ceiling 13,400 ft (4085 m)

Westland Sea King

A mid-1960s agreement with Sikorsky for licence production of the S-61 resulted in four US-built examples (c/ns 61-393 to 396) being shipped to Westland as pattern aircraft. The first **Sea King** was a navalised SH-3D (allocated the serial G-ATYU/XV370), and was flown from Avonmouth docks on 11 October 1966. The other three (XV371-373) were used for British ASW systems trials for **Sea King HAS.Mk 1** (Specification HAS.261) development for the RN.

The first of 56 production HAS.Mk 1s (XV642-677/XV695-714) began flying on 7 May 1969, followed by 13 **HAS.Mk 2**s with uprated Rolls-Royce Gnome H.1400 turboshafts and six-bladed tail rotors from mid-1976, and the first 15 **HAR.Mk 3**s for RAF SAR roles from September 1977. Eight more HAS.Mk 2s from early 1979 included a prototype **HAS.Mk 5** ASW upgrade conversion, many of the earlier RN Sea Kings also being converted to **HAS.Mks 5/6** or **HAR.Mk 5** standards. New-build HAS.Mks 5 and 6 followed from mid-1980, eventually increasing overall RN ASW Sea King deliveries to 113. The HAS.Mk 5 introduced Thorn-EMI Sea Searcher radar in a large, flat-topped radome, Racal MIR-2 Orange Crop ESM, new sonobuoy dropping equipment and LAPADS acoustic processing. The cabin was enlarged to make room for the new equipment. The HAS.Mk 6 has a further enhanced ASW suite and reduced equipment weight, resulting in a 30-minute extension to endurance. The Orange Crop ESM system is raised to Orange Reaper standard, and the dunking depth of the sonar is increased from 245 ft (75 m) to 700 ft (213 m), among other improvements.

Three more HAR.Mk 3 SAR versions in 1985 brought RAF procurement to 19 (including one for ETPS at Boscombe Down in 1980) for three squadrons. Two SAR-tasked HAR.Mk 3s of No. 78 Sqn (based in the Falkland Islands) are equipped with chaff dispensers and RWRs. Another £50 million-plus early 1992 RAF order added six upgraded **HAR.Mk 3A**s, reopening Sea King production for more Wessex replacements.

Development of a non-amphibious Sea King variant as the Commando assault, tactical and general transport (described separately) began in mid-1971. The Royal Navy subsequently placed orders from 1979 for 41 **HC.Mk 4** Commando helicopters. Two **Mk 4X** Sea Kings (ZB506/ ZB507) were built by Westland as DRA avionics, rotor and systems test aircraft for EH.101 development, bringing overall UK service procurement of all variants to 175.

Although designated Commando Mk 3s, the aircraft of Qatar's No. 8 Anti-Surface Vessel Squadron have full Sea King systems and sponsons. Like Pakistani aircraft, they can carry Exocet anti-ship missiles.

Ten of the Royal Navy's Sea Kings serve with No. 849 Sqn in AEW.Mk 2A configuration. Searchwater radar is mounted on a swivelling strut, and is protected by an inflatable radome. The AEW system was also sold to Spain for its Sikorsky-built Sea Kings.

Westland has supplied 147 Sea Kings (and the related Commando) to overseas customers. German Sea Kings were converted from SAR to anti-ship roles from 1986 with Ferranti Seaspray Mk 3 radar and BAeD Sea Skua AShMs, which also arm Indian navy Mk 42Bs, while some Pakistani and Qatari Sea Kings/Commandos are equipped to launch Aérospatiale AM39 Exocet anti-ship missiles. The Indian navy's **Sea King Mk 42B**s are **Advanced Sea King**s, with 1,465-shp (1092-kW) Gnome H.1400-1T turboshafts, composite main and tail rotors, improved avionics and a take-off weight of 21,500 lb (9752 kg).

The Royal Navy's lack of airborne early-warning capability in the 1982 Falklands War resulted in the hurried conversion in May 1982 of two HAS Sea Kings (XV650 and 704) to **AEW.Mk 2A** standard with Thorn-EMI Searchwater radar and associated equipment, including anti-Exocet I-band jammers and Racal MIR-2 Orange Crop ESM. This involved fitting a large radome suspended to starboard of the cabin and swinging back through 90° for ground stowage. Both AEW.Mk 2A development aircraft began flying in July 1982, and were deployed in August on *Illustrious* for postwar Falklands service with No. 824 Sqn. Eight further Sea Kings were modified as AEW.Mk 2As and equipped No. 849 Sqn, the FAA's historic AEW unit, shore-based at RNAS Culdrose and in RN V/STOL carrier

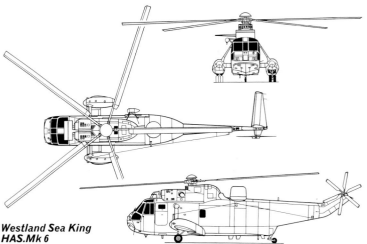

Westland Sea King HAS.Mk 6

Westland Sea King

Left: The RAF operates the HAR.Mk 3 on dedicated SAR duties. Two serve in the Falklands, wearing a dark grey 'combat SAR' camouflage.

Right: India's Mk 42Bs are virtually to HAS.Mk 5 standard, and feature the square-topped fuselage radome for the Sea Searcher radar. They can launch the Sea Eagle anti-ship missile.

flights from 1 November 1984. Three similar radar systems were also sold to Spain in 1984 for AEW conversions of some of the AAA's Sikorsky SH-3H Sea Kings.

WEAPON OPTIONS

Up to four Mk 46, A244S or Sting Ray torpedoes can be carried externally, or four Mk 11 depth charges. The Sea King can also field BAe Sea Eagle or Exocet anti-ship missiles for anti-surface vessel duties. Pintle-mounted 7.62-mm GPMGs (general-purpose machine-guns) can be fitted in the starboard door.

SPECIFICATION

Westland Advanced Sea King
Rotor system: main rotor diameter 62 ft 0 in (18.90 m); tail rotor diameter 10 ft 4 in (3.16 m); main rotor disc area 3,019.07 sq ft (280.47 m2); tail rotor disc area 83.86 sq ft (7.79 m2)
Fuselage and tail: length overall, rotors turning 72 ft 8 in (22.15 m), fuselage 55 ft 10 in (17.02 m), with main rotor blades folded 57 ft 2 in (17.42 m) and with main rotor blades and tail pylon folded 47 ft 3 in (14.40 m);

height overall 16 ft 10 in (5.13 m) with rotors turning, 15 ft 11 in (4.85 m) with rotors stationary, and 15 ft 6 in (4.72 m) to top of rotor head; wheel track 13 ft 0 in (3.96 m); wheel base 23 ft 5 in (7.14 m)
Powerplant: two Rolls-Royce Gnome H.1400-1T turboshafts each rated at 1,660 shp (1238 kW) for take-off and 1,465 shp (1092 kW) for continuous running
Weights: basic empty 11,891 lb (5393 kg) with sponsons or 11,845 lb (5373 kg) without sponsons; empty equipped 16,377 lb (7428 kg) for the ASW role, or 16,689 lb (7570 kg) for the ASV role, or 17,143 lb (7776 kg) for the AEW role, or 13,760 lb (6241 kg) for the SAR role, or 12,594 lb (5712 kg) for the troop transport role, or 12,536 lb (5686 kg) for the freight role or 15,917 lb (7220 kg) for the VIP role; maximum take-off 21,500 lb (9752 kg)
Fuel and load: internal fuel 817 Imp gal (981 US gal; 3714 litres) plus provision for 190 Imp gal (228 US gal; 863 litres) of auxiliary fuel in a fuselage tank; external fuel none; maximum ordnance 2,500 lb (1134 kg)
Speed: never exceed speed at sea level 122 kt (140 mph; 226 km/h); maximum cruising speed at sea level 110 kt (126 mph; 204 km/h)
Range: ferry range 940 nm (1,082 miles; 1742 km) with auxiliary fuel; range 800 nm (921 miles; 1482 km) with standard fuel
Performance: maximum rate of climb at sea level

2,030 ft (619 m) per minute; service ceiling 4,000 ft (1220 m) with one engine out; hovering ceiling 6,500 ft (1980 m) in ground effect and 4,700 ft (1435 m) out of ground effect

Westland Sea King AEW.Mk 2A
generally similar to the Westland Advanced Sea King except in the following particulars:
Powerplant: two Rolls-Royce Gnome H.1400-1 turboshafts each rated at 1,660 shp (1238 kW)
Weights: maximum take-off 21,000 lb (9526 kg)
Speed: maximum cruising speed at optimum altitude 90 kt (104 mph; 167 km/h)
Performance: service ceiling 10,000 ft (3050 m)

OPERATORS

Export customers for all variants of Sea King are:
Australia: HAS.Mk 50/50As (12 delivered, seven remaining) serving with HS-817 at RAN Nowra in utility transport/ASW role
Belgium: five Mk 48s with 40 Sm/Esc at Coxyde on SAR duties
Egypt: five Commando Mk 1s, 17 Mk 2s, two VIP Mk 2Bs, four ECM Mk 2Es, six (five remaining) Sea King HAS.Mk 47s

Germany: 22 SAR/anti-ship Mk 41s serving with 1/MFG 5 at Kiel-Holtenau
India: 12 (eight remaining) Mk 42s and three Mk 42As for ASW with INAS 330 at Dabolim, 20 Mk 42Bs for ASW with INAS 336 at Cochin and six Mk 42Cs for assault transport with INAS 339 at Margar
Norway: 10 (eight remaining) Mk 43s, one Mk 43A and one Mk 43B for SAR with 330 Skvadron at Bodø, Banak, Ørland and Sola. Mk 43B features nose radar and FLIR, others being similarly upgraded
Pakistan: six ASW/ASV Mk 45s with No. 111 Sqn at PNS Mehran
Qatar: three Commando Mk 2As, one Mk 2C with No. 9 Squadron for assault/VIP transport, eight Mk 3s with No. 8 Squadron for anti-ship
United Kingdom (RN): deliveries were 56 HAS.Mk 1s, 21 HAS.Mk 2s, 40 HC.Mk 4s, 30 HAS.Mk 5s and five HAS.Mk 6s. Current force consists of 10 AEW.Mk 2As (No. 849 Sqn), five Nos 707, 772, 845 and 846 Sqns), five HAR.Mk 5s (No. 771 Sqn), 29 HAS. Mk 5s (Nos 706, 771 and 891 Sqns) and 41 HAS.Mk 6s (Nos 810, 814, 819 and 820 Sqns)
United Kingdom (RAF/MoD PE): 19 HAR.Mk 3s and six HAR.Mk 3As (on order) with Nos 22, 78 and 202 Sqns, headquartered at St Mawgan, Mount Pleasant and Boulmer, respectively. Two Mk 4Xs serve with DRA and one HC.Mk 4 with ETPS

Westland Sea King HC.Mk 4/Commando

Development of a non-amphibious transport version of the Sea King lacking flotation sponsons (but normally retaining flotation bags on the wheel hubs) and ASW equipment began in mid-1971, resulting in the **Westland Commando** assault, tactical and general transport. The aircraft was based on the Sea King HAS.Mk 2, with the same engines, gearbox and six-bladed tail rotors. In this form the helicopter could carry 7,500 lb (3402 kg) of equipment or 28 fully armed troops. No interest was expressed initially by the British armed forces, but a number of overseas customers placed orders. The first of these was the **Egyptian air force**, which received five **Commando Mk 1s (Sea King Mk 70s)** in early 1974, ordered by Saudi Arabia on its behalf. These aircraft were not, in fact, true Commandos, being based on the engine/airframe of the HAS.Mk 1 but with ASW equipment removed and provision for the carriage of troops or cargo. The Commando Mk 1s were

followed by 19 full-standard **Commando Mk 2s** based on the Sea King HAS.Mk 2. Two of the aircraft were fitted out as VIP transports and were designated **Commando Mk 2B**. All were delivered by February 1976. Four more aircraft, designated **Commando Mk 2E** and equipped for ECM operations with huge spherical radomes on the fuselage sides, were delivered during 1979-80. All but the Commando Mk 1s were fitted with intake dust filters.

Before Egypt took delivery of its Mk 2s, another customer for the aircraft was found. The **Qatar Emiri air force** bought four aircraft based on the Sea King HAS.Mk 2, delivered in 1975/76. Three (designated **Commando Mk 2A**) were 27-seat utility transports, while the fourth was a **VIP** transport designated **Commando Mk 2C**. Qatar later ordered a second batch of eight aircraft with the H.1400-IT engines of the Advanced Sea King, designed to carry Exocet ASMs, SURA or SNEB rockets or podded 0.5-in machine-guns. These **Com-

mando Mk 3s**, retaining Sea King-style undercarriage sponsons, were delivered from November 1982 to January 1984.

Royal Navy interest in the Commando began in 1978, when the aircraft was first considered as a potential 'off-the-shelf' replacement for the Wessex HU.Mk 5s then in use with the Commando ('Junglie') squadrons. Essentially a Commando Mk 2, the RN aircraft retained the Sea King name with the designation **HC.Mk 4**. An initial order for 15 was placed and the first made its maiden flight in November 1979. Further orders brought total HC.Mk 4 procurement to 41, one of these going to the ETPS at Boscombe Down, and another to the Aeroplane and Armament Experimental Establishment as a navigation and radio trials aircraft at the same base. Two basically similar **Sea King Mk 4Xs** were built by Westland for the RAE as avionics, rotor and systems test aircraft, and were extensively used for EH.101 development work. Over 50 RN Sea Kings of Nos 820, 824, 825, 826 and 846 Sqns played a prominent part in the 1982 Falklands War in the ASW, SAR, assault, transport, anti-ship missile decoy, and general fleet support roles, five being lost in action. One HC.Mk 4 was destroyed by its crew after landing an SAS surveillance party near the southern Argentine base at Punta Arenas. Sea King HC.Mk 4s of Nos 845, 846 and 848 Squadrons played a part in Operation Desert Storm, and aircraft from Nos 845 and 846 Squadrons were involved in humanitarian relief and UN support duties in Bosnia during 1993, the latter flying from RFA Argus.

Qatar's Commando Mk 2As serve with No. 9 Multi-Role Squadron, which also flies the Mk 2C VIP transport.

SPECIFICATION

Westland Commando Mk 2
Rotor system: main rotor diameter 62 ft 0 in (18.90 m); tail rotor diameter 10 ft 4 in (3.16 m); main rotor disc area 3,019.07 sq ft (280.47 m2); tail rotor disc area 83.86 sq ft (7.79 m2)
Fuselage and tail: length overall, rotors turning 72 ft 8 in (22.15 m), fuselage 55 ft 10 in (17.02 m); height overall 16 ft 10 in (5.13 m) with rotors turning, and to top of rotor head 15 ft 6 in (4.72 m); wheel track 13 ft 0 in (3.96 m); wheel base 23 ft 8 in (7.21 m)
Powerplant: two Rolls-Royce Gnome H.1400-1T turboshafts each rated at 1,660 shp (1238 kW) for take-off and 1,465 shp (1092 kW) for continuous running
Weights: operating empty 12,390 lb (5620 kg) with two crew; normal take-off 21,000 lb (9526 kg); maximum take-off 21,500 lb (9752 kg)
Fuel and load: internal fuel 817 Imp gal (981 US gal; 3714 litres) plus provision for 190 Imp gal (228 US gal; 863 litres) of auxiliary fuel in a fuselage tank; external fuel none; maximum payload 8,000 lb (3629 kg)
Speed: never exceed speed at sea level 122 kt (140 mph; 226 km/h); maximum cruising speed at sea level 109 kt (126 mph; 204 km/h)
Range: ferry range 940 nm (1,082 miles; 1742 km) with auxiliary fuel; range 800 nm (921 miles; 1482 km) with maximum standard fuel or 214 nm (246 miles; 396 km) with maximum payload
Performance: maximum rate of climb at sea level 2,030 ft (619 m) per minute; service ceiling 4,000 ft (1220 m) with one engine out; hovering ceiling 6,500 ft (1980 m) in ground effect

Westland Sea King HC.Mk 4

Westland Wasp

Simultaneously with its development of the Scout for service with the UK Army Air Corps, Westland began work to evolve from the same source (the Saunders-Roe P.531) a five-seat general-purpose helicopter optimised for operation to and from ships at sea. The Royal Navy ordered the type into production as the **Sea Scout HAS.Mk 1**, with two pre-production aircraft required for familiarisation. The first of these (XS463) was flown initially on 28 October 1962, by which time the aircraft's designation had been changed to **Wasp HAS.Mk 1**.

Westland produced a total of 133 Wasp HAS.Mk 1s, comprising 98 for the Royal Navy (these aircraft have been retired) and 35 Wasps built for export (for Brazil, the Netherlands, New Zealand and South Africa). The Wasp could carry a pair of Mk 44 ASW torpedoes, or a single Mk 46. A range of depth charges could be carried, or for surface attack two Aérospatiale AS12 wire-guided missiles (with roof-mounted sight). No sensors were fitted, the design of the Wasp being intended for rapid reaction to known threats.

New Zealand maintains seven Wasps in airworthy condition for service from 'Leander'-class frigates. Several non-flying airframes provide spares.

Current users are **Indonesia** (nine of 10 ex-Netherlands aircraft) operated by 400 Skwadron at Surabaya, **Malaysia** (six ex-RN aircraft operated by 499 Sqn at Lumut) and **New Zealand**, which has seven (of a total of 17 new and ex-RN deliveries) serving with No. 3 Sqn at Hobsonville.

SPECIFICATION

Westland Wasp HAS.Mk 1
Rotor system: main rotor diameter 32 ft 3 in (9.83 m);

tail rotor diameter 7 ft 6 in (2.29 m); main rotor disc area 816.86 sq ft (75.89 m²); tail rotor disc area 44.18 sq ft (4.10 m²)
Fuselage and tail: length overall, rotors turning 40 ft 4 in (12.29 m) and fuselage 30 ft 4 in (9.24 m); height overall 11 ft 8 in (3.56 m) with tail rotor turning, and to top of rotor head 8 ft 11 in (2.72 m); wheel track 8 ft 0 in (2.44 m); wheel base 8 ft 0 in (2.44 m)
Powerplant: one 1,050-shp (783-kW) Rolls-Royce (Bristol Siddeley) Nimbus Mk 503 turboshaft derated to 710 shp (530 kW)
Weights: manufacturer's empty 3,452 lb (1566 kg); maximum take-off 5,500 lb (2495 kg)

Fuel and load: internal fuel 1,240 lb (562 kg); external fuel none; maximum ordnance 540 lb (245 kg) or maximum payload 1,500 lb (680 kg)
Speed: maximum level speed 'clean' at sea level 104 kt (120 mph; 193 km/h); maximum and economical cruising speed at optimum altitude 96 kt (111 mph; 179 km/h)
Range: 263 nm (303 miles; 488 km); typical range 235 nm (271 miles; 435 km) with four passengers
Performance: maximum rate of climb at sea level 1,440 ft (439 m) per minute; service ceiling 12,200 ft (3720 m); hovering ceiling 12,500 ft (3810 m) in ground effect and 8,800 ft (2680 m) out of ground effect

Westland Wessex

Turboshaft-powered versions of the Whirlwind had given Westland a good appreciation of the capability of a helicopter with such a powerplant, leading to licence negotiations with Sikorsky for manufacture of the S-58. Westland believed that its larger size, allied with a turboshaft powerplant, would make possible the development of an ASW aircraft combining the hunter and killer activities of the two-aircraft Whirlwind team, but such hopes proved to be premature. However, following receipt of a single S-58 sample aircraft from Sikorsky, Westland began by replacing its standard Wright R-1820 piston engine with an 820-kW (1,100-shp) Napier Gazelle NGa.11 turboshaft, with which it flew for the first time on 17 May 1957 to become the company's demonstrator (XL722).

Satisfactory testing led first to a Westland-built prototype (XL727) and two pre-production examples of what was to be named the **Westland Wessex**, all powered by the 1081-kW (1,450-shp) Napier Gazelle Mk 161, as was the initial production **Wessex HAS.Mk 1** helicopter, of which about 130 were built. These were used by the Royal Navy as 'hunter-killer' pairs in the ASW role, and by the Royal Marines as transports carrying up to 16 fully-equipped commandos. A similar **Wessex HC.Mk 2** for **Royal Air Force** deployment in ambulance, transport and utility roles featured an important difference in the introduction of two coupled Bristol Siddeley Gnome turboshafts, each rated at 1007 kW (1,350 shp) and interconnected so that in the event of an engine failure the remaining engine could continue to drive the rotors.

The Navy's next variant, the **HAS.Mk 3**, introduced the more powerful Napier Gazelle NGa.22 turboshaft and, more importantly, a new AFCS that allowed an entire

The RAF support helicopter fleet has adopted a two-tone green camouflage.

ASW search or strike mission, from lift-off to positioning for landing, to be flown automatically. Later versions included two **Wessex HCC.Mk 4** VIP transports (similar to the HC.Mk 2) for The Queen's Flight; the **Wessex HU.Mk 5** (similar to HC.Mk 2) troop-carrying assault helicopter for the Royal Marine Commandos; and a civil version of the HC.Mk 2, designated **Wessex Mk 60** and designed for use as 10-passenger civil transports, as an air ambulance with eight stretchers, two sitting casualties and a medical attendant, or to carry 15 survivors in a rescue operation.

The **Wessex HAS.Mk 31**, exported to the Royal Australian Navy, was similar to the HAS.Mk 1 except for a Napier Gazelle NGa.13/2 flat-rated at 1148 kW (1,540 shp); these were later given upgraded ASW systems and other improvements to become redesignated **HAS.Mk 31B**. Finally, versions of the HC.Mk 2 were built for Iran, Ghana and Brunei under the respective designations **Wessex Mk 52, Mk 53** and **Mk 54**. It is now over 35 years since the Westland-built Wessex prototype first flew, yet many of these multi-role helicopters continue to provide useful service.

The RAF is the sole current Wessex operator. Around 60 HC.Mk 2s are flown by No. 22 Sqn on SAR duties, No. 28 Sqn in Hong Kong, No. 60 Sqn at Benson and No. 72 Sqn in Northern Ireland. Aircraft of the latter two squadrons are often equipped with Nitesun searchlights, countermeasures and GPMGs mounted in the cabin door. The rotary-wing training unit at Shawbury, 2 FTS, also operates this variant. A pair of HCC.Mk 4s continues to serve with The

Right: The RAF's five HC.Mk 5Cs all serve with No. 84 Sqn at Akrotiri. These wear a blue band in recognition of their UN peacekeeping role in Cyprus. They are being replaced by HC.Mk 2s from mid-1994.

Queen's Flight at Benson, although they will transfer to Northolt as part of No. 32 Squadron in April 1995. No. 84 Sqn at Akrotiri operates five **HC.Mk 5Cs** converted from ex-RN machines.

SPECIFICATION

Westland Wessex HC.Mk 2
Rotor system: main rotor diameter 56 ft 0 in (17.07 m); tail rotor diameter 9 ft 6 in (2.90 m); main rotor disc area 2,643.01 sq ft (228.81 m²); tail rotor disc area 70.88 sq ft (6.58 m²)
Fuselage and tail: length overall, rotors turning 65 ft 9 in (20.04 m) and fuselage 48 ft 4.5 in (14.74 m); height overall 16 ft 2 in (4.93 m) and 14 ft 5 in (4.39 m) to top of rotor head; wheel track 12 ft 0 in (3.66 m)

Powerplant: two Rolls-Royce (Bristol Siddeley) Gnome Mk 110/111 turboshafts each rated at 1,350 shp (1007 kW)
Weights: operating empty 8,304 lb (3767 kg); maximum take-off 13,500 lb (6123 kg)
Fuel and load: internal fuel 300 Imp gal (360 US gal; 1364 litres) plus provision for 200 Imp gal (240 US gal; 909 litres) of auxiliary fuel; external fuel none; maximum payload 4,000 lb (1814 kg)
Speed: maximum level speed at sea level 115 kt (132 mph; 212 km/h); maximum cruising speed at optimum altitude 105 kt (121 mph; 195 km/h)
Range: ferry range 560 nm (645 miles; 1040 km) with auxiliary fuel; range 415 nm (478 miles; 769 km) with standard fuel
Performance: maximum rate of climb at sea level 1,650 ft (503 m) per minute; hovering ceiling 4,000 ft (1220 m) out of ground effect

Left: The Wessex HC.Mk 2 is a regular sight in Britain's mountainous and coastal regions. They are being replaced in the search and rescue role by further procurement of Sea King HAR.Mk 3s.

Right: Helping to police the colony of Hong Kong until 1997 are the Wessex HC.Mk 2s of No. 28 Sqn, which fly from Sek Kong.

Westland WS-70

A single example of the Sikorsky S-70 (an S-70A-16) battlefield helicopter was imported into Britain after Westland acquired production rights from United Technologies, and flew initially in June 1986, powered by RTM 322 turboshafts. The first Westland-assembled **WS-70A** (Sikorsky S-70A-19) demonstrator was first flown on 1 April 1987. Equivalent to the US Army's **UH-60A Black Hawk**, it is powered by two 1,560-shp (1151-kW) General Electric T700-GE-701 turboshafts. An order for 88 **WS-70L**s was provisionally included in the Saudi Arabian Al Yamamah II (Peace Bird II) programme outlined in July 1988. The future of this order remains unclear, pending the completion of final contracts.

The single WS-70L has worn a number of paint schemes to attract customers with varying needs.

Xian H-6

Xian Aircraft Company
PO Box 140, Xian, Shaanxi 710000
People's Republic of China

As its most ambitious licence-building programme, in September 1957 the Chinese aircraft manufacturer acquired from the Soviet Union production rights to the Tupolev Tu-16 strategic medium bomber. It was decided that the aircraft would be built jointly by factories at Xian and Harbin. The first data reached **China** in February 1959, and were followed by two pattern aircraft together with one example of the Tu-16 disassembled and another in CKD (component knock-down) kit form. The first aircraft was reassembled at Harbin within 67 days, and was flown on 27 September 1959. Two years later, all work was transferred to what was to become the Xian Aircraft Manufacturing Company (XAC), work on production tooling commencing in 1964. The first completely Chinese-manufactured bomber flew as the **H-6A** on 24 December 1968.

The H-6A was powered by two 20,944-lb st (93.17-kN) Xian (XAE) WP8 turbojets, carried six crew members, featured a defensive armament of dorsal, ventral and tail twin-gun barbettes and, in its initial form, had a normal internal bomb load of 6,614 lb (3000 kg). The development of a maritime strike version, the **H-6D**, commenced in 1975, this flying in prototype form on 29 August 1981. The H-6D has a new under-nose radome housing an unidentified target acquisition and missile guidance radar and provision for C-601 anti-shipping missiles on underwing pylons, the maximum offensive load totalling 19,841 lb (9000 kg).

An impressive line-up of standard H-6 bombers rests at a People's Liberation Army Air Force base.

A dedicated nuclear bomber and a variant with a second-generation navigation and bombing system have also been produced. H-6s also serve as drone carriers, ECM platforms and engine testbeds.

Low-tempo production of the H-6 – averaging four aircraft annually – continued into the early 1990s, and in excess of 100 H-6s in various versions are reportedly currently serving with the People's Republic of China air force and navy. Four H-6Ds were exported to **Iraq** as **B-6D**s.

SPECIFICATION

Xian H-6 'Badger'
Wing: span 34.189 m (112 ft 2 in); aspect ratio 7.09; area 164.65 m² (1,772.34 sq ft)
Fuselage and tail: length 34.80 m (114 ft 2 in); height 10.355 m (33 ft 11.75 in); tailplane span 11.75 m (38 ft 6.5 in); wheel track 9.77 m (32 ft 0.75 in); wheel base 10.57 m (34 ft 8 in)
Powerplant: two Xian (XAE) Wopen-8 (Mikulin AM-3M-500) turbojets each rated at 93.16 kN (20,944 lb) thrust
Weights: empty equipped 38530 kg (84,943 lb); maximum take-off 75800 kg (167,110 lb)
Fuel and load: internal fuel 36600 kg (80,688 lb); external fuel none; maximum ordnance 9000 kg (19,841 lb) of bombs or 4880 kg (10,7598 kg) in the

form of two C-601 anti-ship missiles
Speed: maximum level speed 'clean' at 19,685 ft (6000 m) 992 km/h (535 kt; 616 mph); cruising speed at optimum altitude 786 km/h (424 kt; 488 mph) with two C-601 missiles
Range: 4300 km (2,320 nm; 2,672 miles); combat radius 1,800 km (971 nm; 1,118 miles)
Performance: maximum rate of climb at sea level 2,513 ft (1140 m) per minute; service ceiling 39,370 ft (12000 m); take-off run 2100 m (6,890 ft) with maximum warload; landing run 1540 m (5,052 ft) at normal landing weight

Left: This H-6 is used for engine tests, complete with an icing rig in front of the intake.

Right: The large undernose radome and wing pylons identify the H-6D anti-ship variant.

Xian JH-7

Revealed publicly in model form at the 1988 Farnborough air show, the **JH-7** (Jianjiji Hongzhaji – fighter-bomber) is a high-performance interdictor and anti-ship aircraft with a maximum take-off weight in the 27,500-kg (61,000-lb) class. The aircraft has a high-set anhedralled swept wing with a large dog-tooth notch at mid-span, sharply-swept tail surfaces with low-set tailplanes and two lateral intakes feeding side-by-side turbofans. A crew of two sits on tandem HTY-4 ejection seats. Offensive weapons (such as the C-801 anti-ship missile) and fuel tanks are carried on four underwing pylons, while for self-defence there are wingtip launch rails for AAMs and a nose-mounted 23-mm twin-barrelled cannon. A Chinese terrain-following radar is fitted.

The first prototype is believed to have flown in early 1989, powered by Xian WS9

An artist's impression shows the JH-7 in anti-ship form, with missiles on the inboard pylons and self-defence AAMs on wingtip launchers.

(licence-built Rolls-Royce Spey Mk 202) turbofans. Production aircraft are expected to feature a Liming engine of 138.3 kN (31,085 lb) afterburning thrust. Service entry was due for 1992-93, but this is likely to have slipped due to developmental problems. Variants for the **PLA air force** (interdictor)

and **PLA navy** (maritime attack) may feature different avionics items.

Xian Y-7

The **Y-7** is essentially an unlicensed copy of the An-24 'Coke'. Development began in October 1966, and a design team was formed from engineers from Xian, Nanchang, Harbin and a collection of research institutes. The prototype made its maiden flight on 25 December 1970 and was certificated in July 1982. The aircraft entered service in early 1984, by which time production had switched to the improved **Y7-100**, developed by Hong Kong Aircraft Engineering Company. This was built to Western airworthiness standards, introduced Western avionics and was fitted with winglets. The

Chinese paratroops board Y7Hs for an air assault exercise. Up to 39 paratroops can be carried by each aircraft. The Chinese air force has about 20 Y7Hs in service.

Y7-200A is a derivative with Pratt & Whitney Canada PW124 turboprops and a Collins EFIS, while the **Y7-200B** is an indigenously powered version for the domestic market. Originally designated **Y-14-100**, the **Y7H-500** is a Chinese-built version of the An-26 'Curl', and features a rear-loading ramp. A handful of Y-7s and Y-7Hs are in military service, mostly with **China**, in both air force and navy service.

SPECIFICATION

Xian Y-7
Wing: span 29.20 m (95 ft 9.5 in); aspect ratio 11.37; area 74.98 m² (807.10 sq ft)
Fuselage and tail: length 23.7 m (77 ft 9.5 in); height 8.55 m (28 ft 0.75 in); tailplane span 9.08 m (29 ft 9.5 in); wheel track 7.90 m (25 ft 11 in); wheel base 7.90 m (25 ft 11 in)
Powerplant: two Dongan (DEMC) Wojiang-5A-1

turboprops each rated at 2080 kW (2,790 shp) and one MNPK 'Soyuz' (Tumanskii) RU-19-300 turbojet (or Chinese-built equivalent) rated at 8.83 kN (1,984 lb st)
Weights: operating empty 14235 kg (31,382 lb); maximum take-off 21800 kg (48,060 lb)
Fuel and load: internal fuel 4790 kg (10,560 lb) plus provision for auxiliary fuel in four centre-section tanks; maximum payload 4700 kg (10,362 lb)
Speed: maximum level speed 'clean' at optimum altitude 518 km/h (280 kt; 322 mph); maximum cruising speed at 4000 m (13,125 ft) 478 km/h (258 kt;

297 mph); economical cruising speed at 6000 m (19,685 ft) 423 mph (228 kt; 263 mph)
Range: ferry range 2420 km (1,306 nm; 1,504 miles) with auxiliary fuel; range 1900 km (1,026 nm; 1,181 miles) with standard fuel, or 910 km (491 nm; 565 km) with maximum passenger payload
Performance: maximum rate of climb at sea level 458 m (1,504 ft) per minute; service ceiling 8750 m (28,705 ft); take-off run 1248 m (4,095 ft) at maximum take-off weight; landing run 620 m (2,035 ft) at normal landing weight

Yakovlev **Yak-11 'Moose'**

Moscow Machine-building Factory 'Skorost', named after A.S. Yakovlev
68 Leningradsky Prospekt
Moscow 125315, Russia

Derived directly from the wartime Yak-3 fighter, the **Yak-3UTI** tandem two-seat trainer first flew in 1945. Subsequently designated **Yak-11**, a slightly refined variant flew in 1946. Deliveries of an eventual 3,859 began in 1947, and 707 more were licence-built in Czechoslovakia as the **LET**

C-11. Sub-variants included the **Yak-11U**, which had a nosewheel undercarriage for training pilots destined for modern jets. Very widely exported, only a handful now survive in military service, probably in **Afghanistan**, **Mali**, **North Korea**, **Somalia**, **Vietnam** and **Yemen**.

SPECIFICATION

Yakovlev Yak-11 'Moose'
Wing: span 9.40 m (30 ft 10 in); aspect ratio 5.74; area 15.40 m² (165.77 sq ft)
Fuselage and tail: length 8.50 m (27 ft 10.7 in);

height 3.28 m (10 ft 9 in)
Powerplant: one Shvetsov ASh-21 radial piston engine rated at 570 hp (425 kW)
Fuel and load: internal fuel 230 kg (507 lb); external fuel none; maximum ordnance 200 kg (440 lb)
Speed: maximum level speed 'clean' at 2500 m (8,200 ft) 465 km/h (251 kt; 289 mph)

Yakovlev **Yak-18 'Max'**

While the Yak-11 was intended as an advanced trainer, and was based on the wartime Yak-3 fighter, the **Yak-18** was intended primarily as a basic trainer and was derived from the pre-World War II Yak UT-2. Although the prototype had a fixed landing gear, subsequent aircraft had aft-retracting mainwheels and a fixed, castoring tailwheel. The 160-hp (119-kW) Shvetsov M-11FR radial engine was closely cowled, with distinct bulges over each of the five cylinders.

The **Yak-18U** introduced a tricycle undercarriage, with the nosewheel retracting aft and the mainwheels retracting forward. When retracted, half-wheels remained

exposed, giving the unusual possibility of a damage-free wheels-up landing if the propeller was stopped in the horizontal position. The aircraft also had a longer nose and increased dihedral on the outer wings. Heavier weight seriously degraded performance characteristics.

The **Yak-20** was powered by the more powerful 260-hp (194-kW) Ivchenko AI-14R engine in a long-chord smooth cowling, and featured structural strengthening, increased internal fuel capacity, a redesigned tail unit, a deeper canopy and improved avionics and systems. Later redesignated **Yak-18A**, it became the most widely used military train-

ing variant and served as the basis for the Chinese **Nanchang CJ-6**, which is described separately.

The **Yak-18P**, **Yak-18PM** and **Yak-18PS** were dedicated competition aerobatic machines, development of which led to the Yak-50 series. The **Yak-18T** was an extensively redesigned cabin version, with side-by-side seats for the pilots, and accommodation behind for passengers or cargo. Some of the latter may remain in military service with **Afghanistan**, **Mali**, **Mongolia**, **Romania** and **Vietnam**.

SPECIFICATION

Yakovlev Yak-18T
Wing: span 11.16 m (36 ft 7.25 in); aspect ratio 6.64;

area 18.75 m² (201.83 sq ft)
Fuselage and tail: length 8.35 m (27 ft 4.75 in)
Powerplant: one VMKB (Vedeneyev) radial piston engine M-14P rated at 360 hp (269 kW)
Weights: empty 1200 kg (2,646 lb); normal take-off 1500 kg (3,307 lb); maximum take-off 1650 kg (3637 lb)
Fuel and load: internal fuel more than 150 kg (331 lb); external fuel none; ordnance none
Speed: maximum level speed 'clean' at optimum altitude 295 km/h (159 kt; 183 mph); maximum cruising speed at optimum altitude 250 km/h (135 kt; 155 mph)
Range: standard range 900 km (485 nm; 559 miles)
Performance: maximum rate of climb at sea level 300 m (984 ft) per minute; service ceiling 5500 m (18,045 ft); take-off run 330 m (1,085 ft) at maximum take-off weight; landing run 400 m (1,315 ft) at normal landing weight

Yakovlev **Yak-28 'Brewer'**

The **Yak-28** was a supersonic bomber developed from the Yak-25 and Yak-27, with similar configuration, but with increased wing and tailplane area and span, and with new 12,676-lb (56.4-kN) R-11AF-300 engines. The **Yak-28R 'Brewer-D'** was developed in 1963 as a dedicated tactical reconnaissance aircraft. A derivative was the **Yak-28PP 'Brewer-E'**, a dedicated ECM jammer designed to escort bombers and strike aircraft. The 'Brewer-E' could be externally distinguished by the replacement of its 'Short Horn' ventral radome with a broader, flatter, rectangular radome, and by the prominent cylindrical fairing projecting from the former bomb bay. Various other antennas, dielectric panels and heat ex-

The 'Brewer-E' was the last variant in front-line service, operating as an electronic warfare platform.

changer inlets and outlets proliferate, and the cannon seems to have been deleted. Rocket pods were frequently carried outboard of the underwing fuel tanks, perhaps indicating a secondary direct defence suppression role. Like late 'Brewer-Ds', the Yak-28PP has smaller, less heavily framed nose glazing, with a vertical aft edge.

Yak-28s were finally retired from the important Group of Soviet Forces in Germany during early 1989. A handful of 'Brewer-Ds' and 'Brewer-Es' may still remain in service in **Russia** and **Ukraine**.

No longer serving as front-line ECM-escort aircraft or reconnaissance platforms, these have probably been relegated to trials and

training roles. Most Yak-28s have now been replaced by dedicated Sukhoi Su-24 'Fencer' variants.

Yakovlev **Yak-38 'Forger'**

Development of a V/STOL fighter for the **Soviet navy**'s new 'Kiev' class of aircraft-carriers began during the early 1960s. Intensive studies bore fruit in the shape of a number of **Yakovlev Yak-36 'Freehand'** research aircraft, with a bicycle undercarriage under the fuselage augmented by wingtip outriggers. The aircraft is believed to have been powered by a pair of 8,267-lb (36.78-kN) Koliesov engines, each with a rotating nozzle. These gave a tremendous thrust margin, and powerful autostabilisers gave a rock-steady hover, using reaction control 'puffer jets' in the tail, wingtips and at the tip of a long nose-probe.

Despite carrying UV-16-57 rocket pods at Domodyedovo, the Yak-36 was not an oper-

ational aircraft although it did lead directly to the **Yak-38**. This first flew during 1971 (reportedly as the **Yak-36MP**), and was first seen during trials of the *Kiev* in the Black Sea during 1975, and afterwards

Two Yak-38U two-seat trainers are usually deployed on each carrier. The Yak-38U features an unusual drooping nose and has a constant-section rear fuselage plug to compensate for the longer nose.

when the same vessel passed through the Bosphorus into the Mediterranean. Required by international treaty to declare details of the vessel's complement, the USSR described its new shipborne fighters as 'Yak-36s', leading to some confusion among Western analysts until 1984, when East European magazines began to use the type's correct Yak-38 designation.

Powered by a single 68-kN (15,300-lb st) Soyuz/Tumanskii R27V-300 turbojet with twin rotating nozzles, the Yak-38 also has a pair of 30-kN (6,725-lb st) Koliesov/Rybinsk RD-36-35FVR lift jets mounted in tandem immediately aft of the cockpit. The vectoring nozzles are controlled by a separate lever, but this is linked to the throttle by a gate which limits nozzle movement angles

Yakovlev Yak-38 'Forger'

Having served for many years in dark blue, many Yak-38s now wear this light grey air defence scheme.

according to the throttle setting.

Up to four pylons can be fitted under the inboard sections of the wing, and these can carry a theoretical maximum weapon load of about 2000 kg (4,409 lb), although two pylons are normally left empty. Yak-38s have been seen armed with UV-16-57 and UV-32-57 rocket pods, R60 (AA-8 'Aphid') AAMs, bombs of up to 500 kg (1,102 lb), and various cannon pods. Auxiliary fuel tanks can be carried by some modernised and late production aircraft, which bear the designation **Yak-38M**.

The Yak-38's unique operating and handling characteristics made the construction of a two-seat trainer essential. The resulting **Yak-38U** has tandem cockpits under sepa-

rate sideways-hinging canopies, with the longer nose having a pronounced 'droop'. A constant-section plug in the rear fuselage compensates for the longer nose, but fin area is not increased. The Yak-38U lacks underwing pylons, IR sensor and ranging radar, and thus has no combat capability.

Improvements during service included the provision of auxiliary blow-in doors in the sides of the main intakes, and fore-and-aft fences on each side of the upper fuselage intake for the lift jets. The basic colour scheme worn by these aircraft is also changing. The dark green anti-corrosion paint used on the undersides is retained, but the dark blue topsides are giving way to grey upper surfaces.

The Yak-38 has often been proposed as a land-based attack aircraft (like Britain's Harrier) and has been demonstrated operating from a lorry-towed take-off and landing platform. With the aircraft's wings folded, the platform folds up to become a trailer. During 1980/81 a handful of Yak-38s were deployed to Afghanistan for operational trials and evaluation against the Su-25. The Yak's limited payload and high accident rate made the result a foregone conclusion.

Production of the 'Forger' was limited to about 90 aircraft, and of these 37 are known to have been lost, resulting in 32 ejections (19 automatic) all of which were successful. When deployed, each carrier had a squadron with 12 single-seaters and two trainers. Reports that the Yak-38 has been retired from service or permanently withdrawn from deck operations are almost certainly premature since, although *Minsk* and *Novorossiysk* are being mothballed, another of the 'Kiev'-class carriers (*Gorshkov*, formerly *Baku*) remains in service and *Kiev* itself is under repair. Certainly the Yak-38's replacement, the Yak-141 'Freestyle', is nowhere near service entry, and the portion of the **AV-MF** which remains under Russian control is unlikely to be willing to give up its only operational shipborne strike fighter.

SPECIFICATION

Yakovlev Yak-38 'Forger-A'
Wing: span 7.32 m (24 ft 0.2 in); width folded 4.88 m (16 ft 0.1 in); aspect ratio 2.9; area 18.50 m² (199.14 sq ft)
Fuselage and tail: length 15.50 m (50 ft 10.3 in); height 4.37 m (14 ft 4 in); tailplane span 3.81 m (12 ft 6 in); wheel track 2.90 m (9 ft 6 in); wheel base 5.50 m (18 ft 0 in)
Powerplant: one MNPK 'Soyuz' (Tumanskii) R-27V-300 turbojet rated at 66.68 kN (14,991 lb st) and two RKBM (Koliesov) RD-36-35FVR lift jets each rated at 31.87 kN (7,175 lb st)
Weights: operating empty 7485 kg (16,501 lb) including pilot; normal take-off 11700 kg (25,794 lb) for vertical take-off; maximum take-off 13000 kg (28,660 lb) for short take-off
Fuel and load: internal fuel about 2900 litres (766 US gal); external fuel up to two 600-litre (158.5-US gal) drop tanks; maximum ordnance 2000 kg (4,409 lb)
Speed: maximum level speed 'clean' at 11000 m (36,090 ft) 1009 km/h (544 kt; 627 mph) and at sea level 978 km/h (528 kt; 608 mph)
Range: combat radius 370 km (200 nm; 230 miles) on a hi-lo-hi attack mission with maximum warload, or 240 km (130 nm; 150 miles) on a lo-lo-lo attack mission with maximum warload, or 185 km (100 nm; 115 miles) on a hi-hi-hi patrol mission with AAMs and drop tanks for a 75-minute loiter
Performance: maximum rate of climb at sea level 4500 m (14,764 ft) per minute; service ceiling 12000 m (39,370 ft)

Yakovlev **Yak-40 'Codling'**

The **Yak-40** was designed as a feederliner to replace the Lisunov Li-2 (the Soviet-built DC-3) and Il-14 in Aeroflot service. The prototype first flew on 21 October 1966. Good short-field performance was achieved by using a lightly-loaded high-lift wing, and three powerful tail-mounted engines, which also kept cabin noise levels low. A hydraulically actuated ventral door with a built-in airstair allows passenger access without external steps, and an APU allows self-starting. Accommodating up to 32 passengers, the Yak-40 has become a popular military staff and VIP transport and serves with the air forces of **Bulgaria, Cambodia, Cuba, Ethiopia, Guinea Bissau, Laos, Poland, Syria, Vietnam,**

Yugoslavia and **Zambia**. A proposed twin-fan Yak-40 conversion, the **Yak-40TL**, has not yet won any military orders.

SPECIFICATION

Yakovlev Yak-40 'Codling'
Wing: span 25.00 m (82 ft 0.25 in); aspect ratio 8.93; area 70.00 m² (753.50 sq ft)
Fuselage and tail: length 20.36 m (66 ft 9.5 in); height 6.40 m (21 ft 4 in); tailplane span 7.50 m (24 ft 7.25 in); wheel track 4.52 m (14 ft 10 in); wheel base 7.465 m (24 ft 6 in)
Powerplant: three ZMDB Progress (Ivchyenko) AI-25 turbofans each rated at 14.71 kN (3,307 lb st)
Weights: empty 8580 kg (18,916 lb); normal take-off

13150 kg (28,990 lb); maximum take-off 13700 kg (30,203 lb)
Fuel and load: internal fuel 3000 kg (6,614 lb); external fuel none; maximum payload 2790 kg (6,151 lb)
Speed: maximum level speed 'clean' at optimum altitude 600 km/h (324 kt; 373 mph); maximum cruising speed at optimum altitude 550 km/h (297 kt;

342 mph); economical cruising speed at optimum altitude 500 km/h (270 kt; 311 mph)
Range: 1600 km (863 nm; 994 miles)
Performance: take-off run 340 m (1,115 ft) at normal take-off weight or 360 m (1,181 ft) at maximum take-off weight; take-off distance to 15 m (50 ft) 1310 m (4,298 ft) at normal take-off weight or 450 m (1,476 ft) at MTOW; landing run 340 m (1,115 ft)

Poland's Yak-40s are operated by the 38th Special Transport Regiment based at Warsaw-Okecie. The unit has absorbed many aircraft from the national airline, LOT, into its fleet.

Yakovlev **Yak-42 'Clobber'**

Although sharing the same basic configuration as the Yak-40, the **Yak-42** 'Clobber' is an all-new design accommodating up to 120 passengers, and features a swept wing. The first prototype, with only 11° leading edge sweep, flew on 7 March 1975 and was followed by a second with 23° sweep, like the production aircraft. A number of Yak-42s serve as testbeds, including the **Yak-42E-LL** propfan development aircraft and the **Yak-42F**, which carries huge underwing equipment pods and is used for earth resources work and electro-optical research. A handful may be in use as military transports.

Yakovlev **Yak-44**

The status of the **Yak-44** is unknown. A twin turboprop aircraft, the Yak-44 is similar in appearance and concept to the US Navy's E-2C Hawkeye and may have been selected for service on the *Kuznetsov* after the An-74 'Madcap' was abandoned.

Yakovlev **Yak-50/52/53**

Derived from the Yak-18, the **Yak-50** was a single-seat competition aerobatic aircraft designed for the 1976 World Aerobatic Championship. A tricycle undercarriage two-seat training version, the **Yak-52**, was built by IAv Bacau in Romania (described separately under Aerostar), along with the similar (but single-seat) **Yak-53**. Yak-52s serve in large numbers with **Russia**'s paramilitary DOSAAF, which is adminis-

tered by the CIS air force and is used as the basic flying training organisation for military and civilian pilots.

The **Yak-54** and **Yak-55** are two- and single-seat versions of a high-performance aerobatic design.

Yakovlev **Yak-41 'Freestyle'**

The **Yak-41** was developed as a supersonic replacement for the Yak-38 for service aboard the Soviet navy's 'Kiev'-class carriers. Development began during 1975. Spotted by a Western satellite at Zhukhovskii during the mid-1980s, the new (and still unflown) aircraft was assigned the reporting name **'Ram-T'** before the standard reporting name **'Freestyle'** was adopted in 1988. The first of two flying prototypes (in addition to two static test airframes) made its maiden flight in March 1989, in the hands of chief test pilot Andrei Sinitsin, under the bureau designation **Yak-141**. If it enters service, the designation **Yak-41** will be used.

The flight test programme progressed smoothly (apart from some early recirculation problems) until October 1991, when the second prototype, coded '77', was badly damaged in a landing accident on the *Gorshkov*. The rear fuselage suffered damage from an engine fire, and the forward fuselage was reportedly damaged when the pilot ejected. It was at one time suggested that it would be rebuilt as the prototype **Yak-41M**, but this was not funded.

The **Yak-141** is powered by a single 152-kN (34,150-lb st) Koptychenko R-79V-300 lift-cruise engine. The engine produces about 20 per cent less thrust in the hover mode. The main nozzle can be rotated

Westland Wasp

Simultaneously with its development of the Scout for service with the UK Army Air Corps, Westland began work to evolve from the same source (the Saunders-Roe P.531) a five-seat general-purpose helicopter optimised for operation to and from ships at sea. The Royal Navy ordered the type into production as the **Sea Scout HAS.Mk 1**, with two pre-production aircraft required for familiarisation. The first of these (XS463) was flown initially on 28 October 1962, by which time the aircraft's designation had been changed to **Wasp HAS.Mk 1**.

Westland produced a total of 133 Wasp HAS.Mk 1s, comprising 98 for the Royal Navy (these aircraft have been retired) and 35 Wasps built for export (for Brazil, the Netherlands, New Zealand and South Africa). The Wasp could carry a pair of Mk 44 ASW torpedoes, or a single Mk 46. A range of depth charges could be carried, or for surface attack two Aérospatiale AS12 wire-guided missiles (with roof-mounted sight). No sensors were fitted, the design of the Wasp being intended for rapid reaction to known threats.

New Zealand maintains seven Wasps in airworthy condition for service from 'Leander'-class frigates. Several non-flying airframes provide spares.

Current users are **Indonesia** (nine of 10 ex-Netherlands aircraft) operated by 400 Skwadron at Surabaya, **Malaysia** (six ex-RN aircraft operated by 499 Sqn at Lumut) and **New Zealand**, which has seven (of a total of 17 new and ex-RN deliveries) serving with No. 3 Sqn at Hobsonville.

SPECIFICATION

Westland Wasp HAS.Mk 1
Rotor system: main rotor diameter 32 ft 3 in (9.83 m); tail rotor diameter 7 ft 6 in (2.29 m); main rotor disc area 816.86 sq ft (75.89 m2); tail rotor disc area 44.18 sq ft (4.10 m2)
Fuselage and tail: length overall, rotors turning 40 ft 4 in (12.29 m) and fuselage 30 ft 4 in (9.24 m); height overall 11 ft 8 in (3.56 m) with tail rotor turning, and to top of rotor head 8 ft 11 in (2.72 m); wheel track 8 ft 0 in (2.44 m); wheel base 8 ft 0 in (2.44 m)
Powerplant: one 1,050-shp (783-kW) Rolls-Royce (Bristol Siddeley) Nimbus Mk 503 turboshaft derated to 710 shp (530 kW)
Weights: manufacturer's empty 3,452 lb (1566 kg); maximum take-off 5,500 lb (2495 kg)

Fuel and load: internal fuel 1,240 lb (562 kg); external fuel none; maximum ordnance 540 lb (245 kg) or maximum payload 1,500 lb (680 kg)
Speed: maximum level speed 'clean' at sea level 104 kt (120 mph; 193 km/h); maximum and economical cruising speed at optimum altitude 96 kt (111 mph; 179 km/h)
Range: 263 nm (303 miles; 488 km); typical range 235 nm (271 miles; 435 km) with four passengers
Performance: maximum rate of climb at sea level 1,440 ft (439 m) per minute; service ceiling 12,200 ft (3720 m); hovering ceiling 12,500 ft (3810 m) in ground effect and 8,800 ft (2680 m) out of ground effect

Westland Wessex

Turboshaft-powered versions of the Whirlwind had given Westland a good appreciation of the capability of a helicopter with such a powerplant, leading to licence negotiations with Sikorsky for manufacture of the S-58. Westland believed that its larger size, allied with a turboshaft powerplant, would make possible the development of an ASW aircraft combining the hunter and killer activities of the two-aircraft Whirlwind team, but such hopes proved to be premature. However, following receipt of a single S-58 sample aircraft from Sikorsky, Westland began by replacing its standard Wright R-1820 piston engine with an 820-kW (1,100-shp) Napier Gazelle NGa.11 turboshaft, with which it flew for the first time on 17 May 1957 to become the company's demonstrator (XL722).

Satisfactory testing led first to a Westland-built prototype (XL727) and two pre-production examples of what was to be named the **Westland Wessex**, all powered by the 1081-kW (1,450-shp) Napier Gazelle Mk 161, as was the initial production **Wessex HAS.Mk 1** helicopter, of which about 130 were built. These were used by the Royal Navy as 'hunter-killer' pairs in the ASW role, and by the Royal Marines as transports carrying up to 16 fully-equipped commandos. A similar **Wessex HC.Mk 2** for **Royal Air Force** deployment in ambulance, transport and utility roles featured an important difference in the introduction of two coupled Bristol Siddeley Gnome turboshafts, each rated at 1007 kW (1,350 shp), and interconnected so that in the event of an engine failure the remaining engine could continue to drive the rotors.

The Navy's next variant, the **HAS.Mk 3**, introduced the more powerful Napier Gazelle NGa.22 turboshaft and, more importantly, a new AFCS that allowed an entire

The RAF support helicopter fleet has adopted a two-tone green camouflage.

ASW search or strike mission, from lift-off to positioning for landing, to be flown automatically. Later versions included two **Wessex HCC.Mk 4** VIP transports (similar to the HC.Mk 2) for The Queen's Flight; the **Wessex HU.Mk 5** (similar to HC.Mk 2) troop-carrying assault helicopter for the Royal Marine Commandos; and a civil version of the HC.Mk 2, designated **Wessex Mk 60** and designed for use as 10-passenger civil transports, as an air ambulance with eight stretchers, two sitting casualties and a medical attendant, or to carry 15 survivors in a rescue operation.

The **Wessex HAS.Mk 31**, exported to the Royal Australian Navy, was similar to the HAS.Mk 1 except for a Napier Gazelle NGa.13/2 flat-rated at 1148 kW (1,540 shp); these were later given upgraded ASW systems and other improvements to become redesignated **HAS.Mk 31B**. Finally, versions of the HC.Mk 2 were built for Iran, Ghana and Brunei under the respective designations **Wessex Mk 52**, **Mk 53** and **Mk 54**. It is now over 35 years since the Westland-built Wessex prototype first flew, yet many of these multi-role helicopters continue to provide useful service.

The RAF is the sole current Wessex operator. Around 60 HC.Mk 2s are flown by No. 22 Sqn on SAR duties, No. 28 Sqn in Hong Kong, No. 60 Sqn at Benson and No. 72 Sqn in Northern Ireland. Aircraft of the latter two squadrons are often equipped with Nitesun searchlights, countermeasures and GPMGs mounted in the cabin door. The rotary-wing training unit at Shawbury, 2 FTS, also operates this variant. A pair of HCC.Mk 4s continues to serve with The

Right: The RAF's five HC.Mk 5Cs all serve with No. 84 Sqn at Akrotiri. These wear a blue band in recognition of their UN peacekeeping role in Cyprus. They are being replaced by HC.Mk 2s from mid-1994.

Queen's Flight at Benson, although they will transfer to Northolt as part of No. 32 Squadron in April 1995. No. 84 Sqn at Akrotiri operates five **HC.Mk 5Cs** converted from ex-RN machines.

SPECIFICATION

Westland Wessex HC.Mk 2
Rotor system: main rotor diameter 56 ft 0 in (17.07 m); tail rotor diameter 9 ft 6 in (2.90 m); main rotor disc area 2,643.01 sq ft (228.81 m2); tail rotor disc area 70.88 sq ft (6.58 m2)
Fuselage and tail: length overall, rotors turning 65 ft 9 in (20.04 m) and fuselage 48 ft 4.5 in (14.74 m); height overall 16 ft 2 in (4.93 m) and 14 ft 5 in (4.39 m) to top of rotor head; wheel track 12 ft 0 in (3.66 m)

Powerplant: two Rolls-Royce (Bristol Siddeley) Gnome Mk 110/111 turboshafts each rated at 1,350 shp (1007 kW)
Weights: operating empty 8,304 lb (3767 kg); maximum take-off 13,500 lb (6123 kg)
Fuel and load: internal fuel 300 Imp gal (360 US gal; 1364 litres) plus provision for 200 Imp gal (240 US gal; 909 litres) of auxiliary fuel; external fuel none; maximum payload 4,000 lb (1814 kg)
Speed: maximum level speed at sea level 115 kt (132 mph; 212 km/h); maximum cruising speed at optimum altitude 105 kt (121 mph; 195 km/h)
Range: ferry range 560 nm (645 miles; 1040 km) with auxiliary fuel; range 415 nm (478 miles; 769 km) with standard fuel
Performance: maximum rate of climb at sea level 1,650 ft (503 m) per minute; hovering ceiling 4,000 ft (1220 m) out of ground effect

Left: The Wessex HC.Mk 2 is a regular sight in Britain's mountainous and coastal regions. They are being replaced in the search and rescue role by further procurement of Sea King HAR.Mk 3s.

Right: Helping to police the colony of Hong Kong until 1997 are the Wessex HC.Mk 2s of No. 28 Sqn, which fly from Sek Kong.

Westland WS-70

A single example of the Sikorsky S-70 (an S-70A-16) battlefield helicopter was imported into Britain after Westland acquired production rights from United Technologies, and flew initially in June 1986, powered by RTM 322 turboshafts. The first Westland-assembled **WS-70A** (Sikorsky **S-70A-19**) demonstrator was first flown on 1 April 1987. Equivalent to the US Army's **UH-60A Black Hawk**, it is powered by two 1,560-shp (1151-kW) General Electric T700-GE-701 turboshafts. An order for 88 **WS-70L**s was provisionally included in the Saudi Arabian Al Yamamah II (Peace Bird II) programme outlined in July 1988. The future of this order remains unclear, pending the completion of final contracts.

The single WS-70L has worn a number of paint schemes to attract customers with varying needs.

Xian H-6

Xian Aircraft Company
PO Box 140, Xian, Shaanxi 710000
People's Republic of China

As its most ambitious licence-building programme, in September 1957 the Chinese aircraft manufacturer acquired from the Soviet Union production rights to the Tupolev Tu-16 strategic medium bomber. It was decided that the aircraft would be built jointly by factories at Xian and Harbin. The first data reached **China** in February 1959, and were followed by two pattern aircraft together with one example of the Tu-16 disassembled and another in CKD (component knock-down) kit form. The first aircraft was reassembled at Harbin within 67 days, and was flown on 27 September 1959. Two years later, all work was transferred to what was to become the Xian Aircraft Manufacturing Company (XAC), work on production tooling commencing in 1964. The first completely Chinese-manufactured bomber flew as the **H-6A** on 24 December 1968.

The H-6A was powered by two 20,944 st (93.17-kN) Xian (XAE) WP8 turbojets, carried six crew members, featured a defensive armament of dorsal, ventral and tail twin-gun barbettes and, in its initial form, had a normal internal bomb load of 6,614 lb (3000 kg). The development of a maritime strike version, the **H-6D**, commenced in 1975, this flying in prototype form on 29 August 1981. The H-6D has a new under-nose radome housing an unidentified target acquisition and missile guidance radar and provision for C-601 anti-shipping missiles on underwing pylons, the maximum offensive load totalling 19,841 lb (9000 kg).

An impressive line-up of standard H-6 bombers rests at a People's Liberation Army Air Force base.

A dedicated nuclear bomber and a variant with a second-generation navigation and bombing system have also been produced. H-6s also serve as drone carriers, ECM platforms and engine testbeds.

Low-tempo production of the H-6 – averaging four aircraft annually – continued into the early 1990s, and in excess of 100 H-6s in various versions are reportedly currently serving with the People's Republic of China air force and navy. Four H-6Ds were exported to **Iraq** as **B-6D**s.

SPECIFICATION

Xian H-6 'Badger'
Wing: span 34.189 m (112 ft 2 in); aspect ratio 7.09; area 164.65 m² (1,772.34 sq ft)
Fuselage and tail: length 34.80 m (114 ft 2 in); height 10.355 m (33 ft 11.75 in); tailplane span 11.75 m (38 ft 6.5 in); wheel track 9.77 m (32 ft 0.75 in); wheel base 10.57 m (34 ft 8 in)
Powerplant: two Xian (XAE) Wopen-8 (Mikulin AM-3M-500) turbojets each rated at 93.16 kN (20,944 lb) thrust
Weights: empty equipped 38530 kg (84,943 lb); maximum take-off 75800 kg (167,110 lb)
Fuel and load: internal fuel 36600 kg (80,688 lb); external fuel none; maximum ordnance 9000 kg (19,841 lb) of bombs or 4880 kg (10,7598 kg) in the form of two C-601 anti-ship missiles
Speed: maximum level speed 'clean' at 19,685 ft (6000 m) 992 km/h (535 kt; 616 mph); cruising speed at optimum altitude 786 km/h (424 kt; 488 mph) with two C-601 missiles
Range: 4300 km (2,320 nm; 2,672 miles); combat radius 1,800 km (971 nm; 1,118 miles)
Performance: maximum rate of climb at sea level 2,513 ft (1140 m) per minute; service ceiling 39,370 ft (12000 m); take-off run 2100 m (6,890 ft) with maximum warload; landing run 1540 m (5,052 ft) at normal landing weight

Left: This H-6 is used for engine tests, complete with an icing rig in front of the intake.

Right: The large undernose radome and wing pylons identify the H-6D anti-ship variant.

Xian JH-7

Revealed publicly in model form at the 1988 Farnborough air show, the **JH-7** (Jianjiji Hongzhaji – fighter-bomber) is a high-performance interdictor and anti-ship aircraft with a maximum take-off weight in the 27500-kg (61,000-lb) class. The aircraft has a high-set anhedralled swept wing with a large dog-tooth notch at mid-span, sharply-swept tail surfaces with low-set tailplanes and two lateral intakes feeding side-by-side turbofans. A crew of two sits on tandem HTY-4 ejection seats. Offensive weapons (such as the C-801 anti-ship missile) and fuel tanks are carried on four underwing pylons, while for self-defence there are wingtip launch rails for AAMs and a nose-mounted 23-mm twin-barrelled cannon. A Chinese terrain-following radar is fitted.

The first prototype is believed to have flown in early 1989, powered by Xian WS9

An artist's impression shows the JH-7 in anti-ship form, with missiles on the inboard pylons and self-defence AAMs on wingtip launchers.

(licence-built Rolls-Royce Spey Mk 202) turbofans. Production aircraft are expected to feature a Liming engine of 138.3 kN (31,085 lb) afterburning thrust. Service entry was due for 1992-93, but this is likely to have slipped due to developmental problems. Variants for the **PLA air force** (interdictor)

and **PLA navy** (maritime attack) may feature different avionics items.

Xian Y-7

The **Y-7** is essentially an unlicensed copy of the An-24 'Coke'. Development began in October 1966, and a design team was formed from engineers from Xian, Nanchang, Harbin and a collection of research institutes. The prototype made its maiden flight on 25 December 1970 and was certificated in July 1982. The aircraft entered service in early 1984, by which time production had switched to the improved **Y7-100**, developed by Hong Kong Aircraft Engineering Company. This was built to Western airworthiness standards, introduced Western avionics and was fitted with winglets. The

Chinese paratroops board Y7Hs for an air assault exercise. Up to 39 paratroops can be carried by each aircraft. The Chinese air force has about 20 Y7Hs in service.

The remarkable Yak-141 has all the features of a modern supersonic fighter, yet incorporates V/STOL technology. Air defence and anti-shipping were the intended roles.

through 95° to give some forward thrust for braking or to move backwards in the hover. The main engine is augmented by a pair of 39-kN (8,767-lb) Rybinsk/Kuznetsov RD-41 (also quoted as RD-36) lift jets mounted in tandem, inclined about 15° aft. To facilitate the transition to forward flight, the nozzles can be vectored further aft to about 24°, and to give thrust braking can be angled forward to 2°. Retractable intake and exhaust doors are located above and below the fuselage immediately behind the cockpit.

A short take-off is achieved by rotating the nozzle of the main engine to 65° during the take-off roll, simultaneously increasing the thrust of the lift jets. An even shorter take-off roll (claimed as 5 m/16.4 ft) can be achieved by rotating the nozzle to 65° before take-off. Because afterburner is used during such short take-offs, runway surfaces can suffer heat damage. For this reason, steel matting is usually used in preference to a concrete runway.

The 'Freestyle's' controls are actuated by a triplex full-authority digital FBW control system with mechanical backup. Yakovlev claims that this gives a level of agility broadly comparable with that enjoyed by the MiG-29 but, in fact, manoeuvrability is considerably less impressive, although the main engine can be vectored in forward flight (VIFFed) to reduce turn radius or make

an unpredictable change in the plane of flight. Harrier operators have found VIFFing to be a valuable combat technique, although it does have the disadvantage of killing energy at an alarming rate, and must be used with caution.

The Yak-141 is claimed to have 'the same radar as the MiG-29', but whether this means the elderly N-019 of the basic 'Fulcrum' or the N-010 of the MiG-29M is uncertain. The aircraft also features a laser/TV target designator, a helmet-mounted sighting system, and avionics systems similar to the MiG-29 and Su-27. Four underwing weapons pylons are provided, all of them inboard of the wing fold, and a fifth pylon is provided under the centre fuselage. This can carry a 2000-litre (440-Imp gal) conformal fuel tank. Provision is made under the port side of the fuselage for a single GSh-30-1 30-mm cannon, with a 120-round ammunition tank.

Yakovlev began studies of a redesigned

Yak-141 following Operation Desert Storm, hoping to produce a land-based STOL fighter of the kind which might have been able to operate from Iraqi airfields even after coalition air attacks. This, it was hoped, would appeal to the Russian air force. The new version would have a new, more powerful version of the R-79 engine, a strengthened undercarriage and uprated brakes (to allow a shorter 120-m/394-ft landing run), and increased internal fuel capacity. The wing is redesigned to be trapezoidal in shape, similar to that of the YF-22, and the LERXes are extended forward to the intake lips. A wraparound windscreen and bubble canopy would also be added.

Funding difficulties have led Yakovlev to seek international partners for further development of all variants of the aircraft, discussing the project with Indian and South African aerospace companies, and perhaps with China and Abu Dhabi.

SPECIFICATION

Yakovlev Yak-141 'Freestyle'
Wing: span 10.10 m (33 ft 1.75 in); width folded 5.90 m (19 ft 4.25 in)
Fuselage and tail: length 18.30 m (60 ft 0 in); height 5.00 m (16 ft 5 in)
Powerplant: one MNPK 'Soyuz' R-79V-300 rated at 107.67 kN (24,206 lb st) dry and 152.00 kN (34,171 lb st) with afterburning, and two RKBM RD-41 each rated at 41.78 kN (9,392 lb st) dry
Weights: maximum take-off 19500 kg (42,989 lb) for short take-off
Fuel and load: maximum ordnance 2600 kg (5,732 lb)
Speed: maximum level speed 'clean' at 11000 m (36,090 ft) 1800 km/h (971 kt; 1,118 mph)
Range: 2100 km (1,133 nm; 1,305 miles) after STO with drop tanks or 1400 km (755 nm; 870 miles) after VTO with internal fuel
Performance: service ceiling more than 15000 m (49,215 ft)

Zlin Aircraft Moravan Aeronautical Works
CR-765 81 Otrokovice
Czech Republic

Zlin 42/43

Featuring side-by-side seating and a 180-hp (134-kW) Avia M 137AZ engine, the **Zlin Z 42** basic trainer first flew on 17 October 1967 and was adopted by the East German air force as its primary trainer. The **Z 43**, flown 10 December 1968, provided two additional seats behind the pilots and a 210-hp (157-kW) Avia M 337A engine. Small batches of Z 43s were acquired by East Germany and **Hungary**, and by the **Czechoslovakian air force** for liaison duties, and the type remains operational with the latter two. The **Zlin 142** and **143** are current production versions of the Z 42 and Z 43, with several variants available, including the **Zlin 242L** with Lycoming engine. The latter is operated by **Slovenia**.

Hungary operates four of the four-seat Zlin Z 43s on liaison duties. They serve with 2 Flight.

Fuselage and tail: length 7.75 m (25 ft 5 in); height 2.91 m (9 ft 6.5 in); tailplane span 3.00 m (9 ft 10 in); wheel track 2.44 m (8 ft); wheel base 1.75 m (5 ft 9 in)
Powerplant: one Avia M 337 AK piston engine rated at 210 hp (156.5 kW)
Weights: equipped 730 kg (1,609 lb); maximum take-off 1350 kg (2,976 lb)
Fuel and load: internal fuel 130 litres (28.5 Imp gal)
Speed: maximum level speed 'clean' at sea level 235 km/h (127 kt; 146 mph); cruising speed 210 km/h (113 kt; 130 mph)
Range: standard range 610 km (325 nm; 375 miles);

SPECIFICATION

Zlin 43
Wing: span 9.76 m (32 ft 0.2 in); area 14.50 m² (156.1 sq ft)

Performance: maximum rate of climb at sea level 330 m (1,082 ft) per minute; service ceiling 5000 m (16,405 ft); take-off run 220 m (722 ft) at normal take-off weight; take-off distance to 15 m (50 ft) 540 m

(1,772 ft) at maximum take-off weight; landing run 190 m (624 ft) at normal landing weight
g limits: -3.5 to +6 at aerobatic weight, -3 to +5 at normal take-off weight and -1.5 to +3.8 at MTOW

Zlin 326 and 526

The **Zlin Z 26** family was launched with a prototype first flight in 1947 and remained in production for some 30 years until 1980, with nearly 2,000 built. Successive variants ranged from the **Z 126** to the **Z 726**, the latter appearing in 1973, and included single-seat and tandem two-seat models, and versions with fixed or retractable undercarriages. Principal military users, of the **Z 326** and **Z 526** variants, included the air forces of **Czechoslovakia**, **Cuba**, **Egypt**, East Germany and **Mozambique**. Small-scale use continues with these air forces except in Germany, and possibly at the Air Force Academy in the former **Yugoslavia**, where the Z 526 has been used for liaison and recreational flying.

SPECIFICATION

Zlin 526 Trener-Master
Wing: span 10.60 m (34 ft 9 in); aspect ratio 7.26; area 15.45 m² (166.31 sq ft)
Fuselage and tail: length 7.80 m (25 ft 7 in); height 2.06 m (6 ft 9 in)
Powerplant: one Walter Minor 6-III piston engine rated at 160 hp (119 kW)
Weights: empty equipped 680 kg (1,499 lb); normal take-off 940 kg (2,072 lb) for aerobatics; maximum take-off 975 kg (2,150 lb)
Fuel and load: internal fuel 97 litres (25.6 US gal); external fuel up to two 68-litre (18-US gal) tip tanks; ordnance none
Speed: maximum level speed 'clean' at sea level

238 km/h (157 kt; 181 mph); cruising speed at optimum altitude 205 km/h (110 kt; 127 mph)
Range: ferry range 980 km (529 nm; 609 miles); standard range 580 km (313 nm; 360 miles)
Performance: maximum rate of climb at sea level 300 m (984 ft) per minute; service ceiling 5000 m

(16,405 ft); take-off run 230 m (755 ft) at normal take-off weight; landing run 135 m (443 ft) at normal landing weight

Egypt retains a few Zlin 326s for training and aerobatics.

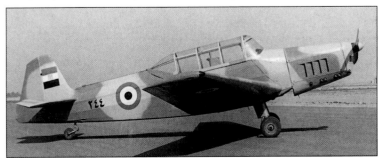

INDEX